CROWDFUNDING

CROWDFUNDING
Fundamental Cases, Facts, and Insights

DOUGLAS J. CUMMING

College of Business, Florida Atlantic University, Boca Raton, FL, United States

SOFIA A. JOHAN

College of Business, Florida Atlantic University, Boca Raton, FL, United States

ACADEMIC PRESS

An imprint of Elsevier

British Library Cataloguing-in-Publication Data
A catalogue record for this book is available from the British Library

Library of Congress Cataloging-in-Publication Data
A catalog record for this book is available from the Library of Congress

ISBN: 978-0-12-814637-8

For Information on all Academic Press publications
visit our website at https://www.elsevier.com/books-and-journals

Publisher: Brian Romer
Acquisition Editor: Brian Romer
Editorial Project Manager: Ruby Smith
Production Project Manager: Nirmala Arumugam
Cover Designer: Christian J. Bilbow

Typeset by MPS Limited, Chennai, India

Working together
to grow libraries in
developing countries

www.elsevier.com • www.bookaid.org

Dedication

For
Sasha Adeline
and
Dylan Jedi

Contents

Part III

Crowdinvesting

8. Equity crowdfunding, valuation, and cases

9. Equity crowdfunding and governance

10. Signaling in equity crowdfunding

11. Are equity crowdfunders sensitive to distance?

Part IV

Crowdfunding regulation and policy

Part V

Conclusion

Preface and Acknowledgments

This book is intended for advanced undergraduate and graduate students in business, economics, law, and management. This book is also directed at practitioners and policymakers with an interest in crowdfunding and related topics in fintech.

This book is not intended to be region specific. We consider data from more than 80 countries around the world. The coverage of different countries is focused on countries that include the United States, Canada, the United Kingdom, Australia, and continental Europe, as there is a longer history and available data from crowdfunding in some countries relative to others.

Selected chapters in this book are based on previously published material, as summarized next:

Chapters 2 and 3:

Cumming, D. J., & Johan S. A. (2009). *Venture capital and private equity contracting: An international perspective.* Elsevier Science Academic Press.

Chapter 5:

Cumming, D. J., Leboeuf, G., & Schwienbacher, A. (2019). Crowdfunding models: Keep-it-all versus all or nothing. *Financial Management*, forthcoming. See https://onlinelibrary.wiley.com/doi/abs/10.1111/fima.12262.

Chapter 6:

Cumming, D. J., Leboeuf, G., & Schwienbacher, A. (2017). Crowdfunding cleantech. *Energy Economics, 65*, 292–303.

Chapter 7:

Cumming, D. J., & Johan, S. J. (2016). Chapter 5: Crowdfunding and entrepreneurial internationalization. In N. Dai, & D. Siegel (Eds.), *Entrepreneurial finance: Managerial and policy implications.* The World Scientific Publishers.

Chapter 9:

Cumming, D. J., Vanacker, T. R., & Zahra, S. A. (2019). Equity crowdfunding and governance: Toward an integrative model and research agenda. *Academy of Management Perspectives*, forthcoming. See https://journals.aom.org/doi/10.5465/amp.2017.0208.

Chapter 10:

Ahlers, G. K. C., Cumming, D. J., Guenther, C., & Schweizer, D. (2015). Signaling in equity crowdfunding. *Entrepreneurship Theory and Practice, 39*, 955–980.

Chapter 11:

Guenther, C., Johan, S., & Schweizer, D. (2018). Is the crowd sensitive to distance? Differences in investment decisions by investor types. *Small Business Economics*, *50*(20), 289–305.

Chapter 12:

Cumming, D. J., Meoli, M., & Vismara, S. (2019). Investors' choices between cash and voting rights: Evidence from dual-class equity crowdfunding. *Research Policy*, 48(8), 103740.

Chapter 13:

Cumming, D. J., Meoli, M., & Vismara, S. (2019). Does equity crowdfunding democratize entrepreneurial finance?. *Small Business Economics*, forthcoming. See https://link.springer.com/article/10.1007/s11187-019-00188-z.

Chapter 16:

Cumming, D. J., & Johan, S. A. (2013). Demand driven securities regulation: Evidence from crowdfunding. *Venture Capital: An International Journal of Entrepreneurial Finance*, *15*, 361–379.

Chapter 17:

Cumming, D. J., Johan, S., & Zhang, Y. (2018). Public policy towards entrepreneurial finance: Spillovers and the scale-up gap. *Oxford Review of Economic Policy*, *34*, 652–675.

Chapter 18:

Cumming, D. J., & Schwienbacher, A. (2018). Fintech venture capital. *Corporate Governance: An International Review*, *26*(5), 374–389.

Chapter 19:

Cumming, D. J., Johan, S. A., & Pant, A. (2019). Regulation of the crypto-economy: Managing risks, challenges, and regulatory uncertainty. *Journal of Risk and Financial Management*, 12(3), 126.

We are indebted to Gerrit Ahlers, Christina Guenther, Gael Leboeuf, Michele Meoli, Anshum Pant, Denis Schweizer, Armin Schwienbacher, Tom Vanacker, Silvio Vismara, Yelin Zhang, and Shaker Zhara for the generosity in allowing us to use the material upon which Chapters 5, 6, 9–13, and 17–19 are based, as that work was developed jointly with these excellent coauthors.

Each chapter of the book ends with a list of key terms and a number of discussion questions. PowerPoint lecture slides for each chapter are available online at the Elsevier webpage that accompanies this book.

## PART I

Introduction to Crowdfunding

1

Introduction

Crowdfunding involves individuals, typically entrepreneurial oriented, or entrepreneurial firms raising capital through (typically) online Internet platforms from large numbers of small investors. Crowdfunding is a cheap and effective way for entrepreneurs to raise capital at their earliest stages of starting and growing their ideas and products. Almost all crowdfunding campaigns involve less than $1 million in total capital raised, and many campaigns seek smaller amounts up to $10,000, although total amounts raised in exceptional circumstances have been as high as $10 million.

There are four main types of crowdfunding:

- donations (e.g., Gofundme.com, Crowdhelps.com)[1] whereby (typically) individuals raise money from other individuals for charitable causes;
- rewards (e.g., Kickstarter and Indiegogo) whereby entrepreneurs raise money from crowdfunders in exchange for a promise to receive a reward (e.g., a yet to be made product);
- debt [including peer-to-peer (P2P), such as Lending Club, and marketplace landing, such as Funding Circle] whereby individuals (in the case of P2P lending) or firms (in the case of marketplace lending) raise money from individuals in exchange for a debt security that pays a specified rate of interest; and
- equity (e.g., Crowdcube) whereby firms raise money from individuals in exchange for ownership in the firm.

In this book, we focus on crowdfunding that is arguably more entrepreneurial oriented, namely, rewards and equity crowdfunding and marketplace lending (individuals lending to firms). P2P loans can facilitate entrepreneurial activity as well, and hence we provide a discussion herein as well alongside our review of marketplace lending. We briefly consider donations crowdfunding alongside rewards crowdfunding.

---

[1] Gofundme is a generalist platform, whereas crowdhelps is a platform specifically targeting women's issues.

3

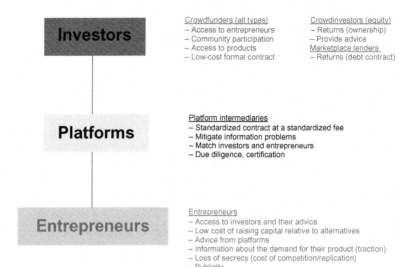

FIGURE 1.1 Crowdfunding financial intermediation. Source: *Adapted from Agrawal, A., Catalini, C., & Goldfarb, A. (2013). Some simple economics of crowdfunding,* Innovation Policy and the Economy, *14, 63−97.*

Broadly framed questions addressed in this book include, but are not limited to, the following:

- What do crowdfunding platforms do, and how much do they charge?
- Which types of entrepreneurs engage in crowdfunding in terms of their characteristics and capital needs?
- Does crowdfunding democratize access to capital?
- What do crowdfunding portals do to mitigate risks for investors?
- How do the platform rules and practices influence crowdfunding outcomes?
- How much equity should entrepreneurs give away in crowdfunding?
- Is it helpful for entrepreneurs to issue dual-class shares and keep special voting rights in the case of equity crowdfunding?
- What interest rates are commonly seen with lending crowdfunding?
- How common is crowdfunding fraud?
- How is crowdfunding related to other forms of entrepreneurial finance?
- How should crowdfunding regulation be designed?
- How should policymakers use crowdfunding to promote entrepreneurship?

Crowdfunding platforms are intermediaries between the entrepreneur or entrepreneurial firm and their investors (Agrawal, Catalini, & Goldfarb, 2013) (see Fig. 1.1). The platform typically does a variety of due diligence checks (background checks, site visits, credit checks, cross-checks, account monitoring, and third-party proof) to ensure that the entrepreneur is of sufficiently high quality and not of ill repute before enabling the campaign to go ahead. Some platforms offer additional potentially value-added services, such as prelisting evaluation, strategic guidance, business planning, contract help, and promotion services. Platforms charge different fee levels and terms. The most common fee arrangement observed in Cumming, Johan, and Zhang's (2019) dataset of Canadian crowdfunding platforms, for example, a fixed percentage of the capital raised only if the campaign is successful (almost one-fourth of platforms in their data, and this fee is commonly set between 4% and 5% of the total amount of capital raised[2]), although it is likewise almost as common to observe platforms charging a fixed percentage of capital raised regardless of whether the funding was successful. Other platforms charge onetime listing fees, periodical subscriptions at different levels/tiers, and management fees and carry percentages.

Fig. 1.1 further highlights that investors in crowdfunding projects benefit not merely by getting access to a product (rewards crowdfunding) or a financial return (equity crowdfunding and marketplace lending), but they also benefit by being able to gain access entrepreneurs, participate in the community, and carry out their investment with the entrepreneur at a low cost. Other forms of finance, such as angel finance, could lead to the same total dollar capital raise but would be much more expense in terms of legal fees arranging financial contracts. For example, anecdotally, we have discussed with entrepreneurs that on angel investments of $150,000, legal fees can amount to 40%−45% of the capital raised. The main drawback, however, is that by posting a project on an Internet platform, it is much harder to keep secret the things that the entrepreneur is engaged in. Entrepreneurs nevertheless obtain capital much more cheaply and can source capital from a wider array of investors than that which might otherwise have been possible through their personal networks. Moreover, the geographic scope of the investors, and diversity of investors, could enable the entrepreneurial team to develop and grow their business and obtain subsequent rounds of financing. And entrepreneurs can demonstrate "traction" or interest in their product to subsequent investors by virtue of the interest in their crowdfunding campaign by the take-up from crowdfunders.

The process sounds easy at a first look, but there are hurdles that entrepreneurs, platforms, and investors have to cross. Not all entrepreneurs are of high quality, and it is difficult for entrepreneurs to signal that their quality is superior to others in a way that investors will appreciate. And there is potential for entrepreneurs without substantial oversight to misuse the money that they raise without investors knowing about it, or at least until it is too late. Without some level of governance and regulation, the crowdfunding market might break down through scandals and a lack of investor confidence. Information asymmetries, signaling, and agency problems are the common theme that link the topics covered in this book. Crowdfunding enables entrepreneurs to seek capital at a very early stage of development when there is scant track record and scant information disclosure requirements and regulation. Successful crowdfunding, therefore, requires effective handling of information asymmetries and agency problems. This book will show how entrepreneurs and investors allocate risks, incentives, and rewards. This book will further show tools entrepreneurs and platforms can use to ensure successful crowdfunding outcomes and success.

[2] In the case of initial public offerings (IPOs), by contrast, the listing fee is commonly set at 7% of capital raised for large IPOs, and this fee can be much higher in the case of smaller IPOs (see Cumming & Johan, 2013).

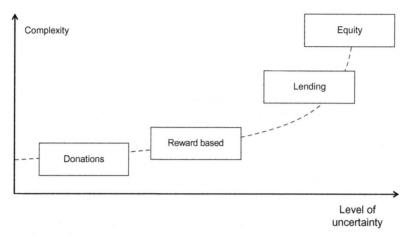

FIGURE 1.2 Uncertainty and complexity in different types of crowdfunding. Source: *Based on an earlier working paper version of Ahlers, G.K.C., Cumming, D.J., Günther, C., & Schweizer, D. (2015) Signaling in equity crowdfunding,* Entrepreneurship Theory and Practice, 39(4), 955—980.

Different types of crowdfunding have different degrees of uncertainty and complexity. Fig. 1.2 summarizes the differences. Donations crowdfunding has a minor degree of uncertainty as reflected in media reports of "crowd thieving"[3] due to scams, such as fake medical scams,[4] such as a notorious one where an individual claimed to have cancer and raised $38,000 for fake medical bills.[5] But the issues are typically transparent as long as the donors in the crowd carry out due diligence to ensure the campaign they are giving to represent a real need and not a scam. Rewards crowdfunding is more complicated, as it typically involves the creation of a good or service, and the funding is used for advance access to capital for the entrepreneur to create that good or service. The entrepreneur needs to set a campaign goal and design the incentives for different levels of commitment by different crowdfunders. There is uncertainty regarding whether or not the entrepreneur will actually develop what is promised and possible fraud (see also Chapter 15: Introduction to crowdfunding regulation and policy). Debt crowdfunding carries more uncertainty and complexity as the terms of the loan need to be set, such as interest rates on loan. And there is financial information that needs to be understood by the crowd investors (see Chapter 14: Marketplace lending). Finally, equity crowdfunding typically involves the most uncertainty and complexity since the equity share, valuation of the company, and financial and business model of the company need to be set by the entrepreneur and understood by the crowd. Part III of this book explains these equity terms in extensive detail.

Data comprise the central tool in this book to shed light on industry practices in crowdfunding. A dataset is a collection of individual cases. We likewise refer to select cases on

---

[3] https://www.consumerreports.org/crowdfunding/be-careful-about-donating-through-crowdfunding/

[4] https://www.dailydot.com/irl/manchausen-internet-rise-medical-crowdfunding-scams/

[5] https://clark.com/family-lifestyle/donating-volunteering/fake-cancer-woman-gofundme-crowdfunding/

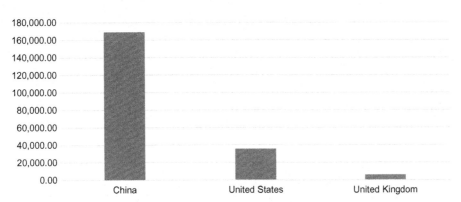

FIGURE 1.3 Estimates crowdfunding volume around the world, all types, $ millions, averaged 2015–16, three largest countries by all types of total crowdfunding volume. Source: *Created from statistics provided in Rau, P. R. (2018). Law, trust, and the development of crowdfunding. Working Paper, University of Cambridge* (August 1, 2018).

different topics to highlight specific issues that arise in crowdfunding. Sometimes cases are outliers, and other times cases are reflective of the typical industry practice; but without an examination of data, it is hard to tell outliers from typical practice.

Rau (2018) estimates that total crowdfunding volume around the world (averaged 2015–26) was $214.3 or $290 billion in 2016, which comprised $3 billion from equity crowdfunding and $208.4 billion in debt crowdfunding (both P2P and marketplace lending). China, the United States, and the United Kingdom are the three largest markets, representing $243 (83%),[6] $35 (12%), and $7 billion (7%). Crowdfunding was only at $0.5 billion in 2011. Growth in crowdfunding has been exponential. Based on Rau's (2019) estimates, the growth rate per year has been over 250%.[7] A large part of the China's crowdfunding market around this time is due to its P2P market, which was $218 billion,[8] or more than that of the rest of the world combined. The massive differences in the scale of crowdfunding around the world are graphically depicted in Figs. 1.3 and 1.4.

In 2015 Massolution[9] estimated that lending crowdfunding around the world comprised 75.6% of all crowdfunding (driven by the massive size of China's P2P market); followed by donation crowdfunding around the world, which comprised 8.56% of all crowdfunding; followed by reward (8.1%) and equity (7.7%). Massolution noted that crowdfunding has surpassed investment by angel investors in 2015 and was set to overtake venture

---

[6] As at 2019, the Chinese P2P market is expected to shrink in size with new regulatory restrictions; see https://www.bloomberg.com/news/articles/2019-01-02/china-s-online-lending-crackdown-may-see-70-of-businesses-close. The change reflects recent scandals and a lack of a unified risk rating system; see https://www.ft.com/content/c71eea4a-c198-11e8-84cd-9e601db069b8.

[7] See Chapter 3, Overview of institutional contexts and empirical methods, for a discussion of these survey data used by Rau (2019).

[8] https://www.finextra.com/blogposting/17107/the-rise-and-fall-of-p2p-lending-in-china

[9] https://www.forbes.com/sites/chancebarnett/2015/06/09/trends-show-crowdfunding-to-surpass-vc-in-2016/#1dace16b4547

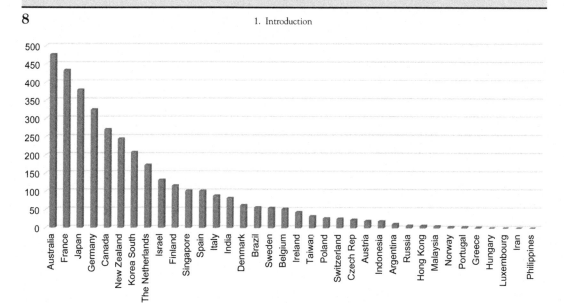

FIGURE 1.4 Estimates crowdfunding volume around the world, all types, $ millions, averaged 2015–16, selected countries, all types crowdfunding. Source: *Created from statistics provided in Rau, P. R. (2018). Law, trust, and the development of crowdfunding. Working Paper, University of Cambridge* (August 1, 2018).

capital (VC) investment around the world in 2016. As discussed in Chapter 3, Overview of institutional contexts and empirical methods, aggregate statistics are hard to assemble in these markets, but by all independent measures crowdfunding has been growing at an exponential rate and has become at least as important as other forms of entrepreneurial finance, such as VC and angel investment.

It is important and relevant to review data to show real outcomes from crowdfunding campaigns and explain how entrepreneurs design campaigns, and how portals have a nontrivial role, in facilitating entrepreneurial campaign goal success. Without analyzing data, we would at best be limited to our best guesses from specific cases, which is not the intention here. The data considered in this book are international in scope, with a focus on Australia, Canada, Europe, and the United States. It is important to consider data from a multitude of countries to understand how and why crowdfunding markets differ around the world. As well, idiosyncratic features of certain countries and platforms distort our understanding of how crowdfunding works in practice.

In short, by considering international datasets and not data from just one country, such as the United States, we are able to gain a significant amount of insight into how crowdfunding markets operate in relation to their legal and institutional environment. Each chapter in this book, where possible and appropriate, will refer to and analyze data. Note however that crowdfunding platforms, entrepreneurs, and investors are neither compelled to publicly report data nor are they willing to do so. As such, there is always more data that can be collected. It is the author's hope that this book will not only provide an understanding of how crowdfunding markets operate but also will inspire further empirical work in the field so that we may better understand the nature and evolution of crowdfunding markets in years to come.

Part I of this book comprises three chapters. Chapter 1, Introduction, briefly refers to aggregate industry statistics on crowdfunding around the world to compare the size of the markets in different countries. Chapter 2, Overview of agency and signaling theory in crowdfunding, describes information asymmetries and agency problems in crowdfunding. The intention of the chapter is to provide a framework for working through the data and concepts in the subsequent chapters. Chapter 3, Overview of institutional contexts and empirical methods, provides an overview of the empirical methods considered in this book. The description of the statistical and econometric techniques used is intended to be user friendly so that all readers can follow along each of the chapters regardless of background. In addition, the chapter provides an overview of the institutional and legal settings in the countries considered in the different chapters. A central theme in this book is that differences in crowdfunding markets are attributable to international differences in legal and institutional settings. Finally, the chapter is an overview of empirical valuation methods insofar as they pertain to crowdfunding campaigns.

Part II of this book (Chapters 4–7) considers rewards-based crowdfunding. Chapter 4, An overview of rewards-based crowdfunding, explains the mechanics of rewards-based crowdfunding. It explains what do entrepreneurs need to do to prepare a campaign. Also, it provides example cases to highlight cases that have worked well versus cases that have failed.

Chapter 5, Crowdfunding models: keep-it-all versus all-or-nothing, explains that reward-based crowdfunding campaigns are commonly offered in one of two models via fundraising goals set by an entrepreneur: "keep-it-all" (KIA), where the entrepreneur keeps the entire amount raised regardless of achieving the goal, and "all-or-nothing" (AON), where the entrepreneur keeps nothing unless the goal is achieved. The chapter hypothesizes that AON forces the entrepreneur to bear greater risk and encourages crowdfunders to pledge more capital-enabling entrepreneurs to set larger goals. The chapter further hypothesizes that AON is a costly signal of commitment for entrepreneurs yielding a separate equilibrium with higher quality and more innovative projects with greater success rates. Empirical tests are provided in the chapter in support of these hypotheses.

Chapter 6, Crowdfunding cleantech, examines crowdfunding of new alternative energy technologies. This chapter shows that cleantech crowdfunding is more common in countries with low levels of individualism and more common when oil prices are rising. Cleantech crowdfunding campaigns are more likely to have higher capital goals, more photos, a video pitch, and longer text descriptions of the campaign. Relative to nonclean-tech campaigns, the success of cleantech campaigns, in terms of achieving funding goals, is more economically sensitive to the campaign's goal size, being not-for-profit, and having a video pitch. The evidence is consistent with the view that while alternative energies are viewed as being more risky and investors face greater information asymmetries relative to other types of investment projects, there are mechanisms for entrepreneurs to mitigate these information problems and be at least as successful in cleantech crowdfunding markets.

Chapter 5, Crowdfunding models: keep-it-all versus all-or-nothing, and Chapter 6, Crowdfunding cleantech, are based on data from Indiegogo. Indiegogo is the world's second largest rewards-based crowdfunding platform behind Kickstarter. Indiegogo is an interesting setting, which studies rewards-based crowdfunding but has an additional interesting feature that does not exist on Kickstarter, namely, the KIA versus the AON option. These data in Chapter 5, Crowdfunding models: keep-it-all versus all-or-nothing, and Chapter 6, Crowdfunding cleantech, comprise crowdfunding campaigns on Indiegogo from over 80 countries around the world. Chapter 7, Crowdfunding to internationalize, thereafter considers how entrepreneurs have used other crowdfunding platforms to internationalize their entrepreneurial start-up activities. Specifically, the chapter examines case studies and portals where entrepreneurial internationalization is facilitated by crowdfunding. It also discusses opportunities, challenges, and future research opportunities that pertain to crowdfunding and internationalization.

Part III of this book (Chapters 8−14) presents information pertinent to equity crowdfunding. Chapter 8, Equity crowdfunding, valuation, and cases, provides an overview of equity crowdfunding. It explains how entrepreneurs value their projects, what proportion of equity to give up, and things that need to be included in an equity crowdfunding campaign. Also, it provides some perspective on selecting between debt and equity crowdfunding. Chapter 9, Equity crowdfunding and governance, provides an overview of equity crowdfunding models and various theoretical perspectives on equity crowdfunding.

Chapter 10, Signaling in equity crowdfunding, uses data on equity crowdfunding from the Australian Small Scale Offerings Board (ASSOB), one of the first equity crowdfunding platforms in the world, to study the role of signaling in equity crowdfunding. It considers the effectiveness of signals that entrepreneurs use to induce (small) investors to commit financial resources to equity crowdfunding campaigns. It examines the impact of venture quality (human capital, social (alliance) capital, and intellectual capital) and uncertainty on fundraising success. These data highlight that retaining equity and providing more detailed information about risks can be interpreted as effective signals and can therefore strongly impact the probability of funding success. Social and intellectual capitals, by contrast, have little or no impact on funding success. The chapter discusses the implications of the results for theory, future research and practice.

Chapter 11, Are equity crowdfunders sensitive to distance?, presents data, also from ASSOB, on the role of distance between investors and the entrepreneur. Data on cash flow versus control rights in equity crowdfunding are presented in the chapter. It considers the role of the influence of geographic distance among retail, accredited, and overseas investors and venture location in an equity crowdfunding context. By analyzing investment decisions, the chapter shows that geographic distance is negatively correlated with investment probability for all home country investors. The comparison of home country and overseas investors in the chapter reveals that overseas investors are not sensitive to distance. However, when comparing only home country investors (subdivided into retail and accredited), the chapter documents that both investor types are similarly sensitive to the distance of possible ventures. Evidence from other entrepreneurial financing contexts, such as VC is consistent with the view that a wider geographic scope of investors is very helpful for lowering the cost of capital and expanding future exit opportunities, including the probability of an initial public offering (IPO) or an acquisition (Cumming, Knill, & Syvrud, 2016).

As explained in Chapter 12, Cash flow and control rights in equity crowdfunding, some platforms enable the entrepreneur to issue nonvoting shares in crowdfunding campaigns. The chapter considers whether or not this type of offering is advisable. It examines dual-class equity crowdfunding as a digital ownership model. Unique to this context, companies can set an investment threshold under which no voting rights are granted, making the issuance of Class A versus Class B shares, depending on individual investors. Using a sample of 491 offerings on the UK platform Crowdcube from 2011 to 2015, the chapter shows that a higher separation between ownership and control rights lowers the probability of success of the offering, the likelihood of attracting professional investors, as well as the long-run prospects. Different from small investors, professional investors care about the implementation of a threshold for the attribution of voting rights and often bid the Class A threshold exactly. Family businesses, although less attractive to small investors, are relatively safer investments, because of their lower chances of failure.

Finally, Chapter 13, Does equity crowdfunding democratize access to entrepreneurial finance?, explains the importance of equity crowdfunding for democratizing access to capital. With a growing number of equity crowdfunding campaigns that are targeting traditionally disadvantaged communities,[10] it is natural to wonder whether equity crowdfunding equalizes access to capital. Specifically, the chapter investigates whether gender, age, ethnicity, and geography affect the choice of equity crowdfunding offerings versus IPOs on traditional stock markets and whether these characteristics increase the likelihood of a successful offering. Using 167 equity offerings in Crowdcube and 99 equity offerings on London's Alternative Investment Market raising between £300,000 and £5 million, the chapter shows that companies with younger top management team members are both more likely to launch equity crowdfunding offerings than IPOs and have higher chances to successfully complete an equity crowdfunding offering. Remotely located companies are more likely to launch equity crowdfunding offerings than IPOs and have higher chances to successfully complete an equity crowdfunding offering. On the contrary, female entrepreneurs do not have higher chances to raise funds in equity crowdfunding. Minority entrepreneurs do not have higher chances of successfully raising capital but do attract a higher number of investors. Overall, the evidence in this chapter provides empirical guidance for the first time to the oft-repeated policy claim that equity crowdfunding democratizes entrepreneurial finance by providing access to funding to underrepresented groups of potential entrepreneurs.

Chapter 14, Marketplace lending, discusses marketplace lending, including the typical interest rates in marketplace lending (debt crowdfunding where entrepreneurial firms raise money from individual investor), and which types of marketplace lending campaigns attract more investor interest. Also, it explains, with reference to evidence from Germany, that marketplace lending investors pay attention to easy-to-understand ratings of borrowers (provided by platforms) instead of complicated financial information.

In view of the evidence in Parts II and III, Part IV (Chapters 15–19) discusses crowdfunding regulation and public policy. Chapter 15, Introduction to crowdfunding regulation and policy, provides an introduction to regulation in the crowdfunding setting. It explains what crowdfunding platforms do (such as due diligence that includes background checks, site visits, credit checks, cross-checks, account monitoring, and third-party proof), and how platforms and their investors can mitigate adverse selection and agency

---

[10] See for example the LGBTQ + targeted campaign of You & Sundry: https://wefunder.com/you-and-sundry?auto_login_token = 9wpX7PSkzg8AgMXO&utm_swu = 5264.

costs. Also, it provides some evidence on crowdfunding fraud and the frequency of fraud. We explain that fraud cases are less common than what we might have otherwise expected relative to the frequency of fraud among publicly traded companies. Further, we explain that fraud is more common among campaigns with entrepreneurs that do not have a social media presence (e.g., LinkedIn, Facebook, and Twitter), have hard-to-read campaign pitches, have lots of enticements in terms of reward levels, and are not repeat crowdfunders.

Chapter 16, Demand driven crowdfunding regulation, discusses investor, platform, and entrepreneurial views toward crowdfunding regulation. Specifically, the chapter considers the evolution of crowdfunding regulation from the perspective of the race-to-the-bottom/race-to-the-top debate. The empirical setting in the chapter is based on survey data from Canada in 2013(Q1) when equity crowdfunding was not permitted but was openly contemplated by regulators. These data show some tension toward a race to the bottom insofar as start-ups prefer fewer restrictions on their ability to crowdfund, and portals prefer fewer disclosure requirements and fewer restrictions on free trading of crowdfunded shares. However, this evidence is tempered by the fact that investors demand more disclosure, limits on amounts entrepreneurs can raise, and lower thresholds for audited financial statements, among other things. Based on the ease with which the Internet facilitates cross-jurisdictional investment, we infer from these data that investor demands will give rise to a race to the top in the crowdfunding space. Interestingly, in the Canadian case and after the collection of these data in the chapter, the approved crowdfunding regulations were so strict that no entrepreneurs actually took up the equity crowdfunding exemption to raise capital over the subsequent 5-year period after they were introduced.

Chapter 17, Public policy toward entrepreneurial finance: spillovers and scale-up, puts crowdfunding as part of a broader portfolio of other types of entrepreneurial finance and explains that an appropriate set of regulatory and public policy goals consider regulation not in isolation, but in terms of how there is an interplay between different forms of entrepreneurial finance. That is, research in the area of public policy toward entrepreneurial finance has traditionally been focused on financing gaps and whether or not government programs successfully address or mitigate those financing gaps. More recently, a growing literature has identified externalities across different forms of entrepreneurial finance. These externalities include but are not limited to spillovers from one form of finance to another (such as from crowdfunding to VC), spillovers from domestic to international investment, and spillovers from early stage to late stage investment. Sometimes these externalities are positive and other times they are negative. In this chapter, we review what is known about these spillovers and highlight a need to better understand these spillovers for the optimal design of a government's portfolio of policy toward entrepreneurial finance.

Chapter 18, Regulation and investment in fintech ventures, shows how regulatory developments that are perhaps overly stringent can lead to entrepreneurial activity to develop in regions that are not overly constrained by regulation. The chapter examines the context of fintech (crowdfunding is just one component of fintech, and it is broader than crowdfunding in its coverage of activity) VC investments taking place around the world and the role of institutional factors in the international allocation of fintech VC. The evidence in the chapter shows a notable change in the pattern of fintech VC investments around the world relative to other types of investments after the global financial crisis. We show that fintech VC investments are relatively more common in countries with weaker regulatory enforcement and without a major financial center after the financial crisis. Also, we show the fintech boom is more pronounced for smaller private limited partnership VC that likely have less experience with prior VC booms and busts. These fintech VC deals are substantially more likely to be liquidated, especially when located in countries without a major financial center. The chapter builds on the institutions and corporate governance literatures by showing the importance of enforcement in driving relative differences in investment patterns and investor participation. For entrepreneurial start-ups, regulatory arbitrage drives investment into countries with a dearth of enforcement and regulatory costs. It argues that the spike in fintech VC in certain countries is attributable to differential enforcement of financial institution rules among start-ups versus large established financial institutions after the financial crisis. Regulatory arbitrage in the context of fintech VC can spur booms and busts. Less experienced VC seem more prone to undertake investments that exacerbate boom and bust cycles. National governance is strengthened by the enforcement of regulatory standards, and corporate governance, through investor experience and oversight, can mitigate these swings and facilitate better investment outcomes.

Chapter 19, Crypto regulation, discusses regulation around an unusual but popular type of crowdfunding, that is, cryptocurrencies. Specifically, we examine initial coin offerings (ICOs), and how this application of crowdfunding mechanism has the promise for economic innovation. The distributed ledger technology, also known as blockchain, is gaining traction globally. Riding on the magnanimous promises of the blockchain secure validation mechanism and decentralized mass collaboration, cryptocurrencies are the newest asset class being introduced to investors worldwide and are being used by companies to raise capital to further their development of the advancement of blockchain technology via ICOs. The substantial inflow of unregulated capital into a transactional and transnational industry has aroused interest from not just investors but also national securities and monetary regulatory agencies. In the chapter we explore the potential for blockchain to exacerbate the already decentralized economy. We review the Security and Exchange Commission's initial statements on ICOs to illustrate the potential problems with applying a dated legal framework to an ever-evolving ecosystem. Recognizing the inability of enforcement within existing regulatory frameworks, we argue for the regulation of the crypto asset class and internal collaboration between government agencies and developers in the establishment of an ecosystem that integrates investor protection and investment.

Finally, in Part V, the last part of the book, we offer a summary and conclusion remarks in Chapter 20, Summary, conclusion, and looking forward. We highlight the lessons for entrepreneurs in running successful crowdfunding campaigns, for platforms in running efficient forums for enabling the matching between entrepreneurs and their investors, and for investors in terms of doing due diligence and making suitable decisions in the crowdfunding market. Finally, we discuss lessons from regulation and lessons for regulators.

2

Overview of agency and signaling theory in crowdfunding

2.1 Introduction

This chapter provides an overview of the agency theory and signaling theory in the context of crowdfunding.

The term "agency cost" generally refers to things that parties to a contract might do, which are in their own self-interest but against the interest of the other party. If agency problems did not exist, crowdfunding would likely be much more commonplace insofar as it offers enables capital raising at potentially lower transaction costs; that is, there would be a scant need for expensive intermediaries, such as banks, venture capitalists, private equity funds, and other investors with the expertise to minimize problems associated with the provision of capital to entrepreneurs, to facilitate entrepreneurial finance. Much of the investor and regulatory concerns around crowdfunding is associated with agency costs. Mechanisms by which agency costs can be mitigated are through financing terms and due diligence from platforms, investors who invest in projects, and "the crowd," in general, that has an interest in crowdfunding but may not have invested in specific projects for which agency problems are potentially pronounced. Hence, the analysis of crowdfunding in this book is focused on agency theory, and in this analysis, it makes sense to begin by providing a primer on agency costs. One type of agency cost is adverse selection, and hence, we also provide a discussion of signaling theory in this chapter.

In this chapter, we provide an overview of agency costs in the context of the two main different forms of finance (debt and common equity) used in crowd investing. Many agency principles can be illustrated within this context. While there are other forms of finance used in other contexts, such as venture capital (convertible debt, preferred equity, convertible preferred equity, and other forms), those securities are scantly used in crowdfunding and hence are not discussed here.[1]

This book is focused on entrepreneurial firms raising capital. In crowdfunding markets, there are two types of debt crowdfunding. First, there is "marketplace lending," which

---

[1] See Cumming and Johan (2013) for a discussion of these other forms of finance.

15

refers to individuals making loans to entrepreneurial firms via online platforms, and "peer-to-peer" lending, which refers to individuals making loans to other individuals. Our focus in this book is on crowdfunding by entrepreneurial firms, and as such, we will not be discussing work on peer-to-peer lending.

In this chapter we will

- review what the two main forms of securities (debt and common equity) in crowd investing actually entails;
- analyze how different types of agency problems arise when different forms of finance are used;
- consider how mitigating agency problems can enhance firm value;
- consider how signaling can mitigate costs associated with agency problems; and
- provide direction for subsequent chapters in this book on topics that include but are not limited to how crowdfunding investors, platforms, and entrepreneurs can mitigate agency problems and enhance value.

2.2 Forms of finance

Debt is known as a "fixed claim" as it provides the investors with a fixed return on the investment so long as the entrepreneur is able to repay obligation in full. Common equity is known as a "residual claim" as the investor shares in the upside as the entrepreneurial firm increases in value. Fixed claims versus residual claims are one of the most fundamental distinctions in terms of different forms of finance.

2.2.1 Debt

Debt claims enable higher priority over common equity holders to the investor. Debt typically comes with stipulated interest payments (typically annual or semiannual), but it is theoretically possible to have a "zero-coupon" debt instrument in which there are no interest payments. When interest payments are not made on time and in full, it might be possible for the investor to force the entrepreneurial firm into bankruptcy. If there are no other debt holders or stakeholders to the firm, who have senior claims, a debt holder can force the entrepreneurial firm to repay the interest by liquidating the firm's assets, and this may be done formally in bankruptcy proceedings. Debt holders have a higher priority in bankruptcy than common equity holders.

The payoff to a debt holder is illustrated in Fig. 2.1. If a debt holder is paid in full, he receives the principal (the amount borrowed) and the stream of interest payments from the entrepreneurial firm. The value of a debt contract is the present value of the interest and principal (accounting for the time value of money). If the entrepreneurial firm is sufficiently successful, such that it is able to repay the interest and principal on debt, increases in the value of the entrepreneurial firm do not have any effect on the value of a debt claim. For this reason, the payoff to debt is a straight horizontal line after the level of the preset value of the principal and interest payments. However, if the entrepreneurial firm is not successful and worth less than the present value of the principal and interest, the value of

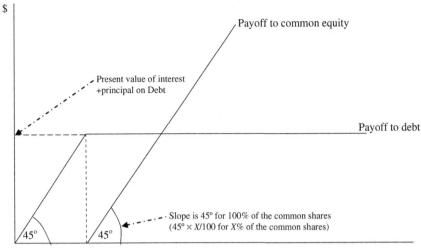

FIGURE 2.1   Payoff functions.

the debt claim varies depending on the value of the entrepreneurial firm. In this type of bankruptcy situation, if there are no other claimants to the firm's assets (such as unpaid wages), the value of the debt claim varies in direct proportion with the value of the entrepreneurial firm. For this reason, we draw a 45% line from the origin in Fig. 2.1 up to the level that represents the present value of the interest and principal.

If a firm has preferred equity, its payoff function would be similar to that of debt (illustrated below in subsection 2.3.4 in Figs. 2.3 and 2.4). Preferred equity is a fixed claim to a stream of preferred dividends for which an investor cannot force a firm into bankruptcy if payment is not made (albeit payments must be made in advance of any common dividends). Preferred equity is not an ownership claim, unlike common equity.

2.2.2 Common equity

Common equity shares enable rights of ownership to the investor. Common equity holders are, however, last in priority behind debt in the event of a bankruptcy. Dividends are not prespecified with common equity (unlike preferred equity). Some firms rarely or almost never pay common equity dividends (Microsoft Corporation, which was founded in 1975, incorporated in 1981, and floated in 1986, announced its first ever dividend payment on January 16, 2003), while other firms more frequently pay dividends. The value of common equity depends on expected dividend payments and capital appreciation. Common equity is a claim to the residual value of the firm: after interest, the principal on debt and preferred dividends are paid, and capital appreciation of the firm enhances the value of common equity shares. For successful entrepreneurial firms that start small but grow to be large companies, the most valuable security is common equity.

2.2.3 Rewards-based crowdfunding

Rewards-based crowdfunding offers neither debt nor common equity to the crowdfunders. Instead, a promise is given to offer a "reward" for the capital contribution. The reward can include the (yet to be made) product that is the subject of the crowdfunding campaign, an opportunity to participate in the development or design of the product and/or a token of appreciation (a small gift or public recognition on a webpage). Often there are multiple levels of rewards depending on the terms of the offering. Typically, companies that go bankrupt after a successful rewards-based crowdfunding campaign will not have completed the project and delivered the product or rewards to the consumers. Products that are completed are delivered upon completion. If a dispute arose in the event of liquidation within a company that had debt and rewards-based crowdfunded obligations, whether or not the crowd received the product or if the product went to unpaid debt holders, it would depend on whether the debt was secured against the inventory. Regardless, obligations of delivering product to crowdfunders would come ahead of any payment that equity owners would expect to receive.

2.3 Agency problems

A principal–agent problem arises when a principal hires an agent under conditions of incomplete and asymmetric information. An agent is responsible for and takes actions that affect the financial returns to the principal. An agent may, however, have either pecuniary or nonpecuniary interests in doing things that are against the interest of the principal. These potentially adverse actions of the agent are referred to as *agency problems*. Contracts can be designed to enable a principal to mitigate agency problems, but agency problems can never be fully eliminated (Farmer & Winter, 1986). The central issue considered in this book is how crowdfunding terms can be designed to mitigate agency problems as best possible.

A common example of the principal–agent relationship is the employer–employee relationship. Since it is impossible to continually monitor the activities of an employee, the employee can do many things that are against the interests of his or her employer. As one example, an employee might shirk responsibilities or not work as efficiently as possible when he or she is not being monitored. Employment contracts can be structured in a way to mitigate agency problems. For example, an employee on a fixed salary has a greater incentive to shirk responsibilities than an employee working on commission or who receives a performance bonus. Since many actions by employees are observable but not verifiable, it is not possible to write contracts that anticipate and address all aspects of an employer–employee relationship, and therefore agency problems will exist to some extent regardless of the structure of the contract. The key to writing a good contract is to recognize that contracts are by definition incomplete and that while every possible eventuality cannot be foreseen, agency problems that can be anticipated must be addressed while mitigating the capacity for other potential agency problems to develop.

The crowdfunding market is particularly interesting for investigating agency problems. Fig. 2.2 illustrates the agency relationships that exist in a typical (albeit simplified) crowdfunding context. Fig. 2.2 considers one crowdfunding platform. There are two

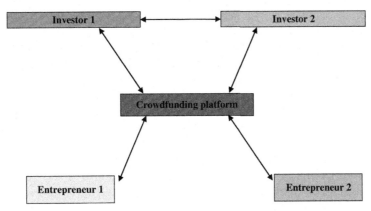

FIGURE 2.2 Principal ↔ agency relationships in crowdfunding, through the platform as an intermediary, abstracting from direct agency relations between entrepreneurs and their investors.

investors. The crowdfunding platform is enabling financing for two entrepreneurial firms. The agency relationships in Fig. 2.2 are presented with the use of arrows, whereby the direction of the arrow points to the agent from the principal. In Fig. 2.2, there are, in fact, 10 distinct agency relationships between different principals and different agents.

Principal	Agent
1. Investor 1	Crowdfunding platform
2. Investor 2	Crowdfunding platform
3. Crowdfunding platform	Investor 1
4. Crowdfunding platform	Investor 2
5. Investor 1	Investor 2
6. Investor 2	Investor 1
7. Entrepreneur 1	Crowdfunding platform
8. Entrepreneur 2	Crowdfunding platform
9. Crowdfunding platform	Entrepreneur 1
10. Crowdfunding platform	Entrepreneur 2

The crowdfunding platform takes steps on behalf of the investors to make sure that the companies listed on the platform are sufficiently high-quality companies by doing various due-diligence checks (agency relationships 1 and 2) (Cumming & Zhang, 2016). The investors on the platform also take steps to make sure that the platform runs a successful business model (agency problems 3 and 4). For example, the Wiseed equity crowdfunding platform in France operates as a membership, whereby each member votes on the projects before they can be listed on the platform. The investors should make an honest effort to evaluate the proposed projects and rank them on different areas (quality of product, management, intellectual property) and suggest a hypothetical investment in the company if the project were to actually go forward (Cumming, Hervé, Manthé, & Schwienbacher, 2017). Members of the crowd in other contexts are viewed more generally to have a social contract to not spread false information about the projects on the platform and to share negative information (including suspected frauds) about the crowdfunding company when they learn about it. For example, a member of the crowd caught the Kobe Beef Jerky fraud, and media on the case reported that "Kickstarter relies on its community to self-police...".[2] As different members of the crowd may take these steps to different degrees affecting each other's well-being, there are agency problems across different investors (agency problems 5 and 6 in the previous table).

Crowdfunding platforms take steps on behalf of their entrepreneurs (agency problems 7 and 8). Some platforms also offer advice and services to improve the quality of the company before it lists on the platform (Cumming & Zhang, 2016). Platforms must also keep the money provided by crowdfunders in the course of a crowdfunding campaign and ensure proper and timely transfer of the funds in the event of a successful offering. Platforms carry out various marketing functions and engage in proper business practices to attract investors to the platform. Platforms charge a fee for these services, and the nature or structure of the fees charged may influence the quality of the services that they offer.

Finally, entrepreneurial firms take steps that affect the crowdfunding platforms (agency problems 9 and 10). Entrepreneurs may make dishonest claims, or even honest mistakes, which in turn affect the reputation and ability of the platform to offer a viable business model. The more successful and honest the entrepreneur with projects that are completed on time and investors who are satisfied, the better-off the platform is in terms of attracting more investors and future entrepreneurs to list with the platform.

Fig. 2.2 highlights the complexity of the agency relationships for a typical, very simplified crowdfunding campaign. For a single transaction, there are numerous agency relationships. Platforms are, of course, much larger and as a business scales up, the scope for agency problems becomes significantly larger. The parties have large stakes invested (in terms of financial, effort, and reputational commitment) over lengthy periods of time involving many interested parties, and there is significant scope for the parties to act in ways that are potentially detrimental to each other's interests.

For ease of presentation, Fig. 2.2 abstracts from the agency problems that exist directly between the investors and the entrepreneurs, and instead focuses on the agency problems through the crowdfunding platform as an intermediary. After crowdfunding is successfully completed, the role of the platform is diminished, and a financial agreement exists between the entrepreneur and the investors. As such, there is a bilateral agency problem between the entrepreneur and each of the investors.

In the next section, we highlight some of the common agency problems that exist in crowdfunding campaigns. The ways in which entrepreneurs and investors can act against each other's interests can be categorized into different areas, and these areas are listed later under the following headings[3]: moral hazard, bilateral moral hazard, multitask moral hazard, adverse selection, free riding, holdup, trilateral bargaining, window dressing, underinvestment, asset

---

[2] https://money.cnn.com/2013/06/17/technology/kickstarter-scam-kobe-jerky/.

[3] Practitioners might refer to these terms as academic jargon, but these terms do enable us to identify the particular agency problem at hand.

stripping, and risk shifting. These agency problems are explained in the context of the use of different securities identified earlier in Section 2.2.

2.3.1 Moral hazard

The term *moral hazard* most commonly refers to the prospect of an agent not exerting the best effort (against the interest of the principal) in view of his diminished accountability. This effort will, in turn, affect the expected payoff of the principal. It is not possible to write a contract to enforce effort. Effort is potentially observable but not verifiable and therefore unenforceable (it would generally be implausible to sue someone for "a lack of effort"). It is, however, possible to write contracts to incentivize effort, which is very important in financing contexts where the effort of each party affects the expected value of the entrepreneurial venture (including crowdfunding but also angel finance and venture capital finance).

Recall the different securities identified earlier in Section 2.2. An agent's effort is an increasing function of her residual claim (share in the profits) to the venture.[4] The intuition is straightforward. The entrepreneur and the investors take unobservable actions that affect the expected payoff to be divided between them. The effort of each agent yields a positive externality on the other party, but such an effort is costly to both parties. As such, when bankruptcy is not expected, the entrepreneur's effort into a venture is a decreasing function of the relative amount of common equity provided to the investor. A sharing rule that provides a greater equity share to the investor yields more (less) investor (entrepreneurial) effort. If the contracting objective is to mitigate moral hazard costs (and abstracting from all other possible contracting objectives and other types of agency problems) and the investor is not expected to provide effort, it makes sense to provide the investor with a fixed claim security (crowdlending or rewards-based crowdfunding). If the investor is expected to provide effort, it makes sense to provide the investor with at least some common equity.

Moral hazard is also apparent in the contract terms with the crowdfunding platform. Platforms that charge a fixed fee regardless of the crowdfunding outcome may not provide as great an effort in carrying out due diligence as a platform that takes a percentage fee relative to the funds raised by the campaign. Many platforms, for example, charge a fee of (approximately) 5% of the capital raised by each campaign.

In short, moral hazard tells us that an agent's incentive in maximizing effort is an increasing function of the agent's residual claim to the entrepreneurial venture.

2.3.2 Bilateral moral hazard

Situations that involve agency relationships, such as that the contracting parties are both principals and agents, are referred to as *bilateral agency relationships*. In Fig. 2.2, crowdfunding platforms are in a bilateral moral hazard relationship with both their investor and their entrepreneurs. Also, the investors in Fig. 2.2 are in a bilateral moral hazard relationship with one another.

---

[4] See, for example, Tirole (1998: 35–36).

2.3.3 Multitask moral hazard

Multitask moral hazard refers to situations that involve multiple tasks the agent may undertake, and only a subset of these tasks benefit the principal (Holmstrom & Milgrom, 1991). A common example of multitask moral hazard involves the entrepreneurs as principals and the crowdfunding platform as the agent. The crowdfunding platform will have more than one entrepreneur on the platform and hence has multiple tasks as an agent for different entrepreneurial firms. The platform may spend comparatively more time helping a specific entrepreneurial firm on the platform. Also, the platform with too many listed firms per employee may not take appropriate steps to do proper due diligence checks before listing all of the firms (i.e., they are too busy).

2.3.4 Adverse selection

Moral hazard, bilateral moral hazard, and multitask moral hazard refer to agency problems that may arise after a contract is initiated between a principal and agent (ex post). An agency problem also exists even before a contract is signed (ex ante). This agency problem is known as *adverse selection*. The seminal work on adverse selection by George Akerlof, Michael Spence, and Joseph Stiglitz led to their joint Sveriges Riksbank Prize in Economic Sciences in Memory of Alfred Nobel in 2001 (also known as the Nobel Memorial Prize in Economic Sciences).[5]

At a general level, in the context of contracting, adverse selection refers to the problem that offers of different types of contracts attract different types of parties to the contract. This problem is usefully illustrated in the context of offers of nonconvertible debt versus common equity finance. An investor that offers debt finance will attract a different type of entrepreneur than an investor that offers equity finance (DeMeza & Webb, 1987; Stiglitz & Weiss, 1981). We illustrate this proposition by considering two examples. In the first example, we consider entrepreneurs that differ by their level of risk and not their expected mean return. In the second example, we consider entrepreneurs that differ by their expected return and not by their level of risk.

First, let us consider entrepreneurial firms that have the same expected value but different expected risk. In statistics, we would say that the entrepreneurial firms have the same first moment (expect return) but different second moments (expected risk) of the returns distribution. This situation is illustrated in the top part of Fig. 2.3, which presents probability distribution functions (graphs of the expected value of the entrepreneurial firm under different states of nature). In Fig. 2.3, Entrepreneur 1 is riskier than Entrepreneur 2. There is a high probability than Entrepreneur 1 will be very valuable (a "home run"), but also a high probability that Entrepreneur 1 will go bankrupt. Entrepreneur 2, by contrast, has a high probability of a modest value and a low probability of being a home run and going bankrupt. Due to the high risk, Entrepreneur 1 is referred to as a "nut" in the work by

---

[5] See http://nobelprize.org/nobel_prizes/economics/laureates/2001/public.html. Akerlof's (1970) work was in the context of the market for lemons (such as that for used cars). Spence's (1973) work was in the context of job market signaling. Stiglitz's work was largely in the context of contracting (see, e.g., Stiglitz & Weiss, 1981), which is of course primarily our interest in this book.

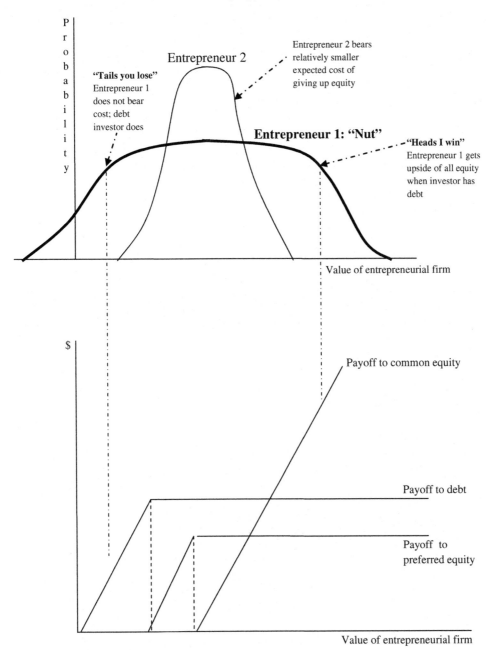

FIGURE 2.3   Debt attracts nuts.

Stiglitz and Weiss (1981) and related work. In practice, we might think of Entrepreneur 1 as a high-tech firm or an internet startup and Entrepreneur 2 as a manufacturing firm for a generic product that has a stable demand from consumers.

Entrepreneur 1 is more likely to be attracted to offers of (straight or nonconvertible) debt financing or rewards-based crowdfunding than offers of common equity financing. If Entrepreneur 1's venture turns out to be successful, he/she is better-off by holding all of the common equity and not sharing common equity with the investor. In Fig. 2.3, this is indicated at the point labeled "Heads I win," which is what Entrepreneur 1 says (to himself in reference to the investor) if the project turns out successfully and the investor has nonconvertible debt. If Entrepreneur 1 had common equity financing, he/she would have to share the upside of the successful project with the investor and thereby significantly dilute the profits that he/she would enjoy as an owner. In the payoff diagram below the probability distribution functions in Fig. 2.3, notice the difference between the value of common equity and nonconvertible debt.

The case of "Heads I win" is perhaps best exemplified in practice by the Kickstarter rewards-based crowdfunding campaign of Oculus Rift.[6] The campaign raised $2.4 million on Kickstarter in 2012, but then the entrepreneurs sold the company for $2 billion in March 2014 on Facebook.[7,8] A few days after the sale, media reported "fury" among the crowd insofar as the crowd financed the venture but was inappropriately compensated.[9]

Now suppose Entrepreneur 1's venture turns out to be unsuccessful. If Entrepreneur 1 is financed by debt, the investor is able to reclaim any value left in the firm in bankruptcy. In Fig. 2.3, this point is labeled "Tails you lose," which is what Entrepreneur 1 says (to himself in reference to the investor) if the investor is left with little or no salvage value of the firm's assets in bankruptcy (see the payoff diagram in the lower part of Fig. 2.3). Entrepreneur 1 is not personally liable in bankruptcy and only loses the value of his or her investment. Discharge from bankruptcy is effective almost immediately in many countries (see Armour & Cumming, 2008, for details across Canada, Europe, and the United States), which means the entrepreneur is able to immediately start another business.[10]

Entrepreneur 2 has a much lower expected opportunity cost of giving up common equity to the investor than Entrepreneur 1. There is a very low probability than Entrepreneur 2 will be extremely valuable, and hence, Entrepreneur 2 does not lose as much as Entrepreneur 1 from giving up common equity to the investor. In fact, Entrepreneur 2 may have an incentive to sell common equity to the investor to encourage

---

[6] https://www.kickstarter.com/projects/1523379957/oculus-rift-step-into-the-game.

[7] https://www.inc.com/walter-chen/how-oculus-vr-crowdfunded-their-way-to-a-2-billion-business-a-6-step-checklist.html.

[8] https://arstechnica.com/gaming/2014/03/facebook-purchases-vr-headset-maker-oculus-for-2-billion/.

[9] https://www.theguardian.com/technology/shortcuts/2014/mar/26/oculus-rift-facebook-fury-kickstarter-funders.

[10] In part, this will involve a reputation cost. However, some investors have been known to view an entrepreneur's experience with bankruptcy as a valuable experience. See Armour and Cumming (2006, 2008).

the investor in taking steps to increase the expected value of the venture (recall the earlier moral hazard problem with the investor as the agent).

In short, an adverse selection problem of offering debt financing is that debt attracts nuts under conditions in which entrepreneurs differ in terms of their expected risk but not in terms of the expected value.

The adverse selection problem is rather different; however, if entrepreneurs diverge in terms of their expected value and not in terms of their risk. This situation is illustrated in Fig. 2.4.

In Fig. 2.4, Entrepreneur 3 is a "lemon" with a low expected value. Entrepreneurs 3 and 4, however, do have the same expected risk in that the second moment of the probability distribution (the width of the probability distribution functions) is the same for Entrepreneurs 3 and 4. In this case, Entrepreneur 4 is relatively more attracted to offers of debt financing and Entrepreneur 3 is relatively more attracted to offers of equity financing. First, note that at point A in Fig. 2.4, Entrepreneur 3 has a comparatively low expected opportunity cost of giving up equity for the probability at point A relative to the same probability level for Entrepreneur 4 at point B. Conversely, at point C, Entrepreneur 3 is in bankruptcy, and there is a high probability that Entrepreneur 3 is also in bankruptcy. If the investor holds debt at point C, Entrepreneur 3 faces a permanent loss in decision rights over the firm in bankruptcy (in terms of a reorganization or complete liquidation), and loses all priority to the investor that holds debt. Overall, therefore debt is much less attractive to Entrepreneur 3 than to Entrepreneur 4, and the opportunity cost of giving up common equity is much lower for Entrepreneur 3 than Entrepreneur 4. In fact, Entrepreneur 3 may have an incentive in giving common equity to the investor for encouraging him/her to take steps in increasing the expected value of the venture (recall the earlier moral hazard problem with the investor as the agent) and shift the probability distribution of Entrepreneur 3 to the right.

In short, an adverse selection problem of offering common equity financing is that common equity attracts lemons, under conditions in which entrepreneurs differ in terms of their expected value but not in terms of their risk.

Empirical evidence is consistent with the view that equity crowdfunding attracts, on average, lemons (Blaseg, Cumming, & Koetter, 2019). The theory and evidence are discussed further in Chapter 15, Introduction to crowdfunding regulation and policy. In short, the average equity-crowdfunded project is of lower quality, but nevertheless, there are outliers with large returns that make investment highly attractive in some instances. In some ways, it is a bit like "lottery stocks" in junior stock markets such as the Alternative Investment Market in the United Kingdom and the Toronto Venture Exchange in Canada, whereby the average quality may be lower, but the outlier returns can be very pronounced (Carpentier, Cumming, & Suret, 2012).

Empirical evidence is also consistent with entrepreneurs' signaling their ability in mitigating the costs of adverse selection. Chapter 10, Signaling in equity crowdfunding and Chapter 11, Are equity crowdfunders sensitive to distance? present theory and evidence. An effective signal is one that is costly, and the cost cannot be easily replicated by lower quality entrepreneurs. For example, potential signals of quality include establishing a highly educated board of directors, developing a patent, or committing to not undertake the project (and returning the money to the crowdfunders) unless the campaign goal is reached.

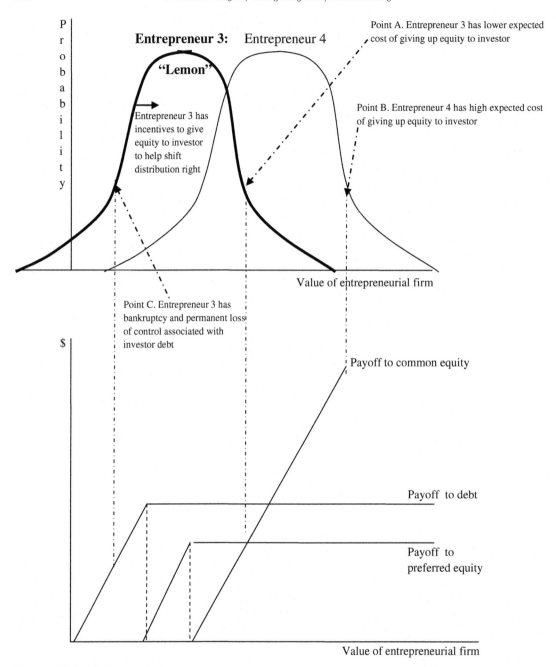

FIGURE 2.4   Equity attracts lemons.

2.3.5 Free riding

Free riding is an agency problem that exists in the context of ventures in which the effort of different agents is substitutable. For example, in the context of a crowdfunded investment, one investor may free ride off the due diligence efforts of another syndicated investor.

2.3.6 Holdup

Holdup refers to situations of expropriation in which there is unequal bargaining power between different parties to a contract. The terms of the original contract may be renegotiated if the party with stronger bargaining power decides to "hold up" the other party.

In some situations the entrepreneur may hold up the investors. Suppose the investor contributes a very large amount of capital to finance the venture, and the entrepreneur is the only person capable of ensuring the success of the venture. Suppose the entrepreneur receives an attractive employment offer by another company after receiving financing from the investor. If the entrepreneur accepts the offer, the venture fails. In this case, the entrepreneur is in a position to renegotiate the initial terms of the investment with the investors. For this reason, many venture capital contracts incorporate terms, whereby the entrepreneur's stock options do not become effective until 3 (or more) years after the initial contract or upon achieving a significant milestone such as public floatation (Cumming & Johan, 2013a). In equity-crowdfunded campaigns, however, such terms are scantly observed. In other situations the investors may hold up the entrepreneur; however, with dispersed investments across a large crowd, it is significantly less plausible (although theoretically possible) to observe coordinated strategic investor behavior.

2.3.7 Trilateral bargaining

Consider an equity-crowdfunded campaign. Suppose the entrepreneur has control over the firm and the ability to decide whether to sell the right of control to a different investor (a third party). The entrepreneur might consider selling control to a third party in situations where the entrepreneurial firm is approaching the possibility of bankruptcy unless the entrepreneur is able to lower its cost of capital. By selling control to a third party, the entrepreneur is able to obtain cheaper external capital and mitigate the possibility of bankruptcy. By mitigating bankruptcy the entrepreneur is better-off, and by gaining control rights, the third party is better-off (the deal between the entrepreneur and the third party is voluntary, and therefore by definition the entrepreneur and third party are better-off). The initial crowdfunded investors, however, are potentially harmed by this transaction. The initial investor did not undertake the initial investment in the entrepreneur to have decisions made by an unknown third-party investor. It is possible that the third-party investor makes decisions about the future of the firm that counter the interests of the initial investor, such as selling assets or investing over a different time horizon than initially contemplated, among other things.

These situations of third-party sales are referred to as trilateral bargaining, which have been studied in the theoretical literature in contracting (Aghion & Bolton, 1992) and specifically in the theoretical literature in venture capital contracting (Berglöf, 1994). Contracts can be written in a way to mitigate the possibility of a trilateral bargaining agency problem arising. On the contrary, with large dispersed investors, such contracts would have to be standardized with the platform that arranges the offering. Alternatively, regulation could be put in place, which limits the scope-permissible actions by the entrepreneur in contexts such as this one.

2.3.8 Window dressing

At a general level, window dressing refers to making one look better on the surface relative to what lies beneath. Much of corporate fraud has been some form of window dressing or another; for example, the accounting scandals (cooking the books) that led to the demise of Enron and Arthur Andersen (among other things of course). Window dressing typically has short-term benefits (such as attracting more capital from external investors) but longer term costs (when investors realize that circumstances are not what they initially appeared to be).

2.3.9 Underinvestment

Underinvestment does *not* refer to investors providing too little capital. Rather, it refers to entrepreneurs who do not have sufficient incentives to provide effort in ensuring project success. Underinvestment is an agency problem associated with debt finance. In Fig. 2.5, consider an entrepreneur financed by debt and currently at point A. An investment opportunity comes along, which would enable the value of the firm to increase from point A to point B. The entrepreneur will have to work to ensure that this investment opportunity comes to fruition. Will the entrepreneur undertake the opportunity? Not likely. The entrepreneur's income as a common equity holder is not improved at all by putting forth effort in increasing the value of the firm from A to B. Only the debt holder benefits from the

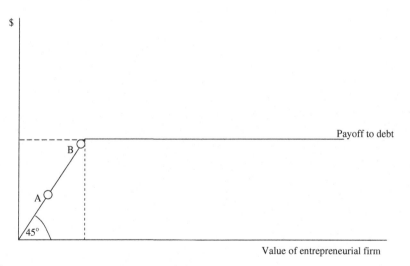

FIGURE 2.5   Agency problem of underinvestment.

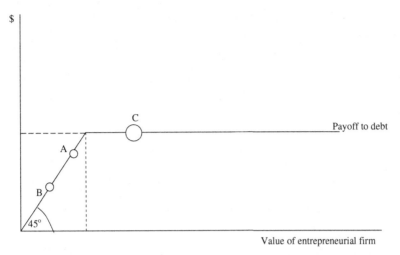

FIGURE 2.6   Agency problem of asset stripping.

entrepreneur's effort. This is viewed as an agency problem since the move from A to B is a positive net-present-value project, which is beneficial to the investor (principal) but not carried out by the entrepreneur (agent).

2.3.10 Asset stripping

Asset stripping is an agency problem, which is most pronounced with external debt finance. Suppose in Fig. 2.6, the entrepreneur believes the firm is at point A, but the entrepreneur has superior information about the prospects of the firm than the investor. The entrepreneur tells the investor that the firm is at point C. Thereafter the entrepreneur starts to remove assets from the firm (e.g., computers, office supplies), travels to unnecessary scientific conferences in Hawaii and the Caribbean (unnecessary from the perspective of adding value to the entrepreneurial firm) at the firm's expense, and throws an extravagant Christmas party for all of the employees (again at the firm's expense). All of these activities are against the interest of the debt investor. Suppose the company goes bankrupt 6 months after these activities transpire. The firm could have been at point A if these activities had not taken place, but because they did, the firm is now at point B. Essentially, by stripping assets in these different ways, the entrepreneur steals from the investor. On the contrary, this type of asset stripping is difficult to prove in a court of law as the burden is on the investor to prove that not only were the actions taken outside the course of ordinary business and outside the entrepreneur's authority but also that the entrepreneur knew the firm was facing bankruptcy when these decisions were made.

2.3.11 Risk shifting

Risk shifting is very similar to the agency problem of adverse selection (discussed earlier), with the difference being that adverse selection is an ex ante contract agency problem while risk shifting is an ex post contract problem. Risk shifting is most pronounced for firms that are debt financed (Green, 1984). Suppose an entrepreneur has a business plan that fits with the profile of Entrepreneur 2 in Fig. 2.3. Then, after obtaining debt financing, the entrepreneur changes the profile of the firm by undertaking projects that have significantly greater risks but potentially greater payoffs. Entrepreneurs that are debt financed capture the increase in expected value associated with the increase in risk, because they gain in the expected upside without having to share the proceeds of the gain with the debt investor. Conversely, if the gamble of changing the firm's profile does not work out and the firm goes bankrupt, it is the investor that bears the cost.

By analogy, consider a friend, a jockey who borrows money from you to buy a stallion. Instead of using the money to buy the stallion, the friend takes the money to Las Vegas and bets it all on a hand of poker. If the friend wins the hand, you get paid back (but do not expect anything extra in terms of a share of the winnings). If the friend loses, you do not get paid back.

Examples in entrepreneurial finance are not so extreme but nevertheless present. Consider for instance a biotechnology firm that seeks to develop additives for foods based on natural (nongenetically modified) processes. After receiving financing, the firm then decides to take on the extra risk of working on engineering genetically modified organisms (GMOs). The production of GMOs is inherently more risky and may give rise to consumer controversies that limit returns to the investment (increasing the downside risk) (Cumming & MacIntosh, 2000a, 2000b). At the same time, however, incorporating GMOs in the product line increases the potential profit margins.

In short, firms financed by debt have greater incentives to make decisions that increase the risk profile of the firm to transfer expected wealth from the debt holders (investor) to the equity holders (the entrepreneurs).

2.4 Does mitigating agency problems enhance firm value?

Firms with lower expected agency problems have higher expected values. For seminal work on the topic, see Jensen and Meckling (1976) and Jensen (1986, 2001, 2004).

The literature on optimal capital structure and firm value originated with Modigliani and Miller (1958). Modigliani and Miller showed that in an ideal world without taxes and without agency problems, capital structure is irrelevant. The intuition is easily understood with the help of one of Yogi Berra's famous quotes: "You better cut the pizza in four pieces because I'm not hungry enough to eat six." In terms of financing a firm, how you divide up the claims between investors does not affect value. The irrelevance of capital structure is depicted graphically by the horizontal line in Fig. 2.7.

Miller and Modigliani (1963) published a correction of their original hypothesis upon recognition that interest on debt is tax deductible. In effect, firms that take on more debt reduce their tax burden and hence increase firm value. This is depicted graphically by the constant upward sloping line in Fig. 2.7.

Since firms are almost never financed by 100% debt, the Miller and Modigliani (1963) story is incomplete. Jensen and Meckling (1976) argue that there are agency costs associated with different capital structures. Indeed, numerous examples were provided in this

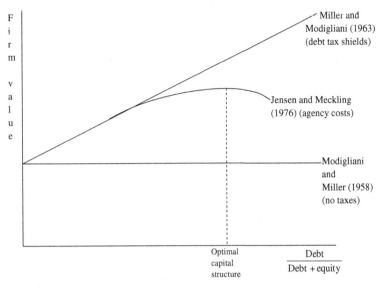

FIGURE 2.7   Capital structure and firm value.

chapter. As agency costs of debt increase (along with risk of bankruptcy), firm value will eventually decline when a firm takes on too much debt. This effect is depicted in Fig. 2.7. Numerous empirical studies support the Jensen and Meckling (1976) thesis, and as such Jensen and Meckling (1976) is one of the most cited academic papers in economics and finance.

In addition to capital structure choices, there are other mechanisms by which agency problems can be mitigated in the context of crowdfunding. These mechanisms include the use of contractual voting rights, and national regulation, for example. The various mechanisms are discussed throughout this book.

In sum, there is ample theory and evidence in support of the view that agency problems are paramount in crowdfunding.

Agency costs are a highly theoretical concept. Theory can only take us so far... at the end of the day, we seek to apply theory to practice to see what is relevant in the real world. To this end, this book makes use of a large amount of data in each of the ensuing chapters. Chapter 3, Overview of institutional contexts and empirical methods, therefore reviews the statistical and econometric tools used in the data analyses in the subsequent sections of this book.

2.5 Summary and steps forward in the remaining chapters

In this chapter, we explained the payoffs to investing with debt and common equity versus rewards-based crowdfunding. We then reviewed a menu of different agency problems in entrepreneurial finance and used payoffs with different securities to illustrate when these agency problems might be more pronounced. Thereafter we explained that mitigating agency problems is a central mechanism by which firm value can be enhanced.

A central objective of the remainder of this book is to consider ways in which agency problems in entrepreneurial finance can be mitigated through various mechanisms through contracting, due diligence, and regulation. We will argue and empirically provide evidence that the effective due diligence, signaling, and regulation translates into more successful crowdfunding campaigns. To this end, it is important to have a good grasp of agency problems identified in this chapter prior to considering further the rest of this book.

While this chapter focused on agency theory and, to a lesser extent, signaling theory, there are other theories that have been advanced in crowdfunding research, which have been viewed to be pertinent in various contexts. These theories include, but are not limited, to observational learning theory (Colombo, Franzoni, & Rossi-Lamastra, 2015; Vismara, 2018) (which highlights a role of attention, retention, reproduction, and motivation in learning), social capital theory (Vismara, 2016) (how a person's position and participation within a group forms, is influenced by, and influences others), and social network theory (Polzin, Toxopeus, & Stam, 2018) (the interaction of people within a network). A full discussion of those theories is beyond the scope of this chapter, but they do lend themselves naturally to the crowdfunding context and hence periodically consider ideas related to these theories.

Key terms

Debt
Rewards-based crowdfunding
Common equity
Fixed claimant
Residual claimant
Capital structure
Security design
Monitoring
Agency cost
Information asymmetry
Moral hazard
Bilateral moral hazard
Multitask moral hazard
Adverse selection
Lemon
Nut
Free riding
Holdup
Trilateral bargaining
Window dressing
Underinvestment
Asset stripping
Risk shifting

Discussion questions

2.1. True/False/Uncertain: "Agency costs associated with financing entrepreneurial firms can be completely eliminated."

2.2. True/False/Uncertain: "Rewards-based crowdfunding gives investors a residual claim to the entrepreneurial firm."

2.3. True/False/Uncertain: "Agency problems are more pronounced for equity crowdfunding than marketplace lending and rewards-based crowdfunding."

2.4. How might social capital, social networks, and learning affect agency problems and the ability to signal ability?

2.5. Describe and explain the following agency problems in the context of financing an entrepreneurial firm:

    a. Adverse selection

    b. Asset stripping

    c. Free riding

    d. Holdup

    e. Moral hazard

    f. Multitask moral hazard

    g. Risk shifting

    h. Trilateral bargaining

    i. Underinvestment

    j. Window dressing

    Use graphs where appropriate.

Overview of institutional contexts and empirical methods

3.1 Introduction and learning objectives

This chapter comprises two main parts. The first part of this chapter provides an overview of international differences in the institutional and legal settings in different countries around the world from which data are considered in this book. This material provides a basis for understanding potential sources for differences in crowdfunding markets across countries. International differences across countries are quantified with the use of indices to reflect differences in legal standards, which enables empirical comparisons of crowdfunding markets across countries in the subsequent chapters of this book.

The second part of this chapter then summarizes the statistical and econometric methods used in each of the chapters herein. The statistics and econometrics review is nontechnical and accessible for all readers regardless of background, so that all readers may follow along each of the subsequent chapters. It is important to review large datasets from multiple countries to draw generalizable lessons about crowdfunding markets in practice. Without considering data, propositions about the apparent efficient capital raising in crowdfunding might be inaccurate or at least inapplicable to practice. Without considering data from a multitude of countries, inferences drawn might be attributable to the institutional context in a single country and not generalizable to other markets.

In this chapter we will

- provide an overview of the legal and institutional context considered in the different countries studied in the ensuing chapters of this book;
- review basic statistical and econometric methods for empirically studying crowdfunding markets.

3.2 An overview of the international institutional context

Differences in crowdfunding across countries might be attributable to a variety factors, including but not limited to

- law, such as legal origin (English, French, German, and Scandinavian), as well as the degree to which a country's rules protect minority shareholders and creditors;
- culture, such as differences in the extent to which societies are individualistic versus supportive of one another, and the degree to which people in society are risk averse, or have a long-term orientation;
- economic conditions, such as GDP per capita or the size of a country's stock market.

Some of the main legal differences across the countries considered in this book are summarized in Table 3.1. There are numerous established indices of law quality around the world. Legal origin is perhaps the most widely recognized benchmark for international legal differences, following La Porta, Lopez-de-Silanes, Shleifer, and Vishny (1997; La Porta, Lopez-de-Silanes, Shleifer, & Vishny, 1998). The primary legal origins are English, French, German, and Scandinavian legal origin. French, German, and Scandinavian legal origin countries follow the civil law tradition, while English legal origin countries follow the common one. La Porta et al. (1998) explain that civil laws afford weaker legal protection than common law countries. Common law countries do not enable rules that block shares for block shareholder meetings, more often have laws protecting oppressed minorities, require relatively little share capital to call an extraordinary shareholder meeting, and enable stronger enforcement of these and other shareholder rights (La Porta et al., 1998). Similarly, common law countries offer creditors stronger legal protections against managers in terms of being more likely to guarantee priority rules in bankruptcy for secured creditors and precluding managers from unilaterally seeking court protection from creditors (La Porta et al., 1998). Furthermore, common law systems afford greater flexibility and react faster to new developments and governance mechanisms relative to civil law systems.

As well, within and across different legal origins, there is significant variance in law quality on a country-by-country basis. Common measures of law quality include the strength of minority investor protection (thereby spurring minority equity investors) and strength of creditor rights (thereby spurring lending markets). These measures are widely reported and updated annually by the World Bank at doingbusiness.org; see also La Porta et al. (1998). These indices are briefly summarized in Table 3.1. For these legal indices a higher index value indicates better substantive legal content pertaining to investing the quality and likelihood of enforcement. Note that legal indices refer to the laws of the country of residence of the entrepreneurial firm. Rau (2018) notes that from surveys of different platforms in different countries around the world, total crowdfunding volume is explained by different legal indices and is less closely connected to measures of social factors.[1]

---

[1] Rau's (2019) data are in part summarized in Table 3.1. Note, however, that these data are not completely exhaustive of all of the crowdfunding data in each country; for example, there are less than half of the number of platforms in Canada in Rau's (2019) data than that which are reported by https://ncfacanada. org/canadian-crowdfunding-directory/. See also *infra* note 2 and accompanying text.

TABLE 3.1 Legal, cultural, and economic conditions around the world.

Country	Legal origin					Legal indices		Hofstede indices						GDP per capital (2018)	Est. crowdfunding volume ($ millions, averaged 2015–16) (Rau, 2019)	Countries in which data are from in this book
	English	French	German	Scandinavian	Communist	Strength of minority investor protection (0–100)	Strength of insolvency framework index (0–16)	Power distance index	Individualism index	Masculinity index	Uncertainty avoidance index	Long-term orientation index	Indulgence index			
Argentina	0	1	0	0	0	61.67	9.5	49	46	56	86	20	62	$11,653	11.07	5,6,18
Australia	1	0	0	0	0	60	11	38	90	61	51	21	71	$57,305	476.45	5,6,9,10,15,18
Austria	0	0	1	0	0	68.33	11	11	55	79	70	60	63	$51,513	19.14	5,6,18
Belgium	0	1	0	0	0	61.67	11.5	65	75	54	94	82	57	$46,556	52.80	5,6,18
Brazil	0	1	0	0	0	65	13	69	38	49	76	44	59	$8921	56.78	5,6,18
Canada	1	0	0	0	0	78.33	11	39	80	52	48	36	68	$46,125	270.8	5,6,7,15,16,18,19
China	0	0	1	0	0	55	11.5	80	20	66	30	87	24	$9771	169,007.54	5,6,18,19
Czech Rep	0	0	1	0	0	58.33	14	57	58	57	74	70	29	$22,973	22.55	5,6,18
Denmark	0	0	0	1	0	66.67	12	18	74	16	23	35	70	$60,596	62.58	5,6,18
Finland	0	0	0	1	0	58.33	14.5	33	63	26	59	38	57	$49,960	115.86	5,6,18
France	0	1	0	0	0	66.67	11	68	71	43	86	63	48	$41,464	433.56	5,6,18
Germany	0	0	1	0	0	58.33	15	35	67	66	65	83	40	$48,196	325.15	5,6,7,14,15,18
Greece	0	1	0	0	0	63.33	12	60	35	57	112	45	50	$20,324	2.00	5,6,18
Hong Kong	1	0	0	0	0	78.33	6	68	25	57	29	61	17	$48,717	6.70	5,6,15
Hungary	1	0	0	0	0	50	10	46	80	88	82	58	31	$15,939	0.43	5,6,18
Indonesia	0	0	0	1	0	80	8.5	78	14	46	48	62	38	$3894	18.81	5,6,18
India	1	0	0	0	0	63.33	10.5	77	48	56	40	51	26	$20,016	82.04	5,6,18,19
Iran	0	1	0	0	0	33.33	5	58	41	43	59	14	40	$5628	0.16	5,6,18
Ireland	1	0	0	0	0	75	10.5	28	70	68	35	24	65	$77,450	43.73	5,6,15,18
Israel	1	0	0	0	0	73.33	12.5	13	54	47	81	38	NA	$41,614	131.27	5,6,18
Italy	0	1	0	0	0	58.33	13.5	50	76	70	75	61	30	$34,318	88.11	5,6,18
Japan	0	0	1	0	0	60	14	54	46	95	92	88	42	$39,287	379.34	5,6,18

(*Continued*)

TABLE 3.1 (Continued)

Country	Legal origin					Legal indices		Hofstede indices						GDP per capital (2018)	Est. crowdfunding volume ($ millions, averaged 2015–16) (Rau, 2019)	Countries in which data are from in this book
	English	French	German	Scandinavian	Communist	Strength of minority investor protection (0–100)	Strength of insolvency framework index (0–16)	Power distance index	Individualism index	Masculinity index	Uncertainty avoidance index	Long-term orientation index	Indulgence index			
Luxembourg	0	1	0	0	0	48.33	7	40	60	50	70	64	56	$114,340	0.17	5,6,18
Malaysia	1	0	0	0	0	81.67	7.5	104	26	50	36	41	57	$11,239	5.82	5,6,18
Netherlands	0	1	0	0	0	58.33	11.5	38	80	14	53	67	68	$52,978	172.31	5,6,18
New Zealand	1	0	0	0	0	81.67	8.5	22	79	58	49	33	75	$41,966	245.51	5,6,7,18
Norway	0	0	0	1	0	75	11.5	31	69	8	50	35	55	$81,807	3.47	5,6,18,19
Philippines	0	1	0	0	0	40	14	94	32	64	44	27	42	$3103	0.06	5,6,18
Poland	0	0	1	0	0	61.67	14	68	60	64	93	38	29	$15,424	26.91	5,6,18
Portugal	0	1	0	0	0	60	14.5	63	27	31	104	28	33	$23,146	3.38	5,6,18
Russia	0	0	0	0	1	61.67	11.5	93	39	36	95	81	20	$11,289	6.71	5,6,18
Singapore	1	0	0	0	0	80	8.5	74	20	48	8	72	46	$64,582	101.75	5,6,18
Korea South	0	0	1	0	0	73.33	12	60	18	39	85	100	29	$31,363	208.74	5,6,18
Spain	0	1	0	0	0	70	12	57	51	42	86	48	44	$30,524	101.28	5,6,15
Sweden	0	0	0	1	0	68.33	12	31	71	5	29	53	78	$54,112	55.03	5,6,18,19
Switzerland	0	0	1	0	0	50	12	34	68	70	58	66	66	$82,839	25.88	5,6,18
Taiwan	0	0	1	0	0	73.33	10.5	58	17	45	69	93	49	$24,971	32.65	5,6,18
United Kingdom	1	0	0	0	0	75	11	35	89	66	35	51	69	$42,491	5829.85	5,6,7,12,13,15,18,19
United States	1	0	0	0	0	64.67	15	40	91	62	46	26	68	$62,641	35,356.36	5,6,7,15,18,19

Note that the same set of countries is not simultaneously considered in each chapter in this book. The primary reason is data availability. Unlike companies listed on stock exchanges, crowdfunding companies are not compelled to report their information to the public. Some information is available from crowdfunding platforms and associations in different countries, while more detailed information typically must be hand collected through the use of surveys or web-scraping techniques. These issues are discussed further in Section 3.3. Despite general data limitations in studying crowdfunding, the data presented in this book represent some of the largest and most detailed crowdfunding datasets available from anywhere in the world.

Apart from legal standards, culture may influence international differences in crowdfunding markets. Hofstede (1991, 2001, 2011) characterizes culture in a number of different dimensions, including power distance, individualism, masculinity, uncertainty avoidance, long-term orientation, and indulgence. These national cultural traits may explain international differences in crowdfunding practices. For example, in low power distance societies, people strive to equalize the distribution of power and might, therefore, be more inclined to equalize access to capital through crowdfunding, while in high power distance society there is a greater adherence to inequalities and less democratization in the access to capital. In highly individualistic societies, there may be naturally less interest cultural attraction to crowdfunding. Masculine societies are more include toward competition, while feminine societies are more inclined toward cooperation and sharing, which could be correlated with the extent and type of successful crowdfunding. In more uncertainty avoidance societies, there is more risk aversion, which could negatively affect interest in crowdfunding. Societies that score low on long-term orientation societies prefer to maintain time-honored traditions, while societies that score high on long-term orientation respect the past but also prepare for the future. Indulgent societies are driven by enjoying life and having fun, while societies characterized by restraint suppress gratification in strict social norms, which too could affect the extent and type of crowdfunding that is adopted in a society. It is possible that these cultural forces shape not only crowdfunding market development in different countries but also the types of crowdfunding, as explained in Chapter 6, Crowdfunding cleantech.[2]

Finally, it is important to acknowledge that international differences in crowdfunding markets may reflect differences in the country's economic conditions such as the size of the country's stock market or GDP per capita. Economic and legal conditions are in fact highly positively correlated, which needs to be taken into account in empirical analyses. Techniques for such empirical analyses are described in the next section.

3.3 Statistics and econometrics used in this book

This section summarizes the econometric methods used in each of the chapters in this book. The description of the econometric techniques used is brief and nontechnical for

---

[2] The data in Chapter 6, Crowdfunding cleantech, are based on actual scraping and actual campaigns and not survey replies, in contrast to Rau (2018, 2019). The differences in the type of data and way in which the data are collected can have a strong impact on the results.

ease of reference. The description is provided here to enable a reader who is unfamiliar with statistics and/or econometrics to follow all of the chapters.

3.3.1 Why use statistics and econometrics and not case studies?

Datasets are collections of cases. In this book, we employ statistics and econometrics to study datasets, or collections of cases, as a way to complement discussion of individual cases. This book focuses on data analyses, because we believe it is difficult to draw generalizable lessons from individual cases alone. Individual cases are idiosyncratic and hence do not lend themselves well to forming generalizable principles. Nevertheless, individual cases do highlight the decision-making process in practice and hence are helpful complements to analyses of larger datasets.

Analyses of datasets will enable the reader to study the likely effect of inputs or outputs. For example, to address a generally framed question "what is the optimal structure of a crowdfunding campaign?", or a more specifically framed question "is it appropriate for an entrepreneur to give up cash flow and control rights in a crowdfunding campaign such as voting shares?", it is worthwhile to examine a large amount of crowdfunding data, many different types of campaigns, instead of considering one (or a few) specific case studies. Further, where possible, it is worthwhile to examine data from a multitude of countries as single-country studies are possibly distorted by institutional or legal factors. Large datasets enable one to assess at the same time a multitude of causal factors that might have influenced the outcome of interest.

3.3.2 What are the steps in analyzing data?

Data analyses typically comprise the following five steps and in this order: (1) an assessment of representativeness, (2) a presentation of descriptive statistics of the main variables of interest, (3) comparison tests and univariate correlations, (4) regression analyses, and (5) robustness checks.

3.3.2.1 Representativeness

Ideally, data analyses begin with an assessment of representativeness. Analyses of crowdfunding markets, however, are plagued with an inability or limited ability to claim representativeness. Unlike companies listed on stock exchanges, privately held companies are not compelled to make information public. Hence, it is difficult to assess the characteristics of the population of crowdfunded companies. Industry associations, such as the National Crowdfunding Association of Canada, and various data vendors have helped to assess representativeness. However, coverage in datasets is not 100% and it is difficult to know exactly the extent of coverage. Further, details provided in these datasets are limited. For instance, most of the publicly available datasets from crowdfunding data vendors do not comprise details on other sources of capital secured by the entrepreneur.

In view of limitations in publicly available crowdfunding data, it is necessary to "hand collect" data. Hand collection involves the use of surveys or proprietary access to information via one's own networks and/or efforts to gather detailed information. Surveys where detailed financial information is solicited most often achieve response rates of less than 20%, and often less than 10% (Brau & Fawcett, 2006; Cumming & Zambelli, 2017; Graham & Harvey, 2001). Where possible, one begins with comparison of the sample with the known population. For whatever dimensions from which the sample can be compared to the population, it is desirable to have minimal discrepancies so that the sample considered is representative of the population. If relevant comparisons are not feasible, then at a minimum it is worth qualitatively assessing whether or not response bias is present in data based on the type of information solicited.

3.3.2.2 Descriptive statistics

Once data representativeness is assessed, descriptive statistics of the data analyzed is presented. A presentation of means,[3] standard deviations,[4] medians,[5] and minimum and maximum values enables the reader to assess the relevant statistics in the data. The mean is the average value. The median is the middle value (50% of the observations lie above the median and 50% lie below). The standard deviation measures the dispersion of the values; more disperse values have a greater standard deviation. The mean and median are different for data that have a different degree of dispersion above the median than below.

The descriptive statistics enable a characterization of the data. For instance, for an assessment of the use of nonvoting shares in crowdfunding campaigns and what percentage of equity is sold in equity crowdfunding campaigns, it is worthwhile to know how often such shares are issued. A presentation of descriptive statistics from a dataset on crowdfunding enables the reader to understand the frequency of the use of nonvoting shares and the ownership stake that is typically given up.

3.3.2.3 Comparison tests and correlations

Comparison tests are provided in data analyses to assess differences in one subsample of the data relative to another one. Commonly used comparison tests assess the differences in means, medians, and proportions for different groupings of data. These tests are described at numerous places on the Internet, and some webpages even provide online tests such that one only needs to enter the data.[6]

Comparison tests are a useful first-step at analyzing relationships between variables. Comparison tests, however, are only indicative and not conclusive. That is, they do not control for "other things being equal."

Let's consider an example. Suppose we have a dataset with the following 5 variables and 100 observations in the data.

[3] http://en.wikipedia.org/wiki/Mean

[4] http://en.wikipedia.org/wiki/Standard_deviation

[5] http://en.wikipedia.org/wiki/Median

[6] For instance, see http://www.fon.hum.uva.nl/Service/Statistics.html.

Data observation number	Achieved funding goal (Yes/No)	Cleantech industry (Yes/No)	Goal amount (US$ '000)	Campaign year	Individualism index
1	1	1	100	2017	91
2	1	1	60	2015	20
3	1	0	75	2014	55
. . .					
100	0	0	300	2016	80

Note in this example that the variables "achieved funding goal" and "cleantech industry" are called "dummy variables" in statistics and econometrics, because they can only take on two values: 0 or 1. The value "0" means "no" and the value "1" means "yes." For example, for observation 1 the campaign achieved the funding goal was used, the entrepreneur is in the cleantech industry, the entrepreneur sought to raise $100,000 as the campaign goal, the campaign year was 2017, and entrepreneur is based in the United States (the only country that has an individualism index of 91; see Table 3.1).

Further, note in this example that we would refer to the variable "achieved funding goal" as a "dependent" or an "output" variable, while the other variables "cleantech industry," "goal amount," "campaign year," and "individualism index" are "independent" or "input" or "explanatory" variables, that is, whether or not the funding goal was achieved is an outcome. Factors that may affect this result are the characteristics of the entrepreneur (such as the industry sector), the campaign (such as the goal amount), market conditions (such as an investment year), and country characteristics (such as cultural conditions).

In this example, comparing the proportion of successful campaigns with those that were and were not in the cleantech industry does not conclusively indicate which campaign is more likely to be successful, because it might be the case that some other factor, such as the market conditions in the year of investment, is more directly linked to the success of the campaign. Nevertheless, it is reasonable and appropriate to begin with comparison tests to get a picture of the tendencies in the data and the plausible relationships between variables.

Similarly, with comparison tests, correlation coefficients enable an understanding of the relationships between two variables.[7] Correlation coefficients vary between $+1$ and -1. A correlation of 0 implies that the variables are completely unrelated to one another. A correlation of $+1$ means that the variables move in the same direction at the same time, while a correlation of -1 means that the variables move in the opposite direction at the same time. Correlations cannot exceed $+1$ and cannot be less than -1. Correlation coefficients are typically presented in a matrix to show the relationships between all of the variables of interest in a dataset.

---

[7] http://en.wikipedia.org/wiki/Correlation

A correlation matrix is useful in two respects. First, it enables an assessment between an outcome variable and an input variable. In the example discussed previously, useful statistics are the correlation coefficient between the variables for achieving the campaign goal and cleantech industry, and achieving the funding goal and the goal amount. If the correlation between the former is greater than the latter, then we would infer that campaign success is more closely tied to being in the cleantech industry than it is relative to the goal amount. However, as discussed, this is not conclusive, since it is possible that some other variable is more directly attributable to campaign success, such as market conditions in the year of investment and country characteristics.

Second, a correlation matrix enables an assessment of the relationships across different input variables. If different input variables are highly correlated (either close to $+1$ or -1), then it is difficult to ascertain which of the two input variables is causing the output variables. This second issue is discussed further in the context of regression analyses.

3.3.2.4 Regression analyses

Regression analyses enable an assessment of causal relations between variables while controlling for other things being equal. Following from the previous example, a regression equation can be used to assess the likelihood that a crowdfunding campaign achieved funding goal as per the following hypothetical regression:

$$\text{Achievedfundinggoal} = \beta_0 + \beta_1 \text{cleantechindustry} + \beta_2 \text{goal amount} + \beta_3 \text{campaign year} + \beta_4 \text{individualism index} + \varepsilon$$

As discussed, achieved funding goal is the dependent variable, an outcome variable, which is explained by the independent variables cleantech industry, goal amount, investment year, and the individualism index. The β terms are coefficients. β_0 is a constant, or the value of the intercept if the equation is viewed as representing a line on a graph. β_1 is a coefficient that indicates the sensitivity (i.e., slope) of the relationship between the variable cleantech industry and achieved funding goal. β_2 is a coefficient that indicates the sensitivity (i.e., slope) of the relationship between the variable goal amount and achieved funding goal. β_3 is a coefficient that indicates the sensitivity (i.e., slope) of the relationship between the campaign year and achieved funding goal. β_4 is a coefficient that indicates the sensitivity (i.e., slope) of the relationship between the individualism index and achieved funding goal. ε represents the error, or "residuals," or the portion of the movement in the achieved funding goal variable that is unexplained by the variables cleantech industry, goal amount, campaign year, and the individualism index.

The quality of a regression, or its goodness of fit, is often assessed by a statistic known as "R^2." The R^2 statistic varies between 0 and 1; values closer to 1 mean that the explanatory variables are doing a better job in explaining the movement in the dependent variable. Variants of the R^2 statistic are used for different types of regressions. An adjusted R^2 statistic is used to account for the number of explanatory variables. A pseudo R^2 is used for nonlinear regression models. The interpretation of the different R^2 statistics is similar insofar as they all indicate goodness of fit of the regression model.

Statistical software packages (such as Limdep, STATA, and SAS) are used to estimate regression equations. Key items of interest that are estimated include the value of the coefficients and the R^2 statistic. With respect to the coefficients, it is important to know their sign (positive or negative values) and size. The coefficients give an indication of the magnitude of the effect that one variable has on another; said differently, it indicates "economic significance." Large coefficients are "economically significant"; small ones are "economically insignificant." In addition to the size, econometric programs further assess the probability that the coefficient is estimated accurately. That is, each coefficient has a standard deviation or dispersion measure associated with it. Coefficients that have a relatively high standard error are statistically insignificant.[8] If the coefficient is statistically insignificant, then we would infer that there is no relation between the particular explanatory variable and the dependent variable (regardless of the size of the coefficient). In all regression analyses, it is important to assess both statistical and economic significance.

The type of regression employed depends on the nature of the data examined. In particular, depending on the structure of the dependent variable of interest, it is appropriate to use a different type of regression. Perhaps, the most commonly used type of regression in practice is known as "ordinary least squares" or OLS for short.[9] OLS is appropriate for dependent variables that can take on an infinite range of value from $-\infty$ to $+\infty$. OLS is used in Chapter 5, Crowdfunding models: keep-it-all versus all-or-nothing, Chapter 6, Crowdfunding cleantech Chapter 7, Crowdfunding to internationalize, and Chapter 16, Demand-driven crowdfunding regulation.

Often, the dependent variable of interest can take on only a couple of values. In the previous example the dependent variable achieved funding goal can only take on the values 0 and 1; that is, it is a binary-dependent variable (a dummy variable). In this case, it is appropriate to use a logit[10] or probit[11] regression.[12] As in OLS regressions, logit and probit regressions yield coefficients; however, the economic significance of the coefficients by themselves is difficult to interpret. In order to assess economic significance, it is necessary to compute the "marginal effects" or the effect of a change in the value of the explanatory variable on the probability that the dependent variable takes the value 1. Logit or probit regression equations are used in Chapter 5, Crowdfunding models: keep-it-all versus all-or-nothing, Chapter 6, Crowdfunding cleantech, Chapter 10, Signaling in equity crowdfunding, Chapter 11, Are equity crowdfunders sensitive to distance?, Chapter 12, Cash-flow and control rights in equity crowdfunding, Chapter 13, Does equity crowdfunding democratize access to entrepreneurial finance?, and Chapter 18, Regulation and investment in fintech ventures.

---

[8] *t*-Statistics are used to assess statistical significance. A *t*-statistics is the coefficient value divided by its standard error. *t*-Statistics that are greater than 1.65 in absolute value are statistically significant at the 10% level, that is, they have a *P*-value of 10%, or a 10% chance of inferring that the coefficient is statistically significant when in reality it is not. *t*-Statistics that are greater than 1.96 in absolute value are statistically significant at the 5% level, and *t*-statistics that are greater than 2.59 in absolute value are statistically significant at the 1% level. Regression coefficient estimates are presented with their *t*-statistics and/or standard errors.

[9] http://en.wikipedia.org/wiki/Least_squares

[10] http://en.wikipedia.org/wiki/Logistic_regression

[11] http://en.wikipedia.org/wiki/Probit_model

[12] The use of probit versus logit depends on distribution assumptions of the dependent variable; in practice, the results obtained are extremely similar.

Sometimes, a set of discrete choices can be ranked. For instance, it might be of interest to assess the factors that pertain to preferences in survey data, and variables can take on a few different values such as the highest, middle, and the lowest. If so, an ordered logit model is more appropriate than a binomial logit model.[13] Ordered logit regression models are used in Chapter 16, Demand-driven crowdfunding regulation.

3.3.2.5 Robustness checks

Regression analyses are sensitive to misspecification errors. Indeed, a famous expression indicates that there are "lies, damn lies, and statistics."[14] As such, one never considers a single regression equation. Various regressions assessing the same prediction are used to assess robustness to misspecification error.

Common types of misspecification include omitted variables and collinearity. The problem of omitted variables refers to a deficient set of explanatory in explaining the dependent variable of interest. Exclusion of relevant explanatory variables may give rise to inappropriate inferences about the effect of other included variables on the dependent variable of interest. Collinearity, by contrast, refers to the problem of highly correlated explanatory variables being used in the same regression equation. Where variables are overly correlated, the estimated statistical and economic significance may be highly inaccurate. To assess for problems of omitted variables and collinearity, it is appropriate to consider a variety of regressions to explain the same dependent variable with different sets of included explanatory variables.[15] Ideally, the estimated coefficients are not subject to the included set of explanatory variables.

Heteroscedasticity is common in regression equations as well. Heteroscedasticity refers to a nonnormal distribution of residuals in a regression equation.[16] The resulting statistical significance of the estimated coefficients can be biased when there is pronounced heteroscedasticity. A traditional approach to correct for this problem is to use White's (1980) robust adjusted estimator. A more recent approach involves accounting for clustered standard errors according to specific variables (Petersen, 2009) such as by industry or time period; which was appropriate in the contexts of Chapter 6, Crowdfunding cleantech, Chapter 11, Are equity crowdfunders sensitive to distance?, and Chapter 18, Regulation and investment in fintech ventures.

Another problem that can arise in data analysis involves outlier observations (and possibly measurement error). That is, the estimated coefficients may be subject to the presence of only a few observations in the data which are vastly different from all of the other observations. It is appropriate to assess sensitivity to Winsorizing (see, e.g., Chapter 10: Signaling in equity crowdfunding).[17]

---

[13] http://en.wikipedia.org/wiki/Ordered_logit

[14] http://en.wikipedia.org/wiki/Lies,_damned_lies,_and_statistics

[15] Other diagnostic tests are appropriate as well, but beyond the scope of this chapter. Standard econometric textbooks deal with these issues.

[16] http://en.wikipedia.org/wiki/Heteroskedasticity

[17] http://en.wikipedia.org/wiki/Winsorizing

The issue of endogeneity is perhaps the most common problem in research entrepreneurship and finance, which includes but is not limited to crowdfunding. A typical regression equation, such as the one specified previously, involves the right-hand side (explanatory) variables explaining or causing the left-hand side (dependent) variable. Endogeneity refers to the problem in a regression equation where the right-hand side variables are at least in part caused by the left-hand side variable. The problem of endogeneity arises when the variables on the right-hand side are "choice" variables, or not exogenously determined. In the previous example, it is possible that expected campaign outcomes lead to the decision of where to set the goal amount. This issue comes up in Chapter 5, Crowdfunding models: keep-it-all versus all-or-nothing, for example.

To control for endogeneity, it is customary to use two-step regression methods involving instrumental variables.[18] Instrumental variables are variables that are highly correlated with the potentially endogenous explanatory variable but not correlated with the dependent variable. (In practice, it is typically difficult to find an ideal instrumental variable.) In a two-step regression, first the potentially endogenous variable is regressed on the instruments, and then the fitted values from that regression are used as a new variable in place of the potentially endogenous variable in the second regression. This type of two-step regression is used in Chapter 5, Crowdfunding models: keep-it-all versus all-or-nothing, Chapter 6, Crowdfunding cleantech, and Chapter 11, Are equity crowdfunders sensitive to distance? When a suitable instrumental variable does not exist, another check is to see whether or not the other variables of interest are affected to the inclusion or exclusions of the potentially endogenous variable (see Chapter 18, Regulation and investment in fintech ventures, for example).

Another problem that can arise in regression analyses involves selection effects.[19] For example, this issue arises in the context of assessing the determinants of crowdfunding campaign success. For example, an entrepreneur may list on one platform or another, and the outcomes of campaigns on the platform might be attributable to which firms came to the platform and not the characteristics of the campaign itself. To account for such selection biases, it is appropriate to use statistical methods developed by Heckman (1976, 1979). This issue arises in Chapter 12, Cash-flow and control rights in equity crowdfunding.

A further way to assess problems of selection effects and other confounding factors involves the use of propensity score matching. Propensity score matching involves creating a matched dataset based on items that are deemed relevant or similar, with the exception of outcome variables of interest. For example, in the case of crowdfunding campaigns, propensity scoring could be used to match similar campaigns across size and industry across different platforms. See Chapter 5, Crowdfunding models: keep-it-all versus all-or-nothing, Chapter 6, Crowdfunding cleantech and Chapter 14, Marketplace lending, for applications of propensity score matching techniques.

Further details on the econometric methods used in this book are provided in each of the chapters. The statistics and econometrics used are intended to be as user friendly as

---

[18] http://en.wikipedia.org/wiki/Instrumental_variable

[19] http://en.wikipedia.org/wiki/Selection_bias

possible. Empirical analyses of crowdfunding datasets from a multitude of countries are provided where possible to enable generalizable inferences. The data are exciting aspects and a central feature of this book and we do not wish to detract from the interest with technical details. Data enable us to ascertain whether or a specific case represents the typical scenario, or whether or not the case is an outlier.

3.4 Summary

Because a central objective of this book is to empirically examine crowdfunding decisions and outcomes in different countries around the world, this chapter provided an explanation of institutional differences across countries. In particular, we described legal, cultural, and economic differences.

Also, we provided a brief review of the statistical and econometric techniques methods in this chapter to help the flow in the ensuing chapters. The data presented in each chapter are intended to be user friendly. It is important and worthwhile to examine data so that readers are familiar with crowdfunding outcomes in the real world and not just from a theoretical lens or from a selective set of cases. Analyses of large datasets enable generalizable insights, unlike studying one-off cases. Similarly, analyses of international datasets are useful, where possible, since single-country datasets may be attributable to an institutional context which is inapplicable to another country.

Key terms

Common law
Civil law
Creditor rights
Minority shareholder protection
Power distance
Individualism
Masculinity
Uncertainty avoidance
Long-term orientation
Indulgence
Trust
Culture

Key statistical and econometric terms

Collinearity
Comparison test
Correlation
Dependent variable

Economic significance
Endogeneity
Heteroscedasticity
Independent variable
Instrumental variables
Logit
Mean
Median
Ordered logit
Ordinary least squares
Outliers
Probit
Propensity score matching
Representativeness
Sample selection
Standard deviation
Statistical significance

Discussion questions

3.1. Do you think legal protection or culture would play a more important role in explaining crowdfunding levels across countries?

3.2. Which types of legal protections and cultural conditions should matter more for the development of equity crowdfunding markets?

3.3. What types of statistical methods should be used to evaluate the importance of imprecise or incomplete aggregation of crowdfunding data within and across countries?

Rewards crowdfunding

An overview of rewards-based crowdfunding

4.1 Introduction

Part II of this book comprises Chapters 4–7 and covers the topic of rewards-based crowdfunding. Rewards-based crowdfunding is carried out through online platforms such as Kickstarter.com and Indiegogo.com. Investors are individuals who contribute small amounts of money in exchange for a reward. The reward is often the advance purchase of a product, but certainly it could involve other things as small as a "thank you" on the entrepreneur's webpage.

The following typical set of things included in a crowdfunding campaigns:

- a description of the product or service that the entrepreneur (or entrepreneurial team) is seeking to raise money for, which can be as short as a few works, or as long as thousands of words;
- the entrepreneur's biography;
- the rewards (crowdfunding campaigns are typically structured with a number of different rewards levels to entice the crowd to larger contributions);
- The entrepreneur's location, and where the rewards will be shipped to, and the expected time taken to shipment;
- The entrepreneur's social media links (such as Facebook, Linkedin, and Twitter);
- Pictures;
- Videos[1];
- A campaign horizon (time remaining to contribute to the campaign);
- A campaign goal (the amount of money desired);

---

[1] And there is much guidance on the web as to how to produce a video that will lead to funding success. See for example this advice from Indiegogo https://entrepreneur.indiegogo.com/education/guide/campaign-video-creation-guide/, which also states that campaigns are on average four times more successful with a video (see also Chapter 5, Crowdfunding models: keep-it-all versus all-or-nothing, and Chapter 6, Crowdfunding cleantech, for a more rigorous analysis on this point that considers other things in a comprehensive setup).

- A choice (known to the crowd) of whether or not the entrepreneur gets to keep the money raised regardless of whether the campaign goal is reached (at the, or whether or not the money is returned from the platform to the entrepreneur after the campaign);
- Updates made by the entrepreneur during the campaign;
- Comments that can be entered by investors (or other members of the crowd) during the campaign;
- A real-time listing of the number of backers, and the amount backed; and
- Any information provided by the platform (including whether or not the campaign has been suspended in the case of fraud).

To motivate the range of possible things that can be crowdfunded, and to show how campaigns look, we begin with the one of the more famous crowdfunding campaigns ever: "I'm making potato salad" as shown in Exhibit 4.1. This campaign is of course quite unusual, as it highlights the excitement over crowdfunding and the unusual subculture that is part of crowdfunding. The intention of the campaign was perhaps to be funny, and to be the first to do something so unusual. The entrepreneur's goal was to raise $10. The campaign went "viral" so-to-speak at least relative to its goal, with 6911 individuals contributing in total $55,492. There were 10 different reward levels for commitment amounts of $1, $2, $3, $5, $10, $20, $25, $35, $50, and $110. The different rewards are explicitly listed from the entrepreneur's description in Exhibit 4.1. The project description is extremely short (I'm making potato salad) relative to that of most campaigns, which are typically thousands of words, see Chapter 5: Crowdfunding models: keep-it-all versus all-or-nothing.

In the remaining parts of this chapter, we review the following. In Section 4.2, we explain the advantages of rewards-based crowdfunding relative to other types of crowdfunding and other forms of finance. In Section 4.3, we explain the trade-offs associated with using some of the different rewards-based platforms. In Section 4.4, we provide cases of successful rewards-based campaigns. In Section 4.5, we provide cases of failed rewards-based campaigns. The concluding section summarizes and provides an overview of the remaining chapters in Part II of this book.

4.2 Why rewards-based crowdfunding?

There are a number of advantages associated with using rewards-based crowdfunding relative to other ways of raising capital. These advantages, from the perspective of the entrepreneur, include as follows:

1. The entrepreneur does not have to give up equity in his or her firm. As such, the entrepreneur does not have to share ownership and keeps all of the profits associated with crowdfunding, with the exception of the payment for the production and delivery of the promised rewards.
2. The entrepreneur does not have to repay debt. A debt contract comes with a contractual obligation to repay the investor at a certain point in time and with a certain interest rate. Debt may have other conditions as well, such as collateral that might have to be

EXHIBIT 4.1 "I'm making potato salad"

Funded! This project was successfully funded on August 2.

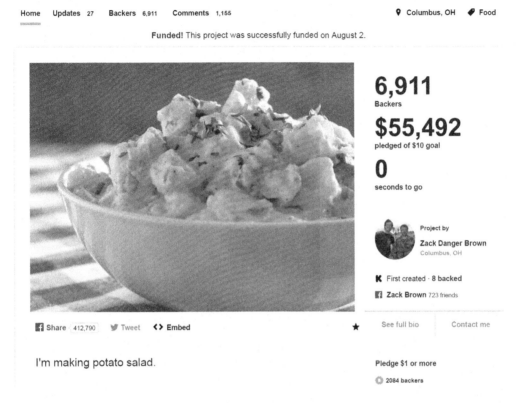

6,911
Backers

$55,492
pledged of $10 goal

0
seconds to go

Project by
Zack Danger Brown
Columbus, OH

K First created · 8 backed
f **Zack Brown** 723 friends

f Share 412,790   🐦 Tweet   <> Embed   ★   See full bio   Contact me

I'm making potato salad.   Pledge $1 or more
                                                  ⚙ 2084 backers

Rewards:

Pledge $1 or more
2084 backers
With your help, we will be on our way to a successful potato salad. You will get a "thank you" posted to our website and I will say your name out loud while making the potato salad.
Estimated delivery: Dec 2014

Pledge $2 or more
1253 backers
Receive a photo of me making the potato salad, a "thank you" posted to our website, and I will say your name out loud while making the potato salad.
Estimated delivery: Dec 2014
Ships anywhere in the world.

Pledge $3 or more
1272 backers
Receive a bite of the potato salad, a photo of me making the potato salad, a "thank you" posted to our website, and I will say your name out loud while making the potato salad.

Estimated delivery: Dec 2014
Ship anywhere in the world.

Pledge $5 or more
589 backers
DELUXE PACKAGE: PACKAGE: Choose a potato-salad-appropriate ingredient to add to the potato salad, receive a bite of the potato salad, a photo of me making the potato salad, a "thank you" posted to our website and I will say your name out loud while making the potato salad.
Estimated delivery: Dec 2014
Ship anywhere in the world

Pledge $10 or more
464 backers
PLATINUM LEVEL: Hang out in the kitchen with me while I make the potato salad, choose a potato-salad-appropriate ingredient to add to the potato salad, receive a bite of the potato salad, a photo of me making the potato salad, a "thank you" posted to our website, and I will say your name out loud while making the potato salad.
Estimated delivery: Dec 2014
Ship anywhere in the world

Pledge $20 or more
4 backers All gone!
POTATO MADNESS: Receive a potato-salad themed haiku written by me, your name carved into a potato that will be used in the potato salad, a signed jar of mayonnaise, the potato salad recipe, hang out in the kitchen with me while I make the potato salad, choose a potato-salad-appropriate ingredient to add to the potato salad, receive a bite of the potato salad, a photo of me making the potato salad, a "thank you" posted to our website, and I will say your name out loud while making the potato salad.
Estimated delivery: Dec 2014
Ship anywhere in the world

Pledge $25 or more
289 backers
THE HAT: Receive a potato-salad themed hat along with a bite of the potato salad, a photo of me making the potato salad, a "thank you" posted to our website, and I will say your name out loud while making the potato salad.
Estimated delivery: Dec 2014

Pledge $35 or more
585 backers
THE HOMAGE T-SHIRT: Receive a limited edition t-shirt designed and printed by Columbus, Ohio t-shirt company Homage (http://www.homage.com). Also receive a bite of the potato salad, a photo of me making the potato salad, a "thank you" posted to our website, and I will say your name out loud while making the potato salad.
Estimated delivery: Dec 2014
Ship anywhere in the world

Pledge $50 or more

106 backers

POTATO SALADS OF THE WORLD: Receive a recipe book with potato salad recipes inspired by each country where we have a backer along with a bite of the potato salad, a photo of me making the potato salad, a "thank you" posted to our website, and I will say your name out loud while making the potato salad. The recipe book will have a dedication page with the name of each of our backers.

Estimated delivery: Dec 2014

Ship anywhere in the world

Pledge $110 or more

21 backers

THE PLATINUM POTATO: Receive the recipe book, the shirt and the hat along with a bite of the potato salad, a photo of me making the potato salad, a "thank you" posted to our website and I will say your name out loud while making the potato salad.

Estimated delivery: Dec 2014

Ships anywhere in the world

---

given up in the event of nonpayment. Failure to meet debt obligations may further result in liquidation of the entrepreneurial firm.

3. The entrepreneur may never deliver the promised product or reward. It is possible to claim "mistake" and deliver late,[2] fail to deliver, and typically without penalty.

4. The entrepreneur gains "traction" or a track record of demonstrating interest in the product. This information is very useful for entrepreneurs seeking subsequent financing as the firm develops.

5. There is a marketing and promotional benefit associated with crowdfunding, as the product and entrepreneurial team are advertised widely through the crowdfunding campaign.

6. The entrepreneur is able to raise capital cheaply. The contract terms through the platform are fixed and standardized. By contrast, with angel or venture capital investment, there are significant legal expenses associated with the negotiation and production of financial contracts. A crowdfunding platform typically charges a fixed percentage of the capital raised only if the campaign is successful (this fee is commonly set between 4% and 5% of the total amount of capital raised); other types of fee arrangements include a fixed percentage of capital raised regardless of whether the funding was successful, one-time listing fees, periodical subscriptions at different levels/tiers, and management fees and carry percentages (Cumming, Johan, & Zhang, 2019).

7. The entrepreneur receives services from the platform, including showing due diligence to investors (background checks, site visits, credit checks, cross-checks, account monitoring, and third-party proof) and providing advice to the entrepreneur (prelisting evaluation, strategic guidance, business planning, contract help, and promotion services) (Cumming, Johan, & Zhang, 2019).

[2] It has been noted that 84% of the Kickstarter projects are delivered later than that which was promised in the campaign. See https://money.cnn.com/2012/12/18/technology/innovation/kickstarter-ship-delay/index.html?iid = EL.

8. The entrepreneur receives advice from investors. Investors participate in crowdfunding campaigns often provide feedback to entrepreneurs. Some entrepreneurs even actively encourage feedback to better inform their product development.
9. The entrepreneur gains an access to a wider scope of investors, including a wider geographic scope of investors, which can enable growth of the entrepreneur's business and expansion of the range of customers and improve sales.

There are, however, a number of disadvantages associated with rewards-based crowdfunding. These disadvantages include but are not limited to the following:

1. Theft: Posting an entrepreneurial opportunity on a well-publicized webpage may lead to replication of the idea by other investors. A number of cases have been reported where Kickstarter campaigns led to replication in China and was on sale in China before the Kickstarter campaign was even finished, such as a smartphone case that unfolds into a selfie stick,[3] spice grinders,[4] personalized air conditioners,[5] and gadgets for android devices.[6]
2. Future investors may be dissuaded from investing in a company that has been through crowdfunding. This issue, however, appears to be more of a concern with equity crowdfunding than rewards-based crowdfunding, as discussed in Chapter 17, Public policy towards entrepreneurial finance: spillovers and scale-up.
3. The costs of reporting to and communicating with a large number of crowdfunders can be large. And failure to report (or improper communication) and failure to deliver (or improper delivery) to crowdfunders could lead to legal consequences, as discussed in Chapter 15, Introduction to crowdfunding regulation and policy.

4.3 Where to do a rewards-based crowdfunding campaign?

There are generalist crowdfunding platforms and specialist crowdfunding platforms. The two most popular generalist crowdfunding platforms are Kickstarter and Indiegogo. The advantage of using a generalist crowdfunding is that they have a large investor base that pays attention to their offerings. The difference between Kickstarter and Indiegogo is that on Kickstarter, if the entrepreneur does not meet the stated funding goal, all of the money raised in the campaign is returned to the investors ("all-or-nothing" or "AON" model). By contrast, on Indiegogo, if the entrepreneur wants to, they can elect to not to use the AON model and instead use the "keep-it-all" or "KIA" model where the

[3] https://qz.com/771727/chinas-factories-in-shenzhen-can-copy-products-at-breakneck-speed-and-its-time-for-the-rest-of-the-world-to-get-over-it/

[4] https://www.scmp.com/property/hong-kong-china/article/2086394/designers-turn-crowdfunding-sites-bring-ideas-life

[5] https://www.scmp.com/property/hong-kong-china/article/2086394/designers-turn-crowdfunding-sites-bring-ideas-life

[6] https://technode.com/2014/01/26/crowdfunding-sites-makes-copied-in-china-even-easier-all-is-needed-is-a-photoshopped-image/

entrepreneur keeps all of the money raised regardless of whether or not the funding goal was reached. Chapter 5, Crowdfunding models: keep-it-all versus all-or-nothing, presents evidence that 95% of the entrepreneurs using Indiegogo go with the KIA model. Chapter 5, Crowdfunding models: keep-it-all versus all-or-nothing, also shows important differences in the characteristics of entrepreneurs that go with KIA versus AON.

Table 4.1 presents the top 10 most successful (in terms of capital raised) campaigns on Kickstarter and Indiegogo. The projects cover sectors that include technology, games, animation, design, education, and 3D printing. Table 4.2 presents a similar list of example projects (not necessarily the largest) involving social innovation. That is, the projects involve some improvement to the quality of life beyond merely the returns to the entrepreneur and their investors. Social innovations are discussed and analyzed in more detail in Chapter 6, Crowdfunding cleantech.

Specialist crowdfunding platforms target unique market niches and hence may be able to secure a more dedicated and loyal investor base relative to a generalist platform. For example, Sellaband is a platform based in Amsterdam, which promotes new music groups, and had been quite successful (Agrawal, Catalini, & Goldfarb, 2015). Another example involves universities crowdfunding projects, lectures, and other things that intersect universities to the broader community, such as the Carleton University platform in Ottawa, Canada.[7] Additional examples involve crowdfunding platforms that enable funding for the arts[8] and fashion.[9] Similarly, there is now a platform specifically for equity- and debt-based crowdfunding in cleantech.[10]

Whether or not a specialist or generalist platform is appropriate depends at least in part on the degree to which a project is likely to catch a wide array of interests, and not be specific solely to a particular interest. Also, it depends on the services that are offered by the platform and the fees charged.

In Sections 4.4 and 4.5, we provide examples of successful and failed crowdfunding campaigns, respectively.

4.4 Cases of successful rewards-based crowdfunding campaigns

4.4.1 Star Citizen

Star Citizen[11] is a multiplayer combat game. It was first crowdfunded in over a 32-day funding period in October and November 2012 and raised $2,134,374, or more than 4 times the goal of $500,000. It offered 19 different rewards levels ($5, $10, $30, $30, $35, $37, $40, $60, $60, $60, $110, $110, $110, $125, $125, $250, $500, $1000, $2500, and $5000).

---

[7] https://futurefunder.carleton.ca/

[8] For example, http://artsfunding.ca/

[9] For example, https://www.luevo.com/

[10] https://gridshare.com/

[11] https://www.kickstarter.com/projects/cig/star-citizen

TABLE 4.1 Top 10 most successful Kickstarter and Indiegogo projects.

Title	Amount raised ($)	Platform	Category	Brief description	Campaign webpage
Kickstarter					
Pebble Time—Awesome Smartwatch, No Compromises	20,338,986.00	Kickstarter	Design	Smart watch with removable face	https://www.kickstarter.com/projects/597507018/pebble-time-awesome-smartwatch-no-compromises
Coolest Cooler: 21st Century Cooler that's Actually Cooler	13,285,226.00	Kickstarter	Technology	Innovative cooler for the beach	https://www.kickstarter.com/projects/ryangrepper/coolest-cooler-21st-century-cooler-thats-actually
Pebble 2, Time 2 + All-New Pebble Core	12,779,843.00	Kickstarter	Design	Smart watch with removable face	https://www.kickstarter.com/projects/getpebble/pebble-2-time-2-and-core-an-entirely-new-3g-ultra
Kingdom Death: Monster 1.5	12,393,139.00	Kickstarter	Games	Video game	https://www.kickstarter.com/projects/ouya/ouya-a-new-kind-of-video-game-console
Critical Role: The Legend of Vox Machina Animated Special	11,385,449.00	Kickstarter	Animation	Vidao, animation, sound	https://www.kickstarter.com/projects/criticalrole/critical-role-the-legend-of-vox-machina-animated-s
Pebble: E-Paper Watch for iPhone and Android	10,266,845.00	Kickstarter	Design	Smart watch with removable face	https://www.kickstarter.com/projects/597507018/pebble-e-paper-watch-for-iphone-and-android
The World's Best TRAVEL JACKET with 15 Features ‖ BAUBAX	9,192,055.00	Kickstarter	Design	Better jacket for traveling	https://www.kickstarter.com/projects/597538543/the-worlds-best-travel-jacket-with-15-features-bau/description
Exploding Kittens	8,782,571.00	Kickstarter	Games	A card game	https://www.kickstarter.com/projects/elanlee/exploding-kittens
OUYA: A New Kind of Video Game Console	8,596,474.00	Kickstarter	Games	A video game	http://www.kickstarter.com/projects/ouya/ouya-a-new-kind-of-video-game-console
Snapmaker 2.0: Modular 3-in-1 3D Printers	7,850,866.00	Kickstarter	3D printing	3D printing	https://www.kickstarter.com/projects/snapmaker/snapmaker-20-modular-3-in-1-3d-printers
Indiegogo					
Flow Hive: Honey on Tap Directly From Your Beehive	12,212,833.00	Indiegogo	Technology	Honey, easier on beekeeper and easier on the bees	https://www.indiegogo.com/projects/flow-hive-honey-on-tap-directly-from-your-beehive
Sondors Electric Bike	5,832,467.00	Indiegogo	Technology	Electric bike	https://www.indiegogo.com/projects/sondors-electric-bike

Project	Amount	Platform	Category	Description	URL
Restore King Chapel Now. Every Day & Dollar Counts	5,048,213.00	Indiegogo	Technology	Martin Luther King Chapel	https://www.indiegogo.com/projects/restore-king-chapel-now-every-day-dollar-counts
An Hour of Code for Every Student	5,022,911.00	Indiegogo	Education	Student programming/coding education	https://www.indiegogo.com/projects/an-hour-of-code-for-every-student
Super Troopers 2	4,473,983.00	Indiegogo	Film	Movie involving state troopers	https://www.indiegogo.com/projects/super-troopers-2
KAISR Original: The Ultimate Inflatable Air Lounge	4,091,621.00	Indiegogo	Design	Inflatable lounge chair for beach or cottage	https://www.indiegogo.com/projects/kaisr-original-the-ultimate-inflatable-air-lounge
MATE. The coolest and most affordable eBike EVER	3,932,434.00	Indiegogo	Technology	Bicycle	https://www.indiegogo.com/projects/mate-the-coolest-and-most-affordable-ebike-ever-bicycle/
ONAGOfly: The Smart Nano Drone	3,463,604.00	Indiegogo	Technology	Small drone	https://www.indiegogo.com/projects/onagofly-the-smart-nano-drone-2/
Con Man	3,156,334.00	Indiegogo	Video/Web	Comedy film	https://www.indiegogo.com/projects/con-man
Pulse Audio: A CrowdsourcedHigh-Rez Sound System	2,900,553.00	Indiegogo	Technology	High-resolution sound system	https://www.indiegogo.com/projects/pulse-audio-a-crowdsourced-high-rez-sound-system

Source: Based on <https://crowdfundingblog.com/most-successful-crowdfunding-projects/> Accessed July 2019; page was last updated June 28, 2019 at the time of access.

TABLE 4.2 Examples of successful crowdfunding campaigns for creating a better world.

Title	Amount raised ($)	Platform	Category	Brief description	Campaign webpage
Rainforest Connection	167,299	Kickstarter	Social innovation	A sensor network of recycled smartphones uses built-in mics to thwart loggers by guarding vast areas of jungle (one square mile a piece)	https://www.kickstarter.com/projects/topherwhite/rainforest-connection-phones-turned-to-forest-guar
EcoQube	454,000 (over 2 campaigns)	Kickstarter	Social innovation	Eco-based high yield farming technique requires less than 2% of water of traditional farming approaches; modern, small-scale farming	https://www.kickstarter.com/projects/kevinzl/ecoqube-c-your-window-to-nature-0
WakaWaka Base: A Power & Light First Aid Kit	764,000	Kickstarter	Social innovation	Portable, cheap, solar LED light	https://www.kickstarter.com/projects/wakawaka/wakawaka-base-a-power-and-light-first-aid-kit
Hydaway	263,086	Kickstarter	Social innovation	Alternative to single-use plastic bottles	https://www.kickstarter.com/projects/hydaway/hydawaytm-a-pocket-sized-water-bottle-fit-for-any/posts
Global Village Construction Set	63,573	Kickstarter	Social innovation	Low-budget housing in impoverished parts of the world	https://www.kickstarter.com/projects/622508883/global-village-construction-set
Bombas Kids Socks. Better Socks. Better World. Bee Better	25,884	Indiegogo	Social innovation	Better kids socks	https://www.indiegogo.com/projects/bombas-kids-socks-better-socks-better-world-bee-better#
Nowlight: the next generation GravityLight	162,939	Indiegogo	Social innovation	Pull cord to generate light	https://www.indiegogo.com/projects/nowlight-the-next-generation-gravitylight/coll
Solar Lights that are Changing the World!	71,209	Indiegogo	Social innovation	Solar lights to help Puerto Rico	https://www.indiegogo.com/projects/solar-lights-that-are-changing-the-world#
Cleantech SuperHero Mission—Innovating to Zero Emissions! Together We Can	9780	Indiegogo	Social innovation	Funding to attending university program to empower entrepreneur to build a disruptive cleantech venture from scratch	https://www.indiegogo.com/projects/cleantech-superhero-mission-innovating-to-zero-emissions-together-we-can#
Greentown Grows	32,200	Indiegogo	Social innovation	Create an incubator for clean energy entrepreneurs	https://www.indiegogo.com/projects/greentown-grows#

Source: Based on <https://inhabitat.com/10-successful-kickstarters-creating-a-better-world/>, and authors' own searches.

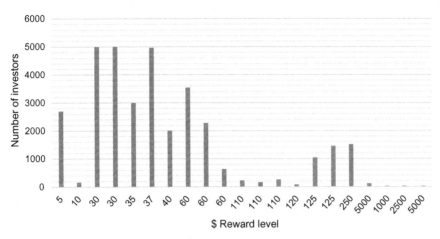

FIGURE 4.1 Number of investors at different reward levels for Star Citizen 2012 crowdfunding on Kickstarter. Source: *Based on data from <https://www.kickstarter.com/projects/cig/star-citizen>. Less visible are the 22, 3, and 1 investors in the top three rewards categories.*

The rewards corresponded to different features offered by the game (including different features at the repeated amounts for $60 and $110 that the funders could pick).

There are two striking things about Star Citizen that lead us to highlight this case. First, Star Citizen never stopped crowdfunding after the experience on Kickstarter. By the end of 2018, Star Citizen had raised over $200 million from over 2 million backers,[12] making it one of the all-time most successful crowdfunded companies in history.

Second, Star Citizen has used feedback received from its users to evolve the game. Put differently, Star Citizen has been engaged in *crowdfunding* alongside *crowdsourcing* of ideas. This approach of crowdsourcing alongside crowdfunding is a widely recognized way to gain long-term customer loyalty and improve traction from empowered consumers.[13] Also, by involving the crowd in the development of the game, the approach serves to mitigate most of the agency problems in Chapter 2, Overview of agency and signaling theory in crowdfunding, including expected costs associated with the risks of adverse selection, moral hazard, risk shifting, and window dressing.

Some of the keys to funding success involved rewards which enabled users to show with their use of the game that they funded the game (starting at the $5 reward), and a copy of the game (starting at the $30 reward) (see Fig. 4.1).

4.4.2 Oculus Rift

Oculus Rift[14] raised $2,437,419 from 9522 over a 30-day funding period in August 2012. There were 14 reward categories offering different levels ($10, $15, $25, $35, $75, $275,

[12] https://www.eurogamer.net/articles/2018-11-17-star-citizen-shoots-through-the-USD200m-raised-barrier

[13] https://www.fundable.com/learn/resources/guides/crowdfunding/the-benefits-of-crowdfunding

[14] https://www.kickstarter.com/projects/1523379957/oculus-rift-step-into-the-game

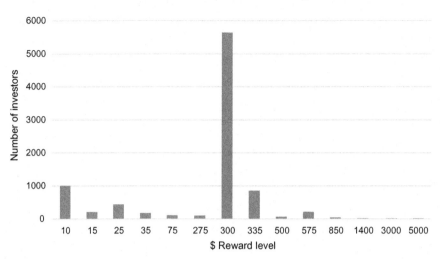

FIGURE 4.2 Number of investors at different reward levels for Oculus Rift 2012 crowdfunding on Kickstarter. Source: *Based on data from <https://www.kickstarter.com/projects/1523379957/oculus-rift-step-into-the-game>. Less visible are the 7 investors in the top two rewards categories.*

$300, $335, $500, $575, $850, $1400, $3000, and $5000) and offering early product access to funders. The key reward level that attracted funders was $300, which was the minimum commitment that enabled the reward of a developer's kit (see Fig. 4.2).

One of the most interesting things about Oculus Rift was the $2 billion sale to Facebook in March 2014,[15] which outraged the crowdfunders that did not financially benefit from the sale.[16] The outrage led many commentators to argue that the inability of the US entrepreneurs and investors to use equity crowdfunding at that time was unfair and afforded undue rewards to entrepreneurs at the expense of their investors that did not finally benefit from the upside of their capital contributions to the development of the product.[17] Put differently, those in the crowd expressed anger regarding the unequal equity sharing, which would exacerbate moral hazard problems and limit investor participation in future rewards-based offerings of this type. It was not until the JOBS Act of June 2014 was equity crowdfunding permitted in the United States.[18]

---

[15] https://www.theguardian.com/technology/shortcuts/2014/mar/26/oculus-rift-facebook-fury-kickstarter-funders

[16] https://www.theguardian.com/technology/shortcuts/2014/mar/26/oculus-rift-facebook-fury-kickstarter-funders. See also https://www.fastcompany.com/3028249/oculus-rift-kickstarter-and-the-delicate-line-between-growing-fast-and-selling and https://money.cnn.com/2014/03/26/investing/oculus-vr-kickstarter-backlash/, among numerous other news stories around that time.

[17] https://www.theverge.com/2014/3/28/5557120/what-if-oculus-rift-kickstarter-backers-had-gotten-equity

[18] The JOBS Act was signed into law on April 5, 2012, but rules permitting equity crowdfunding were not established and effective until October 30, 2015. See https://www.sec.gov/news/pressrelease/2015-249.html.

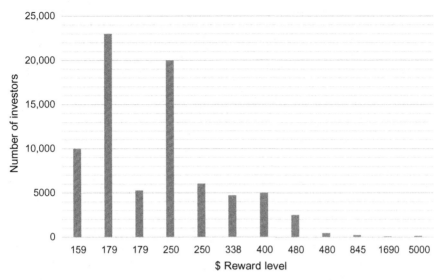

FIGURE 4.3 Number of investors at different reward levels for Pebble Watch 2012 crowdfunding on Kickstarter. Source: *Based on data from <https://www.kickstarter.com/projects/getpebble/pebble-time-awesome-smartwatch-no-compromises>. Less visible are the 451, 237, 82, and 142 investors in the top 4 rewards categories.*

4.4.3 Pebble Watch

Pebble Watch was crowdfunded over 31 days in February–March 2015. It received $20,338,986 from 78,471, making it Kickstarter's most successful campaign of all time (see Table 4.1).

A notable feature of the Pebble Watch campaign was the use of cutoffs for the number of rewards. That is, only a certain number (10,000) of rewards (one free watch) were allowed at the lowest reward level, and then the minimum price went up. At the $338 level a crowdfunder could obtain two Pebble Watches. In total, there were 12 reward categories: $159, $179, $179, $250, $250, $338, $400, $480, $480, $845, $1690, and $5000. Having a large number of reward categories mitigates the ability of the entrepreneur to risk shift (Chapter 2: Overview of agency and signaling theory in crowdfunding), as it limits the scope of actions that the entrepreneur can take in the future since deviations would make delivery of the rewards possibly more problematic and also motivates the backers in the crowd to participate at different levels that best fits their interests. The number of crowdfunders at each level is shown in Fig. 4.3.

Unfortunately for Pebble Watch, long-term success was not to be, due to the introduction of the Apple Watch. Nevertheless, Fitbit purchased Pebble Watch[19] and continues to support the watch through a new Rebble product.[20]

---

[19] https://www.digitaltrends.com/outdoors/fitbit-extends-pebble-support/

[20] https://www.digitaltrends.com/mobile/rebble-web-services-for-pebble-smartwatch-news/

4.4.4 Nowlight: the next generation GravityLight

The Indiegogo campaign "nowlight: the next generation GravityLight" offered a product that would "Create instant light and power with the pull of a cord. 1 minute pulling generates 2 hours of light!."[21] The features appear to be very useful for people around the world, as it is "The World's Most Efficient Manually-Powered Light: nowlight generates instant renewable light & power, simply with the pull of a cord! 1 SECOND MANUAL CHARGING = UP TO 2 MINUTES OF LIGHT. 1 MINUTE = 15 MINUTES TALK TIME ON YOUR MOBILE." Certainly, in the developing world, such a power source could have remarkable benefits to over 1.1 billion people around the world without access to electricity.

Indiegogo shows that nowlight raised $101,422 from 1260 backers as of July 1, 2018, and as at July 2019 had raised $162,939 from 1838 backers.[22] The campaign offered eight rewards levels ($5, $50, $74, $90, $140, $625, $1250, and $6000). It is noteworthy that the $90 reward is featured at the top of the Indiegogo webpage, and on as a "discount" of 14% off the regular price of $105. Further, as you scroll down the page, the $74 reward level was on at a discount as well from the original $90, or 17% off. The rewards are interesting as well as they are a mix of rewards and donations. Specifically, the $90 reward level allows the backer to get the best product offered, while the $74 offers fewer product options, and the $5 affords only fairy lights. The $50 allows empowering a refugee family. The higher reward levels offered to ship different numbers of products to impoverished families. These other reward levels for donations to impoverished families were not offered at a "discount," while the $74 and $90 rewards for personal consumption were offered at a discount (perhaps, it is possible a backer does not as greedy or guilty about buying something for oneself versus for a needy person when the discount is only available for personal consumption). The number of backers at each level is shown in Fig. 4.4. It is interesting as it allows a direct comparison and contrast of consumption versus donation, and marketing of new product development with charitable actions.

Additional projects in the area of "doing well by doing good" from Indiegogo and Kickstarter are featured in Table 4.1. Further, Chapter 6, Crowdfunding cleantech, in this book examines in detail a complete set of cleantech crowdfunded projects and the systematic differences for that industry versus other industries.

4.4.5 Meet the pilot: smart earpiece language translator

This campaign was one of Indiegogo's[23] most successful technology campaigns, which raised $1 million in only 2 hours,[24] and $2,385,157 from 10,648 in their first campaign in June 2016, and $4,462,205 from 19,940 backers by the end of their second campaign. Some details regarding rewards levels and funding amounts at different rewards levels are no

---

[21] https://www.indiegogo.com/projects/nowlight-the-next-generation-gravitylight#/

[22] https://www.indiegogo.com/projects/nowlight-the-next-generation-gravitylight#/

[23] https://www.indiegogo.com/projects/meet-the-pilot-smart-earpiece-language-translator#/

[24] https://go.indiegogo.com/blog/2017/05/1m-2-hours-creators-pilot-share-crowdfunding-secrets.html

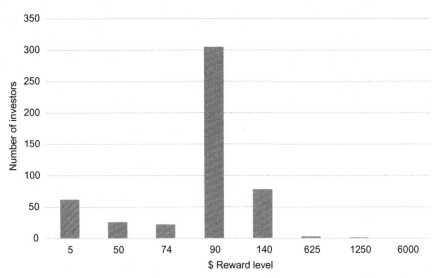

FIGURE 4.4 Nowlight: the next generation GravityLight 2018 on Indiegogo. Source: *Based on data from <https://www.indiegogo.com/projects/nowlight-the-next-generation-gravitylight#/comments>. Less visible are the 3, 1, and 0 investors in the top 3 rewards categories.*

longer on Indiegogo, but Indiegogo highlights a number of successful points on this campaign. Specifically, there is a featured article from the management team that explains why they felt their campaign was successful; while their exposition of their lessons do not specifically refer to the agency problems reviewed in Chapter 2, Overview of agency and signaling theory in crowdfunding, they clearly focus on minimizing information asymmetries between the investors and entrepreneurs to alleviate expected adverse selection costs and demonstrating their actions and goals to minimize expected moral hazard problems. Based on their experience, the entrepreneurs prepared a 12-point outline for a successful rewards-based crowdfunding campaign[25]:

1. "Have an exciting thumbnail and enticing headline
2. Emphasize social media shares
3. Showcase media/press for social proof
4. Show how it works w/ detailed product pics and walkthroughs (copy, photos, video)
5. Simplify the idea for the average person to understand
6. Testimonials of real people, especially social influencers
7. List the features and specs of what it does
8. Reveal technological magic of how it works as proof
9. Call to Action — lay out company history and difficulties/hard work put in, and ask for help to make the dream a reality

---

[25] https://medium.com/indiegogo/how-we-used-crowdfunding-to-raise-4-4m-and-pre-sale-23-000-units-6bc68f58e008

10. Compelling Rewards — infographic with clear/concise reward tiers (a) small $1 tier for an easy pledge, (b) pricing tiers of high, medium and low rewards — price anchoring, (c) humor and intrigue into right panel pricing tiers to show personality, (d) scarcity & FOMO of limited rewards without running out of rewards, (e) photos and samples of what each reward tier includes, (f) infographic and "map" of reward tiers, (g) quality of reward tiers vs quantity of reward tiers — don't make it too, (g1) simple menu including featured rewards, favorite of creators/backers and easiest choice, (h) consistency of reward tiers with overall product
11. History and Roadmap/Timeline
12. Showcase Team"

4.5 Cases of failed rewards-based campaigns

There are many cases of failed crowdfunding campaigns. Many campaigns do not reach their funding goal. In fact, only 36.84% of the Kickstarter campaigns reach their funding goal,[26] which means that under Kickstarter's AON rules, 63.16% of the campaigns involve Kickstarter returning the money to their investors. Typical reasons for failure include a poorly structured or incomplete campaign (such as without a video, pictures, badly worded text, and scant information about the entrepreneurs such as a bio and social media links); see Chapter 5, Crowdfunding models: keep-it-all versus all-or-nothing, Chapter 6, Crowdfunding cleantech, and Chapter 15, Introduction to crowdfunding regulation and policy. These problems may be correlated with expected agency problems such as those outlined in Chapter 2, Overview of agency and signaling theory in crowdfunding; said differently, failure to properly structure a campaign may be a signal of expected future agency problems.

In this section, we present four cases of successful funding in terms of meeting the funding goal, but unsuccessful in terms of failed or inappropriate product delivery. Surveys of Kickstarter users show 1 out of 10 projects fail (8% of dollars committed were toward failed projects), investors receive a refund 13% of the time, 9% of projects never deliver a reward, 7% of crowdfunders did not receive their chosen reward.[27] Moreover, it was the smallest projects of under $1000 capital goals that failed most often (up to 15%).[28] Sections 4.5.1–4.5.4 present some cases that illustrate these failures. While they might appear to be frauds, these cases are not examples of crowdfunding fraud. Cases of crowdfunding fraud are presented in Chapter 15, Introduction to crowdfunding regulation and policy.

Also, in this section, we present a case of a failed campaign in terms of not reaching its funding goal. The failure is attributable to not properly structuring the campaign, unlike the example in Section 4.4.5. Further to this case, Chapter 5, Crowdfunding models: keep-it-all versus all-or-nothing, and Chapter 6, Crowdfunding cleantech, establish

---

[26] https://www.statista.com/statistics/235405/kickstarter-project-funding-success-rate/

[27] https://www.theverge.com/2015/12/7/9865112/kickstarter-9-percent-failure-rate-survey

[28] https://www.theverge.com/2015/12/7/9865112/kickstarter-9-percent-failure-rate-survey

statistical evidence as to what leads to crowdfunding success and failure in terms of meeting the funding goal.

4.5.1 Coolest Cooler

The Coolest Cooler is the second most successful campaign on Kickstarter (Table 4.1). It raised $13,258,226 from 62,642 backers over 52 days in July–August 2014.[29] However, the company failed to deliver a substantial number of those coolers and still had over 20,000 undelivered coolers by June 2018.[30]

The Coolest Cooler fiasco is not exactly one of fraud, but perhaps more one of mistake and being ill suited toward mass production. Consumers were of course nevertheless angry, and in a settlement with the Oregon Department of Justice, consumers received approximately $20 on a roughly $200 contribution for their cooler.[31]

A well-documented concern among crowdfunding commentators is that crowdfunding enables entrepreneurs to directly pay themselves a handsome salary and then never deliver the product with the explanation of "sorry, we made a mistake." (Essentially, an extreme form of the agency issues reviewed in Chapter 2: Overview of agency and signaling theory in crowdfunding.) It is of course unclear in any given case where there is improper or completely absent delivery of the promised rewards or product as to whether there is frustration or mistake, or if indeed there was some element of pronounced agency problems or fraud. The legal decision in this case is highly suggestive that there were problems that were not completely innocent.

4.5.2 Torquing Group Drone

Torquing Group's "ZANO—Autonomous. Intelligent. Swarming. Nano Drone." Kickstarter campaign received £2,335,119 from 12,075 backers over 45 days in November 2014–January 2015.

The drone was never delivered, and the company filed for bankruptcy. Fraud was never proven in this case, as an investigator did find evidence that the company really did try to make the nano drone that fit in the palm of your hand.[32] The main problem was the apparent lack of financial resources.[33] Backers did not receive anything for their contributions and still complain about it regularly on the Kickstarter webpage, even up to the time of writing this chapter in July 2019.[34] As at July 2019, there were 10,536 comments, and most of them appear to be about the lack of delivery. Again, the concerns are indicative of extreme agency problems as indicated in Chapter 2, Overview of agency and signaling

---

[29] https://www.kickstarter.com/projects/ryangrepper/coolest-cooler-21st-century-cooler-thats-actually

[30] https://www.oregonlive.com/business/2018/06/kickstarter_fiasco_coolest_coo.html

[31] https://www.oregonlive.com/business/2017/06/coolest_coolers_settlement_cou.html

[32] https://www.digitaltrends.com/cool-tech/biggest-kickstarter-and-indiegogo-scams/

[33] https://www.digitaltrends.com/cool-tech/biggest-kickstarter-and-indiegogo-scams/

[34] https://www.kickstarter.com/projects/torquing/zano-autonomous-intelligent-swarming-nano-drone/comments

theory in crowdfunding, and highlight the need for investor due diligence and regulatory oversight, as well as transparent documentation of how crowdfunded funds have been spent.

4.5.3 Central Standard Timing

Central Standard Timing raised $1,026,292 from 7658 backers over 45 days in January–February 2013. It claimed to be the world's thinnest watch (0.80 mm).[35] In 2015 the company filed for bankruptcy.[36] The claim and report from the company was that there was a dispute with the manufacturer, which suggests the issue is not exactly one of fraud but could be interpreted as frustration or mistake. As of July 2019, there are 3789 comments on the Kickstarter page, and most appear to be from backers that want their money back expressing outrage for matters that are consistent with the entrepreneurs not acting in the best interests of their backers (i.e., agency problems as per Chapter 2: Overview of agency and signaling theory in crowdfunding). People in the crowd, particularly backers but not only backers, continue to post such comments in 2019, similar to the ZANO drone case immediately discussed earlier.

4.5.4 FND Films

FND Films crowdfunded a film "IT'S ALL GOOD" on Indiegogo in 2014, raising $77,915 from 605 backers.[37] It was their second successful Indiegogo campaign, where their first was a film in 2012 for which they raised $11,100 of their $10,000 capital goal in 2012.[38] However, it was their last. It's All Good was not all good. It was a farce. The campaign video talks about the need for funds for travel and production and asks to "give us your f_&$*#*_ing money!"[39] And in the end, they did deliver a film, but it was about the promoters blowing it on partying in Europe and Mexico as a way to troll the crowdfunders. Needless to say, the backers were not happy about it, where, for example, one backer complains about being broke and in college and had hoped to spend the money on food if they were otherwise not serious about making a movie.[40] Commentators in media were equally unimpressed.[41]

In an extraordinary way the case of FND films not only highlights some of the agency problems overviewed in Chapter 2, Overview of agency and signaling theory in crowdfunding, but also it even shows the entrepreneurs mocking how pronounced those problems can be through their own maliciously designed farcical campaign, and how little

[35] https://www.kickstarter.com/projects/1655017763/cst-01-the-worlds-thinnest-watch

[36] https://www.digitaltrends.com/cool-tech/biggest-kickstarter-and-indiegogo-scams/

[37] https://www.indiegogo.com/projects/it-s-all-good-by-fnd-films#/

[38] https://www.indiegogo.com/projects/punching-by-fnd-films#/

[39] https://www.youtube.com/watch?v = Kfy2iaVpEKI

[40] https://www.indiegogo.com/projects/it-s-all-good-by-fnd-films#/comments

[41] See, for example, https://www.theverge.com/tldr/2016/9/29/13106770/its-all-good-indiegogo-crowdfunding-troll and https://www.digitaltrends.com/movies/its-all-good-indiegogo/.

the crowd can do to figure them out in advance. In a strange way the entrepreneurs did deliver a product. But the vague description of what that product was going to be enabled them to deliver a product that mocked their backers and the entire crowdfunding process. The case highlights the importance of product specificity in the description to mitigate the ability of entrepreneurs to change the scope or content of what they will deliver.

If there is one positive outcome from this case, it seems fair to say that these entrepreneurs would have a tough time crowdfunding again. Likewise, it would be interesting as well to imagine what their career trajectories would have been in the absence of creating this campaign, particularly, with such a notorious and well-publicized campaign that is permanently visible on the web.

4.5.5 Art Gallery of Ontario's Infinity Room

An example of a failed crowdfunding campaign is the Art Gallery of Ontario's (AGO's) Infinity Room Art Exhibit in 2018 with a $1.3 million campaign goal.[42] The initial campaign had minimal rewards levels, with just one option of $25 to see the exhibit and $100 to get a tax receipt[43] (in sharp contrast to the cases of successful crowdfunding from Section 4.4 with multiple rewards levels with enticing incentives). It was crowdfunded not through a crowdfunding platform but instead through the AGO's own webpage. The campaign failed, raising just half of its desired goal, despite some media coverage.[44] The AGO nevertheless secured the funding in the end from other sources and even created a permanent one to say thanks to the 4700 donors.[45]

Chapter 5, Crowdfunding models: keep-it-all versus all-or-nothing, and Chapter 6, Crowdfunding cleantech, of this book explore in more detail how different attributes of a campaign design can influence fundraising success.

4.6 Summary and overview of the remaining chapters in Part II of this book

This chapter overviewed the components of successful rewards-based crowdfunding. We highlighted the importance of campaign design with text, videos, social media connections, pictures, and rewards levels in achieving funding goals. We further provided cases where crowdfunding was successful as well as a failure.

Chapter 5, Crowdfunding models: keep-it-all versus all-or-nothing, explores in more detail exactly how relevant different decision variables are in a campaign in order to successfully fundraise through rewards-based crowdfunding. Chapter 6, Crowdfunding cleantech, thereafter considers the specialized context of cleantech crowdfunding campaigns. Finally, Chapter 7, Crowdfunding to internationalize, presents information and cases on the use of crowdfunding for entrepreneurial internationalization to complete

[42] https://canadianart.ca/features/hard-lessons-from-the-agos-kusama-crowdfunding-problems/

[43] https://canadianart.ca/news/art-gallery-of-ontario-crowdfund-kusama-infinity-room/

[44] https://nowtoronto.com/culture/art-and-design/ago-kusama-crowdfunding-infinity-room/

[45] https://ago.ca/infinityago-thankyou

Part II of this book. Part III starts in Chapter 8, Equity crowdfunding, valuation, and cases, with an introduction to equity crowdfunding and marketplace lending.

Key terms

Adverse selection
Agency costs
Campaign goal
Generalist platform
Moral hazard
Specialist platform
Reward levels
Social innovation
Traction

Discussion questions

4.1. Discuss the advantages associated with rewards-based crowdfunding. What precisely are the advantages to the entrepreneur versus the backers?

4.2. Explain the possible problems with rewards-based crowdfunding? How do the possible problems differ between the entrepreneurs versus the backers?

4.3. What elements are typically found in successful rewards-based crowdfunding campaigns? Which do you think are most important? Would you expect the parts of the campaign to differ depending on the industry sector?

4.4. What are some advantages and disadvantages associated with mixing rewards- and donations-based crowdfunding together in the same campaign?

4.5. What distinguished a failed crowdfunding campaign from a fraudulent crowdfunding campaign? Provide some examples of failed crowdfunding campaigns and explain why you think they did not amount to fraud.

4.6. Relate the agency problems of Chapter 2, Overview of agency and signaling theory in crowdfunding, to some of the cases presented in this chapter. Were the successful cases in some way related to signaling or mitigating expected agency problems? And were failed cases in some ways related to failure to signal or mitigate expected agency problems?

4.7. How do rewards levels in crowdfunding campaigns relate to moral hazard problems discussed in Chapter 2, Overview of agency and signaling theory in crowdfunding?

4.8. How do pictures, videos, social media connections, and text in crowdfunding campaigns relate to adverse selection problems discussed in Chapter 2, Overview of agency and signaling theory in crowdfunding?

4.9. Are information asymmetries and agency costs more likely to be more pronounced on specialists or generalist crowdfunding platforms?

4.10. How would entrepreneurs mitigate the costs of idea replication associated with posting a crowdfunding campaign?

Crowdfunding models: keep-it-all versus all-or-nothing

5.1 Introduction

Standardized Internet platforms that act as two-sided markets through the participation of a large crowd have facilitated the rise of crowdfunding. These platforms enable clear mechanisms through which individuals can provide money for, or even invest in, early stage entrepreneurial firms (Belleflamme, Lambert, & Schwienbacher, 2014; Mollick, 2014b; Vismara, 2016). Understanding how crowdfunding works has attracted increasing interest from research scholars (Burtch, Ghose, & Wattal, 2015; Chemla & Tinn, 2017; Iyer, Khwaja, Luttmer, & Shue, 2015; Kuppuswamy & Bayus, 2018; Roma, Petruzzelli, & Perrone, 2017; Stanko & Henard, 2017; Yu, Johnson, Lai, Cricelli, & Fleming, 2017). However, most of this research abstracts from the fact that platforms differ significantly from each other. Some of these differences likely affect the capacity of entrepreneurs to attract crowdfunders and share risk with them. In this chapter, taking the entrepreneurial perspective, we provide new theory and supporting evidence as to how the design of the crowdfunding mechanism can influence the risks and benefits associated with crowd participation.

Most policies that stimulate entrepreneurial financing are based on tax incentives, friendlier bankruptcy laws, and publicly funded incubator centers that all lower the risks to entrepreneurs and their investors (Grilli & Murtinu, 2014; Milosevic, 2018). There is comparatively less focus in the literature on whether or not shifting risk between the entrepreneur and investors facilitates entrepreneurial financing and innovation, particularly at the seed stage of development.[1] On the one hand, less risk for the entrepreneur encourages exploration (Manso, 2011). On the other hand, less risk for the investor encourages larger capital investment, and more capital enables entrepreneurship and innovation. It is unclear whether enabling an alteration of risk between investors and seed stage entrepreneurs ultimately helps or hinders entrepreneurial financing. In this

---

[1] Throughout this chapter, we use the term risk alteration instead *of risk sharing* or risk transfer. As discussed later, entrepreneurs and investors often bear different risks that cannot be simply transferred such as insurance policies or derivative contracts.

chapter, we shed light on this question by examining a unique crowdfunding setting where entrepreneurs self-select into higher risk taking.

Kickstarter and Indiegogo are reward-based crowdfunding platforms through which entrepreneur's state capital raising goals. In exchange, individuals are offered a reward for participating.[2] In most cases the reward is the product that is eventually produced by the entrepreneur with the money raised during the campaign. In practice, two types of funding models have emerged: "all-or-nothing" (AON) and "keep-it-all" (KIA). In the AON model, entrepreneurial firms set a capital raising goal below which the entrepreneurial firm does not keep any of the pledged funds, and the crowd does not receive any reward. In contrast, in the KIA model, the entrepreneurial firm can keep the entire pledged amount, albeit at higher fees, regardless as to whether or not the stated capital raising goal is reached. In this chapter, we consider whether these two fundraising models are associated with different types of entrepreneurial firms and projects, and whether this choice impacts the likelihood of campaign success. Moreover, we explore whether the choice of funding model leads to different sensitivity of crowdfunders to information released by the entrepreneurs.

Most crowdfunding campaigns do not achieve their funding goals.[3] Thus choosing the right funding model is a crucial strategic choice as it not only affects the capacity of the entrepreneur to collect the pledges but also affects how the risk of underfunding is allocated between the crowd and the entrepreneur. One critical problem plaguing these entrepreneurs is the inherent difficulty in conveying the true quality of the project and the capacity of the entrepreneur to deliver leading to information asymmetry (Ahlers et al., 2015; Hildebrand, Puri, & Rocholl, 2017).

We theorize that entrepreneurs who self-select the AON model do so in order to signal to the crowd that they are committed to only undertake the project if enough capital is raised reducing the crowd's risk that undercapitalized projects will be undertaken, as under the KIA model. Thus crowdfunders are less reluctant to pledge money under the AON model as they are sure to receive their money back if the funding goal is not achieved. As such, AON projects are expected to attract more backers and be more successful. Entrepreneurs will only bear this risk if they have a highly valuable project, and the signal of choosing AON is credible. Entrepreneurs with less valuable projects do not choose the same funding model. In contrast, KIA projects are selected by entrepreneurs who have less promising projects, as AON is too costly a signal. These entrepreneurs may prefer using a more flexible funding model that allows them to collect small amounts. This may occur if the degree of underfunding is not so excessive that the crowd avoids bearing a greater risk of not receiving anything. Conversely, the AON model involves the entrepreneur taking more risk (i.e., they have "skin in the game") and, as such, has a

---

[2] Other forms of crowdfunding platforms exist, such as equity-, loan-, and donation-based crowdfunding platforms. These platforms attract different types of crowdfunders as incentives for participation are not based on receiving a product.

[3] Throughout the analysis, we define "success" as having achieved the funding goal at the end of the campaign. This definition is consistent with most of the prior literature. Kickstarter offers a success rate of 36% (source: https://www.kickstarter.com/help/stats), while Indiegogo does not communicate statistics. The data in this chapter indicate a success rate of 18% for Indiegogo.

greater chance of successful funding. This makes the choice of funding model a credible and costly signal (the so-called Spence Condition; Spence, 1973). The KIA model, while offering an overall lower chance of success, may be optimal for entrepreneurs with less valuable projects or when the signal is not credible, especially if the higher risk involved in AON is not compensated by sufficiently higher success rates.

To test these propositions, we extracted a sample of 22,850 fundraising campaigns from the Indiegogo platform (www.indiegogo.com) from 2011 to 2013. Unlike other major platforms, Indiegogo has offered entrepreneurs the option of selecting either the AON or the KIA model since December 2011. Thus Indiegogo offers a unique setting to investigate our research questions. The data indicate that 94.8% of the fundraising campaigns used the KIA model, while only 5.2% used the AON model. Campaigns using the AON model, on average, sought to raise $31,397 (with a median of $16,485), while campaign goals for KIA were, on average, $20,478 (with a median of $10,000). AON campaigns had an average completion ratio (i.e., the ratio of total pledges over goal in a percentage) of 64%, while KIA campaigns had a completion ratio of 42%. Put differently, 34% of all AON campaigns were successfully completed (i.e., they had a completion ratio of 100% or higher), while only 17% of all KIA campaigns achieved their funding goals. AON campaigns had, on average, 189 backers (with a median of 43), while KIA campaigns, on average, attracted 76 backers (with a median of 33).

The data further indicate that there is a positive relationship between the funding goal and usage of the AON model, in line with the prediction that the AON model constitutes a commitment device thereby reducing the risk to the crowd as underfunded projects are not undertaken with AON. Consistent with existing studies on crowdfunding success (Belleflamme, Lambert, & Schwienbacher, 2013; Mollick, 2014a; Mollick & Kuppuswamy, 2014), campaigns with larger fundraising goals are less successful. Controlling for size differences, our data indicate that AON campaigns are more likely to achieve their goals, despite the fact that their goals are larger, on average. Taken together, these results are consistent with the view that choosing to use AON is a clear signal to the crowd that the entrepreneur will not commit to undertaking the project if the necessary funds are not raised. This represents a potential cost to the entrepreneur who may not be able to undertake the project. Thus the AON model reduces the risk to the crowd enabling AON entrepreneurial firms to set higher goals, raise more money, and more likely reach their stated goals. Opting for the AON model allows entrepreneurs to alleviate constraints on their fundraising goals induced by the negative impact of their funding goals on success. In contrast, KIA projects tend to be less successful, in general, despite their lower goals when compared to AON campaigns. Under a KIA campaign the crowd bears the risk when an entrepreneurial firm undertakes a project that is underfunded and, more likely to eventually fail, making the crowd more reluctant to pledge. However, these conclusions do not imply that AON is systemically superior as AON entails significantly higher risk for the entrepreneur, something only entrepreneurs with the most promising projects are willing to bear. Our findings support the view that entrepreneurs are often willing to reduce their own risk by opting for a KIA model at the expense of achieving higher funding amounts and reducing their chances of achieving these goals. These findings are robust to a number of specification tests including controls for the endogenous choice of the fundraising goal and propensity score matching.

The remainder of the chapter is structured as follows. The following section provides information regarding the structure of the Indiegogo platform. Our theoretical predictions are then explained and summarized. The subsequent sections introduce the data and provide empirical tests. A discussion and concluding remarks are provided in the last section.

5.2 The structure of the Indiegogo platform

Launched in 2007, Indiegogo has become the second largest crowdfunding platform worldwide (with more than 800,000 projects launched and more than $1.3 billion raised since 2007), after Kickstarter (with 420,127 launched projects since 2008, among which 151,602 were successfully funded for a total amount raised of $3.49 billion).[4,5] Indiegogo offers entrepreneurs the possibility of launching their online reward-based crowdfunding campaign in three categories: Creative, Innovative, or Social, subdivided into 24 subcategories (see the full description in Table 5.1). Entrepreneurial projects presented on the platform are quite varied ranging from eyeglasses that stream first person videos through social media, classified in the Creative category and the design subcategory, to a brain-sensing headband classified in the Innovative category and the technology subcategory, to a training center for rescue dogs classified in the Social category and the animals subcategory.[6,7,8] The website is available in English, French, German, and Spanish, but project leaders may be located in any country throughout the world. Entrepreneurs must have a fundraising goal of at least 500 U in any accepted currency (USD, EUR, GBP, CAD, or AUD). An individual, a group of persons, a registered business, a nonprofit institution, a community, or even a religious or political organization can post projects. Campaigns can last up to 60 days for AON and up to 120 days for KIA. During the campaign the platform collects pledges from backers. Once the campaign ends, the money is transferred to the entrepreneur via PayPal.

One of the main differences between Indiegogo and most other platforms is the possibility for the entrepreneur to choose between a KIA funding model and an AON model.[9] Other major platforms, such as Kickstarter, FundedByMe, or PeopleFund.it, only offer the

---

[4] *Source*: https://expandedramblings.com/index.php/indiegogo-facts-statistics/ (last viewed on October 9, 2018).

[5] *Source*: https://www.kickstarter.com/help/stats (last viewed on October 9, 2018).

[6] https://www.indiegogo.com/projects/social-video-glasses#/

[7] https://www.indiegogo.com/projects/muse-the-brain-sensing-headband#/

[8] https://www.indiegogo.com/projects/a-brighter-future-for-dogs-in-need#/

[9] There are other platforms offering choices between the KIA and AON models, such as Community Funded and Crowdtilt. Indiegogo, however, is by far the larger and more widely known platform according to the Google page rank (from 0 up to 10), which assigns a value of 7 for Indiegogo, 4 for Community Funded, and 6 for Crowdtilt. By comparison, Kickstarter's Google page rank is seven and Wikipedia is nine. When compared to these other platforms that also offer the choice between the KIA and AON models, Indiegogo is also larger in terms of the number of projects posted and the volume pledged.

TABLE 5.1 Description of variables.

Project characteristics variables	Definition
All-or-Nothing Dummy	Dummy variable equal to one if the entrepreneur chooses an "all-or-nothing" funding model and zero for the "KIA" funding model
Verified Nonprofit	Dummy variable indicating whether the entrepreneur is a US registered nonprofit organization
Goal	The crowdfunding campaign goal in USD set by the entrepreneur. For campaigns based on a currency other than USD, we converted the amount into USD at the annual average exchange rate
Reward Levels	Number of reward levels offered by the entrepreneur for his campaign
Risk for the Entrepreneur	Interaction term of "All-or-Nothing Dummy" and "Goal"
Team Size	Number of members in the team leading the project
Duration	Duration of the funding campaign in days and set by the entrepreneur prior to starting the campaign
Innovative Dummy	Dummy variable indicating whether the project belongs to the "Innovative" category (as defined by Indiegogo), which includes the following subcategories: technology, small business, food, and sports
Creative Dummy	Dummy variable indicating whether the project belongs to the "Creative" category (as defined by Indiegogo), which includes the following subcategories: art, dance, film, gaming, music, photography, theater, transmedia, writing, comic, design, fashion, and video/web
Social Dummy	Dummy variable indicating whether the project belongs to the "Social" category (as defined by Indiegogo), which includes the following subcategories: animals, community, education, environment, health, politics, and religion

Soft information variables	
Catch Phrase Length	Length (in number of characters) of the project catch phrase. Indiegogo allows a maximum of 120 characters. This sentence is found in the index description of the project and in the heading of the project page
Gallery Items	Number of pictures or videos presented in the media gallery
Video Pitch Dummy	Dummy variable indicating if a video pitch of the project is provided
Full Text Length	Length (in characters) of the full text of the project description on the project's main page
Social Networks	Number of external links to social networks (such as Facebook, Twitter, or any other community website)
ARI	The "ARI" score based on the full text of the project description. This value is expressed in US grade levels. For instance, Grade 1 indicates text for children of 6–7 years old and Grade 12 for high school students of 17–18 years old. This index is based on the following formula: $[5.71 \times (characters/words) + 0.5 \times (words/sentences) - 21.43]$

(Continued)

II. Rewards Crowdfunding

TABLE 5.1 (Continued)

Project characteristics variables	Definition
Campaign outcome variables	
Total Pledge	Sum of all pledges made by backers
Completion Ratio	Ratio between the total pledge and campaign goal (i.e., the ratio of the variables Total Pledge over Goal)
Success Dummy	Dummy variable equal to one if the completion ratio is at least equal to one and zero otherwise. The project is thus considered fully financed
Extended Success	This variable is an extension of the Success Dummy variable. It is equal to one, also for all KIA projects with a completion ratio higher or equal to 0.8, considering the funding as almost complete for KIA projects. For AON projects, we keep the threshold value of completion ratio at unity as for Success Dummy
Total Backers	Number of backers having pledged money to the project
Instrumental variables	
Med. Goal by Subcat. of Succ. Proj. in s-1	For each project, this is the median goal of successful projects in the same subcategory during the semester previous to the campaign start date
Med. Completion Ratio by Subcat. in s-1	For each project, this is the median completion ratio of projects in the same subcategory during the semester previous to the campaign start date

AON, All-or-nothing; *ARI*, automated readability index; *KIA*, keep-it-all.

possibility of running AON campaigns. Other platforms, such as RocketHub, GoFundMe, or Sponsume, only allow use of the KIA model. In an AON crowdfunding campaign the entrepreneur sets a fixed fundraising goal. If the total money pledged is smaller than the goal at the end of the campaign period, all of the pledges are canceled and the entrepreneur does not receive anything. On Indiegogo, this type of campaign is called "fixed funding," and the platform takes a 4% success fee on the money received by the entrepreneur in the case of a successful campaign. In a KIA campaign the entrepreneur also sets a fixed fundraising goal. However, whatever the outcome at the end of the campaign, the entrepreneur can choose to keep all the money pledged by backers, even if the goal is not reached. On Indiegogo, this type of campaign is called "flexible funding." In this case the platform charges a 4% fee for successful campaigns (as in AON campaigns) and a 9% fee for an unsuccessful campaign if the entrepreneur chooses to call the pledged money. Thus there is a cost to the entrepreneur for setting the funding goal too high.[10] The costs of too high of a goal are even larger for AON projects as the entrepreneur then needs to abandon their project. While all of the campaigns were based on the KIA model in the first years of the platform's existence, Indiegogo started offering entrepreneurs the option of choosing between KIA and AON from November 2011 onward. In Table 5.2, we present very similar projects financed through the AON or the KIA funding model for comparison.

[10] In addition to these success fees, Indiegogo also charges 3% third-party fees for credit card processing for both models.

TABLE 5.2 Examples of similar projects financed through different funding models.

Project type	All-or-nothing		Keep-it-all	
Home furniture	Title: Exhale	URL: https://www.indiegogo.com/projects/tesla-inspired-bladeless-ceiling-fan#/	Title: Canary	URL: https://www.indiegogo.com/projects/canary-the-first-smart-home-security-device-for-everyone#/
	Goal: $35,000	Pledged: $46,458	Goal: $100,000	Pledged: $1,961,663
Mobile phone accessory	Title: BRIGHT	URL: https://www.indiegogo.com/projects/bright-solar-lamp-phone-charger#/	Title: CulCharge	URL: https://www.indiegogo.com/projects/culcharge-smallest-usb-charge-data-cable#/
	Goal: $50,000	Pledged: $54,583	Goal: $15,000	Pledged: $94,311
3D printer	Title: The Peachy Printer	URL: https://www.indiegogo.com/projects/the-peachy-printer-the-first-100-3d-printer-scanner#/	Title: Tantillus	URL: https://www.indiegogo.com/projects/tantillus-portable-3d-printer-5#/
	Goal: $50,000	Pledged: $74,167	Goal: $30,000	Pledged: $10,450
Bluetooth speaker	Title: TMI Stereo	URL: https://www.indiegogo.com/projects/tmi-stereo-the-best-split-wireless-bluetooth-speakers	Title: Boombot REX	URL: https://www.indiegogo.com/projects/boombot-rex-limited-edition#/
	Goal: $22,000	Pledged: $42,307	Goal: $50,000	Pledged: $13,090
Video game	Title: Starship Corporation	URL: https://www.indiegogo.com/projects/starship-corporation#/	Title: Caravaneer 2	URL: https://www.indiegogo.com/projects/caravaneer-2#/
	Goal: $6000	Pledged: $20,550	Goal: $5000	Pledged: $5723
Card game	Title: Sushi Go!	URL: https://www.indiegogo.com/projects/sushi-go-a-super-fast-sushi-card-game#/	Title: Waste Not	URL: https://www.indiegogo.com/projects/waste-not-card-online-game#/
	Goal: $5000	Pledged: $7626	Goal: $25,000	Pledged: $1695
Graphic novel	Title: Magpies	URL: https://www.indiegogo.com/projects/magpies-the-graphic-novel#/	Title: Modo: Ember's End	URL: https://www.indiegogo.com/projects/modo-ember-s-end#/
	Goal: $20,000	Pledged: $30,566	Goal: $15,000	Pledged: $17,631

In this chapter, we focus on data from Indiegogo as the only platform offering a choice between KIA and AON. We recognize that there is a preliminary choice of platform. We use propensity score matching, in part, to tackle the question of whether or not the choice of platform affects the inferences drawn from the data.[11] Entrepreneurs can choose among a large set of national and international platforms, although Indiegogo and Kickstarter are certainly by far the largest platforms worldwide. Ultimately, we can only speculate why an entrepreneur might choose Indiegogo, but some differences between the two platforms are likely to affect the choice. First, Indiegogo was launched approximately 1 year before Kickstarter. In addition, Kickstarter was initially a pure US-based platform, and a US social security number was required to post a project. The Kickstarter platform eventually gave access to individuals located outside of the United States, although it is still not available in all countries (crowdfunders can be based anywhere, either in or outside of the United States). In contrast, Indiegogo was, from its beginning, a truly international platform that attracted projects from everywhere allowing for different currencies and languages of presentation. Thus for a long time, the choice between using Indiegogo and Kickstarter was only possible for the US residents. Moreover, Indiegogo charges slightly lower fees and allows a greater variety of types of projects than Kickstarter. For example, Kickstarter does not allow all of the projects that Indiegogo labels as "social." Thus Indiegogo is more of a generalist platform than Kickstarter. Later, our propensity score matching (PSM) procedure only includes a subset of the projects including Creative and Innovative categories that are common to both platforms.

In sum, two important decisions must be considered by the entrepreneur when setting up their campaign: the funding structure (an AON model vs a KIA model) and the fundraising goal. These two variables are set simultaneously at the beginning of the campaign and are potentially endogenous, as we discuss and control for in our empirical analyses next. Each project also indicates a reward scale. The entrepreneur sets one or more pledge levels (based on the pledged amount) for which they will offer different rewards to the backers. Rewards offered can be as simple as a "thank you" on the project page. Usually, the main reward offered is the project's main product combined with some extras (dedication, personalization, etc.). These rewards offer no legal obligation for the entrepreneur or guarantee for the backers, even in case of project success. In addition to this hard information, Indiegogo also permits an entrepreneur to provide "soft" information about their project, similar to other crowdfunding platforms. While some information is provided before the campaign starts, other information flow accrues only over time. The entrepreneur can update, whenever they need or want, the project page with additional information during the campaign, usually by posting comments.

5.3 Theory and hypotheses

Prior empirical and theoretical work on crowdfunding has focused on the factors that affect success on reward-based crowdfunding platforms that only offer AON

---

[11] The structure of our data does not fully allow for other approaches. We encourage other researchers to investigate the choice of platform questions more fully in future work. Almost all of the papers on crowdfunding to date are based on a single platform. Our look at propensity score matching across two platforms is a small step toward understanding how platform differences may affect inferences drawn from crowdfunding data.

crowdfunding including Kickstarter (Belleflamme et al., 2014; Chemla & Tinn, 2017; Colombo et al., 2015; Mollick, 2014a; Mollick & Kuppuswamy, 2014). Our theoretical setting differs from prior and contemporaneous work on crowdfunding and signaling (Chakraborty & Swinney, 2019) by examining the role of funding model choice as a signal in the crowdfunding campaign. While most prior studies focus on crowd and project characteristics, such as gender (Greenberg & Mollick, 2017) or geographical origin (Agrawal et al., 2013, 2015; Lin & Viswanathan, 2015), our contribution lies in examining the choice of AON versus KIA relative to different project characteristics, the impact on the crowd's willingness to pledge money, and the ultimate campaign outcome. This chapter complements Wei and Lin (2016), which examines how the choice of the market allocation mechanism in online peer-to-peer lending affects crowd participation and outcomes. However, their setting is very different and considers which investors participate in the loan depending upon whether or not the platform uses an auction or a first come, first served allocation mechanism. This chapter further complements the one by Iyer et al. (2015) that studies the contributions of individuals in the form of loan-based crowdfunding, evidencing that peer lenders are good at predicting default risk and are able to assess the risk of crowdfunded projects.

5.3.1 Choosing the funding model

Two important assumptions are required for the funding model to qualify as a "costly signal" that conveys information (following the view of Spence, 1973). First, we assume entrepreneurs know more about the true cost structure of the project (e.g., the amount of fixed costs involved) than the crowd. Under this assumption the entrepreneur may undertake an underfunded project if, relative to fully funded projects, such a project can only be completed at a lower probability of success or a lower final quality of the good produced. In the absence of information asymmetry, signaling is useless. In addition, to ensure the AON funding model is a credible signal in the sense that only entrepreneurs with good projects opt for it (i.e., other entrepreneurs have no incentive to mimic them), we require the costs related to the signal to be higher for low-quality projects than high-quality projects. By cost, we mean higher risk. This means that entrepreneurs need to "have sufficient skin in the game" to convince the crowd as entrepreneurs with low-quality projects find it too costly to adopt the same strategy. In other words, signaling costs must be negatively correlated with project quality (Spence, 1973). If this were not the case, even entrepreneurs with high-quality projects would prefer the KIA model.[12]

These assumptions imply that there is greater risk under AON for the entrepreneur as they get nothing if the funding goal is not met. However, there exists potential for greater return for the entrepreneur from the project once it is undertaken. At the same time, under KIA, there is greater risk for the crowdfunders as they can potentially contribute to an underfunded project that will not be successfully completed. Thus crowdfunders are less willing to contribute, though not

[12] In technical terms, this means we obtain a pooling equilibrium in which all entrepreneurs select the KIA model. The Spence Condition is a necessary (but not sufficient) condition for obtaining a separating equilibrium, where only entrepreneurs with good projects opt for the costly signal (Spence, 1973).

completely unwilling, since underfunded projects can be undertaken albeit at a lower probability of product delivery relative to fully funded projects.

Note that we are referring to different types of risks for the entrepreneur and the crowdfunders so that it does not represent a pure type of risk transfer as typically studied in finance (and that deals within financial markets with derivatives and other types of financial contracts). For the crowdfunders, there is the risk of not being able to receive the product that they funded. For the entrepreneur, there is the risk of not being able to complete the project due to lack of sufficient funding. Thus when the KIA funding model is chosen instead of the AON funding model, crowdfunding, in general, alters the risk between the entrepreneur and the crowdfunders. Given that the latter takes on a different risk than the former, we use the term "risk alteration" and not "risk transfer."[13]

The funding choice also affects the crowd's expected gains and incentives. By imposing an AON model, individual backers are more likely to pledge since they know they will become crowdfunders for the project, but only if a sufficient number of other crowdfunders with similar preferences also contribute. This ensures that an underfunded project is stopped. Thus the level of the funding goal plays the role of a costly mechanism that ensures the entrepreneur will limit the risk faced by the crowd only by starting the project with sufficient financial resources. This maximizes the chances that the entrepreneur will be able to deliver the promised reward to the crowdfunders. In contrast, the KIA model forces crowdfunders to bear the risk of the entrepreneur undertaking the project, even if the goal is not met.[14]

By selecting the AON model, entrepreneurs have the ability to signal the quality and feasibility of the project. If an entrepreneur leads a project with a high capital goal, they must attract more crowdfunders and/or try to convince each of them to pledge larger amounts. To do so the entrepreneur must offer some sort of guarantee to the crowdfunders. Based on the notion that incompletely funded projects are riskier than projects that begin fully financed, setting an AON campaign demonstrates to the potential crowdfunders that the project will start if and only if the funds are sufficient. The decision to seek AON financing imposes a larger risk for the entrepreneur of being unable to start the project at all, making the choice of AON a costly and credible signal for the entrepreneur (consistent with the Spence Condition that any signal must be costly to be credible; Spence, 1973). Such campaigns may then be considered less risky for the backers and may, as such, attract more backers and larger amounts. These arguments lead to our first hypothesis, as follows:

---

[13] We owe our gratitude to an anonymous reviewer for this helpful comment.

[14] Strausz (2017) studies the choice of funding goals in the presence of entrepreneurial moral hazard. Here, in line with other empirical studies on the topic, we assume the funding goal to be exogenous (although we do test for possible endogeneity) as it is primarily driven by the cost structure of the project. This is because entrepreneurs continue to sell their product in the aftermarket. If this were not the case and the entrepreneur should raise more than what is needed to kick start the project, they would carry even greater risk. Setting the funding goal freely may then constitute a second signaling mechanism, which, following Strausz (2017), may be hampered by moral hazard. Thus the overall impact on fundraising is then ambiguous. An interesting study on entrepreneurial moral hazard in crowdfunding is provided by Lin and Pursiainen (2018) that indicates that moral hazard leads to lower success rates.

Hypothesis 5.1: *Projects with high capital goals are more likely to opt for all-or-nothing crowd-funding campaigns.*

5.3.2 Likelihood of success under all-or-nothing versus keep-it-all

Given this prediction on the choice of funding models, especially in light of the discussed signaling theory, we further expect outcomes to be affected in terms of achieving (or not achieving) the campaign goal. Considering the risk alteration under the different funding models, entrepreneurs will never pursue riskier AON campaign strategies unless the average success level associated with the riskier campaign strategy is higher. If success were, on average, higher under KIA campaigns, entrepreneurs would never select AON campaigns because there is no reward for taking the extra risk (Spence, 1973). In contrast, we expect KIA projects to be less successful since the crowd bears the risk of an entrepreneurial firm undertaking a project that is underfunded and more likely to fail. Thus the crowd is less willing to participate. All things being equal, entrepreneurs will use the riskier AON method only if they are certain they have a viable project. In this case, using the AON model represents a credible signal and an optimal choice for the entrepreneur.

In sum, in view of the signaling theory, we expect the following hypothesis:

Hypothesis 5.2: *All-or-nothing campaigns are, on average, more likely to be successful (i.e., achieve the stated funding goal) than keep-it-all campaigns.*

5.3.3 Disclosure of soft information

The risks entrepreneurs face in terms of an underfunded AON project are much more pronounced than an underfunded KIA project since no money is obtained in the first case. As such, we expect entrepreneurs to spend more effort and expense (in terms of money and time) on preparing the campaign prior to its launch. These expenses are primarily in the form of soft information, such as employing longer catch phrases, more photos, a video pitch, and longer project descriptions.

Hypothesis 5.3: *Entrepreneurs pursuing riskier campaign strategies will make greater use of soft information to mitigate the uncertainty faced by the crowd.*

5.4 Data and summary statistics

Our dataset was extracted directly from the Indiegogo website. Data were collected page by page in October 2013. On Indiegogo, all finished projects stay visible on the website regardless as to whether the campaign was successfully funded or not. Our initial sample consisted of all 47,139 finished campaigns that took place from the beginning of Indiegogo in 2008 to October 2013. Computer automated data collection led to a loss of less than 5% of data that is due to missing or erroneous key values or inconsistencies in data provided on the Indiegogo website. There is no evidence that these missing data were linked to specific project characteristics. Thus it seems reasonable to assume that these missing projects were randomly distributed and that our initial sample is representative of the full population of projects launched on Indiegogo.

Since the database includes projects with five different currencies (USD/EUR/CAD/AUD/GBP), we converted all monetary values (goals, pledges, and rewards) to USD to make them comparable. The exchange rate is the yearly average exchange rate. For campaigns running over two subsequent calendar years, the ending date was retained. We excluded 5727 campaigns that took place between 2007 and November 2011 since the choice between the AON and KIA model was only introduced in December 2011. As such, our hypotheses could not be tested on these campaigns. Following previous empirical research on crowdfunding (Mollick, 2014), we excluded projects with a fundraising goal under $5000. Such projects typically rely on money from family, friends, and relatives and cannot be compared with projects relying on backers (i.e., the crowd) outside the close network of the entrepreneur. We also excluded projects with a goal higher than $200,000, which corresponds to the 99th percentile of our distribution. Indeed, some projects had very large fundraising goals (12 projects had a goal higher or equal to $10m). Consistent with the approach adopted by Mollick (2014a) for Kickstarter data, we considered these few observations as outliers, distinct from the traditional type of projects proposed on the platform. Our final sample was composed of 22,850 campaigns. A full description of the variables available in our dataset is provided in Table 5.1. Variables are classified as three types: project characteristics, soft information provided at the beginning of and during the campaign, and campaign output.

We control for other factors that can affect the choice of funding model and ultimate campaign success including, but not limited to, the information provided by the entrepreneur, other project characteristics, the team size, and the structure of the rewards. The level of information provided prior to the fundraising campaign may affect the probability of success.

The number of reward levels can further affect the probability of success as it affects the compensation of the crowdfunders. More reward levels increase the utility of crowdfunders when they have different preferences for how the final product should look (e.g., the color or design) as each crowdfunder can select the most appropriate reward type for themselves. This greater choice, in turn, increases the total amount of pledges as more backers may want to participate. From the perspective of the entrepreneur, more reward levels reduce the risk of failure. While the overall effect on the choice of the funding model is unclear, it is important to control for the structure of the rewards as this affects crowd participation and, ultimately, the entrepreneur's risk. We further expect that campaigns with more reward scales are more likely to succeed since these campaigns are more likely to match the preferences of the crowd due to a broader variation in the amount that can be invested and the reward to be received.

The recorded project characteristics are mandatory information and prior to the start of the campaign, all of the entrepreneurs set them once and for all. While some variables including the category/subcategory and the location are intrinsic to the project itself, others, such as the goal, the funding model, the number of rewards, the level of each reward (the suggested amount a backer should give), and the duration, are set freely by the entrepreneur. The additional "soft" information is a set of descriptive information provided to inform the crowd about the project. It consists of text, pictures, video pitches, and additional comments and updates, as well as any other information that the entrepreneur discloses to potential backers either at the beginning of or during the campaign. As these pieces of information are primarily of a qualitative nature, we limited ourselves to those that could be measured quantitatively. For instance, information, such as the number of words/pictures/items and the presence or not of some items, allowed us to observe the implication of the entrepreneur in their project and the degree of preparedness associated with success (Mollick, 2014a). Where it is difficult or costly for the entrepreneur to provide information that is more than empty talk, campaigns that offer greater information (e.g., providing a video, not only a textual description of the project) are more likely to be successful.

Given that this information is intended for a wide audience, we include the automated readability index (ARI) as a control variable. Readability indexes are designed to gauge the understandability of written text. This index uses the full text of the project description as described in Table 5.1. The ARI offers an index expressed in US grade levels making it easy to interpret economically. For instance, Grade 1 indicates text for children who are 6—7 years old, while Grade 12 indicates text for high school students who are 17—18 years old.[15]

We include subcategory, month, and country fixed effects in all our regressions to control for other unobservable characteristics in order to mitigate possible omitted-variable biases. For instance, projects from different subcategories may differ in terms of the importance of fixed costs, which drives up the costs of undertaking an underfunded project. Projects with absolutely no fixed costs can be started with any number of backers as long as the required pledge covers the product's marginal cost of production. Similarly, these projects may differ in their variable costs. Moreover, projects in some subcategories may find it easier to pursue a scaled-down project due to the nature of the product being produced. Examples include books (e.g., a subset of the proposed chapters or a comic book without color), music albums with fewer tracks than expected, and video games with fewer levels and less options (e.g., less items, no digital voices, or less sophisticated graphics). The subcategory, month, and country information are readily available on the project website.

Finally, we consider campaign output based on observable information at the end of the campaign. These output measures consist of the total amount pledged by backers, the total number of backers, and the completion ratio. These output measures define the success of the campaign. We used the total number of backers since prior work in a non-crowdfunding context has established that a larger and diversified investor base improves financial access and opportunities in the future, lowers the cost of capital, and facilitates corporate financing decisions (Corwin & Schultz, 2005; Huang, Shangguan, & Zhang, 2008; Huang & Zhang, 2011; Stulz, 1999). Thus the number of investors has likewise been

---

[15] In unreported analyses, we also considered an alternate measure of readability called the Coleman—Liau index, which is based on the notion that the length of words is a better predictor of readability than syllable counts. We obtained qualitatively similar results as both measures are highly correlated. When both measurements are included in the same regression, the ARI takes all the significance leading us to prefer this measurement over the Coleman—Liau index.

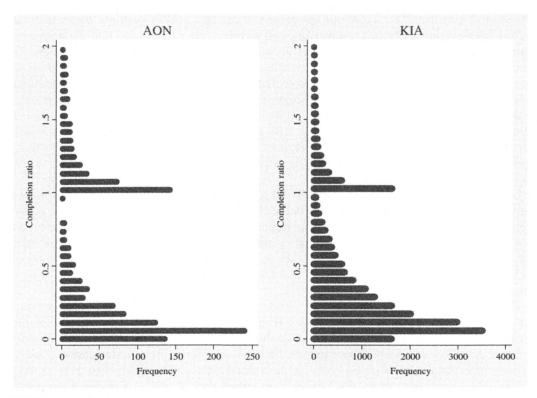

FIGURE 5.1   Histogram of completion ratio by funding model.
This Fig. 5.1 illustrates, separately, the frequency (in number of campaigns) of the Completion Ratio for each funding model. Statistics are based on the final sample of projects, but the histogram shown is truncated at a completion ratio of two to enhance readability.

adopted as a measure of success in a crowdfunding context (Ahlers et al., 2015). We define the variable *Completion Ratio* as the ratio of the total amount pledged over the funding goal set by the entrepreneur. Our primary measure of success is a dummy variable called *Success Dummy*, which takes a value of one if the *Completion Ratio* is equal to or greater than one and zero otherwise. Fig. 5.1 illustrates the distribution of the *Completion Ratio* for AON and KIA (up to a value of 2) and highlights that the distribution is highly weighted on zero and one. The shape of this distribution lends support to our decision to use a dummy variable as our primary measure of campaign success. In unreported analyses, we considered the *Completion Ratio* an alternative-dependent variable to the *Success Dummy*, and our obtained conclusions are qualitatively similar. Thus we do not report them next.

As demonstrated in Table 5.3, Panel A, 56.2% of the projects in our final sample belong to the Creative category, 13.3% to the Innovative category, and 30.5% to the Social category. The AON model is becoming increasingly popular and now represents more than 5% of new campaigns (Panel A). Especially innovative projects choose the AON model more often, consistent with the view that these projects may be subject to information asymmetry problems due to their innovative nature. In Table 5.3, Panel B indicates that

TABLE 5.3 Sample distribution.

Panel A. Number of projects by category and by model

	By category			By funding model	
	Creative	Innovative	Social	All-or-nothing	Keep-it-all
2011	496	48	161	5	700
	70.4%	6.8%	22.8%	0.7%	99.3%
2012	5787	1156	3281	503	9721
	56.6%	9.4%	32.3%	4.9%	95.1%
2013	6559	1827	3535	692	11,229
	55%	15.3%	29.7%	5.8%	94.2%
Total	12,842	3031	6977	1200	21,650
	56.2%	13.3%	30.5%	5.2%	94.8%

Panel B. Financing model by category

	All-or-nothing (%)	Keep-it-all (%)
Creative	5.3	94.7
Innovative	11.7	88.3
Social	2.4	97.6
Total	5.2	94.8

Panel A reports the distribution of projects in each category and the funding model year by year for our final sample. Values are given in the number of projects and in the percentage of total projects. Panel B presents the use of funding models (in percent) by category and in total.

innovative projects are more likely to be AON projects (11.7% are AON vs 88.3% KIA), while social projects are more likely to be KIA projects (2.4% are AON vs 97.6% KIA) with creative projects falling in the middle (5.2% AON vs 94.8% KIA).

Table 5.4 presents the summary statistics for our final sample and for the two subsamples, AON and KIA. *t*-Tests for the difference of the mean and the median between both subsamples are provided in the last two columns.

KIA campaigns offer fewer reward levels. The first reward level is, on average, 13% smaller for AON campaigns and equal to $1 in 19% of the cases, while only 12% of the KIA campaigns have a first reward equal to $1 (not reported in Table 5.3). All verified not-for-profit organizations (the variable *Verified Nonprofit*) use the KIA model suggesting that this form of fundraising constitutes a typical way nonprofit organizations raise money on a regular basis. Supporting our signaling hypothesis, AON projects demonstrate 53% higher capital goals (the variable *Goal*), on average, than KIA and a 65% higher median. With an average of 2.4 team members, team size (the variable *Team Size*) is not statistically different between the two subsamples.

TABLE 5.4 Summary statistics by funding model.

Variables	All projects			All-or-nothing			Keep-it-all				
	Mean	Std. dev.	Median	Mean	Std. dev.	Median	Mean	Std. dev.	Median	Mean diff. test	Median diff. test
Project characteristics											
Goal	21,052.00	26,601.00	10,000.00	31,397.00	36,878.00	16,485.00	20,478.00	25,792.00	10,000.00	1.1e+04***	6500.00***
Verified Nonprofit	0.10	0.30	0.00	0.00	0.00	0.00	0.11	0.31	0.00	−0.11***	n.a.
Reward Levels	7.44	3.94	8.00	8.74	3.72	9.00	7.37	3.94	8.00	1.37***	1.00***
Team Size	2.40	2.03	2.00	2.40	2.05	2.00	2.40	2.03	2.00	0.00	0.00
Duration	48.32	22.61	45.00	40.27	13.22	40.00	48.77	22.94	45.00	−8.50***	−5.00***
Soft information											
Catch Phrase Length	115.20	38.68	125.50	115.10	35.24	123.00	115.2	38.86	126.00	−0.12	−3.00**
Gallery Items	6.80	10.52	3.00	7.81	11.29	4.00	6.75	10.48	3.00	1.07***	1.00***
Video Pitch Dummy	0.79	0.41	1.00	0.85	0.36	1.00	0.78	0.41	1.00	0.07***	n.a.
Full Text Length	4658.00	3439.00	3809.00	6098.00	4474.00	5068.00	4579.00	3354.00	3763.00	1519.59***	1306.00***
Social Networks	3.29	31.53	3.00	3.28	1.91	3.00	3.29	32.39	3.00	−0.01	0.00
ARI	15.26	4.62	14.95	14.77	2.88	14.54	15.29	4.69	14.98	−0.52***	−0.43***
Campaign outcome											
Completion Ratio	0.44	1.20	0.22	0.64	1.16	0.21	0.42	1.20	0.22	0.22***	−0.01
Success Dummy	0.18	0.38	0.00	0.34	0.48	0.00	0.17	0.37	0.00	0.18***	n.a.
Total Backers	82.36	413.50	33.00	188.70	803.00	43.00	76.47	379.60	33.00	112.22***	10.00***
Total Pledge	6583.00	29,851.00	2502.00	15,323.00	56,995.00	3903.00	6098.00	27,497.00	2465.00	9224.00***	1451.00***
Observations	22,850			1200			21,650			22,850	

This table presents the summary statistics for the variables included in our database. All of the variables are defined in Table 5.1. We provide means, standard deviations, and medians for the full sample of 22,850 campaigns and for the two subsamples based on funding models. The last two columns provide difference-in-mean tests and difference-in-median tests between the two subsamples. Significance levels are based on two-tailed tests (*P*-value): * $P < .1$, ** $P < .05$, and *** $P < .01$.ARI, Automated readability index.

As the risk of not collecting any funds is higher for an AON campaign, it seems that entrepreneurs provide additional information to increase their chances of attracting more backers. Indeed, project descriptions are longer (the variable *Full Text Length*) and easier to read (*ARI*), and more pictures and video pitches are provided. These differences are consistent with the idea that providing more detailed information and preparing a video is costly, and that these costs are more likely to be borne by entrepreneurs when they opt for the AON model as a signaling mechanism. There is no difference in the number of external social network pages available for both types of projects suggesting that setting up a page on a social network requires little effort to generate extra information. This can also be explained by the fact that social networks are a base constituent of crowdfunding and, as such, considered by a majority of entrepreneurs as a must do before even starting the crowdfunding campaign itself.

Outcomes also differ between subsamples. AON campaigns seem to be more successful (34% vs 17% for KIA campaigns) and attract almost three times more backers (see the variable *Backers* that corresponds to the number of backers at the end of the campaign) providing support for Hypothesis 5.2. This difference in success will be confirmed in the multivariate analysis provided in the next section.

Table 5.5 offers summary statistics based on outcome (i.e., whether the campaign was successful or not in terms of achieving the funding goal). As expected, more information is provided in successful campaigns (longer text, more video pitches, and more pictures in the galleries). Of course, successful projects imply, on average, more backers and a higher average of pledges by backers. Here, too, there is no difference in the social network presence between the two groups suggesting that presence does not mean popularity. The readability of the campaign descriptions does not seem to affect outcomes. The two groups have approximately the same typology of texts. At best, unsuccessful projects are easier to read. However, readability may be driven by the differences in project categories. It is worthwhile to note that the values obtained here are quite high as they correspond to text designed at the undergraduate level. Recall that the ARI score corresponds to the US educational system level, with 12 being the last grade level of secondary education before college and 14 being a second-year undergraduate. Thus an average level of 15 indicates text written (intentionally or not) at a third-year undergraduate level.

Table 5.6 provides further insight into Hypothesis 5.2 on funding outcomes. Panel A of Table 5.6 reports the mean of the *Completion Ratio* and the standard deviation of the *Completion Ratio* for the full sample, the KIA subsample, and the AON subsample, as well as for Innovative, Creative, and Social KIA and AON campaigns. Panel B of Table 5.6 provides the same information for the amount pledged (the variable *Total Pledge*). In these two panels, we use winsorized variables at the 99th percentile to make the different amounts comparable (the same range for each variable) and to avoid excessive outliers at the higher end. The data and figures in Panels A and B as in Table 5.6 show a clear, positive relationship between the standard deviation and mean of the *Completion Ratio*. Thus greater risk for the entrepreneur is associated with a higher average success level.[16]

---

[16] Note that we do not present the same pictures in Table 4.4 for the *Success Dummy* variable as a higher mean for this variable is mechanically related to a higher standard deviation.

TABLE 5.5 Summary statistics by outcome.

Variables	Successful (Success Dummy = 1)			Unsuccessful (Success Dummy = 0)			Mean diff. test	Median diff. test
	Mean	Std. dev.	Median	Mean	Std. dev.	Median		
Project characteristics								
All-or-Nothing Dummy	0.10	0.30	0.00	0.04	0.20	0.00	− 0.06***	n.a.
Goal	13,477.00	16,702.00	8500.00	22,678.00	28,012.00	11,667.00	9200.73***	3167.00***
Verified Nonprofit	0.13	0.33	0.00	0.10	0.29	0.00	− 0.03***	n.a.
Reward Levels	7.99	4.00	8.00	7.32	3.92	7.00	− 0.67***	− 1.00***
Team Size	2.74	2.27	2.00	2.33	1.96	2.00	− 0.41***	0.00
Duration	44.62	20.71	42.00	49.12	22.92	45.00	4.50***	3.00***
Soft information								
Catch Phrase Length	114.00	37.96	123.00	115.50	38.83	126.00	1.40**	3.00***
Gallery Items	8.63	12.38	5.00	6.41	10.04	3.00	− 2.22***	− 2.00***
Video Pitch Dummy	0.82	0.38	1.00	0.78	0.42	1.00	− 0.05***	n.a.
Full Text Length	4990.00	3704.00	4083.00	4587.00	3375.00	3757.00	− 402.70***	− 326.00***
Social Networks	3.33	15.68	3.00	3.28	33.98	3.00	− 0.05	0.00
ARI	15.37	5.01	14.94	15.24	4.53	14.95	− 0.13	0.02
Campaign outcome								
Completion Ratio	1.40	2.60	1.07	0.23	0.20	0.16	− 1.17***	− 0.91***
Total Backers	267.20	953.50	107.00	42.67	59.75	26.00	− 224.56***	− 81.00***
Total Pledge	21,787.00	68,243.00	10,103.00	3318.00	4728.00	1885.00	− 1.8e + 04***	− 8218.00***
Observations		4039			18,811			22,850

This table reports the summary statistics for the variables included in our database. All of the variables are defined in Table 5.1. We provide means, standard deviations, and medians for the subsamples of successful (Success Dummy = 1) and unsuccessful (Success Dummy = 0) campaigns. The last two columns provide difference-in-mean tests and difference-in-median tests between the two subsamples. Significance levels are based on two-tailed tests (*P*-value): * $P < .1$, ** $P < .05$, and *** $P < .01$. ARI, Automated readability index.

Table 5.7 provides a comprehensive correlation matrix that includes the most relevant variables. In particular, the reported correlations offer preliminary support for Hypothesis 5.1 on the funding goal. The correlation of the *Goal* and the *All-or-Nothing Dummy* is 0.0916 and is also significant at the 1% level. As for our prediction for success, we find a correlation of 0.1033 between the *Success Dummy* and the *All-or-Nothing Dummy* supporting the

TABLE 5.6 Risk and return analysis.

Panel A. Completion Ratio

Std. dev	Std. dev	Std. dev	Std. dev	Std. dev	Std. dev
Final sample	22,850	0.403	0.441	0.00	2.22
KIA	21,650	0.396	0.429	0.00	2.22
AON	1200	0.541	0.603	0.00	2.22
Innov. KIA	2677	0.337	0.454	0.00	2.22
Innov. AON	354	0.432	0.584	0.00	2.22
Creat. KIA	12,161	0.409	0.411	0.00	2.22
Creat. AON	681	0.617	0.630	0.00	2.22
Social KIA	6812	0.394	0.447	0.00	2.22
Social AON	165	0.464	0.475	0.00	1.58

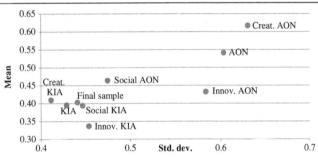

Panel B. Total Pledge

	Obs	Mean	Std. dev.	Min	Max
Final sample	22,850	5402	8370	0	56,461
KIA	21,650	5165	7867	0	56,461
AON	1200	9674	14,086	500	56,461
Innov. KIA	2677	5990	10,209	0	56,461
Innov. AON	354	10,234	15,699	500	56,461
Creat. KIA	12,161	5046	7252	0	56,461
Creat. AON	681	9827	13,805	503	56,461
Social KIA	6812	5055	7846	0	56,461
Social AON	165	7845	11,218	500	56,461

(Continued)

TABLE 5.6   (Continued)

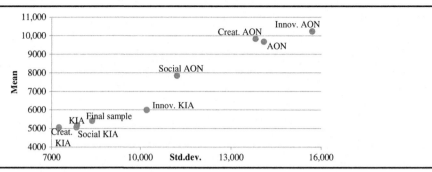

This table presents additional statistics on the risk (standard deviation) and return (mean) of campaign outcomes for various subsamples. Panel A is based on the output variable Completion Ratio, while Panel B is based on Total Pledge. The value of some observations employed here differs from the rest of the analysis as we have winsorized the variables at the 99th percentile to eliminate excessive outliers. *AON*, All-or-nothing; *KIA*, keep-it-all.

TABLE 5.7   Correlation matrix of main variables.

	Goal	All-or-Nothing Dummy	Verified Nonprofit	Reward Levels	Team Size	Duration	Catch Phrase Length	Gallery Items
Goal	1							
All-or-Nothing Dummy	0.0916*	1						
Verified Nonprofit	0.0021	− 0.0791*	1					
Reward Levels	0.1274*	0.0777*	0.0079	1				
Team Size	0.0927*	0.0004	0.0973*	0.1944*	1			
Duration	0.1000*	− 0.0839*	− 0.0090	− 0.0965*	0.0102	1		
Catch Phrase Length	0.0430*	− 0.0007	0.0511*	0.0548*	0.0234*	− 0.0813*	1	
Gallery Items	0.0727*	0.0226*	− 0.0017	0.1874*	0.2217*	0.0477*	0.0444*	1
Video Pitch Dummy	0.0588*	0.0361*	0.0441*	0.3457*	0.1385*	− 0.0542*	0.0512*	0.1214*
Full Text Length	0.1778*	0.0986*	− 0.0116	0.3141*	0.1817*	− 0.0007	0.1142*	0.2333*
Social Networks	0.0034	− 0.0001	0.0047	0.0259*	0.0070	0.0034	0.0136	0.0190*
ARI	0.0270*	− 0.0250*	0.1040*	0.0365*	0.0685*	0.0108	0.0412*	0.0161
Completion Ratio	− 0.0829*	0.0408*	0.0114	0.0119	0.0321*	− 0.0491*	− 0.0080	0.0616*
Success Dummy	− 0.1319*	0.1033*	0.0375*	0.0650*	0.0768*	− 0.0758*	− 0.0143	0.0805*

(Continued)

TABLE 5.7   (Continued)

	Goal	All-or-Nothing Dummy	Verified Nonprofit	Reward Levels	Team Size	Duration	Catch Phrase Length	Gallery Items
Total Backers	0.0982*	0.0605*	− 0.0027	0.0632*	0.0473*	− 0.0304*	0.0082	0.0616*
Total Pledge	0.1491*	0.0689*	0.0093	0.0728*	0.0669*	− 0.0150	0.0182*	0.0931*

	Video Pitch Dummy	Full Text Length	Social Networks	ARI	Completion Ratio	Success Dummy	Total Backers	Total Pledge
Video Pitch Dummy	1							
Full Text Length	0.1639*	1						
Social Networks	0.0214*	0.0012	1					
ARI	0.0523*	0.1246*	0.0478*	1				
Completion Ratio	0.0104	0.0397*	− 0.0003	− 0.0046	1			
Success Dummy	0.0438*	0.0447*	0.0007	0.0105	0.3731*	1		
Total Backers	0.0301*	0.0886*	0.0015	− 0.0125	0.7102*	0.2072*	1	
Total Pledge	0.0389*	0.1213*	0.0019	0.0002	0.4880*	0.2360*	0.6922*	1

This table presents pair-wise correlations between the main variables. All of the variables are defined in Table 5.1. A star indicates a significance level of 1% based on two-tailed tests. *ARI*, Automated readability index.

hypothesis that AON projects are more successful, on average, in achieving their goal. The next section tests and confirms these findings in a multivariate setting.

5.5 Results

5.5.1 Choice of all-or-nothing versus keep-it-all crowdfunding models

Table 5.8 addresses the issue as to what drives entrepreneurs to opt for AON. To test Hypothesis 5.1, we consider that the decision between KIA and AON will depend upon some characteristics intrinsic to the project that exist prior to the campaign launch including the category of the project and the goal amount of the funding campaign. We also expect the size of the team leading the project to have an impact on this choice.

The first method used is a probit regression as our dependent variable *All-or-Nothing Dummy* is binary. However, the goal of the campaign is set at the same time as the funding model and is, therefore, linked. This can cause a problem of endogeneity between our

TABLE 5.8 Choice of funding model for crowdfunding campaigns.

	(1) Probit	(2) First stage (dep. var. = ln(Goal))	(3) IV probit (second stage)	(4) 2SLS
ln(Goal)	0.014***		0.051***	0.085***
Team Size	− 0.001	0.053***	− 0.004***	− 0.005***
IVs				
Med. Goal by Subcat. of Succ. Proj. in s-1 (log)		0.084***		
Med. Completion Ratio by Subcat. in s-1		− 1.132***		
Country F.E.	Yes	Yes	Yes	Yes
Subcategory × Month F.E.	Yes			
Category/industry/semester F.E.		Yes	Yes	Yes
Observations	18,751	22,850	22,850	22,850
Adj./pseudo R^2	0.185	0.078		
			Tests for Weak Instr., *Over-id., and Exog.*	
Over Identif. test			0.076	
Over Identif. P-val			0.782	
First stage F-stat			27.590	
Wald chi^2 test of Exog.			8.252	
Wald chi^2 P-val			0.004	

This table reports the factors influencing the funding model decision. The dependent variable in regressions (1), (3), and (4) is the "All-or-Nothing Dummy," a dummy variable that is equal to one if the model used is "all-or-nothing," and zero if the "keep-it-all" model is used. All of the variables are defined in Table 5.1. Regressions (3) and (4) control for the endogeneity of the variable "ln(Goal)" using a two stage IV probit regression in Model 3 and a 2SLS regression in Model 4. The instrumented variable for the first step [see regression (2)] is "ln(Goal)," and the two instrumental variables used are as follows. The first is the median goal of successful projects in the same subcategory for the semester prior to the campaign launch, and the second is the median Completion Ratio for projects in the same subcategory during the semester prior to the campaign launch. All of the regressions include country, category, industry, and semester fixed effects. Standard errors are robust to heteroskedasticity. Significance levels are based on two-tailed tests (P-value): * $P < .1$, ** $P < .05$, and *** $P < .01$. IV, Instrumental variables.

goal variable and the *All-or-Nothing Dummy*. The campaign goal is primarily determined by real needs, though most likely adjusted for strategic purposes that are based on the desire to signal commitment and on the expectations of the entrepreneur about their capability to attract the crowd's interest. To control for the possible endogeneity of the goal amount, we also use two-step [instrumental variable (IV) probit] regressions in which the first equation estimates the *ln(Goal)* and the second equation estimates the choice of the funding model (*All-or-Nothing Dummy*).

Moreover, all of our models control for fixed effects due to the country of origin of the project initiator, the project category, the industry category (whether it is a multimedia project or not), and the semester of the campaign launch.[17] In the probit regression, we include interactions between subcategories and month fixed effects. We could not include these interaction dummies in the IV regressions as our instruments use similar variations. However, the variable *Verified Nonprofit* is not included as all nonprofit projects use KIA. Hence, there is no variation in the sample. Table 5.8 presents the results for our regressions under various specifications.

Our main explanatory variable of interest is the logarithm of goal. As shown in Table 5.8, the impact of *ln(Goal)* is positive and statistically significant such that a one standard deviation increase in *ln(Goal)* gives rise to a 1.2% (Model 1) increase in the probability of the use of AON. Note that we have carried out several robustness checks that are not reported (but available on request from the authors) in the tables for succinctness. Among other actions, we have also split our sample into projects with a "high funding goal" and a "low funding goal" (either relative to the median or the average), and the results were similar. Moreover, we have split our sample in bins based on the size of the funding goal (with bins of various sizes). These alternative measures do not alter our conclusions.

We now turn to our second estimation methodology, the two-step IV probit regressions (Models 2–4 in Table 5.8). The first stage regression in Model 2 used to estimate the goal is based on two IVs that are linked to the goal of the project but are independent of the decision of the funding model. The first IV is the median goal of successful projects in the same subcategory in the semester prior to the campaign launch, and the second is the median completion ratio for projects within the same subcategory for the semester prior to the campaign launch. We present statistics in Table 5.8 indicating that these are statistically valid instruments (see the discussion below). In terms of the intuition, these variables for the median previous period's goal size of the same subcategory and the median previous period's completion ratio of the same subcategory are likely to affect the goal levels selected by current entrepreneurs seeking crowdfunding. It would be unusual for an entrepreneur to have a vastly different goal amount than a similar, successful entrepreneur in a prior period unless a similar entrepreneur in the prior period was unsuccessful in achieving that goal. We see that higher goals set by previously successful projects [*Med. Goal by Subcat. of Succ. Proj. in s-1 (log)*] positively impact current goals consistent with recent success stories driving follow-up entrepreneurs to undertake more ambitious projects. In contrast, the high completion ratios of previous projects (*Med. Completion Ratio by Subcat. in s-1*) negatively impact current goals, which can be explained by entrepreneurs

---

[17] For the time period, we considered a half year (semester) to be a better choice given that campaigns typically last a few months. Thus entrepreneurs can only assess the completion ratios for a longer time period. One month would not be enough as projects within this shorter time period just started. Funding goals can obviously be assessed on a shorter time period, but we consider that entrepreneurs will likely look for a longer time period, especially if they want to obtain other key indicators (such as the completion ratio of recently finished projects). As for industry fixed effects, we consider two industry dummies: digital (with the following project categories reported by entrepreneurs on Indiegogo: comic, film, gaming, music, photo, transmedia, video/web, and writing) and nondigital (all other categories). A digital industry is able to deliver the product quickly, at no variable extra costs (all costs are generally borne by the first unit), and to a large number of people. Also, they may be supplied partially complete. E-books are a good example.

taking less risk by setting lower goals (consistent with Hypothesis 5.1 as signaling becomes less important). We use the estimated goal [$ln(Goal)$] of the first regression (Model 2) for the estimation of the second regression (Model 3). As a robustness check, Model 4 presents results based on a 2SLS regression (i.e., using ordinary least squares (OLS) for the second equation) that yield qualitatively similar results. The results observed in Table 5.8 confirm our findings in the first probit specification (Model 1) in terms of the statistical significance and show higher economic significance, whereby a one standard deviation increase in ln (Goal) gives rise to a 7.3% (Model 4) increase in the probability of AON. In short, even if we were only partly dealing with endogeneity in these tests, the findings are very stable under different specifications. As such, we have no reason to believe that the results are being significantly affected by endogeneity. If anything, controlling for endogeneity strengthens the inferences that can be drawn from the data.

In addition to these regressions, we created some tests to address concerns about the validity of our IV probit methodology. The first test of endogeneity follows the specification of Durbin–Wu–Haussmann testing the difference between the two estimates. The null hypothesis tests whether the regressor of interest [the variable $ln(Goal)$] is exogenous. As the null hypothesis is rejected in our tests, the variable $ln(Goal)$ is indeed endogenous. Thus ordinary probit estimates are inconsistent, and the IV probit estimates are appropriate. The second test determines whether or not the instruments are weakly correlated with our endogenous variable. Based on the F-statistic values of our first stage, we can assume that our instruments are not weak. We can compare the values with the minimal recommended value of 11.59 for two IVs in Stock, Wright, and Yogo (2002). A third assumption for IV's validity is the exclusion restriction, which refers to the exogeneity of our instruments. Since the exclusion restriction cannot be directly tested, we need to find insights in line with our assumption of exogenous instruments. A first argument usually accepted in the literature is the J-test for the over-identifying restriction computed by the Amemiya–Lee–Newey score following the procedure described by Lee (1992). This test verifies the exogeneity of all instruments assuming that at least one of the instruments is exogenous. The results of this test are provided at the bottom of Table 5.8 and indicate that the null hypothesis cannot be rejected. Thus our instruments seem valid. However, this test may fail to detect the case where all of the instruments are endogenous. To consolidate our confidence in the chosen instruments, we also tested for an existing significant direct impact of our instruments on the funding model by including the instruments directly into the second step equation. These tests are not included in the chapter but are available on request from the authors. By combining these results, we have no evidence that our instruments may fail to satisfy the exclusion restriction.

5.5.2 Outcome of crowdfunding campaigns

Table 5.9 examines the factors that affect the outcome of crowdfunding campaigns in terms of the probability of success for the campaign. We provide results based on different measures of success. The first one is the binary variable *Success Dummy* that is equal to one when the funding goal is achieved. The data indicate that AON campaigns are

TABLE 5.9 Outcome of crowdfunding campaigns.

Panel A

	(1) Success	(2) Backers	(3) Extended Success	(4) Success (after PSMatch)	(5) Backers (after PSMatch)	(6) Extended Success (after PSMatch)
Project characteristics						
All-or-Nothing Dummy	0.168***	56.370**	0.163***	0.214***	41.702	0.203***
ln(Goal)	− 0.115***	35.590***	− 0.121***	− 0.124***	89.289***	− 0.128***
Verified Nonprofit	0.049***	− 0.298	0.064***	0.131***	42.350	0.162***
Reward Levels	0.007***	2.491**	0.007***	0.010***	− 4.248	0.009***
Team Size	0.014***	5.528***	0.015***	0.018***	11.925	0.016***
Duration	− 0.001***	− 0.616***	− 0.001***	− 0.002**	− 0.643	− 0.002***
Soft information						
Catch Phrase Length	− 0.000***	− 0.116	− 0.000***	0.000	− 0.107	− 0.000
Gallery Items	0.002***	1.244***	0.002***	0.005***	1.518	0.005***
Video Pitch Dummy	0.028***	2.257	0.028***	− 0.011	− 12.041	− 0.008
Full Text Length	0.000***	0.006***	0.000***	0.000***	0.025***	0.000***
Social Networks	− 0.002	− 1.169	− 0.002*	− 0.000	10.093	0.002
ARI	0.001	− 1.580**	0.001	0.005	− 14.370**	0.004
Subcategory × Month & Country F.E.	Yes	Yes	Yes	Yes	Yes	Yes
Observations	21,913	22,656	22,108	1839	2364	1839
Adj./pseudo R^2	0.121	0.023	0.12	0.254	0.184	0.252

Panel B

Variable	Unmatched (U)/ matched (M)	Mean		Bias %	% Reduction Bias	t-Test		V(T)/V(C)
		AON	KIA			t	P > t	
Goal	U	31,397.00	20,478.00	34.30		13.90	0.00	2.04[a]
	M	31,415.00	32,665.00	− 3.90	88.60	− 0.80	0.43	0.88[a]
Reward Level	U	8.74	7.37	35.80		11.79	0.00	0.89[a]
	M	8.80	8.67	3.10	91.30	0.77	0.44	0.90
Team Size	U	2.40	2.40	0.20		0.06	0.96	1.02
	M	2.41	2.36	2.60	− 1471.80	0.65	0.52	1.11
Gallery Items	U	7.81	6.75	9.80		3.41	0.00	1.16[a]
	M	7.82	7.56	2.30	76.10	0.59	0.56	1.23[a]

Panel B

| Variable | Unmatched (U)/ matched (M) | Mean | | | % Reduction | t-Test | | |
		AON	KIA	Bias %	Bias	t	P > t	V(T)/V(C)
Full Text Length	U	6098.10	4578.60	38.40		14.97	0.00	1.78[a]
	M	6170.00	5863.70	7.70	79.80	1.70	0.09	1.05
ARI	U	14.77	15.29	− 13.30		− 3.76	0.00	0.38[a]
	M	14.77	14.76	0.20	98.70	0.06	0.95	1.05

[a]*Variance ratios that exceed the 2.5th and 97.5th percentiles.*
Panel A presents the results regarding the impact of the success of a crowdfunding campaign. In Model 1 the dependent variable is the Success Dummy, in Model 2 the dependent variable is the number of backers, and in Model 3 the dependent variable is our extended success measure (including KIA projects with at least 80% completion). Models 4, 5, and 6 are similar to Models 1, 2, and 3, but with matched subsamples (every AON project is matched with one KIA project, and all unmatched KIA projects are dropped). All of the variables are defined in Table 5.1. All of the regressions include country and subcategory × month interaction fixed effects. Standard errors are robust to heteroskedasticity. Significance levels are based on two-tailed tests (P-value): * P < .1, ** P < .05, and *** P < .01. Panel B presents t-tests for equality of means between the all-or-nothing and keep-it-all campaign subsamples before and after propensity score matching for matched variables. It also reports the standardized percentage bias (percentage of the square root of the average of the sample variances in AON and KIA groups) and the variance ratio between the two subsamples. AON, All-or-nothing; ARI, automated readability index; KIA, keep-it-all.

significantly more successful, on average (16.8% in Model 1), and this effect is statistically significant at the 1% level.

The variable *ln(Goal)* is negative and significant at the 1% level, such that a one standard deviation increase in *ln(Goal)* is associated with approximately a 9.9% reduction in the likelihood of success (Model 1). *Verified Nonprofits* are 5.9% more often completed. In line with previous research (Kuppuswamy & Bayus, 2018; Mollick, 2014a), *Duration* is negatively and significantly associated with success. A one standard deviation increase in *Duration* gives rise to a 2.3% reduction in the probability of success. Other statistically significant variables are *Team Size, Catch Phrase Length, Gallery Items, Video Pitch,* and *Full Text Length*.

The next models use alternative measures of success by looking at the number of backers (Model 2) and by the binary variable *Extended Success* (Model 3). This alternative dummy variable takes into account that a completion ratio of slightly less than 100% may still be a relative success for KIA projects as they are funded when they "almost" reach their goal. Thus this alternative measure is equal to one if the completion ratio is 100% for AON projects, but 80% for KIA projects and zero otherwise. The results are mostly in accordance with previous findings in Model 3 for *Extended Success* in terms of the economic and statistical significance. But there are a few pronounced differences with the number of backers. Most notably, there is a positive impact of the project size (goal) on the number of backers where a one standard deviation increase in *ln(Goal)* is associated with a 38.4% increase in the number of backers relative to the average of 82.4. Further, AON projects receive 68.4% more backers relative to the average. A one standard deviation increase in *Reward Levels* is associated with an 11.9% increase in the number of backers relative to the average. A one standard deviation increase in *Team Size* is associated with a 13.6% increase in the number of backers relative to the average.

A one standard deviation increase in *Duration* is associated with a 16.9% reduction in the number of backers relative to the average.

According to Table 5.4, there is, on average, a significant difference in project size between KIA and AON. Since the goal is a key variable of our hypotheses and impacts the decision for the funding model, and since the goal is also a determinant of the completion ratio and, by extension, *Success Dummy*, which is our dependent variable, we wanted to be sure that the difference in the goals between the subsamples was not affecting our results. Using a propensity score matching methodology (Rosenbaum & Rubin, 1983), we are able to weight projects in the KIA subsample to match more closely with the average size of the projects between both subsamples. This methodology links all of the AON projects one by one with the closest KIA project (matching projects based on the campaign start date, category, goal, number of rewards, team size, number of items in the gallery, length of the text, and readability index). In the process, since there are fewer AON projects, all of the AON projects must have at least one KIA equivalent. All KIA projects were dropped that did not match with any AON project. At the end of the matching process, we found a number of observations equivalent in both subsamples (1200 in each, equivalent to the total of the AON projects).

After running the same regression models presented in Model 1 of Table 5.9 on the new matched samples, we were able to confirm that the sign and statistical significance of our results are robust.[18] The findings with matched samples are reported in Models 4 and 6 of Table 5.9. In the economic significance of the results between Models 1 and 4, there are some differences as follows. Relative to Model 1, the marginal effect for the *All-or-Nothing Dummy* is 27.4% higher, the *ln(Goal)* is 7.8% higher, the *Verified Nonprofit* is 267% larger, the *Reward Levels* is 42.8% larger, the *Team Size* is 28.5% larger, and the *Duration* is two times larger in the matched sample in Model 5. The marginal effects for *Gallery Items* and the *ARI* are 2.5 and 5 times larger, respectively, in Model 4 relative to Model 1. The marginal effects for the other soft information variables are statistically insignificant in Model 5. The economic significance for the estimates in Model 6 for *Extended Success* is very similar to the estimates in Model 3. The primary difference was that there are fewer significant variables for soft items in Model 6, and the soft information variables that are significant are *Gallery Items* and *ARI* (analogous to Model 4). In Model 5, for the number of backers after the propensity score matching, the coefficient of *ln(Goal)* is positive and statistically significant such that a one standard deviation increase in *ln(Goal)* is associated with a 37.6% increase in the number of backers relative to the average number.

To account for the possible endogeneity of AON to success, Table 5.10 provides a robustness check for the results presented in Table 5.9 by using predicted values, instead of observed values, of AON from Table 5.8. By using Model 1 provided in Table 5.8, we are able to estimate the fitted values of the *All-or-Nothing Dummy* in the first step. In Table 5.9, we use these estimated values to run 2SLS regressions on our three outcome variables (*Success*, *Backers*, and *Extended Success*, respectively, in Models 1, 2, and 3). These models display very similar results with AON campaigns being more successful (a 29.2%

---

[18] To further test for robustness, we performed the analysis on subsamples based on goal levels (instead of the matched sample approach in Table 4.7). The findings are similar.

TABLE 5.10 Outcome of crowdfunding campaigns—two-step approach.

	(1) Success	(2) Backers	(3) Extended Success
All-or-Nothing Dummy	0.292***	316.560***	0.266***
ln(Goal)	−0.089***	35.935***	−0.096***
Verified Nonprofit	0.059***	7.245	0.073***
Team Size	0.018***	7.573***	0.019***
Constant	0.959***	−294.770***	1.039***
Observations	22,850	22,850	22,850
R^2	0.054	.	0.057

Similar to Table 5.9, this table presents the results of the impact of the success of a crowdfunding campaign. In Model 1 the dependent variable is the Success Dummy, in Model 2 the number of backers, and in Model 3 the alternative success measure "Extended Success" (that considers KIA projects with at least 80% completion as being successful). In all three models the All-or-Nothing Dummy is now estimated using the probit regression presented in Model 1 of Table 5.8, which also includes all of the fixed effects. All of the variables are defined in Table 5.1. Significance levels are based on two-tailed tests (P-value): * $P < .1$, ** $P < .05$, and *** $P < .01$.

increase in the probability of *Success* in Model 1, a 26.6% increase in the probability of *Extended Success* in Model 3, and 316.56 more backers in Model 2). Furthermore, Table 5.10 indicates that there is a positive effect of the campaign's goal on the number of backers, despite the negative effect on the chances of reaching the funding goal.

Even when controlling for category fixed effects, our analysis may still suffer from an omitted variable bias. Campaigns may show very different characteristics depending upon the type of product being financed. Therefore in Table 5.11, we restrict the sample to innovative projects to show robustness within a more homogenous project sample. In doing so, we exclude entrepreneurial projects of a social or artistic nature. Panel A reports similar analysis to that we observed in Table 5.8. The impact of *ln(Goal)* is still positive and statistically significant in line with Hypothesis 5.1. In fact, the marginal impact is even larger than for the full sample suggesting that innovative projects face a greater need to signal their quality as information asymmetry could be arguably greater. Panel B demonstrates that *AON Dummy* is associated with a statistically significant increase in the probability of success by 8.7%. This is consistent with Hypothesis 5.2. Here, too, the variable *ln(Goal)* is negative and significant at the 1% level.

In Table 5.12, we match all of the innovative projects from the Indiegogo platform with the innovative projects from the Kickstarter platform (e.g., matching projects based on variables that are available in both databases: the goal, text length, gallery items, and the presence of a video pitch). Since Kickstarter only offers the AON funding model, this could suggest that the selection of the funding model can be closely linked to the selection of the platform. The results presented in this table confirm our previous findings regarding the positive impact on campaign success of the AON funding model, even when controlling for the platform choice where the project is presented.

TABLE 5.11 Robustness table: innovative projects.

Panel A

	(1) Probit	(2) First stage	(3) IV probit	(4) 2SLS
ln(Goal)	0.028***		0.178***	0.172***
Team Size	0.000	0.075***	− 0.009**	− 0.008*
IVs				
Med. Goal by Subcategory of Succ. Projects in S-1		0.051		
Med. % of Completion Ratio by Subcat. in S-1		− 2.375***		
Country F.E.	Yes	Yes	Yes	Yes
Subcategory × Month F.E.	Yes			
Category/Industry/Semester F.E.		Yes	Yes	Yes
Observations	2558	2934	2848	2934
Adjusted R^2	0.093	0.095		
		Tests for Weak Instr., Over-id., and Exog.		
Overidentification test			0.13	
Overidentification P-val			0.72	
First Stage F-stat			9.30	
Wald chi^2 test			26.29	
Wald chi^2 P-val			0.00	

Panel B

	(1) Success	(2) Backers	(3) Extended Success	(4) Success (after PSMatch)	(5) Backers (after PSMatch)	(6) Extended Success (after PSMatch)
Projects characteristics						
All-or-Nothing Dummy	0.087***	42.663	0.078***	0.122***	93.365	0.115***
ln(Goal)	− 0.104***	23.833**	− 0.107***	− 0.106***	24.006	− 0.114***
Reward Levels	0.069**	− 10.643	0.090***	0.175	− 24.139	0.152
Team Size	0.009***	4.849	0.010***	0.011**	8.850	0.013***
Duration	0.016***	12.069	0.017***	0.022***	48.030	0.023***
Soft information						
Catch Phrase Length	0.000	− 0.042	0.000	0.000	0.281	0.000
Gallery Items	0.004***	2.185*	0.004***	0.008***	4.202	0.008***
Video Pitch Dummy	0.028	6.620	0.029	− 0.003	24.155	− 0.019

Panel B

	(1) Success	(2) Backers	(3) Extended Success	(4) Success (after PSMatch)	(5) Backers (after PSMatch)	(6) Extended Success (after PSMatch)
Full Text Length	0.000***	0.015**	0.000***	0.000	0.010	0.000
Social Networks	− 0.004	− 2.215	− 0.004	− 0.005	− 11.717	− 0.003
ARI	0.000	− 2.438	− 0.001	0.004	4.675	0.002
Country & Subcategory × Month F.E.	Yes	Yes	Yes	Yes	Yes	Yes
Observations	2765	2996	2810	541	699	541
Adj./pseudo R^2	0.179	0.012	0.177	0.292	0.140	0.291

Panel A. Choice of funding model for crowdfunding campaigns: This table is similar to Table 5.8, but limited exclusively to the subsample of innovative projects. It presents factors influencing the decision on the funding model. The dependent variable in regressions (1), (3), and (4) is the "all-or-nothing dummy," a dummy variable that is equal to one if the model used is "all-or-nothing" and zero if the "keep-it-all" model is used. All of the variables are defined in Table 5.1. Regressions (3) and (4) control for the endogeneity of the variable "ln(Goal)" using a two-stage IV probit regression in Model 3 and a 2SLS regression in Model 4. The instrumented variable for the first step [see regressions (2)] is "ln(Goal)," and the two instrumental variables used are as follows. The first is the median goal of the successful projects in the same subcategory for the semester prior to the campaign launch, and the second is the median Completion Ratio for the projects in the same subcategory during the semester prior to the campaign launch. All of the regressions include country, category, industry, and semester fixed effects. Standard errors are robust to heteroskedasticity. Significance levels are based on two-tailed tests (*P*-value): * $P < .1$, ** $P < .05$, and *** $P < .01$. ARI, Automated readability index.

Panel B. Outcome of crowdfunding campaigns: This table is similar to Table 5.9, limited exclusively to the subsample of innovative projects. It present results regarding the impact of the success of a crowdfunding campaign. In Model 1 the dependent variable is the Success Dummy, in Model 2 the dependent variable is the number of backers, and in Model 3 the dependent variable is our extended success measure (including KIA projects with at least 80% completion). Models 4, 5, and 6 are similar to Models 1, 2, and 3, but with matched subsamples (every AON project is matched with one KIA project, and all unmatched KIA projects are dropped). All of the variables are defined in Table 5.1. All of the regressions include country and subcategory × month interaction fixed effects. Standard errors are robust to heteroskedasticity. Significance levels are based on two-tailed tests (*P*-value): * $P < .1$, ** $P < .05$, and *** $P < .01$. IV, Instrumental variables.

5.5.3 Soft information disclosure and entrepreneurial risk

Thus far, we have examined the strategic choice of a funding model and the extent to which it affects campaign outcome. However, other parameters can be set by the entrepreneur, either at the beginning of or during the campaign. We now test Hypothesis 5.3 regarding the usage of soft information by the entrepreneur to minimize uncertainty for the crowd. This is directly linked to the amount of effort that the entrepreneur has spent on preparing the campaign. The disclosure of soft information refers to the amount of information disclosed and the quality of the text itself in terms of accessibility. Following Hypothesis 5.3, we expect that the amount and structure of the information disclosed will be related to the funding model as the model may reduce the overall risk the entrepreneur will bear. Thus the analysis in this section examines whether information disclosure and the funding model are linked.

In Table 5.13, we examine whether the risk taken by the entrepreneur is related to the amount of soft information provided. We consider that the entrepreneur incurs a higher

TABLE 5.12 Robustness table: propensity score matching with Kickstarter.

Panel A

Variable	Unmatched (U)/ matched(M)	Mean		Bias %	Bias reduction %	Mean diff. test	Variance ratio
		Treated	Control			*t*-Stat	
Goal	U	31,936.00	30,433.00	4.30		2.15***	1.07
	M	31,936.00	32,557.00	− 1.80	58.70	− 0.66	0.97
Video Pitch Dummy	U	0.80	0.75	11.80		5.69***	
	M	0.80	0.83	− 8.40	28.80	− 3.45***	
Gallery Items	U	7.00	6.06	10.10		5.14***	1.15[a]
	M	7.00	7.90	− 9.70	3.70	− 3.61***	1.01
Full Text Length	U	5248.90	3308.20	57.00		30.91***	1.61[a]
	M	5248.90	5374.10	− 3.70	93.50	− 1.22	0.86[a]

Panel B

	(1) Success IGG-KS matched	(2) Total Pledge IGG-KS matched	(3) Total Backers IGG-KS matched
Project characteristics			
All-or-Nothing Dummy	0.872***	977.215	47.996
ln(Goal)	− 0.635***	10,566.766***	44.463***
KS Dummy	0.295**	9923.781***	45.766
Soft information			
Full Text Length	0.000***	1.581***	0.012***
Video Pitch Dummy	1.119***	4780.531***	62.685***
Gallery Items	0.042***	1141.708***	8.079***
Constant	2.753***	− 113,750.483***	− 511.088***
Observations	5868	5868	5868
Adj./pseudo R^2	0.126	0.064	0.053

[a]*Variance ratios that exceed the 2.5th and 97.5th percentiles.*
Panel A. Matching accuracy: This table reports the *t*-tests for the equality of means between the Indiegogo and Kickstarter project subsamples before and after propensity score matching for the matched variables. It also provides the standardized percentage bias (percentage of the square root of the average of the sample variances in the Indiegogo and Kickstarter groups) and the variance ratio between the two subsamples. *, **, and *** indicate significance at the 10%, 5%, and 1% levels, respectively. *Panel B. Regressions using propensity score matching*: This table provides the regressions for the campaign success, the total pledge, and the total backers. The sample is composed of 2934 projects presented on Indiegogo matched with 2934 projects presented on Kickstarter. All of the projects are from the Innovative category. The propensity score matching is based on the project size (goal), the presence of a video pitch, the number of items in the picture gallery, and the length of the text describing the project. *, **, and *** are significant at the 10%, 5%, and 1% levels, respectively. The variables are as defined in Table 5.1. KS Dummy is a dummy that is equal to one if the project was presented on the Kickstarter platform.

TABLE 5.13 Soft information disclosure in crowdfunding campaigns.

	(1) Full Text Length (OLS)	(2) Full Text Length Goal < Median	(3) Full Text Length Goal ≥ Median	(4) Full Text Length Innovative	(5) Full Text Length Creative	(6) ARI	(7) ARI Innovative	(8) ARI Creative	(9) Rewards Levels
All-or-Nothing Dummy	412.376***	253.435	544.106**	771.754**	396.812*	−0.424***	−0.350	−0.578***	0.518***
ln(Goal)	456.669***	534.780***	331.938***	416.627***	519.385***	0.162***	0.048	0.117*	0.779***
Verified Nonprofit	−45.693	63.674	−114.299	−82.535	178.463	1.267***	1.121***	1.317***	−0.082
Reward Levels	234.964***	205.092***	256.484***	282.777***	219.336***	0.028**	0.003	−0.014	
Team Size	167.541***	127.526***	183.549***	194.767***	165.203***	0.081***	0.108***	0.071**	0.293***
Duration	2.197*	3.873**	1.106	3.172	1.112	0.002	0.006	0.002	−0.007***
Constant	316.715	350.622	2083.623*	−6663.967***	−2375.906**	9.299***	14.849***	15.128***	−2.558
Country & Subcategory × Month F.E.	Yes	Yes	Yes	Yes	Yes	Yes	Yes	Yes	Yes
Observations	22,850	10,711	12,139	3031	12,842	22,656	2996	12,725	22,850
Adjusted R^2	0.195	0.168	0.193	0.257	0.165	0.033	0.042	0.016	0.292

This table presents the results on the impact of the quantity of information provided by the entrepreneur in the crowdfunding campaign. The main variables of interest are the two risk parameters ln(Goal) and all-or-nothing dummy. All of the variables are defined in Table 5.1. All of the regressions include country and subcategory × month interaction fixed effects. Standard errors are robust to heteroskedasticity. Significance levels are based on two-tailed tests (P-value): * $P < .1$, ** $P < .05$, and *** $P < .01$. ARI, Automated readability index.

risk of not obtaining any funding in the AON model. Similarly, entrepreneurial risk goes up with the funding goal. In Table 5.11, Models 1–5 demonstrate that these two risk factors for the entrepreneur are related to the amount of soft information provided to the crowd in that the text length is longer. In Model 1, AON projects have 8.8% more text relative to the average project. A one standard deviation increase in $ln(Goal)$ for the entrepreneur is associated with an amount of text provided that is larger by 392 characters or 8.4% relative to the average project. Similarly, AON campaigns have a text length that is longer than KIA campaigns by 412 characters. When compared to the average length observed (4658 characters, Table 5.4), this represents an increase of 8.8%. These effects for AON and $ln(Goal)$ are statistically significant at the 1% level in Model 1 and Models 3–5. The economic significance of AON effects is more pronounced for larger and more innovative projects (Models 3 and 4), while the economic significance of $ln(Goal)$ is more pronounced for small and creative projects (Models 2 and 5) relative to that for the average project in Model 1.

In Table 5.13, Models 6–8 provide analogous regressions to Models 1, 4, and 5 with the difference in terms of the dependent variable being the ARI score in Models 6–8. A higher ARI score suggests that the text is more complicated (more characters per word and more words per sentence; see Table 5.1 for the formula). Table 5.13 indicates that AON campaigns (which are riskier for the entrepreneur) present a lower readability score (the text is easier to read for a greater number of people). This effect is significant at the 1% level in Models 6 and 8 for the full sample and creative projects, respectively. The economic significance is such that an AON campaign is associated with a 2.7% reduction in the readability index for the average project in Model 6. Furthermore, the ARI readability index is positively associated with being a *Verified Nonprofit* (significant in Models 6–8 at the 1% level), *Reward Levels* (positive and significant at the 5% level in Model 6, positive and insignificant in Model 7, and negative and insignificant in Model 8), and *Team Size* (significant at the 1% level in Models 6 and 7 and at the 5% level in Model 8). In Model 6, *Verified Nonprofits* are associated with an 8.3% higher ARI score, on average. A one standard deviation increase in *Reward Levels* and *Team Size* is associated with a 0.7% and 1.1% increase in ARI, respectively.

Model 9 offers a similar test for reward levels. The greater the amount of risk taken by the entrepreneur (either in the form of choosing the AON model or setting a higher goal), the more likely the entrepreneur will provide greater effort by offering more reward levels in order to attract more backers. The results support this prediction. The economic significance is that AON projects have 7% more reward levels relative to the average project. A one standard deviation increase in $ln(Goal)$ is associated with a 9.0% increase in the number of reward levels relative to the average number. Finally, Model 9 also indicates that a one standard deviation increase in *Team Size* and *Duration* is associated with an 8.03% increase and a 2.1% decrease in the number of reward levels relative to the average, respectively.

5.6 Discussion and future research

As a result of the emergence of Internet platforms, crowdfunding has become accessible to a large number of entrepreneurs as an alternative form of funding. While the standardization in crowdfunding platforms offers clear benefits in terms of comparability across projects and readability, it also reduces the extent to which entrepreneurs can tailor their offer according to their specific needs. One important dimension of standardization has been the adoption of AON and KIA models by the major reward-based platforms. The choice of model clearly affects the fee structure paid by the entrepreneurs (since the platforms charge different fees), and how pledges are transformed into funding for the entrepreneur.

In this chapter, we compare the AON versus the KIA models in terms of the types of companies that use these methods for raising capital, their disclosures, and their success. An analysis of the Indiegogo platform offers a unique opportunity to examine the choice between the two forms of crowdfunding models as the platform offers entrepreneurs the option to choose between the two models along with the fundraising goal of their project. Our findings offer support to the prediction that AON models offer a guarantee to the crowd that the entrepreneur does not start a project with unrealistically low funding. Overall, AON fundraising campaigns involve substantially larger capital goals and are much more likely to be successful at achieving their goals. These findings are robust to controls for self-selection and endogeneity and robust to propensity score matching. Furthermore, we find that AON fundraisers disclose more information than KIA fundraisers, and that this information is more easily understandable for a broader audience.

These findings have implications for entrepreneurs. First, funding models enable entrepreneurs with the most promising projects to signal the quality of their projects. By having skin in the game, they are able to attract more backers. However, this affects the risk-taking of entrepreneurs as they may end up with nothing if the funding goal is not achieved. More generally, the choice of funding models affects the allocation of risk between the entrepreneur and backers. Relying on the signaling effect appears to be more valuable when larger amounts need to be raised. From a theoretical perspective, projects must be of better quality to induce entrepreneurs to opt for AON. In addition, in order to reduce the risk of not achieving the goal under AON, entrepreneurs need to undertake considerable prep work by drafting larger project descriptions, posting more updates during the campaign, and making the text accessible to more people. This more extensive preparation helps to compensate for the increased risk of choosing the AON funding model.

In terms of implications for the platforms, these findings offer support that providing flexibility to entrepreneurs, in terms of a choice of a funding model, may be an interesting selling point for platforms and a way to differentiate themselves in this rapidly growing market. This may also explain the success of Indiegogo (the major platform that offers this choice) as many entrepreneurs may prefer to raise funds on Indiegogo due to the possibility of opting for the KIA model. The fact that this platform offers this choice magnifies the signaling effect of AON compared to other platforms, such as Kickstarter, where this choice is not possible (and, as such, cannot be a "signaling" mechanism).

This chapter offers avenues for future research, including determining the chances for the success of the projects themselves, beyond the campaign's success. Our analysis examines success during the fundraising campaign but is silent about what happens afterward. Such an analysis would especially be useful to better understand the ultimate source of the information asymmetry (i.e., whether it is about the project quality itself or the entrepreneurial skills employed to execute the project). For instance, Mollick and Kuppuswamy (2014) report that 75% of the projects successfully funded on Kickstarter deliver late. However, based on the conclusion offered in this chapter, one could expect this percentage to vary according to the fundraising models (KIA vs AON) used during the campaign as the latter is related to the amount raised. Projects that are started with sufficient funds are more likely to produce the promised product and eventually deliver on time, an issue that is worth investigating in future research.

If more data become available in the future, further research may focus on other mechanisms to signal quality. For instance, one possible mechanism is related to the difficulties that arise when managing a large number of funders. Since KIA is riskier for the crowd, there will be a price discount compared to AON. This price discount is meant to compensate funders for the risk taken. This further implies that the entrepreneur must attract even more funders for a given amount needed as lower prices indicate that each funder provides less. Thus on the basis of an equally matched funding amount for AON and KIA, we would expect more funders for each dollar raised through KIA. Managing a greater number of funders implies greater costs on the firm in terms of delivering rewards, product- and firm-level communication, and the coordination of the stakeholders for the future direction of the enterprise. These issues, in turn, suggest that the KIA mechanism makes future success more difficult for the enterprise.

Another worthwhile research question is whether certain models are more prone to fraud. Concerns have recently been raised by regulators and academics (Griffin, 2013; Hildebrand et al., 2017; Hornuf & Schwienbacher, 2017a, 2017b) that crowdfunding simply shifts the risk to the crowd, and some entrepreneurs may exploit an unsophisticated crowd. In the context studied here, one can extend this analysis by determining whether projects funded with a KIA model are more prone to fraud. Under KIA the funding goal can be arbitrarily set as the entrepreneur can keep the money anyway and the project can continue. If the entrepreneur does not get what they need to do a proper job on the project, then the entrepreneur is more likely to abscond with the funds. To the extent that data are available, however, there appears to be substantially less fraud on Indiegogo than Kickstarter (Cumming, Hornuf, Karami, & Schweizer, 2016). Thus the preliminary evidence is suggestive that the KIA model does not exacerbate the moral hazard. However, future research is warranted.

Key terms

All-or-Nothing
AR Index
Campaign Duration
Campaign Goal
Campaign Success
Campaign Extended Success Measure
Catch Phrase Length
Completion Ratio
Creative Campaign

Gallery Items
Innovative Campaign
Keep-It-All
Propensity Score Matching
Social Campaign
Social Networks
Soft Information
Video Pitch

Discussion questions

5.1. Are campaign goals typically larger with keep-it-all crowdfunding campaigns? Discuss why.

5.2. Are campaign success rates typically higher with all-or-nothing campaigns? Discuss with.

5.3. Are social, creative, or innovative crowdfunding campaigns the riskiest? Which types are most commonly observed? Which of these categories of campaigns tends to have the highest level of fundraising success? Explain why.

5.4. How does the use of soft information affect crowdfunding success? What types of soft information are the most important for crowdfunding success? Explain why.

5.5. Which type of campaign tends to use more soft information: all-or-nothing campaigns or keep-it-all campaigns? Why is the role of soft information more pronounced for different types of crowdfunding campaigns?

5.6. What types of campaign details are endogenous to the campaign outcome? How would you evaluate statistical information that related campaign details to campaign outcomes that did not account for this potential endogeneity?

5.7. How might project scalability be related to the choice of a keep-it-all versus all-or-nothing campaign? Why?

5.8. Are nonprofit campaigns more often employing the keep-it-all or the all-or-nothing model? Why?

5.9. Are keep-it-all campaigns typically over a longer duration than all-or-nothing campaigns? Why?

5.10. Are keep-it-all campaigns typically better worded than all-or-nothing campaigns? Explain why you think there might be a difference.

Crowdfunding cleantech

6.1 Introduction

New technologies such as cleantech present unique opportunities and challenges for investors. Cleantech encompasses four main sectors: energy, transportation, water, and minerals, and these sectors include projects such as green energy, renewable energy, recycling, wind power, solar power, biomass, hydroelectric, photovoltaic, geothermic, biofuel, green transport, gray water, and electric motors (Pernick & Wilder, 2007; Sadorsky, 2011). Many of these sectors have recently been characterized as generating the best opportunities for private investments (Aguilar & Cai, 2010).

Cleantech projects are characterized as encompassing a public good with positive externalities in terms of a cleaner environment; as such, cleantech often has higher costs for consumer adoption, where consumers may pay more in view of positive feelings associated with cleantech use (Bloomberg New Energy Finance, 2010, 2012). Therefore the importance of cleantech investments is likely to vary from one country to another as a result of cultural differences in the sensitivity to environmental issues (Cameron, Brown, & Chapman, 1998; Kountouris & Remoundou, 2016), social responsibility, and socially responsible consumption (Liobikienėa, Mandravickaitėb, & Bernatonienėc, 2016). Such cultural traits may promote support for green product and cleantech initiatives (Romani, Grappi, & Bagozzi, 2016). Cleantech is likewise characterized as having high risks in terms of being disrupted or becoming quickly obsolete (Hart & Milstein, 1999); therefore investors face high information asymmetries with respect to evaluating not only the science underlying cleantech but also the market opportunities of cleantech investments (Bloomberg New Energy Finance, 2010, 2012).

Prior work on energy finance has largely been focused on studies of commodities markets with the use of exchange data (e.g., Dewally, Ederington, & Fernando, 2013; Henderson, Pearson, & Wang, 2015) and on examining the financial performance of environmental mutual funds (Muñoz, Vargas, & Marco, 2014). There have been fewer studies of private companies in energy markets, arguably due to the scant availability of data, except in the case of venture capital studies of energy finance. Venture capitalists around the world have expertise in evaluating new technologies (Megginson & Weiss, 1991; Megginson, 2004; Nahata, 2008; Nahata, Hazarika, & Tandon, 2014); therefore there has

107

been much hype about the intersection between cleantech and venture capital in recent years (Crifo & Forget, 2013; Cumming et al., 2013; Ghosh & Nanda, 2010; Marcus, Ellis, & Malen, 2012; Wüstenhagen, Wuebker, Bürer, & Goddard, 2009). Cleantech was one of the fastest growing sectors in the venture capital industry from 2000 to 2013, comprising more than 10% of all venture capital deals in 2010–13. In 2007 Nobel Peace Prize winner Al Gore was hired by Kleiner Perkins, one of the world's leading venture capital funds.[1] While early signs of cleantech venture capital looked promising (Bürer & Wustenhagen, 2009), many funds that ventured into cleantech have lost a significant amount of their invested capital, including industry leaders such as Kleiner Perkins.[2]

Moreover, the fall in oil prices in late 2014 made cleantech investment substantially less attractive.[3] The combination between low oil prices and failed cleantech deals led many venture capitalists to think of cleantech as a "dirty word."[4] These industry developments have given rise to the need for alternative energies to seek alternative forms of funding outside of the mainstream alternative sources such as venture capital. Indeed, while Kumar, Managi, and Matsuda (2012) have found little evidence on established firms (based on stock prices), many of the pathbreaking technologies in renewable investments are also made outside large firms.

One such new alternative form of funding on the rise is crowdfunding. Crowdfunding has grown exponentially in recent years worldwide from a $2 billion market in 2011 to $6 billion in 2012, and $16 billion in 2014. It is expected to reach $95 billion by 2025.[5] Standardized platforms such as Indiegogo have facilitated the growth of crowdfunding by enabling entrepreneurs to reach out to large numbers of investors to fund projects through Internet portals. In the United States, these projects are funded through rewards- and donations-based crowdfunding to retail investors, while equity crowdfunding is only available to accredited investors in the United States (Agrawal et al., 2015; Bayus, 2013; Belleflamme et al., 2013; Belleflamme et al., 2014; Boudreau & Jeppesen, 2015; Burtch, Ghose, & Wattal, 2013; Colombo et al., 2014; Mollick, 2014; Mollick & Kuppuswamy, 2014; Mollick & Nanda, 2015; Schwienbacher & Larralde, 2012).[6] In other countries, such as Australia (Ahlers et al., 2015) and European Union member states (Hornuf & Schwienbacher, 2014; Vismara, 2016), entrepreneurs may sell shares and other forms of securities over Internet portals in the form of equity crowdfunding. Unlike venture capital markets, in which control rights are transferred to investors to mitigate costs associated

---

[1] http://money.cnn.com/2007/11/11/news/newsmakers/gore_kleiner.fortune/. See also http://www. washingtonpost.com/politics/decision2012/al-gore-has-thrived-as-green-tech-investor/2012/10/10/ 1dfaa5b0-0b11-11e2-bd1a-b868e65d57eb_story.html

[2] http://www.reuters.com/article/2013/01/16/us-kleiner-doerr-venture-idUSBRE90F0AD20130116

[3] http://www.cnbc.com/id/102279652#. See also Hamilton (2011).

[4] http://www.bloombergview.com/articles/2014-11-14/vcs-think-cleantech-is-a-dirty-word

[5] http://www.crowdsourcing.org/

[6] The Securities and Exchange Commission has recently implemented Title III of the JOBS Act in the United States so that equity crowdfunding platforms can now also solicit nonaccredited investors. However, the US equity crowdfunding platforms have been slow to take advantage of this opportunity, unlike in other countries, where equity crowdfunding has been commonplace for several years.

with information asymmetries (Cumming, 2008) and in unique ways for socially responsible investments (Scarlata & Alemany, 2010), crowdfunding markets are characterized by limited loss of control by the entrepreneur and a pronounced role for signaling by the entrepreneur. Since crowdfunders invest smaller amounts of money, they typically take into account not only tangible benefits but also societal ones, such as the extent to which these projects solve social and environmental problems. The large number of projects is offered through crowdfunding platforms, and the large number of investors offers a unique learning environment to study the information asymmetries offered by new technologies, such as alternative cleantech energy projects, and the usefulness of mechanisms on crowdfunding platforms to mitigate such information asymmetries.

In this chapter, we examine the Indiegogo platform. Indiegogo is a US-based platform but employs entrepreneurs from a very large number of countries around the world that engage in fundraising campaigns. These countries vary extensively in terms of cultural differences and concerns about environmental problems. Most of the campaign goals are between $5000 and $200,000. We study 22,786 campaigns over the period 2011−13, where 1864, or 7.4% of the campaigns, involved cleantech projects.

We find that cleantech crowdfunding is more common in countries with low levels of individualism and more common when oil prices are rising. These findings are consistent with cultural traits that value the long term, possess a greater awareness regarding social responsibility, and have high alternative energy costs. Cleantech crowdfunding campaigns are more likely to have higher capital goals, more photos, a video pitch, and longer text descriptions than other campaigns. Relative to non-cleantech campaigns, the success of cleantech campaigns, in terms of achieving funding goals, is more economically sensitive to the campaign's goal size, being not-for-profit, and having a video pitch. Overall, these data are consistent with the view that cleantech projects have pronounced information problems investors must face. Cleantech entrepreneurs can make use of mechanisms on crowdfunding platforms to significantly mitigate the investors' information asymmetries in ways that make cleantech campaigns no less successful than their non-cleantech counterparts.

This chapter is organized as follows. Section 6.2 discusses the testable propositions in view of the institutional setting of the Indiegogo platform. Section 6.3 presents the data. Multivariate analyses are presented in Section 6.4. The concluding section discusses the implications for practice, policy, and future research.

6.2 Hypotheses

In this section, we derive four testable hypotheses regarding cleantech crowdfunding. While these predictions have not been discussed or tested in prior literature, they are, nevertheless, closely aligned with prior work on the cleantech literature and other related fields on institutions and entrepreneurial finance. Our first two predictions are focused on the drivers of cleantech crowdfunding. Our third and fourth predictions pertain to the use of soft information and the success of cleantech crowdfunding campaigns compared to campaigns of other project types.

Cleantech projects are unique in a number of ways (Bloomberg New Energy Finance, 2010, 2012; Hall and Milstein, 2003; Henriques, Husted, & Montiel, 2013; WCED, 1987). First, there is a high chance that they may give rise to disruptions in traditional industries related to energy. This type of disruptive technology has the potential to give rise to very large payoffs; but, at the same time, there is a high risk that the cleantech project could itself be disrupted by other competing cleantech projects. Second, cleantech often involves high risks for consumer adoption, insofar as there are costs to switching from one energy source to another. Sadorsky (2012) provides evidence on the correlation between renewable energy stocks and oil prices, making the holding of such stock a hedge in the crude oil futures market. Inchauspe, Ripple, and Trück (2015) provide further evidence for the impact of oil prices on investments in renewable energy. Thus oil price changes tend to affect cleantech adversely. Third, in view of the positive benefits of cleantech developments on the environment, many projects are costly, but consumers are nevertheless willing to pay higher prices to support green technologies that show corporate and environmental and social responsibilities. The more costly the use of traditional energy sources for consumers, the more likely it is that cleantech projects will be initiated as the potential profits to cleantech rise.

With the existence of positive externalities arises from cleantech, economic forces are likely to drive investments into renewable energy and, in particular, the opportunity costs of relying on more traditional, crude oil. This view is consistent with empirical findings of Sadorsky (2012), Inchauspe et al. (2015) on investments made in renewable energy. Crude oil prices drive the opportunity costs of renewable energy, since crude oil (and gas in some countries) are crucial alternative sources of energy for households. Thus we expect cleantech projects to be more readily funded in periods of rising oil prices.

Hypothesis 6.1: *Cleantech crowdfunding campaigns are more common in periods of rising oil prices.*

There are ample reasons to expect cleantech crowdfunding levels to reflect soft institutional characteristics across countries. It is well established that cultural traits are in line with sensitivity to environmental issues and societal responsibility (Vitell, Nwachukwu, & Barnes, 1993). Since the cultural environment is reflected in the proenvironmental behavior of households (Milfront and Schultz, 2016), we expect that cleantech campaigns are more likely to originate in countries where there is a less dominant influence from established energy sources and a culture of low *power inequality* and *lower masculinity* (as defined by Hofstede, 1991, 2001; formal definitions are also provided, next). Masculine cultures focus on ambition and ego, while feminine cultures value the service toward others and the quality of life. As cleantech offers benefits to others and society at large, it is a much better fit with feminine societies than masculine societies. Similarly, lower power inequality cultures value equal opportunity for all individuals in society. Cleantech disrupts power held by established energy providers such as oil producers; hence, cultures that value low power distance are more likely to have a preference for cleantech.

There is exacerbated uncertainty regarding the science underlying cleantech, since much scientific research is funded by organizations such as oil companies that have an incentive to create a false impression about the need for and benefits of cleantech.

For example, prominent scientific work debating the role of the oil industry in spurring global warming has been revealed to have been funded from the oil industry.[7] These types of nondisclosure, improper debate, and confusion in scientific journals exacerbate the uncertainty associated with cleantech and the information asymmetry faced by cleantech investors. For these reasons, we would expect cultures with high levels of *uncertainty avoidance* to be less likely to engage in cleantech crowdfunding.

Cultural characteristics other than power inequality, masculinity, and uncertainty avoidance can matter for cleantech as well. Specifically, we may expect more cleantech crowdfunding investment in countries with a *long-term orientation*, less *indulgence*, and less *individualism*. Cleantech will benefit individuals for many years in the future, and even generations that are not yet born, which will generate more utility amongst individuals that have longer term, less indulgent characteristics. Furthermore, the benefits for consumer adoption of cleantech can give rise to positive externalities, and the consumption of cleantech may be nonexcludable and nonrival, in that other consumers can benefit without paying for the benefit. As such, societies that are more *collective* and less *individualistic* will show greater support of cleantech in view of the nonrival and nonexcludable nature of cleantech consumption.

Hypothesis 6.2: *Cleantech crowdfunding campaigns more often originate from countries with low power distance, low individualism, low masculinity, low uncertainty avoidance, low indulgence, and high long-term orientation.*

Our third hypothesis pertains to the mechanisms that can be used in crowdfunding campaigns, often referred to as the disclosure of "soft information," to mitigate information asymmetries between the entrepreneur and potential investors. In the context of crowdfunding the use of soft information is costly for the entrepreneur to prepare and hard to replicate by others, if the intrinsic qualities of the entrepreneur and the project are low. Specifically, entrepreneurs can post extensive photo gallery items and a professional video, if their project is well developed with prototypes, and if there exist equipment and facilities for developing the project further. Consistent with Spence (1973), entrepreneurs with a higher quality project, and entrepreneurs with better writing skills, can post lengthy project descriptions, and better worded project descriptions, in order to mitigate information problems faced by their new backers. Therefore they convey a costly signal by exerting more effort in preparing the campaign. Empirical evidence consistent with this view has been recently provided in crowdfunding (Mollick, 2014a, see also Chapter 5: Crowdfunding models: keep-it-all versus all-or-nothing, and Chapter 10: Signaling in equity crowdfunding), showing that the disclosure of pictures, videos, and lengthier texts contributes to the success of crowdfunding campaigns. As cleantech projects are riskier, with potentially abstracting benefits to society at large, these mechanisms that transfer soft information about cleantech projects to potential investors are particularly important.

---

[7] http://www.washingtonpost.com/news/energy-environment/wp/2015/02/23/no-the-sun-isnt-driving-global-warming/

Hypothesis 6.3: *Cleantech crowdfunding campaigns are more likely to make use of more detailed soft information to mitigate information problems, including more gallery items, video pitches, longer project descriptions, and better worded project descriptions.*

Our fourth hypothesis pertains to the success of crowdfunding projects. We have no reason to expect a priori that cleantech projects will be more or less successful, particularly in view of the mechanisms that can be used to mitigate information problems faced by investors. However, we would expect campaign success to be more sensitive to the use of soft information for cleantech projects when there are pronounced information problems faced by cleantech investors. As cleantech projects are, on average, riskier than non-cleantech, and the benefits to society need clarification and justification to entice a crowd to invest, the success of cleantech crowdfunding projects is more likely dependent on the use of gallery items, video pitches, and the length and quality of project descriptions.

Hypothesis 6.4: *The success of cleantech crowdfunding campaigns is more sensitive to the use of soft project information.*

6.3 Data and summary statistics

We use data from the rewards-based crowdfunding platform Indiegogo. It was launched in 2008 and is now the second largest rewards-based platform worldwide, right after Kickstarter, which is more than twice as large in terms of projects started. One particularity of Indiegogo compared to Kickstarter is that entrepreneurs can choose between a flexible [so-called keep-it-all (KIA)] funding mechanism and a fixed [all-or-nothing (AON)] one (Chapter 5, Crowdfunding models: keep-it-all versus all-or-nothing); while on Kickstarter and most other rewards-based platforms, only the latter one is possible. Under the flexible mechanism the entrepreneur gets to keep whatever the crowd has pledged, even if the minimum goal was not achieved by the end of the campaign. Under the fixed mechanism the entrepreneur only collects the pledges if the minimum goal is achieved. As mentioned in Chapter 5. Crowdfunding models: keep-it-all versus all-or-nothing, this has implications on the allocation of risk between the entrepreneur and the crowd, since, under the flexible mechanism, the crowd bears the risk that the project is undertaken, although it is underfunded. In contrast, the crowd's risk is reduced under an AON mechanism. Campaigns generally last between 2 and 4 months, depending on the funding mechanism chosen and the decision of the entrepreneur on total duration at the beginning of the campaign. As for other platforms, Indiegogo only earns fees if the campaign is successful. The success fee may vary between 4% and 9%.

Our dataset comprises all campaigns launched on the Indiegogo platform since it began until October 2013, when the data were extracted. Indiegogo leaves all the projects on its website, except those that do not achieve at least 500 currency units. Since it is an international platform, entrepreneurs may post amounts in USD, euros, Canadian dollars, Australian dollars, or British pounds. Whenever currency other than USD is used, we convert all values into USD using a yearly average exchange rate. Our original sample comprises 47,139 campaigns.

We apply filters before performing analyses. We first drop all campaigns that were launched before November 2011, because there were very few projects at the beginning, and because the platform did not allow an entrepreneur the choice between the "AON" or "KIA" model before that date. This filter is important here, since we explicitly control for the choice of funding model (consistent with Chapter 5, Crowdfunding models: keep-it-all versus all-or-nothing). We further exclude all projects with a campaign goal below USD 5000, since they often target friends and family members (consistent with Mollick, 2014a). A final filter concerns the largest projects, where we exclude projects with a campaign goal beyond the 99-percentile of the distribution (which corresponds to a goal close to USD 200,000). These projects are very different in nature than the rest and may result in extreme outliers. This leads to a final dataset of 22,786 project campaigns.

To identify cleantech projects, we perform a text analysis by searching for the following words in the project description: "green energy," "cleantech," "recycle," "wind power," "solar power," "biomass," "renewable energy," "hydroelectric," "photovoltaic," "geotherm," "sustainable," "biofuel," "green transport," "environmental footprint," "gray water," and "electric motor." Since there is not clear consensus about what constitutes the "cleantech" industry, this list of words is directly derived from the definition of cleantech available on Wikipedia and other web pages such as http://www.cleantech.com/ (consistent with Cumming et al., 2013). This led to a sample of 1864 cleantech projects.

Appendix 6.1 and Figs. 6A.1 and 6A.2 summarize the projects by country. The projects originated from 81 countries around the world. The most common countries in the dataset include the United States, Canada, the United Kingdom, Australia, Germany, Italy, Israel, France, and The Netherlands (Appendix 6.1). For countries with more than 90 campaigns the highest percentage of deals that are cleantech are from The Netherlands, South Africa, Mexico, and India (Fig. 6A.1). For countries with more than five projects, and where at least 25% are cleantech, the countries with the highest proportion of cleantech projects are Liberia (67%), Sierra Leone (50%), Vietnam (50%), Zambia (50%), and Ecuador (44%) (Fig. 6A.2). Finally, cleantech projects became more common over time, from 6.81% in the second semester of 2011 to 7.84% in the second semester of 2013 (Fig. 6A.3).

A full description of variables available in our dataset is provided in Appendix 6.2, and summary statistics are provided in Table 6.1. Variables are classified in five types: project characteristics (subcategory, goal, duration, etc., as well as additional soft information provided either at the beginning of the campaign or during the campaign); measures of campaign output (number of backers or rewards left, etc.); macroeconomic and legal conditions; and, finally, cultural conditions.

The recorded project characteristics are mandatory information, and all entrepreneurs set them once and for all prior to the campaign start. Although some variables are intrinsic to the project itself (the category/subcategory, the location), others are set freely by the entrepreneur (the goal, the funding model, the number of rewards, and the level of each reward—the amount a backer should give to choose the defined reward, the duration, etc.). The additional "soft" information is a set of descriptive information provided to inform the crowd about the project. It consists of text, pictures, video pitches, additional comments, and updates, as well as any other information that the entrepreneur discloses to potential backers. As these pieces of information are mostly of qualitative nature, we decided to limit ourselves to those that could be measured quantitatively. For instance,

TABLE 6.1 Summary Statistics.

Variables	Non-cleantech					Cleantech				Mean difference test
	Mean	SD	Median			Mean	SD	Median		
Project characteristics										
Verified nonprofit	0.10	0.30	0			0.13	0.34	0		− 0.03***
Goal	20,635	26,160	10,000			26,095	30,764	15,000		− 5500***
Keep-it-all dummy	0.95	0.22	1			0.93	0.25	1		0.02***
Reward's levels	7.38	3.96	8			8.27	3.56	8		− 0.89***
Digital output dummy	0.45	0.50	0			0.17	0.37	0		0.29***
Team size	2.36	2	2			2.89	2.31	2		− 0.53***
Duration	48.32	22.77	45			48.33	20.52	45		− 0.01
Soft information and success										
Catch phrase length	114.8	38.75	125			120.8	36.48	131		− 5.97***
Updates	5.05	8.88	2			5.68	7.85	3		− 0.63***
Comments	29.91	227.7	13			30.07	105.8	14		− 0.16
Gallery's items	6.63	10.46	3			9.04	11.10	5		− 2.41***
Video pitch dummy	0.78	0.41	1			0.85	0.36	1		− 0.07***
Full-text length	4510	3302	3707			6554	4366	5349		− 2000***
Social networks	3.27	32.80	3			3.48	2.07	3		− 0.21
AR index	15.15	4.69	14.83			16.54	3.21	16.22		− 1.39***
Completion ratio	0.44	1.21	0.22			0.44	1.06	0.23		− 0.002

Success dummy	0.18	0.38	0	0.19	0.39	0	− 0.02
Total pledge	6478	30,318	2460	7900	23,695	3088	− 1400*
Total backers	81.37	415.8	33	94.28	381.6	38	− 12.91
Macroeconomic conditions							
Oil price evolution in 6 months	1.77	10.70	4.14	2.52	10.17	4.87	− 0.75***
Oil price at start	95.74	7.15	95.25	95.93	7.19	95.34	− 0.19
Oil price at end	95.97	7.04	95.25	96.28	7.23	95.61	− 0.31*
Gas price evolution in 6 months	0.18	0.85	0.39	0.24	0.85	0.43	− 0.059***
Gas price at start	3.3	0.58	3.39	3.35	0.58	3.43	− 0.052***
S&P 500 evolution in 6 months	119.3	76.35	119.05	123.19	74.41	122.78	− 3.895**
S&P 500 at start	1496.91	132.36	1472.34	1505.94	129.79	1513.17	− 9.032***
Cultural dimensions							
Power distance	40.81	7.74	40	41.99	10.22	40	− 1.18***
Individualism	86.21	13.04	91	83.12	18.58	91	3.09***
Masculinity	60.09	7.48	62	59.28	8.93	62	0.81***
Uncertainty Avoidance	47.91	9.43	46	48.91	11.21	46	− 1.00***
Long-term orientation	29.86	11.22	25.69	30.31	11.97	25.69	− 0.45
Indulgence	66.54	8.18	68.08	65.97	9.38	68.08	0.57***
Legal conditions							
Strength of minority investors protection index	6.62	0.56	6.60	6.46	0.85	6.60	0.16***
Observations	21,102				1684		

The table provides summary statistics for the subsample of cleantech versus non-cleantech projects. The last column shows results of the mean difference test between both subsamples. *, **, *** Significant at the 10%, 5%, and 1% levels, respectively. Variables are as defined in Appendix 6.2.

information such as number of words/pictures/items and presence or not of some items allow us to observe the implication of the entrepreneur in the project and the degree of preparedness, as it is associated with success (Mollick, 2014a, 2014b).

Given that this information is intended for reading by a wide audience, we also include a readability index as a control variable for evaluating crowd perception. Readability indexes are designed to gauge the understandability of written text. We use the automated readability index (ARI) that uses the full text of the project description, as described in Appendix 6.2. The ARI offers an index expressed as a US grade level. For instance, Grade 1 indicates text for children of 6/7 years, and Grade 12 indicates text for high school students of 17/18 years old.

Finally, we consider campaign outputs based on observable information at the end of the campaign. It consists in total amount pledged by backers, total number of backers, and the completion ratio. These output measures define the success of the campaign. Our primary measure of success is the completion ratio, which corresponds to the ratio of total amount pledged over the goal set by the entrepreneur.

Table 6.1 indicates several statistical differences in the characteristics of cleantech versus non-cleantech investments. In total, there are 1684 cleantech campaigns and 21,102 non-cleantech campaigns. Cleantech deals are more likely to be nonprofit (13% for cleantech and 10% for non-cleantech) and have high-target goals on average ($26,095 for cleantech and $20,635 for non-cleantech). Cleantech is less likely to be associated with the KIA-funding model (93% for cleantech and 95% for non-cleantech). Cleantech has, on average, more reward levels (8.3 for cleantech vs 7.4 for non-cleantech). Cleantech projects are less likely to generate a digital output (17% for cleantech and 45% for non-cleantech), whereby the project size can be adjusted and still undertaken with partial funding. We do not find any significant difference in the length of cleantech versus non-cleantech campaigns, where both are approximately 48 days, on average. Finally, cleantech projects are done by larger teams, on average (2.89 persons vs 2.36 for non-cleantech projects).

Cleantech deals provide significantly more detailed soft information, on average. The catch phrase length is 120.8 words, on average, for cleantech versus 114.8 for non-cleantech. Cleantech projects have 5.68 updates, on average, compared to 5.05 updates for non-cleantech. Cleantech campaigns post 9.04 gallery items, on average, compared to 6.63 for non-cleantech; and 85% of the cleantech campaigns involve a video versus 78% for non-cleantech. The full-text length is 6554 words for cleantech versus 4510 for non-cleantech, and the cleantech readability score is significantly higher at 16.54 compared to 15.15 for non-cleantech. However, there are neither significant differences for the number of comments for cleantech versus non-cleantech (both 30, on average) nor for the use of social networks (the median is 3 networks for both cleantech and non-cleantech).

Cleantech projects, on average, are not significantly more successful. The completion ratio is 44% for cleantech and non-cleantech. Funding success, in terms of meeting the goal, is 19% for cleantech and 18% for non-cleantech. However, cleantech projects, on average, attract a significantly higher total pledge ($7900) than non-cleantech ($6478), as well as more backers (94.28 for cleantech vs 81.37 for non-cleantech, though this latter difference is not statistically significant).

On average, cleantech deals are significantly more common over periods when there has been an increase in oil prices over the prior 6 months ($2.52 for cleantech vs $1.77 for non-cleantech), and higher oil prices at the end of the campaign ($96.28 for cleantech and $95.97 for non-cleantech), consistent with Hypothesis 6.1.

Cleantech deals are significantly associated with different Hofstede's cultural indices. Cleantech deals are more common in countries with higher power distance scores (41.99 for cleantech vs 40.81 for non-cleantech), lower individualism scores (83.12 for non-cleantech and 86.21 for cleantech), lower masculinity scores (59.28 for cleantech and 60.09 for cleantech), higher uncertainty avoidance scores (48.91 for cleantech and 47.91 for non-cleantech), and lower indulgence scores (65.97 for cleantech and 66.54 for non-cleantech). These findings offer preliminary support for Hypothesis 6.2. Finally, Table 6.1 shows that cleantech deals are more likely in countries with lower legal protection scores (6.46 for cleantech and 6.62 for non-cleantech).[8]

Table 6.2 provides a correlation matrix. The correlations are consistent with the comparison tests in Table 6.1 for cleantech versus non-cleantech. Also, note from Table 6.2 that there are high correlations across some of the variables in the data, including, the country-level measures. As such, in the next section, we consider robustness to excluding different variables in the alternative specifications (reported and otherwise available on request). We further checked the values of variance inflation factors in our analyses to ensure lack of multicollinearity in the specifications shown below (the highest value of some variables being below 4, but most below 2).

6.4 Multivariate analyses

Our regression analyses proceed in three steps. First, we study the frequency of cleantech crowdfunding campaigns to test Hypotheses 6.1 and 6.2. Second, we examine the factors that affect the use of soft information for cleantech versus non-cleantech campaigns to test Hypothesis 6.3. Finally, we examine the effect of soft and other information on crowdfunding success for cleantech versus non-cleantech campaigns. Each model is estimated with heteroscedasticity robust standard errors. Alternative specifications with clustered standard errors by time period and/or industry and/or country did not materially change any of the results reported next and are available on request.

Table 6.3 presents an analysis of factors that affect the likelihood that a crowdfunding campaign will involve a cleantech project. The determinants of cleantech crowdfunding are a function of oil prices and cultural variables, as well as fixed effects for the different time periods. Several control variables are included, among which the extent to which investors are protected (consistent with finding of Kim and Park, 2016, on the impact of financial development on investments in renewable energy projects) and the general economic conditions (the measures S&P 500 evolution in 6 months and S&P 500 at start).

---

[8] In unreported analysis, we have considered a variety of other country variables, such as legal and policy variables. For instance, we have investigated policy differences proxied by ICRG indices on government stability, socioeconomic conditions, existence of external conflicts, and corruption. These directly pertain to the political and legal environments. Their inclusion does not alter our main conclusions on the hypotheses.

TABLE 6.2 Correlation matrix.

	Success	Cleantech dummy	Goal	Verified nonprofit	Keep-it-all dummy	Gallery's items	Video pitch dummy	Full-text length	Social networks	AR index	Oil price evolution in 6 months
Success	1										
Cleantech dummy	0.0109	1									
Goal	-0.1722*	0.0705*	1								
Verified nonprofit	0.0374*	0.0292*	0.0251*	1							
Keep-it-all dummy	-0.1036*	-0.0203*	-0.0915*	0.0790*	1						
Gallery's items	0.0803*	0.0600*	0.1048*	-0.0017	-0.0225*	1					
Video pitch dummy	0.0439*	0.0449*	0.0964*	0.0442*	-0.0362*	0.1215*	1				
Full-text length	0.0446*	0.1550*	0.2176*	-0.0117	-0.0983*	0.2334*	0.1635*	1			
Social networks	0.0007	0.0017	0.0061	0.0047	0.0001	0.0191*	0.0215*	0.0012	1		
AR index	0.0105	0.0788*	0.0374*	0.1039*	0.0252*	0.0160*	0.0524*	0.1247*	0.0476*	1	
Oil price evolution in 6 months	0.0166*	0.0185*	0.0091	0.0961*	0.0119	-0.0510*	0.0558*	0.0471*	0.0004	0.0265*	1
Oil price at start	0.0078	0.007	0.0064	0.0490*	0.0160*	-0.0690*	0.0334*	0.0410*	-0.0041	0.0171*	0.7902*
Oil price at end	0.0188*	0.0115	0.0148*	0.0855*	0.0074	-0.0392*	0.0341*	0.0478*	-0.0009	0.0204*	0.5095*
Gas price at start	0.0273*	0.0229*	0.0707*	0.1356*	-0.0311*	0.0087	0.0661*	0.0708*	0.0102	0.0296*	0.1388*
Gas price evolution in 6 months	0.0114	0.0175*	0.0735*	0.0567*	-0.0476*	0.0526*	0.0253*	0.0393*	0.0089	0.0059	-0.3630*
S&P 500 at start	0.0272*	0.0173*	0.0775*	0.1316*	-0.0371*	-0.0309*	0.0812*	0.0877*	0.007	0.0287*	0.5026*
S&P 500 evolution in 6 months	0.0171*	0.0131*	0.0332*	0.0843*	-0.0186*	-0.0058	0.0621*	0.0520*	0.0031	0.0181*	0.6341*
Power distance	-0.0085	0.0381*	0.0064	-0.0253*	-0.0017	0.0272*	-0.0001	0.0694*	-0.0009	0.0449*	0.0108
Individualism	0.0108	-0.0585*	-0.0218*	0.0999*	0.0602*	-0.0649*	-0.0259*	-0.1187*	0.0012	-0.0726*	-0.0142*
Masculinity	-0.004	-0.0274*	-0.0159*	0.0772*	0.0626*	-0.0288*	-0.0206*	-0.0446*	0.001	-0.0005	-0.0231*
Uncertainty avoidance	-0.0168*	0.0268*	0.0168*	-0.0567*	-0.0547*	0.0632*	0.0204*	0.1137*	0.0003	0.0680*	0.0158*
Long-term orientation	0.0068	0.0102	0.0340*	-0.1157*	-0.0979*	0.0851*	0.0405*	0.1501*	0.0002	0.0544*	0.0134*
Indulgence	0.0071	-0.0176*	-0.0295*	0.0465*	0.0453*	-0.0686*	-0.0223*	-0.1034*	0.0004	-0.0486*	-0.0123
Minority investors protection index	0.0140*	-0.0715*	-0.0097	-0.0503*	-0.0118	-0.0197*	0.0024	-0.0142*	0.0007	-0.0254*	-0.0069

	Oil price at start	Oil price at end	Gas price at start	Gas price evolution in 6 months	S&P 500 at start	S&P 500 evolution in 6 months	Power distance	Individualism	Masculinity	Uncertainty avoidance	Long-term orientation	Indulgence
Oil price at end	0.4681*	1										
Gas price at start	−0.0235*	0.3421*	1									
Gas price evolution in 6 months	−0.4146*	−0.1254*	0.6759*	1								
S&P 500 at start	0.4853*	0.4744*	0.6872*	0.3476*	1							
S&P 500 evolution in 6 months	0.3824*	0.3731*	0.2549*	−0.0116	0.6766*	1						
Power distance	0.0061	0.0158*	0.0206*	0.0143*	0.0177*	0.0108	1					
Individualism	−0.0082	−0.0165*	−0.0109	−0.0062	−0.0135*	−0.0127	−0.6470*	1				
Masculinity	−0.0156*	−0.0235*	−0.0253*	−0.0097	−0.0316*	−0.0307*	−0.0688*	0.4099*	1			
Uncertainty avoidance	0.0038	0.0114	0.0155*	0.0084	0.0192*	0.0255*	0.4092*	−0.5899*	−0.2135*	1		
Long-term orientation	0.0051	0.0134*	0.0008	−0.0132*	0.0043	0.0164*	0.2780*	−0.5715*	−0.2308*	0.3316*	1	
Indulgence	−0.0007	−0.0088	−0.0228*	−0.009	−0.0164*	−0.0160*	−0.5280*	0.5607*	0.1317*	−0.4438*	−0.6173*	1
Minority investors protection index	−0.0009	−0.0104	−0.0210*	−0.0167*	−0.0197*	−0.0144*	−0.2994*	0.2417*	0.0438*	−0.3869*	0.0882*	0.2254*

The table provides correlations for the main variables in the sample. * Significant at the 5% level. Variables are as defined in Appendix 6.2.

There are five alternative probit regression models to assess the statistical and economic significance of the results to alternative control variables.

The data in Table 6.3 highlight some of the main robust factors that affect the likelihood that a campaign involves a cleantech project. To begin, there is evidence that oil prices matter, and, in particular, the evolution of oil prices over the 6 months prior to the start of the campaign (oil price evolution in 6 months). This effect is statistically significant at the 1% level in Models 1 and 5 and at the 5% level in Model 4. Model 5 shows that the results are robust to the inclusion of a control variable for general economic conditions (S&P 500 evolution in 6 months and S&P 500 at start), which may strongly affect oil price movements. In terms of the economic significance, the results show that a 1-standard deviation increase in the change in oil prices over the prior 3 months gives rise to a 0.8% increase ($=0.0008147 \times 10.17 = 0.008285499$) in the probability of a cleantech crowdfunding campaign, based on the Model 5 estimate. Since the average probability of a crowdfunding campaign is 7.98% in the data, a 0.8% increase is equivalent to an increase by 9.7% ($=0.0798/0.082$).[9] This effect is, therefore both statistically and economically significant, strongly supporting Hypothesis 6.1. The impact of oil prices at the start of the campaign is also significant at the 5% level in Model 5, but this effect is not robust to other specifications (Models 1 and 4).

To stress the robustness of these results, we use country-adjusted oil price changes. As crude oil is only naturally present and available in a few countries but traded worldwide in USD, when it comes to final users, the price may vary greatly from one country to another. For instance, differences may result from currency conversions or from country-specific taxes on energy. The website globalpetrolprices.com offers a country index of oil-derived products prices. We use their gasoline index to adjust the price at a country level. More specifically, we multiply the oil prices used so far for our analysis by their adjustment factor to obtain country-adjusted prices. Results are provided in Model 6 of Table 6.3. We obtain qualitatively similar results for our primary measure of oil price changes. Similarly, we use gas price changes as a possible alternative driver, since, in many countries, gas is widely used as a source of energy by households. Again, we obtain similar results (see Model 7).

The cultural variables highlight one significant factor that affects the probability of a cleantech deal. Individualism is negatively associated with the probability of cleantech deals, and this effect is statistically significant at the 1% level in the specifications. A 1-standard deviation increase in individualism is associated with a 1.3% reduction in the probability of a cleantech campaign, which is a drop by 16.7%, relative to the average frequency of cleantech deals. Uncertainty avoidance is partially also significant, however, at the 10% level only and only in Models 4, 5, and 6. Note, as well, that the cultural variables are highly correlated with each other; as such, we replicated the regressions with each of the cultural variables considered separately. The results are not materially different for individualism. The cultural variable for individualism on its own has a coefficient of -0.000789 and is significant at the 1% level, which is just slightly less than the estimate of

---

[9] In unreported analysis, we also examined the impact of a short window of 3 months. The impact is weaker. However, given the time required to prepare a cleantech project, a longer window, such as 6 months, seems more appropriate for the analysis.

−0.001 as shown in Table 6.3. The uncertainty avoidance variable coefficient, however, is not robust. As such, the data provide the strongest support for the importance of low levels of individualism in facilitating crowdfunding. In other words, in view of the externalities of cleantech discussed in Section 6.2, with respect to being nonexcludable and nonrival, individualism is the most important cultural factor affecting the frequency of cleantech crowdfunding campaigns. This evidence strongly supports Hypothesis 6.2, at least with respect to the individualism cultural trait.

Finally, the data in Table 6.3 show some support for the role of legal protections in facilitating cleantech crowdfunding campaigns, but this effect is significant in Model 3 (when estimating without macroeconomic and cultural variables) and not robust in the other models.

Table 6.4 presents regressions for the characteristics of the crowdfunding campaign for cleantech versus non-cleantech, controlling for other project characteristics, macroeconomic conditions, cultural conditions, and legal conditions. Several fixed effects are also included. Regression 1 presents an analysis of factors that affect the size of the campaign goal. Cleantech goals are, on average, much more likely to be higher goals, and this effect is significant at the 1% level. In terms of the economic significance, cleantech deals are, on average, 16.0% higher than the average goal of $21,039. Model 2 shows that cleantech deals have, on average, 32.1% more gallery items relative to the average level of 6.81 items, and this effect is significant at the 1% level. Model 3 shows that video pitches are 8.7% more likely for cleantech versus non-cleantech deals. Model 4 shows that cleantech deals have, on average, 1947.11 more words than non-cleantech deals in the full-text description, which is 41.8% higher than the 4661 average number of words across all campaigns. Finally, Model 5 shows that cleantech deals have a readability score that is 1.2 higher, on average, which is 7.7% higher than the average readability score of all campaigns. Overall, therefore the data highlight the fact that cleantech campaigns are significantly different than other campaigns. The data are consistent with the view that entrepreneurs use more detailed information to mitigate the risk associated with the campaigns.

The control variables in Table 6.4 are significant in ways that we might expect. For example, KIA projects are associated with smaller goals, less use of video pitches, and shorter full-text length. These results are consistent with the view that the KIA-funding model is used in smaller and less risky projects (Chapter 5: Crowdfunding models: keep-it-all versus all-or-nothing). Note that we do not use goal size as a factor that explains the other left-hand-side variables in Models 2–5, because it is arguably endogenous; but, when we do include the goal size variable, the cleantech variable's statistical significance is not affected, and there is merely a trivial effect on its economic significance. One thing to note in Table 6.4 is that the only factor that consistently affects all five left-hand-side variables is the cleantech variable. Overall, therefore the data strongly support Hypothesis 6.3.

Table 6.5 presents further robustness checks on the models presented in Table 6.4. In particular, we use propensity score matching on the campaign goal, funding model, subcategory, and date, to ascertain whether or not the findings still hold. The matching was made based on the cleantech sample: every cleantech project was matched with the closest non-cleantech project in terms of the subcategory, campaign goal, funding model, and date. In Panel A, we report measures of the accuracy of our matching process. The standardized percentage bias, expressed as the percentage of the square root of the average of

TABLE 6.3 Cleantech-based crowdfunding campaigns.

	(1)	(2)	(3)	(4)	(5)	(6)	(7)
Macroeconomic conditions							
Oil price evolution in 6 months	0.0008147***			0.0007496**	0.0009841***		
Oil price at start	−0.0007698*			−0.0008314	−0.0010828**		
Oil price at end	0.0001763			−0.000111	−0.000059		
Country-adjusted oil price evolution in 6 months						0.0006125**	
Country-adjusted oil price at start						−0.0001074	
Gas price evolution in 6 months							0.0126354**
Gas price at start							0.0063454
S&P 500 evolution in 6 months					−0.0000738	−0.0000461	0.0000244
S&P 500 at start					0.0000648	0.0000405	−0.0000026
Cultural dimensions							
Power distance		−0.0000894		−0.0001581	−0.0001593	−0.0002325	−0.0001727
Individualism		−0.0009883***		−0.0010163***	−0.0010154***	−0.0010838***	−0.0010216***
Masculinity		−0.0000842		−0.0000736	−0.0000721	−0.0000749	−0.0000563
Uncertainty avoidance		−0.0002628		−0.0003505*	−0.0003464*	−0.0003416	−0.0003526*
Long-term orientation		−0.0001899		−0.0001485	−0.0001459	−0.0000476	−0.000138
Indulgence		0.000166		0.0002213	0.000222	0.0002423	0.0002214
Legal conditions							
Strength of minority investors protection index			−0.0246323***	−0.0053462	−0.0052851	−0.0060293	−0.0054862
Semester fixed effect				Yes	Yes	Yes	Yes
Observations	22,875	22,014	22,768	22,014	22,014	21,972	22,014
Pseudo R-squared	0.001	0.004	0.008	0.005	0.005	0.005	0.005

The table provides marginal effects in probit regressions for the determinants of cleantech campaigns. The dependent variable is "cleantech dummy." Regressions 1, 2, and 3 show results respectively for macroeconomics conditions, cultural dimensions, and legal conditions. Regressions 4 shows results for all the independent variables taken together with semester fixed effect. Regression 5 adds control for world economic evolution. Regression 6 uses oil prices adjusted at the country level, and regression 7 tests our hypothesis on gas as an alternative fossil energy source. Standard deviations are estimated robust to heteroscedasticity. *, **, *** Significant at the 10%, 5%, and 1% levels, respectively. Variables are as defined in Appendix 6.2.

TABLE 6.4 Crowdfunding campaign presentation.

	(1) Ln(goal)	(2) Gallery	(3) Video pitch	(4) Full-text length	(5) ARI
Project characteristics					
Cleantech dummy	0.159***	2.188***	0.087***	1947.117***	1.172***
Keep-it-all dummy	− 0.201***	0.430	− 0.027**	− 692.923***	0.397***
Verified nonprofit	0.167***	0.909***	0.060***	132.147*	1.384***
Macroeconomic					
Oil price evolution in 6 months	0.001	− 0.041***	0.001**	2.946	0.006
Oil price at start	− 0.002	0.028	− 0.002***	− 5.656	− 0.006
Oil price at end	− 0.002	0.012	− 0.001*	2.621	− 0.003
Cultural dimensions					
Power distance	0.020*	− 0.221	− 0.036***	50.860	− 0.049
Individualism	− 0.002	− 0.057	− 0.009***	11.781	− 0.024
Masculinity	− 0.010	0.393	0.047***	8.584	0.134
Uncertainty avoidance	− 0.012**	0.115	0.015***	38.873*	0.111***
Long-term orientation	− 0.003	− 0.028	− 0.006***	− 4.216	− 0.022
Indulgence	0.015	− 0.406**	− 0.040***	− 23.915	− 0.153
Legal conditions					
Strength of minority investors protection index	0.369***	− 2.883**	− 0.229***	439.102	− 0.699
Constant	6.834***	32.910**	3.815***	− 2590.033	20.530***
Subcategory fixed effect	Yes	Yes	Yes	Yes	Yes
Semester fixed effect	Yes	Yes	Yes	Yes	Yes
Country fixed effect	Yes	Yes	Yes	Yes	Yes
Observations	22,014	22,014	22,014	22,014	21,838
R-Squared	0.095	0.048	0.122	0.113	0.044
Adjusted R-squared	0.091	0.044	0.118	0.109	0.040

The table provides OLS regressions for the campaign goal (1), number of gallery items (2), the length of the text describing the campaign (4), and the readability score of the text (5), and a probit regression for the probability of the use of a video pitch (3). *, **, *** Significant at the 10%, 5%, and 1% levels, respectively. Variables are as defined in Appendix 6.2. *ARI*, Automated readability index.

TABLE 6.5 Crowdfunding campaign presentation based on propensity score matching.

Panel A: Matching accuracy

Variable	Unmatched (U) Matched (M)	Mean Cleantech	Mean Non-cleantech	% Bias	% Reduction Bias	Mean difference test t-Stat	Variance ratio
Keep-it-all dummy	U	0.93144	0.94878	− 7.3		− 3.08***	n.a.
	M	0.93144	0.93913	− 3.2	55.7	− 0.91	n.a.
Goal	U	26,080	20,643	19		8.10***	1.38[a]
	M	26,080	25,373	2.5	87	0.68	1.06
Start date (days relative to 01.01.1960)	U	19,365	19,350	7.7		3.04***	0.96
	M	19,365	19,366	− 0.7	90.9	− 0.21	1.03

Panel B: Regressions using propensity score matching

	(1) Gallery	(2) Gallery	(3) Video pitch	(4) Full-text length	(5) ARI
Project characteristics					
Cleantech dummy	1.622***	1.476***	0.078***	1823.094***	1.161***
Keep-it-all dummy		− 1.797*	− 0.076***	− 1154.574***	0.047
Verified nonprofit		1.702**	0.099***	− 341.915*	1.089***
Macroeconomic conditions					
Oil price evolution in 6 months		− 0.093**	− 0.001	2.756	0.016
Oil price at start		0.068	− 0.003	4.215	− 0.002
Oil price at end		0.006	0.000	− 9.623	− 0.004
Cultural dimensions					
Power distance		1.453	0.052***	536.335	0.006
Individualism		− 1.09	0.003	− 281.587	0.059
Masculinity		0.491	− 0.010***	140.388	− 0.047
Uncertainty avoidance		1.485	0.001	445.220	− 0.238
Long-term orientation		− 0.853*	− 0.011***	− 246.141	− 0.001
Indulgence		4.877	0.051**	1528.664	− 0.424
Legal conditions					
Strength of minority investors protection index		− 53.577	0.002	− 16,328.982	7.388
Constant	7.414***	− 13.894	− 3.980**	− 10,057.679	3.749
Subcategory fixed effect	No	Yes	Yes	Yes	Yes

Panel B: Regressions using propensity score matching

	(1)	(2)	(3)	(4)	(5)
	Gallery	Gallery	Video pitch	Full-text length	ARI
Semester fixed effect	No	Yes	Yes	Yes	Yes
Country fixed effect	No	Yes	Yes	Yes	Yes
Observations	3384	3151	3151	3151	3151
R-Squared	0.004	0.088	0.091	0.15	0.127
Adjusted R-squared	0.004	0.064	0.067	0.128	0.105

[a]*Variance ratios that exceed the 2.5th and 97.5th percentiles.*

Panel A: Matching accuracy: The table shows t-tests for equality of means between cleantech and non-cleantech projects subsamples before and after propensity score matching for matched variables (except for subcategories). It also reports the standardized percentage bias (percentage of the square root of the average of the sample variances in cleantech and non-cleantech groups) and the variance ratio between the two subsamples. *, **, *** Significant at the 10%, 5%, and 1% levels, respectively.

Panel B: Regressions using propensity score matching: The table provides OLS regressions for the campaign number of gallery items, the length of the text describing the campaign, the readability score of the text, and a probit regression for the probability of the use of a video pitch. The sample is composed by 1684 cleantech projects matched with 1684 non-cleantech projects. The propensity score matching is based on the project subcategory, size (goal), the funding model (keep-it-all or all-or-nothing), and the project launch date. *, **, *** Significant at the 10%, 5%, and 1% levels, respectively. Variables are as defined in Appendix 6.2. *ARI*, Automated readability index.

the sample variances in the cleantech and non-cleantech groups (Rosenbaum & Rubin, 1985), is now reduced by 87%, 56%, and 91%, respectively, for the goal, funding model, and start date. Differences in mean t-tests between cleantech and non-cleantech projects are, thus, no longer significant for matched samples in terms of the project size (goal), funding model, and start date. The results reported in Panel B are very consistent with those reported in Table 6.4. Likewise, other matching criteria (considered and available on request), such as for cultural and legal conditions, do not change the main findings.

Finally, Table 6.6 presents an analysis of project success for cleantech versus non-cleantech projects. Seven alternative specifications are provided to highlight robustness. Models 1–5 examine the full sample to ascertain whether, on average, cleantech projects are, more or less, successful than non-cleantech projects, using the following measures of success: the total amount pledged by backers, the number of backers, the completion ratio, and the success dummy (i.e., whether the completion ratio is at least equal to 1). We find no evidence of any significant effect, with the sole exception of Model 1, where there is suggestive evidence that is significant at the 10% level (but not robust to alternative specifications considered and available on request). Models 6 and 7, therefore present regressions for the separate subsample of cleantech (Model 6) versus non-cleantech (Model 7) subsamples. Models 6 and 7 are very informative, as they highlight the differences in the sensitivity of different factors of success in terms of achieving the funding goal in ways that are consistent with Hypothesis 6.4.

Models 6 and 7 in Table 6.6 show that, relative to non-cleantech campaigns, the success of cleantech campaigns, in terms of achieving funding goals (the variable success dummy), is 9.1% more economically sensitive to the campaign's goal size, 86.2% more sensitive to being not-for-profit, 11.5% more sensitive to being an AON campaign, and 105.5% more sensitive to having a video pitch. However, the data also indicate that cleantech success is 31.4% less sensitive to the gallery items and 34.4% less sensitive to the full-text length,

TABLE 6.6 Success of cleantech projects.

	(1)	(2)	(3)	(4)	(5)	(6)	(7)
	Pledged	Backers	Completion ratio	Success	Success	Success – cleantech	Success – non-cleantech
Project characteristics							
Cleantech dummy	− 1685.142*	− 13.162	− 0.021	0.016	0.016		
ln(Goal)	3673.846***	34.874***	− 0.192***		− 0.093***	− 0.101***	− 0.092***
Verified nonprofit	1026.573***	− 1.340	0.074***		0.056***	0.097***	0.052***
Keep-it-all dummy	− 4567.670***	− 64.447***	− 0.210***		− 0.203***	− 0.224***	− 0.201***
Gallery's items	198.511***	1.602***	0.008***		0.003***	0.002*	0.003***
Video pitch dummy	505.621*	8.329	0.040		0.040***	0.077***	0.038***
Full-text length	0.699***	0.007***	0.00002***		0.000006***	0.000004*	0.000006***
Social networks	− 158.900**	− 0.332	− 0.005		0.0001	0.004	− 0.00008
AR index	− 54.369*	− 1.517**	− 0.0006		0.0010	− 0.004	0.001
Macroeconomic conditions							
Oil price evolution in 6 months	41.924	0.845	0.0005		0.0006	− 0.0008	0.0008
Oil price at start	− 127.544**	− 3.068**	− 0.006		− 0.001	0.004	− 0.001*
Oil price at end	113.922***	0.49	0.001		0.0002	0.0007	0.0002
Cultural dimensions							
Power distance	− 67.400	− 0.145	− 0.024***		− 0.039***	0.025	− 0.038***
Individualism	91.343***	1.223***	0.0002		− 0.003**	0.001	− 0.003*
Masculinity	− 2.538	− 3.666	0.026***		0.047***	− 0.000006	0.043***
Uncertainty avoidance	45.553	0.075	0.012***		0.021***	− 0.014	0.020***

	(1)	(2)	(3)	(4)	(5)	(6)	(7)
Long-term orientation	5.146	0.386	0.0004		− 0.0007	− 0.012	− 0.0005
Indulgence	− 38.844	1.613	− 0.025***		− 0.042***	0.011	− 0.040***
Legal conditions							
Strength of minority investors protection index	− 3070.032***	− 12.772	− 0.301***	0.176***	− 0.429***	0.142	− 0.416***
Constant	− 12,002.847	154.306	5.099***		4.887***	− 1.109	4.819***
Subcategory fixed effect	Yes	Yes	Yes	No	Yes	Yes	Yes
Semester fixed effect	Yes	Yes	Yes	No	Yes	Yes	Yes
Country fixed effect	Yes	Yes	Yes	No	Yes	Yes	Yes
Observations	21,838	21,838	21,838	22,875	21,838	1530	20,308
R-Squared	0.047	0.026	0.028	0.000	0.072	0.121	0.071
Adjusted R-squared	0.042	0.021	0.024	0.000	0.068	0.074	0.067

The table provides OLS regressions for the success of the campaigns. Regressions 1, 2, and 3 show success as proxied by the total amount pledged, the number of backers, and the percent funded. Models 4, 5, 6, and 7 show results of probit regressions for the probability of success in terms of meeting or exceeding the funding goal. Regressions 4 and 5 are based on the full sample, and regressions 6 and 7 compare subsamples of cleantech and non-cleantech campaigns. *, **, *** Significant at the 10%, 5%, and 1% levels, respectively. Variables are as defined in Appendix 6.2.

implying that excessive photos and excessive wordiness are less relevant in cleantech campaigns. Apart from these project characteristics, the macroeconomic, cultural, and legal condition variables as shown in Table 6.6 are statistically insignificant in Model 6 for cleantech investments. Overall, this evidence in Table 6.6 is consistent with the findings in Tables 6.4 and 6.5; cleantech campaigns must overcome more pronounced information asymmetries, and, as such, cleantech entrepreneurs are more successful when they make better use of mechanisms to mitigate such information asymmetries.

In other robustness checks for Table 6.6, we considered other specifications, such as propensity score matching, as done in Table 6.5 relative to Table 6.4. The findings were not materially different and, therefore not explicitly reported, but they are available on request. Finally, we have considered other macroeconomic and institutional variables from the World Bank for each of the tables, but the results were not materially different.

6.5 Conclusion

This chapter provided, for the first time, an empirical analysis of crowdfunding in the cleantech or alternative energy sector. We examined more than 20,000 different projects from 81 countries around the world on the Indiegogo platform, where 7.4% were cleantech campaigns. Cleantech campaigns are more common when oil prices are rising and in countries with low levels of individualism. The evidence further shows that cleantech entrepreneurs make more use of soft information to inform the crowd about their projects, which is consistent with the view that alternative energies are viewed as being more risky, so investors face greater information asymmetries relative to other types of investment projects. Finally, these data are consistent with the view that cleantech entrepreneurs who use these soft mechanisms to mitigate these information problems are more likely to have a successful fundraising campaign. The mere fact that a project is a cleantech, however, does not affect the campaign outcome in itself.

Our analysis extends the prior literature in a few important respects. We extend the analysis of the financing of alternative energies from other investors, such as the publicly listed market and the venture capital market, to the crowdfunding arena. Crowdfunding is a relatively new area of study, and no prior paper has examined crowdfunding of alternative energies. By examining the crowdfunding marketplace, we can infer from the wisdom of the crowd the factors that influence success for alternative energies. Furthermore, the analysis of crowdfunding allows an analysis of entrepreneurial actions regarding the use of mechanisms to mitigate information asymmetries faced by investors. Crowdfunding is particularly interesting with respect to studying the financing of technologies, such as alternative energies that have nonrival and nonexcludable properties. Also, the fact that crowdfunders are not directly seeking financial returns on this type of platform allows us to study support cleantech projects beyond the traditional support from financial markets.

As the crowdfunding market grows over time and different types of crowdfunding are adopted in different countries and on different platforms, further analyses of the crowdfunding of alternative energies can be carried out. We hope that this type of analysis in future work can help to inform entrepreneurs, investors, academics, and policymakers to get the most out of the financing of alternative energies so that cleantech can fill a greater role in society in the coming years.

Key terms

Cleantech
Indulgence
Long-term orientation
Masculinity
Minority investor protection
Power distance
Soft information
Uncertainty avoidance

Discussion questions

6.1. What is "cleantech?" Why might crowdfunding be a natural fit for financing cleantech ventures? Explain why and provide examples based on information in Chapter 4, An overview of rewards-based crowdfunding, and current chapter.

6.2. Why might oil prices affect the volume of cleantech crowdfunding projects? Explain the intuition and discuss the existing statistical evidence.

6.3. Is soft information in crowdfunding campaigns more or less important for the success of cleantech crowdfunding campaigns relative to the typical non-cleantech campaign? What type of soft information might be more important in typical cleantech campaigns? Why?

6.4. Explain the main different national cultural conditions and cultural indices developed by Hofstede. Which of these different cultural dimensions is more important for understanding cleantech crowdfunding frequency and success? Explain the intuition and discuss the existing statistical evidence.

6.5. Are legal or cultural conditions across countries more important for cleantech crowdfunding frequency and success? Explain the intuition and discuss the existing statistical evidence.

6.6. In which countries are there a higher proportion of cleantech crowdfunding projects than non-cleantech? Why do you think cleantech crowdfunding is more common in some countries relative to others?

6.7. Are cleantech crowdfunding campaigns more likely to be nonprofits? Explain why and discuss the existing evidence.

6.8. Do cleantech crowdfunding campaigns typically use more rewards levels? Explain why and discuss the existing evidence.

6.9. Are cleantech crowdfunding campaigns more likely to be scalable? Do cleantech crowdfunding campaigns more often use the all-or-nothing or keep-it-all funding model? Explain why and discuss the existing evidence.

6.10. Are cleantech crowdfunding campaigns typically larger and more successful than their non-cleantech counterparts? Explain why and discuss the existing evidence.

Appendix 6.1 Cleantech crowdfunding data by countries and time

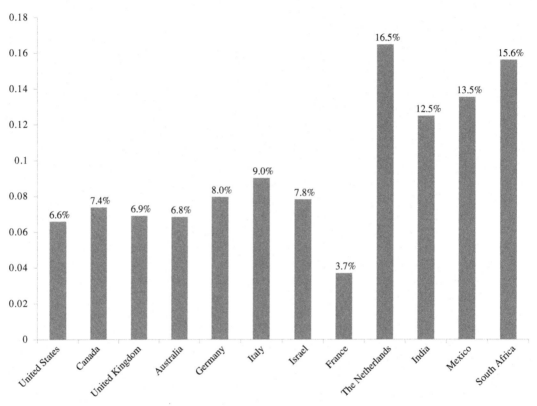

FIGURE 6A.1 Cleantech projects by country.
The chart shows the percentage of campaigns financing cleantech, for countries with more than 90 projects. Countries are ordered by total number of projects presented on the platform (from higher on the left to lower on the right).

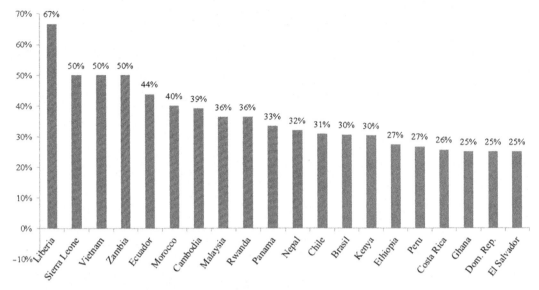

FIGURE 6.A2   Countries with a high proportion of cleantech projects.
The chart shows the percentage of campaigns financing cleantech for countries where such projects account for more than 25% of presented projects and with a total number of projects higher than 5.

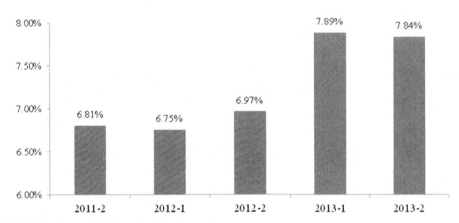

FIGURE 6A.3   Cleantech projects by semester.
The chart shows the overall proportion of cleantech projects for each semester.

II. Rewards Crowdfunding

Appendix 6.2 Variables definitions

Project characteristics

Cleantech dummy	Dummy variable indicating if the project description indicates a cleantech project (based on a list of words: "green energy," "cleantech," "recycle," "wind power," "solar power," "biomass," "renewable energy," "hydroelectric," "photovoltaic," "geotherm," "sustainable," "biofuel," "green transport," "environmental footprint," "gray water," "electric motor")
Goal	The crowdfunding campaign goal in USD set by the entrepreneur. For campaigns based on a currency other than USD, we convert the amount into USD at an annual average exchange rate
Verified nonprofit	Dummy variable indicating if the entrepreneur is a registered nonprofit organization
Keep-it-all dummy	Dummy variable equal to one if the entrepreneur chooses a "keep-it-all" and zero for the "all-or-nothing" funding model
Gallery's items	Number of pictures or videos presented in the media gallery
Video pitch dummy	Dummy variable indicating if a video pitch of the project is provided
Full-text length	Length (in characters) of the full text of the project description on the project main page
Social networks	Number of external links of the project to social networks (like Facebook, Twitter, or any other community website)
ARI	The "ARI" score, based on the full text of project description. This value is expressed in a US grade level. For instance, Grade 1 indicates text for children of 6/7 years, and Grade 12 for high school students of 17/18 years. This index is based on the following formula: [4.71 × (characters/words) + 0.5 × (words/sentences) − 21.43]
Categories	Projects are classified by category, which are classified in several subcategories (shown in brackets): innovative (technology, small business, food, sports); creative (art, dance, film, gaming, music, photography, theater, transmedia, writing, comic, design, fashion, video/web); and social (animals, community, education, environment, health, politics, religion)

Project outcome

Success	Dummy variable equal to one if the funding percentage is greater or equal to 100%, and zero otherwise. The project is thus considered fully financed and the crowdfunding campaign successful
Pledged	Sum of all pledges made by backers
Backers	Number of backers having pledged money to the project
Completion ratio	Ratio between the total pledge and campaign goal

Macroeconomic conditions

Oil price evolution in 6 months	Difference in spot price for crude oil between the day of campaign's launch and 6 months earlier
Oil price at start	Crude oil spot price at campaign's launch
Oil price at end	Crude oil spot price at campaign's end

Country-adjusted oil price evolution in 6 months	Difference in spot price for crude oil between the day of campaign's launch and 6 months earlier adjusted at the country level. The crude oil price is multiplied by a country-specific factor that takes into account the difference in oil cost for final users in each country. The adjusting factors range from 0.13 to 1.74 and are calculated based on globalpetrolprices.com country-specific prices
Country-adjusted oil price at start	Country-adjusted crude oil spot price at campaign's launch. The crude oil price is multiplied by a country-specific factor that takes into account the difference in oil cost for the final user in each country. The adjusting factors range from 0.13 to 1.74 and are calculated based on globalpetrolprices.com country-specific prices
Gas price evolution in 6 months	Difference in spot price for natural gas between the day of campaign's launch and 6 months earlier
Gas price at start	Natural gas spot price at campaign's launch
S&P 500 evolution in 6 months	Difference in S&P 500 index between the day of campaign's launch and 6 months earlier
S&P 500 at start	S&P 500 index at campaign's launch
Legal conditions	
Strength of minority	This is the average of the extent of conflict of interest regulation index and the extent of shareholder governance index
Investor protection index (World Bank Index)	The index ranges from 1 to 10, rounded to the nearest decimal place, with higher values indicating stronger minority investor protections. This methodology was developed by Djankov, La Porta et al. (2008)

Hofstede (1991, 2001, 2011) national cultural dimensions[a]

Power distance	This dimension expresses the degree to which the less powerful members of a society accept and expect that power is distributed unequally. The fundamental issue here is how a society handles inequalities among people. People in societies exhibiting a large degree of power distance accept a hierarchical order in which everybody has a place and which needs no further justification. In societies with low power distance, people strive to equalize the distribution of power and demand justification for inequalities of power
Individualism	The high side of this dimension, called individualism, can be defined as a preference for a loosely knit social framework in which individuals are expected to take care of only themselves and their immediate families. Its opposite, collectivism, represents a preference for a tightly knit framework in society in which individuals can expect their relatives or members of a particular in-group to look after them in exchange for unquestioning loyalty. A society's position on this dimension is reflected in whether people's self-image is defined in terms of "I" or "we"
Masculinity	The masculinity side of this dimension represents a preference in society for achievement, heroism, assertiveness, and material rewards for success. Society at large is more competitive. Its opposite, femininity, stands for a preference for cooperation, modesty, caring for the weak, and quality of life. Society, at large, is more consensus-oriented. In the business context, Masculinity versus Femininity is sometimes also referred to as "tough versus gender" cultures

II. Rewards Crowdfunding

Uncertainty avoidance	The uncertainty avoidance dimension expresses the degree to which the members of a society feel uncomfortable with uncertainty and ambiguity. The fundamental issue here is how a society deals with the fact that the future can never be known: Should we try to control the future or just let it happen? Countries exhibiting strong UAI maintain rigid codes of belief and behavior and are intolerant of unorthodox behavior and ideas. Weak UAI societies maintain a more relaxed attitude in which practice counts more than principles
Long-term orientation	Every society must maintain some links with its own past while dealing with the challenges of the present and the future. Societies prioritize these two existential goals differently. Societies who score low on this dimension, for example, prefer to maintain time-honored traditions and norms while viewing societal change with suspicion. Those with a culture which scores high, on the other hand, take a more pragmatic approach: they encourage thrift and efforts in modern education as a way to prepare for the future. In the business context, this dimension is referred to as "(short term) normative versus (long term) pragmatic" (PRA). In the academic environment the terminology monumentalism versus flexhumility is sometimes also used
Indulgence	Indulgence stands for a society that allows relatively free gratification of basic and natural human drives related to enjoying life and having fun. Restraint stands for a society that suppresses gratification of needs and regulates it by means of strict social norms

[a]These definitions are the interpretations offered by the Hofstede Center (https://geert-hofstede.com) for the measures of cultural dimensions as defined by Hofstede (2011).
ARI, Automated readability index; UAI, Uncertainty Avoidance Index.

7

Crowdfunding to internationalize

7.1 Introduction

This chapter examines how crowdfunding can be used not only for corporate finance purposes but potentially also for both development and trade initiatives. Examples of products, companies, and nongovernmental organizations (NGOs) that have used crowdfunding are presented to illustrate our suggestions. While we acknowledge that research in the area of crowdfunding is still in its infancy, we note that prior work has not connected crowdfunding to entrepreneurial internationalization. It is our hope that this chapter, which offers a descriptive look at this connection, is a first step toward developing this newly emerging literature on crowdfunding and entrepreneurial internationalization.

The seminal work of Oviatt and McDougall (1994) identified four necessary and sufficient conditions for successful new venture internationalization: "(1) organization formation through internalization of some transactions, (2) stronger reliance on alternative governance structures to access resources, (3) establishment of foreign location advantages, and (4) control over adequate resources." Subsequent research, such as Zahra (2014) has refined some of these criteria to consider the interaction between strong versus weak public governance at the national level and corporate governance at the firm level. Here, in this chapter, we argue that crowdfunding may facilitate that control over adequate resources, which is an important component of entrepreneurial firm internationalization.

Crowdfunding is an umbrella term used to describe an increasingly widespread form of fundraising whereby groups of people pool money, typically (very) small individual contributions, to support a particular goal (Bayus, 2013; Belleflamme et al., 2013, 2014; Colombo, Franzoni, & Rossi-Lamastra, 2014; Mollick, 2014a, 2014b; Mollick & Kuppuswamy, 2014; Schwienbacher & Larralde, 2012). It is increasingly widespread as social networks created on the World Wide Web have enabled fundraising to be carried out through online portals. The portal acts as an intermediary between the large groups of investors and the firms or individuals raising money. Fundraising is carried out in numerous ways. Donations-based crowdfunding simply involves donations made by crowdfunders to the organization, firm, or individual raising money where there is no expectation of a return other than feeling good about the gesture. Examples include crowdfunding for disaster relief, not-for-profit organizations, charities, helping individuals fund medical or legal fees, and even raising money for rebels in war torn countries (Becker & Myers, 2015). Rewards-based crowdfunding involves small rewards to the crowdfunders, such as a product or some other small token of appreciation from the firm or individual raising money. Lending-based crowdfunding involves peer-to-peer loans from one individual to another whereby matching is facilitated by the portal. Equity-based crowdfunding is a form of equity financing in which entrepreneurs make an open call for funding on the platform, hoping to attract a large group of (small) investors (Chapter 10: Signaling in equity crowdfunding).

In this chapter, we first explain in Section 7.2 that the market for crowdfunding is becoming increasingly popular around the world. Moreover, restrictions on access to crowdfunding are loosening over time. Then in Section 7.3, we explain the economic incentives to engage in crowdfunding. We review in detail the incentives of investors, portals, and entrepreneurs. In Section 7.4, we review the problems and pitfalls that may arise in crowdfunding markets and some of the regulatory responses to crowdfunding. In Section 7.5, we provide evidence that access to finance is an important part of the resources needed for firms to internationalize. In Section 7.6, we provide examples of products, companies, and NGOs that have used crowdfunding. In Section 7.7, we explain how international investors in other types of small- and medium-sized enterprise (SME) financing markets have added value, such as the venture capital market. Finally, Section 7.8 concludes and suggests avenues for future research.

7.2 Why care about crowdfunding for entrepreneurial internationalization?

Crowdfunding, albeit a relatively new phenomenon for entrepreneurial firms raising funds or firm equity capital, is growing rapidly around the world. Massolution[1] estimates that the crowdfunding market around the world was US$3 billion in 2012, $6 billion in 2013, and $16 billion in 2014 (based on Q3 2014 figures). In 2012 crowdfunding raised $1.6 billion in North America, $945 million in Europe, and $110 million in the rest of the world. Crowdfunding expanded at a 63% compound annual growth rate (CAGR) from 2009 to 2012: donation-based platforms exhibited a CAGR of 43%, reward-based platforms exhibited a CAGR of 524%, lending-based platforms exhibited a CAGR of 78%, and equity-based platforms exhibited a CAGR of 114%. This will continue to grow as in 2014, $16.2 billion in global crowdfunding was raised and it is thought that in 2015 the crowdfunding market is on its way to raising $34.4 billion.

This growth will undoubtedly continue as crowdfunding markets become more open over time, especially for equity-based platforms. The increasing activity within the crowdfunding market may be attributed to more recent acceptance by crowdfunders to escalate their activities from low to nil expectation—based donation fund, to the increasingly higher expectation rewards-, lending-, and equity-based crowdfunding. There is increasing familiarity within crowdfunding circles, and such familiarity is breeding trust. As there are more crowdfunders seeking to fund projects or finance firms with innovative projects, more portals are being established to meet this demand. With more portal choice,

---

[1] www.massolution.com

innovators and firms find it much easier to look to crowdfunding portals to facilitate fund or firm capital raising. This increasing acceptance by the general public across the world of crowdfunding that in part has resulted in the United States enacting the Jumpstart Our Business Startups (JOBS) Act in March 2012 (and became effective and implemented in June 2015), which essentially removed restrictions in place for equity sales or placements. Also, in Canada, general equity crowdfunding rules were established in more than half of the Canadian provinces in April 2015.[2]

7.3 What are the economic incentives to engage in crowdfunding?

Identifying the growth of this market is arguably easier than determining why the market is growing in the first place. In any market, it is possible to determine the economic incentives for market participants, just as it is possible to identify ensuing disincentives which result in market failure.

Recall from Fig. 1.1 (Chapter 1: Introduction) that crowdfunding is a form of financial intermediation between investors and entrepreneurs. In Chapter 1, Introduction, we introduced some incentives and disincentives to engage in crowdfunding alongside Fig. 1.1. Raising external funding, especially equity finance, can be an inefficient exercise for innovators and entrepreneurial firms. For example, we are aware of an entrepreneur from Saskatchewan that recently obtained Can$150,000 in angel capital for his start-up and had legal fees amounting to $70,000 for the deal. In view of information asymmetries and agency costs between entrepreneurs and their fund providers and investors, external finance is not only uncertain but also costly (Cosh, Cumming, & Hughes, 2009). It is a result of this information asymmetry and agency costs that most investors, especially retail investors, are restricted from making equity investments in firms that are not approved for public trading on regulated exchanges. Equity investments in high risk early stage companies have until recently been limited to sophisticated investors, mainly private equity investors, institutional investors, and high net worth individuals. While the authors, to a certain extent, appreciate the need for such regulations to protect nonsophisticated investors, we also appreciate that this has hampered retail investors' investment in private equity which is widely known as a form of alternative investment which is prominently used to diversify investment portfolios (Cumming & Johan, 2006). Crowdfunding is thus increasingly appealing to potential crowdfunders as it enables them to diversify their

---

[2] The Globe and Mail, November 29, 2012
- "Regulators struggle with crowdfunding model. . . ."
- "Ontario looked upon as key to setting pace. . . ."
- "Using our existing regulatory framework to deal with something like equity crowdfunding is like trying to jam a round peg into a square hole"

Lawyers' Weekly, April 19, 2013 issue
- "Regulators Unveil Crowdfunding Rules for Startups"

The Globe and Mail March 20, 2014
- "Ontario examines ways to loosen [equity] crowdfunding rules"

savings or retirement portfolios. The demand for funding and the swelling supply only serve to make it advantageous for portals to act as intermediaries.

Crowdfunding can be extremely useful for innovators and firms because of particular ease of access to funds. One-stop online portals provide access to an audience of eager donors, fund providers, and investors from around the world (Agrawal et al., 2015). Such access to an eager audience not only lowers the cost of marketing the innovative product or firm but also benefits from escalation by crowdfunders, or the potential for a donation crowdfunder to be more comfortable to take the extra step to provide equity crowdfunding instead. The access to such a diverse audience of crowdfunders also enables the bundling of reward and equity. Rewards-based crowdfunding is known to provide proof of concept to innovators, or proof that the service or product offered has a demand and the funds raised are used to meet this demand. With a hybrid reward—equity base, not only are innovators and firms able to obtain crowdfunder validation or proof of concept, but the innovators and firms are able to exploit this traction, signal of quality, and the ensuing lowering of information asymmetry to obtain equity funding (Agrawal et al., 2013). With reference to our earlier example, the amounts involved in crowdfunding are relatively small compared to traditional lending or equity finance-sophisticated investors, and therefore direct costs of crowdfunding are lower and do not involve significant legal bills and costs of giving up control rights. This is generally because crowdfunders are either not expecting any rewards, place more value on the personal or the community benefits (Schwienbacher & Larralde, 2012) rather than financial benefits of crowdfunding, or are aware that their relatively small contribution may not entitle them to legal certainty in the case of equity crowdfunding. These somewhat altruistic incentives to being a part of the crowdfunding community also result in crowdfunders being more willing to constructively contribute to the innovation process. This provision of advice provides valuable feedback and information regarding the success or even failure of the product or fundraising exercise, which increases the ease of fund or equity raising for innovators and firms (Lauga & Ofek, 2009). This sense of community among crowdfunders enables news about projects or firms to be circulated cost effectively, resulting in what Agrawal et al. (2013, 2015) refers to herding behavior among crowdfunders. A result of herding behavior is media exposure which in turn attracts more crowdfunders doe to the publicity. Like the venture capital industry, which crowdfunding is often compared to, publicity, especially good publicity, only serves to increase project or firm value due as a result of reduced information asymmetry. Just as venture capitalists would grandstand their investments, or take their investments public early, to take advantage of the resulting publicity, firms seeking crowdfunding will also benefit from media coverage.

This ease of access to capital and diminishing cost of raising funds are also a result of the increasing number of portals that have launched to take advantage of the network effects of crowdfunding. In 2013 the World Bank determined that there were 45 nations in North America, Latin America, Europe, the Middle East and North Africa, Sub-Saharan Africa, and Asia that have active crowdfunding platforms (World Bank, 2013). The ease of access to capital, advice provided, information gathered, and publicity garnered as a result of crowdfunder activity only serve to make their function as intermediary easier and less costly to implement. First, we need to understand what these portals are. They are basically online platforms (e.g., Kickstarter and Crowdcube) that provide the means, or the conduit, for the transactions to be carried out. The portals are incentivized to provide the means as revenue can be earned either based on transaction value or firm performance (Agrawal et al., 2013). They could be said to do what other equity exchanges do, such as setting the legal groundwork within which investments (or in this case donations and loans) could be made, preselection of the innovators or firms, providing a forum for the innovators or firms to market their products or services, and the ability to process financial transactions. The difference is that they are relatively unregulated, and the extent to which any of the abovementioned functions are carried out to ensure a fair and efficient market differ across platforms and across countries. They are in essence matchmakers for investors and innovators/firms seeking crowdfunding. These portals help mitigate information asymmetry issues for crowdfunders first by providing certification of chosen innovators and firms availed to the portal audience. As portals mature, they are able to identify the determinants of potentially successful, or unsuccessful, projects or firms and are more sophisticated in their due diligence and screening (Agrawal et al., 2013). The more sophisticated portals get, the better they become at differentiating themselves among the numerous portals available to both crowdfunders and innovators/firms, and this will further strengthen the signaling effects of portal choice.

Just as many firms seek to be listed on the New York Stock Exchange or NASDAQ, many innovators and firms will aim to be listed on Kickstarter or Indiegogo, portals of repute. The strong reputation of the portal will provide invaluable endorsement of risky projects and nascent firms seeking funding. Research finds that there is a strong sense of community participation among crowdfunders (Schwienbacher & Larralde, 2012); therefore many crowdfunders would prefer to take part on a portal of like-minded crowdfunders that enables them to access appropriate projects and firms. Crowdfunding has also proven to be an easy way for nonsophisticated donors, lenders, and investors to access new causes, innovative products, and firms. As the funding amounts are relatively small, and the expectation for returns very low in most cases, the investment risk is small. Especially with regard to equity crowdfunding, crowdfunders are able to invest in new innovative firms directly without facing prohibitive due diligence and legal costs. Due diligence is essentially carried out collectively within the community of crowdfunders, wisdom of the mass essentially, and it is within this community that crowdfunders share advice and other information that will reduce information asymmetry and other agency problems faced by investors (Agrawal et al., 2015). Crowdfunders who are especially interested in investing early in nascent firms find the removal of restrictions for nonsophisticated investors from investing in private equity timely.

7.4 Problems with crowdfunding

With every incentive for crowdfunders, portals and innovator, and firms to participate in the burgeoning crowdfunding market, there are as many disincentives that may potentially lead to market failure (see, e.g., Ruiz, 2015). Innovators might find that the audience of eager crowdfunders within portals might have such differing expectations from the project or firm. Because the projects or firms seeking crowdfunding are in their early stages, many innovator sand firms find it overwhelming to deal with the sudden barrage of information requests and offers of advice from their new community of funders and investors. Escalation of expectation may not be able to be met by the project or firm as it gets overwhelmed. Also, while rewards-based crowdfunding is known to provide proof of concept to innovators, the same barrage of demand might prove to be detrimental to a project. For example, as of 2012, more than 50% of the Kickstarter projects were unable to meet project deadlines (Agrawal et al., 2014). The small amounts involved in crowdfunding serve to incentivize crowdfunders, but at the same time, innovators and firms might find it not worth their while as more media attention is directed to the projects that have failed to deliver and the legal woes and social harassment faced by innovator sand firms as a result disappointed crowdfunders (Lewis-Kraus, 2015). The issue of potentially disclosing too much information leading to innovative ideas being stolen and copied, potentially sabotaging any chance of the innovator or firm obtaining further funding from more sophisticated investors is discussed in Agrawal et al. (2014). This same sense of community among crowdfunders that enables news about projects or firms to be circulated cost effectively, resulting in what Agrawal et al. (2014) refers to herding behavior among crowdfunders, is the same behavior that may terminate a project or firm even before it has taken off. Herding may not necessarily be logical, and it is said that bad news always travels faster than good news.

For crowdfunders, crowdfunding has also proven to be an easy way for them to access new causes, innovative products, and firms. As the funding amounts are relatively small, and their expectation for returns very low in most cases, the investment risk is small. However, there is still a risk of fraud. There have been many documented cases highlighted in the media such as the infamous beef jerky case, but more recently, the United States Federal Trade Commission on June 11, 2015 announced a settlement in its first crowdfunding case. The case involved a project initiated in May 2012 which involved the production of a board game "The Doom That Came to Atlantic City," that raised more than US$120,000 from 1246 crowdfunders on the online portal Kickstarter. The innovator of the board game essentially failed to produce the game within the agreed 6 month period and spent the money on personal expenses, including rent. The case resulted in a $111,794 judgment, however, as the innovator was unable to pay, the judgment was suspended. Due diligence is thought to be easier and cheaper in crowdfunding as it is carried out collectively within the community of crowdfunders. Unfortunately, in this case that we know of, it failed. Rules and regulations regarding fundraising are put in place to mitigate risk of misrepresentation and fraud, and with the loosening of such rules, crowdfunders have to be even more vigilant.

Portals that rely on increasing demand for crowdfunding and supply of crowdfunders are cognizant of this need to help the market participants mitigate their risks. Over time, the portals that aim to improve their services have implemented additional rules to ensure that the innovators and firms at least disclose sufficient information in their marketing material to manage crowdfunder expectations. There is increasing sophistication in portal due diligence of potential projects and firms seeking funding. There is also increased recognition from the community of crowdfunders that due diligence is their responsibility as it is, at the end of the day, their money they are giving away or investing.

7.5 Crowdfunding for internationalization

As discussed earlier, many commentators believe that crowdfunding will serve to mitigate the funding gap for many innovators, charities, and nascent firms. What we would like to discuss in this section, however, is to what extent crowdfunding may be able to go beyond closing this gap and possibly help innovators, charities, and firms in other ways. In view of the fact that one of the main incentives for crowdfunding participants is the global access to funds and projects/firms, we find of interest to what extent crowdfunding could help in the internationalization of projects and firms. Is it possible to use crowdfunding to also help entrepreneurs to sell their products and services internationally, and/or raise financing internationally?

The cross-jurisdictional feature of donations-based crowdfunding is well understood. Many donations- and rewards-based crowdfunding projects are development oriented, and it is said that this development-oriented crowdfunding is the catalyst for the integrated market as we know it now. Granted, the more unusual efforts, such as the project to raise money for rebel fighters in the Ukraine, we mentioned earlier are the ones getting more media attention, but portals specifically focusing on poverty alleviation such as Benevolent. net have benefitted many in this world. Escalating from disaster relief and poverty alleviated, a lesser known form of donation and perhaps rewards-based crowdfunding is for education purposes. Many universities use crowdfunding to fund student scholarships. For example, on January 10, 2015, it was reported that a student at the University of Calgary used crowdfunding to finish her PhD. According to her, crowdfunders supporting her included those from Germany, Slovakia, and the United Kingdom (UK).[3] An example of a portal is Futurefunder.carleton.ca that facilitates the crowdfunding of a variety of different projects. Academics are also using sites such as Indiegogo to not only fund research projects but also to get advice on potentially research and commercial projects. However, while donations, rewards- and equity-based campaigns typically get the media coverage, it is lending-based crowdfunding that dominates the industry. Massolution (2015) finds that lending-based crowdfunding raised $11.08 billion dollars in 2014.

What is interesting about lending-based crowdfunding is that it is said to fill the void left between microfinance and sophisticated investors. By extending the network effects or social mechanics of donation- and rewards-based crowdfunding, lending-based crowdfunding enables crowdfunders to provide larger amounts of capital to innovators and nascent firms. Crowdfunders are able to help fund high-growth start-ups, frequently in the high-technology sector, or to provide expansion capital to existing businesses, but yet still mitigate their investment risks. Lending- and equity-based crowdfunding could arguably lead to more buy-in for the future success of the project or the firm as crowdfunders are more invested in the future success of the project or firm. Foreign crowdfunders may help Canadian firms internationalize. Crowdfunders may help with market intelligence, localization of products and provide local knowledge pertinent to internationalization of products and services. Canadian innovators and firms are responsive to international

---

[3] See Grad student Erin Baerwald seeks crowdfunding to finish bat research thesis (http://www.cbc.ca/news/canada/calgary/grad-student-erin-baerwald-seeks-crowdfunding-to-finish-bat-research-thesis-1.2896528).

investors and provide sufficient information to enable them to participate in Canadian entrepreneurial ventures that may be unfamiliar to them. The concept of using information derived from a crowd, or crowdsourcing, to seek market intelligence of information on travel-related problems, restrictions, and even spread of disease is not new, as portals such as Open.Canada.ca and thefunded.com becomes more popular.

Unfortunately, we do not have any direct empirical evidence on whether crowdfunding matters for facilitating international trade. For indirect evidence, we can refer to a recent working paper where Timmis (2013) shows that Internet adoption improves exports by 32%−36% in developing economies. We are aware of US evidence of impediments faced by both large firms and SMEs. Suominen and Lee (2015) show that smaller firms face higher constraints or impediments related to not only financing, which is listed as the leading constraint, but also language and cultural barriers, difficulty in locating sales targets, difficulty in finding foreign partner firms, and establishing affiliates in foreign markets. These difficulties in obtaining funding and establishing networks could, we believe, be mitigated by crowdfunding.

7.6 Examples of products, companies, and nongovernmental organizations that have used crowdfunding to internationalize

Direct empirical evidence of the internationalization benefits that crowdfunding may bring to innovators and firms in addition to fundraising may be unavailable, but we are able to provide examples of products, firms and NGOs that have used crowdfunding. We refer to examples in specific jurisdictions that have had a longer history of crowdfunding: the UK, the United States, New Zealand, Germany, and finally Canada.

7.6.1 The United Kingdom

SME firms in the UK face similar impediments to US SMEs, yet such impediments are increasingly being overcome as illustrated by the following examples of firms that have been able to access the funds they need to meet production needs, build new distribution networks, and promote their products in unfamiliar markets (Lang, 2014). In 2013 East End Manufacturing, a company producing clothing in London's East End needed to move to new premises and raised £150,000 in equity on platform Crowdcube.com. It raised a further £250,000 to finance its international expansion. As a result, the company now sells its clothing in 240 countries through Asos.com. Another firm producing salad dressing, Righteous, also used the Crowdcube portal to raise an initial £75,000 for marketing efforts. Its efforts were successful enough to enable it to seek a further round of funding of £150,000 to meet production demands for overseas orders. The salad dressing is now sold at major US retailers such as Costco and Whole Foods. Another example of a firm using crowdfunding to raise funds and internationalize its operations is The London Distillery Company. In March 2012 it used Crowdcube.com to raise £250,000 from 44 investors for up to 45% equity in the company. The funds enabled it to enter untapped international markets, increase brand awareness, and ramp up production. It now exports to 17 countries including Germany, Sweden, Singapore, Italy, Australia, and China.

7.6.2 The United States

To meet increasing demand for not only funding but also value-added assistance or services for innovators and firms that are attempting to globalize their markets, operations and production capability, a new crowdfunding portal called TradeUp Capital Fund[4] was launched in 2014. According to the portal, it is a first-in-class debt and equity crowdfunding platform for globalizing companies, bringing together savvy investors with high-growth globalizing companies to fuel international growth and expansion. By crowdfunding through TradeUp, firms are not only able to raise US$100,000 to $20 million in debt-, equity-, or royalties-based financing, but more significantly, the portal provides access to services that also help firms access and aggregate prescreened international trade service providers, such as export consultants, trade lawyers, and shippers. This is crucial for nascent firms seeking to globalize as these are services that are arguably more difficult to access that funds alone. Successful globalization on the part of the firms will allow investors to diversify their portfolios into an exceptionally attractive investment with global growth potential and mitigated downside risk.

7.6.3 New Zealand

Innovators and firms in New Zealand have faced the same funding constraints as others around the world. In a 2012 survey of 169 businesses with less than 50 employees in New Zealand, 32% of the respondents considered access to capital a real constraint. In response to this a change in legislation was made to permit firms in New Zealand to raise up to NZ $2 million in any 12-month period through licensed equity-based crowdfunding platforms. As a result, the equity crowdfunding portal, Snowball Effect was created in August 2014. New Zealand's first successful equity crowdfunding was raised by Renaissance Brewing, which raised $700,000 in less than 2 weeks, with 287 investors investing an average of $2436 each. It is interesting to note that while the average was $2436, it also attracted a single investment of over $50,000 therefore demonstrating that equity crowdfunders may not necessarily be using this platform to only make small investments. Of most interest is the recognition that crowdfunders come with a wide range of experience and expertise that the investee firm can draw upon. Snowball Effect enables crowdfunders to make their skills visible to a potential investee. This may enable innovators and firms to seek more value-added resources in addition to funding. This model essentially allows investee firms to harness the power of the crowd and investors to be more engaged directly with the projects they back.

---

[4] https://www.crunchbase.com/organization/tradeup-capital-fund.

7.6.4 Germany

Germany offers a fun example of crowdfunding and internationalization. There is growing concern around the world about surveillance technology and the loss of privacy.[5] Crowdfunding was therefore used by Boris Kartheuser to raise money to sue the government over export of their surveillance technology.[6] It is easy to see how this campaign was popular in that there is mass appeal and interest in the loss of privacy.

7.6.5 Canada

The best Canadian example of internationalization and crowdfunding from Canada comes from Pebble watch. Unfortunately for Canada, the "internationalization" part meant that the entrepreneur relocated from Waterloo in Ontario to Silicon Valley in California. There was not sufficient financing in Canada, and by relocating to the United States and starting a Kickstarter Campaign (April 11, 2012 to May 18, 2012) the entrepreneur raised $10.3 million.[7] By December 2014, Pebble has sold more than 1 million smart watches. In 2014, in another campaign on Kickstarter, Pebble had 68,929 backers that pledged a total of $10,266,845, one of Kickstarters most successful campaigns ever. The case in one that is often cited by Canadians as a classic example as to the problems with not having sufficient domestic financing.

7.7 Broader view of the ecosystem and whether or not international investors add value

A potential benefit of crowdfunding is that entrepreneurs and investors may come from all over the world. The Indiegogo platform, for example, has crowdfunding projects from more than 91 countries around the world (see Chapter 5: Crowdfunding models: keep-it-all versus all-or-nothing and Chapter 6: Crowdfunding cleantech). While it is preliminary to assess whether or not international investors are useful in the crowdfunding space, there is a small literature on international investment in venture capital and its value to venture capital-backed companies. This growing importance of international investment is evidenced from countries such as Canada where there has been increasing presence of international venture capital investors.[8]

Internationalization of an investor base provides diversity, thereby lowering the cost of capital (Cumming et al., 2016; Dai, Jo, & Kassicieh, 2012). Nevertheless, there are potential costs to international investors, including possible political interference, cultural clashes, legal uncertainty, and agency problems (Johan, Knill, & Mauck, 2013). On the balance,

---

[5] For example, see http://www.scu.edu/ethics/publications/briefings/privacy.html.

[6] http://onlinejournalismblog.com/2015/01/27/guest-post-crowdfunding-a-lawsuit-against-the-german-government-to-unveil-the-export-of-surveillance-technology-to-dictatorships.

[7] https://www.kickstarter.com/projects/597507018/pebble-e-paper-watch-for-iphone-and-android.

[8] For details, see http://www.cvca.ca/research-resources/industry-statistics/.

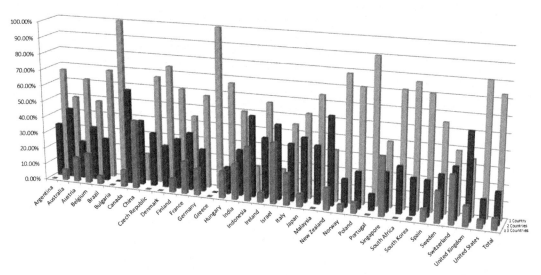

FIGURE 7.1   Success of international VC deals.
This figure shows the percentage of successfully exited venture capital deals via and IPO or acquisition with investors from 1, 2, or 3 or more countries. The countries listed on the horizontal axis reflect the location of the entrepreneur at the time of first venture capital investment. The data span venture capital over the years span investments. *IPO,* Initial public offerings; *VC,* venture capitalist. Source: *Based on Cumming, D., Knill, A., & Syvrud, K. (2016). Do international investors enhance private firm value? Evidence from venture capital.* Journal of International Business Studies, 47(3), 347–373.

however, the available data are consistent with the view that internationalization of the investor based enhances private firms' value. The broadest set of evidence on topic is presented by Cumming et al. (2016) who show that a large proportion of successful investments comprise private investors from multiple countries (see Fig. 7.1).

While this evidence on international investment and success in venture capital is not conclusive or necessarily extendable or applicable to crowdfunding, it nevertheless is quite suggestive that there are potentially large benefits for new ventures that are seeking to internationalize through crowdfunding. Crowdfunding enables firms to directly gain traction in consumer markets around the world, and across wide distance (Chapter 11: Are equity crowdfunders sensitive to distance?). Future research is warranted as more time passes and new large datasets are assembled to better address this topic in empirical work.

7.8 Conclusion

This chapter provided a review of some recent work on crowdfunding and extended this work by discussing the opportunities for crowdfunding to aid in the internationalization of new ventures. We provided a number of examples of how crowdfunding is being used in international initiatives in different countries around the world. There are likely other types of initiates that will be seen in future years, including trade and development initiatives, and the use of crowdfunding by universities and NGOs to expand internationally.

Future research could examine more broadly the ecosystem and policies for stimulating international entrepreneurship and international entrepreneurial finance. Future work could also compare internationalization with crowdfunding and other forms of entrepreneurial assistance, such as business incubators (see, e.g., Cumming & Fischer, 2012; Cumming, Fischer, & Peridis, 2015) and venture capital funds (see Cumming, Knill, & Syvrud, 2016).

Key terms

Cost of capital
Crowdsourcing
Internationalization
Market intelligence
TradeUp

Discussion questions

7.1. What are the economic incentives to internationalize, both in terms of the entrepreneur's investor base, or in terms of the entrepreneur's sales? Explain how crowdfunding might be used to achieve those internationalization goals. How might internationalization with crowdfunding compare to internationalization with some other forms of finance for a start-up, such as venture capital?

7.2. What are some examples of crowdfunding portals that encourage entrepreneurial internationalization? Do you think it is better to use a specialized internationalization crowdfunding portal, or a generalist portal? What are the advantages and disadvantages of each, with reference to internationalization and other possible entrepreneurial goals?

7.3. What types of projects have used crowdfunding to internationalize? What are some of the potential problems or pitfalls associated with entrepreneurial internationalization, and the use of crowdfunding to internationalize?

7.4. How might policymakers make use of crowdfunding to complement existing government programs to encourage entrepreneurial internationalization? Discuss and provide examples from different countries around the world.

7.5. Does crowdfunding potentially mitigate or exacerbate information asymmetries and agency costs associated with internationalization? How might internationalization affect an entrepreneur's cost of capital? Why?

Crowdinvesting

8

Equity crowdfunding, valuation, and cases

8.1 Introduction

Part III of this book comprises this chapter and Chapters 9—14 and covers the topic of equity-based crowdfunding (this chapter and Chapters 9—13) and marketplace lending (Chapter 14: Marketplace lending). This introductory chapter is focused on equity-based crowdfunding. As we cover marketplace lending in one chapter, we focus that discussion in Chapter 14, Marketplace lending. Some of the valuation materials in this chapter are nevertheless useful for marketplace lending, and the concepts in this chapter and Chapters 9—13 are useful to review before reviewing marketplace lending.

Equity-based crowdfunding is carried out through online platforms such as the Australian Small Scale Offerings Board in Australia (the world's first equity crowdfunding platform founded in 2004, and now rebranded as EnableFunding),[1] and EquityNet in the United States (the first crowdfunding platform in the United States, founded in 2005),[2] Crowdcube[3] in the United Kingdom, and OurCrowd in Israel.[4]

Equity crowdfunding allows entrepreneurs to raise small amounts of less than $100,000 and larger amounts of $10 million or more. But the average capital raise for many platforms around the world is around $300,000, as discussed in this chapter and Chapters 9—13.

There are things that entrepreneurs need to do before equity or debt crowdfunding, as indicated on a number of resource pages on the web,[5] including (1) form a company (establish location, form legal structure, register business name, get tax ID number, register for state or local taxes, obtain a business license, research legal needs for hiring),

---

[1] https://www.enablefunding.com/

[2] https://www.equitynet.com/

[3] https://www.crowdcube.com/

[4] https://www.ourcrowd.com/

[5] https://www.equitynet.com/blog/category/startups/

(2) prepare legal documentation (prepare articles of incorporation, file with state and securities agencies, become familiar with securities laws including solicitation), (3) prepare financial documentation (prepare a business plan, prepare pro form financials, prepare a valuation with scenario analysis), (4) create brand and marketing materials (logos, company webpage, promotional video, social media, press releases), (5) set fundraising goals [campaign funding goal, funding type (debt, equity, rewards), select platform, horizon, equity share if equity crowdfunding, voting or not voting shares if equity crowdfunding depending on whether platform offers], and (6) prepare a crowdfunding campaign (create company profile, upload materials including text, some financials, pictures, and video).

This chapter is focused on the financial decisions associated with equity crowdfunding. This chapter covers the following topics. In Section 8.2, we explain the different crowdfunding platforms in different countries around the world and introduce some of the tradeoffs associated with the use of different platforms. Section 8.3 provides information and methods on valuation of projects for equity crowdfunding. Section 8.4 explains the methods associated with selecting the extent of ownership that can be given up in equity crowdfunding and the signaling effects associated with different ownership levels. These signaling effects are discussed and analyzed further to a much more extensive degree in Chapter 10, Signaling in equity crowdfunding. Section 8.5 discusses a number of successful equity crowdfunding cases, while Section 8.6 considers failed equity crowdfunding cases. A summary and roadmap for Chapters 9–14 is provided in Section 8.7.

8.2 Features of different equity crowdfunding platforms

Different equity crowdfunding platforms offer different economic opportunities and governance models. Three common examples include a direct model, a nominee model, and a coinvestment model. The direct model is offered on platforms such as Crowdcube in the United Kingdom, which involves investors making direct investments into the entrepreneurial firms that list on the platform. The nominee model, such as that follows by Seedrs in the United Kingdom follows a nominee structure where crowd investors invest in a special purpose vehicle and are not direct shareholders. The coinvestment model is an investment model that combines a professional investor (an angel investor or a venture capitalist) that invests alongside crowd investors and is used by platforms such as SyndicateRoom in the United Kingdom. Chapter 9, Equity crowdfunding and governance, reviews these alternative governance models with equity crowdfunding in further detail.

Within each platform there are specific rules associated with the offering structure. Most equity crowdfunding platforms follow the all-or-nothing rule (e.g., Wefunder in the United States) but follow the keep-all rule (such as WiSeed in France, but a minimum threshold must be met; see Cumming, Herve, Manthe, & Schwienbacher, 2017c); some allow a choice between the two (such as Indiegogo discussed in Chapter 5: Crowdfunding models: keep-it-all versus all-or-nothing and Chapter 6: Crowdfunding cleantech and which now offer the opportunity to engage in equity crowdfunding after the JOBS Act was implemented in the United States, discussed further below). The WiSeed platform has a unique feature, whereby the 70,000 + members must vote in favor of the entrepreneurial campaign before it is listed on the platform (Table 8.1). While many votes do not materialize in terms of subsequent investment,[6] these votes are collectively good predictors of entrepreneurial success (Cumming et al., 2017c).

Some platforms offer only one class of shares, while other platforms offer an array of share structures. For example, the Crowdcube platform in the United Kingdom enables issues of both voting and nonvoting shares (see Chapter 12: Cash-flow and control rights in equity crowdfunding). The dual class share offerings on Crowdcube are interesting, as there is debate in the academic and policy literature as to whether or not dual class offerings are good or bad for private firms, public firms, and newly public firms in initial public offerings (IPOs). Most IPOs in the United States since the global financial crisis of August 2017−19 have been dual class IPOs (Davis, 2016). Stock exchanges that do not allow dual class IPOs have had a harder time attracting firms to list on their exchange. Alibaba for instance had considered going public in Hong Kong but eventually did not due to the HKEX no dual class shares rule. Alibaba did its $25 billion IPO in New York, which led HKEX to revisit that rule.[7] One rationale for allowing start-ups and new IPOs to have dual class shares is that they insulate the entrepreneurial CEO from external takeover and related threats and allow them to focus on long-term shareholder value maximization. On the flip side, they may exacerbate agency costs such as those highlighted in Chapter 2, Overview of agency and signaling theory in crowdfunding, as controlling CEOs are insulated from shareholder governance. In turn, shareholders may be less willing to invest in dual class structures, as analyzed in Chapter 12, Cash-flow and control rights in equity crowdfunding.

It goes without saying that different equity crowdfunding platforms have to adhere to the national securities rules in the country in which they are based. These rules are outlines in Chapter 15, Introduction to crowdfunding regulation and policy. Likewise, the regulatory barriers also limit the geographic coverage of the investors but not completely (see Chapter 11: Are equity crowdfunders sensitive to distance?).

A list of various equity-based crowdfunding platforms around the world is provided in Table 8.1. The list also highlights some of the distinctive features on each platform. In addition to platforms, there are a number of service providers that go along with platforms, including marketing service providers, ratings agencies, and share transfer agents. A list of service providers in Canada and the United States is maintained on the National Crowdfunding Association of Canada's directory.[8] And Table 8.2 lists some of the main marketing service providers in the United States

---

[6] Cumming et al. (2017c) show that on WiSeed for every €1 at the preliminary nonbinding voting stage, only €0.18 is subsequently invested when the campaign goes ahead. The figure is higher for women (approximately €0.38) than for me (approximately (€0.13), and higher amongst the subsets of members that are more educated, and are middle-class (voters in the poorest and richest areas are less likely to subsequently invest after positively voting).

[7] https://www.ft.com/content/6f0e9914-fa96-11e7-a492-2c9be7f3120a

[8] https://ncfacanada.org/canadian-crowdfunding-directory/

TABLE 8.1 Select equity crowdfunding platforms around the world.

Platform name	Webpage	Twitter followers	Total invested	# Companies funded	Prospective investors (or exclusive members for some platforms)	Founded/ launched	Notable features
Australia							
EnableFunding	https://www.enablefunding.com/		$148,211,341	176	250,000 +	Founded 2004, launched 2007	Formerly ASSOB, or Australian Small Scale Offerings Board, First Equity Crowdfunding Platform in the world
Equitise	https://equitise.com/	1900	AU$25 million	54	8000 +	2014	Investors can join syndicates to coinvest with VC's and investment clubs, in exchange for carry
OnMarket	https://www.onmarket.com.au/	3600	AU$74.5 million	126	47,622	2015	Funds both listed and unlisted companies through all aspects of capital raising, from seed, Series A and Equity Crowdfunding, to IPOs through to follow-on placements
Birchal	https://www.birchal.com/	500	AU$70 million		610,000	2018	Free for investors and if a company is successful in meeting their minimum target, a 6% fee is collected
Belgium							
Spreds	https://www.spreds.com/en	3800	€69,473,141	152	41,457	2017	Entrepreneurs can consider private and/or public fundraising campaigns. The minimum campaign on Spreds is €100,000 for a loan and €150,000 for equity
Canada							
FrontFundr	https://www.frontfundr.com/	3500		42		2015	Being an Exempt Market Dealer, FrontFundr is directly overseen by the securities regulators in Canada
Vested	https://vested.ca/	300	$1.086 million	35	3098		If you decide that you would like to cancel your investment, you will have a 48-h period to do so

Finland						
Invesdor	https://www.invesdor.com/en	6200	€67,200,000	139	2012	Europe's first crowdfunded company (Heeros Oyj) to subsequently go public in Europe
France						
WiSeed	https://www.wiseed.com/fr	10,400	€107,000,000	433	2008	Campaigns only listed if a sufficient number of members vote in favor of it in advance
Germany						
Seedmatch	https://www.seedmatch.de/	5800	€45,167,500	125	2011	The average funding is €360,219 from 323 investors over 75 days
Aescuvest	https://www.aescuvest.de/	900	€6,868,550	125	2014	Aescuvest cooperates with Touwho—China's largest crowdfunding platform for medicine and biotechnology
Companisto	https://www.companisto.com/en	3000	€64,668,417	125	2012	Only around 1% of all companies who apply make it to the platform
Italy						
BacktoWork24	https://www.backtowork24.com/	5700			2012	Investors will be asked a short questionnaire in order to verify the appropriateness of the investment in relation to investor profile, as required by the CONSOB Regulation. Whatever the result of the questionnaire, the investor can still decide to proceed with the investment
MamaCrowd	https://mamacrowd.com/	700	€33,500,000	211	2011	The preselection and the support of the incubators determine a higher probability of success of the projects
Malaysia						
CrowdPlusAsia	https://www.crowdplus.asia/	450		18		Successful entrepreneurs and managers act as QMI to help mentor companies

(Continued)

TABLE 8.1 (Continued)

Platform name	Webpage	Twitter followers	Total invested	# Companies funded	Prospective investors (or exclusive members for some platforms)	Founded/ launched	Notable features
The Netherlands							
Oneplanetcrowd	https://www. oneplanetcrowd.com/en	3700	€11,000,000	120	18,000	2012	All companies on Oneplanetcrowd contribute to one or more sustainable development goal (s)
Symbid	https://www.symbid.com/	5200	€31,775,117	212	54,343	2013	Invest in companies with equities or convertible bonds
New Zealand							
Snowball Effect	https://www.snowballeffect.co.nz/	2000	NZ $53,000,000	60	18,000	2014	Snowball Effect facilitates public offers, private offers, and wholesale investor offers
PledgeMe	https://www.pledgeme.co.nz/	4900	NZ $38,000,000	1350	115,000	2015	70% success rate for investment campaigns
Spain							
The Crowd Angel	https://www.thecrowdangel.com/	4800	€13,202,421	44	15,626	2012	Only around 2% of all companies who apply make it to the platform
Startupxplore	https://startupxplore.com/en	22	€6,400,000	27	17,429	2014	Investors coinvest alongside Startupxplore and a professional investor
Sweden							
FundedByMe	https://www.fundedbyme.com/en/	7000	SEK60,507,723	500	250,000	2011	In June 2018, UNITI became the first official FundedByMe unicorn after being valued at over a billion SEK. The innovative electric vehicle company launched their equity crowdfunding campaign on FundedByMe in 2016 and raised €1.2 million
United Arab Emirates							
Eureeca	https://eureeca.com/	3900			24,848	2013	Eureeca is licensed to operate in three different continents—Europe, Middle East, and South East Asia

Country / Platform	URL					Year	Description
Israel							
OurCrowd	https://www.ourcrowd.com/	8600	$1.1 billion	180	33,000	2013	With OurCrowd, investors can diversify their investment portfolio with multiple funds by their preferred sector, stage, geography, or investment thesis
Fundit	https://www.fundit.co.il/	100	NIS37,000,000	900		2011	Fundit charges 4% of the total funding for raising debt and 7% of the total funding for raising equity funding
United Kingdom							
Crowdcube	https://www.crowdcube.com/	43,700	£690 million	883	764,801	2014	Direct model
Seedrs	https://www.seedrs.com/	31,800	£645 million	850			Nominee model
SyndicateRoom	https://www.syndicateroom.com	4700	NZ$53 million	60	18,000	2014	Coinvestment model
Crowd for Angels	https://crowdforangels.com/	4900				2014	Companies can raise finance through the issue of shares (equity), crowd bonds (debt) and tokens (cryptocurrency)
Envestors	https://www.envestors.co.uk	50	£100 million	700	8000	2004	This platform connects investment networks from across the United Kingdom, India, EMEA, and China and enables the Syndication model
United States							
EquityNet	https://www.equitynet.com/	6908	$500 million +	15,000 +	50,000 + Accredited investors, plus retail investors	Founded 2005, launched 2007	Mixes retail and accredited investments since 2015
Fundable	https://www.fundable.com/	25,800	$563 million				Companies raising funds may be headquartered elsewhere as long as they are registered in the United States
Indiegogo	https://equity.indiegogo.com/	341,000	$1.5 billion +	800,000 +	9 million	Founded 2008 Equity funding 2016–18	No longer issuing Reg CF shares

(Continued)

TABLE 8.1 (Continued)

Platform name	Webpage	Twitter followers	Total invested	# Companies funded	Prospective investors (or exclusive members for some platforms)	Founded/ launched	Notable features
StartEngine	https://www.startengine.com/	25,700	$90 million +	265 +	200,000 + Prospective Investors		An equity crowdfunding platform and broker-dealer, with a planned expansion to become an Alternative Trading System offering a secondary market where investors can trade their securities
Wefunder	https://wefunder.com/	6626	$98.5 million	295	261,578	2013	Direct investment in Reg CF, Reg D, and Reg A + shares
SeedInvest	https://www.seedinvest.com/	19,200	$150 million +	150 +	250,000	2012	The SeedInvest Selections Fund invests $200,000 alongside each company that successfully raises capital on SeedInvest[1] under Reg D
Republic	https://republic.co/	8400		78		2016	Republic was founded by alumni of AngelList, the world's largest online investment platform for accredited investors
Localstake	https://localstake.com/	1700					Revenue share loan funding model
MicroVentures	https://microventures.com/	1233	$200 million	189	10,000	2009	Coinvestment model. Full-service online platform for VC investments that is open to the public. Advertises that they take the best parts of VC (connections, research, deal flow, mentoring) and combine it with the best aspects of Equity Crowdfunding (open access, ease of use, diversification) to give investors the best of both worlds

Note: Funding statistics are from inception to July 2019 based on various searches on the web (e.g., https://startupfundingsecrets.io/equity-crowdfunding-sites/), either from the platform itself or other media reports of the platform. The list of platforms here is not intended to be exhaustive. For EquityNet, the funding statistics from Johan and Zhang (2019) for the years 2007–16 for 6584 firms. Items left blank where insufficient information was available as at July 2019. For the direct model, nominee model, and coinvestment model, see Table 9.2 and accompanying text. *IPOs*, Initial public offerings; *QMI*, qualified matching investor; *VCs*, venture capitalists.

TABLE 8.2 Crowdfunding marketing service agencies.

Name	Webpage	Services	Price
INVENTUREX	https://inventurex.com	Full-service crowdfund marketing agency for Kickstarter & Indiegogo	$5000–$15,000 + 10% of sales. Official partner with Shark Tank's Kevin Harrington. InventureX partners with select entrepreneurs and inventors to crowdfund new products and ideas [Read More]
METRIC THEORY ADS	http://metrictheory.com	Facebook ads agency	Fee on ad budget spend (minimum $20,000)
FINN PARTNERS	https://finpartners.com	Public relations firm	Marketing fees range from $15,000 to $25,000 in total
HAWKE MEDIA	https://hawkemedia.com/	Digital marketing agency	$8000 monthly retainer + $10,000 minimum ad budget
CROWDFUND MAFIA	https://crowdfundmafia.com/	Crowdfund marketing and design agency	$16,000–$32,000 upfront fee
EVENTY PARTNERS	https://enventyspartners.com/	Crowdfund marketing and advertising	$15,000 fee + $10,500 ad budget minimum
RON STONE CREATIVE	https://ronstonecreative.com/	Crowdfund marketing agency	$5000 euro upfront fee + 40% of your total funding raised
JC MEDIA	http://juliecarrmedia.com/	Branding and digital marketing agency	$7500 retainer for ads only
AGENCY 20	https://www.agency20.com/	Crowdfund advertising firm	$15,500 upfront fee + 40% of your total funding raised
THE BERMAN GROUP	http://www.bermangrp.com/	PR & marketing agency	$8900 monthly retainer for PR only

Reproduced from https://crowdfundusa.org/launch-your-idea-with-these-top-crowdfunding-services-now/.

8.3 How to value a start-up for equity crowdfunding?

To overgeneralize, a typical equity crowdfunding campaign raises $300,000. Even across countries, the average amount of capital raised in regions such as Australia (see Chapter 10: Signaling in equity crowdfunding, with data from ASSOB), France (Cumming, Herve, Manthe, & Schwienbacher, 2018, with data from WiSeed), the United Kingdom (see Chapter 12: Cash-flow and control rights in equity crowdfunding, with data from Crowdcube), and the United States (Johan & Zhang, 2019, with data from EquityNet) is consistently around $300,000. The range of capital that can be raised is quite large. For example, EquityNet advertises capital raises between $10 thousand and $10 million are common. Some crowdfunding webpages in the United States report statistics along the lines that it takes 9 weeks to be fully funded with equity crowdfunding, and 5 weeks with marketplace lending.[9] Some specific detailed data, however, show different statistics in other countries such as Australia (where a successful equity crowdfunding takes 7–374 days, and on average 135 days; see Chapter 10: Signaling in equity crowdfunding).

Key questions for entrepreneurs in deciding whether equity crowdfunding is appropriate are (1) what is my business or business idea worth, and (2) what share of my business would I have to sell in an equity crowdfunded offering. This subsection addresses the first of these two questions, and Section 8.4 addresses the second. The analysis of valuation in this section begins with comparables valuation in Section 8.3.1 and then continues with net present value (NPV) valuation in Section 8.3.2. Section 8.3.3 presents real options valuation as an alternative method that accounts for future uncertainty. Thereafter in Section 8.3.4, we discuss other methods and refer to online tools at crowdfunding webpages where investors and entrepreneurs have ready access to valuations that could become increasingly standardized.

8.3.1 Comparables valuation

In valuing a private business, the most common starting point is to carry out a comparables valuation. Comparables valuations make use of information from publicly traded companies because publicly traded companies have market determined prices of their shares and hence readily available valuations of their companies. The comparables method is atheoretical, as it is merely based on accounting ratios. There is no underlying basis to select one accounting method over another. So, normally a number of different accounting measures are used to form derive a range of possible valuation numbers as a starting point for further analyses, such as an net-present value valuation as discussed immediately hereafter. The comparables valuation method indicates a range of possible valuations that could apply to the private business based on what others are paying for similar businesses.

An example of a comparables valuation is presented in Table 8.3. Very simplified information is presented from a balance sheet, an income statement, and some market data. The key missing item for the crowdfunded company is the price/earnings ratio, as there is no ready market price for the crowdfunded company prior to crowdfunding. We can infer what that price could possibly be from the five ratios presented at the bottom of Table 8.3. The example here only involves two comparable companies for illustrative purposes only. In practice, using more comparable companies is better as long as the companies are in fact comparable. With only two companies, it is possible that inferences drawn from the analysis are highly skewed if one or both are statistical outliers due to issues such as extraordinary growth, or impending doom from a lawsuit or regulatory breach, or some other fact not rendering the companies as following the normal course of business.

The first ratio in Table 8.3 is the price–earnings (P/E) ratio. The P/E ratio from comparable companies 1 and 2 are 18 and 14, respectively, and the average is therefore 16. Net income (E) of the crowdfunded start-up is 0.333 million. Hence, the implied valuation of the crowdfunded startup is $P/E \times E$, or $16 \times 0.333 = \$5.33$.

---

[9] See, for example, https://www.equitynet.com/blog/funding-finish-line/.

TABLE 8.3 Comparables valuation.

	Crowdfunded start-up	Comparable company 1	Comparable company 2
Balance sheet			
Assets	4	40	20
Long-term debt	0.167	15	2
Net worth	2.333	19	11
Income statement			
Revenues	4.4	41	22
EBITDA	1	8	5
Net income	0.333	3	2.5
Market data			
Price−earnings ratio (times)	NA	18	14
Shares outstanding (m)	0.167	2	2.5
Number of members	5000	40,000	30,000

	Comparable company 1	Comparable company 2	Average	Private crowdfunded start-up implied value ($m)
Price−earnings ratio	18.00	14.00	16.00	5.33
Market value/EBITDA	6.75	7.00	6.88	6.88
Market value/sales	1.32	1.59	1.45	6.40
Market value/book value of equity	2.84	3.18	3.01	7.03
Market value/members ('000)	1.35	1.17	1.26	6.29

EBITDA, Earnings before interest, tax, depreciation, and amortization.
This valuation example is adapted from an example in Lerner, J., Hardymon, F., & Leamon, A. (2012). Venture capital and private equity: A casebook *(5th ed.). Wiley.*

The second, third, fourth, and fifth ratios use the market value of the comparable companies in the numerator. The market value of Comparable Company 1 is $P/E \times E$, or $18 \times 3 = 54$. The market value of Comparable Company 2 is $P/E \times E$, or $14 \times 2.5 = 35$. The average market value/EBITDA (earnings before interest, tax, depreciation, and amortization)[10] of both comparable companies is $(54/8 + 35/5)/2 = 6.88$, and then the implied value of the crowdfunded start-up is 6.88 times its EBITDA of 1.0, which is 6.88. Similarly,

[10] EBITDA refers to earnings before interest, tax, depreciation, and amortization. EBITTDA is common used in financial analysis because it reflects earnings from regular operations of the business and not from accounting concepts such as depreciation and financial and tax concepts which are possible extraordinary and nonrecurring items.

the average market value/sales of both comparable companies is $(54/41 + 35/22)/2 = 1.45$, and then the implied value of the crowdfunded start-up is 1.45 times its sales (revenues) of 4.4, which is 6.40. The average market value/book value of both comparable companies is $(54/19 + 35/11)/2 = 3.01$, and then the implied value of the crowdfunded start-up is 3.01 times its book value of 2.33, which is 7.03. Finally, the average market value/members[11] of both comparable companies is $(54/40 + 35/30)/2 = 1.26$, and then the implied value of the crowdfunded start-up is 1.26 times its members of 5 thousand, which is 6.29.

From this example in Table 8.3, the range of possible valuations is $5.33–$7.03. Since the start-up is relatively more illiquid (harder to sell and convert the investment into cash), a lack of marketability discount of up to 25%–30% could apply depending on the context. But there could be other factors that may be associated with different expected rates of growth to apply in this context which could lead to higher valuations. In the end, comparables is merely a starting point to ascertain a range of possible values to provide context and guidance when considering results from other valuations methods.

8.3.2 Net present value valuation

Perhaps the most common approach in business valuation is the NPV method. NPV discounts future cash flows generated by the firm, assuming the firm will continue forever. Normally, future cash flows are forecasted for 5 years (or possibly only 3 years), and then from years 5 to infinity, a set of assumptions is used to infer the remaining discounted value from a Taylor Series known as the "terminal value" (TV). An example of an NPV valuation is provided in Table 8.4 and the steps are explained here.

To begin, an NPV valuation requires cash flow projections. Cash flows are typically forecasted in one of two ways. A top-down forecast asserts the overall market value of the industry, and the entrepreneur claiming that s/he can secure (often) 1% of it. That type of forecasting is not often respected.[12] A bottom-up forecast starts with explaining how just one sale is generated. From that sale, and the sales force expansion rate and geographic coverage, a set of revenues and costs can be constructed. For example, if sales are generated by doing "lunch-and-learn" presentations among two sales staff, then the number of presentations per year could be ascertained for a geographic region, with expected call back rates (that may differ by the quality of the presenter or other factors) and expected call back conversion and expected value of the conversions. Bottom-up forecasts are typically much more believable and detailed than top-down forecasts.

Cash flows can be inferred from pro forma financial statements. The income statement has some noncash flow numbers, and the balance sheet has some cash flow numbers, so the creation of a cash flow statement is not completely straightforward. From the income statement, depreciation amounts and any other noncash item must be accounted for (i.e.,

---

[11] Market value/members are a useful ratio only where firms have a stable number of members or clients.

[12] For example, in 10–15 minutes presentations of business plans to angel investor groups, the investors might play "bingo" whereby they write down a letter every time they hear the entrepreneur say something that they do not believe. And if they say five false or misleading things in the 10- to 15-minute presentation then one of the investors will should out "bingo!"

TABLE 8.4 Net present value valuation.

WACC calculation						
Tax rate	40%					
$R_m - R_f$	6.00%					
E/V	100%					
Bu	1.5					
10-year treasury bond	4.00%					
WACC	13.00%					

Cash flows						
Terminal growth rate	3.00%					
Year	0	1	2	3	4	5
Revenues		3	3.5	3.9	4.4	4.8
Less: costs		4	3.5	3	3	3
EBIT		−1	0	0.9	1.4	1.8
Less: tax		0	0	0	0.52	0.72
EBIAT		−1	0	0.9	0.88	1.08
Less: change NWC		0.3	0.05	0.04	0.05	0.04
Free cash flow		−1.3	−0.05	0.86	0.83	1.04
Discount factor		0.8850	0.7831	0.6931	0.6133	0.5428
PV (cash flow)		−1.1504	−0.0392	0.5960	0.5091	0.5645
PV (cash flows)	0.4799					
Terminal value						10.7120
PV (terminal value)						5.8140

Net present value and sensitivity analysis				**WACC**		
				12%	**13%**	**14%**
PV (cash flows)	0.4799	Terminal	2%	$6.55	$5.71	$5.02
PV (terminal value)	5.8140	Growth	3%	$7.28	$6.29	$5.49
Net present value	6.2940	Rate	4%	$8.20	$7.00	$6.05

(Continued)

TABLE 8.4 (Continued)

Tax calculation					
EBIT	-1	0	0.9	1.4	1.8
NOLs used	0	0	0.9	0.1	0
NOLs added	1	0	0	0	0
Tax	0	0	0	0.52	0.72
Beginning NOLs	0	1	1	0.1	0
Ending NOLs	1	1	0.1	0	0
Net working capital (10% sales)					
Beginning NWC		0.3	0.35	0.39	0.44
Ending NWC	0.3	0.35	0.39	0.44	0.48
Change in NWC	0.3	0.05	0.04	0.05	0.04

NWC, Net working capital; WACC, weighted average cost of capital. $ Amounts are in millions.
This valuation example is adapted from an example in Lerner, J., Hardymon, F, & Leamon, A. (2012). Venture capital and private equity: A casebook *(5th ed.). Wiley.*

added back in the case of depreciation). From the balance sheet, working capital and larger asset purchases must be deducted, and asset sales need to be added to cash flows. Table 8.4 shows an example of how to treat inventory requirements at 10% of sales. For example, in year 1 sales are 30, so inventor needed is $3 \times 0.1 = 0.3$ and subtract beginning inventories (0 in starting year) which is 0.3. In year 2, sales are 3.5, so inventory required is $0.35 - 0.3 = 0.05$, and so on as shown at the bottom of Table 8.4.

Losses are carried forward in NPV valuations, since most countries around the world have a loss carry forward rule, whereby past losses are offset by future gains and shield the entrepreneurial firm from taxation. The loss carry forward calculations are shown in Table 8.4. The firm has a loss of 1.0 in year 1, which is offset against the next year's income (0), and the years 3 and 4 income. The first year where there are no loss carry forwards is year 5 where the full 40% tax rate is applied in this case.

The discounted cash flows in Table 8.4 are calculated as follows:

$$\text{NPV} = \frac{CF_0}{(1+r)^0} + \frac{CF_1}{(1+r)^1} + \frac{CF_2}{(1+r)^2} + \frac{CF_3}{(1+r)^3} + \frac{CF_4}{(1+r)^4} + \frac{CF_5}{(1+r)^5} + \frac{((CF_5 \times (1+r))/(r-g))}{(1+r)^5}$$

The first term is the current period cash flows at date 0 (today, or CF_0), which are technically not discounted since anything to the power of 0 is just 1. In the example in Table 8.4, there are no current period cash flows. The "discounting" in each of the denominator terms adjusts for the preference to have cash now, such that cash in the future is valued less than it is today, and each year the drop in value is compounded.

The terms for years 1–5 are the discounting of the forecasted cash flows for those years 1–5 (CF_1–CF_5). The cash flows are forecasted in the ways explained above. The discount rate r is calculated at the weighted average cost of capital, or WACC. WACC is calculated as the cost of equity (r_e) multiplied by the proportion of equity (E) used by the firm relative to its total debt and equity (D + E), plus the after-tax (1 − t) cost on debt (because

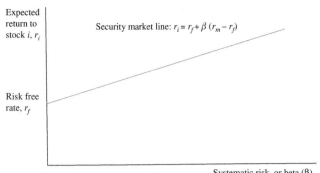

Expected return to stock i, r_i

Security market line: $r_i = r_f + \beta\,(r_m - r_f)$

Risk free rate, r_f

Systematic risk, or beta (β)

FIGURE 8.1 Capital asset pricing model.

interest on debt is tax deductible and dividends on equity is not tax deductible) times the cost of debt (or the interest rate on debt held by the firm, r_d) times the proportion of debt held by the firm, as indicated by the following formula:

$$\text{WACC} = \frac{E}{E+D} r_e + \frac{D}{E+D} r_d (1 - t)$$

The cost of debt is known from the borrowing contracts held by the firm. The cost of equity has to be estimated from comparables. For all valuation methods used for private firms, comparables are brought in at some stage by necessity. There is no way to complete the NPV valuation of a private firm without using comparables due to the need to compute the cost of equity and the inability of ascertain the cost of equity from the private firm itself. The most common way to estimate the cost of equity is to use the capital asset pricing model (CAPM), which is derived from a set of assumptions[13] that give rise to the following implication: the cost of equity is equal to the risk-free rate plus the "beta" on a stock multiplied by the market risk premium (the difference in the return to the S&P index net of the risk-free return). The risk-free rate used in practice is the rate on 10-year government bonds. The beta is the systematic risk, which can be derived from a regression of daily returns to a stock on a constant and market returns (such as that from the S&P 500 Index).[14] The formula for the CAPM is given by the following formula, which represents the equation for the security market line as shown in Fig. 8.1:

$$r_i = r_f + \beta(r_m - r_f)$$

[13] These assumptions include economic agents that diversified, risk averse, and rational investors that seek to maximize their utility, that cannot influence prices, that can borrow or lend at the risk-free rate, do not face transaction costs, can trade any divisible quantity of an asset, have homogenous expectations, and complete information.

[14] The formal equation from such a regression is $\beta_i = \text{cov}(r_m, r_i)/\text{var}(r_m) = \rho_{i,m}\sigma_i/\sigma_m$, where $\text{cov}(r_m, r_i)$ refers to the covariance between the return to the market and the return to stock i, $\text{var}(r_m)$ refers to the variance the market return, $\rho_{i,m}$ is the correlation coefficient between the return to stock i and the return to the market, σ_i is the standard deviation of stock I's returns, and σ_m is the standard deviation of the market returns. On popular webpages such as Google Finance https://www.google.com/finance, 3-year betas for stocks are readily available on each stock's specific page.

Since betas for private firms are not available, it is necessary to obtain betas from publicly traded firms. As many comparable betas as possible is appropriate. For example, picking betas of firms that are in the same industry as comparables is a good starting point. Adjustments to beta could be made for differences in leverage. For example, if the comparable firms had debt while the private crowdfunded firm to be valued had no debt, one could adjust (lower) beta by multiplying the average comparable betas by the comparable firms' ratio of equity to debt + equity to infer an approximate value of an unlevered beta (assuming a linear relation between the use of debt and a firm's systematic risk).[15] Similar adjustments in a variety of different ways depend on the assumptions underlying the valuation model.[16]

In the valuation example in Table 8.4 the tax rate is 40%, the market risk premium $(r_m - r_f)$ is 6%, the firm has no debt, the unlevered beta is 1.5, and 10-year government bonds yield 4%. Hence, the WACC is simply the cost of equity, which is $4\% + 1.5 \times 6\%$, or 13%.

For years 6 to infinity, it is implausible to accurately forecast cash flows and unnecessary to repeatedly discount each year's cash flows. Instead, if we assume that cash flows grow at a constant rate (g) after year 5 and discount rates are the same each year (13% in this example) then we can estimate the remaining discounted value of the firm, or the TV after year T (5 in this case) through the use of a Taylor Series[17] as follows:

$$TV = \frac{CF_T(1 + g)}{(r - g)}$$

In the example in Table 8.4, TV is estimated at 10.712, and discounting it back to today [dividing by $(1 + 0.13)^5$] gives 5.814.

The NPV of the firm in Table 8.4 is the sum of the discounted cash flows in years 1−5 (0.4799) plus the discounted TV (5.8140) which equals 6.2940 million. Table 8.4 likewise calculates the NPV 8 more times for growth rates of 2% and 4% and WACC estimates of 12% and 14%. The sensitivity of the results to different assumptions is important and useful to ascertain. Here, we see that small changes in the assumptions can lead to large changes in the resulting valuations, which in Table 8.4 ranges from $5.02 million to $8.20 million.

A variant of the NPV model is the "adjusted net present value model" or "APV." The APV approach is useful for firms with large changes in capital structure over time and for firms with significant loss carry forwards. The APV approach discounts loss carry forwards at the cost of debt, and the tax shields on debt (the value of the firm attributable to the fact that interest on debt is tax deductible[18]) at the cost of debt and not WACC

---

[15] As an alternative, you could adjust the levered beta as follows to calculate an unlevered beta
$\beta_u = \beta_L / \left(1 + (1 - t)\left(\frac{D}{E}\right)\right)$. See http://pages.stern.nyu.edu/~adamodar/New_Home_Page/valquestions/apv.htm.

[16] See generally the webpage of Aswath Damodaran http://pages.stern.nyu.edu/~adamodar/ which has a number of useful valuation resources, discussions of different modeling techniques, and current data that can be used for valuing private companies.

[17] https://www.encyclopediaofmath.org/index.php/Taylor_series

[18] See Fig. 2.8 and accompanying text in this book.

[because obtaining that tax benefit is certain and hence the cost of (risky) equity is theoretically too high]. A complete treatment of the APV model is found in a variety of sources (e.g., Lerner, Hardymon, & Leamon, 2012), including many online.[19] Large changes in capital structure over time are perhaps more common for private equity turnaround investments (those that were once profitable and are no longer so, hence now being recapitalized and turned around). It is perhaps less applicable to the typical equity crowdfunding context, and hence, we do not discuss it in full here.

8.3.3 Real options valuation

Real options offer a theoretically more appealing valuation method than NPV or comparables insofar as it accounts for the fact that the firm has different probabilities of doing well or poorly (and possibly ending in bankruptcy). Here, we explain how real options can be used in valuation in the classic case when all of the investment in the firm does not have to be made up front, and instead part of the investment can be delayed until a period after which some uncertainty is revealed.

Let's revisit the NPV example from Table 8.4 and change the cash flows slightly. Suppose we have no cash flows in years 1 and 2, and the cash flows are the same in years 3, 4, and 5. Let's keep the same discount rate (13%) and same terminal growth rate (3%). Then the present value of the positive cash flows generated by the project are $7.96 million $= 0.86/(1.13^3) + 0.83/(1.13^4) + 1.04/(1.13^5) + (1.04 \times 1.03)/(0.13 - 0.03)/(1.13^5)$. If this project required an $8 million investment today, we would not go ahead with the investment since the NPV is $ - 0.52$ million.

Instead now suppose we can break the investment outlay into two cash flows. The first is a $1 million investment required today, and the second is a $7 million investment in year 2, which the entrepreneur may or may not take on depending the resolution of some uncertainty between years 0 and 2 (such as that with market conditions, technological changes, and actions of potential competitors). If this uncertainty with cash flows is distributed normally (i.e., a normal distribution), we can value the firm with the standard Black–Scholes valuation model.[20] The model considers the $7 million as the cost of exercising the option (X), which may or may not be exercised in year 2 (hence, the time to expiration relative to today, $T - t$, is equal to 2). The valuation is based on the present value of the cash flows generated by the project (S_t), and the risk-free rate (r, or 0.04 following the above NPV example in Table 8.4), and the riskiness of the underlying assets (σ). The riskiness of the underlying assets needs to be proxied from comparables (analogous to the use of comparables to estimate beta in the NPV example above). For the purpose of our example below, we assume comparables gives us a σ of 0.6.[21]

---

[19] See for example http://pages.stern.nyu.edu/ ~ adamodar/New_Home_Page/valquestions/apv.htm.

[20] For a practical discussion and application, see also http://people.stern.nyu.edu/adamodar/pdfiles/country/option.pdf.

[21] A good source of searching for comparables is in the data section at http://pages.stern.nyu.edu/ ~ adamodar/.

The value of the call option (C) is given by the Black–Scholes formula:

$$C = S_t N(d_1) - X e^{-r(T-t)} N(d_2)$$

where

$$d_1 = \frac{\ln(S_0/X) + (r + 0.5\sigma^2)(T - t)}{\sigma\sqrt{T - t}}$$

and

$$d_2 = d_1 - \sigma\sqrt{T - t}$$

We begin the calculations with d_1, which is $[\ln(7.48359/7) + (0.04 + (0.5(0.6)^2 2))]/[0.6 \times (2)^{0.5}] = 0.60$. Then, d_2 is $0.60 - (0.6 \times 2^{0.5}) = -0.25$. To convert these standard normal values d_1 and d_2 values to their $N(.)$ based on the normal distribution, an easy approach is to use Excel's NORMSDIST(.) function, which is the standard normal cumulative distribution function.[22] In this example the standard normal value for values d_1 and d_2 are 0.73 and 0.40, respectively.

The value of C in our example is therefore $(7.4836 \times 0.7257) - 7 \times e^{-0.04(2)} \times 0.4013 = 2.73$ million.[23] Adjusting for the initial cost of purchasing the option in year 0 for $1 million, the net value is 1.73 million.

Note that in any real options valuation exercise, the value goes up when volatility is higher. Just as we considered sensitivity to the cost of equity and growth inputs with the NPV example above, a prudent valuer would likewise consider sensitivity to different assumed underlying volatilities of the underlying assets.

Of course, it may be unrealistic to assume that future uncertainty can be characterized by a normal distribution. Alternative approaches are of course possible with different underlying assumptions in the case of options valuation or any of the valuation methods. The main issue is to have a meeting of the minds so to speak, whereby all of the parties agree to the resulting valuation number. To that end, in Section 8.3.4, we discuss the fact that some equity crowdfunding pages offer online tools to quickly and easily come up with a valuation based on a quick set of inputs.

8.3.4 Online valuation resources

There are an increasing number of webpages that allow the user to plug in financial values and other firms-specific information to quickly arrive at a valuation estimate. One such resource on an equity crowdfunding webpage is seen at EquityNet.

To begin, let's consider EquityNet's survival probability calculator in Table 8.5. It enables its user to calculate the probability a start-up firm will be out of business depending on capital needs, time to requiring additional capital, growth, and the manager's and team's preparation (evaluation of cash flows, degree of business planning, and experience). EquityNet does not provide its precise formula (presumably it is proprietary), but

---

[22] An alternative is to use a standard normal table, such as that which is online here https://byjus.com/maths/z-score-table/. The calculations in the text here use this normal values from the table.

[23] The value of e is approximately 2.71828.

TABLE 8.5 EquityNet start-up 5-year survival probabilities.

Scenario	About how much debt and equity capital has been provided to your business? (in $)	How long do you think it would take to obtain additional funding for your business?	How often do you evaluate your cash flow status or plan? (in months)	What is your degree of business planning? Rate 1–7: 1 = no plan, 7 = very detailed plan?	What's the approximate annual growth rate of your market?[a]	How many years of management experience do you or your team have? (in years)	How many years of industry experience do you or your team have? (in years)	5 year likelihood of survival (%)
1	1,000,000	1 year	6	7	30	5	5	41
2	1,000,000	6 months	6	7	30	5	5	44
3	1,000,000	1 month	6	7	30	5	5	47
4	1,000,000	1 year	3	7	30	5	5	42
5	1,000,000	1 year	1	7	30	5	5	43
6	300,000	1 Year	6	7	30	5	5	40
7	300,000	6 months	6	7	30	5	5	43
8	300,000	1 month	6	7	30	5	5	46
9	300,000	1 year	3	7	30	5	5	41
10	300,000	1 year	1	7	30	5	5	41
11	300,000	1 year	6	4	30	5	5	37
12	300,000	1 year	6	1	30	5	5	34
13	300,000	1 year	6	7	10	5	5	33
14	300,000	1 year	6	7	0	5	5	33
15	300,000	1 year	6	7	30	3	5	40
16	300,000	1 year	6	7	30	1	5	39
17	300,000	1 year	6	7	30	5	3	39
18	300,000	1 year	6	7	30	5	1	38

[a]In this question there are five possible answers: 0% no growth, 5% low growth, 10% moderate growth, 20% high growth, 30% extreme growth.

Source: The table was produced using the survival probability calculator at https://www.equitynet.com/crowdfunding-tools/startup-risk-calculator.aspx in July 2019.

one can infer the importance of different inputs by running a variety of scenarios like the ones presented in Table 8.5. And it is important, not necessarily because it is precise, but if other entrepreneurs and crowd investors rely on it, it then facilitates a meeting of the minds to enable parties to come to terms and do a deal.

Table 8.5 focuses on the 5-year survival probabilities, since the 5-year horizon is used as an input in EquityNet's valuation calculator (described later). We see from Table 8.5 that at $1 million of capital and 1 year to additional capital, a 6-month evaluation of cash flows and ranking of 7 on business valuation, 30% growth, 5-year management and industry experience, the 5-year survival probability of a new start-up is 41%[24] (the 1 year survival probability is 83%, 2-year is 70%, 3-year is 59%, and 4-year survival probability is 49%).[25] Changing capital from $1 million to $300,000 does not significantly affect the 5-year survival probability, but lowering growth rates and lowering industry experience does have a more pronounced effect (see Table 8.5). Across all 18 scenarios, the average 5-year survival probability is 40.06% in Table 18.5.

Table 8.6 presents similar calculations from EquityNet's valuation calculator. Again, the formula is not provided by EquityNet, but one can infer the relative importance of the different inputs by running a number of different scenarios. The calculator requires inserting the probability of the business surviving in 5 years (see Table 8.5), the industry sector, cash and other assets on hand, liabilities, revenues today and in 5 years, profits today and in 5 years. Table 8.6 shows the valuations are very sensitive to assets, profits, and survival probabilities and less sensitive to liabilities and revenues. There are some differences depending on industry sector. Again, the issue here is not necessarily the precision of the formula or worksheet, but its ability to enable crowd investors and entrepreneurs to come to terms.

8.4 What percentage of equity gets sold in equity crowdfunding?

Given the premoney valuation of a start-up (i.e., the valuation prior to the new capital that may come from the investors currently evaluating the company), now we need to ask what percentage of the company should be sold. One way to do so is as follows.[26] Continuing from a representative firm used in the comparables and NPV valuations described above, suppose the firm is expected to earn $4.8 million 5 years from now and

---

[24] For scenario 1, EquityNet reports "Your relatively long lead time to gain access to additional capital (1 year +) makes it more likely that you'll exhaust your capital resources prior to reaching profitability or a liquidity event. A lackadaisical approach to managing cash flow has hurt your chances for survival. Your answer to this question (every 6 months) suggests that you do not keep updated and accurate records on a regular basis and that you lack discipline regarding managing expenses and cash resources."

[25] For scenario 2, the survival probabilities are 85%, 73%, 62%, and 52%, respectively, for years 1−4. For scenario 3, the survival probabilities are 87%, 73%, 65%, and 55%, respectively, for years 1−4. For scenario 4, the survival probabilities are 84%, 70%, 59%, and 50%, respectively, for years 1−4. For scenario 5, the survival probabilities are 84%, 71%, 60%, and 50%, respectively, for years 1−4.

[26] This approach is often used by venture capitalists; see Lerner et al. (2012).

TABLE 8.6 EquityNet start-up valuations.

Scenario	What are the odds of your business surviving in 5 years? (in %)	What is the industry sector of your business?	How much cash and other assets does your business have, including property and equipment? (in $)	How much liabilities does your business have, including bill payables, loans, and debt? (in $)	How much revenue do you expect your business produce this year? (in $)	How much revenue do you expect your business will produce 5 years from now? (in $)	How much operating profit (loss) do you expect your business will generate this year? (in $)	How much operating profit do you expect your business will generate 5 years from now? (in $)	Valuation ($)
1	50.00	Consumer products	3,000,000	100,000	500,000	15,000,000	300,000	3,000,000	6,200,000
2	47.00	Consumer products	3,000,000	100,000	500,000	15,000,000	300,000	3,000,000	6,000,000
3	33.00	Consumer products	3,000,000	100,000	500,000	15,000,000	300,000	3,000,000	5,100,000
4	40.00	Biotech, Pharma, and Healthcare	3,000,000	100,000	500,000	15,000,000	300,000	3,000,000	4,800,000
5	40.00	Computers	3,000,000	100,000	500,000	15,000,000	300,000	3,000,000	5,400,000
6	40.00	Consumer products	3,000,000	100,000	500,000	15,000,000	300,000	3,000,000	5,500,000
7	40.00	Consumer products	1,000,000	100,000	500,000	15,000,000	300,000	3,000,000	4,200,000
8	40.00	Consumer products	6,000,000	100,000	500,000	15,000,000	300,000	3,000,000	9,200,000
9	40.00	Consumer products	3,000,000	200,000	500,000	15,000,000	300,000	3,000,000	6,100,000
10	40.00	Consumer products	3,000,000	10,000	500,000	15,000,000	300,000	3,000,000	6,300,000
11	40.00	Consumer products	3,000,000	100,000	1,000,000	15,000,000	300,000	3,000,000	6,300,000
12	40.00	Consumer products	3,000,000	100,000	250,000	15,000,000	300,000	3,000,000	6,200,000
13	40.00	Computers	3,000,000	100,000	500,000	30,000,000	300,000	3,000,000	6,200,000
14	40.00	Computers	3,000,000	100,000	500,000	7,500,000	300,000	3,000,000	6,100,000
15	40.00	Computers	3,000,000	100,000	500,000	15,000,000	600,000	3,000,000	6,300,000
16	40.00	Computers	3,000,000	100,000	500,000	15,000,000	150,000	3,000,000	6,100,000
17	40.00	Computers	3,000,000	100,000	500,000	15,000,000	300,000	6,000,000	9,200,000
18	40.00	Computers	3,000,000	100,000	500,000	15,000,000	300,000	1,500,000	4,600,000

Source: The table was produced using the start-up valuation calculator at https://www.equitynet.com/crowdfunding-tools/startup-valuation-calculator.aspx in July 2019.

is in an industry with an average PE ratio of 16. Suppose that to be enticed to invest, based on the risk of default and bankruptcy (Section 8.3.4), investors need to be offered a 50% rate of return. So the discounted TV is as follows:

$$\text{Discounted terminal value} = \frac{\text{Terminal value}}{(1+\text{target rate})^{\text{years}}} = \frac{4.8 \times 16}{(1+50\%)^5} = \$10.11 \text{ million}$$

And for a $1 million investment, investors will therefore demand a 9.89% ownership share:

$$\text{Required percent ownership} = \frac{\text{Investment}}{\text{Discounted terminal value}} = \frac{1 \text{million}}{10.11 \text{ million}} = 9.89\%$$

If there are currently 500,000 shares outstanding prior to crowdfunding, the equity crowdfunding offering will need to be an additional 54,863 shares:

$$\text{Number of new shares} = \frac{500,000}{(1 - 9.89\%)} - 500,000 = 54,863 \text{ new shares}$$

And the price per new share will be $18.23:

$$\text{Price per new share} = \frac{\$1,000,000}{54,863} = \$18.23 \text{ per share}$$

The value of the company prior to the $1 million crowdfunding goal will be $9.12 million:

Implied pre money valuation $= 500,000 \text{ shares} \times 18.23 \text{ per share} = 9.12 \text{ million}$

And the postmoney valuation will be exactly $1 million higher:

Implied post money valuation $= 554,863 \text{ shares} \times 18.23 \text{ per share} = 10.12 \text{ million}$

In this example, if we changed the capital raise from $1 million to $500,000, the equity sold would change to 4.94%, and the new shares issues change to 26,005, and the price per share would be $19.23. The premoney valuation would be $9.62 million and postmoney valuation would be $10.12 million.

Conversely, in this example, if we changed the capital raise from $1 million to $2 million, the equity sold would change to 19.78%, and the new shares issues change to 123,250, and the price per share would be $16.23. The premoney valuation would be $8.12 million and postmoney valuation would be $10.12 million.

Finally, note that there could be more than one equity crowdfunding round (see Section 8.5 for examples). In each round, there will be further dilution. For example, if there are two more rounds of capital raising, one with a 10% dilution and another with a 5% dilution, the equity retained (retention ratio) is $1/(1.1)/(1.05)$ or 86.6%. As such, an entrepreneur would be giving up more than the 9.89% share calculated above through these subsequent rounds (and changes to the original equity offered might be desired by the entrepreneur).

As in Section 8.3.4, it is instructive to see EquityNet's fundraising statistics by industry, in terms of fundraising goals and premoney valuations. Across all industries, the average funding goal is $1.42 million and average premoney valuation is $6.80 million.

The average equity share is 32% (for investors). Additional statistics and variations by industry are available in Table 8.7. The statistics should be interpreted with the perspective that EquityNet is a United States based platform where equity crowdfunding was not possible for retail investors until 2015, and as such, the amounts are geared toward larger investments and larger accredited or institutional investors for most of the operation of the platform (dating back to 2007). The fundraising statistics for platforms geared toward retail investors tend to show average capital raises around $300,000, as discussed above and in Chapters 9–13. Also, the average share amounts offered to investors is much lower on equity crowdfunding portals focused on retail investors, typically around 10%–15%.

It is important to keep in mind that selling a larger equity stake is not necessarily good for attracting investors. We discuss the reasons why at length in Chapter 10, Signaling in equity crowdfunding, and Chapter 12, Cash-flow and control rights in equity crowdfunding, with reference to large sample datasets. Before doing so, in Sections 8.5 and 8.6 next, we examine some motivating or interesting cases of success and failure, respectively. Then in Section 8.7, we present a summary of the information in this chapter and a roadmap for the subsequent Chapters 9–14 in this part III of the book on crowd investing.

8.5 Successful equity crowdfunding cases

Equity crowdfunding of course does not always result in massive successes. And recall Chapter 2, Overview of agency and signaling theory in crowdfunding, where we explained that theoretical Nobel Prize winning work by Ackerlof, Spence, and Stiglitz is consistent with the notion that equity crowdfunding would on average attract "lemons" that do not have a high expected value. So here, we introduce six cases of equity crowdfunding success. And then in Section 8.6, we present cases of equity crowdfunding failure. The cases here are perhaps limited in the sense that it would be much more instructive to evaluate the very long run performance of equity crowdfunded companies 10 or 20 years from crowdfunding after a sufficient amount of time had passed. Here, we are unable to do so because equity crowdfunding has not been around long enough. But these cases represent a start to our body of knowledge. And the data in the ensuing chapters in this Part III of this book bring a first look at the collective evidence to date and explain what is needed in the future.

8.5.1 ReWalk

One of the most celebrated equity crowdfunding cases ever is ReWalk, a crowdfunded company on the Israel equity crowdfunding platform OurCrowd. ReWalk manufacturer robotic exoskeletons for paraplegics. Importantly, ReWalk was the first company to obtain US FDA approval to offer such a product for personal use.[27] Videos of their product have been viewed hundreds of thousands of times, and it is easy to see from these videos how

---

[27] https://www.roboticsbusinessreview.com/health-medical/
rewalk_robotics_eyes_future_after_36m_ipo/

TABLE 8.7 EquityNet campaign statistics by industry averages.

	Funding goal ($)	Premoney valuation ($)	Investor equity share (%)	Prior year revenue ($)	Current year revenue ($)	Revenue growth rate (%)	Market size ($)	Market growth rate (%)	Age of company	Number of employees	Data representation (%)
Biotech, pharma, and healthcare	1,737,022	9,091,846	26.71	441,345	713,446	24	263,888,051	16.08	7.29	7.47	13
Business products and services	893,994	5,495,162	29.56	423,115	603,048	28	202,797,479	19.07	5.82	12.24	22
Communications	1,720,766	6,433,646	36.42	694,036	952,071	30	195,633,972	23.15	7.04	7.30	4
Computers and control systems	1,202,134	6,923,747	30.14	3,350,094	1,053,666	24	265,185,260	18.83	5.34	4.49	2
Consumer products and services	724,824	3,196,424	33.89	325,045	512,245	22	169,671,968	16.60	4.38	7.97	24
Electronics and instrumentation	1,081,529	7,403,207	27.03	358,291	895,273	35	299,611,238	18.66	8.6	8.54	1
Energy and utilities	2,331,671	11,490,207	30.04	554,446	1,141,702	16	317,635,469	22.01	6.19	7.69	4
Financial services and real estate	1,963,696	6,861,749	40.40	625,469	988,588	22	225,127,713	15.86	4.29	8.68	12
Industrial and manufacturing	1,577,148	5,970,500	33.59	775,142	1,475,021	21	249,832,058	16.78	6.57	12.11	4
Media and entertainment	1,017,244	5,460,480	32.21	160,644	302,943	25	177,469,037	22.32	3.96	6.88	9
Software	NA	NA	NA	NA	NA	NA	NA	NA	NA	NA	NA
Transportation and distribution	1,386,379	6,429,781	32.95	567,910	973,702	24	233,685,130	14.66	4.22	13.74	4

These statistics were extracted from https://www.equitynet.com/crowdfunding-statistics.aspx in July 2019.

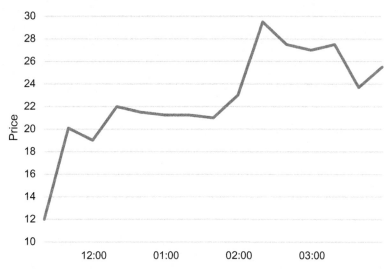

FIGURE 8.2   Underpricing of ReWalk's Nasdaq (RWLK: NASDAQ) IPO, September 12, 2014. Source: *Based on https://www.crowdfundinsider.com/2014/09/49550-ourcrowd-portfolio-company-ReWalk-lists-nasdaq-shares-rocket/.*

excitement in the crowd could be infectious and truly inspiring.[28] ReWalk raised $1.3 million on OurCrowd in June 2013.[29] ReWalk raised another $2.1 million on OurCrowd in a subsequent crowdfunding campaign prior to its IPO (Nasdaq:RWLK) on September 12, 2014.

ReWalk raised an estimated $36 million in its IPO (after deducting underwriting fees, commissions, and offering expenses) by selling $3 million shares for $12 each, implying the company valuation of $136 million.[30,31] ReWalk's IPO shares were "underpriced" in the short run (first trading day), insofar as the end of day first price climbed higher (to $25.60 per share; see Fig. 8.2) than its original offer price. The tendency of an IPO closing day price to be higher than its offer price in the morning is not unusual; in fact, anything but is unexpected.[32] But the magnitude in this case of over 100% underpricing is certainly an outlier.

It is noteworthy that OurCrowd investors had invested alongside professional venture capitalists, including Pontifax, Israel Health Care Ventures, and SCP Vitalife, and the Japanese Robotics giant YASKAWA.[33] ReWalk's CEO Larry Jasinski praises OurCrowd publicly and has been quoted as saying, for example, "I have enjoyed the professional and comprehensive approach of OurCrowd and its investors and believe they have added value to our efforts."[34]

---

[28] See, for example, https://www.youtube.com/watch?v = 2Xd27c-pz4Y.

[29] https://blog.ourcrowd.com/ourcrowds-portfolio-company-ReWalk-featured-in-forbes/

[30] https://www.roboticsbusinessreview.com/health-medical/
ReWalk_robotics_eyes_future_after_36m_ipo/

[31] https://blog.ourcrowd.com/ourcrowds-ReWalk-ipo/

[32] See https://site.warrington.ufl.edu/ritter/ipo-data/. Explanations for short run IPO underpricing are reviewed in Cumming and Johan (2013, Chapter 19: Crypto regulation).

[33] https://blog.ourcrowd.com/ourcrowds-ReWalk-ipo/

[34] https://blog.ourcrowd.com/ourcrowds-ReWalk-ipo/

As at July 31, 2019, RWLK was trading at $3.72 per share.[35] The tendency of IPOs to perform poorly over the long run (1−5 years after the IPO) is very common and widely regarded as "IPO overpricing."[36] ReWalk is certainly consistent with the typical IPO case, although the magnitude of long run overpricing could be considered an outlier relative to typical IPOs.[37] Specifically, over 42% of IPOs in the United States have buy-and-hold returns of less than −50%, and the average 3-year buy-and-hold return for IPOs in the United States has been −10% (−45.3% market adjusted, and −29% style adjusted) for IPOs of firms with sales of less than $10 million.[38] At the end of July, 2019, ReWalk's 3-year monthly beta was 2.06 (reflecting a high degree of systematic risk) and its total market capitalization was $25.88 million.[39]

8.5.2 Heeros Oyj

Heeros Oyj is a Finnish growth company that specializes in cloud-based financial management software solutions. Heeros Oyj is the first European IPO of a company that was previously crowdfunded. Heeros raised €660,000 in equity crowdfunding round from almost 200 shareholders on Invesdor in late 2015. Shares were initially priced at €2.70. Heeros raised a further €3.4m from more than 700 investors on Invesdor on October 19, 2016 to November 4, 2016.[40] On November 10, 2016, Heeros went public on Nasdaq First North Helsinki, at €3.10 and raised approximately €10.5 million.[41]

Notably, Heeros was the first exit (i.e., liquidity event, allowing investors to cash out) for shareholders on Invesdor.[42] Invesdor CEO Lasse Mäkelä is quoted as saying,[43] "[e]quity crowdfunding needs to show that it can generate exits for investors; this is the only way the industry can sustain its growth. While growth companies are generally long term investments, having the possibility to exit is crucial for investors' confidence in the system.... ... Crowdfunding platforms can be convenient tools for IPOs due to their efficiency in reaching retail investors and processing share subscriptions. If I was planning an IPO, I would consider using crowdfunding platforms as cost-efficient distribution channels."

---

[35] https://www.google.com/search?q = rwlk&tbm = fin#scso = _zw46XazgCIK0tQX-i5KABw6:0

[36] See https://site.warrington.ufl.edu/ritter/ipo-data/. Explanations for long run IPO overpricing are reviewed in Cumming and Johan (2013, Chapter 19: Crypto regulation).

[37] https://site.warrington.ufl.edu/ritter/ipo-data/

[38] https://site.warrington.ufl.edu/ritter/files/2019/04/IPOs2018_Longrun-Returns.pdf

[39] https://finance.yahoo.com/quote/RWLK?ltr = 1

[40] https://home.invesdor.com/en/blog/2016/11/10/the-first-crowdfunding-backed-public-company-starts-trading-today

[41] https://home.invesdor.com/en/blog/2016/11/10/the-first-crowdfunding-backed-public-company-starts-trading-today

[42] https://medium.com/@InnFin/heeros-ipos-a-year-after-crowdfunding-on-invesdor-8dc6971ef493

[43] https://home.invesdor.com/en/blog/2016/11/10/the-first-crowdfunding-backed-public-company-starts-trading-today

Heeros CEO Matti Lattu has likewise publicly stated that there is a value associated with obtaining retail and institutional investment prior to an IPO. Specifically Matti Lattu commented,[44] "I am happy about the result of the IPO and about the interest shown towards Heeros. Both retail and institutional investors have understood our growth potential in the digitizing market of financial management software. I want to thank all our investors for their trust."

The Heeros case is an interesting one as it is suggestive of the benefit of reaching retail shareholders pre-IPO for the purpose of gaining their confidence in an IPO for better IPO performance or at least from that which would have otherwise been possible without the opportunity to raise capital in equity crowdfunding. To date, however, there have been too few crowdfunded companies that have gone public to carry out a rigorous statistical assessment of this claim. And the but-for exercise is quite tough to assess with a few cases at hand.

Heeros is trading on the Frankfurt stock exchange on December 26, 2016, at €3.08. As at July 31, 2019, Heros was trading at €2.12, with a monthly 3-year beta of 1.00 and market capitalization of €9.744 million.[45]

Invesdor is a pan-European equity crowdfunding platform but based and focused in Finland.[46] It is noteworthy that Invesdor presents an index of returns to crowdfunding on their webpage.[47] The index as at July 31, 2019 is presented in Fig. 8.3. Invesdor explains that for their index[48]:

- Companies will be removed in the event of bankruptcies and M&As.
- Companies are added to the index quarterly if they "reach the cumulative capital amount of the smallest component."
- "New additions will decrease the weight of existing constituents in the index. In case the new addition has executed smaller rounds previously, they are retrospectively taken into account." "Only capital invested via Invesdor is included in weightings."
- "The index is a proxy for performance of euros invested in the big deals via Invesdor."
- "The index is updated using valuation in new financing rounds plus publicly available data."

Clearly, there have been some impressive companies financed through Invesdor, as indicated by the Heeros case. But clearly the performance statistics in Fig. 8.3 can be somewhat misleading of average performance statistics, due to the nature of the index creation. This type of reporting has been found in other industries such as venture capital, where fund managers tend to exaggerate their performance statistics to attract additional investment (Cumming & Johan, 2006; Cumming & Walz, 2010; Johan & Zhang, 2015). It is unclear as to whether an average retail investor might be somewhat mislead as to what the performance numbers in Fig. 8.3 represent.

---

[44] https://home.invesdor.com/en/blog/2016/11/10/the-first-crowdfunding-backed-public-company-starts-trading-today

[45] https://finance.yahoo.com/quote/HER.F?p = HER.F&.tsrc = fin-srch

[46] https://home.invesdor.com/en/

[47] https://home.invesdor.com/en/invesdor-digital-fundraising-index

[48] https://home.invesdor.com/en/invesdor-digital-fundraising-index

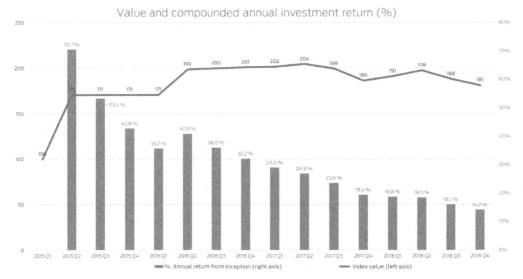

FIGURE 8.3   Invesdor's Equity Crowdfunding Index.
Note: Invesdor explains that the Index is comprised as at 2018 Q4 as follows: Invesdor Oy 13%, Cityvarasto Oyj 4%, Helsinki Allas Oy 5%, Ägras Distillery Oy 3%, Heeros Oyj 15%, Siili Solutions Oyj 2%, Friends & Brgrs Ab 3%, WordDive Oy 4%, Transfluent Oy 3%, Injeq Oy 6%, Ezylet Ltd 3%, Yepzon Oy 4%, Prasos Oy 10%, Wello Oy 7%. Parking Energy Oy 3%, Mekitek Oy 6%, FaFa's 4%, Naturvention Oy (Naava) 7%.

8.5.3 Beta bionics

Wefunder is one of the most successful equity crowdfunding platforms to date in the United States (Table 8.1). One of Wefunder's more successful campaigns has been Beta Bionics.[49] Beta Bionics is based in Boston; perhaps it is not surprising, as Route 128 outside of Boston has had the largest cluster of biotech start-ups for decades.[50] Beta Bionics builds bionic pancreas to improve the lives of people suffering from type 1 diabetes. Specifically, its product iLet is a pocket-sized, wearable medical device that autonomously manages blood sugar levels in people with diabetes. The iLet technology has the ability to continuously monitor and adapt to the ever-changing insulin needs of people with diabetes and in effect serves as an "irrevocable bridge to the ever-elusive cure."[51]

Beta Bionics raised $1 million from 817 investors in August 2016 on a $100 million valuation. Beta Bionics has had significant press coverage and commentaries from established university professors in biomechanical engineering, the New York Times, Time Magazine, BBC, Business Insider, among others.[52]

[49] https://wefunder.com/beta.bionics

[50] https://www.digitalrealty.com/blog/bostons-technology-corridor

[51] https://www.digitalrealty.com/blog/bostons-technology-corridor

[52] https://www.digitalrealty.com/blog/bostons-technology-corridor

Beta Bionics is likewise interesting for its exit outcome. Normally, the biotechnology industry is notorious for a "long runway," or a substantial amount of time from first investment to exit. But Time Magazine reported on April 1, 2016, that Beta Bionics had recently received a $5 million investment from Eli Lilly.[53] It is suggestive that crowdfunding to subsequent rounds of capital and M&A exits could be feasible exit outcomes. But again, more time is needed to allow more cases to develop and large sample statistical evidence to be gathered and analyzed to see if there is a benefit of equity crowdfunding over other types of entrepreneurial finance.

8.5.4 Sondors Electric Car

Emoryville, CA, based Sondors Electric Car[54] raised $999,996 of its $70,000 to $1 million goal on a $32.4 million valuation on StartEngine (by November 2016 they reached their goal of $600,000 according to their update on the StartEngine platform).[55] Sondors is an electric car company, and as such, it is not surprising that it is based proximate to Silicon Valley which is the leading cluster in this industry.[56] Shares were priced at $12 per share, for a $33 million valuation. Sondors has a track record of selling over 17,000 electric bikes. The car crowdfunding project is geared toward producing $10,000 electric cars.

As at July 31, 2019, Sondors is on a capital raise for $20 million on same platform StartEngine.[57] Sondors presents an interesting case study as the evolution of a new technology alongside a new way of raising capital. Also, the staged rounds for electric cars versus other types of technologies on crowdfunding versus other types of entrepreneurial finance and other platforms offers interesting angles for further statistical analyses as more time passes and more data are available.

8.5.5 Hopsters Brewery

Hopsters Brewery[58] raised $1.3 million on a $4 million valuation from 713 investors in first offering on Wefunder in 2017 and was last funded to $1,699,901 from 860 investors as at March 2019. It is brewpub restaurant based on Boston, with $1.3 million in annual sales reported in 2018, and a 75% gross margin (90% margin on Hopsters-brewed beer served on site), net income of 20% of EBITDA (which they highlight is more than five times as profitable as a standard restaurant), and 50% COGS (cost of goods sold). They report corporate events with leading institutions to maintain or boost sales, including corporate events with Google, HP, John Hancock, PWC, Vertex, GE, HubSpot, and Harvard.

[53] https://time.com/4278068/bionic-pancreas-company/

[54] https://www.startengine.com/sondors-electric-car

[55] https://www.startengine.com/sondors-electric-car

[56] https://www.eenews.net/stories/1060102493

[57] https://www.startengine.com/sondorscar

[58] https://wefunder.com/hopsters

Thanks in part to this capital from Wefunder investors, in 2019, Hopsters ranked 15th of the 50 fastest growing craft breweries in the United States.[59] It has been reported that they are seeking future equity of $5.5 million with a premoney valuation of $25.5 million.[60] As with Sondors, it will be interesting to compare the success of different multiple rounds of equity crowdfunding in different sectors on different platforms as more time passes.

8.5.6 Wolfprint

Wolfprint[61] is an Estonian company that raised $604,640.00 on a $4.5 million valuation on the US equity platform SeedInvest in 2016. Wolfprint does 3D printing and uses virtual reality. It develops a global network of 3D scanners and uses a database of 3D scans that grows by more than 70% per month.

Certainly Wolfprint is notable for a few reasons. First, it is pioneering a new technology and making use of the novel equity crowdfunding route to do so. Second, Wolfprint used a US-based platform, despite being an Estonian start-up. Referring back to Chapter 7, Crowdfunding to internationalize, it would be interesting to see how different types of start-ups can use these new funding mechanisms to be "born global" over the coming years.

There are numerous other cases of successful equity crowdfunding success stories. Some of them are featured in various news stories.[62] Noteworthy cases include Legion M. Entertainment, a fan-owned Hollywood studio, which raised $1 million on a $12.6 million valuation on Wefunder; Hops & Grain Brewing, an Austin Texas brew company, which raised $1 million on Wefunder; Liquid Piston, a Bloomfield Connecticut motor designer, which raised $759,351 on a $25 million valuation on Wefunder; Green Sense Farms, a Portland (Indiana) vertical indoor farming company, which raised $641,100 on a $56.3 million valuation on StartEngine; and SwitchPitch, a District of Columbia−based start-up social network company, which raised $505,000 on a $4.5 million valuation.[63]

Chapters 10−13 examine in more detail systematic evidence of the determinants of fundraising success and failure in terms of large-scale statistical evidence. Section 8.6 immediately below first considers specific cases of equity crowdfunding failure.

8.6 Failed equity crowdfunding cases

This section presents three cases in Sections 8.6.1−8.6.3 of failed equity crowdfunding outcomes. Section 8.6.1 presents a case of a successful equity crowdfunding fundraising campaign, but a failed long-term outcome after crowdfunding. Sections 8.6.2 and 8.6.3 present cases of failed equity crowdfunding fundraising attempts. We do not discuss here

[59] https://wefunder.com/hopsters

[60] https://ec2-52-3-80-236.compute-1.amazonaws.com/

[61] https://www.seedinvest.com/wolfprint.3d/seed

[62] See, for example, https://www.toptal.com/finance/fundraising/us-equity-crowdfunding-market.

[63] See, for example, https://www.toptal.com/finance/fundraising/us-equity-crowdfunding-market.

crowdfunding fraud; that topic is addressed in Chapter 15, Introduction to crowdfunding regulation and policy.

8.6.1 Rebus

Rebus,[64] founded in 2010, raised over £816,790 on Crowdcube in 2015 by selling a 6.63% stake in its firm to 109 investors. One investor invested £135,000. The case is memorable as a failed equity crowdfunding company that went into bankruptcy because Rebus sold itself as helping investors that bought into "flawed complex financial solutions—a market which is estimated to be £55 billion."[65] Rebus had a CEO with a track record of success in a similar type of company (Ask Jeeves) and had significant traction with clients at the time of fundraising (29 employees, 1700 claims, total value of £930 million).

Crowdcube notes that Rebus is its biggest bankruptcy and states that 6% of successfully funded companies have failed in bankruptcy.[66] Commentators have used Rebus to express concern that there is deficient public understanding of the risks associated with equity crowdfunding, and there is need for more investor education.[67]

8.6.2 Alchemiya Media

Alchemiya Media[68] is a start-up founded in 2013 in the similar space as Netflix but with a focus on Muslim-oriented programing. The campaign goal was £60,000 on Crowdcube in 2015. It sought to retain 98% of the ownership for the founders (among the top). Alchemiya offered nonvoting shares and was among the bottom half of companies on Crowdcube in respect of having significant ownership without any voting rights offered to investors. In the end, Alchemiya obtained 72 investors but only raised 81% of their target capital raise.

It is worth contrasting Alchemiya with Property TV. Property TV was founded in 2012 and campaigned on Crowdcube in 2015 for £200,000. Property TV offered 18% equity to crowd investors (higher than the average on Crowdcube) and no nonvoting shares (unusual for Crowdcube). Property TV secured 290 investors and reached £320,000 (160% of its fundraising target).[69] Relative to Alchemiya, the high-equity share

---

[64] https://www.crowdfundinsider.com/2016/02/81305-rebus-called-biggest-uk-crowdfunding-failure-to-date-as-firm-files-for-bankruptcy/

[65] https://www.crowdfundinsider.com/2016/02/81305-rebus-called-biggest-uk-crowdfunding-failure-to-date-as-firm-files-for-bankruptcy/

[66] https://www.crowdfundinsider.com/2016/02/81305-rebus-called-biggest-uk-crowdfunding-failure-to-date-as-firm-files-for-bankruptcy/

[67] https://www.crowdfundinsider.com/2016/02/81305-rebus-called-biggest-uk-crowdfunding-failure-to-date-as-firm-files-for-bankruptcy/

[68] https://www.crowdcube.com/companies/alchemiya-media

[69] https://propertyindustryeye.com/new-property-tv-station-has-crowdfunding-pitch-pulled/

for the crowd and/or the use of voting shares only may have been attractive to the crowd, leading to a successful fundraising. But the case of Property TV is particularly interesting not only because it contrasts with Alchemiya Media's campaign but also because Property TV's fundraising success appears to have been ill deserved. In particular, in response to concerns with the management of Property TV on social platforms, Crowdcube investigated further (more than their usual due diligence). The case highlights the importance of the "wisdom of the crowd" alongside an active platform like Crowdcube that does its due diligence (see also Chapter 15: Introduction to crowdfunding regulation and policy). Crowdcube sent to its investors notification of their decision to cancel a letter, one of which is shown in Fig. 8.4.

The example is interesting, as it shows retaining a high-equity share for the entrepreneur and/or offering nonvoting shares may be less desirable for attracting equity crowdfunding investors, despite its underlying quality. In Chapter 12, Cash-flow and control rights in equity crowdfunding, we examine large-scale evidence to address this issue in detail. But first we present a further set of contrasting cases in the next section.

FIGURE 8.4 Crowdcube's removal of Property TV.
Note: The Property TV campaign was successful raising 160% of the capital goal, but Crowdcube decided to not disburse the funds to Property TV following social media comments and Crowdcube's further due diligence reviews. *TV*, Terminal value. Source: *https://www.propertytribes.com/ben-rogers-is-simon-zutshi-correct-t-13842-6.html#pid229060.*

8.6.3 Buy2Let

Buy2Let, a property buy to rent service founded in 2012, tried to raise £150,000 on Crowdcube in 2014.[70] It offered a significant ownership stake to investors (25% in aggregate), which places it at the top 10% of crowdfunding campaigns on Crowdcube in terms of equity share sold. Also, it offered substantial nonvoting shares (also in the top 10%). In the end, the capital raise was unsuccessful (only £35,670).

By contrast, Jewel Street, an original jewelry company founded in 2012, had a campaign goal of £100,000 on Crowdcube in 2014.[71] It only offered a 15.83% equity stake to the crowd investors on a £1,000,110 valuation, and did not sell any nonvoting shares. The campaign was successful with the entrepreneurs raising £188,120 of their intended £100,000 capital goal.

The Alchemiya Media and Buy2Let failed campaigns are interesting next to their counterparts that did succeed. They are suggestive that the ownership stake sold and the extent to which voting versus voting shares are sold may influence fundraising success. But it is hard to be certain from a few cases. Chapter 10, Signaling in equity crowdfunding and Chapter 12, Cash-flow and control rights in equity crowdfunding, examine these issues with large sample evidence.

8.7 Summary and roadmap for Chapters 9–14

This chapter provided an overview of different equity crowdfunding platforms around the world. We explained how private companies that are considering crowdfunding can be valued with comparables, NPV, and options valuations methods. We explained how to calculate the extent of equity that an entrepreneur may seek to give up. We gave examples of how online resources are being used to facilitate transparent valuations for entrepreneurs and investors alike. We provided a number of cases of crowdfunding success and crowdfunding failure, in both the short run in terms of the campaign fundraising success, and in the long run in terms of the outcome of the company. Sometimes companies that used crowdfunding eventually become successful IPOs and others fail in bankruptcy. Reporting of crowdfunding outcomes on public webpages may not entirely represent a clear picture of the potential rewards and risks.

Chapter 9, Equity crowdfunding and governance, provides a more complete discussion of the different types of equity crowdfunding models that are used by different platforms. Different models have associated with them different governance standards that may possibly mitigate failure and enhance the probability of success. Chapter 10, Signaling in equity crowdfunding, considers empirical evidence on the determinants of successful fundraising based on the first-ever equity crowdfunding platform in the world, ASSOB, from Australia. Chapter 11, Are equity crowdfunders sensitive to distance?, examines the interaction between distance and crowdfunders with the ASSOB data.

[70] https://www.insidermedia.com/insider/southeast/108015-property-entrepreneur-seeks-150k-build-business

[71] https://www.crowdcube.com/companies/jewelstreet/pitches/bd5dmq

Chapter 12, Cash-flow and control rights in equity crowdfunding, examines additional evidence on fundraising and long-term success in equity crowdfunding from Crowdcube in the United Kingdom. Chapter 13, Does equity crowdfunding democratize access to entrepreneurial finance?, investigates differences across Crowdcube and the Alternative Investment Market (he junior or small cap market of the London Stock Exchange) to see if crowdfunding enables a more balanced access to capital (a "democratization" of access to capital) than traditional equity markets. At the end of Part III, Chapter 14, Marketplace lending, reviews marketplace lending and contrasts the risks and rewards of individuals lending to companies versus investing as equity investors.

Key terms

Comparables
Cost of capital
Cost of debt
Cost of equity
Equity share
Net present value (NPV)
Options valuation
Postmoney valuation
Premoney valuation
Standard deviation
Weighted average cost of capital

Discussion questions and exercises

8.1. One of your early assignments at your new place of employment at an equity crowdfunding platform is to assess the value of companies that are seeking listing on the platform. A new start-up presents itself with the following cash flow projections. You consider using NPV and option pricing methods to value this company. All amounts are in thousands.

	Year 0	Year 1	Year 2	Year 3	Year 4	Year 5
Cash flow except CapEx	0	0	0	15	15	50
Capital expenditure	−130	0	0	0	0	0
Total cash flow	−130	0	0	15	15	50

WACC = 25%, terminal growth rate = 3%. Initial investment: $30 thousand for R&D equipment and personnel. The $100 thousand expenditure on the plant could be undertaken any time in the first 2 years (whenever the project would be undertaken, the present value of the plant construction expenditures would total $100 thousand in today's dollars). The entrepreneur pursues the $100 thousand expenditure only if the first stage investment is successful. The Valuation decision now based on a $30 thousand investment bundled with a 2-year European call option and priced using the Black–Scholes model. Time to expiration $(T - t) = 2$ years. Risk-free rate $(r_f) = 7\%$. Exercise price (X) = present value of the investment to build the plant = $100 thousand. Stock price (S) = discounted cash flows generated by the underlying assets associated with the expansion opportunity can be computer for year 0 using a discount rate of 25% and a terminal growth rate of 3% per year. The standard deviation (σ) based on comparables is 0.6. Do you think listing this company on your equity crowdfunding platform would be good for its reputation and long-term success of the start-up, and for the platform? Why? Or why not?

8.2. Your start-up is considering raising money through equity crowdfunding. The goal is to raise $400,000, and you need to decide on what share of the company you should sell. You project the company will have Net Income in year 5 of $1.8 million. Similar profitable Internet ventures listed on stock exchanges are trading at an average price–earnings Ratio of 14. The company currently has 100,000 shares outstanding. In view of the risk of failures in this industry sector, you promote that in the event of a successful outcome, investors should expect to receive a 30% rate of return. What share of the company should you offer for sale, and how many shares would that offering comprise in an equity crowdfunding campaign? What would be the appropriate price per share? Would your answer change if you expected a second equity crowdfunding round with another 10% of equity sold? And can you identify possible problems with using the average price–earnings ratios of current publicly trading Internet companies for the purposes of valuing your start-up?

8.3. What are the benefits and costs associated with offering a higher equity share to the crowd in equity crowdfunding cases? What is a typical equity share that is offered in crowdfunding?

8.4. What are benefits and costs associated with issuing nonvoting shares in equity crowdfunding? What might be some benefits for retail investors associated with investing alongside a professional or accredited investor?

8.5. Which equity crowdfunding platforms are the most successful in the world? What might have contributed to their success? What are some examples of successful companies that have listed on these platforms? What are some examples of failed crowdfunding campaigns? What is the difference between long-run and short-run success in evaluating crowdfunding cases?

8.6. How are returns to equity crowdfunding promoted on select webpages? Are there any agency problems associated with such promotions? If so, explain how? What might be done to improve investor education and protection?

Equity crowdfunding and governance

9.1 Introduction

Attention to corporate governance has intensified over the last three decades, reflecting changes in ownership structures, the globalization of financial markets, and the occurrence of the global financial crisis (Wright et al., 2013). Some have taken a relatively narrow view of corporate governance, defining it as "the ways in which suppliers of finance to corporations assure themselves of getting a return on their investment" (Shleifer & Vishny, 1997: 737). Others have taken a broader perspective, defining it as "the determination of the broad uses to which organizational resources will be deployed and the resolution of conflicts among the myriad participants in organizations" (Davila, Foster, & Gupta, 2003: 371). While much of governance research has focused on public firms (Hart, 1995; Shleifer & Vishny, 1997), more recently, private firms, including family firms and entrepreneurial start-ups, have also gained increasing attention (Audretsch & Lehmann, 2004; Filatotchev & Wright, 2005; Schulze et al., 2001; Uhlaner et al., 2007; Zahra et al., 2009). Clearly, governance research has become broader in scope, covering a multitude of organizational forms and actors.

Particularly after the global financial crisis, people have searched for new ways of financing entrepreneurship that have the potential to democratize entrepreneurial financing (Mollick & Robb, 2016), by engaging larger segments of the investing public. With the recent emergence of equity crowdfunding as "a method of financing, whereby an entrepreneur sells a specified amount of equity or bond-like shares[1] in a company to a group of (small) investors through an open call for funding on Internet-based platforms" (Chapter 10: Signaling in equity crowdfunding), a new "hybrid" organizational form has developed. Equity-crowdfunded (ECF) firms usually combine the characteristics of public firms that have a large number of (small) shareholders with those of privately held entrepreneurial firms in which ownership and control largely overlap because entrepreneurs retain a large share of the equity.

---

[1] In some countries (e.g., Germany) the sale of shares carrying voting rights through crowdfunding platforms has not been permitted, but profit-participating arrangements are possible. These bond-like shares do not carry voting rights (Vismara, 2016).

Today, equity crowdfunding plays an increasingly important role in entrepreneurial finance. For instance, since 2012 the global equity crowdfunding market has roughly doubled in volume each year (Massolution, 2015) and if this growth continues, this market could reach $36 billion by 2020, thereby surpassing the size of the venture capital market (Barnett, 2015). In the United Kingdom an estimated 20% of all early stage investments already occur through equity crowdfunding platforms (Beauhurst, 2015). The emergence of ECF firms as a new, hybrid organizational form poses challenges to existing theories and systems of governance, requiring new thinking about structuring the relationships among different actors with different incentives and time horizons. Indeed, in agency theory, the focus is on how external investors should device governance mechanisms to control agency problems, but small equity crowdinvestors may have limited incentives and power to do so (Chapter 10: Signaling in equity crowdfunding). Thus there is a need to better understand the different mechanisms that different actors could use to ensure effective participation in equity crowdfunding, while also ensuring ECF firm success.

To address these issues, we develop a conceptual model that highlights the multitude of governance mechanisms that (potentially) operate in equity crowdfunding markets. Our model and related discussion underscore the crucial importance of corporate governance for ECF firms and the viability of the equity crowdfunding market. Without effective governance, this market may eventually fail, and opportunities for further growth may be missed. Moreover, we call for a shift in research on equity crowdfunding from an almost exclusive focus on the funding success and funding dynamics on platforms to study the governance of ECF firms and how it is related to ECF firm success. To achieve this purpose, we develop a research agenda on governance and equity crowdfunding and, more specifically, on how corporate governance may help in the selection and development of viable ECF firms.

Even though different forms of crowdfunding exist (e.g., Mollick, 2014), we focus on equity crowdfunding for good reasons. First, equity crowdfunding allows for a more direct comparison with more traditional external financiers of entrepreneurship that include venture capitalists (VCs) and angel investors. Similar to these financiers, in equity crowdfunding, potential monetary returns and the reduction of information asymmetries related to entrepreneurs' skills and firms' prospects are primary concerns (Chapter 10: Signaling in equity crowdfunding; see also Cholakova & Clarysse, 2015; Vismara, 2018). Second, while other forms of crowdfunding are often launched by *individuals* or represent "artistic" *projects*, in equity crowdfunding the proponents are by definition *firms* (Vismara, 2018). Third, unlike the other forms of crowdfunding, equity crowdfunding may introduce a large set of new shareholders—with divergent secondary interests (besides realizing monetary returns) and time horizons—in firms, making corporate governance issues particularly salient (Bruton, Khavul, Siegel, & Wright, 2015).

The current chapter contributes to the governance and equity crowdfunding literature in several ways. First, with the rising prominence of ECF firms, there is a need to better understand their governance. Despite the paucity of empirical evidence, the types and importance of governance mechanisms to which "traditional" public and privately held firms are subject are likely to differ from those of ECF firms. For instance, while public firms may have strong track records and reputations that could explain why managers often deliver on their promises even when they cannot be forced to (Shleifer & Vishny, 1997), these mechanisms are generally lacking in young ECF firms. Also, public firms are actively monitored, tracked, and evaluated by information intermediaries, such as stock analysts (Healy & Palepu, 2001), but this is not the case for ECF firms and much less in-depth information is available on them. Moreover, in contrast to public firms, the shares of ECF firms cannot be sold (easily) given the lack of liquid secondary markets (Signori & Vismara, 2018), thereby limiting capital market discipline. There are also important differences with privately held firms that raise other sources of external equity finance such as venture capital and are subject to due diligence, extensive contracts, and monitoring (e.g., Amit, Brander, & Zott, 1998; Sapienza, Manigart, & Vermeir, 1996). ECF firms, however, raise funding from small so-called "amateur" investors that may lack the knowledge, incentives, and power to conduct a due diligence, write extensive contracts, and monitor entrepreneurs (Chapter 10: Signaling in equity crowdfunding). Thus we cannot simply generalize findings from prior work on public firms with dispersed ownership or private firms with concentrated ownership to ECF firms. In other words, what works in public firms or in privately held firms might not work in ECF firms, and other governance mechanisms may be at play that are specific to the equity crowdfunding context.

Second, we present an integrative model of governance mechanisms that (potentially) operate in equity crowdfunding markets. For this purpose, we draw on an information economics perspective. The most influential perspective in governance research, namely, agency theory, originates from information economics (Eisenhardt, 1989). However, agency theory has focused on how "*the principal* should seek to avoid or mitigate the agency problem" (Arthurs & Busenitz, 2003: 148, emphasis added) and portrays entrepreneurs as "potential thieves or deadbeats" and investors as "police officers enforcing the law" (Arthurs & Busenitz, 2003: 156). An information economics perspective argues that there are "good" and "bad" entrepreneurs and focuses on the role of investors (e.g., the crowd), intermediaries (e.g., crowdfunding platforms), country institutions, and even entrepreneurs themselves to minimize informational asymmetry problems that are the root cause of many agency issues. These problems include "hidden information," which leads to adverse selection problems, and "hidden action," which leads to moral hazard problems (Amit et al., 1998). Thus we offer an encompassing conceptual model of how different actors and environments could minimize informational asymmetry problems.

Third, current equity crowdfunding research has almost exclusively investigated the factors related to funding "success" (Chapter 10: Signaling in equity crowdfunding, and Chapter 12: Cash-flow and control rights in equity crowdfunding; see also Block, Hornuf, & Moritz, 2018; Block, Colombo, Cumming, & Vismara, 2018; Lukkarinen et al., 2016; Mamonov & Malaga, 2018; Mohammadi & Shafi, 2018; Vismara, 2016, 2018) and the funding dynamics on equity crowdfunding platforms (e.g., Hornuf & Schwienbacher, 2018; Vismara, 2018). This research focus is probably driven by the unique data that is often more or less readily available on the equity crowdfunding platforms. Though it is undeniably important for entrepreneurs to raise financing, the implications for investors, other stakeholders, and eventually even entrepreneurs themselves may be limited if equity crowdfunding does not allow for the selection of promising firms that develop into viable businesses. This highlights the need for a broader investigation, where scholars examine the governance mechanisms that may lead to the selection of the most promising firms *and* benefit the postcampaign performance of ECF firms, leading to the development of viable businesses that create new jobs and value for society at large.

Two recent studies illustrate that such a shift in research focus may be necessary and timely. Walthoff-Borm, Vanacker, and Collewaert (2018) show that firms search for equity crowdfunding as a "last resort"—that is—when they lack internal funds and lack access to (additional) debt financing. Thus equity crowdinvestors have only access to a relatively narrow set of firms that are often highly unprofitable. This should not necessarily be a concern as venture capital-backed and angel-backed firms are also often high unprofitable, and eventually fail, but we also have many examples of such firms that develop into some of the largest "celebrity" firms in our modern economies. However, Signori and Vismara (2018) show that most current exits in equity crowdfunding are bankruptcies, and there are few successful exits so far. Even though some of the surviving ECF firms could eventually develop into the leading firms of the future, they could equally (and probably more) likely develop into "empty shells" or "zombie firms." This suggests that while corporate governance has the potential to stimulate the development of viable ECF firms, we currently lack insights into the governance mechanisms that (potentially) operate in equity crowdfunding markets and in particular their effectiveness for creating viable businesses.

Having defined the objective and scope of our study, in the next section, we develop the idea why corporate governance is crucial in equity crowdfunding markets and then summarize the broad range of mechanisms that have been advanced in extant corporate governance research. We then discuss specific governance mechanisms that (potentially) operate in the equity crowdfunding markets, detail how these mechanisms can tackle the information asymmetry issues described earlier, and how future research can contribute to answering some key questions that remain unaddressed. In so doing, we hope our discussion helps to set up an agenda for future governance work in the equity crowdfunding context and illustrates how this research can also make meaningful theoretical contributions while influencing policy.

9.2 Information economics and the need for governance in equity crowdfunding markets

The information economics literature became particularly prominent after the seminal work of Akerlof, Spence, and Stiglitz (e.g., Akerlof, 1978; Spence, 1973; Stiglitz & Weiss, 1981). It focuses on the extent to which imperfect information, which can lead to adverse selection and moral hazard problems (Chapter 2: Overview of agency and signaling theory in crowdfunding), influences decision-making in the marketplace (Amit et al., 1998). Imperfect information is also a major cause for agency problems because it precludes the writing of complete contracts that stipulate the behavior of entrepreneurs in all eventualities, making corporate governance particularly salient (Hart, 1995).

When investing in young, entrepreneurial firms, external investors confront several *hidden information problems* that may lead to adverse selection, where they invest in low-quality projects that have been presented to them as high quality (Amit et al., 1998). This is possible because entrepreneurs, who are intimately involved in their firms and their internal systems and operations, often have more information on the quality of their firms compared to external investors, who can only assess the average quality of firms on the market. Entrepreneurs may also have incentives to misrepresent the information they have to their advantage when searching for financing. For instance, they may highlight visible signs of progress on specific projects while withholding information about other projects or tensions within firms that could undermine the viability of firms. Consequently, the information-disadvantaged investors may only be willing to buy shares at a discount, which reflects their information disadvantage. This behavior may lower the average quality of the firms that sell shares because entrepreneurs of above average quality firms have no incentive to sell their shares at a discount and thus withdraw from the market, which could ultimately lead to market failure.

When investing in young, entrepreneurial firms, external investors are also facing *hidden action problems* because they cannot perfectly observe the effort and actions of entrepreneurs (e.g., Amit et al., 1998). This situation may lead to moral hazard problems, especially if the goals of entrepreneurs and investors are not perfectly aligned. Entrepreneurs, for instance, may shirk effort, invest in "pet" projects (e.g., research projects with limited commercial value) to achieve private benefits at the expense of external investors and sometimes even take actions that not only harm external investors (and other stakeholders) but also themselves (Schulze et al., 2001). The risk of this occurring in entrepreneurial firms is particularly high given their focus on exploration and experimentation, often outside known boundaries. Entrepreneurs are also rule breakers, who do not do things in conventional ways, increasing the causal ambiguity surrounding their intentions and actions (Harris et al., 2009).

Traditional external equity financiers have developed a range of mechanisms to reduce informational asymmetry, related agency problems, and incomplete contracts (Amit et al., 1998). For instance, VCs and angel investors engage in detailed due diligence preinvestment and active monitoring postinvestment (Fried & Hisrich, 1994; Sapienza et al., 1996). They also prefer to invest locally (Cumming & Dai, 2010) and rely on preexisting direct and indirect ties between themselves and entrepreneurs to reduce informational asymmetry (Shane & Cable, 2002). However, equity crowdinvestors may individually neither have the required experience nor the incentives (given their average small investments) to conduct a detailed due diligence (Chapter 10: Signaling in equity crowdfunding). Equity crowdinvestors are also investing without meeting the entrepreneurial team in person. Moreover, equity crowdinvestors may be too small and numerous to monitor their investments on a day-to-day basis, and again it does not make economic sense for any individual investor to bear large monitoring costs. As a result, an information economics perspective suggests that there is a clear danger of adverse selection and moral hazard in the equity crowdfunding context, making effective corporate governance crucial.

The corporate governance literature has proposed a broad range of governance mechanisms to address the problems that arise from hidden information and hidden action, aiming to protect investors and help them create value. These mechanisms can operate within (*internal* mechanisms) or outside to the firm (*external* mechanisms) (Davila et al., 2003). The most examined corporate governance mechanisms include the board of directors and large investors (or ownership concentration), which serve as internal governance mechanisms that allow to both control and influence management (Shleifer & Vishny, 1997; Uhlaner et al., 2007). Also regularly examined are laws that protect investors against expropriation, which serves as an external governance mechanism (La Porta et al., 2000; Shleifer & Vishny, 1997). In their survey of the corporate governance literature, Shleifer and Vishny (1997: 769) propose that "legal protection of investors and some form of concentrated ownership are essential elements of a good corporate governance system." While there has been significant attention to the *formal* governance mechanisms that are described earlier, there can also effective *informal* governance mechanisms (Chrisman et al., 2018; Mustakallio et al., 2002). For instance, the external market for corporate control, that is, the threat of a hostile takeover might discipline management. Moreover, reputations (Shleifer & Vishny, 1997) and trusting relationships (Arthurs & Busenitz, 2003) may significantly reduce the probability of opportunistic behaviors by entrepreneurs.

Moreover, a key goal of some corporate governance mechanisms is to avoid *adverse selection* problems. These mechanisms are often more temporal in nature and are "triggered" by specific events, such as financing rounds or transactions. For instance, before providing financing, traditional external equity investors carry out a detailed due diligence to reduce the risk that they provide their valuable resources to low-quality firms. The primary goal of other corporate governance mechanisms is to reduce *moral hazard* problems. These mechanisms are often more enduring in their effect once "installed." For instance, traditional investors often take an active role in the board of directors of the firms they fund or have regular meetings with management. The purpose is to reduce the risk that entrepreneurs misuse the valuable resources they provided after the investment. Other governance mechanisms, such as a country's institutions, have the potential to address both adverse selection and moral hazard issues.

Ultimately, a combination of governance mechanisms will need to operate in equity crowdfunding markets in order to reduce adverse selection *and* moral hazard problems. These mechanisms can operate within and outside ECF firms and can be formal or informal in nature. An information economics perspective suggests that without an effective bundle of governance mechanisms, the equity crowdfunding market is unlikely to remain a viable alternative in entrepreneurial finance. Thus the role of corporate governance in equity crowdfunding should become a central part of the future research agenda.

9.3 Governance mechanisms (potentially) embedded in equity crowdfunding markets

Drawing on the governance as well as the broader management (e.g., Certo, 2003; Filatotchev & Wright, 2005), entrepreneurship (e.g., Uhlaner et al., 2007; Wright et al., 2013), and finance (e.g., La Porta et al., 2000; Shleifer & Vishny, 1997) literature, we develop a conceptual model of the multitude of governance mechanisms that may operate in equity crowdfunding markets. These mechanisms start with the crowd (investors) but also cover entrepreneurs, the crowdfunding platform, and the national level. As the discussion to follow and related Table 9.1 make clear, these mechanisms vary in terms of their formality (vs informality) and whether they are internal or external. Next, we discuss the effectiveness of these mechanisms in addressing adverse selection and moral hazard problems, respectively. We also identify a large range of issues for future research to examine, especially in reference to how these governance mechanisms may influence ECF firm success.

TABLE 9.1 Governance mechanisms that potentially operate in equity crowdfunding markets.

Governance mechanism	Adverse selection	Moral hazard
Crowdinvestors		
Wisdom of the crowd	++	0
	When markets are wise, this mechanism might be very effective in reducing adverse selection problems	The wisdom of the crowd mechanism may reveal moral hazard issues. However, the diversity in backgrounds, goals, and time horizons of equity crowdinvestors may provide more discretion to entrepreneurs, thereby fostering moral hazard problems. Ultimately, other governance mechanisms will be required to control moral hazard issues
Entrepreneurs		
Signaling	+	0 to +
	Entrepreneurial signaling may decrease adverse selection and minimize the need for formal regulations that increase information availability	Signaling is unlikely to be effective to reduce moral hazard, unless it is combined with other governance mechanisms, such as active secondary markets or strong investor protection laws
Platforms		
Due diligence	+	0
	If the wisdom of the crowds mechanism functions, probably most important to reduce fraud cases and assure that information provided on platform represents the facts	Should be ineffective
Shareholder structure	0 to +	0 to +
	Both direct and nominee shareholder structures do not directly address adverse selection issues. In the coinvestment structure, however, crowdinvestors may benefit from the due diligence efforts of others	The direct shareholder structure might be more problematic in dealing with moral hazard problems, but the nominee structure and coinvestment structure might be more effective because of shareholder concentration
Secondary markets	0	+
	Should be ineffective	May be effective through creating a form of market discipline
Country institutions		
Formal	+	+ to ++
	Laws that increase information availability may be important but can also be problematic as they raise the cost of firms that search for equity crowdfunding	Strong investor protection laws may be important to curtail self-dealing and other moral hazard problems. The effectiveness of these laws may dependent on how elaborate shareholder agreements are between crowdinvestors and the ECF firm
Informal	+	+
	Informal institutions such as country-level trust may be efficient to reduce both adverse selection and moral hazard problems. Informal and formal institutions may have complementary or substitutive effects	

Notes. ++ = potentially very effective, + = potentially somewhat effective, and 0 = likely ineffective. *ECF*, Equity-crowdfunded.

9.3.1 Crowdinvestors

In successful equity crowdfunding campaigns, firms typically attract funding from several hundreds of small investors (i.e., "the crowd") (Vismara, 2016). This is different from the traditional entrepreneurial finance model, where firms generally raise financing from one or a few investors. Traditional external equity financiers who support entrepreneurship, such as VCs and angel investors, generally rely on formal, extensive, and costly due diligence processes that usually occur before (potentially) making an investment, aiming to minimize adverse selection issues in the entrepreneurial finance market (Fried & Hisrich, 1994). As Arthurs and Busenitz (2003: 150) note, "the due diligence process is a form of insurance against potential adverse selection." Through a detailed analysis of investee firms' business plans, meetings with entrepreneurs and other activities, investors, and their external consultants aim to separate high-quality firms from low-quality firms. Nevertheless, these due diligence activities entail fixed costs that do not vary with the investment size. As a consequence, the cost of these activities for individual equity crowdinvestors would be prohibitively expensive relative to their small investments.[2]

The equity crowdfunding market, however, rely on another, external and more informal governance mechanism aiming to minimize adverse selection risks: the "wisdom of the crowd" (Table 9.1). The wisdom of the crowd principle (e.g., Surowiecki, 2005) suggests that crowds have more diverse sources of information and expertise than any individual (even when that individual is an expert), which can be leveraged through group decision-making (Schwienbacher & Larralde, 2012). Although there is noise in the decision-making of each individual, this noise is canceled out because of a large number of individuals in the investor crowd. Ultimately, this approach is believed to lead to better decision-making by the crowd as a whole than decision-making by the smartest individual from the crowd or an expert (e.g., Mollick & Nanda, 2016). Thus the crowd might be more effective in minimizing adverse selection issues relative to the traditional financiers of entrepreneurship.

The wisdom of the crowd mechanism in equity crowdfunding relates closely to the idea that public equity markets are efficient at least in a semistrong form. This idea implies that while each individual investor may lack the full set of publicly available information on firms, the stock prices reflect all publicly available information and expectations about the future. As Jensen (1978: 96) notes, "Indeed, the [the Semi-strong Form of the] Efficient Market Hypothesis progressed from the state of a curiosity taken seriously by only a few scientists in the economics and finance communities, to that of a dominant paradigm in finance." One key difference with public equity markets, however, is that much less information is publicly available on small and young ECF firms.

---

[2] Isenberg (2012) suggests that venture capital investors "spent about $50,000 just in legal fees, and sometimes hundreds of hours studying the ventures' markets, engaging in business model discussions, talking to prospective customers, interviewing industry experts, studying the technology and intellectual property, and talking to each founder's references, sometimes ten or more per founder." Such due diligence costs are excessive given that the average investment by an individual investor on Crowdcube—a leading UK-based equity crowdfunding platform—for instance, is only about £20,000 ($26,500) (Vismara, 2016).

To date, we lack empirical evidence on the potential utility of the wisdom of the crowd in equity crowdfunding, relative to the traditional due diligence activities performed by professional investors to reduce adverse selection problems.[3] There may certainly be constraints to the wisdom of the crowds, leading some critics to talk about the "madness of crowds." Isenberg (2012), for instance, observes that "crowds bring us tulip crazes, subprime meltdowns, the Kitty Genovese scandal, Salem witch trials, and other tragedies." Social psychologists and cognitive scientists have also pointed out problems with group decision-making such as groupthink (Janis, 1982) and social loafing (Latané, Williams, & Harkins, 1979). However, we are also much aware of problems with venture capital decision-making. VCs, for instance, maybe overconfident, which may negatively affect their decision accuracy (Zacharakis & Shepherd, 2001). VCs also often overemphasize an entrepreneurial team's human capital when making investment decisions (Baum & Silverman, 2004). Thus both the decision-making of crowds and experts may be imperfect. Scholars will need to investigate under which conditions either one of them (or potentially a combination of both) will work better to reduce adverse selection problems.

Next to addressing adverse selection problems, we need also to consider the possible role of the crowd in addressing moral hazard issues (Table 9.1). Contrary to external equity financiers who write detailed contracts and are also involved in postinvestment monitoring activities (by taking seat in the board of directors, holding frequent meetings with management and similar approaches) to reduce moral hazard problems (e.g., Sapienza et al., 1996), it might be economically infeasible for individual equity crowdinvestors to bear such contracting and monitoring costs. Also, free rider problems are especially acute because if one equity crowdinvestor actively monitors (and bears the full cost), this investor must share the benefits with others who do not bear a cost. Finally, the crowd represents a diverse group of investors with distinct backgrounds, who may have very different secondary motives besides realizing financial gains, including investing for fun or social purposes. As a result, they may also have different time horizons. These differences make coordination difficult as crowdinvestors may disagree among themselves on how the firm should evolve.

The abovementioned problems are similar to what dispersed shareholders in public firms experience (e.g., Hart, 1995). While there are several mechanisms that protect dispersed shareholders against moral hazard issues in public firms, the wisdom of the crowd mechanism by itself may not be very effective in reducing moral hazard problems after the investment in ECF firms. One reason is that in public firms, information intermediaries, such as stock analysts and specialized media, often actively track the behavior and performance of listed firms and their management teams (Healy & Palepu, 2001; Pollock & Rindova, 2003; Pollock et al., 2008). These intermediaries bring information to dispersed public shareholders in a more efficient way than when each shareholder

---

[3] There is some evidence on the wisdom of crowds in rewards-based crowdfunding and lending-based crowdfunding (e.g., Iyer et al., 2015; Mollick and Nanda, 2016). Nevertheless, while predicting the likelihood that firms will provide specific rewards that fulfill a funder's expectations or repay their debts is also difficult, informational asymmetry is especially high in the equity crowdfunding context (Chapter 10: Signaling in equity crowdfunding). Thus the ability to select high-quality entrepreneurial firms with no (or a limited) track record may be particularly challenging (Isenberg, 2012).

would monitor individually. However, these intermediaries do not focus on ECF firms which often remain "under the radar." Another reason is that even when equity crowdinvestors observe specific moral hazard issues in ECF firms, they might lack the power to influence entrepreneurs' (or managers') behaviors. Indeed, contrary to investors in public firms who can sell their shares on public capital markets and thus enforce market discipline, equity crowdinvestors invest in illiquid shares that are very difficult, if not impossible to sell (Signori & Vismara, 2018). A final reason is that while there is always the possibility of a (hostile) takeover risk for public firms with dispersed ownership so that management can be replaced (Schneper & Guillén, 2004), entrepreneurs in ECF firms generally retain a significant ownership percentage, which makes such actions infeasible. Overall, although the crowd might be wise in that it spots moral hazard problems, without other governance mechanisms the crowd will be extremely constrained in addressing these problems.

9.3.2 Entrepreneurs

In agency theory, informational asymmetry problems may allow entrepreneurs to engage in opportunistic behaviors. As a result, an important task of the principal (shareholders) is to device corporate governance mechanisms that minimize adverse selection and moral hazard problems (Arthurs & Busenitz, 2003). However, in an information economics perspective, particularly high-quality entrepreneurs can (and do) also take actions that reduce information asymmetry problems related to their own abilities, the quality of their projects, and the prospects of their firms.

One important way entrepreneurs can reduce potential adverse selection issues, for example, is through signaling—where entrepreneurs provide credible pieces of information on firms' unobservable quality and intentions including strategic moves (e.g., Connelly, Certo, Ireland, & Reutzel, 2011; Porter, 1980). As indicated in Table 9.1, signaling by entrepreneurs may serve as an internal, informal governance mechanism that gets activated as entrepreneurs engage in the acquisition of equity crowdfunding (or other external resources). Because entrepreneurs may have incentives to positively bias information or withhold negative information when they search for external financial resources, simply stating that they are "good" or of high quality will not be effective (Amit et al., 1998). In signaling theory (Spence, 1973), which has its roots in information economics as well, observable attributes function as a credible signal of unobservable quality, when these attributes are correlated with unobservable quality and are costly or difficult to obtain for low-quality firms relative to high-quality firms. Thus by signaling, high-quality entrepreneurs can potentially differentiate their firms from low-quality entrepreneurs, thereby reducing adverse selection issues.

Extensive research has shown how entrepreneurs and managers engage in signaling to ease resource attraction, for example, when making decisions about their boards' structures by having prominent board members (e.g., Certo, 2003; Certo et al., 2001) and with endorsement relationships, including prominent VC investors and alliance partners (e.g., Colombo et al., 2018; Stuart, Hoang, & Hybels, 1999), among others. Equity crowdfunding research further suggests that entrepreneurs signal unobservable firm quality to equity crowdinvestors, aiming to increase their fundraising success (Chapter 10: Signaling in equity crowdfunding, and Chapter 12: Cash-flow and voting rights in equity crowdfunding;

see alsoVismara, 2016; Vulkan et al., 2016). One consistent finding, for instance, is that when entrepreneurs retain more equity, this serves as an important signal that positively impacts the probability of funding success (Chapter 10: Signaling in equity crowdfunding, and Chapter 12: Cash-flow and voting rights in equity crowdfunding; Vismara, 2016). Moreover, Chapter 10: Signaling in equity crowdfunding shows that when entrepreneurs provide more detailed information about risks they increase the probability of funding success. Vismara (2016) also shows that social capital influences the probability of funding success.

Nevertheless, existing studies on equity crowdfunding—just like signaling studies in the management literature more broadly—examine how signals influence resource attraction, but this does *not* provide direct evidence that these signals are effective mechanisms in reducing adverse selection issues. Further, existing research has not fully leveraged insights from signaling theory in information economics. More specifically, for signals to separate high-quality from low-quality entrepreneurs and their firms, the signal's expectations (i.e., the correlation between the observable characteristic and unobservable quality) should eventually get confirmed (Bergh, Connelly, Ketchen, & Shannon, 2014). However, we lack evidence on whether specific signals are eventually correlated with firm success and might be an effective governance tool for entrepreneurs to reduce adverse selection concerns. The growing availability of data in the crowdfunding context should allow scholars to address these important issues in future studies and provides the potential to make important contributions to signaling theory as well.

Moreover, as detailed earlier, existing studies have shown how entrepreneurs can signal with prominent broad members, or prominent exchange partners (Certo, 2003; Stuart et al., 1999). An important question that remains, however, is how entrepreneurs of very early stage firms can assemble the resources needed to attract managerial talent or prominent affiliates and stack their boards with industry leaders (e.g., Shane, 2003) with which entrepreneurs can signal their unobservable quality. Moreover, many early stage firms do not have formal boards (Uhlaner et al., 2007). Given these factors, the equity crowdfunding context provides an ideal setting in which to examine these important issues. Chapter 10: Signaling in equity crowdfunding, for instance, presents evidence that equity crowdinvestors also rely on "cheap talk" or nonbinding, nonverifiable, and costless claims made by entrepreneurs (Farrell & Rabin, 1996). Specifically, claims by entrepreneurs that they envisage an initial public offering (IPO) exit (48% of entrepreneurs in their sample do) increases the odds of a successful equity crowdfunding campaign. This finding suggests that equity crowdinvestors rely not only on credible signals but also on other types of communication. Thus there is a possibility that equity crowdinvestors react to communications that do not present the facts, which may actually foster adverse selection problems in the equity crowdfunding context. This evidence provides opportunities for further research that examines how entrepreneurs combine credible signaling and other forms of communication, why the investors would rely on cheap talk, and when different types of signals or other types of communications become more impactful for subsequent resource attraction and firm success.

Finally, just like equity crowdfunding studies have focused on possible signaling by entrepreneurs around the time of the equity crowdfunding campaign (e.g., Chapter 10: Signaling in equity crowdfunding), entrepreneurial finance scholars have generally investigated signaling around specific events, including VC fundraising or an IPO (e.g., Certo, 2003; Colombo et al., 2018; Ko & McKelvie, 2018). However, more substantive actions that relate to firm professionalization with which entrepreneurs signaled to raise early funds, such as setting up a formal board of directors, may have a more long-standing impact on firm behavior and success. Moreover, high-quality entrepreneurs may have incentives to engage in signaling across time, and low-quality entrepreneurs can also (deliberately or not) provide signals that reveal their true nature (Arthurs and Busenitz, 2003). For instance, by providing timely and accurate information and professionalizing their boards, high-quality entrepreneurs can signal their trustworthiness. By doing so, these entrepreneurs can also reduce the need for formal governance mechanisms discussed earlier. However, the question remains how equity crowdinvestors can take corrective actions when they receive signals of low-quality, inappropriate behavior, or suboptimal behavior after the investment has taken place. Given that crowdinvestors obtain shares that are illiquid and cannot be easily traded, this suggests that while signaling by entrepreneurs may be a valuable informal governance mechanism, it is not sufficient by itself to minimize moral hazard problems (Table 9.1).

9.3.3 Crowdfunding platforms

When entrepreneurs decide they want to raise funding through a specific equity crowd-funding platform, their firms will not be automatically listed on these platforms. Rather, equity crowdfunding platforms play an increasingly important role in filtering firms for their audiences (Younkin & Kashkooli, 2016; Cumming, Johan, & Zhang, 2019). These platforms also play a key role in determining the way in which the relationship between firms and equity crowdinvestors will be structured. In some cases, for example, crowdinvestors become direct shareholders in the firms they wish to fund, but other platforms have used alternative structures.

There are a host of equity crowdfunding platforms active across the globe and even within single countries (Dushnitsky, Guerini, Piva, & Rossi-Lamastra, 2016). For instance, in Italy, there are 10 active equity crowdfunding platforms, and some of these platforms come from abroad. Consequently, there will be a strong pressure for reputation building (e.g., Petkova, 2012) and professionalization by crowdfunding platforms to attract the best projects, retain a large base of equity crowdinvestors, and withstand competition from peers (Fleming & Sorenson, 2016). If people observe many outright fraud cases or failures on specific platforms, these platforms may experience a significant drop in the number of entrepreneurs who want to list their firms on these platforms and a similar significant drop in crowdinvestors who want to contribute funds through the platforms. Such a situation may threaten the very survival of an equity crowdfunding platform. Moreover, competition from traditional entrepreneurial finance markets, including venture capital and angel markets, may further push the equity crowdfunding market and individual platforms to professionalize and consolidate.

Such reputational concerns by equity crowdfunding platforms and competition from alternative forms of financing may give equity crowdfunding platforms strong incentives to preselect the highest quality firms. To mitigate adverse selection problems, different crowdfunding platforms carry out due diligence (Table 9.1), although there is great variance in the extent of such due diligence across platforms. Crowdfunding platform due diligence comprises background checks, site visits, credit checks, cross-checks, account monitoring, and third-party proof on funding projects. Cumming, Johan, and Zhang (2019) find evidence of more due diligence performed by Canadian platforms that have fewer projects per employee (the busyness of platform employees constrains the ability to carry out due diligence) and incentive fee structures (platforms with fixed fees regardless of campaign outcomes carry out less due diligence). Also, they provide empirical evidence that equity crowdfunding platforms conduct more due diligence than rewards-based crowdfunding platforms. Because due diligence screens lower quality projects, Cumming, Johan, and Zhang (2019) also find that more extensive due diligence by platforms is associated with a higher percentage of successful campaigns and larger capital raises on these platforms. Subsequent research (Rossi & Vismara, 2018) from investment-based platforms in France, Italy, Germany, and the United Kingdom is supportive of these findings.

While some equity crowdfunding platforms engage in due diligence to reduce adverse selection issues, we currently lack compelling evidence if this due diligence is effective and ultimately leads to more successful firms being funded (and not just firms that raise more financing on these platforms). Such questions are important also because more detailed due diligence by crowdfunding platforms may also be at odds with the wisdom of the crowd mechanism, as discussed earlier. Specifically, if the crowds are wise, the primary role of equity crowdfunding platforms would be to avoid outright fraud cases getting on the platforms and assure that the information provided in the crowdfunding campaign represents the facts. However, if equity crowdfunding platforms increasingly mirror the selection criteria typically used by traditional investors in entrepreneurial ventures, this may limit the possibility of equity crowdfunding to democratize entrepreneurial finance.

Different equity crowdfunding platforms further employ different shareholder structures—that is, how they structure the relationship between crowdinvestors and firms—that may influence the incentives and power of equity crowdinvestors to reduce moral hazard problems after their investments (Table 9.1). However, how these different structures influence ECF firm actions and performance remain virtually unexplored, although there may be significant variability in their effectiveness to address moral hazard problems. In Table 9.2, we provide more insights on the most prominent structures adopted by equity crowdfunding platforms, their potential advantages, and disadvantages.

Some platforms use a direct shareholder model where each equity crowdinvestor individually becomes a direct shareholder in a firm. In the case of Crowdcube, a leading UK-based equity crowdfunding platform, depending on the presence of a possible investment threshold, crowdinvestors may receive A-shares with voting and preemptive rights when they invest at or above the threshold or receive B-shares without voting and preemptive rights when they invest below the threshold (Cumming, Johan, & MacIntosh, 2017). Crowdcube does not recommend any shareholders' agreement for the crowd. The direct shareholder model most closely resembles the private firm with dispersed ownership, where an informational economics perspective suggests that shareholders may have little incentive and power to monitor (Hart, 1995). As we highlighted before, the wisdom of the crowd by itself might have limited ability to limit moral hazard problems. While this shareholder structure might be less effective in reducing moral hazard problems, it also has advantages. For instance, it might foster "the feeling of belonging" (Belleflamme et al., 2014: 589) by being more directly connected to the ECF firm.

TABLE 9.2 Shareholder structures employed by equity crowdfunding platforms.

	Direct model	Nominee model	Coinvestment model
Definition:	Equity crowdinvestors become direct shareholders in the ECF firm	Equity crowdinvestors invest in a "special purpose vehicle" and thus are not direct shareholders in the ECF firm. A "nominee" manages the shares of all equity crowdinvestors	The equity crowdfunding platform requires that next to a commitment by the crowd, a professional investor (venture capitalist or business angel) also commits funding
Advantages:	Fosters a sense of belonging by the crowd	Limits coordination problems between crowdinvestors. Increases the power and incentives to monitor entrepreneurs	Detailed due diligence and monitoring by the professional investor
Disadvantages:	Limited power and incentives for individual crowdinvestors to monitor and influence entrepreneurs	May hamper the sense of belonging by crowdinvestors. Potential differences in goals between the nominee and the crowd may create new agency issues	Potential principal–principal problems between the crowd and professional investors
Example:	Crowdcube	Seedrs	SyndicateRoom

ECF, Equity-crowdfunded.

Other platforms use a nominee structure. In this case, equity crowdinvestors do not become direct shareholders in firms, but they invest in "special purpose vehicles" that combine all equity crowdinvestors and are managed by nominees (i.e., the platform itself or an external individual). For instance, in the case of Seedrs—another prominent UK-based equity crowdfunding platform—the platform does not appoint external nominees, but the management board of Seedrs Limited acts as a nominee. Seedrs develops subscription agreements with ECF firms that generally include consent rights that cover issues such as the winding-up of ECF firm, issuing preference shares, transferring assets out of the ECF firm, making certain loans, or increasing director salaries beyond an agreed level. The management board of Seedrs Limited is authorized to take votes and issue consents on behalf of each individual investor that provided funds through Seedrs. However, Seedrs Limited does not take a seat on the board of their portfolio companies. Because nominees generally share in the value created at an exit, they have incentives to monitor, and free rider problems among individual crowdinvestors are avoided. The nominee structure further reduces shareholder dispersion and decreases coordination costs, giving the nominee the power to influence entrepreneurs' behaviors. A potential disadvantage of this structure is that it decreases crowdinvestors' feeling of belonging by creating a wedge between the crowd and the ECF firm.

Other platforms (e.g., SyndicateRoom) require firms to also obtain cofunding from VCs or angel investors. In this case the equity crowdinvestors benefit from the detailed due diligence and monitoring activities by the professional (lead) investor (Agrawal, Catalini, & Goldfarb, 2016). This structure resembles syndication in venture capital investments, with the difference that nonleading venture capital investors also conduct their own detailed due diligence and monitor the portfolio companies as well (Baeyens, Vanacker, & Manigart, 2006). While this structure may seem to combine the best of two worlds (detailed due diligence and monitoring by a professional investor and the wisdom of the crowds), it also raises new concerns related to harmful coinvestments, and principal–principal problems (e.g., Morck & Yeung, 2003). For example, there is the risk that more powerful venture capital investors expropriate wealth from less powerful crowdinvestors. Still, venture capital investors often care about their reputations, which are crucial in their industry, and as such, they might refrain from taking actions that harm other minority shareholders in ECF firms.

Another recent development is that some equity crowdfunding platforms, including Crowdcube and Seedrs, have started to experiment with the creation of secondary markets to increase liquidity (Table 9.1). Currently, the shares of ECF firms are illiquid and difficult to trade (Signori & Vismara, 2018). Some crowdfunding platforms, for example, enable investors to trade shares at "fair value" to current investors in a given firm (e.g., Seedrs). Others have organized an on-platform secondary share trade (e.g., Crowdcube). More liquid secondary markets may increase the information available through the share price. When minority shareholders are unhappy with firms' plans or actions, they can sell their shares. When entrepreneurs cannot convince other prospective investors of the value of their plans or actions, entrepreneurs will see the value of their shares decreasing. Overall, such market discipline might influence entrepreneurial behavior and minimize moral hazard issues.

9.3.4 Country institutions

Countries' formal (i.e., the codified rules and standards) and informal institutions (i.e., the collective meanings, values, and understandings shared by its inhabitants) define or enforce socially acceptable behavior and thereby influence firm performance (Holmes et al., 2003, 2016; North, 1990; Scott, 1995). Some of these institutions may limit the adverse selection and moral hazard problems, as indicated in Table 9.1. For instance, stronger investor protection enshrined in a country's legal codes and regulatory frameworks may limit managers' ability to engage in self-dealing, including executive perquisites, excessive compensation, or even outright theft of corporate assets (Djankov et al., 2008; Shleifer & Vishny, 1997). There are also important differences between national cultures and dominant values. For instance, higher country-level trust might reduce opportunistic behavior by individuals (Arthurs & Busenitz, 2003; La Porta et al., 1997a). Such informal institutions also support and reinforce formal institutions; together, they can significantly reduce informational problems, thereby fostering the growth of financial markets and the performance of firms.

An influential stream of research in the "law and finance" tradition draws on the seminal work of La Porta et al. (1997b). It advances that countries that are characterized by stronger shareholder protection (e.g., United Kingdom or United States) have significantly larger and broader public equity markets. This insight has led scholars not only to focus on the role of formal institutions for public equity market development but also examine how formal and informal institutions influence the behavior of venture capital investors and the development of venture capital markets as a whole. For instance, cross-country differences in legality have a significant impact on the governance structure of investments in the venture capital industry: better laws facilitate faster deal screening and deal origination, lower the probability of potentially harmful coinvestment, and facilitate investor board representation (Cumming, Schmidt, & Walz, 2010). Cultural distance between venture capital investors and entrepreneurs may also hamper deal screening, contracting, and postinvestment involvement and monitoring (Li et al., 2014). Ultimately, formal institutions and informal national cultural constraints can even influence the development of venture capital markets as a whole (Armour and Cumming, 2006; Li & Zahra, 2012).

Several scholars have provided a descriptive picture of the formal legal institutions related to equity crowdfunding markets and, more specifically the laws that regulate access to equity crowdfunding for firms and crowdinvestors (e.g., Vismara, 2016; Horváthová, 2019). Legal restrictions on public offerings of shares to the general public have constrained the development of equity crowdfunding markets in many countries (Bruton et al., 2015). For instance, to date, equity crowdfunding has played a trivial role in the United States, probably because the Securities and Exchange commission (SEC) regulations require entrepreneurial firms that solicit equity investments from nonaccredited investors to register for a disproportionately costly public offering. With the SEC approval of Title III of the Jumpstart Our Business Startups act, nonaccredited, amateur investors will now be able to invest in such entrepreneurial firms.[4] Other studies have begun to investigate how formal (e.g., regulations) and informal (e.g., individualism) institutions influence the size of specific crowdfunding markets (e.g., Chapter 6: Crowdfunding cleantech; see also Rau, 2018).

Chapter 15: Crowdfunding regulation and policy, Table 15.1 (see also Horváthová, 2019, Table 28.1) summarizes equity crowdfunding regulation in 42 countries around the world. Countries with specific crowdfunding regulations as at 2017 include Austria (2015), Canada (2015), China (2015), Finland (2016), France (2014), Germany (2015), Israel (2017), Italy (2012), Japan (2014), Lithuania (2016), The Netherlands (2016), New Zealand (2014), Portugal (2015), Spain (2015), the United Kingdom (2000), and the United States (2012, 2015). Countries without specific crowdfunding regulations normally have securities regulations that are pertinent to crowdfunding activities, including Australia, Belgium, Brazil, Bulgaria, Croatia, Cyprus, Czech Republic, Denmark, Estonia, Greece, Hong Kong, Hungary, Iceland, Ireland, Malta, Poland, Romania, Slovakia, Slovenia, Sweden, and Switzerland. And some countries have crowdfunding legislation recently proposed but not yet signed into law, including Australia, Israel, Latvia, and Luxembourg. And other countries such as Russia have recently put together working groups to develop crowdfunding rule proposals.

However, existing research has only skimmed the surface of how country institutions may limit adverse selection and moral hazard issues in equity crowdfunding markets. One may wonder why there is such limited research, given the widespread interest in institutions. We believe this lack of evidence again relates to the current focus in equity crowdfunding research on "funding success." Thus as highlighted before, while some studies have started to study how institutions influence the size of equity crowdfunding

---

[4] Hornuf and Schwienbacher (2017a) provide an excellent overview of regulatory reforms in several countries across the globe related to equity crowdfunding.

markets as a whole, we particularly lack empirical evidence on how bundles of country-level institutions might influence the development of viable ECF firms in different countries. In addressing such questions, scholars need to address several complex issues.

One common issue is that scholars often talk about "laws" but typically ignore heterogeneity in the scope and goals of the laws (Table 9.1). Specifically, some laws focus on allowing firms to raise equity crowdfunding (or not) and regulate the amounts of money that firms can raise or the maximum amount of money investors can invest in equity crowdfunding campaigns. For instance, in the United Kingdom, there is an aggregate investment limit of 10% of the net investable financial assets that can be allocated to equity crowdfunding by individual investors (Hornuf & Schwienbacher, 2017a). In essence, these laws might have limited effects on reducing potential adverse selection and moral hazard problems but do limit the exposure of investors to the risks involved in equity crowdfunding.

Other laws focus on increasing the flow of information toward equity crowdinvestors. Consequently, these laws might limit potential adverse selection and make it more likely that equity crowdinvestors detect moral hazard problems in ECF firms. However, they might still be hampered in taking corrective actions against such behaviors. Using a theoretical model, Hornuf and Schwienbacher (2017a) provide interesting insights on the impact of exemptions to prospectus regulations on entrepreneurs' fundraising decisions. Specifically, they argue that restrictive exemptions may create a funding gap for small firms. Yet, insights from laws that increase (or decrease) the information requirements for firms that search for equity crowdfunding (and thus impact the costs of firms that search for equity crowdfunding) are not necessarily generalizable to investor protection laws in general.

Indeed, still other laws focus on the rights that shareholders have vis-à-vis the assets of the firm and how shareholders can appeal to the courts and enforce their rights when entrepreneurs violate the terms of the contract (Shleifer & Vishny, 1997) (note that these laws do not necessarily increase the costs for entrepreneurs that search for equity crowdfunding when they stick to the shareholders' agreement). While we lack empirical evidence, these laws may be effective in minimizing moral hazard problems, thereby improving ECF firm performance. Overall, this suggests that we need a much finer-grained understanding of how distinct aspects of laws may influence the development of viable ECF firms, which can also bring important contributions to the law and finance literature.

A related issue is that scholars often borrow and employ legal measures that have been developed for a specific set of firms (e.g., public firms with dispersed ownership). However, the legal reality can be very different for another set of firms (e.g., firms with concentrated ownership). As Bebchuk and Hamdani (2009: 1263–1264) argue:

> The impact of many key governance arrangements depends considerably on companies' ownership structure: measures that protect outside investors in a company without a controlling shareholder are often irrelevant or even harmful when it comes to investor protection in companies with a controlling shareholder, and vice versa. Consequently, governance metrics that purport to apply to companies regardless of ownership structure are bound to miss the mark with respect to one or both types of firms.

For instance, several elements of the widely used Anti-Director Rights Index (La Porta et al., 1997b) are not relevant for firms with a controlling shareholder. More specifically, elements of the Anti-Director Rights Index, such as shareholders' ability to vote by mail or to call a special meeting, will be ineffective in protecting the rights of minority shareholders (e.g., crowdinvestors) in firms where entrepreneurs hold the majority of shares. Indeed, in such a situation, the crowd (or any other minority shareholder) will lack power to fundamentally influence or challenge entrepreneurs, as majority shareholders. The Anti-Self-Dealing Index (Djankov et al., 2008), however, does focus on elements that protect minority shareholders from firms with a controlling shareholder. In a similar vein, scholars have sometimes paid disproportionate attention to corporate bankruptcy laws, while personal bankruptcy laws may be theoretically more impactful in an entrepreneurial setting (Armour & Cumming, 2008).

Our preceding observations suggest that, as we move forward, it will be particularly important to develop appropriate legal measures that take heterogeneity in laws and contexts—with different informal institutions as well—into account to increase our understanding of how bundles of country institutions could foster the development of viable ECF firms.

9.4 Governance as the protection of value and the creation of value

The idea that entrepreneurs have an information advantage with respect to the quality of their firms, projects, and own abilities, over external stakeholders, including investors, is well established in the literature (Amit et al., 1998). Consequently, entrepreneurs can use this information advantage to the detriment of other stakeholders. Up to this point, our analysis has primarily focused on the role of corporate governance in avoiding adverse selection and moral hazard problems (Table 9.1) or, in other words, the role of governance in protecting shareholders' wealth. This focus is commonplace in the corporate governance literature (e.g., Uhlaner et al., 2007).

However, scholars have also highlighted situations in which entrepreneurs lack information about their industry, their competitors, and the new capabilities that will be required as their firms grow (Zahra & Filatotchev, 2004). These "blind spots" in the information, knowledge, and experiences of entrepreneurs are one of the main reasons why professional equity investors often spend significant effort and time on their so-called "coach" function (e.g., Colombo & Grilli, 2010; Sapienza et al., 1996). There is increasing recognition in the governance literature that governance could also serve as a source of wealth creation in firms (e.g., Filatotchev & Wright, 2005; Zahra et al., 2009). For instance, firms' board of directors or advisory boards may help entrepreneurs to collect new information about their industry and competitors, helping entrepreneurs to make more effective strategic choices (Zahra et al., 2009).

Thus while entrepreneurs may have certain information advantages relative to other stakeholders, some stakeholders may also have specific information advantages relative to entrepreneurs. Ultimately, the exchange of information among key actors in the corporate governance systems of firms will be crucial for their long-term success (e.g., Zahra & Filatotchev, 2004). However, we currently lack insights on how the governance mechanisms in the equity crowdfunding market—and particularly the wisdom of the crowd— may bring new information to entrepreneurs, allowing them to potentially make not only better strategic decisions that benefit firm development but also the potential downsides of these mechanisms. We propose that the equity crowdfunding market and equity crowdinvestors may provide both opportunities and threats to information exchange and, as a result, value creation in ECF firms.

More specifically, crowdfunding campaigns can play a key role in bringing new information and knowledge to entrepreneurs that provide them with important insights into opportunities and how to best pursue them (Afuah & Tucci, 2012). This role can be performed in multiple ways. First, the equity crowdfunding market may provide a "laboratory" for entrepreneurs and equity crowdinvestors alike. Entrepreneurs can pitch their business ideas to a broad set of individuals. Significant investment interest by the crowd indirectly provides information to entrepreneurs about the viability of their ideas. For equity crowdinvestors, it further allows spreading the risk related to funding early stage, potentially innovative ideas. Second, entrepreneurs may also acquire valuable information in a more direct way. Individual equity crowdinvestors, for example, not only contribute (small) amounts of money, but they are also frequently active in providing comments, feedback, and innovative ideas to entrepreneurs. The indirect and direct information flows from equity crowdinvestors to entrepreneurs might provide the latter with more confidence in their business ideas and provide new information to better pursue existing opportunities, while at the same time pointing toward new opportunities.

However, the diversity of equity crowdinvestors—in terms of background, possible secondary motives to invest next to financial gains, and time horizons—might also bring significant challenges for ECF firms. Effective governance systems require an understanding of the motives of its key players (Zahra & Filatotchev, 2004), but the crowd could be so diverse that such an understanding is very difficult to obtain for entrepreneurs. The different feedback, comments, and ideas provided by a very diverse group of people can also lead to "information congestion." It is also likely that when entrepreneurs choose a specific strategic action that pleases some equity crowdinvestors, it makes others feel disgruntled. Finally, the information flows between equity crowdinvestors and entrepreneurs often occur in public. Such a situation may lead to the release of sensitive information that may ultimately harm the ECF firm. Thus despite the potential value of the vast amount of information that is embedded in the crowd for ECF firms, the same crowd also raises important challenges.

Overall, we not only call for more research on how governance mechanisms may limit informational asymmetry and related adverse selection and moral hazard issues in equity crowdfunding but also believe that it will be crucial for future scholarship to increase our theoretical and empirical understanding of how equity crowdinvestors may help to create value in ECF firms. From our abovementioned discussion, it should be clear that equity crowdinvestors can both contribute to, but also hamper, effective governance that creates value for ECF firms.

9.5 Discussion and conclusion

The equity crowdfunding context brings an important conundrum to the surface. On the one hand, practically, the global equity crowdfunding market is growing exponentially and has the potential to democratize entrepreneurial finance. On the other hand, theoretically, the equity crowdfunding market is expected to be replete with informational asymmetry problems, such as adverse selection and moral hazard, which may eventually cause market failure. In such a context, corporate governance can play a crucial role to diminish adverse selection and moral hazard problems and thereby sustain the growth of the global equity crowdfunding market.

Extant corporate governance research, however, has primarily focused on large and public firms. More recently, governance research has also embraced other, more common-place, organizational forms, such as small- and medium-sized enterprises and entrepre-neurial firms. Still, our understanding of what works (or does not work) in one type of firm may not simply generalize to other types of firms (Audretsch & Lehmann, 2014), including ECF firms. For example, relative to shareholders in public firms, shareholders in ECF firms obtain illiquid shares, which should limit capital market-based corporate gover-nance mechanisms. Or, relative to professional venture capital investors in entrepreneurial firms, the large number of small online crowdinvestors in ECF firms may have limited incentives and power to conduct a detailed due diligence and actively monitor their port-folio firms.

The current chapter calls for a fundamental shift in the focus of equity crowdfunding research, which has almost exclusively focused on the factors that drive funding success on equity crowdfunding platforms (e.g., Ahlers et al., 2015; Block, Hornuf, et al., 2018; Block, Colombo, et al., 2018; Guenther et al., 2018; Lukkarinen et al., 2016; Mamonov & Malaga, 2018; Mohammadi & Shafi, 2018; Vismara, 2016, 2018; Vulkan et al., 2016) and the funding dynamics on these platforms (e.g., Hornuf & Schwienbacher, 2018; Vismara, 2018). It is undeniably important to understand how entrepreneurs can more successfully raise funds on equity crowdfunding platforms. However, if entrepreneurs do not create viable businesses with the money raised, investors and society at large will ultimately obtain limited benefits. Thus it is probably even more important to understand what is happening after the equity crowdfunding campaign and, more specifically, how corporate governance can improve the viability and long-term success of these firms.

For this purpose, we have developed a conceptual model of mechanisms that could operate in the equity crowdfunding context to minimize adverse selection and moral hazard problems (see Table 9.1). We move beyond the most used theoretical framework in corporate governance, agency theory, which has largely focused on how shareholders (i.e., principals) should take actions to reduce agency problems created by entrepreneurs. Drawing on an information economics perspective, we suggest that a combination of actors can trigger or install a host of (internal or external, formal or informal) governance mechanisms to reduce adverse selection and moral hazard. These actors include crowdin-vestors, entrepreneurs themselves, equity crowdfunding platforms, and governments (see Table 9.1).

First, wisdom of the crowd effects may explain why equity crowdinvestors can select firms that are equally (more) likely to create value than professional investors, even when it does not make economic sense for crowdinvestors to conduct a detailed due diligence given their relatively small investments. Still, we lack evidence on wisdom of the crowd effects in equity crowdfunding markets. While empirical work on the possibility that equity crowdinvestors are (not) wise may not reach the contribution to theory threshold at many entrepreneurship/management journals, there is an increasing receptivity by lead-ing journals for replication-style studies (e.g., Bettis et al., 2016). Finance journals have also been more receptive for studies that examine important aspects of a specific phenomenon. For instance, hundreds of empirical papers have been published on the question whether (and the extent to which) public capital markets are efficient. However, by demonstrating the possible boundary conditions of wisdom of the crowd effects, there is still significant room for scholars to provide important theoretical contributions as well.

Second, entrepreneurs often provide credible signals to reduce adverse selection and moral hazard issues. While extant crowdfunding research has addressed how such signals could influence the ability of entrepreneurs to raise equity crowdfunding (e.g., Chapter 10: Signaling in equity crowdfunding), we argue that future research should also examine how these signals eventually relate to firm success. Some of these signals, such as setting up a formal board of directors and appointing prominent directors, may not only have a signaling value at the time of raising funds but could also have more substantive effects of ECF firm behavior and success after the investment. To address such questions, scholars will need to collect data not only from equity crowdfunding platforms but they will also need to collect firm-level data on the actions, strategies, and success after an equity crowd-funding campaign. With the increasing maturity of equity crowdfunding markets, we now have sufficient firms that can be tracked across time. Moreover, the increasing availability of data on private firms may provide significant benefits (e.g., Vanacker, Heughebaert, & Manigart, 2014). For instance, in several European countries (such as Belgium, France, Italy, Spain, and the United Kingdom), even the smallest and youngest firms report detailed financial accounts data.

Third, equity crowdfunding platforms may play an important role in assuring that the information firms provide on their platforms represents the facts, thereby reducing adverse selection problems. Different platforms also have different modes of operating—with some platforms, for example, allowing crowdinvestors to become direct shareholders in firms, while others use a nominee structure—which may have important consequences for ECF firm governance and subsequent firm performance. Unfortunately, to date, scholars have primarily focused on data from one specific platform (e.g., Dushnitsky & Fitza, 2018; Dushnitsky & Zunino, 2018). To increase our understanding of how platform structures and platform diversity influence firm performance, scholars will need to rely on broader datasets that include firms that were listed on different platforms. Obviously, entrepreneurs themselves may self-select by applying for a listing on specific platforms that fit best with their characteristics and the characteristics of their firms, which should make scholars wary of such self-selection effects.

Finally, governments set "the rules of the game" for equity crowdfunding, and the effectiveness of these rules, in combination with national cultures, could also significantly diminish adverse selection and moral hazard problems. The development of alternative factor markets such as the size and development of the venture capital and angel market might also be impactful. Existing crowdfunding research, however, has generally focused on funding success on a specific platform operating in a specific country. More recent research has also started to explore how formal and informal country institutions influence the size of equity crowdfunding markets. But, this focus has constrained our understanding of how national institutions influence the decisions and outcomes of ECF firms themselves. Again, we not only need evidence on the institutions and factor markets that influence the size of equity crowdfunding markets but also how they can influence the success of ECF firms. We call for research that uses cross-country datasets to examine how ECF firms develop and perform relative to similar firms that do not attract crowdfunding, and how national institutions moderate this relationship.

9.6 Additional avenues for future research

While in the core of the current chapter, we have already presented a research framework on the governance of ECF firms and its impact on firm success, we here present some additional avenues for future research.

First, our framework suggests that some governance mechanisms will probably be more effective than others in addressing adverse selection and moral hazard problems, respectively (Table 9.1). We also discussed these governance mechanisms in a largely sequential manner. However, it is important to acknowledge that any mechanism in isolation is unlikely to be completely effective in reducing severe adverse selection and moral hazard issues. Still, governance research is general has often focused on a specific governance mechanism, such as the board of directors, in isolation (e.g., Audretsch & Lehmann, 2014). The equity crowdfunding context opens up opportunities to examine how governance mechanisms at different levels (i.e., firm-platform-country) interact and impact firm development—an issue that remains underexplored in the broader governance literature (e.g., Aguilera, Filatotchev, Gospel, & Jackson, 2008; Vanacker et al., 2014; Strange, Filatotchev, Buck, & Wright, 2009). For example, a promising avenue for future research would be to examine how the heterogeneity in the strength of contracts between crowdinvestors and ECF firms (often linked to the choice of crowdfunding platform on which entrepreneurs will list their projects) and the national governance systems have a complementary or substitutive effect.

Second, our framework in Table 9.1 has primarily focused on governance mechanisms as value protection safeguards, a focus that is consistent with the broader governance literature. However, work on how corporate governance mechanisms can potentially create value in ECF firms is lacking. Equity crowdinvestors can provide ECF firms with more than money. Equity crowdinvestors often also provide feedback, and they could serve as ECF firm "ambassadors." The question of how entrepreneurs can attract valuable crowdinvestors remains unaddressed. We know that entrepreneurs can communicate with potential crowdinvestors through the platforms on which they are listed, but we do not know whether differences in entrepreneurial behavior allow firms to attract funding from a crowd with distinct characteristics and backgrounds—and whether this matters for ECF firm outcomes. Recent theoretical work indicates that firms may obtain distinct competitive advantages from engaging with online communities (Fisher, 2018). Still, to date, we lack evidence on whether, how and when equity crowdinvestors can add extra financial value to ECF firms.

Third, the current wave of research on crowdfunding and equity crowdfunding more in particular has further strengthened the already heavily segmented entrepreneurial finance literature (Cumming & Johan, 2016). Entrepreneurs generally use several sources of financing in order to form and grow their ventures (Cosh et al., 2009). Still, academic papers generally focus on one specific source of finance (or two sources at a maximum).

For instance, we have a relatively established literature on venture capital, angel financing, bank financing, trade debt, and now a growing stream of work on crowdfunding. However, cross-fertilization between these literatures remains very limited. The question of how entrepreneurs choose between these different sources of financing also remains largely unexplored. Existing equity crowdfunding research, for instance, has generally focused on the firms that are already listed on specific platforms (e.g., Walthoff-Borm, Vanacker, et al., 2018). We need a better theoretical and empirical understanding of why entrepreneurs search for specific sources of financing, how they combine different sources of financing, and how their bundle of financing sources influences firm behaviors and outcomes. Overall, we need more work that crosses the largely distinct literatures that are segmented by financing sources within the entrepreneurial finance literature.

9.7 Policy implications

While we currently lack evidence on the governance of ECF firms and its impact of firm performance, our conceptual framework provides some guidance and implications for policy-makers.

The need for governments to craft stricter regulations that reduce adverse selection problems in equity crowdfunding markets may be limited. Specifically, there are sufficient mechanisms at the crowd level and crowdfunding platform level that could be effective in dealing with adverse selection. At the crowd level, wisdom of the crowd effects can lead to the selection of firms that are equally, if not more, likely to create value relative to those firms selected professional investors. Even when future empirical work would suggest that crowds are not "wise," one can wonder whether it is the role of governments to protect the crowd against their "madness." It is probably sufficient for governments to craft "soft" regulations that limit crowdinvestors to invest excessive portions of their total wealth exclusively in equity crowdfunding. Besides this, crowdinvestors will learn with their own money whether the potential returns are worthwhile for the risk they take. Moreover, specific crowdinvestors may also value other benefits besides monetary returns such as supporting entrepreneurship. Furthermore, at the platform level, there are also some mechanisms that could reduce adverse selection issues. Platforms can perform more thorough due diligence to screen out the lowest quality firms. Platform managers have strong reputational incentives to device mechanisms that reduce adverse selection because over time more failures of ECF firms funded through their platforms are likely to reduce the inflow of new deals, thereby hampering the survival of their own business.

However, the role for governments to craft regulations that discourage moral hazard problems in ECF firms may be more critical. Once invested, even "wise" crowdinvestors obtain largely illiquid shares. In essence, they are locked in until an exit can be realized several years after their investment. Some platforms also take a relatively passive attitude after the crowdfunding campaign. While some platforms device more professional contracts and manage the shares of the crowd, they are not necessarily active in a board of directors. Platforms can also create coinvestment structures, where they require the crowd to coinvestment with professional investors, who have more incentives to monitor. Still, in all these cases, minority investors require efficient courts and investor laws that protect them against opportunistic behaviors by entrepreneurs, who often remain controlling shareholders. Fostering the development of capital market-based governance mechanisms, such as active secondary markets for the shares of ECF firms, could also be instrumental.

Governments not only serve as regulators of equity crowdfunding markets but also often provide individuals with tax reductions when they invest in early stage firms through equity crowdfunding platforms or other means. The general reason behind tax shelter initiatives is that they might activate the significant amounts of savings that otherwise just remain on savings accounts, thereby providing an increased stimulus to entrepreneurship and economic growth. Governments hence require research that informs them on whether the costs to support the development of equity crowdfunding market are worthwhile, given the benefits it creates. The question whether equity crowdfunding markets can create viable businesses and how this market can be governed to create more successful businesses is crucial from a policy perspective. If equity crowdfunding markets, however, mainly create firms "zombie firms" or "empty shells," this could not only imply the ineffectiveness of tax shelter initiative but actually entails that governments indirectly hamper the productivity of existing firms.

We see both opportunities and threats related to the developing equity crowdfunding market. We hope that the chapter forms starting point for significantly more research that increases our theoretical and empirical understanding of ECF firm governance and how it impacts ECF firm success. To date, we are left almost completely in the dark about these important topics.

Key terms

Adverse selection
Coinvestment model
Direct model
Due diligence
Formal governance
Hidden action
Hidden information
Informal governance
Moral hazard
Nominee model
Secondary markets
Shareholder structure
Wisdom of the crowd

Discussion questions

9.1. Explain the coinvestment model in equity crowdfunding. Which platforms use the model? What agency problems does it mitigate or exacerbate?

9.2. Explain the nominee model in equity crowdfunding. Which platforms use the model? What agency problems does it mitigate or exacerbate?

9.3. Explain the direct investment model in equity crowdfunding. Which platforms use the model? What agency problems does it mitigate or exacerbate?

9.4. What steps can crowdinvestors, entrepreneurs, and crowdfunding platforms take to mitigate moral hazard and adverse selection problems in equity crowdfunding? Explain in detail with reference to specific agency problems.

9.5. What is the difference between a formal and an informal governance mechanism? How do they mitigate or exacerbate specific moral hazard ad adverse selection problems?

10

Signaling in equity crowdfunding

10.1 Introduction

Crowdfunding is an umbrella term used to describe an increasingly widespread form of fundraising, typically via the Internet, whereby groups of people pool money, usually (very) small individual contributions, to support a particular goal. Despite increased attention by policy makers, regulators, investors, and founders, however, the mechanisms and dynamics of crowdfunding in general, and equity crowdfunding in particular, are not yet well understood (Griffin, 2013). Equity crowdfunding is a form of financing in which entrepreneurs make an open call to sell a specified amount of equity- or bond-like shares in a company on the Internet, hoping to attract a large group of investors. The open call and investments take place on an online platform (e.g., Crowdcube) that provides the means for the transactions (the legal groundwork, preselection, the ability to process financial transactions, etc.).

Small investors, who are often the primary target of start-ups on equity crowdfunding platforms, do not normally have the ability to extensively research and assess potential investments. In order to successfully raise money via an equity crowdfunding platform, therefore, start-ups as well as more mature companies will need to find ways for clearly signaling their value to small investors. Some are very successful, while others are not, as illustrated by two contrasting London-based equity crowdfunding cases, similar to the cases highlighted in Sections 8.6.2 and 8.6.3 in Chapter 8, Equity crowdfunding, valuation, and cases. In December 2011 The Rushmore Group, a start-up that now operates three bars in London, sold 10% of its equity for £1,000,000 to 143 small investors through Crowdcube. The aspiring entrepreneurs of The Rushmore Group accomplished this feat in a little over 2 weeks—a remarkable success story. In early April 2012, another owner and operator of a London bar, Meatballs, offered a 25% equity stake for £300,000 on Crowdcube. Two months after the start of the offering, they had raised only £4750. The comparison of these two cases gives rise to the central question of our chapter: *given different crowdfunding projects characterized by unobservable quality, which observable signals lead (small) investors to invest in certain projects, and not in others?*

This chapter presents a first-ever empirical examination of equity crowdfunding from any platform worldwide. We examine which crowdfunding project's signals and attributes of venture quality are most likely to induce investors to commit financial resources in an equity crowdfunding context. We examine 104 offerings between October 2006 and October 2011 based on data from one of the largest equity crowdfunding platforms, ASSOB (the Australian Small Scale Offerings Board). We believe this platform is very suitable for our purpose because of its size and its location in Australia, a country that permits equity crowdfunding.

Prior work is consistent with the view that potential investors try to evaluate the unobservable characteristics of venture quality by interpreting the signals sent by entrepreneurs as well as, potentially, a company's attributes (Connelly et al., 2011). In a similar context, signaling theory (Spence, 1973) has been used to explain which types of information (board characteristics, top management team characteristics, gender, the presence of venture capitalists or angel investors, founder involvement, etc.) lead investors to invest in start-ups (Ahlstrom & Bruton, 2006; Cosh et al., 2009; Jääskeläinen, Maula, & Seppä, 2006; Robb & Robinson, 2014). This stream of literature has focused predominantly on the signaling of young start-ups toward angel investors or venture capitalists (Mäkelä & Maula, 2006; Schwienbacher, 2007). There is, however, little research on the signaling of start-ups and ventures toward small investors, and in particular, no prior paper has examined signaling in the context of equity crowdfunding (although for related work on crowd financing, see Agrawal, Catalini, & Goldfarb, 2011; Burtch et al., 2013; Colombo et al., 2015; Cumming & Johan, 2013b,c; Schwienbacher & Larralde, 2012; Mollick, 2014).

The way entrepreneurs of, for example, start-ups would signal to (small) investors is likely to be different from the way they would signal to angels or venture capitalists. Corporate finance literature defines small investors as those who (1) invest relatively small amounts of money and (2) receive a relatively small stake of a company in return (e.g., Malmendier & Shanthikumar, 2007). Small investors are likely to lack the financial sophistication and experience of venture capitalists, who are generally highly knowledgeable about valuing start-ups and assessing founding teams (Freear, Sohl, & Wetzel, 1994). Furthermore, relative to their investments, the costs for angel investors and venture capitalists to evaluate ideas and teams are fairly small, but they would be prohibitively high for small investors. For example, it would not make economic sense for a potential investor to spend weeks evaluating the due diligence of a venture investment that may only yield an amount equal to several days' salary.

To this end, in this chapter, we provide theory and supporting evidence of the relative importance of the different types of signals in the equity crowdfunding context. We examine the impact of venture quality [in terms of human capital, social (alliance) capital, and intellectual capital], as well as the level of uncertainty, on fundraising success. Our data highlight that retaining equity and providing more detailed information about risks can be interpreted as effective signals and can therefore strongly impact the probability of funding success. Social (alliance) capital and intellectual capital, by contrast, have little or no impact on funding success.

The remainder of the chapter proceeds as follows. The next sections provide a discussion of the institutional setting and a description of the data in view of the setting. Thereafter we present the theoretical background and develop our hypotheses. We then present empirical evidence, outline promising avenues for further research, and discuss the limitations of our study. The final section summarizes our main results, discusses the policy implications, and provides a conclusion.

10.2 Institutional background of equity crowdfunding

In this section, we introduce the concept of equity crowdfunding as a new form of capital formation. We first give a general outline and highlight the salient differences between equity crowdfunding and its other types such as donations. Thereafter we provide an overview of the equity crowdfunding market.

10.2.1 From crowdfunding to equity crowdfunding

We believe that equity crowdfunding is most relevant, empirically, for studying entrepreneurial signaling to small investors. Equity crowdfunding is in contrast to donation crowdfunding, where factors other than potential monetary returns are important for funders. Information asymmetries surrounding the entrepreneur's or start-up's ability to generate future cash flows are less important in a donation crowdfunding context. Similarly, reward-based crowdfunding is less suitable for our purpose because funders receive a product rather than a share in a company in return for their financial contributions. Funders must evaluate an entrepreneur's ability to produce and deliver a prepurchased product, and we thus believe that reward-based crowdfunding would be more suitable empirically for a prepurchasing study (for similar arguments, see also Belleflamme, Lambert, & Schwienbacher, 2010; for an alternative perspective, see Cholakova & Clarysse, 2015). Lending crowdfunding involves arranging loans for mass investors over the Internet, which could be somewhat appropriate for an empirical analysis of signaling. On the contrary, prior research has questioned whether the essential signal in lending crowdfunding is a company's credit information or something else, because start-up companies often do not have sufficient credit histories (Lin, Prabhala, & Viswanathan, 2009).

The term "equity crowdfunding" has not been specifically defined in previous research. Bradford (2012) explains equity crowdfunding as a model in which funders receive an interest in the form of equity or equity-like arrangements (e.g., profit sharing) in the ventures they fund. Belleflamme et al. (2014) point out that the central difference between equity crowdfunding and traditional capital raising is the funding process itself: entrepreneurs make an open call for funding on a crowdfunding platform, and investors make their decisions based on the information provided therein. Moreover, the crowdfunding platform facilitates the transaction by providing a standardized investment contract and settling the payments. Belleflamme et al. (2014) also note that individual equity crowdfunding investments in start-ups are generally much smaller than venture capital (VC) or angel investments.

Combining these insights, we define equity crowdfunding as follows: *Equity crowdfunding is a method of financing whereby an entrepreneur sells a specified amount of equity- or bond-like shares in a company to a group of (small) investors through an open call for funding on Internet-based platforms.*

10.2.2 An overview of the equity crowdfunding market

The equity crowdfunding market is substantially influenced by the legislative environment of its home country. Furthermore, because it involves the sale of a security (Bradford, 2012) and is thus subject to various regulatory issues, equity crowdfunding has been restricted until now in many countries, including, until recently, the United States.

As of April 2012, there were a total of 39[1,2,3] crowdfunding platforms, which facilitate equity crowdfunding or revenue-sharing models, which is 7.3% of the 452 total crowdfunding sites in existence. Of these 39, 6 offer unconventional revenue-sharing models for investments in music (e.g., My Major Company), films (e.g., Pirate My Film and Slated), arts in general (Sokap), or mobile applications (Appbackr and AppsFunder). The remaining 33 enable entrepreneurs and small enterprises to offer equity or equity-like shares in their companies to a large pool of small investors through open calls for funding on the Internet.

In 2011 the total funding volume of equity crowdfunding platforms was approximately US$88 (US$115) million.[4] In 2011 93% of this volume was raised on five platforms: SeedUps (approximately US$40 million), ASSOB (US$19 million), Grow VC (US$11 million), Buzz Entrepreneur (US$8 million), and Crowdcube (US$4 million). Therefore most of the volume occurred on sites based in Ireland, Australia, the United Kingdom, and France. However, average funding amount per project varied significantly, with US $200,000 for SeedUps, AUD 339,000 (US$347,000) for ASSOB, US$7000 for Grow VC, US $136,000 for Buzz Entrepreneur, and GBP 188,000 (US$250,000) for Crowdcube. Other platforms, such as Innovestment and Seedmatch, tend to have relatively high average project volumes. These figures are likely to increase sharply in the future (Crowdfunding Industry Report, 2013), particularly since the introduction of the JOBS (Jumpstart Our Business Startups) Act in the United States in November 2013. The passage of this legislation allows entrepreneurs to now obtain financing from "nonaccredited" investors in exchange for equity shares through equity crowdfunding.

10.3 Theoretical background and hypothesis development

In this section, we develop a framework (based on Baum and Silverman's (2004) framework) with related hypotheses for how attributes of venture quality and the associated signals, as well as level of uncertainty, are related to funding success. In this context, we define and use four different success measures: (1) whether and how fully funded projects differ from nonfully funded projects, (2) how the number of investors differs, (3) absolute funding amount, and, finally, (4) the speed of investing as a complementary dimension of funding success.

[1] This is according to the Massolution directory of sites. Massolution is a research and advisory firm specializing in the crowdsourcing and crowdfunding industries. As an industry analyst, Massolution tracks both the supply and demand side of each segment. Massolution also edited the Crowdfunding Industry Report (2012).

[2] Several other crowdfunding platforms, such as Sellaband, also facilitate revenue-sharing agreements. However, the focus of these sites is generally the facilitation of prepurchasing, which generally means the preselling of music albums to finance their production. The preselling aspect is more important in these cases, and thus the author categorizes them as reward-based platforms.

[3] Additional equity crowdfunding sites are in the process of being launched. For example, Deutsche Venture Exchange (www.devexo.com) was recently launched in Germany.

[4] By comparison, in 2012, there were an estimated 1 million crowdfunding campaigns worldwide that raised approximately US$2.7 billion. In 2013 both figures roughly doubled (see Gajda & Mason, 2013).

10.3.1 What drives the funding success of venture proposals?

Similarly to VC financing, with ventures, there is also a concern about information asymmetries between investors and entrepreneurs (Connelly et al., 2011). Naturally, an entrepreneur is assumed to be more knowledgeable about a venture's true value than a potential investor (see, e.g., Backes-Gellner & Werner, 2007; Busenitz, Fiet, & Moesel, 2005; Michael, 2009). This is even more pronounced in an equity crowdfunding context, however, because small investors are less likely to have experience evaluating investment opportunities. In an extreme case, one could argue that potential investors may not be able to determine anything concrete about company value, and, as a result, even potentially high-performing ventures may not receive funding.

Thus we observe the problem of adverse selection in entrepreneurial finance as noted in Leland and Pyle (1977), who state that "where substantial information asymmetries exist and where the supply of poor projects is large relative to the supply of good projects, VC markets may fail to exist" (p. 371). For ventures on equity crowdfunding platforms, these information asymmetries are comparably higher, because gathering information, monitoring progress, and providing input are particularly important for early-stage investors, but the costs of these activities are sensitive to distance (see Agrawal et al., 2011).

As we noted earlier, entrepreneurs have been able to raise substantial amounts of funding through platforms such as ASSOB, SeedUps, or Crowdcube. Therefore funders have seemingly been able to infer the quality of listed ventures on platforms by interpreting the information provided therein. In this sense, funders seem to regard at least some of the information as attributes of venture quality or signals, because not all ventures obtain financing. These may derive, for example, from the positive, unobservable qualities of the entrepreneurs (Busenitz et al., 2005; Spence, 1973, 2002). As Stuart, Hoang, and Hybel (1999) state, "[B]ecause the quality of young companies often cannot be observed directly, evaluators must appraise the company based on observable attributes that are thought to co-vary with its underlying but unknown quality. Resource holders therefore assess value by estimating the conditional probability that a firm will succeed, given a set of observable characteristics of the organization" (p. 317).

For funders, one unobservable quality may be the ability of a venture to earn a certain level of cash flows in the future (Ross, 1978). If we assume that funders and entrepreneurs act rationally, the latter will try to signal to the former (Michael, 2009). In this context, Grossman (1981) and Milgrom (1981) show theoretically that funders will infer from entrepreneurs who fail to provide information that their ventures are of below-average quality. This creates a strong incentive, however, to provide information, which can lead to an "unraveling effect," where all firms signal in equilibrium.[5]

Naturally, not all the information on the quality of a venture will ultimately be an effective *signal* to help overcome the problem of information asymmetry. Rather, some information can better be understood as "cheap talk." Effective signals share two characteristics:

---

[5] Neither paper specifically addresses start-ups or young ventures, however. Instead, both papers develop theoretical models and show that the competitive market provides adequate incentives for sellers to reveal information to buyers (Michael, 2009). Grossman (1981) analyzes the informational role of warranties and private disclosures about product quality. Milgrom (1981) develops an abstract model.

observability and signal cost. Observability is the extent to which the signal is noticed and understood by investors; signal cost must be structured so that dishonest signals are not rewarded, and so the cost of *producing* the signal doesn't outweigh its benefits (see, e.g., Connelly et al., 2011).

Within our context, we develop a framework that describes the connection between our independent variables and funding success (see Fig. 10.1). We argue that two channels are mainly responsible for funding success on equity crowdfunding platforms. The first is based on Baum and Silverman's (2004) structure for how investors will most likely be able to use the attributes of *venture quality* provided by entrepreneurs in the offering documents (human capital, social (alliance) capital, and intellectual capital). We argue that projects are more likely to receive funding if they have (observable) characteristics that are generally believed to indicate higher *venture quality*. Consequently, an investment in higher quality projects has a greater likelihood of generating higher returns in the future and therefore represents a favorable investment option.

The second channel is based on investors' concerns about information asymmetries between themselves and entrepreneurs. We specify the *level of uncertainty* in the relationship between the equity share offered on the equity crowdfunding platform and the level of detail for the financial projections. The less (precise) the information provided by entrepreneurs, the more restricted potential investors may be in assessing the proposed venture.

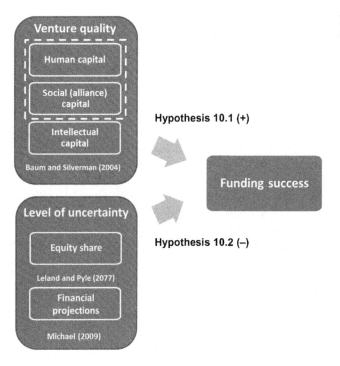

FIGURE 10.1 Determinants of funding success.

In summary, we argue that funding success on equity crowdfunding platforms is positively correlated with *venture quality* and negatively correlated with the *level of uncertainty* as depicted in Fig. 10.1.

10.3.2 Defining funding success

In the context of crowdfunding platforms, funding success is a multifaceted concept. Besides the obvious success measures, that is, whether a project is fully funded, how many investors were attracted, and how much funding was raised, we also consider speed of investment as an important success indicator. Since Penrose's (1959) original "theory of the growth of the firm," where managerial resources were found to play a pivotal role, several factors (such as environmental carrying capacity, market forces, capabilities, culture, and strategy) have been suggested that can affect a venture's growth. Within the field of entrepreneurship, previous research has examined several additional factors and found that funding events are relevant to the evolution of growth (Davila et al., 2003). This is especially important for "high growth" ventures, because they often need to rely on timely execution to take advantage of early-mover advantages; delayed execution can significantly negatively impact their success.

10.3.3 Venture quality

When presenting a project on a crowdfunding platform, entrepreneurs often face the challenge of proving its quality when they are still in a start-up phase. Because unambiguous performance measures are likely to be missing, potential funders should look for alternative indicators of future performance (DiMaggio & Powell, 1983; Podolny, 1993; Baum & Silverman, 2004). Following Baum and Silverman (2004), who analyzed venture capitalists' assessments of startup quality, we argue that there are three major signals/characteristics in the first channel that potential investors on crowdfunding platforms can use to assess project quality: human capital, social (alliance) capital, and intellectual capital.

10.3.3.1 *Human capital*

Following a meta-study by Unger, Rauch, Frese, and Rosenbusch (2011), one of the most robust findings in the entrepreneurship literature is that human capital is associated with venture success (see also Doms, Lewis, & Robb, 2010), even though its magnitude and relative importance are debatable. Generally speaking, "higher" human capital is related to higher capabilities and skills with regard to various aspects of entrepreneurial success: identifying and exploiting business opportunities (e.g., Shane & Venkataraman, 2000), defining and realizing a venture's strategy (Baum, Locke, & Smith, 2001), acquiring additional resources (e.g., financial) (Brush, Greene, & Hart, 2001), and building a positive basis for future learning (Ackerman & Humphreys, 1990; Hunter 1986). In line with this positive relationship between human capital and venture success, Zacharakis and Meyer (2000) found that venture capitalists indicate that experience and management skills are among their most important selection criteria. Similarly, Levie and Gimmon (2008) argue that educational degrees are an effective signal about first-time *"high technology"* venture founders. Human capital is important to experienced investors that conduct significant due diligence or investors that require collateral and other guarantees, such as VC investors, business angels (BAs), and banks (Cosh, Cumming, & Hughes, 2019). Here, we examine the importance of human capital for young ventures in convincing relatively inexperienced investors to contribute funds.

10.3.3.2 Social (alliance) capital

Networks and business linkages are important channels through which firms can access additional and often complementary, resources (e.g., Baum & Silverman, 2004; Chung, Singh, & Lee, 2000; Hoang & Antoncic, 2003). More precisely, networks, and especially social relationships, can provide access to valuable information. According to Granovetter (1973, 1983), this information tends to be more valuable than information accessed through formal channels, because it is supposedly "more useful, reliable, exclusive, and less redundant" (Brüderl & Preisendörfer, 1998, p. 214).

Networks can also provide access to potential suppliers and customers, as well as to financial resources (Brüderl & Preisendörfer, 1998). Moreover, networks can enhance a venture's legitimacy (Baum & Silverman, 2004) and reputation and may thus serve as a signal of venture quality (Hoang & Antoncic, 2003; Stuart et al., 1999). These potential benefits are particularly crucial during the early stages of a venture. But they are not limited to the initial founding phase of a business, referred to as the "network founding hypothesis." Networks can be the basis for a venture's subsequent success; this phenomenon is referred to as the "network success hypothesis" (Brüderl & Preisendörfer, 1998), because they provide a constant source of information, advice, and general support (Hoang & Antoncic, 2003).

10.3.3.3 Intellectual capital

According to Schumpeter (1942) and Baumol (2002), innovation is one of the key determinants of firm survival. It can simultaneously allow new firms to enter the market while helping established firms secure their competitive positions and thus their survival (Cefis & Marsili, 2005).

However, it is obviously not sufficient to just be innovative. Entrepreneurs need to be aware of the importance of protecting their ideas through, for example, patents. In the context of high technology industries such as biotech, making technological claims via patents and pending patent applications, and thereby signaling a firm's innovative capabilities, has been shown to affect both its future survival and its chances of attracting VC funding (Baum & Silverman, 2004; Silverman & Baum, 2002). Moreover, patent ownership can serve as somewhat of a deterrent against future market entrants, which could also be interpreted as a positive signal of a company's strength and quality.

Patents thus clearly fulfill the criteria of a signal as per Spence (1973), who claims that a signal must be costly and able to differentiate among competing projects/start-ups. But the fact that a company holds a patent can reveal even more than its pure technological or innovative capability. According to Cohen and Lemley (2001) and Long (2004), ownership of a patent also delivers technical information to potential investors that would otherwise be difficult to communicate, such as that the organization has reached a certain stage of development, where it has identified and already invested in a possible market positioning or niche, and that it is well managed.

Hypothesis 10.1: *Higher venture quality as reflected in the venture's (A) human capital, (B) social (alliance) capital, and/or (C) intellectual capital, positively affects funding success on equity crowdfunding platforms.*

10.3.4 Level of uncertainty

The second channel of information that investors must assess when deciding whether to invest on an equity crowdfunding platform is level of uncertainty. Daniel Ellsberg introduced his Ellsberg paradox in decision theory in 1961. He emphasized that people generally prefer taking risks when they know the set of possible events and respective probabilities instead of just having an ambiguous alternative. Therefore whenever investors have ambiguous information about an investment opportunity, meaning that they are unable to identify all future outcomes and to clearly allocate probabilities to the outcomes, they are reluctant to invest compared to an equal alternative for which all outcomes and related probabilities are known. We extend this idea in a *monotonic* way and argue that the likelihood of investing decreases with an increase in the level of uncertainty (more ambiguous information). If we translate this theory to the funding situation, entrepreneurs can try to signal the unobservable characteristics of their venture as a way to reduce the ambiguity level (less information asymmetry) for potential investors.

10.3.4.1 Equity share

Leland and Pyle (1977) show that, with the existence of high levels of information asymmetry (high level of uncertainty) between entrepreneurs and investors and a majority of "poor" projects, venture markets may not exist. Therefore higher levels of information asymmetry create a situation for investors in which they have to rely on more ambiguous information to form their investment decision. This reduces the likelihood of investing and in the limit no investments take place at all. Therefore entrepreneurs have to effectively signal the "good" quality of their projects to investors in order to obtain financing (reducing the level of uncertainty). One way to signal quality is to invest indirectly in one's own project and keeping equity. This could demonstrate that the venture's value is positively related to the equity share held by entrepreneurs and thereby reducing the level of uncertainty.

10.3.4.2 Financial projections

Entrepreneurs use the prospectus to provide financial forecasts or projections to potential investors, such as detailed earnings forecasts and/or a disclaimer in which they summarize and explain potential risk factors. If entrepreneurs include neither financial forecasts nor a disclaimer than potential investors are left with a higher level of uncertainty compared to campaigns in which financial forecasts and disclaimer are provided. Thus the prospectus should clearly present their vision and outlook, as well as any potential drawdown risks (see Michael, 2009, for a related study on franchise entrepreneurs). This information can be used by investors to analyze a venture's attractiveness, providing a more precise overview of the risks and opportunities, and helping lessen the risk of asymmetric information. Investors will therefore have a better basis on which to form expectations, which is commonly favored by investors in the sense of Epstein and Schneider (2008), and increase funding success.

Hypothesis 10.2: *The level of uncertainty negatively affects funding success on equity crowdfunding platforms.*

10.4 Data sample

In this section, we introduce the ASSOB platform as the source of our data sample. ASSOB, the Australian platform, has been in business since 2006. With AUD 125 million funded as of April 2012, it is also the equity crowdfunding platform that has raised the largest total amount of capital. Since 2006, over 160 companies have listed on ASSOB, and it is thus one of only a few platforms that currently possess sufficient data for a statistically significant analysis of equity crowdfunding offerings. Moreover, ASSOB operates in a legal environment that permits equity crowdfunding. We can view a study on ASSOB as a forward-looking illustration of how equity crowdfunding may ultimately work in other regions (such as the United States) in the near future.[6]

10.4.1 The Australian Small Scale Offerings Board investment process

ASSOB allows investors to browse small equity offerings of entrepreneurs and to buy shares in these ventures. During registration, potential investors are required to provide certain personal information, including how much they expect to invest, and must confirm awareness of the potential risks involved in capital investments. Once registered, investors can peruse the general information on the offerings on what is called the "Primary Board." This includes company name, listing code, security type (e.g., ordinary shares), industry (e.g., "technology"), status of the capital-raising (e.g., "open"), total funding sought, minimum parcel size, and allocation status. If there is interest in a specific offering, the investor can then access a detailed offering overview.

If the investor wishes to proceed, the next step is to download detailed offering documents. The offering documents are prepared by the entrepreneurs in cooperation with "sponsors," who are typically professional business advisors such as accountants, corporate advisors, business consultants, finance brokers, or lawyers.[7] Although offering

---

[6] We compared offerings on ASSOB with those on RockThePost, which is referred to as an equity crowdfunding platform for accredited investors in the United States. We found that company presentations were very similar on both web sites. We also found strong similarities in the way companies on both sites proffered their investment details. Furthermore, both sites offer, for example, the possibility of providing company news, in order to keep followers and investors informed.

[7] However, companies have no obligation to report sponsors' names in the offering documents. In addition, some include disclaimers similar to the following: "The information contained in this publication has been prepared by or on behalf of the Company. Neither ASSOB as the publisher nor our Sponsor, as the Class Order Operator have undertaken an independent review of the information contained in this publication." Ideally, we would like to have a complete list of sponsors and their respective companies in order to analyze, for example, possible certification effects.

documents are prepared individually for each entrepreneur, all follow a similar structure: (1) key investment highlights, (2) milestones achieved to date, (3) letter from the managing director, (4) business model, (5) market analysis, (6) financial projections, (7) purpose of the capital-raising, (8) offering details, (9) ownership structure, and (10) descriptions of the management team and external board members.

Based on this information, an investor can then apply for shares. A 10% security deposit is required at the time of application, with the remaining 90% due when the equity offering becomes effective, which occurs when the minimum number of shares has been sold. If a minimum number is *not* sold within the prespecified time frame, the equity offering does not become effective, and investors are refunded their 10% deposits. The minimum number of shares is set individually for each venture and can differ significantly from the total funding amount requested.

After founders have successfully financed on ASSOB, they have an opportunity to trade on the secondary market. Unlike common stock exchanges, where there is generally frequent trading (liquidity), ASSOB is a small platform and secondary sales occur very infrequently. Since the formation of ASSOB, only five secondary market transactions have occurred through February 2014. Given that, we do not believe ASSOB can be compared to secondary market exchanges such as the Alternative Investment Market in London.

10.4.2 Dataset construction

Our final sample consists of 104 equity crowdfunding offerings published on ASSOB between October 2006 and October 2011. All of these offerings were either listed for approximately 1 year—the most common offering period on ASSOB—or fully funded beforehand. To the best of our knowledge, this unique sample is the most comprehensive of equity crowdfunding offerings collected so far.

ASSOB provided a list of all 161 offerings for which they had basic information available in their database. We were able to obtain the basic information and the offering documents with the variables in question for 139 of those. Given that not all of the offering documents included all variables, we used a conservative approach, and only included the projects in our final sample and the multivariate analyses that had no missing values. Thus our final sample consists of 104 projects.[8]

According to ASSOB, when it first launched, it did not automatically store offering information, which explains the discrepancy between available listings and the number of total listings published on the site since 2006. However, all offerings were displayed in the same manner on ASSOB's offering overview site, and all follow the general structure described previously, which ensures comparability.

---

[8] In unreported results, we tested if the omitted cases result in biased estimations. We included blocks of variables stepwise and compared the coefficient estimations and statistical significance with the *full* specification (considering all variables). The results are qualitatively highly comparable to those in the *full* specifications in Table 10.4. For sake of brevity, we only report the *full* specifications and other specifications are available from the authors upon request.

For our sample of 104 offerings, we collected seven types of data: (1) human capital, (2) social (alliance) capital, (3) intellectual capital, (4) equity share, (5) financial projections, (6) further control variables, and (6) information on the speed of investment. The descriptive statistics for all variables and the correlation matrix are in Tables 10.1 and 10.2, respectively.

In order to test our hypotheses, we use the following variables:

10.4.2.1 Dependent variables

As explained above, we differentiate between four different success measures. Accordingly, we use four different dependent variables.

Fully funded: This dichotomous variable (0/1) indicates whether a project has received the full target amount. We use this success indicator to assess whether projects that received full funding generally differ significantly from projects that did not.

Number of investors: This variable counts the number of individual investors that invested in the project (excluding founders).

Funding amount: This measure indicates the total funding amount that was generated by the project in millions AUD.

Speed of investment: This complementary success measure uses the number of days a project needed to complete the first round of financing. Because projects are excluded from the platform after about 1 year if they are not funded, we censored this measure after 365 days.

10.4.2.2 Independent variables

Human capital: We obtained management team information, such as composition and qualifications, from the offering documents. Every offering document includes short biographies of executive directors, nonexecutive directors, and, if applicable, key employees. We created a list of all 376 directors (board members) from the 104 offering documents, and noted for each the director type (e.g., executive versus nonexecutive), and whether the director holds an MBA. Based on this listing, we use the *number of board members* to broadly capture the amount of human capital. In addition, we follow Backes-Gellner and Werner (2007) and Levie and Gimmon (2008) and argue that educational degrees, as part of human capital, are an effective signal for a venture's quality. Therefore we choose an MBA degree as a proxy for education. It is observable to (small) investors (e.g., through biographies in the offering documents) and is costly to acquire (both in tuition and in time). Furthermore, it can only be acquired by qualified candidates. Given that most MBA programs require applicants to have work experience, an MBA degree also denotes some professional experience and maturity. In this regard, we include the *share of board members holding an MBA degree* as a second indicator for human capital.

Note that the entrepreneurial founder (and if applicable the other one or two key founding entrepreneurs) is included on the board, because our sample comprises early-stage start-ups, and hence, this measure includes both board entrepreneurs and external board members. Hence, we capture the human capital of the key entrepreneurs based on earlier work (e.g., Schjoedt, Monsen, Pearson, Barnett, & Chrisman, 2013). Also, note that we considered human capital of executive and nonexecutive directors separately and through interaction terms, but these variables were insignificant (possibly due to the sample size in these subcategories), and hence, we do not report them separately.

TABLE 10.1 Descriptive statistics.

	Number of observation	Mean	Std	Min	Max
Dependent variables					
Funding amount	104	318,568 AUD	515,148.7	0 AUD	3540,473 AUD
Number of investors (without founders)	104 (104)	7.52 (7.09)	12.05 (9.58)	0 (0)	88 (57)
Duration of first financing round (if successfully funded)	92	317.72	104.81	7	374
	19	135.37	106.31	7	374
Human capital					
Number of board	104	3.61	1.02	1	8
Percentage of board MBA	104	4.47	11.62	0	50
Social (alliance) capital					
Percentage of nonexecutive board	104	22.91	25.49	0	75
Intellectual capital					
Patent	104	0.20	0.40	0	1
Equity share					
Equity offering	104	21.30	13.25	1.53	90
Financial projections					
Disclaimer_no financial forecast	104	0.15	0.36	0	1
No disclaimer_no financial forecast	104	0.47	0.50	0	1
Additional control					
Number of staff	104	7.16	12.59	0	120
Award	104	0.17	0.38	0	1
Government grant	104	0.019	0.14	0	1
Intended number of rounds	104	2.5	0.59	1	3
Most likely exit-others	104	0.04	0.18	0	1
Most likely exit-trade sale	104	0.48	0.50	0	1
Target funding	104	1778,799 AUD	1421,268 AUD	300,000 AUD	5000,000 AUD
Years in business	104	2.63	4.92	0	30
Years to planned exit	104	3.86	1.15	1	7
Speed of investing					
Funds raised in round 1	92	123,281 AUD	152,812 AUD	0 AUD	650,000 AUD
Parcel size round 1	92	31,304 AUD	20,097 AUD	5000 AUD	200,000 AUD
Share price round 1	92	0.079 AUD	0.11 AUD	0.01 AUD	0.75 AUD

This table shows the mean, std, min, max for all variables. The sample covers 104 crowdfunding projects. *std*, standard deviation; *min*, minimum value; *max*, maximum value.

TABLE 10.2 Correlation matrix.

	(1)	(2)	(3)	(4)	(5)	(6)	(7)	(8)	(9)	(10)	(11)	(12)	(13)
Funding amount (1)	1.0000												
Number of staff (2)	0.0453	1.0000											
	(0.6483)												
Years in business (3)	-0.0696	0.4092***	1.0000										
	(0.4824)	(0.0000)											
Equity offering (4)	-0.1405	0.0395	0.0453	1.0000									
	(0.1549)	(0.6906)	(0.6481)										
Number of board (5)	0.2604***	0.2566***	0.0989	-0.1030	1.0000								
	(0.0076)	(0.0086)	(0.3178)	(0.2983)									
Years to planned exit (6)	-0.2693***	0.0719*	0.2270**	0.1622*	-0.1068	1.0000							
	(0.0057)	(0.4682)	(0.0205)	(0.0999)	(0.2805)								
Percentage of nonexecutive board (7)	-0.0881	0.1781*	0.0943	0.1763*	0.0771	0.1274	1.0000						
	(0.3739)	(0.0705)	(0.3409)	(0.0735)	(0.4364)	(0.1976)							
Percentage of board MBA (8)	-0.0714	-0.1045	-0.0439	0.0276	-0.0629	0.0233	-0.3130***	1.0000					
	(0.4713)	(0.2913)	(0.6579)	(0.7807)	(0.5256)	(0.8147)	(0.0012)						
Number of investors (9)	0.8611***	0.0288	-0.1077	-0.2013**	0.2534***	-0.2833***	-0.1205	0.0050	1.0000				
	(0.0000)	(0.7715)	(0.2765)	(0.0405)	(0.0094)	(0.0036)	(0.2232)	(0.9599)					
Parcel size round 1 (10)	0.1413	-0.0489	-0.0863	0.0852	-0.0217	-0.1599	-0.0666	0.1363	0.0793	1.0000			
	(0.1524)	(0.6222)	(0.3839)	(0.3896)	(0.8267)	(0.1049)	(0.5019)	(0.1677)	(0.4237)				
Share price round 1 (11)	0.5552***	0.0463	-0.0194	-0.1942**	0.1634	-0.1789*	0.0165	-0.0511	0.5694***	0.2264**	1.0000		
	(0.0000)	(0.6408)	(0.8453)	(0.0482)	(0.0974)	(0.0693)	(0.8679)	(0.6067)	(0.0000)	(0.0208)			
Funds raised in round 1 (12)	0.5600***	-0.0065	-0.1749*	0.0562	0.0712	-0.1173	-0.2126**	0.0742	0.5446***	0.1015	0.1007	1.0000	
	(0.0000)	(0.9477)	(0.0757)	(0.5710)	(0.4725)	(0.2356)	(0.0303)	(0.4540)	(0.0000)	(0.3052)	(0.3090)		
Funding sought round 1 (13)	0.2226**	0.1397	-0.0386	0.0797	0.1467	-0.0275	0.1625*	-0.1210	0.2376**	-0.1621	0.0420	0.0316	1.0000
	(0.0232)	(0.1572)	(0.6971)	(0.4213)	(0.1373)	(0.7820)	(0.0993)	(0.2212)	(0.0152)	(0.1003)	(0.6717)	(0.7500)	

This table shows the Pearson correlation coefficients for the variables in Table 10.1—P-values are given in parentheses below the coefficients. ***, **, and * indicate statistical significance at the 1%, 5%, and 10% levels, respectively.

Social (alliance) capital: Human capital and social (network) capital are often intertwined. As argued by Baum and Silverman (2004), larger management teams are not only likely to possess higher human capital, but at the same time, they may have more social capital. Likewise, the variable *share of board members holding an MBA degree* not only serves as a proxy for human capital, but it also indicates the potential for a network surrounding the project, because MBA graduates are often part of exclusive networks. Moreover, we measure the *share of nonexecutive directors on the venture's board* as a proxy for network capital. Nonexecutive directors are often respected industry veterans who act as mentors to ventures. They can add to a venture's legitimacy and can introduce entrepreneurs to potential new stakeholders (such as clients), thus broadening their networks. Experienced managers usually have only a limited amount of time to devote to such efforts. Thus the support of a nonexecutive director may be viewed as a positive attribute of quality that the entrepreneurs have successfully undergone some kind of due diligence process.

Intellectual capital: Regarding intellectual capital, we follow Silverman and Baum (2002) and Baum and Silverman (2004), among others, and use patents as the most common indicator of intellectual capital. More precisely, we use a dummy variable *Granted Patent* to account for whether a venture possesses a granted patent (1), or not (0).

Equity share: Entrepreneurs can effectively signal unobservable characteristics of their venture by the amount of equity they retain after an offering. The rationale is that retaining ownership interests is costly, so entrepreneurs will only retain a "substantial" stake if they expect future cash flows to be high relative to current firm value. A substantial stake in the venture can also help better align the interests of funders and founders. Thus the amount of equity offered is a costly and observable signal, set actively by founders.

Financial projections: Information on the level of uncertainty also comes from the offering documents. Financial forecasts for potential investors generally refer to sales, EBITDA, EBIT, and net earnings forecasts. But there is no standard way to present forecasting information on ASSOB, and companies can decide whether to provide forecasts, and which items to provide if they do. Companies that opt not to provide a forecast can integrate a standard legal disclaimer[9] into their documents. This generally states that the directors believe there is no reasonable basis to forecast future earnings, because the operations of the company are inherently uncertain.

We calculate two dummy variables from the disclosure policy: (1) one dummy variable indicating that the venture has not provided a financial forecast but has included a disclaimer (*disclaimer_no financial forecast*) and (2) one dummy variable indicating that the venture has not provided a financial forecast or a disclaimer (*no disclaimer_no financial forecast*). The group of ventures that has no disclaimer and provides a forecast serves as our reference category in the analyses.

Additional controls: Moreover, in line with Baum and Silverman (2004), we use a set of additional control variables as follows to account for factors that may either influence the

---

[9] The disclaimer reads: "The Directors have considered the matters set out in ASIC Regulatory Guide 130: Prospective Financial Information, and believe that they do not have a reasonable basis to forecast future earnings because the operations of the Company are inherently uncertain. Any forecast or projection would necessarily contain such a broad range of potential outcomes and possibilities that it would be unreliable and, for that reason, the Directors have decided not to include any financial projections or forecasts."

funding process or are related to a venture's future performance. On the ASSOB platform, management has broad set of choices to structure their financing processes. First, fund seekers must indicate the *target amount* (in millions AUD), and the *number of financing rounds* (ranging from one to three) they wish to engage in. Founders who choose to engage in only one financing round may be forgoing two advantages: (1) the benefits of the announcement that they have successfully completed their first round, which is viewed positively by investors and (2) an equal or (in most cases) higher share price in further rounds. These advantages can create a kind of group dynamic for interested investors to observe that only a few parcels are left, which can increase the likelihood of investing.

Second, we use *industry-, year-, and location (big city) fixed effects* to account for unobserved heterogeneity between the projects' attractiveness due to, for example, differing growth potentials between individual industries (eight industry dummy variables), varying degree of crowdfunding platform legitimacy over time (six 1-year dummy variables), or potentially better venture survival prospects in metropolitan areas (four dummy variables for projects located in Sydney, Melbourne, Brisbane, and Perth).

Third, we control for the fact that projects may differ with respect to the announced exit strategy. We therefore categorize projects according to their *planned exit channel* [three dummy variables for most likely exit initial public offering (IPO), trade sale, or other], as well as for the *planned years to exit* (as indicated in the offering documents). Fourth, given that start-ups are not the only businesses seeking funding on the ASSOB platform, we account for a venture's *years in business*, as well as its *number of staff*.

Furthermore, some ventures list government loans (*government grant*) or awards (*award*). We considered a company an award winner if at least one award was mentioned in the offering documents; nominations and finalists were not considered. The spectrum of awards is very broad and ranges from a Highest Achiever Award (e.g., Sonic Grip Ltd.) to the Asia Pacific ICT Alliance Awards: Tools & Infrastructure Category (Incriptus Ltd.) to the Emerging Exporter Award 2006 for South East Queensland (Bantix). However, only 18 companies mentioned awards in their offering documents, and we therefore did not weight the awards with regard to their importance. In our analyses, we use two dummy variables to indicate whether a venture has received an award or a government grant.

Fifth, when we investigate speed of investment, we also control for parcel size for each round and share price. *Parcel size* for each round means that only whole number parcel shares may be purchased by investors within the total amount available per round. To determine whether parcels are still available, on the ASSOB platform, one must check the status of the "squares," whereby one square represents one parcel. A "red square" represents a completed capital-raising parcel. "Grey squares" represent available parcels. The status of individual ASSOB offerings is continually updated, so there is always complete transparency about an offering's status. Ventures that do not reach their minimum threshold for investment after 1 year are delisted.

Given that (potential) investors can observe all previous investments made, early investments are likely to be of greater importance than later ones. Under this circumstance, investors may not be exclusively basing their buying decisions on fundamentals, which is known as the impresario hypothesis (Ritter, 1998). Instead, the price formation of, for example, Investor 1 is driven partly by what Investor 1 thinks Investor 2 is basing his price formation on. In that way, if parcels are sold soon after listing, this could create the appearance of excess demand. Subsequently, other investors may opt to invest because of the perceived demand and not solely because of the information in the offering documents. The last regulatory item for founders is the *share price* in each financing round, which we also control for.

10.5 Empirical analyses

10.5.1 Univariate tests

We begin with a univariate setting. In subsequent analyses, we use multivariate settings to include possible determinants and control factors simultaneously.

Table 10.3 gives the results of our first broad analysis. We explore whether and how fully funded projects differ from nonfully funded projects in terms of the described attributes of venture quality as well as the level of uncertainty. Because we only use a univariate analysis, that is, testing the equality of means between the two groups (with equal or unequal variances, respectively), we use the full sample, which contains basic information as well as offering documents (i.e., 139 projects, as explained in the data construction section).

Within the larger sample of 139 projects, we find missing values for individual variables. We thus exclude these cases from our more detailed analyses in order to keep the results comparable. In subsequent analyses, we use the reduced sample of 104 projects, where all projects offer complete information for all attributes of quality. Most importantly, Table 10.3 shows that higher equity offerings and lower information levels for risks, combined with the omission of a future outlook, are associated with nonfully funded projects (rows 6 and 7), which supports our Hypothesis 10.2. We also find that, within the group of additional control variables, the variables "proposed exit channel" and "shorter time horizons until planned exit" are statistically different for fully and nonfully funded projects. This is somewhat surprising, because we do not have a clear prediction about the relationship with funding success, and we may regard those statements as examples of "cheap talk" instead of credible signals (rows 13 and 17).

We also find that smaller projects are more likely to be financed. And, counterintuitively, award-winning companies tended not to receive full funding (rows 15 and 10). However, we find no initial support for our Hypothesis 10.1 on the value of human capital, social (alliance) capital, and intellectual capital. We do not find a significant difference between fully funded and nonfully funded projects, although our results are derived without controlling for simultaneous effects.

10.5.2 Multivariate tests

We now turn to a more detailed analysis that uses more sophisticated multivariate analyses to evaluate the correlations among venture quality, in the sense of Baum and Silverman (2004), level of uncertainty, and funding success.[10]

[10] We also run all analyses in Table 10.4 "block-wise" as a robustness check. Our results remain qualitatively stable and are available from the authors upon request.

TABLE 10.3   Mean differences between fully funded and not fully funded projects.

	Number of observations	Fully funded (mean)	Not fully funded (mean)	Difference test (fully funded vs not fully funded)
Human capital				
(2) Number of board	139	3.30	3.55	0.25
(3) Percentage of board MBA	137	11.11	3.79	− 7.32
Social (alliance) capital				
(4) Percentage of nonexecutive board members	137	17.22	22.71	5.49
Intellectual capital				
(5) Granted patent	139	0.10	0.17	0.07
Equity share				
(6) Equity offering	139	0.10	0.23	0.13***
Financial projections				
(7) Disclaimer_no financial forecast	139	0.50	0.16	− 0.34***
(8) No disclaimer_no financial forecast	139	0.20	0.48	0.28*
Additional controls				
(9) Number of staff	139	5	9.29	4.29
(10) Award	139	0	0.16	0.16***
(11) Government grant	139	0.10	0.02	− 0.08
(12) Intended number of rounds	139	2.70	2.53	− 0.17
(13) Most likely exit-trade sale	139	0.10	0.44	0.34***
(14) Most likely exit-others	139	0.40	0.13	− 0.27
(15) Target funding	139	848,000	1785,000	937,000***
(16) Years in business	129	3.63	2.65	− 0.97
(17) Years to planned exit	120	2.60	3.94	1.34**
(18) Parcel size	139	33,200.00	31,802.34	− 1397.66
(19) Share price	139	0.22	0.07	− 0.15***

This table presents the comparison of mean test for the fully crowdfunded investment projects (fully funded, number of 10 projects) and partially or not funded investment projects (not fully funded, number of 129 projects). The sample covers 139 crowdfunded projects. Given that we only run a univariate test, we include all projects that include basic information and offering documents in this analysis. As not all projects offer complete information for all variables, the sample used in the subsequent Table 10.4 is reduced to 104. ***, **, and * indicate statistical significance at the 1%, 5%, and 10% levels, respectively.

First, we investigate which factors are related to the *number of investors*. The method of choice should not be ordinary least squares (OLS), because distribution for the number of investors is highly nonnormal and displays a large number of zeros—we have 37 cases for which no investor at all was found to finance a campaign and for one campaign 88 investors supported financially (see Table 10.1). For this data structure, we use the count model zero-inflated negative binomial regressions to investigate which factors influence the number of funders (Table 10.4, Model 1).[11] Given that a substantial share of projects did not attract any investors, we chose this method to control for factors that potentially affect whether a project will ultimately be funded at all, before analyzing in more detail which factors influence the actual number of funders. In particular, we control for the possibility that projects initiated during the earlier days of the platform's existence had a lower probability of attracting investors because crowdfunding was not yet an established investment channel. Thus projects that went unfunded in the past on ASSOB may not have had undesirable characteristics or were of lower quality, but there may have been lower investor experience with this type of fundraising platform. Technically speaking, the excess zeros are modeled independently with a logistic regression (see the results "inflate" of Table 10.4).

Moreover, in addition to the *number of investors*, we use OLS regressions to analyze which factors drive *absolute funding amount* (see Table 10.4, Model 2).[12] Finally, we study the duration until the first financing round is completed and thereby examine factors that affect the *speed of investment* as another success measure (see Table 10.4, Model 3). For this purpose the common method is the cocalled survival analysis. More specifically, we use exponential hazard models (with log relative-hazard forms)[13] to identify which factors reduce the time to completion of the first financing round, measured in days until the target amount for the first round is raised. Survival analysis has the advantage over other regression techniques that it allows the distribution of time-to-event to be nonnormal as well as for censored data (Cleves et al., 2008).

Note that all results are presented in Table 10.4 in Models 1–3, even if different methodologies are applied. This presentation allows a comparison of the results from the three different success measures more easily, because results are presented side by side and the same controlling variables are used. The first set of venture quality attributes we study are summarized under human capital. In line with Hypothesis 10.1 (a), we find statistically significant empirical evidence that the percentage of MBA graduates among executive board members of a founding team is positively related with the number of investors. More precisely, a 1 percentage point increase in board members who hold MBAs coincides with the expected increase in the number of investors by a factor of 1.017, holding all other

---

[11] We have chosen the zero-inflated negative binomial over a zero-inflated Poisson mode, because of the distribution properties of the underlying data. In our case the mean for the *number of investors* is 7.52 and a related variance of $145.20 = 12.05^2$, which exceeds the mean about 19 times (see Table 10.1). This is not in line with the Poisson distribution having equal mean and variance. Therefore our model of choice is the zero-inflated negative binomial model, because due its quadratic variance function, it can rise "faster" and fits the data better at the high end.

[12] In unreported results, we winsorize nondummy variables at the 99% level to control for potential outliers that may be influencing the results. We find none. The results are available from the authors upon request.

[13] We use the Akaike Information Criterion to select the best fitting model, which in our case is the exponential specification (Cleves, Gould, & Gutierrez, 2008).

TABLE 10.4 Success determinants of crowdfunding projects.

	Model 1: Number of investors		Model 2: Funding amount			Model 3: Speed of capital allocation	
	Coefficient	z-Value	Coefficient	Beta	t-Value	Coefficient	z-Value
(1) Constant			− 0.157		− 0.37	− 21.173***	− 2.92
Human capital							
(2) Number of board	0.342**	2.56	0.119*	0.236*	1.93	0.655	1.03
(3) Percentage of board MBA	0.017*	1.74	− 0.002	− 0.045	− 0.52	0.094*	1.83
Social (alliance) capital							
(4) Percentage of nonexecutive board members	− 0.004	− 1.05	− 0.002	− 0.098	− 1.07	0.003	0.12
Intellectual capital							
(5) Granted patent	0.174	0.52	0.076	0.059	0.70	− 1.009	− 1.04
Equity share							
(6) Equity offering	− 0.018***	− 3.08	− 0.003	− 0.075	− 0.77	− 0.165***	− 2.92
Financial projections							
(7) Disclaimer_no financial forecast	0.312	0.94	0.049	0.034	− 0.28	0.863	− 0.78
(8) No disclaimer_no financial forecast	− 0.180	− 0.88	− 0.210**	− 0.205**	− 2.14	− 3.385***	− 3.27
Additional controls							
(9) Number of staff	− 0.003	− 0.38	0.004	0.102	1.34	− 0.113	− 0.83
(10) Award	0.374	1.62	− 0.054	− 0.040	0.45	0.601	0.59
(11) Government grant	0.530	1.30	0.127	0.034	0.38	− 2.425	− 0.86
(12) Intended number of rounds	0.071	0.28	0.078	0.090	1.03	2.910**	2.43
(13) Most likely exit-others	− 1.697***	− 3.63	0.005	− 0.002	− 0.02	− 0.440	− 0.20
(14) Most likely exit-trade sale	− 0.271*	− 1.79	− 0.106	− 0.104	− 1.07	− 1.245	1.38
(15) Target funding	− 0.022	− 0.29	0.025	0.070	0.66	− 0.050	− 0.13
(16) Years in business	− 0.058	− 1.19	− 0.008	− 0.081	− 1.10	0.213**	2.22
(17) Years to planned exit	0.036	0.35	− 0.040	− 0.090	− 0.93	− 0.401	− 0.82
(18) Parcel size						> 0.000***	2.81
(19) Share price						− 1.137	− 0.30
Year fixed effects	Yes		Yes			Yes	
Industry fixed effects	Yes		Yes			Yes	
Big city fixed effects	Yes		Yes			Yes	

(Continued)

TABLE 10.4 (Continued)

	Model 1: Number of investors		Model 2: Funding amount			Model 3: Speed of capital allocation	
	Coefficient	z-Value	Coefficient	Beta	t-Value	Coefficient	z-Value
Inflate							
Offering 2009	1.255	1.61					
Offering 2010	0.576	0.75					
Offering 2011	0.398	0.43					
Constant	− 1.394**	− 2.13					
/lnalpha	− 2.033***	− 5.35					
alpha	0.131						
Number of nonzero observation	67						
Number of zero observation	37						
Log pseudolikelihood	− 253.2365						
Wald $\chi^2(29)$	204.98***						
$F(29,74)$ $[R^2]$			1.59* [54.06%]				
Number of subjects						92	
Number of successful completion of financing round 1						19	
LR χ^2						65.99***	
Log likelihood						− 41.280	

Model 1: The success determinant analyzed in this model is measured by the number of investors. The sample covers 104 crowdfunding projects, and we account for multiple investments by a single investor in a specific project and exclude founders when counting the number of investors. We run zero-inflated negative binomial regressions (using robust standard errors) for the *number of investors* in a crowdfunding project. The fact that 37 projects received no funding at all resulted in a significant number of zeros in our dependent variable. Within the estimation, we control for factors that potentially influence the likelihood of a project attracting at least one investor (0/1 outcome via logit model; depicted in the last part of the table with offerings that began before 2009 as a reference category), because these zeros may be generated by an independent process. The results are presented below "inflate" in Model 1. Exit channel IPO serves as a reference category. *Big city fixed effects* are dummy variables for Sydney, Melbourne, Brisbane, and Perth. We use offering timing as a potential reason why a project received no funding. As a further robustness check (not reported here), we included the additional variables, *equity offering, disclaimer_no financial forecast*, and *no disclaimer_no financial forecast*. Our results remain qualitatively stable. *Model 2*: The success determinant analyzed in this model is measured by the absolute funding amount. The sample covers 104 crowdfunding projects. We run standard OLS regressions (using robust standard errors) to identify the factors that determine *absolute funding amount* in millions and show the coefficient and the standardized coefficient (beta). Exit channel IPO serves as a reference category. *Big city fixed effects* are dummy variables for Sydney, Melbourne, Brisbane, and Perth. In an unreported robustness check, we ruled out the influence of outliers by winsorizing. Absolute Funding Amount and explanatory variables (4), (5), (9)−(14), and (17) are at the 99% and 95% levels. Our results remain qualitatively stable, although the significance of the variable "no disclaimer_no forecast" decreases to the 10% level for winsorizing at the 95% level. Investigating the VIF reveals no multicollinearity, given the mean VIF of 2.01 and all individual values are well below the critical value of 5 (expect for two industry dummy variables with values of 5.21 and 4.53) (see Kutner, Nachtsheim, Neter, & Li, 2005). Excluding one of these borderline cases leads to a mean VIF of 1.65, with all individual values well below 5. However, the exclusion neither changes the results qualitatively nor affects the significance levels of the full model 3. *Model 3*: The success determinant analyzed in this model is measured by the *speed of capital allocation*. The sample covers 92 crowdfunding projects, of which 19 successfully completed their first financing round (i.e., 19 entered a second round of financing after selling all shares offered in round 1). Projects that received no funding or were only partially funded are delisted after 1 year. We run exponential regressions (with log relative-hazard forms) to identify the determinants of the speed of capital allocation (duration of first financing round) by investors measured in days until the target amount for the first round is raised. Exit channel IPO serves as a reference category. *Big city fixed effects* are dummy variables for Sydney, Melbourne, Brisbane, and Perth. ***, **, and * indicate statistical significance at the 1%, 5%, and 10% levels, respectively. *IPO*, Initial public offering; *OLS*, ordinary least squares; *VIF*, variance inflation factors.

III. Crowdinvesting

variables constant (row 3, Table 10.4, Model 1).[14] In addition, we find that a higher number of board members are positive and statistically significant related to funding success for both higher expected number of investors and for higher funding amount. As Table 10.4 shows, an additional member on the board is related to an expected increases in the number of investors by a factor of 1.408 [exp(0.342)] (see row 2, Table 10.4, Model 1), and an expected increase in the total funding amount by 119,000 AUD (0.119 × 1000,000 AUD) (see row 2, Table 10.4, Model 2).

Next, we focus on the impact social (alliance) capital and intellectual capital has on funding success. However, we find no statistically significant impact for the percentage of nonexecutive directors (compare row 4 in Table 10.4, Models 1−3). Similarly to the previous findings, we do not find evidence of a relationship between intellectual capital (measured as patents granted) and funding success (compare row 5, Table 10.4, Models 1−3).

We characterize our empirical findings as support for our Hypothesis 10.1 (a) that higher venture quality, characterized by human capital, has a positive impact on funding success on equity crowdfunding platforms. However, we only find very little evidence in support of Hypothesis 10.1 (b) and (c). A possible explanation could be that our created measures to proxy *intellectual capital* and *social (alliance) capital* are (1) clearly limited to the data availability on ASSOB and (2) those measures are rather crude, meaning, that is, having a patent or not ignores the number of patents and more importantly patent quality (see also our limitation 6 in the next section).

Similarly to the description in the previous section, we expect level of uncertainty to be a highly relevant piece of information for potential investors. As proposed under Hypothesis 10.2, we observe a negative and significant relation between the percentage of offered equity and the expected number of investors (row 6, Table 10.4, Models 1−3). We find that a 1% point increase in equity offered is associated with a decrease in the expected number of investors by a factor of 0.982161 [exp (−0.018)].

This finding is in line with Downes and Henkel (1982), who provide empirical evidence that entrepreneurial ownership is an effective signal in an IPO context. Hypothesis 10.2 is also supported by our finding regarding financial projections of an average statistically significant associated 210,000 AUD decrease in total funding amount, where no disclaimer and no financial forecasts are provided, compared to ventures that include a financial forecast (see row 8, Table 10.4, Model 2). We interpret this to mean there is signaling value in financial forecasts and an inclusion of a disclaimer, because the impact of this investment is larger when information asymmetries are high.

Similar results can also be found for speed of capital allocation as a success measure. We again find a statistically significant positive relationship between a venture's level of uncertainty and financing durations (supporting Hypothesis 10.2). We also find later expected completions of the first financing round among projects with higher percentages of offered equity {an extra percentage of equity offered is associated with a reduction in the expected speed of capital allocation by about 15% [as exp(−0.165) − 1] × 100 = −15.21%} (see Blossfeld, Golsch, & Rohwer, 2007), and less information provided by

---

[14] The expected number of investors changes by the factor of exp(coefficient) for each unit change in the respective predictor, holding all other variables constant. In this case, the expected number of funders increases by a factor of exp(0.017) = 1.01714532.

founders {with no disclaimer and no financial forecasts is associated with a decrease in expected speed of capital allocation by about 97% [as $\exp(-3.385) - 1) \times 100 = -96.61\%$]} as compared to the reference group (see rows 6 and 8, Table 10.4, Model 3).

Unfortunately, the previous argumentation is not supported by the data for campaigns in which a disclaimer is given but no financial forecasts (row 7 in Table 10.4). This means that the latter subgroup is statistically not different from the subgroup providing financial projects. One reason for this outcome could be that all financial projections are highly "optimistic" and potentially overestimate an objectively justifiable future development. When investors anticipate this behavior, they might not differentiate between both subgroups.

Among our additional control variables, we find very limited evidence of stable relationships with funding success. One exception is proposed exit channel. We use the IPO exit channel as our reference category and find that significantly more investors are found than the trade sales exit channel (see row 13 in Table 10.4, Model 1). However, we find no evidence of a relationship between proposed exit channel and absolute funding amount or speed of capital allocation (see row 13 in Table 10.4, Models 2 and 3). This does not provide conclusive evidence that funders regard the exit channel as a valuable signal.

Simultaneously, with the proposed exit channel, founders can also state the number of planned years to exit. However, we again find no empirical evidence that this signal either influences the number of investors or the absolute funding amount. We believe investors may regard this information more as "cheap talk" and not as a valuable signal. Similarly, we find no statistically significant impact from stage of maturity (proxied for by years in business) on the number of investors or the realized funding amount (compare row 16 in Table 10.4, Models 1 and 2). Interestingly, here we find that more mature ventures have a higher likelihood of closing their first financing round earlier (row 16, Table 10.4, Model 3).

In summary, we find strong empirical evidence that effective signals play an important role for investors, especially with respect to the level of uncertainty. The relationships among the aforementioned factors and the number of investors, total funding amount, and speed of the first financing round become apparent on an aggregate project level. But further analysis would be needed to understand the other side of the equation, that is, individual investors' decision-making processes. In particular, we are interested in determining which projects will be perceived as suitable investment alternatives from an individual investor's viewpoint.

10.6 Limitations and avenues for further research

Research on equity crowdfunding has only recently begun, and naturally many interesting questions remain unanswered. In the following, we give a summary of other promising research ideas not covered here and some limitations.

1. We know very little about what drives entrepreneurs to use equity crowdfunding over other financing sources. One reason may be an especially promising investment idea with the potential to inspire a large number of investors. Entrepreneurs should also like and have the skills to handle direct communications with "micro" investors; they

should be using social networks such as Twitter and Facebook actively in their marketing strategies. On the other hand, one could argue that equity crowdfunding is still a funding source of last resort and that more promising projects may have already received, for example, VC.

2. Funders may be motivated by nonmonetary rewards, which are dominant effects in patronage and reward-based crowdfunding (Mollick, 2014). Unfortunately, we could not find appropriate proxies for nonmonetary rewards in the offering documents, but we could consider, for example, classifying investment proposals along dimensions of sustainability.

3. As more data on this investing platform becomes widely available, it may be promising to explore such research questions as which regulatory standards on different platforms foster funding success? And are platform standards related to future project performance? It would also be interesting to conduct a thorough comparison of equity crowdfunded start-ups and VC-funded start-ups in terms of future performance and business risk.

4. We also believe that obtaining information on (1) the length of time investors take to screen the market and thus the platform before they invest in a project and (2) whether the final choice set is restricted to a specific industry, time period, investment pattern, or region would further contribute to our understanding of crowdfunding dynamics. While these questions are clearly beyond the scope of this chapter, our initial inspection of the available ASSOB data for the 104 projects shows that approximately 53% of investors invest in projects that are headquartered in their state of residence. This suggests that geographic distance between investors and entrepreneurs remains an important factor in investor decision-making. Early-stage projects are particularly susceptible, because long distances can create barriers to acquiring information and can increase monitoring costs. Therefore further analyses are necessary to understand whether crowdfunding platforms can indeed eliminate these distance-related economic frictions (Agrawal et al., 2011).

5. As more data become available, it seems promising to investigate whether the effects we find differ for small and large firms, young and old, or technology-based versus nontechnology-based firms, as per Stuart et al. (1999). Unfortunately, we only have 104 projects and 16 explanatory variables, plus *year-*, *industry-*, and *big city fixed effects* as controls. Thus we are rather limited in the extent to which we can split our sample into subsamples, because some of our models would no longer be solvable. For the same reason, we cannot use interaction terms along these groups of firms and the 16 explanatory variables.

6. All of our created measures to proxy, for example, intellectual capital, human capital are clearly limited to the data availability on ASSOB. This could also at least partially explain why we only find little support in the data for Hypothesis 10.1 (b) and (c). For richer datasets, one could probably create better measures, which should be used in subsequent studies on the subject.

7. Finally, it is possible that investors on crowdfunding platforms may be considering other, unobservable, characteristics in their investment decisions, in addition to the venture quality attributes we analyze here. It could be useful to conduct a survey among investors to explore their investment reasons further and perhaps learn more about market dynamics.

10.7 Conclusion

This chapter is the first to conduct an empirical examination of the effectiveness of various venture quality attributes and the level of uncertainty taken from the offering documents that entrepreneurs use to induce (small) investors to commit financial resources in an equity crowdfunding context. The data highlight how important the level of uncertainty is to potential investors, such as the amount of equity offered and whether financial projections are provided. It also demonstrates the importance of human capital (as measured by the percentage of board members with MBA degrees). We also found, somewhat surprisingly, that intellectual capital (as measured by patents) and social (alliance) capital had little or no significant impact on funding success.

Our findings have interesting implications for both practitioners and policy makers. For entrepreneurs that use equity crowdfunding, the data suggest that retaining equity and providing more detailed information about risks can be interpreted as effective signals that can increase the likelihood of funding success. Moreover, internal governance, such as, for example, proper board structure and more highly qualified board members, can enhance the likelihood of attracting investors as well as increase the speed of capital-raising.

With respect to policy implications, our data also highlight the fact that the participants on the equity crowdfunding sites we studied seem to differentiate among attributes of venture quality, and they strongly value credible signals. Crowdfunding investors seem to pay a great deal of attention to the level of uncertainty and the governance material that firms provide. However, at this point, the industry is still in its infancy, and thus our data do not allow us to make a meaningful evaluation of firm outcomes yet. We hope such issues will be explored further as more data become available.

Key terms

Disclaimers
Equity share
Financial projections
Human capital
Intellectual capital
Parcel funding
Planned exit
Signaling
Social (alliance) capital

Discussion questions

10.1. Why might offering a large equity share to crowd investors not help achieve a funding goal? Explain with reference to empirical evidence.

10.2. What are the key requirements for a signal in equity crowdfunding to be effective? Explain with reference to theoretical work on the Nobel Prize winning development of ideas in adverse selection.

10.3. How is social capital pertinent to success in equity crowdfunding? How is social capital different from intellectual capital and human capital? How do these different types of capital affect success in equity crowdfunding?

10.4. What is the typical capital raise in equity crowdfunding? What is the typical campaign goal in capital raising in equity crowdfunding? How long does an equity crowdfunding campaign take? What proportion of entrepreneurial firms that seek capital through equity crowdfunding fail to raise any money at all from crowd investors? What are some of the factors that influence the time to capital raise and the amount of capital raised?

10.5. What is the typical number of investors in equity crowdfunding? What influences the scope of investor participation in a project? Explain with reference to theory and evidence, and differentiate your response relative to the factors that affect the extent of capital raised and time to capital raise. Why might it be helpful for an entrepreneurial firm to have more investors? What are the potential costs to more investors? Explain with reference to agency theory described in Chapter 2, Overview of agency and signaling theory in crowdfunding.

Are equity crowdfunders sensitive to distance?

11.1 Introduction

The open call and investment in equity crowdfunding usually take place on an online platform, such as Crowdcube, which provides the means for the transactions (legal groundwork, preselection, etc.). There are many diverse motivations behind crowdfunding campaigns. Some are charitable in nature; others are entrepreneurial, focusing on raising money to, for example, help bring a new product to market. However, all are positioned as faster and more efficient alternatives to traditional fundraising and lending avenues, such as bank loans. The four primary types of crowdfunding models are donation-based, debt-based, equity-based, and reward-based (Ahlers et al., 2015; Agrawal et al., 2011; Bradford, 2012; Belleflamme et al., 2013, 2014; Burtch et al., 2013; Burtch, Ghose, & Wattal, 2014, 2015; Mollick, 2014; Schwienbacher & Larralde, 2012; Schweizer & Zhou, 2017). See also, for example, Colombo, Franzoni, and Rossi-Lamastra (2015), Mollick (2014), and Moritz and Block (2016) for comprehensive reviews of current crowdfunding literature.

In the aftermath of the recent financial crisis, policymakers around the world have identified crowdfunding as a resourceful approach for promoting projects and young entrepreneurial firms to potential financiers. Equity crowdfunding is considered particularly promising as a means to reduce the funding gap faced by entrepreneurial firms, which have sprung up as venture capitalists (VCs) seek to invest larger amounts in later-stage companies that have the potential to create disruptive technologies or business models. The gaps that were previously filled by VC are increasingly being filled by accredited angel investors. According to the US Small Business Administration, the probability of an entrepreneur obtaining VC funding is about 0.0005. More significantly, the average age of a firm obtaining VC funding is 4 years. Even then, the probability of a mature firm obtaining funding is a minuscule 0.00068. Thus 99.93% of the entrepreneurs will be unable to obtain VC backing (see Rao, 2013).

Crowdfunding, which enables existing angel investors and potential retail investors to invest in entrepreneurial projects, has thus gained great popularity. Equity crowdfunding offers many pronounced potential benefits. Entrepreneurs may obtain needed capital, not available from more traditional sources, such as banks, private equity investors, or VCs, to facilitate their startups and continue their business operations. Indeed, many companies would probably not still be in existence without the option of raising money through crowdfunding. Some well-known examples include Oculus RV, whose entrepreneurs raised US$2.5 million via crowdfunding and which was later acquired by Facebook for US$2 billion. Another example is the Pebble E-Paper Watch, which raised over US$10 million in 37 days, and Pono Music, which raised over US$6 million in 30 days.

However, the potential risks associated with equity crowdfunding are likewise very pronounced. For example, there are lower levels of disclosure required by entrepreneurial firms. Therefore entrepreneurs may squander the proceeds of a funding-round or raise equity capital through crowdfunding and then subsequently issue more shares to themselves, thereby diluting the equity stake held by the crowdfunders. Entrepreneurs may simply pay themselves more and not invest in appropriate projects with the money raised. Investors are certainly not alone in these risks, though as fraudulent activity may also be carried out by crowdfunders or portals themselves (see Cumming, Walz, & Werth, 2016). Nevertheless, it is possible to mitigate such risks through specific conditions imposed on entrepreneurs, portals, and investors, as discussed next.

As mentioned earlier, policymakers have identified crowdfunding as a promising means to cost-effectively bridge geographic boundaries and link investment opportunities with a like-minded entrepreneurial spirit. They hope to at least partially eliminate distance-related economic frictions that are apparent in the early-stage VC market through these types of Internet-based funding platforms (see Agrawal et al., 2011, 2014; Lin & Viswanathan, 2015). Consider the following two contrasting examples, which illustrate the significance of this issue.

Between March 2010 and March 2011, two geographically disparate firms with similar characteristics, Warragundi Beef Co. Queensland Ltd. and Billie Goat Brands Ltd., registered on the Australian Small Scale Offerings Board (ASSOB). Warragundi Beef Co. established itself as a "paddock-to-plate" company providing an integrated high-quality beef supply chain; Billie Goat Brands Ltd. produces a line of goat milk-based skincare and beauty products. Both companies' offerings display similar, easily observable features (e.g., 3–4 years to planned exits, three to four total board members, required total funding of between AU $2 and AU $3.2 million, and total equity offering of above 30%). However, while Billie Goat Brands Ltd. managed to acquire funds through ASSOB, Warragundi Beef Co. Queensland Ltd. did not attract any investors.

Interestingly, the headquarters of Billie Goat Brands Ltd. is in Fountaindale (NSW) in the Central Coast area, which is only a 17-minute car ride away from the larger city of Gosford (population of approximately 160,000), and on the border of the Sydney metropolitan area, the largest city in Australia and approximately a 1-hour car ride away. Warragundi Beef Co. Queensland Ltd., on the other hand, is located in Tamworth (NSW), a small city (population of approximately 50,000), which is 5 hours from Sydney and 6.5 hours from Brisbane by car.

Extant research has established that bridging geographic boundaries is a significant issue for investors. Related research on home bias related to public equity offerings includes Coval and Moskowitz (1999, 2001), Ivković and Weisbenner (2005), Sulaeman (2014), and Seasholes and Zhu (2010). Home bias has been found to impact investor type (e.g., equity and bond) and financial products (see Tesar & Werner, 1995, 1998).

However, this chapter refers primarily to VCs' home bias. In contrast to, for example, mutual funds and hedge funds, VCs tend to invest in early-stage start-ups. And research has found that VC firms seem to prefer local investments (see Chan, Covrig, & Ng, 2005; Cumming & Dai, 2010; Florida & Smith, 1994; Kolympiris, Seele, & Kalaitzandonakes, 2015; Powell, Koput, Bowie, & Smith-Doerr, 2002; Zook, 2002). Sohl (1999) and Harrison, Mason, and Robson (2010) find similar results for the context of business angels. Harrison et al. (2010) conclude that these investors favor local investments for such reasons as, for example, exposure and familiarity to investment opportunities, and direct or indirect knowledge of entrepreneurs.

In crowdfunding, however, equal and close to zero cost access to portals should facilitate exposure, increase familiarity, and improve access to information about entrepreneurial projects for investors. Thus geographic distance should largely cease to matter to investors. For example, Massa and Simonov (2006) suggest that familiarity is information driven. They contrast pure familiarity, where investors tend to rely on what they are most exposed to (either geographically or professionally) even when faced with other information, with information-based familiarity, where investors use familiarity to combat a lack of information. They suggest that, in the case of information-based familiarity, more information should reduce the influence of geographic distance when making investment decisions. We seek to test whether the democratization of information available through Internet-based equity crowdfunding platforms helps to bridge distance-related economic frictions in the early-stage VC market, or will crowdfunding investors remain sensitive to distance?

The VC literature has frequently noted that the likelihood of investing in a venture decreases with geographic distance, because of, for example, due diligence costs and ongoing monitoring efforts (see Sorenson & Stuart, 2001). Equity crowdfunding, which albeit involves a similar type of early-stage financing, nevertheless differs considerably from typical VC investments. With regard to due diligence, for example, crowdfunding investors can only rely on the information provided by the financing portals. Crowdfunded projects are normally at a stage that is too nascent to have received any significant media or industry attention. With regard to monitoring efforts, crowdfunding investors typically make relatively small investments and do not usually obtain the sort of monitoring or control rights that accredited investors such as VCs are granted (Cumming & Johan, 2007; Lerner, 1995).

Moreover, many significant differences exist between the investment behavior of VCs and primarily retail crowdfunders. Consider, for example, the screening methods of each. Moritz, Block, and Lutz (2015), in a qualitative study, show that retail investors appear much less interested in physical meetings with entrepreneurs. They rely more on the "wisdom of the crowd" to screen venture proposals for qualitative facts, such as the level of *comfort* they feel with an entrepreneur after watching the video presentation, how an entrepreneur responds to questions, as well as who has already invested in the project and at what point in time.

However, while crowdfunders have equal access to information, they are not necessarily equally capable of evaluating that information. Investment behavior tends to differ among the various crowdfunding investor types. Such differences are especially pronounced between "accredited" and retail investors, and between foreign and local investors. We question whether crowdfunders are sufficiently incentivized to obtain additional information that may influence their sensitivity to distance from a venture (see Kim & Viswanathan, 2014). Garcia and Strobl (2011) model investors' incentives to acquire correlated information and observe herding behavior on the part of retail investors, who rely on the same information because they care about their wealth relative to their peers. It is possible, therefore, that while crowdfunders may not be homogeneous, they exhibit or mimic similar behavior.

The works most closely related to ours are two recent papers by Agrawal et al. (2011, 2014), who showed that backers were more likely to financially support local bands on a crowdfunding platform called sellaband.com, which specialized in the funding of musicians and bands. However, the authors attribute this finding mainly to family and friends, who are typically geographically closer to a band's location (see also Kuppuswamy & Bayus, 2018, for the importance of family and friends on funding success, and Ordanini, Miceli, Pizzetti, & Parasuraman, 2011, for more details on sellaband.com and the phenomenon of customers becoming supporters).

Lin and Viswanathan (2015) find similar results and document a home bias for financial products on Prosper.com, an online market for unsecured personal loans. Both crowdfunding platforms—sellaband.com and Prosper.com—exhibit some disadvantages for analyzing home bias effects for investments in the early venture market through the Internet, however. For example, sellaband.com in principle provides financial rewards for funders if a band receives US$50,000 to produce an album. In that case, funders would receive a one-third stake of the revenue (prorated according to their investment), and a compact disc (CD). However, from its launch date in August 2006 through 3 years later, only 34 artists out of 4712 listings received the required amount. The average amount invested within those successful campaigns was only US$89 (see Agrawal et al., 2013).

Such low average investment amounts, the low probability of a successful campaign, and highly uncertain distribution even in the case of a successful funding suggest at least some philanthropic component in these investment decisions. On the other hand, the investment amounts on Prosper.com appear to have a clear financial motivation, even though they start as low as US$50. We believe they are too low to have any comparability to typical equity venture investments. Furthermore, the relatively limited borrower information that Prosper.com provides makes the investment decision less complex than typical equity investments in companies. Funders only see the state the borrower resides in, the purpose of the loan, and the requested amount.

For this chapter, we use data from ASSOB, which is a leading equity crowdfunding platform domiciled in Australia on which entrepreneurs offer equity shares of their companies to retail and institutional investors. To date, entrepreneurs on ASSOB have raised more than US$145 million. The minimum investments are also significantly higher than the two aforementioned platforms, and range from AU $5000 to AU $200,000, with an average of AU $31,304. Furthermore, investors have access to a comprehensive prospectus, including a business plan, forecasts, and income statement if available. This situation is highly similar to entrepreneurs presenting documents to VCs to receive financing. It makes ASSOB a near-perfect platform from which to study financial decision making via the Internet in the VC market.

Our findings will be highly relevant for policymakers and practitioners. Given that the SEC approved Title III of the JOBS (Jumpstart Our Business Startups) Act in the United

States in October 2015, entrepreneurs will soon be able to receive funding from so-called nonaccredited (or retail) investors in exchange for an equity stake in their company through Internet-based campaigns on equity crowdfunding platforms. Funding volumes are expected to increase sharply from the relatively low level of about US$115 million in 2012 (see Chapter 11: Signaling in equity crowdfunding).

Our study provides a unique opportunity to study the relationships between various crowdfunding individual investor types—especially "accredited" (or "sophisticated," as they are referred to in Australia) and retail investors—and an equity crowdfunding campaign's geographic distance to determine whether the platforms can successfully reduce market frictions. We believe this will add to the existing literature on home bias established among more sophisticated aggregate investors such as mutual fund managers, hedge fund managers, and VCs. It will also enrich studies related to individual investor behavior.

The crowdfunding issue is particularly relevant today because of the perceived necessity of meeting the financing needs of small- and medium-sized enterprises (SMEs), considered the lifeblood of economies worldwide. Most SMEs experience financing restrictions at various points in their lifecycles, and overcoming them is essential to being able to pursue growth or survive a credit squeeze. A limit on SMEs' financial resources will most likely lead to a limit on economic growth as a whole (Bertoni, Colombo, & Grilli, 2013; Colombo, Croce, & Grilli, 2013). Such obstacles are even more severe in rural areas, far away from more flourishing metropolises (Lipton, 1977; Porter, 2000). In those regions, entrepreneurs face considerable difficulties financing their business ideas, and this is precisely where equity crowdfunding can be most valuable. Its potential to bridge geographic boundaries and bring together investment opportunities with an entrepreneurial spirit would otherwise be virtually impossible. But the question remains, "Is this necessarily happening?", "Is equity crowdfunding fulfilling its potential, and, if not, why not?"

The remainder of the chapter proceeds as follows. The research hypotheses are developed in Section 11.2. We present our dataset construction in Section 11.3. We then describe the applied methodology in Section 11.4 and derive our empirical results in Section 11.5. The final section, Section 11.6, summarizes our main results and concludes.

11.2 Hypothesis development

The home bias phenomenon, which describes investors' propensity to overweight "geographically" close investment opportunities, has been fairly well-established for various contexts in the financial and economics literature (see Ahearne, Griever, & Warnock, 2004; Coval & Moskowitz, 1999; Disdier & Head, 2008; French & Poterba, 1991; Mondria & Wu, 2010; Tesar & Werner, 1995). Several reasons for its existence and persistence have been proffered, which we can broadly categorize into the themes of institutional limitations and investor perceptions. We can break down more detailed explanations within a jurisdiction as follows: (1) better monitoring capabilities and lower associated costs (Coval & Moskowitz, 2001); (2) ambiguity aversion of investors, who subjectively prefer more tangible information that will result in more visible and "familiarity-biased" investments (Franke, Gruber, Harhoff, & Henkel, 2006; Huberman, 2002); and (3) overoptimism toward "home" assets (Lai & Teo, 2008). A number of other studies, including Grinblatt and Keloharju (2000), Feng and Seasholes (2004), and Ivković and Weisbenner (2005), document that investors are more likely to invest in firms that are geographically closer to them.

The Internet has certainly facilitated the flow of information, but it has not resolved some important elements of the home bias, such as a preference for tangible information. For example, consider a bar. Potential investors may frequent the establishment and enjoy the atmosphere. The Internet cannot transcend impressions created through familiarity, and a physical visit creates an opportunity to speak directly to customers and to employees.

Another example is provided by Hortacsu, Martinez-Jerez, and Douglas (2009), who find that the likelihood of a purchase on eBay is inversely related to distance. Agrawal et al. (2011) find that backers on an online crowdfunding platform are more likely to invest in local artists, while Lin and Viswanathan (2015) suggest that lenders prefer geographically close borrowers on Prosper.com, even if they do not have the exact address to, for example, enforce payments. Van Nieuwerburgh and Veldkamp (2009) suggest that investors choose what "home" or "foreign" information to learn about, before deciding what assets to hold. Their model suggests that home bias increases with investors' capacity to process information. More specifically, investors use additional information to build upon their preexisting local knowledge, not necessarily to expand their horizons. Thus if we accept that access to crowdfunding portals increases investors' access to firm information, and increases their information processing capacity, we may find that geographic distance will ultimately influence investment decisions.

Hypothesis 11.1: *A larger geographic distance between home country investors and ventures is negatively correlated with investment probability on equity crowdfunding platforms.*

Research suggests that home bias persists for investments made by sophisticated financial intermediaries, such as mutual fund managers, hedge fund managers, and VCs, as well as by retail investors (see Chan et al., 2005; Cohen, 2009; Coval & Moskowitz, 1999; Cumming & Johan, 2006; Feng & Seasholes, 2004; Grinblatt & Keloharju, 2000; Harrison et al., 2010; Hau & Rey, 2008; Ivković & Weisbenner, 2005; Teo, 2009). For example, Karlsson and Nordén (2007) investigate home bias in the portfolio choices of individual investors. Ritov, Gati, and Tversky (1990) find that households appear to treat familiar gambles as less risky than unfamiliar gambles, even when they assign equal probability distributions to both.

However, this does not necessarily mean that *all* investors are equally affected by geographic distance. Grinblatt and Keloharju (2000) find that the influence of distance is mitigated somewhat among more sophisticated investors. They find that less sophisticated investors have a higher tendency to invest locally than more sophisticated or professional investors.

With reference to the aforementioned research, we seek to differentiate investor sophistication by household wealth. We contrast levels of crowdfunding investor sophistication not by profession, but by a specific examination of the presumably less sophisticated *Retail* investor and the presumably more sophisticated *Accredited* investor. *Accredited* investors are wealthy individuals whose areas of expertise may be within any field, even wholly unrelated to finance, such as medicine or engineering, but who meet certain net wealth or income qualifications (see Section 11.3 for more details). Moreover, Hong, Kubik, and Stein (2004) show that investment decisions are related to social interactions, which are linked naturally to investor communities (see also Vismara, 2015, 2016; Alexy, Block, Sandner, & Ter Wal, 2012, for a discussion on the effect of information cascades). This is especially relevant in a crowdfunding context (see also Chapters 5 and 16 of this book; see also Mollick, 2014), which again leads us to expect less sensitivity to geographic distance among *Accredited* investors.

Hypothesis 11.2: *Accredited investors are less sensitive than retail investors to geographic distance on equity crowdfunding platforms.*

Furthermore, we aim to compare sensitivity to geographic distance between *Overseas* and *Home Country* investors, where additional factors, such as taxes, legal issues, language barriers, and potential information advantages, may play important roles (Coval & Moskowitz, 1999; Ivković & Weisbenner, 2005; Parwada, 2008). Massa and Simonov (2006) suggest that familiarity is information driven. They contrast pure familiarity, where investors, even with more information, tend to rely on what they are exposed to (geographically or professionally), with information-based familiarity, where investors use familiarity to combat a lack of information. They suggest that, in the case of information-based familiarity, more information should reduce the influence of geographic distance when making investment decisions.

A more informed investor would not rely as heavily on publicly available, familiarity-based information, such as geographic proximity. Therefore we assume that those distance-related factors tend to play a subordinate role in the decision-making process, and sensitivity to geographic distance will be lower for *Overseas* investors. However, this does not mean distance is irrelevant. Cultural differences and different economic areas can influence levels of trust and can thus negatively affect investment probability. They should be considered and controlled for in any model to isolate the effect of geographic distance on investment probability (see Grinblatt & Keloharju, 2000; Guiso, Sapienza, & Zingales, 2009). As a result, we expect foreign investors to be less sensitive to distance than *Home Country* investors.

Hypothesis 11.3: *Overseas investors are less sensitive to geographic distance than Home Country investors on equity crowdfunding platforms.*

11.3 Dataset construction

Our dataset is based on the ASSOB equity crowdfunding platform, which has been in operation since 2006. Our analyses include 104 crowdfunding projects over the 2006–June 2012 time period, for which all controlling variables are available (see Chapter 11: Signaling in equity crowdfunding, for a detailed description of the database and sample).

See Table 11A.2 for a list and description of all controlling variables, which are grouped as in Baum and Silverman's (2004) framework and constructed following Chapter 11: Signaling in equity crowdfunding). All company information on investor activities come from ASSOB's client files. However, the organization of those files has changed somewhat over time, and we, therefore, extracted the relevant data from three different types of sources: (1) *Share Application Forms*, filled out by future investors; (2) *Duplicate Share Registers*, compiled by ASSOB and providing an overview of all investors in a company at a specific point in time; and (3) copies of actual *Share Certificates*.

11.3.1 Basic investor information and type

Basic investor information includes (1) name, (2) city of residence, (3) unique investor code, and (4) investor type. Name and city were obtainable through all three sources. To distinguish a backer's level of professionalism, ASSOB categorizes investors as follows according to Section 708 of the Corporations Act of 2001:

Retail—comprises investors with (1) prior contact with the company, (2) any type of professional or related association with the company, or (3) demonstrable interest in the company's Offer.

Accredited—comprises investors in the company who, as per Section 708(8) of the Corporations Act, must meet the following criteria: (1) agree to pay a minimum amount of AU $500,000 for the securities when the company's Offer is accepted and (2) include with the application a *Certification* given by a qualified accountant dated no more than 6 months before the Offer opened. To receive the *Certification* the investor has to have a gross income of AU $250,000 or more per annum in each of the previous 2 years or net assets of at least AU $2.5 million (see Corporations Act 6D.2.03).

Professional—any investor under Section 708(11) of the Corporations Act that has either (1) control of gross assets of at least AU $10 million (including any assets held by an associate under a trust that he manages) or (2) an Australian Financial Services Licensee.

Foreign (overseas)—Individuals domiciled outside Australia who have received the Offer outside Australia [see Corporations Act 708(5)].

Existing shareholder—founding shareholders seeking to consolidate their holdings.

Associate—all those connected with the company, except officeholders and any close relatives of officeholders.

We initially identified 839 individual investors as our starting sample. Basic investor information revealed that 418 are *Retail* investors, 76 are *Accredited*, 5 are *Professional*, 79 are *Foreign*, 25 are *Associates*, and 43 are *Existing Shareholders*. We could find no information available on 193 investors in the *Share Application Forms*, the *Duplicate Share Registers*, or the *Share Certificates*, simply because they did not check the respective box for investor type. Investors in the *Professional* category are presumably the most sophisticated on the platform, which makes them an interesting group to study. However, with only five investments, the sample size is too small from which to draw any meaningful conclusions.

We then matched these investors with the 104 crowdfunding projects identified in Chapter 11: Signaling in equity crowdfunding, with *complete* information. We subsequently eliminated one overseas investor from Papua New Guinea, because Hofstede's (1980) cultural indices are not available there. For all unknown investor types, we then applied the following approach: (1) we classified all investors as *Overseas* if the given address was outside Australia; (2) we classified investors using information available from previous or subsequent order forms; (3) we classified investors specified as *Existing* by ASSOB, even if they subsequently checked a different box, for example, *Retail*; (4) we classified investors with a volume of more than AU $500,000 as *Accredited*; (5) we classified investors as *Professional* if they hold an Australian Financial Services License; and (6) by applying the exclusion principle, we classified the remaining investors as *Retail*.

The cleaned investor classification dataset results in investments made by 409 *Retail* (out of these, 20 investors invested more than once into the same project, including 18 who invested two times in the same campaign, and 2 who invested more than twice into the same project; moreover, we have 1 investor who invested in two different campaigns), 44 *Accredited*, and 34 *Overseas* investors. Note that the following does not consider *Existing Shareholders* or *Associates* because their distance to the venture may be endogenous. Furthermore, the *Professional* group is too small to obtain robust results. This leaves us with a final set of 487 investments.

11.3.2 Distance information

To explore the role of geographic distance in equity crowdfunding of ASSOB companies, we used the information given by the investors and entrepreneurs in the *Share Application Forms* and *Registration Forms*, as described earlier. Entrepreneurs and investors are required to provide this information during the application process. Initially, the city of a company's headquarters and the respective investors' cities of residence were also collected.

To estimate geographic distance, we obtain longitude and latitude for investors and headquarters from Google Maps' APIs (see Table 11.1 and Fig. 11.1). We calculate the linear distance between investors' residences and company headquarters according to Sinnott (1984), which is based on longitude and latitude using spherical geometry as follows:

$$\Delta lon = lon_2 - lon_1$$
$$\Delta lat = lat_2 - lat_1$$
$$a = \left(sin\frac{\Delta lat}{2} \right)^2 + cos(r\Delta lat) \cdot cos(\Delta lon) \cdot \left(sin\frac{\Delta lon}{2} \right)^2 \qquad (11.1)$$
$$log(d) = R \cdot 2 \cdot arcsin \cdot \sqrt{a},$$

where R is 6,371, the radius of the Earth (mean radius in km).[1] We use the logarithm of geographic distance to account for nonlinear transportation costs among the dimensions of time and money (see Sorenson & Stuart, 2001, for a more detailed discussion).

---

[1] The Earth is approximately spherical. Therefore the distance from points on the surface to the center ranges from 6353 to 6384 km. This is why we calculate the mean.

TABLE 11.1 Descriptive statistics.

Variable	Observations	Mean	Std.	Min	Max
Distance—All Investors	50,648	2297.64	3075.48	0.00	17,464.91
Distance—Retail	42,536	1631.66	1348.51	0.00	6753.09
Distance—Accredited	4576	1326.17	1104.59	0.00	3717.92
Distance—Overseas	3536	11,566.20	4423.40	2151.28	17,464.91
Retail Investors	50,648	0.84	0.37	0.00	1.00
Overseas Investors	50,648	0.07	0.25	0.00	1.00
Accredited Investors	50,648	0.09	0.29	0.00	1.00
# Board	50,648	3.61	1.01	1.00	8.00
% Board MBA	50,648	4.47	11.56	0.00	50.00
% Nonexecutive Board Members	50,648	22.92	25.37	0.00	75.00
Granted Patent	50,648	0.20	0.40	0.00	1.00
Equity Offering	50,648	21.30	13.19	1.53	90.00
Disclaimer_No Financial Forecast	50,648	0.15	0.36	0.00	1.00
No Disclaimer_No Financial Forecast	50,648	0.47	0.50	0.00	1.00
# Staff	50,648	7.16	12.52	0.00	120.00
Award	50,648	0.17	0.38	0.00	1.00
Government Grant	50,648	0.02	0.14	0.00	1.00
Intended Number of Rounds	50,648	2.54	0.59	1.00	3.00
Most Likely Exit—Others	50,648	0.04	0.19	0.00	1.00
Most Likely Exit—Trade Sale	50,648	0.48	0.50	0.00	1.00
Years in Business	50,648	2.63	4.89	0.00	30.00
Years to Planned Exit	50,648	3.86	1.15	1.00	7.00
Parcel Size	50,648	31,605.79	19,497.06	5000.00	200,000.00
Share Price	50,648	0.10	0.21	0.01	2.00
Target Funding	50,648	1.78	1.41	0.30	5.00
ΔPDI	50,648	-1.69	9.36	-55.00	16.00
ΔIVC	50,648	2.46	11.40	-1.00	70.00
ΔMVF	50,648	0.77	4.47	-5.00	27.00
ΔUAI	50,648	-0.64	7.91	-44.00	43.00
ΔLTVST	50,648	-2.73	11.40	-62.00	0.00
ΔIVR	50,648	1.92	9.20	-4.00	54.00

The table reports the number of observations, mean, standard deviation (Std.), minimum (Min), and maximum (Max) for all variables. See Table 11A.2 for variable descriptions.

(A)

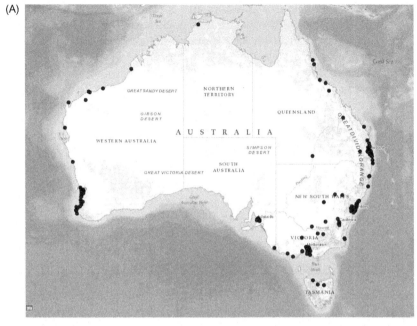

(B)

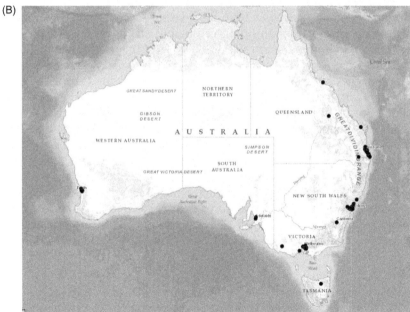

FIGURE 11.1 Geographic distribution of investors and company headquarters.
The geographic distribution of all Australian (*Home Country*) investors (A) and all company headquarters (B) is illustrated. Source: *Created by Adam Schneider using GPSVisualizer (see http://www.gpsvisualizer.com).*

As Fig. 11.1 shows, *Home Country* investors and companies are clearly located throughout the more populous areas, with concentrated pockets on the western and eastern borders, along the Australian coastlines. The more rural northern and central parts of the country have few investors or companies.[2]

Table 11.1 provides an overview of all the data collected and is intended as a first indication of the geographic patterns of crowdfunding investors. See Table 11A.1 for descriptive statistics for the different investor types. Note that *Retail* investors have an average distance of 1632 km from the project they invest in. *Accredited* investors are somewhat closer, with an average distance of 1326 km. *Overseas* investors, on the other hand, are naturally located much further away than the other investor types. On average, they are more than 11,566 km away from their investments, which is approximately five times the average of the entire dataset. The correlations between distance and all considered variables are in Table 11.2.

11.4 Methodology

To analyze investor sensitivity to distance for those who invested in at least one project (and disregarding potential investors who never invested), we apply logistic regressions for each logarithm of distance, analyzing how project distance, among other characteristics, influences investment likelihood from an investor's point of view. Considering only investors who supported a crowdfunding campaign, all derived conclusions are conditional on an investor having made at least one crowdfunding investment.

In a related robustness check, we use distance and its quadratic term in an alternative model. Both approaches are conceptually similar, because they are capable of including nonlinear effects. Generally, the distance between investors and entrepreneurs is considered exogenous, but there are constellations in which one or another actively changes location (see Parwada, 2008), or where unrelated moving impacts investment decisions (Lin & Viswanathan, 2015). Because of our setup, we expect our results to be the least affected by this endogeneity problem, because the entrepreneurs generally do not know their investors before deciding on the location. It is also unlikely that investors will change location to be closer to their ventures. However, institutional investors could strategically decide to be located in "prospering" metropolises in order to be closer to a bigger pool of ventures. We control for this phenomenon by using *Big City* fixed effects on the project level.[3] In addition, we use a number of control variables that are potentially correlated with the financing decision.

---

[2] The 34 *Overseas* investors are located in Germany (2), Hong Kong (2), New Zealand (3), Russia (12), Singapore (2), South Africa (1), Thailand (2), the United Kingdom (6), the United States (3), and Vietnam (1).

[3] For the sake of clarity, we do not explicitly report the coefficients and test statistics for the *Big Cities* (Sydney, Melbourne, Brisbane, and Perth) in Tables 11.3 and 11.4. To summarize, we find a statistically significant effect only for ventures in Brisbane having a higher probability of obtaining investments. This effect is evident in all models in Tables 11.3 and 11.4.

TABLE 11.2 Correlation matrix.

	(1)	(2)	(3)	(4)	(5)	(6)	(7)	(8)	(9)	(10)	(11)	(12)	(13)	(14)	(15)	(16)	(17)	(18)	(19)	(20)	(21)	(22)	(23)	(24)	(25)	(26)
(1) Invest	1.00																									
(2) Log Distance	-0.03	1.00																								
(3) # Board	0.04	0.00	1.00																							
(4) % Board MBA	0.01	0.00	-0.06	1.00																						
(5) % Nonexecutive Board Members	-0.02	0.00	0.08	-0.31	1.00																					
(6) Granted Patent	-0.01	0.01	-0.02	0.10	-0.03	1.00																				
(7) Equity Offering	-0.05	-0.01	-0.10	0.03	0.18	-0.11	1.00																			
(8) Disclaimer_No Financial Forecast	0.07	0.00	-0.23	-0.01	-0.11	-0.02	-0.09	1.00																		
(9) No Disclaimer_No Financial Forecast	-0.01	0.01	-0.09	0.00	0.04	0.01	0.01	-0.40	1.00																	
(10) # Staff	0.01	0.01	0.26	-0.10	0.18	-0.12	0.04	-0.01	-0.08	1.00																
(11) Award	-0.01	0.00	0.03	-0.12	0.00	0.21	0.12	-0.05	0.03	0.08	1.00															
(12) Government Grant	-0.01	0.01	-0.01	0.10	-0.13	-0.07	0.38	-0.06	0.01	0.04	0.12	1.00														
(13) Intended Number of Rounds	0.02	0.00	0.15	-0.12	0.16	0.03	0.08	0.11	-0.21	0.14	0.14	-0.13	1.00													
(14) Most Likely Exit—Others	-0.02	0.00	0.03	0.07	0.00	0.27	-0.15	0.05	-0.09	-0.05	0.04	-0.03	-0.01	1.00												
(15) Most Likely Exit—Trade Sale	-0.02	0.00	-0.20	-0.21	0.11	0.14	0.19	-0.09	0.17	-0.07	0.12	0.01	0.13	-0.19	1.00											
(16) Years in Business	-0.02	0.01	0.10	-0.04	0.09	0.11	0.05	-0.12	-0.09	0.41	0.18	-0.02	-0.04	-0.07	0.02	1.00										

(Continued)

TABLE 11.2 (Continued)

	(1)	(2)	(3)	(4)	(5)	(6)	(7)	(8)	(9)	(10)	(11)	(12)	(13)	(14)	(15)	(16)	(17)	(18)	(19)	(20)	(21)	(22)	(23)	(24)	(25)	(26)
(17) Years to Planned Exit	-0.09	-0.01	-0.11	0.02	0.13	-0.15	0.16	-0.06	-0.03	0.07	-0.10	-0.04	-0.03	-0.19	0.10	0.23	1.00									
(18) Parcel Size	0.05	0.00	-0.02	0.14	-0.07	-0.10	0.09	-0.01	-0.05	-0.05	-0.02	0.04	-0.16	0.06	-0.20	-0.09	-0.16	1.00								
(19) Share Price	0.22	0.01	0.16	-0.05	0.02	-0.09	-0.19	0.19	-0.09	0.05	-0.03	-0.03	0.04	0.07	-0.19	-0.02	-0.18	0.23	1.00							
(20) Target Funding	0.02	-0.01	0.20	0.09	0.04	-0.04	0.18	0.18	-0.20	0.17	0.16	-0.10	0.35	0.16	-0.15	0.00	0.09	0.23	0.26	1.00						
(21) ΔPDI	N.A.	-0.56	N.A.	N.A.	N.A.	N.A.	N.A.	N.A.	N.A.	N.A.	N.A.	N.A.	N.A.	N.A.	N.A.	N.A.	N.A.	N.A.	N.A.	N.A.	1.00					
(22) ΔIVC	N.A.	0.56	N.A.	N.A.	N.A.	N.A.	N.A.	N.A.	N.A.	N.A.	N.A.	N.A.	N.A.	N.A.	N.A.	N.A.	N.A.	N.A.	N.A.	N.A.	-0.89	1.00				
(23) ΔMVF	N.A.	0.47	N.A.	N.A.	N.A.	N.A.	N.A.	N.A.	N.A.	N.A.	N.A.	N.A.	N.A.	N.A.	N.A.	N.A.	N.A.	N.A.	N.A.	N.A.	-0.94	0.88	1.00			
(24) ΔUAI	N.A.	-0.34	N.A.	N.A.	N.A.	N.A.	N.A.	N.A.	N.A.	N.A.	N.A.	N.A.	N.A.	N.A.	N.A.	N.A.	N.A.	N.A.	N.A.	N.A.	0.68	-0.41	-0.71	1.00		
(25) ΔLTVST	N.A.	-0.78	N.A.	N.A.	N.A.	N.A.	N.A.	N.A.	N.A.	N.A.	N.A.	N.A.	N.A.	N.A.	N.A.	N.A.	N.A.	N.A.	N.A.	N.A.	0.84	-0.85	-0.75	0.52	1.00	
(26) ΔIVR	N.A.	0.65	N.A.	N.A.	N.A.	N.A.	N.A.	N.A.	N.A.	N.A.	N.A.	N.A.	N.A.	N.A.	N.A.	N.A.	N.A.	N.A.	N.A.	N.A.	-0.95	0.92	0.87	-0.63	-0.92	1.00

The table shows the correlation between all variables used in the multivariate regressions. See Table 11A.2 for variable descriptions.

TABLE 11.3 Multivariate analysis of geographic distance.

	Model 1: Home country investors only		Model 2: Retail versus accredited investors		Model 3: Overseas investors only	
	Coefficient	z-Value	Coefficient	z-Value	Coefficient	z-Value
Constant	−3.56***	−6.92	−3.11***	−5.33	−11.30***	−4.42
Investor-Related Information						
Log Distance	−0.44***	−20.86	−0.51***	−8.46	0.01	0.12
Retail Investors	−	−	−0.50	−1.63	−	−
Retail Investors × Log Distance	−	−	0.09	1.43	−	−
Human Capital						
# Board	0.06	0.90	0.07	0.92	0.60	1.47
% Board MBA	0.025***	4.29	0.03***	4.30	0.05	1.12
Social (Alliance) Capital						
% Nonexecutive Board Members	<0*	−1.88	−0.01**	−1.88	0.01	0.31
Intellectual Capital						
Granted Patent	−0.27	−1.29	−0.27	−1.29	0.51	0.63
Equity Share						
Equity Offering	−0.01	−0.72	−0.01	−0.73	0.01	0.38
Financial Projections						
Disclaimer_No Financial Forecast	0.56***	2.59	0.57***	2.66	3.578**	2.10
No Disclaimer_No Financial Forecast	0.25	1.58	0.26	1.62	2.31	1.41
Additional Controls						
# Staff	0.01	1.17	0.57	2.66	0.09	1.54
Award	0.50**	2.45	0.26	1.62	−2.72	−1.43
Government Grant	−0.56	−0.87	0.011	1.16	2.29	0.96
Intended Number of Rounds	0.33***	2.86	0.51**	2.49	0.86	1.26
Most Likely Exit—Others	−1.36**	−2.09	−0.55	−0.84	−	−
Most Likely Exit—Trade Sale	0.71***	4.20	0.34***	2.91	−0.08	−0.08
Years in Business	−0.05**	−2.24	−1.37**	−2.10	−0.28	−1.16
Years to Planned Exit	−0.07	−1.08	0.70***	4.18	−0.27	−1.14

(Continued)

TABLE 11.3   (Continued)

	Model 1: Home country investors only		Model 2: Retail versus accredited investors		Model 3: Overseas investors only	
	Coefficient	z-Value	Coefficient	z-Value	Coefficient	z-Value
Parcel Size	>0	0.57	−0.04**	−2.22	>0	0.21
Share Price	1.19***	4.10	−0.07	−1.08	−3.67	−1.51
Target Funding	−0.016	−0.24	1.45e − 06	0.54	−1.00***	−3.34
Year Fixed Effects	Yes		Yes		Yes	
Industry Fixed Effects	Yes		Yes		Yes	
Big City Fixed Effects	Yes		Yes		Yes	
ΔHofstede Distance Measures	N.A.		N.A.		Yes	
Observation	47,112		47,112		3026	
Log Pseudo-Likelihood	−1882.94		−1881.96		−133.38	
Pseudo R²	26.30%		26.33%		28.45%	

We apply logistic regressions to analyze investor sensitivity to geographic distance, where the dependent variable is equal to 1 if the investor funds the project, and 0 otherwise. We cluster standard errors by investor level. In model 1, we restrict investors to solely *Home Country* investors. In model 2, we subdivide the *Home Country* investor base into *Retail* and *Accredited* investors and use the latter as the reference group. Model 3 considers *Overseas* investors only. We exclude associates, professionals, and investors from all models from countries for which no Hofstede (1980) six-dimensional distance measures can be found. See Table 11A.2 for variable descriptions. ***, **, and * indicate statistical significance at the 1%, 5%, and 10% levels, respectively.

In model 1 of Table 11.3, we determine whether a *Home Country* backer invested in an equity crowdfunding campaign by first estimating a logit model, using *Log Distance* as the logarithm of kilometers between backer and venture headquarters to proxy for geographic distance (as well as *Distance* and *Squared Distance* in a robustness check). In model 2 of Table 11.3, we divide the *Home Country* investors by the *Investor Type* dummy variable for *Retail* investors (using *Accredited* investors as the reference group). We also include the interaction term between *Log Distance* and *Retail* investors.

Model 3 is conceptually identical to model 1, except that it considers *Overseas* instead of *Home Country* investors. Further explanatory variables in all models are *Human Capital* (# Board, % Board MBA), *Social* (Alliance), *Capital* (% Nonexecutive Board), *Intellectual Capital* (Patent), *Equity Share* (Equity Offering), *Financial Projections* (Disclaimer_No Financial Forecast, No Disclaimer_No Financial Forecast), and *Additional Control Variables* (# Staff, Award, Government Grant, Intended Number of Rounds, Most Likely Exit—Others, Most Likely Exit—Trade Sale, Target Funding, Years in Business, Years to

Planned Exit, and return on assets (ROA)) (see Table 11A.1 for variable descriptions and calculation methods).[4] The basic structure of our regression equations is as follows:

$$
\begin{aligned}
Investment(0/1) = {} & \alpha + \beta_1 \cdot LogDistance + \beta_2 \cdot InvestorType + \beta_3 \cdot LogDistance \times InvestorType \\
& + \beta_{4,5} \cdot HumanCapital + \beta_6 \cdot Social(Alliance)Capital + \beta_7 \cdot \\
& IntellectualCapital + \beta_8 \cdot EquityShare + \beta_{9,10} \cdot FinancialProjections + \sum_j \gamma_j \cdot \\
& AdditionalControlVariables_j + \xi + \phi + \psi + \sum_k \varpi_k \cdot \Delta HofstedeDistanceMeasure_k + \varepsilon_t,
\end{aligned}
$$

$$(11.2)$$

where ξ are the *Year* fixed effects, ϕ are *Industry* fixed effects, and ψ are *Big City* fixed effects.[5] We omit investment-level notations from Eq. (11.2) for the sake of clarity. In the models investigating *Overseas* investors, we also use the differences among the six Hofstede cultural dimension distance measures (Power Distance Index, Individualism vs Collectivism, Masculinity vs Femininity, Uncertainty Avoidance Index, Long-Term Orientation vs Short-Term Normative Orientation, and Indulgence vs Restraint) in each respective country to the index value of Australia in order to measure cultural distance (see Chapter 3: Overview of institutional contexts and empirical methods; see also Hofstede, 1980; Hofstede, Hofstede, & Minkov, 2010). The Hofstede (1980) indices control for the influence of cultural differences on overseas investors. We use clustered standard errors at the investor level in order to control for the possibility that unobserved investor characteristics influence individual investor decisions, and standard errors are correlated on the investor level (see Bernstein, Korteweg, & Laws, 2017, for a similar argumentation).

11.5 Empirical results

Initial results indicate that investors favor shorter distances over longer ones when looking solely at investors who are Australian residents (*Home Country* investors). This provides support for Hypothesis 11.1 (see Table 11.3, model 1).[6] In model 2, we investigate

---

[4] Consistent with Chapter 11: Signaling in equity crowdfunding, we use the same control variables.

[5] The *Big City* fixed effects are especially useful for addressing a potential selection problem from a higher likelihood that projects will be located in metropolitan areas. We can, therefore, address the higher propensity of projects being born in Sydney, Brisbane, Melbourne, or Perth, while at the same time control for the potentially higher attractiveness of these projects given their location in densely populated areas and for the fact that more potential investors or closer networks may be located in these larger cities.

[6] Given that we only analyze investors who invested at least once into a project, all our results need to be interpreted carefully. We cannot make any statement about whether a larger distance to a project might keep a potential investor from investing in a project altogether. Given this selection bias, our results need to be interpreted conditional on the fact that an investor invested at least in one campaign. Moreover, the clear dominance of the economic activity in the south-east of Australia could potentially lead to spatial autocorrelation.

further whether different groups of Australian residents differ in their sensitivity to distance. More precisely, in Hypothesis 11.2, we argued that *Accredited* investors should react less sensitively than *Retail* investors to distance.

We then differentiate Australian residents further by subdividing them into *Retail* and *Accredited* investors, and introducing an interaction term between *Retail* investors and *Log Distance*. *Accredited* investors serve as our reference group. Contrary to our hypothesis, we find support for the notion that both groups are similarly sensitive to distance, as indicated by the insignificant interaction term on a 10.4% level (see the *t*-statistic for the coefficient *Retail Investors* × *Log Distance* of −1.63, translating into a *P*-value of 10.4% in model 2 in Table 11.3).

Note that this result may be at least partially driven by an opposing trend, namely, that the *Accredited* investor classification does not necessarily correspond with higher levels of investment skill. As per the definition, *Accredited* investors have a certain level of wealth. However, as a recent strand of the literature highlights, wealth can be obtained in several ways. Some of which require no investment knowledge, for example, inheritance (see Lee, 2011). Thus investors meeting the monetary qualifications for being *Accredited* are not necessarily more sophisticated than *Retail* investors.

Model 3 examines the group of *Overseas* investors and their sensitivity to distance. Our Hypothesis 11.3 suggests that *Overseas* investors should react less sensitively to distance than Australian residents, given the likely absence of any local knowledge or face-to-face interaction. Model 3 supports this hypothesis and reveals that *Overseas* investors' investment decisions are not only less sensitive to distance, but they are also not significantly influenced by the distance to the project at all.

In the following robustness check, we replace *Log Distance* with *Distance* and *Squared Distance* as alternatives. Note that both approaches are conceptually similar, because they are capable of including nonlinear effects. Table 11.4 shows that the main results are similar to those using *Log Distance*. *Distance* remains negatively correlated with the probability of investing for Australian residents. However, the quadratic term reveals a reversal point (or tipping point), which means that the negative influence on investment probability decreases for longer distances, given the positive and significant coefficient for the quadratic term (see Table 11.4, model 1b). For *Overseas* investors, we again find no significant influence of distance.

These findings provide valuable insights to practitioners and policymakers. The latter may want to consider that equity crowdfunding (thus far) has not managed to meaningfully eliminate distance-related economic frictions that are apparent in early-stage capital markets within the home country. Hence, it is not yet a "perfect" mechanism for advancing economic development in more rural areas. However, the results also suggest that funding success is higher for companies established in more populous areas. They indicate that highlighting local references in a company's offering documents may increase the perceived familiarity of investors, and may, therefore, improve start-ups' chances of receiving funding.

TABLE 11.4 Multivariate analysis of geographic distance.

	Model 1a: Home country investors only		Model 1b: Home country investors only		Model 2a: Overseas investors only		Model 2b: Overseas investors only	
	Coefficient	z-Value	Coefficient	z-Value	Coefficient	z-Value	Coefficient	z-Value
Constant	-4.72***	-9.06	-3.82***	-7.67	-11.09***	-4.82	-12.843	-4.44
Investor-Related Information								
Distance	-0.001***	-13.64	-0.002***	-10.18	-9.03e-06	-0.37	0.0004	0.94
Squared Distance			2.18e-07***	4.79			-2.16e-08	-0.92
Human Capital								
# Board	0.076	1.10	0.073	1.03	0.60	1.47	0.61	1.47
% Board MBA	0.02***	3.71	0.02***	3.85	0.05	1.12	0.05	1.14
Social (Alliance) Capital								
% Nonexecutual Board Members	-0.01**	-2.36	-0.01**	-2.18	0.01	0.31	0.01	0.33
Intellectual Capital								
Granted Patent	-0.17	-0.80	-0.19	-0.89	0.51	0.64	0.54	0.67
Equity Share								
Equity Offering	-0.01	-0.64	-0.01	-0.58	0.01	0.37	0.01	0.35
Financial Projections								
Disclaimer_No Financial Forecast	0.52**	2.39	0.52**	2.36	3.58**	2.10	3.60	2.13
No Disclaimer_No Financial Forecast	0.28*	1.81	0.27*	1.68	2.31	1.41	2.31	1.43
Additional Controls								
# Staff	0.01	1.37	0.01	1.38	0.09	1.54	0.09	1.55
Award	0.20***	2.10	0.44**	2.18	-2.73	-1.43	-2.74	-1.42
Government Grant	0.57	-1.24	-0.71	-1.19	2.29	0.96	2.29	0.96
Intended Number of Rounds	0.11**	2.31	0.29**	2.50	0.86	1.25	0.83	1.17

(Continued)

TABLE 11.4 (Continued)

	Model 1a: Home country investors only		Model 1b: Home country investors only		Model 2a: Overseas investors only		Model 2b: Overseas investors only	
	Coefficient	z-Value	Coefficient	z-Value	Coefficient	z-Value	Coefficient	z-Value
Most Likely Exit—Others	0.62**	−2.59	−1.56**	−2.48	–	–	–	–
Most Likely Exit—Trade Sale	0.17***	3.66	0.64***	3.82	−0.07	−0.08	−0.05	−0.06
Years in Business	0.02***	−2.58	−0.05**	−2.44	−0.28	−1.17	−0.29	−1.19
Years to Planned Exit	0.06	−0.95	−0.07	−1.10	−0.27	−1.14	−0.27	−1.17
Parcel Size	>0	0.85	>0	0.79	>0	0.21	>0	0.20
Share Price	1.25***	3.94	1.25***	3.92	−3.67	−1.51	−3.68	−1.52
Target Funding	−0.031	−0.48	−0.028	−0.42	−1.00***	−3.34	−1.00***	−3.33
Year Fixed Effects	Yes		Yes		Yes		Yes	
Industry Fixed Effects	Yes		Yes		Yes		Yes	
Big City Fixed Effects	Yes		Yes		Yes		Yes	
ΔHofstede Distance Measures	N.A.		N.A.		Yes		Yes	
Observation	47,112		47,112		3026		3026	
Log Pseudo-Likelihood	−1893.00		−1884.08		−133.38		−132.83	
Pseudo R²	25.87%		26.25%		28.45%		28.75%	

We apply logistic regressions to analyze investor sensitivity to geographic distance, where the dependent variable is equal to 1 if the investor funds the project, and 0 otherwise. We cluster standard errors by investor level. In model 1a, we restrict investors to *Home Country* investors and consider distance as an explanatory variable. Model 1b is based on model 1a but includes squared distance as an explanatory variable. Model 2a considers *Overseas* investors only and uses distance as an explanatory variable. Model 2b is based on model 2a but also includes squared distance as an explanatory variable. We exclude associates, professionals, and investors from all models for which no Hofstede (1980) six-dimensional distance measures can be found. See Table 11A.2 for variable descriptions. ***, **, and * indicate statistical significance at the 1%, 5%, and 10% levels, respectively.

11.6 Conclusion

This chapter is the first to provide evidence of investor sensitivity to the geographic distance between them and a venture's location in an equity crowdfunding context. Our study differs from prior research along several key dimensions. Many previous studies show evidence of home bias among aggregate investors, such as mutual funds, hedge funds, and VCs. Research on individual investors mainly relates to their holding in public market equities and bonds.

In contrast, crowdfunding investors have access to entrepreneurs on equity crowdfunding platforms because they use the Internet as a channel to promote their projects and start-up firms. This gives potential investors the chance to process relevant information for the investment decision at virtually zero cost, while also providing an opportunity to chat with entrepreneurs via, for example, videoconferencing. It is for this reason that policymakers have identified crowdfunding as a resource to cost-effectively bridge geographic boundaries and link investment opportunities with a like-minded entrepreneurial spirit. It may be possible at some point to at least partially eliminate or reduce distance-related economic frictions apparent in the early-stage VC market through such Internet-based funding platforms. The opportunity to gain insight or information about entrepreneurial firms is equal for all investors, irrespective of geographic distance. However, the crowdfunding phenomenon has not managed to alleviate all distance-related sensitivity yet. There remain advantages for investors located close to a venture. For example, they can perhaps assure themselves of venture quality by, for example, visiting a store and speaking personally to employees or entrepreneurs. Such personal contact can help investors familiarize themselves with ventures, and their products/services may appear more tangible, which is commonly perceived to increase investment probability.

Given prior arguments, it is not surprising that geographic distance is negatively correlated with investment probability for *Home Country* investors. This supports the idea of a home bias effect in equity crowdfunding, and that superior access to information due to technological advances has not yet fully overcome distance-related frictions. However, when comparing *Home Country* investors (*Retail* and *Accredited*) only, we were able to document that both investor types are similarly sensitive to distance. This is presumably because, as noted earlier, despite wealth and income differences, *Accredited* investors are not necessarily more sophisticated than *Retail* investors.

Finally, we also show that, in contrast to *Home Country* investors, *Overseas* investors are not sensitive to distance. Intuitively, this makes sense, because it seems unlikely that foreign investors would be able to build an ex ante familiarity with firms, or routinely incur the traveling costs to visit ventures. Thus distance should be of less importance than it is for *Home Country* investors.

We also note that home bias is not necessarily a bad thing. For example, Coval and Moskowitz (2001) and Ivković, Sialm, and Weisbenner (2008) find higher abnormal returns on local stocks in locally biased portfolios versus fully diversified ones. Home biases may be difficult to overcome. However, research shows that the neighboring country advantage can have a similar effect on risks that neighboring countries share and can even lead to increased camaraderie among countries. Ultimately, developing close ties with neighboring countries can be positive and profitable.

Key terms

Accredited investor
Associate
Existing shareholder
Foreign investor
Hofstede cultural conditions
Home bias
Professional investor
Retail Investor

Discussion questions

11.1. Why might distance matter for equity crowdfunding investors if they are conducting business over the Internet? Explain why, with reference to theory and empirical evidence. Is the role of distance in equity crowdfunding different than other financing contexts, such as angel investment, crowdfunding, and mutual fund investment? Why should entrepreneurs care about the geographic scope of their investor base through equity crowdfunding?

11.2. Is the role of distance in equity crowdfunding more or less pronounced for foreign investors? Explain why, with reference to institutional theory and empirical evidence.

11.3. Is the role of distance in equity crowdfunding more pronounced for accredited investors than their nonaccredited counterparts? Explain why, with reference to theory and evidence.

Appendix

TABLE 11A.1 Descriptive statistics by investor type.

	Overseas (#34)				Home Country (#453)				Accredited (#44)				Retail (#409)			
	Mean	Std.	Min	Max	Mean	Std.	Min	Max	Mean	Std.	Min	Max	Mean	Std.	Min	Max
Distance	11,606	4388	2156	16,699	685	1045	0	5780	546	874	0	3682	700	1061	0	5780
# Board	3.24	0.82	1.00	5.00	4.04	1.07	1.00	8.00	3.77	1.08	3.00	6.00	4.07	1.07	1.00	8.00
% Board MBA	14.46	16.58	0.00	33.33	4.37	11.76	0.00	50.00	6.97	13.94	0.00	40.00	4.09	11.49	0.00	50.00
% Nonexecutive Board Members	16.81	26.38	0.00	75.00	16.63	21.03	0.00	75.00	13.64	24.32	0.00	75.00	16.96	20.66	0.00	75.00
Granted Patent	0.47	0.51	0.00	1.00	0.13	0.33	0.00	1.00	0.16	0.37	0.00	1.00	0.12	0.33	0.00	1.00
Equity Offering	18.45	17.61	4.69	90.00	14.44	12.88	1.53	90.00	16.44	9.65	5.78	36.00	14.22	13.17	1.53	90.00
Disclaimer_No Financial Forecast	0.15	0.36	0.00	1.00	0.43	0.50	0.00	1.00	0.18	0.39	0.00	1.00	0.46	0.50	0.00	1.00
No Disclaimer_No Financial Forecast	0.76	0.43	0.00	1.00	0.38	0.49	0.00	1.00	0.48	0.51	0.00	1.00	0.37	0.48	0.00	1.00
# Staff	6.00	5.78	0.00	30.00	8.84	9.43	0.00	120.00	7.07	3.67	2.00	14.00	9.03	9.84	0.00	120.00
Award	0.03	0.17	0.00	1.00	0.15	0.35	0.00	1.00	0.27	0.45	0.00	1.00	0.13	0.34	0.00	1.00
Government Grant	0.03	0.17	0.00	1.00	0.01	0.10	0.00	1.00	0.00	0.00	0.00	0.00	0.01	0.11	0.00	1.00
Intended Number of Rounds	2.79	0.48	1.00	3.00	2.66	0.60	1.00	3.00	2.41	0.79	1.00	3.00	2.68	0.57	1.00	3.00
Most Likely Exit—Others	0.00	0.00	0.00	0.00	0.01	0.08	0.00	1.00	0.00	0.00	0.00	0.00	0.01	0.09	0.00	1.00
Most Likely Exit—Trade Sale	0.47	0.51	0.00	1.00	0.37	0.48	0.00	1.00	0.64	0.49	0.00	1.00	0.34	0.47	0.00	1.00
Years in Business	0.82	1.47	0.00	4.00	1.65	1.91	0.00	20.00	1.43	1.55	0.00	5.00	1.68	1.94	0.00	20.00
Years to Planned Exit	3.44	0.96	2.00	5.00	2.82	1.50	1.00	7.00	3.59	1.06	2.00	7.00	2.74	1.52	1.00	7.00
Parcel Size	26,912	10,942	5000	60,000	43,259	20,564	15,000	72,000	33,864	12,615	15,000	60,000	44,270	21,004	15,000	72,000
Share Price	0.06	0.05	0.02	0.20	0.62	0.88	0.01	2.00	0.05	0.04	0.01	0.20	0.69	0.91	0.01	2.00
Target Funding	1.46	0.94	0.50	4.00	2.10	1.23	0.30	5.00	1.99	1.19	0.50	5.00	2.11	1.23	0.30	5.00

(Continued)

TABLE 11A.1 (Continued)

	Overseas (#34)				Home Country (#453)				Accredited (#44)				Retail (#409)			
	Mean	Std.	Min	Max	Mean	Std.	Min	Max	Mean	Std.	Min	Max	Mean	Std.	Min	Max
ΔPDI	−24.15	27.09	−55.00	16.00	N.A.	N.A.	N.A.	N.A.	N.A.	N.A.	N.A.	N.A.	N.A.	N.A.	N.A.	N.A.
ΔIVC	35.26	26.93	−1.00	70.00	N.A.	N.A.	N.A.	N.A.	N.A.	N.A.	N.A.	N.A.	N.A.	N.A.	N.A.	N.A.
ΔMVF	10.97	13.38	−5.00	27.00	N.A.	N.A.	N.A.	N.A.	N.A.	N.A.	N.A.	N.A.	N.A.	N.A.	N.A.	N.A.
ΔUAI	−9.18	29.04	−44.00	43.00	N.A.	N.A.	N.A.	N.A.	N.A.	N.A.	N.A.	N.A.	N.A.	N.A.	N.A.	N.A.
ΔLTVST	−39.06	21.34	−62.00	−5.00	N.A.	N.A.	N.A.	N.A.	N.A.	N.A.	N.A.	N.A.	N.A.	N.A.	N.A.	N.A.
ΔIVR	27.56	22.83	−4.00	54.00	N.A.	N.A.	N.A.	N.A.	N.A.	N.A.	N.A.	N.A.	N.A.	N.A.	N.A.	N.A.

The table reports the number of observations (#), mean, standard deviation (Std.), minimum (Min), and maximum (Max) for all variables for each investor group separately (*Overseas*, *Home Country*, *Accredited*, and *Retail*). All metrics are based on invested projects only. See Table 11A.2 for variable descriptions.

TABLE 11A.2   Variable definitions.

Variable name	Description and calculation
Distance	
Log Distance	Logarithm of kilometers between backer and venture headquarters.
Distance	Kilometers between backer and venture headquarters.
Squared Distance	Squared kilometers between backer and venture headquarters.
Human Capital	
# Board	Number of directors on a venture's board.
% Board MBA	Percentage of MBA graduates among the executive directors of the board.
Social (Alliance) Capital	
% Nonexecutive Board	Percentage of nonexecutive directors on a company's board.
Intellectual Capital	
Granted Patent	Dummy variable indicating whether a venture quotes a granted patent in an offering document. The variable equals 1 if so, and 0 otherwise.
Equity Share	
Equity Offering	Percentage of equity that a management team plans to sell in an offering prior to the offering. This number is exhibited in the detailed company overview page.
Financial Projections	
Disclaimer × No Financial Forecast	Dummy variable that indicates whether a company's offering documents provide a disclaimer for not including financial forecasts for various reasons. The variable equals 1 for a disclaimer without a forecast, and 0 otherwise.
No Disclaimer × No Financial Forecast	Dummy variable that indicates a company's offering documents do not provide a financial forecast or a disclaimer.
Additional Controls	
# Staff	Total employees at the time of offering. This number is usually provided on the company overview page.
Award	Dummy variable indicating whether a project or a project's product received an award. The variable equals 1 if so, and 0 otherwise.
Government Grant	Dummy variable indicating whether a venture received government grants.
Intended Number of Rounds	Set the number of rounds by founders in the offering documents in which they want to raise money. The number of rounds can vary between one and three.
Most Likely Exit—Trade Sale	Planned exit channel is a trade sale.
Most Likely Exit—Other	Planned exit channel is an LBO, reverse takeover, or not indicated.
Target Funding	Pursued target funding amount in millions AUD.
Years in Business	Number of years a company has been in existence at the time of offering. This number is usually provided on the company overview page.

(Continued)

III. Crowdinvesting

TABLE 11A.2   (Continued)

Variable name	Description and calculation
Years to Planned Exit	Detailed exit plan of a company at the time of offering, if required. This number is usually provided on the company overview page.
Parcel Size	Minimum investment amount in AUD; investors can purchase only whole numbers.
Share Price	Price investors must pay per share.
ΔPDI	Power Distance Index of the respective country minus the Power Distance Index of Australia (see http://geert-hofstede.com/national-culture.html).
ΔIVC	Individualism versus Collectivism of the respective country minus the Individualism versus Collectivism of Australia (see http://geert-hofstede.com/national-culture.html).
ΔMVF	Masculinity versus Femininity of the respective country minus the Masculinity versus Femininity of Australia (see http://geert-hofstede.com/national-culture.html).
ΔUAI	Uncertainty Avoidance Index of the respective country minus the Uncertainty Avoidance Index of Australia (see http://geert-hofstede.com/national-culture.html).
ΔLTVST	Long -Term Orientation versus Short-Term Normative Orientation of the respective country minus the Long-Term Orientation versus Short-Term Normative of Australia (see http://geert-hofstede.com/national-culture.html).
ΔIVR	Indulgence versus Restraint of the respective country minus the Indulgence versus Restraint of Australia (see http://geert-hofstede.com/national-culture.html).

The table gives a detailed description of the data-gathering process and calculation method for all variables.

Cash-flow and control rights in equity crowdfunding

12.1 Introduction

A growing interest in crowdfunding is shared by practitioners, policymakers, the media, and scholars alike. As a new and powerful tool for entrepreneurs, crowdfunding can help push the boundaries of existing theories and help develop new ones (Block, Hornuf, et al., 2018; Block, Colombo, et al., 2018). In fact, new digital technologies have transformed the nature of uncertainty inherent in entrepreneurial processes and outcomes as well as the ways of dealing with such uncertainty (Nambisan, 2017; Nambisan, Lyytinen, Majchrzak, & Song, 2017). While in reward-based crowdfunding backers prepurchase a product or a service, in equity-based crowdfunding, firms raise equity capital from investors who take ownership rights over the business (e.g., Chapter 10: Signaling in equity crowdfunding; see also Hornuf & Schwienbacher, 2018; Vismara, 2016, 2018; Walthoff-Borm, Vanacker, et al., 2018).[1] The implications of this process are significant. In particular, the information asymmetry concerning the start-up's ability to generate future cash flows governs the crowdfunder's decision to become a shareholder. As equity crowdfunders consider becoming minority shareholders, governance concerns arise from the separation between ownership and control. In this chapter, we examine for the first time the implications of the separation of ownership and control through a digital financing platform.

The opportunity to raise public equity has been traditionally granted by stock exchanges. In initial public offerings (IPOs) the ownership base of firms going public is opened, often for the first time, to external shareholders. This typically represents the first event in a firm's history that requires careful consideration of how to deal with the agency conflicts arising from both the separation between ownership and control

---

[1] Equity-based crowdfunding is intrinsically different from donation- and reward-based crowdfunding. First, while the motivations to donate may be philanthropic, a marked characteristic of equity crowdfunding is the possibility to generate financial returns (Vismara, 2016). Second, while in equity crowdfunding the proponent is by definition a company, reward-based campaigns are launched mostly by individuals. Third, the monetary value of an equity crowdfunding offering is also higher on average.

(principal—agent) and between controlling and minority shareholders (principal—principal). Firms undergoing IPOs thus face crucial governance decisions. Coherently, a large body of literature has developed studying the ownership and control of IPO firms. Empirical evidence is supportive of the existence of a positive link between the level of quality of a firm's corporate governance mechanisms and success in securing funding for IPOs.

Equity crowdfunding platforms allow firms to raise capital from a diversified set of shareholders in a similar, though less regulated, way. As sound corporate governance practices are valued by outside investors in IPOs, these attributes should also be decisive in investors' decisions to bid in equity crowdfunding offerings, as they share the same agency concerns. While collective action problems limit investors' monitoring incentives, entrepreneurs can be tempted to engage in self-dealing. Equity crowdfunding offerings are, therefore, a privileged area where we can investigate whether or not the findings of ownership and control studies on traditional stock markets hold in such a loosely regulated context.

To the best of our knowledge, no previous study has investigated the ownership structure of firms raising capital through crowdfunding. This lack is arguably due to the paucity of empirical settings where it is possible to investigate the entry of new shareholders with voting rights. In some countries, such as the United States or Germany, firms are forbidden to offer shares carrying voting rights in crowdfunding. In other countries, such as France and Italy, the number of successful offerings is low. We overcome this limit by focusing on the United Kingdom, where a large number of firms have already raised funds issuing new shares on equity crowdfunding platforms. Crowdcube, on which we focus, provides companies with the possibility of placing both Class A (carrying voting rights) and Class B (not carrying voting rights) shares directly with small investors. Owners of Class B shares do not have voting rights, but they do have equal rights to capital distributions and dividends. The peculiarity of this setting is that it serves as an investment threshold to discriminate between the two classes. Class A differs from Class B shares only in terms of voting and preemption rights attached to A-shares. Those investing more than the threshold set by the company receive A-shares; only B-shares are assigned to investors who bid below the threshold. This approach, in the intention of the platform, strikes a balance between investor protection and capital formation. However, the result is that investors pay the same price for two different asset classes. Equity crowdfunding offerings, indeed, define the ownership and control of firms by opening to outsiders and, at the same time, allowing shareholders to enroll in different classes based on the provision or not of voting rights.

While traditional private deals are limited to a relatively small group of investors, equity crowdfunding allows issuers to advertise to the general public. Differently from what happens in IPOs, however, investors in equity crowdfunding face a general lack of liquidity in secondary markets. Indeed, although equity crowdfunding provides investors with a disintermediated entry into venture financing, the prospects for exiting a successful venture are unclear outside of acquisitions or IPOs. Equity crowdfunding, therefore, is distinct from both IPOs and venture capital (VC) investments, as it occupies a middle space between public and private finance.

Corporate finance studies typically find that firm values increase with the cash-flow rights of controlling shareholders but decrease when voting rights exceed cash-flow rights (e.g., La Porta, Lopez-da-Silanes, Shleifer, & Vishny, 2002). Research also shows that countries where there are more conflicts between minority and majority shareholders usually have a more severe separation of voting power and cash flow (La Porta, Lopez-da-Silanes, & Shleifer, 2006). In line with this literature (e.g., Faccio & Lang, 2002), we measure the degree of separation between ownership and control as the ratio of voting to cash-flow rights, which approximates the divergence from the one-share-one-vote ownership structure. This measure is typically used to proxy for the owner's possibility of extracting private benefits from the firm at the expense of minority shareholders. As a consequence of differentiated voting power, indeed, shareholders without a commensurate economic stake in a corporation are more likely to "tunnel" away a disproportionate part of firm value (Johnson, La Porta, Lopez-da-Silanes, & Shleifer, 2000). Similarly to stock exchange investors, crowdfunding investors may be reluctant to invest in inferior voting shares, because they anticipate the risk of expropriation. Indeed, prior work is largely consistent with the view that separation of ownership from control at the time of an IPO is associated with insiders extracting private benefits and maximizing agency costs (Bebchuk, Kraakman, & Triantis, 2000; Gompers, Ishii, & Metrick, 2010; Smart, Thirumalai, & Zutter, 2008; Bebchuk & Kastiel, 2017). Chemmanur and Jiao (2012), however, argue that the offering of nonvoting shares delivers the opportunity for talented executives to focus on a firm's performance without distractions from outsiders.

The study of dual-class shares is interesting in the context of equity crowdfunding as it provides an additional, novel test-bed to traditional studies on the separation of ownership and control. Second, as mentioned before, we are able to study, for the first time, the behavior of investors who can choose to invest above a threshold in order to obtain voting power. Although our analysis is essentially a firm-level study, we observe and discuss the evidence of investor-level bids. Third, equity crowdfunding is also of great interest for the heterogeneity of investors. Over the last two decades, indeed, three quarters of the IPOs in Europe took place in second markets, such as London's AIM. Most of these IPOs are offered exclusively to institutional investors and are equivalent to private placements, which frequently raise only a few million euros and rarely develop liquid trading (Vismara, Paleari, & Ritter, 2012). With institutional investors being allocated the largest fraction of IPO shares (Aggarwal, Prabhala, & Puri, 2002), crowdfunding investors are likely to be more diverse than shareholders of newly listed companies (Cumming & Vismara, 2017). In particular, equity crowdfunding markets attract bids from both small and professional investors; for example, 11 venture capitalists invested in offerings listed in Crowdcube in 2014 (Signori & Vismara, 2018).

In this chapter, we make use of detailed information on the ownership structure of 491 offerings listed between 2011 and 2015 on Crowdcube, where proponents can decide whether to issue A-shares and, in this case, whether to provide voting rights only to bidders offering an amount greater than a certain threshold. Our goal is to investigate whether the alignment of interests between the entrepreneur and the investors and the separation between ownership and control affects the success of crowdfunding offerings, in terms of probability to successfully reach the target, to attract professional investors, and to achieve long-term success, as proxied by either the ability to raise further financing or to deliver an exit opportunity through IPO or merger and acquisition (M&A).

The structure of the chapter is as follows: Section 12.2 describes the institutional setting and motivates our choice to focus on the UK crowdfunding market. Section 12.3 presents our research design. Section 12.4 reports our results. Section 12.5 concludes the chapter.

12.2 Institutional setting

The United Kingdom, by far the largest market for equity crowdfunding, provides the best opportunity to explore this form of alternative finance.[2] The largest equity crowdfunding platform in the United Kingdom is Crowdcube.[3] Established in 2011, Crowdcube is, as of November 2018, the world's largest platform, with £500 million successfully raised from more than 600,000 investors from over 100 countries. Each project's business plan is vetted before listing (according to Crowdcube statistics, the due diligence team, on average, verifies 28 entrepreneur claims for each admitted project), whereas no ongoing reporting is required to the company. This platform works in an "all-or-nothing" fashion, which means that if the target amount is reached, the campaign is successful, and investors become direct shareholders in the company; otherwise, if the target is not reached, the money is returned at no monetary cost to bidders. Entrepreneurs are, therefore, incentivized to set an achievable target. The overfunding option, however, provides them with the possibility to raise more funds than the initial target. Investors who bid during the overfunding phase have exactly the same rights as investors who invested before the offering became overfunded.

The direct involvement of a large number of small investors makes Crowdcube particularly suitable for studies in corporate finance (e.g., Cumming et al., 2016; Vismara 2016, 2018; Vulkan et al., 2016; Walthoff-Borm, Vanacker, et al., 2018). The choice of this platform is appropriate to study ownership and control of listing firms, as a comparison with alternatives clarifies. SyndicateRoom, the second largest equity crowdfunding platform in the United Kingdom (AltFi.com, 2015), is not a pure equity crowdfunding platform, as it requires at least 25% of the target capital already be committed by institutions and other professional arms-length investors. Both Seedrs and VentureFounders use unified nominee structures, meaning the platforms themselves remain the representative of their investors throughout the investment period, rather than each individual backer becoming a shareholder. The average successful equity offering in Crowdcube, by comparison, gives a direct ownership stake to 145 investors (Signori & Vismara, 2018).

---

[2] The regulation of equity crowdfunding in the United Kingdom is often put forward as an important ingredient of its development, so that it serves as a model for other legislation (Steinhoff, 2015). Some other countries, such as Germany, allow for certain profit-sharing arrangements but forbid the sale of shares carrying voting rights through crowdfunding platforms. In countries where pure equity crowdfunding is permitted, such as France and Italy, the amount of capital raised to date is considerably lower than in the United Kingdom (Vismara, 2016).

[3] Crowdcube has raised more capital than all other competing platforms (AltFi.com, 2015). Different sources agree on the leading role of Crowdcube. Beauhurst names Crowdcube as the leading equity investor in 2015 and the most prolific investor in the e-commerce sector. Crowdsurfer estimates Crowdcube's share in the UK investment crowdfunding market in 2015 at 52%.

The regulation of equity crowdfunding is currently defined in the United Kingdom by the FCA's Policy Statement PS14/4, which delegates the FCA to "mitigate the liquidity risk investors face when investing in the equity or debt securities of small and medium enterprises, which are difficult to price and for which there is no, or only a limited, secondary market." Both professional and retail investors are allowed to trade on crowdfunding platforms. Professional investors include high net worth investors (i.e., annual income over £100,000 or net assets over £250,000) and certified sophisticated investors (i.e., business angels, professionals in the private equity sector, or directors of a company with an annual turnover of at least £1 million).[4] An investor who is neither high net worth nor sophisticated is classified as a "restricted investor." In this case, the fraction of money that he or she can invest in nonreadily realizable investments, including crowdfunded securities, cannot exceed 10% of his or her net assets. In such cases, the platform requires certification that they are informed regarding investment opportunities and risks or have received independent advice.

12.3 Research design

12.3.1 Sample

The initial population of our study is made of 597 equity crowdfunding offerings posted on Crowdcube since its inception in 2011 to the end of 2015. We exclude 12 minibond offerings and 94 equity offerings conducted by companies that had already raised funds in the same platform. The final sample is made of 491 offerings.[5]

12.3.2 Outcome variables

We analyze the impact of ownership and control variables on offering and postoffering outcomes. First, offering success is identified by *offering success*, a dummy variable equal to 1 for campaigns that collected at least the target amount of money. Second, we define the *long-run outcome* of crowdfunding campaigns through a hierarchical criterion: first, failures are identified when firms are insolvent, liquidated, or dissolved following a campaign; alternatively, a firm is identified as successful when, after successfully raising equity in

---

[4] An investor is certified as professional if a qualified firm assesses the investor's capability of understanding the risks associated with engaging in nonreadily realizable investments, or the investor is in presence of a "self-certified professional investor" statement, in which the investor declares him- or herself as a member of a network of business angels, has worked in the business finance sector over the previous 2 years, or has served as a director of a company with at least £1 million in revenues. The definition of the types of investors in equity crowdfunding in the United Kingdom is available on the crowdfunding website. For instance, in Crowdcube, it is available at: www.crowdcube.com/pg/investor-categories-1554.

[5] In the first stage of our analysis a selection mechanism between Crowdcube and Seedrs platforms is performed in order to take into account the potential bias induced by the platform selection mechanism. A sample of 818 offerings listed in the United Kingdom between July 2012 (establishment of Seedrs) and the end of 2015 has been used only in this first step of the analysis.

crowdfunding offerings, it either attracts further equity financing or delivers an exit opportunity to crowdfunding investors, either in the form of IPO or M&A.[6] In order to identify long-run outcomes, we monitor companies in the sample from the closing date of their initial offering to January 2017 using Crunchbase to identify capital infusions following the crowdfunding offering.[7] Crunchbase is a database of startup companies operated by TechCrunch that records information about their characteristics and relevant events. We collect information on the equity offerings carried out by each company, including the type of transaction and identity of the investors. Crunchbase is increasingly used in entrepreneurial finance studies (e.g., Cumming et al., 2016; Hellmann & Thiele, 2015; Signori & Vismara, 2018). This dataset assures a large coverage, as it comprehends all the offerings in Crowdcube, as well as most private equity deals involving crowdfunded companies. Indeed, companies that receive VC financing after crowdfunding have incentives to make this news public, as this contributes to an increase in their visibility and decreases the uncertainty about their quality. Failures are identified using Companies House. We use the first announcement date of the insolvency or liquidation as the failure event.

In addition, we look at how voting and cash-flow rights affect investor participation in crowdfunding offerings. Our main outcome variable here is *professional investors*, a dummy variable equal to 1 if a professional investor (VC or business angels) has participated in the campaign. Professional investors include self-certified sophisticated investors (i.e., business angels, professionals in the private equity sector, or directors of a company with an annual turnover of at least £1 million) and high net worth investors (i.e., annual income over £100,000 or net assets over £250,000). We also consider the *number of investors* participating in the offering as an alternative dependent variable assessing the success in terms of investor participation. In addition, we look at *bid HHI*, a measure of bid concentration, measured as a Hirschman–Herfindahl index, calculated for the bids of all participants in the offering, that is, the sum of squares of all bids, measured as a percentage of the total amount bid in a campaign. This variable allows us to investigate whether and how the delivery of voting rights affects concentrated bids rather than a crowd of small participants. Lastly, *average bid (nonprofessional)* is the average amount bid by nonprofessional investors, identifying the average size of investment for the nonprofessionals.

12.3.3 Ownership and control variables

Our empirical analysis implements ownership and control variables that are uniquely observable for crowdfunding proposals on Crowdcube, where companies are provided

---

[6] This hierarchical criterion is empirically irrelevant in our sample, given that we do not have in our sample cases of refunded firms that went bankrupt over the sampling period. Conceptually, though, this definition allows for the mutual exclusivity of the outcomes. We are thankful to an anonymous referee for pointing this out.

[7] In our framework, older campaigns are observed for a longer time compared to more recent offerings. While this diversity is taken into account by the multilevel, multiprocess hazard model, because hazard rates are estimated on the basis of the changing population available at different point in time, we provide a different approach in our robustness checks, where long-run outcome is defined by monitoring the 2 years following each campaign.

the possibility of placing both Class A (carrying voting rights) and Class B (not carrying vot-ing rights) shares directly with small investors. Companies can set an investment threshold under which no voting rights are granted, making the issuance of Class A versus Class B shares depending on the decision of the individual investor. The variable *A-shares threshold* measures the minimum investment required to obtain A-shares. In our empirical analysis, we use natural logarithms, while, *A-shares threshold/target capital* is used in our robust tests.

We employ two variables to test for the effect of alignment and separation between own-ership and control on the valuation of IPO companies. First, we compute *cash-flow rights* (C) by measuring the controlling shareholder's percentage ownership of the profits and divi-dends of the firm. In corporate governance studies, if there exist multiple chains of owner-ship, the cash-flow rights, along each chain, are the products of all ownership rights in the intermediate companies along that chain. The total cash-flow rights are then equal to the sum of all cash-flow rights from all ownership chains (Faccio & Lang, 2002). In the case of crowdfunding proposals, we define the measure of cash-flow rights to be equal to 1 minus the percentage of equity offered when A-shares are distributed. Second, we measure the controlling shareholder voting rights (V), in accordance with the procedure used by Faccio and Lang (2002). In corporate finance literature, when multiple control chains exist, the vot-ing rights are the sum of the voting rights along each chain with the weakest link among all holding layers. In the case of crowdfunding offerings, V is equal to 1 if no right is distrib-uted (only B-shares are issued). If only A-shares are issued, the calculation of V depends on the existence of a threshold for the attribution of voting rights. If no threshold is set, V is simply given by 1, minus the percentage of equity offered (and is equal to C). If a threshold is set, we cannot determine ex ante whether the offering participants will receive voting shares or not, such that V can be precisely determined only when the proportion of shares sold with voting rights is known.[8] In this case, we calculate the following:

$$V = 1 - [(equity\_offered) \times \gamma] \tag{12.1}$$

where the parameter γ identifies the fraction of shares sold with voting rights, which, in the case of a campaign with a voting threshold, is given by the ratio of shares sold above threshold divided by the total number of sold shares. Such ratio runs from 0 to 1: γ is equal to 0 when no share is sold above threshold, such that V is equal to 1, because the controlling shareholder is distributing no voting rights; γ, vice versa, is equal to 1 when all shares are sold with voting rights (i.e., because all bids were above threshold); therefore V is equal to C, namely, the controlling shareholder's cash-flow right.

The V measure is used to calculate the ratio of the controlling shareholder's *voting to cash-flow rights* (V/C), which approximates the divergence from the one-share-one-vote ownership structure and is used to proxy for the controlling owner's motive to extract wealth from the firm. An alternative measure for the same concept, used in our robustness test, is the *ownership wedge* dummy, equal to 1 if V is greater than C (i.e., the V/C ratio is above 1) and 0 otherwise.

Finally, in accordance with former literature supportive of the importance of controlling shareholders' identities, our analysis implements a dummy variable, *family*, equal to 1 for

---

[8] Indeed, this implies in our empirical model the simultaneous estimation of V/C and Campaign Success, given that investors' choices determine both of them at the same time.

offerings that were posted by family firms. To the best of our knowledge, this is the first empirical study to investigate the family ownership in equity crowdfunding. In line with the empirical literature on family firms, we identify as family businesses those with two members in the top management team (TMT) with the same family name (Kotlar, Signori, De Massis, & Vismara, 2018). This information was collected by scrutinizing the team page on Crowdcube and the business plan of each offering.[9]

12.3.4 Endogenous variables

A number of variables used in our empirical analyses are likely to raise endogeneity concerns, which are dealt with in our research design by implementing instrumental-variable techniques. A large body of corporate governance literature argues that the choice related to the issue of a dual-class share is endogenous with respect to firm value and per-formances (see Gompers et al., 2010). This is why, in the regression analyses, *threshold*, cash-flow rights (*C*), and voting to cash-flow rights (*V/C*) are instrumented with three vari-ables that identify mimicking behavior.[10] Mimicking variables are defined as the reference variable (i.e., *threshold*, *C*, or *V/C*) and measured for each firm as the average of all equity offerings in the same industry in the previous 12 months.[11] Mimicking is a common behavior to achieve legitimacy (Deephouse & Carter, 2005). Mimicking variables have already been used in finance studies on IPOs, in order to instrument ownership and con-trol decisions at the time of the IPO (Bell, Filatotchev, & Rasheed, 2012). Their inclusion in our specification for the potentially endogenous variable allows us to better describe the role of mimicking in crowdfunding offerings and, at the same time, allows identification of our full model.

[9] While we identify family firm ownership, we do not know the exact ownership structure prior to crowdfunding. We note that the ownership structure prior to the deal has been largely neglected in the related literature on VC investments (for a review of related VC work, see Manigart and Wright, 2013; Cumming and Johan, 2006); however, there have been important studies that are indicative of prior ownership based on spin-offs and related topics (Lockett, Siegel, Wright, & Ensley, 2005; Wilson, Wright, & Kaceer, 2018; Wright, Clarysse, Lockett, & Binks, 2006; Wright & Fu, 2015) similar in spirit to our identifying family ownership. Further work may investigate this issue with ownership structures prior to crowdfunding and VC.

[10] With any proposed instrument, it is important to assess whether it satisfies the two criteria for an instrument's validity, namely, (1) relevance and (2) exogeneity and excludability. As far as relevance is concerned, the strength of the instrument is assessed in each of the instrumental regressions by verifying the coefficient significance. As far as exogeneity and excludability are concerned, we regard our variables as fully exogenous, given that our probability measures depend on the choice of competitors; that is, different firms with respect to the reference; our measures are also likely to be excludable, given that we do not expect investors to determine the success of an offering based on the ownership and control mechanisms of competitors.

[11] In order to maximize the number of observations at use, mimicking variables have been set to the average value during the first 12 months covered by our sample for all offerings listed during that period. We also tested the significance of our instruments when dropping these observations and when extrapolating instrument values based on future observations. Results are qualitatively unchanged.

Further, recent crowdfunding literature highlights the potential endogeneity between the *target capital* (viz., the amount of capital to be raised in the offering, in thousands of British pounds) and the likelihood of an offering to be successfully funded (Cumming et al., 2015, 2017). In practice, while the offering target amount is primarily determined by real needs, proponents are likely to make adjustments for strategic purposes based on the desire to signal commitment, as well as on entrepreneurial expectations about their individual capability to attract crowdfunding investments. Therefore following Cumming et al. (2015), we control for the endogeneity of a target amount, which is instrumented with a mimicking variable measured for each firm as the average of all target amounts in the same industry in the previous 12 months.[12]

12.3.5 Control variables

In all our analyses, we include a series of variables concerning the issuing firm, collected through the presentation pages for each project made available by Crowdcube, to control for a potential impact on the different outcome variables in use, along the line suggested by Vismara (2018). *Age* is the proponent company's age (in months). *Positive sales* is a dummy variable equal to 1 if the company has already reported positive sales. *Patents* is a dummy variable equal to 1 if the company owns or is filing patents. *TMT size* is the firm's number of management team members. *Nonexecutive directors* is a dummy variable equal to 1 if at least one member of the board is a nonexecutive member. *Founder experience* is a dummy variable equal to 1 if the founder has previous work experience. *Seed Enterprise Investment Scheme (SEIS)* equals 1 if the offering is eligible for the UK SEIS tax incentive, which is designed to encourage seed investment in early-stage companies with up to £150,000 capital raised. *Exit IPO* equals 1 if the firm declares the intention to conduct an IPO at a future date, according to what the proponents declare at the moment of listing, with regard to exit policies. In all our analyses, we also control for a linear trend, by including a variable set to 0 for 2011 issues (earlier issues in our sample), increasing by 1 each year. Finally, we control for industry starting from Crowdcube classification. Offerings are classified as pertaining to eight industries: (1) art, music, media, and education; (2) environmental and ethical; (3) fitness, leisure, and sport; (4) food and drink; (5) Internet, IT, and technology; (6) manufacturing; (7) professional business and services; and (8) retail and consumer products.

12.3.6 Descriptive statistics

Table 12.1 reports descriptive statistics for our sample of 491 campaigns listed on Crowdcube[13] between 2011 and 2015, distinguishing between campaigns offering A-shares

---

[12] Cumming et al. (2015) do not name their variable as "mimicking behaviour," although their instrument is calculated in accordance.

[13] Table 12.A1 in the "Appendix" section provides additional details on all variables used in our analysis; that is, mean, standard deviation, and max and min values over the full sample. Descriptive statistics comparing our main sample with the sample of 818 offerings on Seedrs, used for the first stage of our analysis, is provided in Table 12.A2 in the "Appendix" section.

TABLE 12.1 Descriptive statistics by share type.

Observations	A-shares 405		B-shares only 86		Test on the difference A- vs B-shares		Successful offerings 189		Unsuccessful offerings 302		Test on the difference Successful vs unsuccessful	
	Mean	Median	Mean	Median	Mean	Median	Mean	Median	Mean	Median	Mean	Median
Panel A. Outcome variables												
Offering success (%)	37.53	0.00	43.02	0.00	−5.49	0.00	1.00	1.00	—	—	—	—
Long-run success (%)	9.13	0.00	9.30	0.00	0.17	0.00	23.80	0.00	—	—	—	—
Failure (%)	5.92	0.00	8.11	0.00	−2.18	0.00	6.35	0.00	—	—	—	—
Professional investors (%)	26.12	0.00	33.93	0.00	−7.81	0.00	41.80	0.00	10.12	0.00	31.68***	0.00
Number of investors	88.70	54.00	129.21	58.50	−40.61**	−4.50	148.48	107.00	62.82	34.5	85.66***	72.5***
Bid concentration (HHI)	6.05	0.00	12.87	0.00	−6.83***	0.00**	7.83	0.00	6.33	0.00	1.50	0.00
Average bid (nonprofessional) (£k)	1.71	1.25	1.69	1.01	0.02	0.24	1.65	1.24	1.78	1.21	−0.13	0.03
Panel B. Ownership and control variables												
A-shares threshold (%)	83.50	100.00	—	—	—	—	80.42	100.00	87.97	100.00	−7.55*	0.00*
A-shares threshold (£k)	9.09	5.00	—	—	—	—	9.60	5.00	8.52	5.00	1.08	0.00
Block threshold (%)	11.89	0.00	—	—	—	—	11.29	0.00	8.59	0.00	2.70	0.00
Threshold/target capital (%)	3.96	2.00	—	—	—	—	5.72	4.00	2.89	0.00	2.82***	4.00***
C (%)	85.55	87.00	86.30	87.50	0.74	−0.50	85.21	86.00	86.22	90.00	−1.01	−4.00*
V/C	1.06	1.10	1.18	1.14	−0.12***	−0.04***	1.05	1.08	1.12	1.11	−0.07***	−0.03***
Ownership wedge (%)	88.15	100.00	100.00	100.00	−11.85***	0.00	80.95	100.00	96.02	100.00	−15.07***	0.00
Target capital (£k)	230.97	150.00	288.40	150.00	−49.87	50.00	249.10	145.00	226.96	150.00	22.13	−5.00
Family (%)	18.02	0.00	19.76	0.00	−1.74	0.00	15.87	0.00	19.86	0.00	−3.99	0.00
Panel C. Control variables												
Age (years)	2.94	2.63	3.09	1.95	−0.15	0.68	2.71	1.97	3.63	2.12	−0.92**	−0.16*

Positive sales (%)	53.05	100.00	51.11	100.00	1.94	0.00	61.29	100.00	39.67	0.00	21.62***	100.00***
Patents (%)	9.16	0.00	2.22	0.00	6.94	0.00	8.06	0.00	8.26	0.00	−0.20	0.00
Nonexecutive directors (%)	9.38	0.00	10.46	0.00	−1.08	0.00	6.62	0.00	14.28	0.00	−7.66***	0.00
Founder experience (no.)	3.49	3.00	5.20	4.00	−1.71***	−1.00***	4.04	3.00	3.28	2.00	0.76*	1.00**
SEIS (%)	39.69	0.00	22.22	0.00	17.47**	0.00**	65.05	100.00	59.50	100.00	5.55	0.00
Exit IPO (%)	21.65	0.00	9.43	0.00	12.22**	0.00	18.30	0.00	23.10	0.00	−4.8	0.00

Descriptive statistics on the sample of 491 Crowdcube offerings between 2011 and 2015. A-shares are firms issuing A-shares both with and without a minimum investment threshold (i.e., granting voting rights). B-shares only are firms issuing shares only without voting rights. Success is a dummy variable equal to 1 for offerings that collected at least the target amount of money. Professional investors is a dummy variable equal to 1 if a professional investor (VC or BA) has participated in the offering. Professional investors include self-certified, sophisticated investors (i.e., business angels, professionals in the private equity sector, or directors of a company with an annual turnover of at least £1 million), and high net worth investors (i.e., annual income over £100,000 or net assets over £250,000). Bid concentration is the Hirschman–Herfindahl index calculated for the bids of all participants in the offering, that is, it is the sum of squares as a percentage of weights for all bids in an offering. Average bid (nonprofessional) is the average amount bid by nonprofessional investors. Long-run success is a dummy variable equal to 1 for all firms that, after successfully raising equity in crowdfunding offerings, either attract further equity financing or deliver an exit opportunity to a crowdfunding investor, either in the form of an IPO or of an M&A, at time t after their first successful offering. Failure is a dummy variable equal to 1 for firms that went insolvent, were liquidated, or were dissolved at time t after their first successful offering. A-shares threshold is the minimum investment required to obtain A-shares, as a percentage of the target amount, or in thousands of British pounds. Block threshold equals 1 in case the threshold is set to £25,000 or higher. Cash-flow rights (C) are measured as the controlling shareholder's percentage of ownership for the profits and dividends of the firm; they are set to 1, minus the equity offered in the proposal, in accordance to the methodology in Faccio and Lang (2002). V/C is the postoffering ratio between the controlling shareholder voting to cash-flow rights, where voting rights are estimated using the procedure used by Faccio and Lang (2002). V is equal to 1 if no right is distributed; 1 minus the equity offered if rights are offered with no threshold; 1 minus equity offered, times γ when a threshold is set for the distribution of rights, where γ is the fraction of shares sold to investors who bid above the threshold. Ownership wedge is a dummy variable equal to 1 if B-shares are issued, or an A-shares threshold is set, and 0 otherwise. Age is the age (in years) of the company. Positive sales equals 1 if the company has already reported positive sales. Patents equals 1 if the company owns or is filing patents. Nonexecutive directors is a dummy variable equal to 1 if at least one member of the board is a nonexecutive member. Founder experience is the founder's number of previous work experiences. SEIS equals 1 if the offering is eligible for the SEIS tax relief. Target capital is the amount of capital to be raised in the offering in thousands of British pounds. Exit IPO equals 1 if the firm declares the intention of conducting an IPO at a future date. *, **, and *** indicate significance at the 10%, 5%, and 1% levels, respectively, of the t-test (z-test for dummy variables) for the difference in means between the two groups. HHI, Hirschman–Herfindahl index; IPO, initial public offering; M&A, merger and acquisition; SEIS, Seed Enterprise Investment Scheme; VC, venture capital.

(i.e., with voting rights) (405 observations) or B-shares only (i.e., with no voting rights provided) (86 cases), as well as between successful cases (189) and unsuccessful cases (302). Looking at the outcome variables in our analysis, successful cases are more frequent among B-shares-only offerings (43%), rather than for A-shares-only offerings (37%), though the difference is not statistically significant. Among successful offerings, we identify 6.35% of failures and 23% of long-run successful offerings, with no statistical difference between A-share and B-share campaigns. In addition, professional investors are more frequent for B-shares-only offerings (34% vs 26%), which are also characterized by a higher concentration of bidders (13% vs 6%). Professionals are also much more frequent in successful campaigns (42% vs 10%).

As far as the use of a threshold for the attribution of voting rights is concerned, this practice characterizes most A-share offerings (83.5%). The average threshold applied is slightly higher than £9000, with the median value being £5000. As reported in Fig. 12.1, the preference for round numbers also applies to values such as £10,000 and £15,000. There is also a handful of offerings requiring more than £25,000 for the attribution of voting rights. The threshold level is, on average, around 4% of the target capital. Interestingly, this value is larger (almost 6%) for successful campaigns than for unsuccessful ones (less than 3%), the difference being significant at less than 1%.

The average crowdfunding offering distributes less than 15% of voting rights, meaning the controlling shareholder cash-flow rights (C) is above 85%. The voting to cash-flow ratio (V/C) is significantly higher for B-shares-only offerings (1.18 vs 1.06), as well as for unsuccessful campaigns (1.12 vs 1.05). The same result is found when comparing groups by the ownership wedge dummy. No statistical difference is found in terms of belonging to a family, which characterizes 16% of successful offerings, 19.86% of other offerings, and target capital (£231,000 vs £288,000).

The average firm in our sample is around 3 years old at the offering. The age is similar for A-share and B-share firms but significantly smaller for successful than for unsuccessful offerings. Successful campaigns are also characterized more frequently (61% vs 40%) by positive sales recorded at the time of the proposal, while no statistical evidence is found

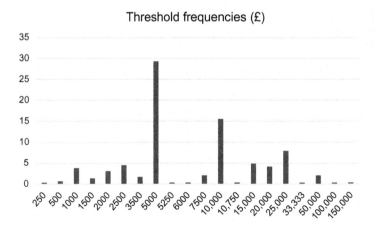

Threshold frequencies (£)

FIGURE 12.1 Number of equity offerings by investment threshold required in each bid to receive A-shares.

with respect to patenting activity. The presence of nonexecutive directors is similar in A-share and B-share offerings but smaller in successful campaigns (6.6%) compared to non-successful campaigns (14%). A-share offerings are characterized by less experienced founders (3.5 vs 5 previous experiences); they are more frequently eligible for SEIS tax relief (40% vs 22%), and they are more frequently aimed at an IPO exit (22% vs 9.4%).

12.3.7 Professional investors and investment thresholds

Preliminary evidence reported before shows that the use of a threshold for the distribution of A-shares is more likely to be found in unsuccessful offerings (88% vs 80%), although successful campaigns are characterized by higher threshold levels, both in absolute values (£9600 vs £8500) and in relative percentage of the target capital (5.7% vs 2.9%). These results provide preliminary evidence that thresholds, like other tools employed to separate ownership and controls, are not attractive, in general, for investors. At the same time, a high threshold level may attract qualified professional investors, who, when selecting the campaign, lead the offering to a likely success.

In order to preliminarily test whether this assertion is grounded in our data, we plot in Fig. 12.2 the frequency of issues characterized by different threshold levels for the attribution of voting rights, distinguishing cases with the participation or not of professional investors. What we find is that professional investors bid in about one-fourth of the offerings that do not deliver voting rights or that deliver voting rights above thresholds of up to £5000. Vice versa, their presence is much more frequent when the threshold is above $5000, where they bid in about half of the offerings.

If professional investors are attracted by the distribution of voting rights, we are likely to find them offering an amount equal to or above the threshold. We thus plot in Fig. 12.3 the amount bid by the professional investors in all offerings characterized by a threshold. We find that professional investors always bid above threshold and, therefore, choose their investment in such a way that grants the attribution of voting rights. In a few cases, professional investors bid the exact amount of the threshold.

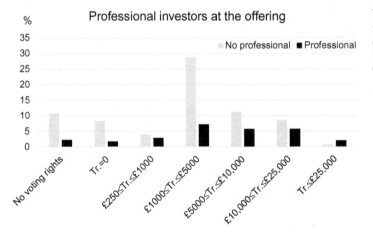

FIGURE 12.2 Levels of investment threshold for Class A shares and investment by professional investors at the crowdfunding offering.

(All thresholds, all professional investors' bids)

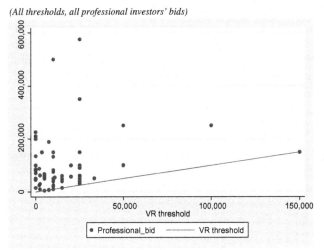

FIGURE 12.3 Relationship between threshold level and professional investors' bids.

(Threshold ≤ £50,000, professional investor's bid ≤ £200,000)

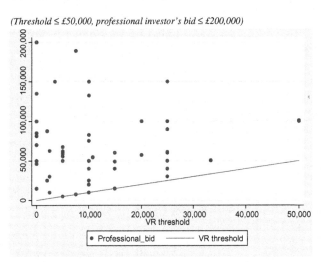

12.3.8 Models

12.3.8.1 Success of equity offerings

Our analysis firstly analyzes whether ownership and control variables affect the likelihood of success for crowdfunding campaigns, that is, to collect at least the target capital. Our first specification is as follows:

$$\text{Offering success} = \alpha_1 + \gamma_{1,1}\text{threshold} + \gamma_{1,2}C + \gamma_{1,3}V/C + \overline{\delta_1}\,\overline{\text{Controls}} + \varepsilon_1 \qquad (12.2)$$

where *offering success* is a dummy variable equal to 1 for offerings that collect at least the target amount of money. *Threshold*, *C* (cash-flow rights), and *V/C* (voting to cash-flow rights) are the main variables we are investigating, whose effects are estimated by the coefficients γ_1 and γ_2, respectively, while $\overline{\delta_1}$ is a vector of coefficients estimated with respect to all control variables, α_1 is a constant, and ε is the vector of regression residuals.

As in all studies of corporate control mechanisms, we need to address endogeneity concerns, and this is why we take an instrumental variable approach. Corporate finance theory maintains indeed that ownership and governance factors should be examined as bundles when determining outcomes (Filatotchev & Wright, 2017). As described in Section 12.3.4, we treat four variables as endogenous in our analyses, namely, the *threshold*, cash-flow rights (C), voting to cash-flow rights (V/C), and *target amount*.

The above-given setup poses two sample selection concerns. First, given that Crowdcube is the only platform allowing proponents to decide whether to issue A-shares, and, in this case, whether to use a threshold, there is the possibility that offering features are preselected. In order to consider this potential source of sample selection bias, we analyze the selection process of offerings posted in Crowdcube with respect to those listed on the main alternative in the United Kingdom: Seedrs. Second, given that the provision of a threshold[14] is available only when the proponent decides to issue A-shares, we need to take into account this second selection process in our analysis. Both selection mechanisms depend on unobservable offering characteristics that are potentially related to the unobservable determinants of offering and postoffering success. These two selection issues can be treated with the standard methods proposed by Lee (1978) and Heckman (1979), if the two selection rules are strictly independent. However, in our case the selection rules (i.e., the likelihood of posting an offering on Crowdcube versus Seedrs and the propensity to issue voting rights) are unlikely to be independent. Indeed, the likelihood of posting an offering in Crowdcube compared with the alternatives might be a determinant of the propensity to issue voting rights. Therefore we are dealing with a double selection rule, which can be addressed with the methodology proposed by Ham (1982) and Tunali (1986). This implies the inclusion of two first-stage equations, to be added to the second stage; that is, the outcome equation described before (Eq. 12.2). In addition, we need four instrumental regressions for the four variables (*threshold, C, V/C*, and *target amount*) that we treat as potentially endogenous.

As far as the two selection equations are concerned, we run a bivariate probit regression on the likelihood of posting an offering on Crowdcube with respect to Seedrs (Eq. 12.3) and on the probability of issuing voting rights in the campaign, that is, A-shares dummy (Eq. 12.4). In order to allow identification, Eq. (12.2) includes a platform preference variable, measured as the number of offerings listed on the Crowdcube, divided by the number of offerings posted on Seedrs, in the same industry, in the 12 months prior to each observation. As far as the second selection process is concerned, we follow Gompers et al. (2010) in choosing possible determinants of rights distribution, and we add *TMT size* (a proxy of internal competition for control), *number of M&As* in the same industry (a proxy of the market for corporate control in the industry), and *mimicking variables* (viz., the

---

[14] The determinants of the provision of a threshold are also analyzed. Results are reported in Table 12.A4 in the "Appendix" section.

probability to issue A-shares calculated as the ratio of crowdfunding offerings which offered voting rights among all previous offerings on the same platform).[15] The two selection equations are used to construct estimates of two Inverse Mills Ratios ($IMR_{platform}$ and IMR_{voting}), to be included in all regressions belonging to the second stage.

The second stage is a system of five equations, where the dependent variables are the *threshold amount* (Eq. 12.5); the controlling shareholder's cash-flow rights, C (Eq. 12.6); the voting to cash-flow rights, V/C (Eq. 12.7); the *target amount* (Eq. 12.8); and the *outcome* variable, the success dummy (Eq. 12.9). The three ownership variables (*threshold*, C, V/C) and *target amount* are treated as endogenous (i.e., instrumented). For each observation, identification variables (i.e., instruments) are measured as the average value of the investment threshold required to receive A-shares (*Pr. threshold*), of the control variable (*Pr. C*), of the separation between ownership and control (*Pr. V/C*), and of the *target amount* (*Pr. target amount*) calculated by using equity offerings in the 12 previous months in the same platform (see Section 12.3.4 for details).

Taken together, our system of equations is as follows:

$$
\begin{cases}
\text{Crowdcube}_{dummy} = \alpha_3 + \beta_{3,1} \text{platform preference} + \overline{\delta_3 \text{controls}} + \varepsilon_3 \\[6pt]
\text{A-shares}_{dummy} = \alpha_4 + \beta_{4,1} \text{TMT size} + \beta_{4,2} \text{M\&As} + \beta_{4,3} \text{mimicking}(\text{A-shares}) + \overline{\delta_4 \text{controls}} + \varepsilon_4 \\[6pt]
\text{Threshold} = \alpha_5 + \beta_5 \text{mimicking variables} + \rho_{5,1} \text{IMR}_{platform} + \rho_{5,2} \text{IMR}_{voting} + \overline{\delta_5 \text{controls}} + \varepsilon_5 \\[6pt]
C = \alpha_5 + \beta_6 \text{mimicking variables} + \rho_{6,1} \text{IMR}_{platform} + \rho_{6,2} \text{IMR}_{voting} + \overline{\delta_6 \text{controls}} + \varepsilon_6 \\[6pt]
\dfrac{V}{C} = \alpha_7 + \beta_7 \text{mimicking variables} + \rho_{7,1} \text{IMR}_{platform} + \rho_{7,2} \text{IMR}_{voting} + \overline{\delta_7 \text{controls}} + \varepsilon_7 \\[6pt]
\text{Target amount} = \alpha_8 + \beta_8 \text{mimicking variables} + \rho_{8,1} \text{IMR}_{platform} + \rho_{8,2} \text{IMR}_{voting} + \overline{\delta_8 \text{controls}} + \varepsilon_8 \\[6pt]
\text{Offering success}_{dummy} = \alpha_9 + \gamma_{9,1} \text{threshold} + \gamma_{9,2} C + \gamma_{9,3} \dfrac{V}{C} + \gamma_{9,4} \text{target amount} \\[6pt]
\qquad + \rho_{9,1} \text{IMR}_{platform} + \rho_{9,2} \text{IMR}_{voting} + \overline{\delta_9 \text{controls}} + \varepsilon_9
\end{cases}
$$

$$(12.3\text{-}12.9)$$

For estimation, we use a generalized structural equation model (GSEM). We opt for a structural equation model due to the need to simultaneously estimate an equation for the selection process, four equations for the instruments,[16] and an outcome equation. The presence of dummy variables among our dependent variables implies a GSEM, whereas (simple) structural equation modeling requires continuous outcomes.

---

[15] As pointed out by Tunali (1986, p. 245), the bivariate selectivity model requires additional exclusion restrictions to properly identify the parameter estimate on the correlation coefficient between the error terms of the selection equations. That is, at least one determinant of each selection process must not be related with the outcome variable (the dependent variable in the second stage). Moreover, in order to allow complete identification, at least one variable included in the second equation must not influence the first selection process, nor the outcome equation.

[16] Among these, V/C is simultaneously determined with *offering success*.

12.3.8.2 Postoffering outcomes

After modeling the determinants of the success of the offerings, our analysis focuses on the effects of ownership and control variables on postoffering outcomes, identifying cases of long-run success and firm failure as possible outcomes. Among the alternative solutions for estimating a competing risk model, we opted for a multilevel, multiprocess hazard model, which has been largely used to adjust regression estimates for both endogeneity (see Section 12.3.4) and selection issues (see Section 12.3.8.1). The multilevel, multiequation modeling framework accommodates the joint estimation of hazard and probit equations to account for the endogeneity of dummy explanatory variables that appear in the hazard equation of primary interest (Lillard, Brien, & Waite, 1995). The joint estimation accounts for the correlation of the random effects and allows us to control for the effects of unobserved offering features (Bartus & Roodman, 2014).

Specifically, in this new setting, we are estimating[17] two equations for the hazard rate of the two potential outcomes, that is, long-run success ($\ln h^{\text{long-run success}}$) and firm failure ($\ln h^{\text{failure}}$) (Eqs. 12.10 and 12.11), while instrumenting four variables, that is, *threshold*, *C*, *V/C*, and *target capital* (as in Eqs. 12.5–12.8). As far as the selection processes are concerned, in order to keep our model parsimonious, we use a single selection equation for *offering success* (Eq. 12.12), given that only successful offerings are observed in our data in the following years. In this equation, identification condition is granted by the inclusion of the number of competing offerings, that is, offerings open in the same equity crowdfunding platform at the time of the opening of each campaign.

$$\ln h^{\text{long-run success}} = \gamma_{10,1} \text{ threshold} + \gamma_{10,2}\, C + \gamma_{10,3}\frac{V}{C}\gamma_{10,4}$$
$$\text{Target amount} + \overline{\delta_{10}\text{controls}} + \varepsilon_{10} \quad \text{if offering success} = 1 \tag{12.10}$$

$$\ln h^{\text{failure}} = \gamma_{10,1} \text{ threshold} + \gamma_{10,2}\, C + \gamma_{10,3}\frac{V}{C}\gamma_{10,4}$$
$$\text{Target amount} + \overline{\delta_{10}\text{controls}} + \varepsilon_{10} \quad \text{if offering success} = 1 \tag{12.11}$$

$$\text{Offering success}_{\text{dummy}} = \alpha_{12} + \beta_{12} \text{ competing offerings} + \text{threshold} + \gamma_{12,2}\, C + \gamma_{12,3}\frac{V}{C}$$
$$+ \gamma_{12,4}\text{target amount} + \varepsilon_{12} \tag{12.12}$$

12.3.8.3 Investor composition

In addition, our analysis aims to test whether the ownership and control variables introduced before influence the participation of professional and other types of investors. Our reference model is the full model with two selection processes and four instrumental

---

[17] Estimation is feasible via the cmp command implemented in Stata by Roodman (2011). The multilevel, multiprocess presented here implies the estimation of a lognormal survival model for the hazard rates, a probit model for the selection equation, and a set of simultaneous instrumental equations for the endogenous variables.

variables described before (Eqs. 12.3–12.9), where we replace the outcome variable *offering success* with the following alternatives: a dummy equal to 1 in case a professional investor has joined the campaign (*professional investors*); the Hirschman–Herfindahl index, calculated for the bids of all offering participants (*bid concentration*); and the average bid offered by nonprofessional investors (*average bid*).

12.3.8.4 Moderating effect of founder experience

While our analysis considers the endogenous determination of the *target amount, ownership*, and *control* variable, it is also interesting to assess whether contingent variables may play a role on the effect of our measure. In particular, extant literature on corporate governance suggests that the separation between *ownership* and *control* may raise investor concerns because of the so-called "entrenchment hypothesis." Indeed, some of the proposal features (i.e., founder experience) could convey signals mitigating such concerns (Ahlers et al., 2015; Vismara, 2018). This is why in all our analyses we consider the role of *founder experience* as a potential moderator of *V/C*, assessing whether this is a signal effectively mitigating investor concerns due to the separation between *ownership* and *control*.

12.4 Results

12.4.1 Success of equity offerings

Table 12.2 reports our results on how ownership variables affect the success of equity crowdfunding offerings.[18] In the first stage, Models 1 and 2 allow analysis of the selection processes. In Model 1, we find that, besides our measure of platform preference, identifying an effect of previous choices within the same industry on the selection of the crowdfunding platform, older proposals seem to prefer Crowdcube, in that *age* has a positive and statistically significant coefficient. As far as the issue of voting rights is concerned, Model 2 shows that the variables chosen to identify the process significantly determine the probability of issuing A-shares; in particular, the larger the *TMT size*, the more likely the probability is for issuing voting rights; conversely, the issuing of A-shares is less frequent in those sectors characterized by active M&A markets. Lastly, we find further evidence that voting rights choices are taken by imitating the behavior in previous offerings, as

---

[18] Table 12.A3 in the "Appendix" section reports a reduced version of this model, where the effect of *Threshold* is ignored, and no selection correction is used. Our results on the role of C and V/C are confirmed on the full sample. This analysis, though, does not consider the selection process due the presence of offerings with or without rights, with or without a threshold. There is a variety of threshold choices represented in our sample: for example, 14% of our sample refers to A-shares issues without thresholds; while 10% of the observations are A-shares issues with a threshold equal or above £25,000. In Table 12.A4 in the "Appendix" section, we report an analysis of threshold determinants (in terms of probability to set a threshold, threshold level, probability to set a threshold above £25,000, and threshold/target capital level). What we find is that founder's experience is positively related to the probability to set a threshold and to set it to a high level. Larger campaigns (in terms of target capital) are more likely to be characterized by threshold, more likely to have a high threshold, indeed with a smaller threshold/target capital ratio.

TABLE 12.2 The effect of voting rights' thresholds on the success of equity offerings.

	(1) Crowdcube	(2) A-shares	(3) Threshold (ln)	(4) C	(5) V/C	(6) Target capital	(7a) Offering success	(7b) Offering success
C	—	—	—	—	—	—	1.138**	1.180**
							(0.548)	(0.530)
V/C	—	—	—	—	—	—	−3.589***	−4.641**
							(1.481)	(2.016)
V/C × founder experience	—	—	—	—	—	—	—	0.468**
								(0.225)
Threshold (ln)	—	—	—	—	—	—	−0.085	−0.096
							(0.136)	(0.141)
Target capital	—	—	—	—	—	—	−0.083	−0.101
							(0.141)	(0.142)
Family	0.556	−0.394	−0.011	0.003*	0.017	−0.011	−0.306	−0.299
	(0.303)	(0.271)	(0.010)	(0.001)	(0.092)	(0.010)	(0.243)	(0.243)
Age	0.781***	−0.108	0.019***	−0.031***	0.016	0.019***	−0.337**	−0.323**
	(0.215)	(0.132)	(0.005)	(0.007)	(0.048)	(0.005)	(0.137)	(0.138)
Positive sales	0.373	0.116	−0.002	0.019*	−0.001	−0.002	0.998***	0.987***
	(0.317)	(0.211)	(0.008)	(0.011)	(0.073)	(0.008)	(0.210)	(0.211)
Patents	−0.173	0.532	−0.026	0.062***	0.264*	−0.026	0.600	0.603
	(0.554)	(0.495)	(0.036)	(0.022)	(0.141)	(0.036)	(0.416)	(0.415)
Nonexecutive directors	0.104	0.155	−0.007	0.026	0.155	−0.007	−0.088	−0.038
	(0.361)	(0.347)	(0.012)	(0.017)	(0.108)	(0.012)	(0.295)	(0.299)
Founder experience	−0.056	−0.100***	0.003	−0.010***	0.007	0.003	−0.006	−0.364
	(0.047)	(0.029)	(0.002)	(0.003)	(0.021)	(0.002)	(0.065)	(0.384)

(Continued)

TABLE 12.2 (Continued)

	(1) Crowdcube	(2) A-shares	(3) Threshold (ln)	(4) C	(5) V/C	(6) Target capital	(7a) Offering success	(7b) Offering success
SEIS	0.209	0.223	-0.019**	0.037***	-0.453***	-0.019**	-0.102	-0.088
	(0.317)	(0.240)	(0.009)	(0.013)	(0.083)	(0.009)	(0.251)	(0.251)
Exit IPO	0.352	0.174	-0.002	-0.006	0.156*	-0.002	0.139	0.122
	(0.357)	(0.284)	(0.010)	(0.015)	(0.093)	(0.010)	(0.255)	(0.256)
Time trend	0.155	-0.136	-0.012	-0.002	-0.203*	-0.012	-0.783***	-0.768***
	(0.218)	(0.209)	(0.013)	(0.018)	(0.117)	(0.013)	(0.171)	(0.171)
Platform preference	0.252**	—	—	—	—	—	—	—
	(0.123)							
TMT size	—	0.091**	—	—	—	—	—	—
		(0.045)						
M&As in the industry	—	-0.215*	—	—	—	—	—	—
		(0.106)						
Pr. A-shares	—	3.275***	—	—	—	—	—	—
		(0.867)						
Pr. threshold	—	—	0.749**	0.134*	0.039	0.042	—	—
			(0.354)	(0.069)	(0.079)	(8.097)		
Pr. C	—	—	-3.123	1.042***	0.048	-1.926	—	—
			(2.468)	(0.302)	(0.117)	(1.920)		
Pr. V/C	—	—	5.555*	-0.386	0.072**	-0.813	—	—
			(2.890)	(0.232)	(0.039)	(2.866)		
Pr. target	—	—	-0.263	-0.186	-0.009	0.744***	—	—
			(0.288)	(0.253)	(0.017)	(0.191)		

IMR$_{platform}$	—	—	0.689	−0.167	0.201	−0.713	−0.187	−1.201
			(1.650)	(0.262)	(0.332)	(1.158)	(0.384)	(1.656)
IMR$_{voting}$	—	—	5.448	−0.159*	0.229**	4.385	2.368	2.233
			(5.022)	(0.081)	(0.103)	(3.735)	(2.226)	(2.197)
Constant	−5.425***	2.895**	0.346	−0.033	2.008***	7.075	11.754**	12.910**
	(1.452)	(1.236)	(0.441)	(0.555)	(0.635)	(6.533)	(5.072)	(5.191)
Log-likelihood	0.148						−412.8	−409.2
Observations	1309					405	405	405

The table reports the results of a double selection model with instrumental variables. The first stage is a bivariate probit model on the likelihood of issuing an offering in Crowdcube, with respect to Seedrs (Model 1) and issuing A-shares (Model 2). The identification conditions are identified as follows: in Model 1, we include platform preference, measured as the number of offerings listed on the Crowdcube, divided by the number of offerings listed on Seedrs, in the same industry, in the 12 months prior to each observation; in Model 2, similar to Gompers et al. (2010); we include TMT size, the number of M&As in the same industry, and a mimicking variable (Pr. A-shares), calculated as the ratio of crowdfunding offerings, which offered voting rights among offerings listed in the previous 12 months on the same platform. The second stage is a system of five equations estimated using a GSEM. The dependent variables are the threshold amount (Model 3), the controlling shareholder's cash-flow rights (Model 4), the voting to cash-flow rights (Model 5), the target capital (Model 6), and the success dummy (Model 7a). Model 7b is a replacement of Model 7a, where the interaction of V/C with founder experience is included (no instrumental equation is reported). Two IMRs are estimated from the first-stage equations and included in all second-stage equations. In the second stage, the ownership and control variables (threshold, C, V/C) are treated as endogenous (i.e., instrumented). For each observation, identification variables (i.e., instruments) are measured as the average value of the investment threshold required to receive A-shares (Pr. threshold), of the control variable (Pr. C), of the separation between ownership and control (Pr. V/C), and of the target capital (Pr. target) calculated using all equity offerings in the same industry in the previous year. When estimating Model 7b, an additional instrumental variable for V/C founder experience is included, as is interaction between Pr. V/C and founder experience. See Table 12.1 for the definition of the variables. Time trend is a variable set to 0 for 2011 issues and increased by 1 each year. Industry effects are included in all regressions, starting from Crowdcube classification. *, **, and *** indicate significance at the 10%, 5%, and 1% levels. GSEM, Generalized structural equation model; IMR, inverse Mills ratio; IPO, initial public offering; M&A, merger and acquisition; SEIS, Seed Enterprise Investment Scheme; TMT, top management team.

testified by the statistical significance of the *mimicking* (Pr. A-shares) variable. Among the control variables, we find that *experienced founders* are less likely to distribute voting rights.

In the second stage, we run a system of five equations, where the *threshold, C, V/C,* and *target capital* are endogenously estimated. These instrumental equations allow us to identify the determinants of ownership and control mechanisms in crowdfunding offerings. Model 3 shows that offering firms mimicked the decisions in previous offerings, carried out within the same industry in the previous year, when deciding where to set *threshold,* so that the amount required for the issuing of A-shares is strongly correlated with the average amount required by previous offerings in the same industry. The *threshold* level is also positively affected by *family,* while *founder experience* is negatively correlated. Interestingly, issues by older companies are likely to show higher C and lower V/C, while issues eligible for SEIS tax incentives show smaller C and higher V/C. As expected, the choices of C and V/C in each offering are largely affected by a mimicking behavior, so much so that levels observed in earlier campaigns (*Pr. C* and *Pr. V/C*) are strongly significant in both equations.

Our results on the success of the offering (Model 7a) show that a higher level of cash-flow rights (i.e., a smaller level of equity offered in the offering) is positively linked to the likelihood of success. The coefficient is 1.138, statistically significant at less than 5%, and implies that, for a one-standard deviation change in cash-flow rights, equal to 7.8%, there would be an increase in the probability of success of by 3.2%. This result shows that the more the interest alignment between proponent and investors (high C), the more likelihood the success. This evidence confirms the validity retained equity as a signal that attracts external investors. The associated increased demand of shares translates in higher valuations and/or higher probability of success of equity offerings (Leland & Pyle, 1977). Our findings extend the evidence from initial or follow-on offerings in stock markets to crowdfunding offerings.

While equity retention has a positive effect, the probability of success is negatively affected by the ratio between voting and cash-flow rights. The coefficient is −3.589, statistically significant at less than 5%, and implies that, for a one-standard deviation change in V/C, equal to 0.08, there would be a decrease in the probability of success by 10.8%. Given that this ratio is a proxy for the separation between *ownership* and *control* (see Faccio & Lang, 2002), this result is evidence that the probability of success for a crowdfunding offering is negatively related to the potential rise of agency cost. As far as the control variables are concerned, our results show that younger issues are more likely to succeed, as well as proposals reporting positive sales in the presentation report. A negative time trend suggests that the increase in the number of recent offers has led to a decrease in the relative probability of success. Across the models, we notice that both selection processes (the choice of Crowdcube and the choice to issue voting rights) affect the results. In particular, unobservable determinants of platform choices are correlated with unobserved determinants of C (positively) and V/C (negatively), while the choice to issue voting rights is correlated both with the separation between ownership and control (V/C) and the likelihood of success.

Lastly, Table 12.2 reports the result for the outcome variable, *success,* introducing an interaction term between the V/C variable and the *founder experience* (selection and instrumental models are not reported for the sake of brevity). The interaction term is positive and significant, showing that the signal provided by an experienced proponent mitigates the concerns arising from the separation between *ownership* and *control*. All other results are qualitatively unchanged.

12.4.2 Postoffering outcomes

Our analysis focuses on postoffering outcomes by analyzing two competing scenarios (i.e., long-run success and failure). We report our results in Table 12.3, where we implement a multilevel, multiprocess hazard model, with two hazard rate equations for long-run success (Model 2) and failure (Model 3), and a selection equation for successful offerings (Model 1). In order to grant identification, Model 1 is enriched with a parameter, *competing offerings*, measuring the number of offerings open in the same equity crowdfunding platform at the time of the opening of each offering. Further, this setting allows us to treat ownership and control variables (*threshold*, C, and V/C,) and *target capital* as endogenous.

Model 1, identifying successful offerings, reports results qualitatively analogous to our previous findings. Model 2a reports our analysis of the likelihood of each offering to be successful in the long run and provides evidence that interest alignment improves the likelihood of postcampaign success, while there is weak evidence that separation between ownership and control reduces such opportunities. *Age* and expectations of IPO exit negatively affect long-run success, while positive sales before the offering increases the likelihood of such a scenario. A positive time trend is statistically significant in describing the phenomenon.

Model 3a presents evidence on the covariates increasing the likelihood of firm failure following the offering: C is strongly negative and V/C weakly positive in affecting this probability. In a complementary way to our previous findings, these results support that C, measuring the interest alignment between controlling shareholders and investors, reduces the likelihood of offering failure in the long-run, while V/C, measuring the separation between ownership and control, increases the probability of such a scenario. Among control variables, we find a negative effect of *target capital*, *family*, *age*, and *positive sales*. These results suggest that larger firms, mature and with a positive sales track record, are less likely to fail.

We find that family businesses launching crowdfunding campaigns are relatively safer investments, as they exhibit higher survival rates ($P < .01$). This is in line with the arguments of family business literature, which has typically portrayed family firms as long-term oriented and more conservative than nonfamily firms (e.g., Westhead & Howorth, 2006; Zellweger, 2007). We argue that this feature is particularly relevant in the context of crowdfunding. Firms raising funds in equity crowdfunding are relatively smaller and younger than in other public equity markets. Hence, the involvement of a family, associated with long-term orientation and risk aversion, might be perceived by external investors as a signal mitigating the uncertainty on the prospects of the firm.

12.4.3 Investor composition

Our analysis also addresses whether decisions on the distribution of voting rights affect investor participation regarding crowdfunding offerings. Table 12.4 reports the results of a

TABLE 12.3　The effect of interest alignment and voting rights' thresholds on postoffering scenarios.

	(1)	(2a)	(3a)	(2b)	(3b)
	Offering success	Long-run success	Failure	Long-run success	Failure
C	1.848*	2.964**	− 6.829**	3.049**	− 4.296*
	(0.973)	(1.347)	(2.886)	(1.284)	(2.459)
V/C	− 4.963**	− 5.923*	5.980*	− 5.409**	7.185*
	(2.698)	(3.119)	(3.197)	(2.575)	(3.991)
V/C × founder experience	–	–	–	0.137	− 3.726*
				(0.523)	(2.103)
Threshold (ln)	− 0.008	0.590	1.614	0.584	0.328
	(0.154)	(0.401)	(1.058)	(0.404)	(0.458)
Target capital	− 0.079	0.063	− 1.961***	0.043	− 1.561***
	(0.154)	(0.363)	(0.499)	(0.346)	(0.549)
Family	− 0.352	− 0.472	− 3.955***	− 0.472	− 4.737***
	(0.268)	(1.151)	(1.129)	(1.153)	(2.054)
Age	− 0.289**	− 1.394**	− 1.547***	− 1.410**	− 1.449*
	(0.138)	(0.646)	(0.487)	(0.679)	(0.835)
Positive sales	1.082***	2.539**	− 2.150***	2.548**	2.164***
	(0.224)	(1.039)	(0.660)	(1.056)	(0.723)
Patents	0.499	0.842	− 2.203	0.840	− 2.455
	(0.377)	(0.714)	(1.577)	(0.705)	(2.209)
Nonexecutive directors	− 0.032	1.964**	2.462	2.009**	3.943
	(0.326)	(0.802)	(1.945)	(0.888)	(2.622)
Founder experience	0.066*	0.085	0.034	− 0.066	− 7.141
	(0.035)	(0.057)	(0.190)	(0.577)	(4.707)
SEIS	− 0.140	0.973	− 0.510	0.983	− 1.243
	(0.247)	(0.871)	(1.024)	(0.850)	(1.535)
Exit IPO	0.178	0.542	− 0.821	0.534	− 0.940
	(0.285)	(0.530)	(1.336)	(0.526)	(1.869)
Time trend	− 0.891***	− 1.470***	0.139	− 1.473***	0.512
	(0.195)	(0.556)	(0.664)	(0.568)	(1.201)
Competing offerings	− 0.019***	–	–	–	–
	(0.006)				

(*Continued*)

TABLE 12.3 (Continued)

	(1)	(2a)	(3a)	(2b)	(3b)
	Offering success	Long-run success	Failure	Long-run success	Failure
Constant	12.669**	–	–	–	–
	(5.683)				
Log-likelihood	– 9.161			0.176	0.181
Observations	491			405	152

The table reports the results of a multilevel, multiprocess hazard model, with two hazard rate equations for long-run success (Model 2a) and failure (Model 3a), a selection equation for offering success (Model 1), and where ownership and control variables (threshold, C, V/C and target capital are treated as endogenous (i.e., instrumented). In Model 1, identification condition is granted by the inclusion of the number of competing offerings; that is, offerings open in the same equity crowdfunding platform at the time of the opening of each offering. For each observation, identification variables (i.e., instruments) are measured as the average value of the investment threshold required to receive A-shares (Pr. threshold), of the control variable (Pr. C), and of the separation between ownership and control (Pr. V/C), calculated using all offerings listed in the previous 12 months on the same platform. The equations for instrumented variables are omitted, as they are qualitatively the same reported in Table 12.2. Time trend is a variable set to 0 for 2011 issues and increased by 1 each year. Models 2b and 3b are replacements of Models 2a and 3a, where the interaction of V/C with founder experience is included. Industry effects are included in all regressions, starting from Crowdcube classification. *, **, and *** indicate significance at the 10%, 5%, and 1% levels. *IPO*, Initial public offering; *SEIS*, Seed Enterprise Investment Scheme.

double selection model with instrumental variables, where the system of Eqs. (12.3)–(12.9) is replicated by replacing the outcome variable *success* with four alternatives: a dummy equal to 1 in case a professional investor has joined the offering (*professional investors*),[19] the number of investors participating in the offering (*number of investors*), the Hirschman–Herfindahl index calculated for the bids of all participants in the offering (*bid HHI*), and the average bid offered by nonprofessional investors (*average bid*, non-Pr.).[20] This set of outcome variables is reported both in the baseline specification (Models 1a–4a) and in a specification including the interaction term between the V/C variable and *founder experience* (Models 1b–4b).

In Model 1a, where the dependent variable is equal to 1 if the equity offering receives bids from professional investors, the *threshold* variable becomes significant, while results related to C and V/C are confirmed. This shows that professional investors are sensitive to interest alignment, through the share of cash-flow rights, to the separation between

[19] The participation of Professional Investors is jointly determined with the success of an offering, and this is why, in this model, we treat it as an alternative outcome variable. According to an alternative view, the participation of professionals may be seen as a determinant of success of an offering. This is why, in Table 12.A5 in the "Appendix" section, we replicate the results reported in Table 12.2, by adding a further endogenous variable (*professional investors*) as a determinant for *success*. The instrumental variable chosen for the identification of this additional endogenous variable is the *TMT size*. Results show that, in this framework, *professional investors* are positively correlated with *success*, also when considering the interaction term between V/C and *Founder Experience*. Most results are qualitatively unchanged.

[20] The table reports only the models for the outcome variables, given that all other results are qualitatively unchanged. All results are, indeed, available on request.

TABLE 12.4 The effect of voting rights' thresholds on the participation of sophisticated and other types of investors.

	(1a) Professional investors	(2a) Number of investors	(3a) Bid HHI	(4a) Average bid (non-Pr.)	(1b) Professional investors	(2b) Number of investors	(3b) Bid HHI	(4b) Average bid (non-Pr.)
C	4.191**	1.895***	0.179	−0.041	4.022**	1.909***	0.112	−0.048
	(2.123)	(0.661)	(0.143)	(2.757)	(2.111)	(0.692)	(0.164)	(2.410)
V/C	−4.715***	−0.108**	−0.096	2.523	−5.815***	−0.145**	−0.084	2.461
	(1.657)	(0.048)	(0.131)	(2.742)	(2.409)	(0.061)	(0.120)	(2.328)
V/C × founder experience	—	—	—	—	0.285**	0.095***	0.012	−0.190
					(0.139)	(0.025)	(0.023)	(0.413)
Threshold (ln)	0.408**	−0.072***	0.016**	−0.061	0.404**	−0.060***	0.015**	−0.048
	(0.201)	(0.016)	(0.007)	(0.50)	(0.205)	(0.006)	(0.007)	(0.57)
Target capital	0.529	0.033**	−0.003	1.151***	0.115	0.409***	−0.003	1.154***
	(0.365)	(0.015)	(0.014)	(0.145)	(0.250)	(0.008)	(0.008)	(0.145)
Family	−0.431	−0.437***	−0.004	−0.300	−0.425	−0.438***	−0.004	−0.298
	(0.541)	(0.020)	(0.015)	(1.604)	(0.539)	(0.020)	(0.015)	(1.609)
Age	0.050	−0.176***	−0.001	0.131	0.037	−0.168***	−0.001	0.129
	(0.245)	(0.008)	(0.008)	(0.133)	(0.247)	(0.008)	(0.008)	(0.133)
Positive sales	0.962**	0.428***	0.007	−0.059	0.973**	0.422***	0.006	−0.058
	(0.420)	(0.014)	(0.012)	(0.211)	(0.424)	(0.014)	(0.012)	(0.211)
Patents	−5.309	0.462***	0.006	−0.566	−5.223	0.455***	0.007	−0.575
	(344.023)	(0.019)	(0.021)	(0.383)	(345.101)	(0.019)	(0.021)	(0.383)
Nonexecutive directors	0.070	0.110***	−0.019	−0.642**	0.120	0.135***	−0.016	−0.663**
	(0.407)	(0.017)	(0.017)	(0.299)	(0.423)	(0.017)	(0.017)	(0.302)

Founder experience	0.159**	0.009***	−0.001	0.017	−0.111	−0.197***	−0.023	0.228
	(0.080)	(0.003)	(0.002)	(0.039)	(0.567)	(0.022)	(0.021)	(0.461)
SEIS	−0.292	−0.131***	−0.009	0.239	−0.267	−0.121***	−0.008	0.231
	(0.445)	(0.018)	(0.014)	(0.249)	(0.450)	(0.018)	(0.014)	(0.250)
Exit IPO	0.493	0.019	−0.003	0.185	0.462	0.006	−0.005	0.196
	(0.365)	(0.015)	(0.015)	(0.251)	(0.370)	(0.015)	(0.015)	(0.252)
Time trend	−0.327	−0.010	−0.007	−0.706***	−0.301	−0.007	−0.006	−0.715***
	(0.310)	(0.011)	(0.010)	(0.195)	(0.316)	(0.011)	(0.010)	(0.196)
IMR$_{platform}$	0.056	−0.460***	0.022	−0.103	0.026	−0.465***	0.022	−0.099
	(0.623)	(0.026)	(0.023)	(0.187)	(0.630)	(0.027)	(0.023)	(0.178)
IMR$_{voting}$	−2.353	−0.231***	−0.058	−0.263	−2.277	−0.256***	−0.057	−0.286
	(2.177)	(0.064)	(0.049)	(0.858)	(2.184)	(0.064)	(0.049)	(0.859)
Constant	−4.155	2.086***	0.179	−13.598***	−2.515	2.897***	0.252	5.486
	(7.870)	(0.279)	(0.241)	(4.090)	(8.577)	(0.294)	(0.251)	(4.598)
Log-likelihood	−411.8	−395.7	−446.1	−409.2	−410.3	−394.2	−446.1	−408.9
Observations	405	405	405	405	405	405	405	405

The table reports the results of a double selection model with instrumental variables. The first stage (omitted) is a bivariate probit model on the likelihood of issuing an offering in Crowdcube, with respect to Seedrs, and issuing A-shares (as in Models 1 and 2 in Table 12.2). The outcome variables in the second stage is, in Model 1a, a dummy equal to 1 in case a professional investor bid shares at the offering; in Model 2a, the number of investors participating in the offering; in Model 3a, a measure of bid concentration, calculated as an HHI (i.e., HHI = 1 if the entire offering is subscribed by only one investor); and in Model 4a, the average bid of nonprofessional investors. In all cases, in the second stage, ownership and control variables (threshold, C, V/C) and target capital are treated as endogenous (i.e., instrumented). Models 1b–4b are a replacement of Models 1a–4a, where the interaction of V/C with founder experience is included (no instrumental equation is reported). For each observation, identification variables (i.e., instruments) are measured as the average value of the investment threshold required to receive A-shares (Pr. threshold), of the control variable (Pr. C), and of the separation between ownership and control (Pr. V/C), calculated using all equity offerings in the same industry in the previous year. When estimating Models 1b–4b, an additional instrumental variable for V/C × founder experience is included, as is interaction between Pr. V/C and founder experience. The equations for instrumented variables are omitted as qualitatively the same as in Table 12.2. Two IMRs are estimated in the first stage and included in all equations of the second stage. See Table 12.1 for the definition of the variables. Time trend is a variable set to 0 for 2011 issues and increased by 1 each year. Industry effects are included in all regressions, starting from Crowdcube classification. *, **, and *** indicate significance at the 10%, 5%, and 1% levels. HHI, Hirschman–Herfindahl index; IMR, Inverse Mills Ratio; IPO, initial public offering; SEIS, Seed Enterprise Investment Scheme.

ownership and *control*, through the voting to cash-flow rights parameter, and they are attracted by issues where a threshold limits the dispersion of ownership. The evidence that professional investors are more likely to bid in offerings in which higher thresholds are required to achieve voting rights point to their preference for more concentrated share ownership. Anecdotal evidence confirms this intuition. In interviews, indeed, a number of professional investors declare that they are more likely to invest in offerings that deliver voting rights above a certain threshold compared to those that deliver voting rights to every investor. Furthermore, if they invest after the offering, they report the preference to repay small investors and provide them with an exit opportunity, so as not to have to deal with them in shareholders meetings.

Results related to control variables are in line with our findings on the success of crowdfunding offerings. Model 2a also shows that the number of investors is positively correlated with C and negatively affected by V/C. Interestingly, the *family* dummy is negatively related to the number of investors. As this variable does not affect the chances for success of crowdfunding offerings nor their attractiveness for professional investors, family businesses appear to be less attractive to small investors.

In Model 3a, coherently with our previous results, we show that the concentration of bids is higher when the threshold is higher. In Model 4a, finally, we show that neither the distribution of voting rights nor the presence of a threshold affects the average size of the bids for nonprofessional investors, which is only sensitive to the size of the offering and to the presence of nonexecutives among the member of the TMT.

Models 1b–4b show that the moderating effect of *founder experience* on V/C is positive and statistically significant both with respect to the presence of professional investors and a large number of investors.

12.4.4 Robustness tests

In this section, we report the outcome of robustness tests run in order to test the sensitivity of our results to the definitions of two key variables and to an alternative specification of long-run outcome.

In Table 12.5, we report the results of our analysis when changing the definition for the threshold level and the ownership variables. First, in Model 1, *threshold/target capital* replaces *threshold* (ln) employed in all former analyses. We report the results for the outcome variable, *success*, here, as in Model 7a, Table 12.2, showing that our results are unaffected. Second, in Model 2, we replace the *voting to cash-flow rights* variable with the *ownership* wedge, a dummy variable equal to 1 when the voting rights are greater than the cash-flow rights. Once again, we report the results for the outcome variable, *success*, as in Model 7a, Table 12.2, showing that our results are also confirmed when changing the proxy for the separation between ownership and control.

Lastly, we assess the robustness of our results when changing the empirical design of the long-run outcome from a survival model (multilevel, multiprocess hazard model) to a multinomial setting. In this analysis, we ignore the time to the event, and rather analyze the determinants of a qualitative outcome, which can take three values: *failure*, identified when firms are insolvent, liquidated, or dissolved within 2 years from the initial

TABLE 12.5 Robustness test on the definition for the threshold level and the ownership variables.

	(1)	(2)
	Offering success	**Offering success**
C	1.031**	1.069**
	(0.485)	(0.491)
V/C	− 4.573**	−
	(2.212)	
Threshold/target	0.064	−
	(0.148)	
Ownership wedge	−	− 0.526**
		(0.251)
Threshold (ln)	−	0.009
		(0.096)
Target capital	− 0.062	− 0.076
	(0.131)	(0.142)
Family	− 0.318**	− 0.307**
	(0.137)	(0.137)
Age	0.973***	0.964***
	(0.210)	(0.210)
Positive sales	0.501	0.520
	(0.419)	(0.419)
Patents	− 0.116	− 0.114
	(0.295)	(0.294)
Nonexecutive directors	− 0.000	− 0.007
	(0.065)	(0.066)
Founder experience	− 0.122	− 0.109
	(0.250)	(0.250)
SEIS	0.177	0.178
	(0.256)	(0.255)
Exit IPO	− 0.318**	− 0.307**
	(0.137)	(0.137)
Time trend	0.973***	0.964***
	(0.210)	(0.210)

(Continued)

TABLE 12.5   (Continued)

	(1)	(2)
	Offering success	**Offering success**
IMR$_{platform}$	−0.156	−0.121
	(0.384)	(0.380)
IMR$_{voting}$	2.156	2.419
	(2.200)	(2.233)
Constant	13.311***	5.246**
	(4.899)	(2.421)
Log-likelihood	−413.0	−412.5
Observations	405	405

These are the same models as in Table 12.3 but with different definitions of ownership variables. In Model 1, *threshold/target* replaces *threshold* (ln). In Model 2, *ownership wedge* replaces (*V/C*). Selection and instrumental equations are not reported, as they are qualitatively analogous to those reported in Table 12.2. *, **, *** indicate significance at the 10%, 5%, and 1% levels. *IMR*, Inverse Mills Ratio; *IPO*, initial public offering; *SEIS*, Seed Enterprise Investment Scheme.

campaigns; among firms that did not fail, a firm is identified as successful (*long-run success*) when it, after successfully raising equity in crowdfunding offerings, either attracts further equity financing or delivers an exit opportunity to crowdfunding investors, either in the form of IPO or M&A; if none of the above-given conditions took place in the 2 years after the initial campaign, a firm is simply identified as surviving (*survival*). In Table 12.6, we report the marginal effects for each outcome (*long-run success, failure*, and *survival*) estimated in a multinomial logit model with a selection equation[21] for *offering success* (identification condition is granted by the inclusion of the number of competing offerings) and where *ownership* and *control* variables (*threshold, C, V/C*) and *target capital* are treated as endogenous (i.e., instrumented), as in the former models presented in the chapter. Results show that C increases the probability of long-run success and decreases the probability of failure, in both cases at a 10% level of significance; V/C decreases the probability of long-run success at 5%, while it increases the probability of failure at 1%; this latter result is mitigated (see Columns 1b and 2b) by the founder's experience. While all these results confirm our earlier findings, here we also have weak evidence that the threshold for the issue of voting rights weakly affects the probability of success. Most results on control variables are qualitatively in line with the model presented earlier in the chapter.

---

[21] We use a single selection equation in order to keep as parsimonious as possible our setting, as well as in analogy to the multilevel, multiprocess hazard model presented earlier in the chapter.

TABLE 12.6 Robustness test on the definition of long-run outcome.

	(1a)	(2a)	(3a)	(1b)	(2b)	(3b)
	Long-run success	Failure	Survival	Long-run success	Failure	Survival
C	0.852*	− 0.568*	− 0.284	0.815*	− 0.328**	− 0.487
	(0.461)	(0.291)	(0.365)	(0.414)	(0.149)	(0.385)
V/C	− 0.890**	1.240***	− 0.350	− 1.671***	2.114***	− 0.443
	(0.357)	(0.468)	(0.309)	(0.617)	(0.701)	(0.372)
V/C × founder experience	−	−	−	0.145**	− 0.159**	0.015
				(0.058)	(0.068)	(0.039)
Threshold (ln)	0.036*	0.033	− 0.069	0.036*	0.033	− 0.069**
	(0.020)	(0.022)	(0.047)	(0.020)	(0.023)	(0.030)
Target capital	0.005	− 0.041**	0.036	0.003	− 0.056**	0.053*
	(0.022)	(0.018)	(0.028)	(0.022)	(0.024)	(0.032)
Family	− 0.009	− 0.447***	0.456	− 0.018	− 0.414***	0.432
	(3.043)	(0.159)	(43.716)	(1.893)	(0.138)	(32.647)
Age	− 0.080***	− 0.033*	0.113***	− 0.083***	− 0.038*	0.121***
	(0.029)	(0.017)	(0.033)	(0.030)	(0.020)	(0.035)
Positive sales	0.161***	0.071	− 0.231***	0.165***	0.091	− 0.256***
	(0.061)	(0.049)	(0.077)	(0.061)	(0.056)	(0.081)
Patents	0.082	− 0.028	− 0.053	0.087	− 0.030	− 0.058
	(0.058)	(0.045)	(0.071)	(0.059)	(0.048)	(0.075)
Nonexecutive directors	0.086**	0.036	− 0.122***	0.091**	0.044	− 0.135***
	(0.035)	(0.032)	(0.046)	(0.036)	(0.039)	(0.052)
Founder experience	0.007	0.002	− 0.009	− 0.009	0.151	0.160
	(0.005)	(0.004)	(0.007)	(0.044)	(0.111)	(0.123)
SEIS	0.044	− 0.083**	0.039	0.044	− 0.112**	0.068
	(0.043)	(0.039)	(0.056)	(0.043)	(0.051)	(0.065)
Exit IPO	0.018	− 0.365	0.347	0.007	− 0.274	0.267
	(2.036)	(31.284)	(29.248)	(1.486)	(27.132)	(25.646)
Time trend	− 0.118**	− 0.027	0.144**	− 0.122**	− 0.045	0.166***
	(0.049)	(0.030)	(0.058)	(0.050)	(0.035)	(0.060)
IMR$_{\text{offering\_success}}$	0.113	0.086	− 0.199	0.125	0.147	− 0.272*
	(0.123)	(0.086)	(0.150)	(0.124)	(0.097)	(0.155)

(Continued)

TABLE 12.6   (Continued)

	(1a)	(2a)	(3a)	(1b)	(2b)	(3b)
	Long-run success	Failure	Survival	Long-run success	Failure	Survival
Log-likelihood	− 62.556			− 58.918		
Observations	405			405		

The table reports the marginal effects after regressing a multinomial logit model, with three possible outcomes 2 years after the offering campaign, that is, long-run success (Model 1a), failure (Model 2a), survival (Model 3a), a selection equation for offering success, and where ownership and control variables (threshold, C, V/C) and target capital are treated as endogenous (i.e., instrumented). In the offering success equation, identification condition is granted by the inclusion of the number of competing offerings, that is, offerings open in the same equity crowdfunding platform at the time of the opening of each offering. For each observation, identification variables (i.e., instruments) are measured as the average value of the investment threshold required to receive A-shares (Pr. threshold), of the control variable (Pr. C), and of the separation between ownership and control (Pr. V/C), calculated using all offerings listed in the previous 12 months on the same platform. The equations for instrumented variables are omitted, as they are qualitatively the same reported in Table 12.2. The offering success equation is omitted, as they are qualitatively equivalent to results reported in Table 12.3. Time trend is a variable set to 0 for 2011 issues and increased by 1 each year. Models 1b, 2b, and 3b are replacements of Models 1a, 2a, and 3b, where the interaction of V/C with founder experience is included. Industry effects are included in all regressions, starting from Crowdcube classification. *, **, and *** indicate significance at the 10%, 5%, and 1% levels. IMR, Inverse Mills Ratio; IPO, initial public offering; SEIS, Seed Enterprise Investment Scheme.

12.5 Conclusion

This chapter investigates for the first time the ownership and control mechanisms in firms raising equity capital through crowdfunding. By using a sample of 491 offerings on Crowdcube from 2011 through 2015, we focus on how the setting of a threshold for voting rights distribution, the concentration of cash-flow rights, and the separation between ownership and control affect the probability of success. This is done both at the offering level and in terms of postoffering outcomes. Our results show that a high separation between ownership and control negatively affects the probability of success of the offering and the likelihood of long-run success, while it decreases the likelihood of survival after the offering. The negative effects due to such separation are mitigated for those issues where the proponent is an experienced founder. Investments in crowdfunding offerings by family firms are safer, as they have lower probabilities of failure. However, they attract a lower number of investors.

Our findings add to the corporate governance literature by providing first-time evidence in the context of equity crowdfunding. By analyzing the impact of cash-flow and voting rights on the probability of success of crowdfunding offering, we find support for the alignment of interest hypothesis and for the entrenchment hypothesis that are validated in extant corporate finance literature for IPOs. While crowdfunding investors rely on the controlling shareholder's cash-flow stake to assess how the potentially divergent interests are aligned, at the same time they are concerned for the potential misbehaviors performed when controlling shareholders control a larger stake with respect to their direct ownership. This is a novel finding that characterizes equity crowdfunding as similar to traditional public equity markets.

Second, our empirical setting allows us to analyze a unique context where it is the individual investor who determines the attribution of voting rights. It is a unique case in which a single price is attributed to two theoretically different asset classes. Indeed, in most offerings, investors can achieve voting rights by investing over a threshold, while the price of the shares is the same between shares carrying or not carrying voting rights. Future corporate finance studies can further investigate entrepreneurs' and investors' choices between ownership and investment. In this respect, our empirical analysis shows that a category of professional investor pays attention to this attribute and often bids the exact amount of money necessary to be assigned A-shares. This finding opens new research perspectives in the growing crowdfunding literature, which has so far considered the demand of shares as originated from a rather homogeneous group of relatively unsophisticated investors. Taking into account the heterogeneity in the experience and background of equity crowdfunding investors, future research should explore whether and how various forms of unaccredited investor experience influences funding rates, performance, and failure in crowdfunded startups.

We believe that our chapter carries important implications for policy and practice. Our evidence contributes to better the understanding of how the features of a crowdfunding platform such as Crowdcube may play a role in stimulating the financing of entrepreneurial activity (Autio, Kenney, Mustar, Siegel, & Wright, 2014) and, in particular, how the provision of voting rights' thresholds enhances the attractiveness for professional investors, a feature that might be of interest for other platform managers as well. Entrepreneurs find evidence that ownership structure decisions affect the outcome of their financial initiatives and, therefore, find support for strategies that try to mitigate investors' concerns by aligning potentially conflicting interests. In this regard, experienced founders are helped in their activity because of the reliability acknowledged for their offering, given that prior acquaintance with a crowdfunding platform significantly decreases concerns, due to the separation between ownership and control. Indeed, mitigating the conditions for access to financing is a topic of dramatic importance, especially for innovative firms, which are, in general, more likely to be turned down for finance than other firms (Lockett, Murray, & Wright, 2002), especially in the wake of the financial crisis (Lee, Sameen, & Cowling, 2015).

From a policy perspective, our chapter may support policymakers who aim to find a balance between the objectives to facilitate capital formation and the need for investor protection. The development of equity crowdfunding can indeed stimulate knowledge ecosystems in technology hotspots (Clarysse, Wright, Bruneel, & Mahajan, 2014). The rapid expansion of crowdfunding has, however, raised concerns regarding the fit of this type of investment opportunity for the crowd, resulting in an active debate whether crowdfunding regimes should promote equity crowdfunding or tighten regulations. We show that differences exist in the investment decisions between professional and small investors. Their exposure to risk is currently constrained by investment limits that are based on income and net worth. The introduction of corporate governance requirements and increased transparency on the contractual terms can further benefit small investors. Indeed, although the use of dual-class shares may be beneficial to entrepreneurs, who encounter fewer distractions than from interacting with numerous small investors, our findings show that small investors are often not able to achieve voting rights.

Admittedly, we need to acknowledge that our results have limitations, due to an important boundary condition, in that firms in our sample chose crowdfunding over alternative options. The choice of focusing on Crowdcube allows for variation in the contractual terms between cash-flow and control rights. However, while our design models the preference for Crowdcube over an alternative platform, at this stage, it is unfeasible to implement a further step back to endogenize the choice of crowdfunding relative to alternatives. Still, we are aware that this choice sets a boundary to the generalization of our results, and we acknowledge this as a limitation for our study. Differently from the case studied in this chapter, other platforms, such as Seedrs, act as a trustee who manages pooled voting rights on behalf of investors. The level of a minimum investment thresholds and coinvestment requirements also vary across platforms. While most platforms ask for symbolic minimum investment thresholds, some require investors to make relatively large investments. In the United Kingdom, SyndicateRoom requires the involvement of accredited investors in order to open the offering to small investors. These differences in the functioning of platforms are likely to affect many aspects of the matching between the supply and demand of entrepreneurial finance (Dushnitsky & Zunino, 2018). The investigation of how the choice of a funding source interacts with the ownership structure design is definitely an interesting topic, and we leave this to further research for investigation.

Key terms

Bid concentration
Block threshold
Class A share
Class B share
Control rights
Instrumental variables
Long-run success
Offering success
Ownership rights
Professional investor
SEIS
Selection model
Threshold
Voting rights

Discussion questions

12.1. What are the potential advantages associated with the separation of ownership and control? What are the potential disadvantages? Explain, with reference to various agency problems outlined in Chapter 2, Overview of agency and signaling theory in crowdfunding. Do you think these advantages and disadvantages would be more pronounced in the context of equity crowdfunding? Why?

12.2. What is the typical ownership share offered in crowdfunding campaigns such as those on Crowdcube? Does offering a higher ownership share improve the probability that the offering will be successful? Does a higher ownership share improve long-run success? Explain, with reference to theory and evidence.

12.3. What is the typical extent to which ownership is separated from voting rights in crowdfunding campaigns on Crowdcube? Does offering a greater separation of ownership and control improve the probability that the offering will be successful? Does a greater separation of ownership and control improve long-run success? Explain, with reference to theory and evidence.

12.4. What are the typical threshold amounts used to obtain voting shares in crowdfunding campaigns on the Crowdcube crowdfunding platform? What affects the decision to set thresholds of different amounts? Explain with reference to theory and evidence.

12.5. What explains the entrepreneur's choice of use of Crowdcube versus one of the other equity crowdfunding platforms in the United Kingdom? Why?

12.6. What explains the decision to issue A-shares versus B-shares on Crowdcube? Why?

12.7. What explains the extent to which equity shares are sold on equity crowdfunding platforms such as Crowdcube? Is the extent to which equity is sold correlated with the extent to which there is a separation of ownership versus control through the issuance of nonvoting shares via Crowdcube? Explain with reference to theory and evidence.

12.8. Do professional investors prefer voting or nonvoting shares on the Crowdcube equity crowdfunding platform? Why? Explain with reference to empirical evidence.

12.9. How important is founder experience for campaign success, and for long-run success of an equity crowdfunded company? Explain with reference to empirical evidence.

12.10. Do tax schemes such as SEIS facilitate successful equity crowdfunded companies? Why? Explain with reference to theory and evidence. What does the evidence say about complementarities (or lack thereof) in the design of public policy for entrepreneurial finance? (See also Chapter 17: Public policy toward entrepreneurial finance: spillovers and scale-up.)

Appendix

TABLE 12.A1 Descriptive statistics.

	Mean	Median	St. dev.	Max	Min
Panel A. Outcome variables					
Offering success (%)	38.49	0.00	48.17	100.00	0.00
Long-run success (%)	9.16	0.00	28.88	100.00	0.00
Failure (%)	6.31	0.00	24.35	100.00	0.00
Professional investors (%)	27.38	0.00	44.65	100.00	0.00
Number of investors	95.79	54.00	183.41	2906	1
Bid concentration (HHI)	7.15	2.00	14.51	100.00	0.01
Average bid (nonprofessional) (£k)	1.70	1.24	1.89	22.90	0.02
Panel B. Ownership and control variables					
A-shares threshold (%)	83.50	100.00	37.19	100.00	0.00
A-shares threshold (£k)	9.09	5.00	4.36	150.00	0.00
Block threshold (%)	11.89	0.00	30.30	100.00	0.00
Threshold/target capital (%)	3.96	2.00	7.06	75.00	0.00
C (%)	86.11	88.00	7.81	0.98	0.15
V/C	1.08	1.04	0.10	1.81	1.00
Ownership wedge (%)	90.22	100.00	29.73	100.00	0.00
Target capital (£k)	277.80	150.00	481.47	6000.00	12.00
Family (%)	18.32	0.00	38.73	100.00	0.00
Panel C. Control variables					
Age (years)	3.05	3.20	2.01	22.44	0.03
Positive sales (%)	52.77	100.00	50.00	100.00	0.00
Patents (%)	8.14	0.00	27.39	100.00	0.00
Nonexecutive directors (%)	9.57	0.00	30.80	100.00	0.00
Founder experience (no.)	3.74	3.00	3.53	30.00	0.00
SEIS (%)	36.92	0.00	48.33	100.00	0.00
Exit IPO (%)	19.76	0.00	39.88	100.00	0.00

Descriptive statistics (mean, median, standard deviation, maximum, and minimum values) on the sample of 491 Crowdcube offerings between 2011 and 2015. *HHI*, Hirschman–Herfindahl index; *IPO*, Initial public offering; *SEIS*, Seed Enterprise Investment Scheme.

TABLE 12.A2 Comparison of Crowdcube and Seedrs samples.

	Crowdcube		Seedrs		Test on the difference	
					Crowdcube vs Seedrs	
Observations	491		818			
	Mean	Median	Mean	Median	Mean	Median
Control variables						
Age (years)	2.97	2.20	3.16	2.59	− 0.19	− 0.39
Positive sales (%)	52.71	100.00	52.20	100.00	0.51	0.00
Patents (%)	7.94	0.00	7.44	0.00	0.54	0.00
Nonexecutive directors (%)	9.57	0.00	8.46	0.00	− 1.08	0.00
Founder experience (no.)	3.79	3.00	4.20	3.00	− 0.41	0.00
SEIS (%)	36.63	0.00	33.57	0.00	3.06	0.00
Exit IPO (%)	19.52	0.00	19.43	0.00	0.03	0.00

Descriptive statistics on the sample of 491 Crowdcube offerings between 2011 and 2015 and on the matched sample of 818 Seedrs UK offerings between 2012 and 2015. Variables are defined as in Table 12.1. Ownership variables are not available for Seedrs offerings. *, **, and *** indicate significance at the 10%, 5%, and 1% levels, respectively, of the *t*-test (*z*-test for dummy variables) for the difference in means between the two groups. *IPO*, Initial public offering; *SEIS*, Seed Enterprise Investment Scheme.

TABLE 12.A3 Determinants of success for the equity offerings (for the full model of issues; no threshold analysis).

| | (1) | (2) | (3) | (4) |
	C	V/C	Target capital	Offering success
C	−	−	−	1.484***
				(0.573)
V/C	−	−	−	− 2.224***
				(0.826)
Target capital	−	−	−	0.004
				(0.115)
Family	− 0.015	0.010*	0.019	− 0.230
	(0.010)	(0.006)	(0.090)	(0.221)
Age	0.018***	− 0.023***	0.024	− 0.268**
	(0.005)	(0.007)	(0.044)	(0.116)
Positive sales	0.003	0.008	0.005	0.889***
	(0.008)	(0.011)	(0.071)	(0.182)

(Continued)

TABLE 12.A3   (Continued)

	(1)	(2)	(3)	(4)
	C	V/C	Target capital	Offering success
Patents	− 0.011	0.022	0.276**	0.307
	(0.014)	(0.021)	(0.129)	(0.323)
Nonexecutive directors	− 0.001	0.009	0.156	− 0.220
	(0.012)	(0.017)	(0.105)	(0.253)
Founder experience	− 0.001	0.003*	0.008	0.043
	(0.001)	(0.002)	(0.010)	(0.027)
SEIS	− 0.014	0.020	− 0.456***	− 0.237
	(0.009)	(0.013)	(0.079)	(0.198)
Exit IPO	0.006	− 0.022	0.170*	− 0.039
	(0.010)	(0.014)	(0.087)	(0.217)
Time trend	− 0.001	0.022	− 0.123	− 0.866***
	(0.010)	(0.014)	(0.087)	(0.139)
Pr. C	1.233***	0.236***	− 0.860*	−
	(0.480)	(0.079)	(0.491)	
Pr. V/C	− 0.139***	0.366***	3.731	−
	(0.055)	(0.097)	(4.308)	
Pr. target	− 0.014**	0.015*	0.891***	−
	(0.006)	(0.008)	(0.052)	
Constant	− 0.386	1.938***	− 2.324	9.253***
	(0.512)	(0.588)	(4.608)	(3.566)
Log-likelihood				− 583.6
Observations				491

The table reports the results of a system of four equations estimated using a GSEM. The dependent variables are the ultimate shareholder's cash-flow rights (Model 1), the separation between ownership and control (Model 2), the target capital (Model 3), and the offering success dummy (Model 4). In Model 4, ownership and control variables (C, V/C) and target capital are treated as endogenous (i.e., instrumented). For each observation, identification variables (i.e., instruments) are measured as the average control (Pr. C), separation between ownership and control (Pr. V/C), and target capital (Pr. target), calculated using all offerings listed in the previous 12 months on the same platform. See Table 12.1 for the definition of the variables. Time trend is a variable set to 0 for 2011 issues and increased by 1 each year. Industry effects included in all regressions, starting from Crowdcube classification. *, **, and *** indicate significance at the 10%, 5%, and 1% levels. *GSEM*, Generalized structural equation model; *IPO*, initial public offering; *SEIS*, Seed Enterprise Investment Scheme.

TABLE 12.A4 Dual-class shares decision and investment threshold.

	First stage		Second step (A-shares threshold)			
	Crowdcube	A-shares	Ln (amount)	Threshold > 0	Block threshold	Threshold/target capital
			(OLS)	(probit)	(probit)	(tobit)
	(1)	(2)	(3)	(4)	(5)	(6)
Family dummy	0.556	− 0.394	0.247*	0.269*	0.333	0.025*
	(0.303)	(0.271)	(0.138)	(0.150)	(0.238)	(0.016)
Age	0.781***	− 0.108	0.017	− 0.067	0.059	− 0.000
	(0.215)	(0.132)	(0.090)	(0.230)	(0.302)	(0.007)
Positive sales	0.373	0.116	0.055	0.144	− 0.248	− 0.006
	(0.317)	(0.211)	(0.136)	(0.361)	(0.469)	(0.011)
Patents	− 0.173	0.532	0.102	− 0.699	− 0.872	0.014
	(0.554)	(0.495)	(0.239)	(0.645)	(0.934)	(0.020)
Nonexecutive directors	0.104	0.155	0.029	− 0.034	− 0.598	− 0.006
	(0.361)	(0.347)	(0.195)	(0.506)	(0.688)	(0.016)
Founder experience	− 0.056	− 0.100***	0.066**	0.080*	0.188**	0.004*
	(0.047)	(0.029)	(0.025)	(0.043)	(0.083)	(0.002)
SEIS	0.209	0.223	− 0.217	0.229	− 0.403	− 0.007
	(0.317)	(0.240)	(0.150)	(0.438)	(0.619)	(0.013)
Exit IPO	0.155	− 0.136	0.017	− 0.318	− 0.013	− 0.012
	(0.218)	(0.209)	(0.090)	(0.431)	(0.552)	(0.013)
Platform preference	0.252**	−	−	−	−	−
	(0.123)					
TMT size	−	−	−	−	−	−
M&As in the industry	−	0.091**	−	−	−	−
		(0.045)				
Pr. A-shares	−	− 0.215*	−	−	−	−
		(0.106)				
Time trend	−	3.275***	0.179	0.108***	− 0.061*	0.010
		(0.867)	(0.113)	(0.041)	(0.033)	(0.009)

(Continued)

TABLE 12.A4   (Continued)

	First stage		Second step (A-shares threshold)			
	Crowdcube	A-shares	Ln (amount)	Threshold > 0	Block threshold	Threshold/target capital
			(OLS)	(probit)	(probit)	(tobit)
	(1)	(2)	(3)	(4)	(5)	(6)
IMR$_{platform}$		−	0.418	1.025**	0.182	0.041*
			(0.260)	(0.459)	(0.438)	(0.021)
IMR$_{voting}$		−	− 0.334	− 0.294	− 0.273	− 0.036
			(0.566)	(0.810)	(0.884)	(0.048)
Constant	− 5.425***	2.895**	4.455***	0.575	− 1.383***	0.209**
	(1.452)	(1.236)	(1.141)	(0.435)	(0.346)	(0.097)
Industry effects	Yes	Yes	Yes	Yes	Yes	Yes
Pseudo (adjusted) R^2	0.142		(0.139)	0.108	0.213	0.195
Observations	1309		405	405	405	405

The table reports the results of a double selection model with instrumental variables using a bivariate probit model on the likelihood of issuing an offer in Crowdcube, with respect to Seedrs (Model 1) and issuing A-shares (Model 2). The identification conditions are identified as follows: in Model 1, we include platform preference, measured as the number of offerings listed on the Crowdcube, divided by the number of offerings listed on Seedrs, in the same industry, in the 12 months prior to each observation; in Model 2, similarly to Gompers et al. (2010), we include the TMT size, the number of M&As in the same industry, and a mimicking variable (Pr. A-shares), calculated as the ratio of crowdfunding offerings that offered voting rights among offerings listed in the previous 12 months on the same platform. The second-stage models the investment threshold required to obtain A-shares. The dependent variables are the log of the monetary value of the threshold (Model 3); a dummy equal to 1 in case the threshold is greater than zero (Model 4); a dummy equal to 1 in case the threshold is set to £25,000 or higher (i.e., a "block threshold") (Model 5); and the ratio between the monetary value of the threshold and the target capital of the proposal (Model 6). The time trend is a variable set to 0 for 2011 issues and increases by 1 each year. Industry effects are included in all regressions, starting with Crowdcube classification. *, **, and *** indicate significance at the 10%, 5%, and 1% levels. *IMR*, Inverse Mills Ratio; *IPO*, initial public offering; *M&A*, merger and acquisition; *OLS*, ordinary least squares; *SEIS*, Seed Enterprise Investment Scheme; *TMT*, top management team.

TABLE 12.A5 Disentangling direct and indirect effect of voting rights' thresholds on the success of equity offerings.

	(1a)	(2a)	(1b)	(2b)
	Professional investors	Success	Professional investors	Success
C	4.132**	0.864*	4.195**	0.912*
	(2.191)	(0.478)	(2.169)	(0.499)
V/C	− 4.761***	− 4.942**	− 4.961***	− 5.414**
	(1.756)	(2.414)	(2.152)	(2.864)
V/C × founder experience	−	−	0.196*	0.473*
			(0.106)	(0.280)
Threshold (ln)	0.388***	− 0.212**	0.271**	− 0.208**
	(0.127)	(0.094)	(0.121)	(0.089)
Target capital	0.144	− 0.089	0.125	− 0.100
	(0.252)	(0.142)	(0.255)	(0.142)
Professional investors	−	0.103**	−	0.121**
		(0.054)		(0.059)
Family	− 0.373	− 0.307	− 0.356	− 0.307
	(0.456)	(0.243)	(0.452)	(0.243)
Age	0.167	− 0.337**	0.199	− 0.336**
	(0.246)	(0.137)	(0.252)	(0.137)
Positive sales	0.942**	0.999***	0.913**	0.999***
	(0.413)	(0.212)	(0.415)	(0.212)
Patents	− 5.807	0.598	− 5.504	0.598
	(275.960)	(0.418)	(121.809)	(0.418)
Nonexecutive directors	0.265	− 0.088	0.234	− 0.088
	(0.420)	(0.295)	(0.423)	(0.295)
Founder experience	0.240	− 0.006	− 0.017	− 0.006
	(0.172)	(0.066)	(0.326)	(0.066)
SEIS	− 0.834	− 0.102	− 0.845	− 0.102
	(0.529)	(0.251)	(0.542)	(0.251)
Exit IPO	0.294	0.141	0.248	0.141
	(0.408)	(0.257)	(0.414)	(0.257)
Time trend	− 0.465	− 0.783***	− 0.407	− 0.783***

(*Continued*)

TABLE 12.A5   (Continued)

	(1a)	(2a)	(1b)	(2b)
	Professional investors	**Success**	**Professional investors**	**Success**
	(0.523)	(0.171)	(0.531)	(0.171)
TMT size	0.083**	–	0.096**	–
	(0.039)		(0.041)	
IMR$_{platform}$	− 0.079	− 1.568	− 0.085	− 0.187
	(0.595)	(1.588)	(0.595)	(0.384)
IMR$_{voting}$	− 5.261	− 1.476	− 6.030	2.367
	(5.737)	(1.467)	(5.909)	(2.226)
Constant	6.844	13.477***	6.348	11.746**
	(12.361)	(5.023)	(12.944)	(5.071)
Log-likelihood		− 413.1		− 410.0
Observations		405		405

The table reports the results of a double selection model with instrumental variables. The first stage (omitted) is a bivariate probit model on the likelihood of issuing an offering in Crowdcube, with respect to Seedrs and issuing A-shares (as in Models 1 and 2 in Table 12.2). The second stage is a system of equations estimated using a GSEM. The outcome variables are a dummy equal to 1 in case a professional investor bid shares at the offering (Model 1a) and the success dummy (Model 2a). Four variables, namely, the threshold amount, the controlling shareholder's cash-flow rights, the voting to cash-flow rights, and the target capital are treated as endogenous. Instrumental equations are not reported, as qualitatively equivalent to Models (3−6) in Table 12.2. Models 1b and 2b are replacements of Models 1a and 2a, where the interaction of V/C with founder experience is included. When estimating Models 1b and 2b, an additional instrumental variable for $V/C \times$ founder experience is included, as is interaction between Pr. V/C and founder experience. The instrument for professional investors is the TMT size. Two IMRs are estimated from the first-stage equations and included in all second-stage equations. See Table 12.1 for the definition of the variables. Time trend is a variable set to 0 for 2011 issues and increased by 1 each year. Industry effects are included in all regressions, starting from Crowdcube classification. *, **, and *** indicate significance at the 10%, 5%, and 1% levels. *GSEM*, Generalized structural equation model; *IMR*, Inverse Mills Ratio; *IPO*, initial public offering; *SEIS*, Seed Enterprise Investment Scheme; *TMT*, top management team.

Does equity crowdfunding democratize access to entrepreneurial finance?

13.1 Introduction

A growing interest in crowdfunding is shared by practitioners, policymakers, the media, and scholars alike. As a new and powerful tool for entrepreneurs, crowdfunding can help push the boundaries of existing theories and help develop new ones. In fact, new digital and information communication technologies (ICT) have transformed the nature of uncertainty inherent in entrepreneurial processes and outcomes as well as the ways of dealing with such uncertainty (Nambisan et al., 2017). ICT can indeed alleviate some of the problems of traditional entrepreneurial finance markets and solve market failure.

As a parallelism, we look at the impact of ICT on urban bike-sharing programs. Already in 1965, Provos released the White Bike Plan in Amsterdam. With no record of who checked out which bike, the plan failed a few weeks after as bikes were often stolen or damaged. After many other attempts, in 1995, a coin-deposit system was established in Copenhagen (Bycyken), with 2000 distinguishable bicycles with docking stations. Nevertheless, the program was terminated due to frequent thefts and damages attributed to customer anonymity. More recently, Shaheen, Guzman, and Zhang (2010) report that in 2009, bike-sharing programs were operating with 150,000 bikes in 125 (mostly European) cities. The estimates have grown to over 1 million bikes in 800 bike-sharing programs in 2014 (Campbell, Cherry, Ryerson, & Yang, 2016). In 2017, Beijing banned new shared bikes as riders can already access 2.5 million. Currently, urban bike-sharing programs run station-less scan&ride systems with real-time monitoring of occupancy, credit scores, and penalties that ultimately allow for selection of users. This parallelism shows that ICT has the potential to lower information asymmetries and alleviate market failure problems.

Similarly, ICT can reduce adverse selection and moral hazard problems in entrepreneurial finance. As far as the availability of finance is a critical element to entrepreneurship, understanding why some categories of individuals are underrepresented in entrepreneurship is a question of both academic and social interest. For instance, the paucity of ethnic entrepreneurs or the unequal access between genders to the necessary resources to establish sustainable new ventures has received increasing media attention. To add to this debate, this chapter investigates whether crowdfunding is as inclusive as often portrayed. The expectation is indeed that by replacing a small set of homogeneous experts with a diverse crowd, the significance of a founder's gender or race will decline. In particular, existing studies have found a more pronounced diversity in sophistication and experience among investors in equity crowdfunding relative to traditional equity offerings (Cumming, McGowan, Farag, & Johan, 2018).[1] While professional investors follow a market logic also when investing in crowdfunding, small, unsophisticated investors are found to consider community logic (Vismara, 2018).

Clear associations between gender, ethnic, or geographic disadvantage and funding are difficult to isolate given that exogenous variables intrude into the process of finance and performance in general. There is, in general, conflicting or scarce evidence regarding whether fundraising via crowdfunding platforms is actually easier for traditionally underrepresented groups. In particular, most of the existing studies focus on a specific aspect, such as gender or geography, in the context of reward-based crowdfunding. Equity-based crowdfunding is, however, intrinsically different from reward-based crowdfunding. While in equity crowdfunding, the proponent is by definition a company, reward-based campaigns are launched mostly by individuals. The motivations to bid for a reward are also likely to be different from those to invest in a company's equity. Coherently, Vismara (2016) finds that offering rewards to investors does not increase the probability of success of equity crowdfunding campaigns. The governance and organizational implications of the process of raising equity capital through crowdfunding are arguably different from those of preselling a product or a service in reward-based crowdfunding (see Chapter 9: Equity crowdfunding and governance). Consistently, prior studies on minorities in crowdfunding are mainly based on consumer theory (e.g., Younkin & Kuppuswamy, 2017).

Crowdfunding platforms allow anyone to view projects posted online, allowing for a more heterogeneous population of backers. This results in a promising path to funding categories that typically find it difficult to deal with business angels or venture capitalists (VCs). Recent research has indeed shown that these private investors bid in equity crowdfunding (Signori & Vismara, 2018). The complementarity between crowdfunding and early-stage private equity makes it more appealing for entrepreneurs to launch a crowdfunding campaign, as the availability of professional investors will help in case low participation by small investors (Schwienbacher, 2018). In private equity the deal is between the entrepreneur and a restricted number of providers of capital. Entrepreneurs can choose who they deal with and are able to negotiate the terms of the contract, including the price and amount of shares. In equity crowdfunding, instead, offerings are open to the public.

---

[1] While the majority of recent IPOs have been offered exclusively to institutional investors, crowdfunding investors are likely to be much more diverse. Over the last two decades, three quarters of the IPOs in Europe took place in secondary markets, such as London's Alternative Investment Market (AIM). Most of these IPOs were offered exclusively to institutional investors (Vismara et al., 2012). Although institutional investors are being allocated the largest fraction of IPO shares (Aggarwal et al., 2002), equity crowdfunding is likely to attract a much more diverse set of investors.

Once the offering is listed on the crowdfunding platform, the price is fixed and the ownership structure is solely defined by investors' demand for shares. For this reason, we believe that traditional initial public offerings (IPOs) represent a more appropriate term of comparison for equity crowdfunding offerings than private equity deals. Interviews with practitioners support this contention. For instance, Marcus Stuttard, Head of AIM and UK Primary Markets at London Stock Exchange Group, has recently declared that both IPOs and equity crowdfunding offerings "democratise how equity investments are made and make it easier for people to invest. Equity crowdfunding was the first step − and, after all, the stock market was one of the original forms of crowdfunding."[2]

While traditional private deals are limited to a relatively small group of private investors, equity crowdfunding allows issuers to broadly solicit and advertise their securities to the general public, thereby increasing the diversification of potential investors. Two decades ago, online auction IPOs were viewed as alternatives to the traditional book-building method of IPO underwriting (Ritter, 2013). However, despite being considered an efficient market mechanism to lower the costs of going public, the expectations of online auction IPOs were never realized. Only one investment bank, W.R. Hambrecht, has developed a platform for online public offerings, and only 20 companies in the United States, most notably Google, have gone public this way, with the last occurring in 2007 (Ritter, 2013). Despite the unmatched expectations of democratization and disintermediation, IPOs in traditional stock markets are the closest term of comparison for equity crowdfunding offerings.

The present chapter is among the first to empirically assess the potential of equity crowdfunding to finance underrepresented categories of entrepreneurs. Specifically, we believe that democratization in entrepreneurial finance should be investigated along four dimensions, namely geography, age, gender, and ethnicity biases. If equity crowdfunding is effectively democratizing access to funding, it should provide means of financing to these four categories that are typically referred to as financially constrained. This chapter, therefore, investigates the democratization potential of equity crowdfunding from a broader perspective than previous studies. Most importantly, this chapter integrates the analysis of the determinants of success of the offerings with a first-stage investigation of the self-selection into equity crowdfunding. We compare a sample of 167 equity offerings in Crowdcube, the world largest equity crowdfunding platform, with 99 IPOs on the loosely regulated London's AIM. These two samples were identified by including only offerings in Crowdcube or on the AIM between 2013 and 2016, raising more than £300,000 and less than £5 million.

The chapter is organized as follows. Section 13.2 reviews previous studies and present our hypotheses. Section 13.3 illustrates the research design. Econometric results are reported in Section 13.4, and conclusion are provided in Section 13.5.

13.2 Literature review and hypotheses

This chapter is not the first to question whether crowdfunding democratizes access to finance, by investigating whether individuals discriminated by traditional financial

[2] https://www.syndicateroom.com/learn/investor-tools-reports/why-aim-needs-crowdfunding-an-interview-with-marcus-stuttard

institutions have more opportunities when targeting crowdfunding. Some previous studies have looked at specific individual characteristics of entrepreneurs such as gender and race (Catalini, Fazio, & Murray, 2016; Pope & Sydnor, 2011; Marom, Robb, & Sade, 2016; Greenberg & Mollick, 2017; Younkin & Kuppuswamy, 2017). In this section, we review the entrepreneurial finance literature with regard to four dimensions, namely gender, age, ethnicity, and geography.

13.2.1 Gender

Gender differences in capital markets do exist. Although there is no evidence of discrimination in terms of approval/turndown rates, few women apply for debt capital (Cavalluzzo, Cavalluzzo, & Wolken, 2002), and they are charged a higher interest rate on their loans or have greater collateral requirements compared to men (Coleman, 2000; Fabowale, Orser, & Riding, 1995; Riding & Swift, 1990). Gender skewness is more evident in accessing external equity, women receive a substantially smaller proportion of VC financing than men do. Part of the motivations points to gender differences in human capital, social capital or growth aspirations, or differences between men's and women's ventures (Carter & Rosa, 1998). Women are less likely to have prior entrepreneurial or/and managerial experience and to participate in networks with high net worth individuals (Verheul & Thurik, 2001). Stereotypically, masculine characteristics associated with leader emergence (Fagenson, 1993) may attract VCs, as they expect a funded venture to grow rapidly in term of sales and profits. In addition, male dominance among VCs and traditions related to investment in male-dominated industries (Greene, Brush, Hart, & Saparito, 2001) impact the gender bias in entrepreneurial finance.[3]

Gender studies in crowdfunding see it as more democratic, at least relative to traditional seed investors such as business angels. In reward crowdfunding, females are more likely to successful raise capital than male founders, all else being equal. Marom et al. (2016) find that women make up about 35% of the project leaders and 44% of the investors on the Kickstarter platform. Using data from a laboratory experiment, Greenberg and Mollick (2017) document that women are more likely to succeed at a reward-based crowdfunding campaign, and this effect primarily holds for female founders proposing technological projects. Radford (2016) uses data from DonorsChoose, a US-based crowdfunding website for public school teachers, to document that inequality only emerges after educators' identities were published. Deanonymization (teachers' identities were hidden until 2008) caused inequality to emerge across all types of gender difference. Using data from a Swedish crowdfunding platform, Mohammadi and Shafi (2018) find that female investors are more likely to invest in projects in which the proportion of male investors is higher.

[3] Brush, Carter, Gatwood, Greene, and Hart (2004) document that although women own more than 30% of US businesses, they receive less than 5% of venture capital funds distributed annually. The angel market predominantly comprises male investors. Only about 10% of VCs and less than 15% of business angels are women. In addition, only 15% of women-led companies were successful in raising capital, as compared with 22% for male-led companies (Stengel, 2015).

Some of the arguments to support the abovementioned studies, however, apply more to reward-based crowdfunding than to equity crowdfunding. While men are guided by agentic goals and, therefore, focus more on the pursuit of personal achievement, women are guided by communal goals and put more emphasis on the development of interpersonal relationships (Carlson, 1972). They also have stronger feelings than men about ethical issues concerning disclosure (Roxas & Stoneback, 2004). The social role theory of leadership (Eagly, Karau, & Makhijani, 1995) contends that female leaders are more likely to show concern for people, whereas male leaders are more likely to possess traits that reinforce competition. This line of thought is in line with the decision to donate or to bid small amounts of money to pledge rewards. The motivations to become costumers in reward-based crowdfunding are indeed likely more linked to ethical motivation than in entrepreneurial financial markets (Vismara, 2018).

For this reason, the equity crowdfunding market offers a complementary perspective, at the crossroad between entrepreneurial and consumer finance. So far, the evidence is rather mixed. In a study of the UK platform Crowdcube, Vismara et al. (2016) find that female investors in female-led businesses are twice those in male-led businesses. Using projects listed on German platforms, Prokop and Wang (2018) find that equity crowdfunding campaigns initiated by women attract fewer investors, as well as lower funding amounts than those initiated by men. In this study, we test whether female-led companies are more likely to launch equity crowdfunding offerings than IPOs and whether they have higher chances to successfully complete an equity crowdfunding offering.

Hypothesis 13.1a*: Female-led companies are more likely to launch equity crowdfunding offerings than IPOs.*

Hypothesis 13.1b*: Female-led companies have higher chances to successfully complete an equity crowdfunding offering.*

13.2.2 Age

Bill Gates founded Microsoft in 1975 at age of 19 years. Just 4 years after the relevant state passed legislation lowering the age of contractual capacity from 21 to 18 years (Manes & Andrews, 1993). More recently, Mark Zuckerberg cofounded Facebook at age of 19 years. These two examples offer an idea of the importance of the young entrepreneurship, which has been so far underinvestigated. On one hand, entrepreneurial intention decrease with age, due to the increasing opportunity cost of time with age (Lévesque & Minniti, 2006). On the other, entrepreneurial opportunities increase with age because of higher accumulated physical, social, and human capital (Lee & Vouchilas, 2016). Coherently, entrepreneurial propensity is found to increase with age in some studies (Fairlie, Morelix, Reedy, & Russell, 2016) but declining in others (Parker, 2009). Zhang and Acs (2018) argue that the relationship between age and entrepreneurship depends on the type of entrepreneurship, as nonnovice and novice entrepreneurs have significantly different skills, competencies, and information. They find that entrepreneurial propensity of novice (versus nonnovice) entrepreneurs has a U-shaped age trend dipping around age of 60 years, while the propensity of full-time (vs part-time) declines from the 30s.

Studies on equity crowdfunding have so far neglected the role of the age of the proponents. On one hand the experience of the founders might be perceived positively by external investors. In a quasiequity crowdfunding context, Piva and Rossi-Lamastra (2018) find that entrepreneurs' entrepreneurial experience significantly contributes to entrepreneurs' success in equity crowdfunding. Nevertheless, crowdfunding has the potential to broaden the categories of individuals raising external equity also with regard to age. Schwartz (2014) argues that teens are well positioned to exploit this new opportunity, with the upshot being that securities crowdfunding may become an important way for youthful entrepreneurs. For these reasons, we hypothesize the following:

Hypothesis 13.2a: *Companies with younger TMT members are more likely to launch equity crowdfunding offerings than IPOs.*

Hypothesis 13.2b: *Companies with younger TMT members have higher chances to successfully complete an equity crowdfunding offering.*

13.2.3 Ethnicity

The role of ethnicity in entrepreneurship and the underrepresentation of minorities among the population of funded ventures (Aldrich & Waldinger, 1990) is the subject of increasing attention. Fairlie and Robb (2007) show that the availability of startup capital is conditioned by race. Similarly, the argument for gender bias, an explanation for this underrepresentation is that resource providers are biased against minority founders, thereby ascribing the bias also to preentry constraints. The theory of statistical discrimination (Arrow, 1998) suggests that prospective supporters use race as a proxy for unobserved traits that indicate the investment is more likely to fail (Morse, 2015). Alternately, taste-based discrimination (Becker, 1957) implies that prospective supporters reject minority founders, irrespective of their qualifications, out of their own distaste for minorities more broadly.

Crowdfunding moves the locus of funding decisions away from a small pool of experts and spreads them out across a much broader population of potential contributors. While crowdfunding platforms presumably remove one of the primary causes of racial disparities in entrepreneurship (access to capital), recent studies indicate that minority founders continue to face significant bias even on these platforms. If, indeed, Herzenstein, Andrews, Dholakia, and Lyandres (2008) find that peer-to-peer (P2P) lenders are less influenced by racial stereotypes than are banks, racial bias is found by Pope and Sydnor (2011) in Prosper.com. Duarte, Siegel, and Young (2012) show that P2P lenders rely on impressionistic short-hand information such as prospects' appearance. Crowdfunding is indeed a context in which the race of the founder is readily apparent and easily identified by potential backers, making it more plausible that founder race influences backer behavior. Younkin and Kuppuswamy (2017) find that minority founders face price discounts, rooted in an assumption that minority founders invest less time and have lesser aspirations. Using experimental data, Younkin and Kuppuswamy (2019) find that despite the promise of crowdfunding, prospective funders remain biased against African-American founders. They explain these results using Becker's (1957) theory of consumer discrimination.

In this chapter, we move from consumer theory to finance, to text for the first time the effect of ethnicity in equity crowdfunding.

Hypothesis 13.3: *Companies with TMT members belonging to minorities have higher chances to successfully complete an equity crowdfunding offering.*

13.2.4 Geography

The VC literature has frequently noted that the likelihood of investing in a venture decreases with geographic distance, because of, for example, due diligence costs and ongoing monitoring efforts (see Sorenson & Stuart, 2001). More broadly, finance literature shows that investors tend to prefer geographically close investment opportunities (see, e.g., French & Poterba, 1991; Sulaeman, 2014). The arguments for such preference, and related "home bias," are related to lower information asymmetries, better monitoring capabilities, and lower associated costs (Coval & Moskowitz, 2001). In crowdfunding, equal and close to zero cost access to portals should facilitate exposure, increase familiarity, and improve access to information about entrepreneurial projects for investors. Thus geographic distance should largely cease to matter to investors. Coherently, policymakers have identified crowdfunding as a promising means to cost-effectively bridge geographic boundaries. They hope to at least partially eliminate distance-related economic frictions that are apparent in the early-stage VC market through these types of internet-based funding platforms (Lin & Viswanathan, 2015). As asserted by Agrawal et al. (2011), the online platform seems indeed to reduce some distance-related economic frictions such as monitoring progress, providing input, and gathering information.

Equity crowdfunding is therefore expected to increase the opportunity of financing for remotely located and less connected individuals. Nevertheless, social connections tend to exist locally not just in physical space but also in social space. Afonso, Kovner, and Schoar (2014) demonstrate that personal interaction is a desirable ingredient in relationship banking. Social network connections between investors and entrepreneurs are found to valuable also in reward-based (Colombo et al., 2015; Polzin et al., 2018) and in equity crowdfunding (Vismara, 2016). Hence, needing real-world connections limits the scope of information advantages in the crowd. Moreover, challenges of investment protection might become an impediment when investing outside of the home country. Despite equity crowdfunding should overcome geographical barriers, the first evidence is that geographical proximity matters. Ordanini et al. (2011) find that investors in reward-based crowdfunding are often located in the same geographical area as the proponent. Chapter 11, Are crowdfunders sensitive to distance?, showed that very few investors and companies are located in rural areas. Burtch et al. (2014) confirm that P2P lenders prefer culturally similar and geographically proximate borrowers.

There are therefore conflicting arguments about the geographical aspects of crowdfunding. However, if distance is not as important as before, as it is online, this means that traditionally constraints business should "tap" this new opportunity. This means that, relative to traditional finance markets, equity crowdfunding should be more attractive for remotely located companies. For this reason, we hypothesize the following:

Hypothesis 13.4a: *Remotely located companies are more likely to launch equity crowdfunding offerings than IPOs.*

Hypothesis 13.4b: *Remotely located companies have higher chances to successfully complete an equity crowdfunding offering.*

13.3 Research design

13.3.1 Sample

Given that our analysis aims, first, to compare the access to alternative sources of financing for young entrepreneurial ventures, namely crowdfunding and IPOs, we need to set up a dataset comprising both types of offerings. In this respect, the UK market is a natural testing bed, given the presence of one of the most popular second markets for IPOs in the world, the AIM, as well as that of a well-developed platform for crowdfunding platform such as Crowdcube. Indeed, extant literature has largely discussed how the AIM is preferred by firms that do not meet the listing requirements of the prime market (Baker, Nofsinger, & Weaver, 2002; Ritter, Signori, & Vismara, 2013; Vismara et al., 2012), and its popularity is largely due to flexible listing requirements. Crowdcube, on the other hand, is by far the largest equity crowdfunding platform in the United Kingdom, which is the largest equity crowdfunding market (Estrin, Gozman, & Khavul, 2018).[4] Established in 2011, Crowdcube is, as of February 2017, the world's largest platform, with £215 million successfully raised from more than 350,000 investors from over 100 countries. Extant literature has discussed how the regulation of equity crowdfunding in the United Kingdom is often put forward as an important ingredient of its development, so that it serves as a model for other legislations (Steinhoff, 2015), and how the specific regulatory framework provided by Crowdcube has allowed a lively participation of crowd as well as professional investors (Chapter 12: Cash-flow and voting rights in equity crowdfunding; Cumming et al., 2018). Moreover, the emergence and the optimal regulation of equity crowdfunding can be achieved only in the presence of developed alternative entrepreneurial finance markets (Hornuf & Schwienbacher, 2017a, 2017b). In summary the contemporaneous existence of AIM and Crowdcube allows an analysis of the choice of sources of entrepreneurial financing.

[4] Crowdcube has raised more capital than all other competing platforms (AltFi.com, 2015). Different sources agree on the leading role of Crowdcube. Beauhurst names Crowdcube as the leading equity investor in 2015 and the most prolific investor in the e-commerce sector. Crowdsurfer estimates Crowdcube's share in the UK investment crowdfunding market in 2015 at 52%.

Indeed, we have to take into consideration the fact that Crowdcube has been recently launched and that an IPO, even on an exchange-regulated market, provides costs that require a minimum investment scale. Therefore in order to identify only those issues that were potentially the object of an offering on the AIM or on Crowdcube, we selected Crowdcube's and AIM's offerings that were placed between 2013 and 2016, raising more than £300,000 and less than £5 million. This procedure has lead us to identify a list of 167 equity offerings offered on Crowdcube and 99 IPOs on the AIM.[5]

13.3.2 Model

Our analysis comes in two stages. In a first stage, we aim to disentangle whether the features traditionally linked to the limited availability of funding (gender, age, and regional remoteness), drive the choice of financing source toward crowdfunding, vis-à-vis IPOs on the AIM. This analysis aims to provide empirical support for Hypotheses 13.1a, 13.2a, and 13.4a. In a second stage, we analyze whether the same determinants are correlated with the success of crowdfunding offerings (in terms of probability to reach the target, or in terms of number of investors). This stage aims to validate Hypotheses 13.1b, 13.2b, 13.3, and 13.4b.

Indeed, the features increasing the likelihood to choose a crowdfunding offering versus an IPO on the AIM may be at the same time determinants of success. Therefore we need to deal with a potential sample selection bias (Heckman, 1979), by estimating the two following system of equations[6]:

$$\begin{cases} Crowdfunding_i = Z_i'\gamma_1 + u_{1i} \\ Success_i = X_i'\beta_1 + \lambda_1 IMR + \varepsilon_{1i} \end{cases} \qquad (13.1-13.2)$$

and

$$\begin{cases} Crowdfunding_i = Z_i'\gamma_2 + u_{2i} \\ No.\ of\ investors_i = X_i'\beta_2 + \lambda_2 IMR + \varepsilon_{2i} \end{cases} \qquad (13.3-13.4)$$

[5] The £300,000 lower boundary has been chosen in order to drop out a 1% share of extremely small IPOs on the AIM. The £5,000,000 upper boundary has been chosen in order to drop out a less than 1% share of extremely large crowdfunding campaigns. In between, we have a sample of 167 equity crowdfunding campaigns (out of our full sample of 643 campaigns) and 99 IPOs on the AIM (out of the population of 224 IPOs), comparable in size. While we are aware that the two subsamples may not perfectly poolable, and this is why we try to control for as many variable as possible, when trying to collect such an amount of money, a venture has had the possibility to opt either for a crowdfunding campaign or for an IPO on the AIM, conditional on several variables. The goal of our first stage is indeed to try and identify how such contextual variables are correlated with the choice of financing mechanism.

[6] Each system is a pair of equation, where the former is the selection equation and the latter the outcome equation. Following Heckman (1979), the two equations are estimated sequentially (first and second stage), in order to grant the correct estimation of the IMR's standard errors.

where *Crowdfunding$_i$* is a dummy variable equal to 1 for firms choosing a crowdfunding offering; *Success$_i$* and *No.of investors$_i$* are the dependent variables in the second stages; Z'_i and X'_i contain the observable determinants of the latent propensity to prefer a crowdfunding offering over a listing on the AIM and of the dependent variables in the second stages, respectively; *IMR* is the inverse Mill's ratio proposed by Heckman, estimated out of the first stage and included in the second stage in order to account for the potential bias caused by the sample selection described above. Given that this *IMR* accounts for the unobservable component in the decision to choose a crowdfunding initiative over a listing in the AIM, we are identifying this parameter as *Prone-to-crowdfunding* in our regression setting.[7]

The second stage measures the success of equity crowdfunding offerings. Therefore we compare both successful and failed crowdfunding campaigns against only successful IPOs. This is done for two reasons. First, differently from what happens in the United States, IPOs are infrequently withdrawn in Europe (Ritter, 2003). In our sample period, less than 5% of the IPOs on the AIM have been withdrawn during the process. Second, while failing to reach the target capital in equity crowdfunding offerings is due to an insufficient demand for shares, an IPO withdrawal can be a positive event, as IPOs are often withdrawn due to superior option for cashing out options for entrepreneurs (Boeh & Dunbar, 2013).

Given that the dependent variable in Eq. (13.2) is a dummy variable, the system composed by Eqs. (13.1 and 13.2) is a probit model[8] with sample selection and can be estimated according to Van de Ven and Van Pragg (1981). By contrast, the dependent variable in Eq. (13.4) is a count variable, such that the system composed by Eqs. (13.3 and 13.4) is a count model, namely a negative binomial regression model, with sample selection, which can be estimated according to Terza (1998).

13.3.3 Variables

In the first stage of our analysis the dependent variable is a dummy identifying crowdfunding initiatives in a sample comprising crowdfunding offerings and IPOs on the AIM. In the second stage, limited to crowdfunding offerings, our analyses are performed with reference to two alternative measures of performance.

First, we investigate the determinants of *Success*, a dummy variable equal to 1 for successful offerings. Second, we look at investor participation in crowdfunding offerings. Our variable here is the *Number of investors* participating in the offering as an alternative dependent variable assessing the success in terms of investor participation.

---

[7] Please consider that, following Heckman (1979), Z'_i should grant identification by an exclusion restriction, that is, there should be at least one parameter excluded from X'_i. In our setting the exclusion restriction is given by the presence in the first stage of industry dummies.

[8] In the case of binary dependent variable, it is common practice to use either logit or probit model, with preference for the one or the other often based on empirical issues. In our case, given that we need to implement a model with sample selection, we need to rely on Heckman (1979) assumption that both error terms (in the selection and in the outcome equation) are normally distributed, in order to calculated and use the Inverse Mill's Ratio. This is why, in line with previous literature, we opt for a probit, rather than a logit model, for both our equations. This choice grants estimation feasibility according to Van de Ven and Van Pragg (1981).

In both stages, our goal is that of identifying the effects of characteristics typically associated with financial constraints. In order to test Hypotheses 13.1a and 13.1b, we use *Female leadership*, a dummy variable equal to one when the majority of the members in the top management team (TMT) are women.[9] We took several steps to code genders based on first names. We first algorithmically used the API of genderize.io. The algorithm returns the gender and a probability that a specific name—gender attribution (male or female) was correct. In a second step a research assistant double-checked the accuracy of the codes and completed the missing variables, with additional help from the pictures displayed on the platform website. Hypotheses 13.2a and 13.2b are tested by including *Age* in our model, namely the average age of all members of the TMT, calculated at the end of 2016, the latest point in our sample. Hypothesis 13.3 is tested by using *Ethnical minority*, a dummy variable, equal to 1 if at least one member of the TMT is non-Caucasian.[10] To obtain such information, we had at least two separate raters visit the project webpage and examine the photo associated with the entrepreneurial team. *Ethnical minority* take the value 1 only if all raters agreed that one of the team members is non-Caucasian, as in Herzenstein et al. (2008). This approach captures the perceived identity of the founder irrespective of self-identification. We used a conservative measure, which requires full agreement. In cases of disagreement the offerings were removed from the study. Last, Hypotheses 13.4a and 13.4b are tested by using *Metropolitan area*,[11] a dummy variable, equal to 1 if the firm belongs to a metropolitan area, according to the Census 2011 classification (i.e., metropolitan areas of London, Birmingham, Manchester, Leeds-Bradford, Liverpool-Birkenhead, Newcastle, Sheffield, South Hampshire, Nottingham-Derby, and Glasgow).

To control for potential variation in the quality of the projects, we include in all our analyses a series of variables concerning the project and its proponents, collected through the presentation pages for each project made available by Crowdcube, and through the prospectus in the case of IPOs: *Equity offered* is the share of equity made available for the crowdfunding campaign, or for the offering on the AIM; *Target* is the amount bid for crowdfunding initiatives, and total proceeds for IPO offerings; *Firm age* is the difference, in years, between the beginning of the crowdfunding campaign, or the offering on the AIM, and the foundation date; *TMT size* is the number of people in the TMT (TMT members are identified in the "team" section of each offering, as reported on the platform's portal); *Positive sales* is a dummy variable equal to 1 if the company has already reported positive sales at the campaign/IPO; *Patents* is a dummy variable equal to 1 if the company owns or is filing patents at the campaign/IPO; and *Population* refers to inhabitants in the

---

[9] The simple presence of women in the TMT is also tested in the robustness analysis, by replacing *Female leadership* with *Female presence*, a dummy variable equal to 1 for all offerings when at least one woman belongs to the TMT of the focal firm.

[10] This variable is not available for our sample of IPOs and is therefore used only in the second-stage analysis.

[11] In the robustness analysis, this variable is replaced with *GDP per capita* and *Unemployment rate*, both measured at the NUTS-3 level.

NUTS-3[12] area where the firm is located. In order to grant the identification conditions required by Heckman (1979), the set of controls in the first stage is increased by the inclusion of industry dummies.[13]

In Table 13.1, a summary of variable description is provided.

Table 13.2 provides descriptive statistics for all the variables employed in our analyses. Our sample is composed of 167 equity offerings on Crowdcube and 99 IPOs on the AIM, each of them raising more than £300,000 and less than £5 million, between 2013 and 2016. 48.5 of crowdfunding campaigns have been successful, with an average of 237.9 investors involved.

Descriptive statistics on the explanatory variables provide univariate evidence on the different attractiveness of crowdfunding and IPOs for financially constrained categories. No statistically significant difference is found for *Female leadership*, though when looking at *Female presence* one can notice how the vast majority of IPOs provides for at least one female member in the TMT (81.3%), differently from crowdfunding offering, where a woman is present in 52.1% of the campaigns. Crowdfunding offerings are preferred by younger teams, with an average age of 42, with respect to 46.2 average years of an IPO's TMT. Further, a large majority of IPOs are performed by firms located in metropolitan areas (57.2%), with respect to a limited 50.4% of crowdfunding campaigns. This corresponds to areas promoting crowdfunding offerings characterized by a smaller population, lower GDP per capita and lower unemployment rates, with respect to the average NUTS-3 are promoting an IPO. Last, crowdfunding offerings campaigns involve ethnical minorities in 16% of cases.

Indeed, crowdfunding and IPOs differ also under several perspectives which are controlled in our analysis. Crowdfunding offerings, on average, offer a smaller percentage of equity (15.7 vs 33.3), are much smaller in size (£925,000 vs £2312.1) and TMT size (3.5 vs 5 members). Firms are similar in age and have reported positive sales in half of the cases both in crowdfunding (49.2%) and IPOs (50.4), although crowdfunding firms have patented less often (19.7% of cases) than IPO counterparts (36.8%).

Correlations among all variables employed in this study are provided in Table 13.A1 in the "Appendix" section.

---

[12] The Classification of Territorial Units for Statistics (NUTS; French: Nomenclature des unités territoriales statistiques) is a geocode standard for referencing the subdivisions of countries for statistical purposes, developed and regulated by the European Union (EU). For each EU member country, a hierarchy of three NUTS levels is established by Eurostat in agreement with each member state. In the United Kingdom, the NUTS-3 level refers to upper tier authorities and groups of unitary authorities and districts: there are 93 NUT-3 areas in England, 12 in Wales, 23 in Scotland, and 5 in Northern Ireland.

[13] We make use of nine dummies, according to the first digit (industry) of the ICB, the Industry Classification Benchmark, a taxonomy launched by Dow Jones and FTSE in 2005 and now owned solely by FTSE International. Notice that ICB is available from prospectuses for IPOs, while it has been manually identified for Crowdcube's campaign, based on the industry description available on the platform. We are aware that the set of industry dummies is likely to potentially affect the outcome of a crowdfunding campaign. Empirically, in our setting we tested for the excludability condition through the Hansen J test. The joint null hypothesis of this test is that the instruments are valid instruments, that is, excludable from the outcome equation, and the P value states the probability that the test statistic is zero, which would imply acceptance of the null hypothesis. Given that P is much greater than 10% in our case, we have evidence supporting our choice.

TABLE 13.1 Variable description.

Dependent variables	
Success	Dummy variable equal to 1 for successfully funded offerings, 0 otherwise
Number of investors	Number of investors in the offering
Explanatory variables	
Female leadership	Dummy variable equal to 1 for firms with the CEO of the firms is a woman, 0 otherwise
Age	Average age of TMT members
Ethnical minority	Dummy variable equal to 1 if at least one TMT member if at least one member of the TMT is non-Caucasian
Metropolitan area	Dummy variable, equal to 1 if the firm belongs to a metropolitan area, according to the Census 2001 classification (i.e., metropolitan areas of London, Birmingham, Manchester, Leeds-Bradford, Liverpool-Birkenhead, Newcastle, Sheffield, South Hampshire, Nottingham-Derby, and Glasgow)
Controls	
Equity offered	Percentage of equity offered
Target	Amount bid for crowdfunding initiatives, and total proceeds for IPO offerings (natural logarithms are used in regression analyses)
Firm age	Difference, in years, between the beginning of the crowdfunding campaign, or the offering on the AIM, and the foundation date
TMT size	Number of people in the top management team
Positive sales	Dummy variable equal to 1 if the company has already reported positive sales at the campaign/IPO, 0 otherwise
Patents	Dummy variable equal to 1 if the company owns or is filing patents at the campaign/IPO, 0 otherwise
Population	Population in the NUTS-3 area where the firm is located (natural logarithms are used in regression analyses)
Additional controls in the selection process	
Industry dummies	Set of dummy variables controlling for industries according to the ICB
Variables included in the robustness analysis	
Female presence	Dummy variable equal to 1 for firms with at least one woman in the TMT
GDP per capita	GDP per capita in the NUTS-3 area where the firm is located (natural logarithms are used in regression analyses)
Unemployment rate	Unemployment rate in the NUTS-3 area where the firm is located
NUTS-1 dummies	Set of dummy variables controlling for the 12 NUTS-1 statistical regions in the United Kingdom

AIM, Alternative Investment Market; *ICB*, Industry Classification Benchmark; *IPO*, initial public offering; *TMT*, top management team.

TABLE 13.2 Descriptive statistics.

	Crowdcube				AIM				Difference in means
	Mean	Std	Max	Min	Mean	Std	Max	Min	
Depedent variables									
Success (dummy, %)	48.5	50.1	1	0	–	–	–	–	–
Number of investors (no.)	237.9	325.8	2209	3	–	–	–	–	–
Explanatory variables									
Female leadership (dummy, %)	31.2	46.4	1	0	36.8	48.2	1	0	5.6
Age (years)	42.0	9.8	72	20	46.2	9.0	79	25	4.2***
Ethnical minority (dummy, %)	16.0	36.9	1	0	–	–	–	–	–
Metropolitan area (dummy, %)	50.4	50.1	1	0	57.2	49.5	1	0	6.8*
Controls									
Equity offered (%)	15.7	8.30	54.3	2.3	33.3	23.3	89.1	9.0	17.6***
Target (£000)	925.0	530.5	3990.0	300.0	2312.1	1392.8	5000	300.0	1387.1***
Firm age (years)	3.1	3.3	20	0	3.4	3.9	22	0	0.8
TMT size (no.)	3.5	1.4	7	1	5.0	1.5	12	2	1.5***
Positive sales (dummy, %)	49.2	45.6	1	0	50.4	50.1	1	0	0.8
Patents (dummy, %)	19.7	39.9	1	0	36.8	48.2	1	0	17.1***
Population (millions)	4.1	3.9	8.8	0.1	4.9	3.8	8.8	0.1	0.8**
Variables included in the robustness analysis									
Female presence (dummy, %)	52.1	50.1	1	0	81.3	39.0	1	0	29.2***
GDP per capita (£000)	58.0	24.5	86.4	24.9	61.7	24.8	86.4	24.9	3.7*
Unemployment rate (%)	4.8	1.1	7.2	2.7	5.1	10.9	7.2	2.7	0.3*

Mean, standard deviation, maximum, and minimum values for all variables employed in the analysis, refereed to the sample of 167 equity offerings on Crowdcube and to the sample of 99 IPOs on the AIM raising more than £300,000 and less than £5 million between 2013 and 2016. The last column reports tests for difference in means (or proportions) between equity offerings on Crowdcube and AIM. ***, **, and * represent statistical significance at 1%, 5%, and 10%, respectively. AIM, Alternative Investment Market; TMT, top management team.

13.4 Results

Our analyses provide validation for our hypotheses with the two-stage models presented in Eqs. (13.1 and 13.2) and (13.3 and 13.4). Hypotheses 13.1a, 13.2a, and 13.4a are tested in the first stage, while Hypotheses 13.1b, 13.2b, 13.3, and 13.4b in the second stages.

First-stage results are reported in the first column of Table 13.3.[14] We find evidence that crowdfunding initiatives are preferred by younger TMTs (the coefficient for *Age* is equal to

[14] A first stage is estimated for all second-stage equation presented. Given that results are qualitatively identical, and numerically extremely close, the first-stage equation is reported only once.

TABLE 13.3 Probability of success.

	Crowdfunding	(1)	(2)	(3)	(4)	(5)	(6)
Female leadership	− 0.416	—	0.602	—	—	—	0.572
	(0.269)		(0.498)				(0.462)
Age	− 0.033**	—	—	− 0.047***	—	—	− 0.045***
	(0.013)			(0.017)			(0.016)
Ethnical minority	—	—	—	—	0.137	—	0.077
					(0.377)		(0.354)
Metropolitan area	0.874***	—	—	—	—	− 0.532*	− 0.480*
	(0.235)					(0.312)	(0.286)
Equity offered	− 5.089***	− 2.502	− 2.857	− 3.607**	− 2.636	− 3.011*	− 4.230**
	(1.183)	(1.723)	(1.798)	(1.691)	(1.767)	(1.746)	(1.789)
Target	− 0.498***	− 1.133***	− 1.180***	− 1.246***	− 1.141***	− 1.177***	− 1.300***
	(0.151)	(0.157)	(0.168)	(0.164)	(0.154)	(0.155)	(0.161)
Firm age	0.035	0.003	0.002	− 0.003	0.005	− 0.003	− 0.009
	(0.046)	(0.042)	(0.041)	(0.042)	(0.042)	(0.042)	(0.042)
TMT size	− 0.584***	− 0.072	− 0.010	− 0.035	− 0.067	− 0.043	0.048
	(0.109)	(0.160)	(0.173)	(0.178)	(0.163)	(0.158)	(0.188)
Positive sales	0.266	0.093	0.044	0.051	0.095	0.037	0.031
	(0.275)	(0.299)	(0.302)	(0.309)	(0.300)	(0.299)	(0.312)
Patents	0.350	0.529	0.518	0.433	0.537	0.450	0.367
	(0.280)	(0.356)	(0.349)	(0.365)	(0.357)	(0.372)	(0.374)
Population	− 0.335***	0.029	0.022	− 0.027	0.023	0.182	0.113
	(0.092)	(0.098)	(0.098)	(0.101)	(0.100)	(0.167)	(0.168)
Prone-to-crowdfunding (IMR)	—	0.134	− 0.975**	− 0.985**	− 0.991**	− 0.906*	− 0.993**
		(0.689)	(0.444)	(0.447)	(0.424)	(0.503)	(0.421)
Industry dummies	Yes***	No	No	No	No	No	No
Constant	− 13.553***	− 14.209***	− 12.410***	− 13.617***	− 16.150***	− 15.231***	− 13.553***
	(2.348)	(2.632)	(2.436)	(2.304)	(3.134)	(3.177)	(2.348)
Observations	266	167	167	167	167	167	167
Pseudo *R*-squared	0.73	0.32	0.34	0.43	0.39	0.42	0.48

The table reports the results of probit models with a selection equation, that is, a two-stage model. The first stage (selection equation) is a probit model on the likelihood to propose a crowdfunding offerings, vis-à-vis a public offering on the AIM, estimated on a sample of 167 offerings offered on Crowdcube and 99 IPOs on the AIM between 2013 and 2016. The identification condition is granted by the inclusion of Industry dummies in the regression specification. The first stage is reported only for the selection equation of Model (1). Results for all the other selection equations are qualitatively the same. The second stage is a probit model on the success of crowdfunding offerings, estimated on a sample of 167 equity offerings offered on Crowdcube, and including the inverse Mill's ratio estimated from the first model. Model (1) is our baseline specification. Model (2) adds Female leadership. Model (3) adds Age. Model (4) adds Ethnical minority. Model (5) adds Metropolitan area. Model (6) adds all variables included in Models (2−5). Robust standard errors in parentheses. ***, **, and * identify significance levels at less than 1%, 5%, and 10%, respectively. *TMT*, Top management team.

−0.033, and statistically significant at a 5% level), and by firms out of metropolitan areas (the coefficient for *Metropolitan area* is equal to −0.874, significant at a 1% level, implies lower probability of crowdfunding for firms located in urban areas, with respect to rural/ remote areas, and vice versa). No statistical significance is found with respect to *Female leadership*. Our results, therefore, provide support for Hypotheses 13.2a and 13.4a, while we do not have statistical evidence in support of Hypothesis 13.1a.

As far as control variables are concerned, we find confirmation of differences highlighted by descriptive statistics, in that crowdfunding initiatives are more likely in the case of smaller equity offered, smaller target, smaller TMT size, and smaller population for the NUTS-3 area of origin.

Models (2)−(6) in Table 13.3 report our result on the determinants of success for the crowdfunding initiatives in our sample. Model (1) reports a baseline specification with all control variables. Models from (2) to (5) include a variable testing for the role of gender, age, ethnical minority, and regional features, respectively, while Model (6) jointly test for the presence of all these characteristics. Our results show that female leadership and presence of ethnical minorities do not statistically impact on the success of crowdfunding offerings, while younger TMTs and campaigns from nonmetropolitan areas are more likely to succeed (as provided by the negative sign of the *Metropolitan area* dummy). Results are confirmed both when separately assessed and when jointly tested and provide support for Hypotheses 13.2b and 13.4b, while we do not have enough statistical evidence to confirm Hypotheses 13.1b and 13.3.

As far as the control variables are concerned, we find confirmation of findings in previous literature in that both the share of equity offered and the target size reduce the probability of success. Interestingly, the coefficient for the inverse Mill's ratio, that is, our measure of how *Prone-to-crowdfunding* is any offering, is negative and statistically significant in all models (either at 5% or 10%). In practice, those features increasing the likelihood to choose a crowdfunding offering over an IPO are negatively correlated to the probability of success.

In Table 13.4, we replicate the former analysis, after replacing *Success* with the *Number of investors* as an outcome dependent variable. Again, model (1) reports a baseline specification with all control variables, Models from (2) to (5) include a variable testing for the role of gender, age, ethnical minority, and regional features, respectively, while Model (6) jointly test for the presence of all these characteristics. Results from the last model show that *Age* is weakly significant in determining the number of participating investors, such that younger TMTs typically attract more the crowd (coefficient = −0.007, significant at less than 10%). Also offerings with a presence of an *Ethnical minority* (coefficient = 0.158, significant at less than 5%) and originated in nonmetropolitan areas (coefficient of *Metropolitan area* = −0.216, significant at less than 5%) have higher likelihood to attract a high number of investors, while no statistically significant effect is found with respect to a *Female leadership*. These results are in support of Hypotheses 13.2b, 13.3, and 13.4b, while again we do not have enough statistical significance in support of Hypothesis 13.1b.

As far as controls are concerned, we find evidence that higher targets typically attract a larger number of investors, while we have weak evidence that a large TMT size reduces the number of investors. Our results also show how Positive Sales and Patents are interesting features in the eyes of investors. Interestingly, the coefficient of the *IMR* is positive and significant, such that features increasing the likelihood of a crowdfunding offering, over an

TABLE 13.4 Number of investors.

	(1)	(2)	(3)	(4)	(5)	(6)
Female leadership	–	0.038	–	–	–	0.035
		(0.156)				(0.146)
Age	–	–	– 0.008*	–	–	– 0.007*
			(0.004)			(0.004)
Ethnical minority	–	–	–	0.149**	–	0.158**
				(0.068)		(0.076)
Metropolitan area	–	–	–	–	– 0.273**	– 0.216**
					(0.115)	(0.103)
Equity offered	– 0.835*	– 0.819	– 0.836*	– 0.684	– 0.703	– 0.519
	(0.492)	(0.507)	(0.492)	(0.501)	(0.473)	(0.488)
Target	0.546***	0.547***	0.546***	0.549***	0.553***	0.556***
	(0.026)	(0.026)	(0.026)	(0.026)	(0.026)	(0.026)
Firm age	0.010	0.010	0.010	0.011	0.010	0.011
	(0.014)	(0.014)	(0.014)	(0.014)	(0.014)	(0.014)
TMT size	– 0.104**	– 0.101*	– 0.105**	– 0.104**	– 0.094*	– 0.089*
	(0.051)	(0.055)	(0.050)	(0.051)	(0.049)	(0.052)
Positive sales	0.273***	0.270***	0.273***	0.281***	0.257***	0.262***
	(0.090)	(0.094)	(0.090)	(0.092)	(0.088)	(0.093)
Patents	0.229**	0.231**	0.229**	0.263***	0.205**	0.241***
	(0.098)	(0.098)	(0.097)	(0.092)	(0.097)	(0.093)
Population	– 0.067**	– 0.066**	– 0.067**	– 0.073***	– 0.009	– 0.011
	(0.026)	(0.026)	(0.027)	(0.026)	(0.038)	(0.036)
Prone-to-crowdfunding (IMR)	0.457***	0.449***	0.457***	0.429***	0.432***	0.390***
	(0.150)	(0.155)	(0.150)	(0.144)	(0.154)	(0.151)
Constant	– 0.014	– 0.043	– 0.025	0.001	– 0.878	– 0.943
	(0.491)	(0.501)	(0.549)	(0.485)	(0.640)	(0.648)
Observations	167	167	167	167	167	167
Pseudo R-squared	0.47	0.49	0.48	0.51	0.52	0.57

The table reports the results of negative binomial regressions with a selection equation, that is, a two-stage model. The first stage (selection equation) is a probit model on the likelihood to propose a crowdfunding offering, vis-à-vis a public offering on the AIM, estimated on a sample of 167 offerings offered on Crowdcube and 99 IPOs on the AIM between 2013 and 2016. The identification condition is granted by the inclusion of Size and Industry dummies in the regression specification. The first stage is not reported, as coefficients are in all cases qualitatively the same as in the model reported in Table 13.3, Model 1. The second stage is a negative binomial regression on the number of investors, estimated on a sample of 167 equity offerings offered on Crowdcube, and including the inverse Mill's ratio estimated from the first model. Model (1) is our baseline specification. Model (2) adds Female leadership. Model (3) adds Age. Model (4) adds Ethnical minority. Model (5) adds Metropolitan area. Model (6) adds all variables included in Models (2–5). Robust standard errors in parentheses. ***, **, and * identify significance levels at less than 1%, 5%, and 10%, respectively. TMT, Top management team.

IPO, are correlated to a larger number of participating investors. This result, interestingly, differs from what has been observed in the former table, highlighting that unobserved determinants of preference for crowdfunding over IPOs positively affect the attraction of investors, but have a (weak) negative impact on the probability to succeed. This may be due to a capability to attract a large number of small investors, that is, by hype creation, while not necessarily attracting enough funds for the success of the campaign.

13.4.1 Robustness analysis

In this section, we provide robustness analysis with respect to the variables employed for testing our hypothesis. First, we test whether the presence of a woman (*Female presence*), rather than the leadership in the team, might have an impact in the choice of a crowdfunding initiative and in the following success. Second, we replace our *Metropolitan area* dummy with variables measuring specific features of the local area, such as the *GDP per capita* and the *Unemployment rate*. Last, our findings with regard to geography might indeed depend on some specificities of the United Kingdom. While we cannot rule out this possibility, we acknowledge that (1) distance might matters less in the United Kingdom than in other countries and (2) the leading role of London as financial center might condition our results. Third, we take into account the specificity of the UK geographical context, repeating our analysis either including dummy variables for the nine NUT-2 regions in the United Kingdom[15] or dropping all observations for firms located in London.

All our robustness checks are reported in Table 13.5. Models A1−5 repeat our first stage when replacing *Female leadership* with *Female presence* (Model A1), *Metropolitan area* with *GDP per capita* (Model A2), *Metropolitan area* with *Unemployment rate* (Model A3), when including regional dummies (Model A4) and when dropping London offerings (Model A5). Results show that *Female presence* is negatively correlated to the probability to choose a crowdfunding initiative over an IPO. This is likely to be due to the larger TMT size of IPO firms, as well as to the greater attention to gender equality in official listing. *GDP per capita* and *Unemployment*, vice versa, are not correlated to the likelihood to prefer a crowdfunding offering, although the signs (negative for *GDP per capita* and positive for *Unemployment*) are coherent with the intuition that disadvantaged areas are more likely to give raise to crowdfunding initiatives.

Models B1−5 and C1−5 report the results of our second stages. Again, we replace *Female leadership* with *Female presence* (Models B1 and C1), *Metropolitan area* with *GDP per capita* (Models B2 and C2), and *Metropolitan area* with *Unemployment rate* (Models B3 and C3), when including regional dummies (Models B4 and C4) and when dropping London offerings (Models B5 and C5). Our results show that *Female presence* does not significantly impact on the success of a crowdfunding campaign, nor on the number of investors. As far as *GDP per capita* and *Unemployment rate* are concerned, coefficients are weakly significant when analyzing the *Number of investors*. Again, the signs support that disadvantaged areas (with

[15] There are 12 NUTS-1 statistical regions in the United Kingdom: Northern Ireland, Scotland, Wales, and 9 regions for England (North East, North West, Yorkshire and the Humber, East Midlands, West Midlands, East of England, Greater London, South East, and South West). Greater London is the reference case. See footnote 10 for details on the NUTS classifications.

TABLE 13.5 Robustness analysis.

	(A1)	(A2)	(A3)	(A4)	(A5)	(B1)	(B2)	(B3)	(B4)	(B5)	(C1)	(C2)	(C3)	(C4)	(C5)
Female leadership	—	−0.331	−0.339	−0.384	−0.362	—	0.581	0.569	0.670	0.352	—	0.034	0.031	0.221	0.165
		(0.222)	(0.222)	(0.270)	(0.298)		(0.475)	(0.491)	(0.604)	(0.297)		(0.149)	(0.150)	(0.202)	(0.200)
Female presence	−0.969***	—	—	—	—	0.093	—	—	—	—	0.048	—	—	—	—
	(0.227)					(0.308)					(0.083)				
Age	−0.029**	−0.026**	−0.025**	−0.026*	−0.019*	−0.045***	−0.046***	−0.045***	−0.068***	−0.057***	−0.008**	0.009**	0.009**	−0.009**	−0.007*
	(0.012)	(0.012)	(0.012)	(0.013)	(0.012)	(0.016)	(0.017)	(0.017)	(0.023)	(0.022)	(0.003)	(0.004)	(0.004)	(0.004)	(0.004)
Ethnical minority	—	—	—	—	—	0.084	0.061	0.068	0.051	0.058	0.157*	0.153*	0.144*	0.188*	0.133*
						(0.353)	(0.353)	(0.378)	(0.521)	(0.523)	(0.086)	(0.087)	(0.089)	(0.106)	(0.076)
Metropolitan area	−0.732***	—	—	−1.331***	−0.393*	−0.446*	—	—	−0.911*	−0.529*	−0.215*	—	—	−0.215*	−0.269**
	(0.231)			(0.390)	(0.218)	(0.243)			(0.490)	(0.294)	(0.113)			(0.118)	(0.105)
GDP per capita	—	−0.208	—	—	—	—	−0.107	—	—	—	—	−0.163*	—	—	—
		(0.398)					(0.581)					(0.068)			
Unemployment	—	—	−1.436	—	—	—	—	1.685	—	—	—	—	−3.615*	—	—
			(1.564)					(1.899)					(2.175)		
Equity offered	−5.361***	−4.513***	−4.423***	−5.721***	−3.644**	−4.031**	−3.897**	−3.978**	−8.612***	−9.127***	−0.503	−0.689	−0.671	−0.235	−0.352
	(1.126)	(1.113)	(1.099)	(1.144)	(1.601)	(1.753)	(1.766)	(1.797)	(3.341)	(2.900)	(0.488)	(0.527)	(0.509)	(0.624)	(0.582)
Target	−0.549***	−0.444***	−0.457***	−0.463***	−0.525**	−1.282***	−1.280***	−1.284***	−1.515***	−1.409***	0.559***	0.551***	0.548***	0.568***	0.546***
	(0.135)	(0.137)	(0.135)	(0.145)	(0.214)	(0.163)	(0.165)	(0.166)	(0.240)	(0.201)	(0.025)	(0.027)	(0.026)	(0.032)	(0.032)
Firm age	0.050	0.051	0.048	0.047	−0.001	−0.007	−0.005	−0.004	−0.013	−0.001	0.011	0.012	0.012	−0.001	−0.001
	(0.042)	(0.047)	(0.047)	(0.046)	(0.058)	(0.043)	(0.042)	(0.041)	(0.058)	(0.052)	(0.014)	(0.014)	(0.014)	(0.015)	(0.015)
TMT size	−0.424***	−0.585***	−0.583***	−0.629***	−0.565***	−0.013	0.026	0.019	0.196	0.044	−0.096**	−0.102*	−0.104*	−0.030	−0.092
	(0.101)	(0.103)	(0.104)	(0.108)	(0.151)	(0.170)	(0.191)	(0.191)	(0.206)	(0.199)	(0.049)	(0.053)	(0.055)	(0.077)	(0.070)

(Continued)

TABLE 13.5 (Continued)

	(A1)	(A2)	(A3)	(A4)	(A5)	(B1)	(B2)	(B3)	(B4)	(B5)	(C1)	(C2)	(C3)	(C4)	(C5)
Positive sales	−0.027	−0.351	−0.351	−0.198	−0.288	0.016	0.002	0.004	0.561	0.290	0.268***	0.270***	0.281***	0.337***	0.317**
	(0.256)	(0.273)	(0.273)	(0.291)	(0.297)	(0.303)	(0.315)	(0.311)	(0.477)	(0.439)	(0.089)	(0.090)	(0.095)	(0.128)	(0.125)
Patents	−0.234	−0.330	−0.326	−0.497	−0.207	0.364	0.437	0.454	0.463	0.431	0.237***	−0.272***	0.261***	0.300**	0.266**
	(0.280)	(0.263)	(0.261)	(0.305)	(0.320)	(0.386)	(0.363)	(0.357)	(0.636)	(0.507)	(0.092)	(0.095)	(0.092)	(0.153)	(0.125)
Population	−0.345***	−0.265**	−0.111	−0.312***	−0.717***	0.104	0.001	−0.144	−0.392	−0.086	−0.009	−0.052	−0.049	0.015	−0.054
	(0.092)	(0.133)	(0.124)	(0.098)	(0.131)	(0.163)	(0.196)	(0.176)	(0.342)	(0.299)	(0.037)	(0.048)	(0.036)	(0.069)	(0.064)
Prone-to-crowdfunding (IMR)	–	–	–	–	–	−0.796*	−0.790*	−0.782*	−1.100*	−0.945	0.390***	0.415***	0.428***	0.466**	0.397***
						(0.401)	(0.403)	(0.420)	(0.575)	(0.651)	(0.145)	(0.149)	(0.153)	(0.193)	(0.136)
Industry dummies	Yes***	Yes***	Yes***	Yes***	Yes***	No	No	No	No	No	No	No	No	No	No
NUTS-1 dummies	No	No	No	Yes***	No	No	No	No	Yes***	No	No	No	No	Yes***	No
Constant	14.896***	11.180***	12.015***	13.432***	20.724***	−14.710***	−12.304***	−12.255***	−10.134**	−13.836***	−1.003	0.416	−0.194	−1.521	−0.207
	(2.424)	(3.656)	(2.472)	(2.512)	(3.618)	(3.055)	(4.460)	(2.652)	(4.966)	(4.966)	(0.653)	(1.365)	(0.552)	(1.022)	(0.958)
Observations	266	266	266	266	159	167	167	167	167	100	167	167	167	167	100
Pseudo *R*-squared	0.74	0.70	0.71	0.79	0.77	0.49	0.47	0.47	0.58	0.56	0.56	0.52	0.54	0.64	0.63

The table reports the results of robustness analysis on the selection equation reported in the first column of Table 13.3—Crowdfunding (Models A1−4), on the success equation reported in Table 13.4, Model 6 (Models C1−4). Models A1−4 are probit models on the likelihood to propose a crowdfunding offering, vis-à-vis a public offering on the AIM. The identification condition is granted by the inclusion of Industry dummies in the regression specification. Models B1−4 are probit models on the success of crowdfunding offerings, including the inverse Mill's ratio estimated from the first model (Models A1−3, respectively). Models C1−4 are negative binomial regressions on the number of investors and including the inverse Mill's ratio estimated from the first model (not reported, but qualitatively equivalent to Models A1−3). In Models A1, B1, and C1, Female presence replaces Female leadership. In Models A2, B2, and C2, GDP per capita replaces Metropolitan area. In Models A3, B3, and C3, Unemployment replaces Metropolitan area. In Models A4, B4, and C4, we include also a set of dummy variables for the 12 NUTS-1 statistical regions. In Models A5, B5, and C5, offerings from London are dropped. The sample size is therefore given by 167 Crowdcube offerings and 99 AIM offerings between 2013 and 2016 in Models A1−4; 100 offerings on Crowdcube and 59 offerings on the AIM in Model A5; 167 offerings on Crowdcube in Models B1−4 and C1−4; 100 offerings on Crowdcube in Models B5 and C5. Robust standard errors in parentheses. ***, **, and * identify significance levels at less than 1%, 5%, and 10%, respectively. *TMT*, Top management team.

lower *GDP per capita* and higher *Unemployment rate*) are more likely to generate a large participation of investors. Signs are coherent, but no statistical significance is found, with respect to the probability of success. Finally, when including regional dummies, our results are qualitatively unchanged, while when removing London offerings, our findings are confirmed, with lower significance in a few cases, probably because of the smaller sample size.

13.5 Conclusion

Although a growing number of studies are exploring the nuances of crowdfunding and its various online platforms, research in this field is rapidly expanding (Block, Hornuf, et al., 2018; Block, Colombo, et al., 2018). The general expectation is that crowdfunding "democratizes" entrepreneurial finance, thereby increasing the possibility of underrepresented categories to raise finance. Gender, age, ethnicity, and geography are among the most important aspects that affect the capacity to gain access to external capital. This problem holds true for both debt and equity financing, where female, minorities, and rural entrepreneurs may face discrimination from external funding sources. Despite such premises, our understanding of whether and how such characteristics of prospective entrepreneurs play in raising funds in equity crowdfunding is still missing.

This study offers a timely contribution to the growing stream of research seeking to unveil the possibilities of equity crowdfunding in facilitating entrepreneurship for those most vulnerable. First, we find that age matters in equity crowdfunding, as companies with younger TMT members are both more likely to launch equity crowdfunding offerings than IPOs, and have higher chances to successfully complete an equity crowdfunding offering. This is a novel result in the crowdfunding literature. Second, we find evidence that equity crowdfunding alleviates some of the distance-related economic frictions between entrepreneurs and investors. Indeed, remotely located companies are more likely to launch equity crowdfunding offerings than IPOs and have higher chances to successfully complete an equity crowdfunding offering. On the contrary, female entrepreneurs, typically considered financially constrained in traditional entrepreneurial markets, do not have higher chances to raise funds in equity crowdfunding. Similarly, minority entrepreneurs do not have higher chances of successfully raising capital. Nevertheless, this type of entrepreneurs is associated with a higher number of investors. We interpret this evidence as a higher sensitivity to ethnicity from small investors, relative to professional investors. Equity crowdfunding offerings, indeed, attract small and professional investors alike. As these two types of investors have been found to have different investment preferences (Signori & Vismara, 2018), their attitude toward ethnicity is likely to be different. Future research might dig deeper in this direction, also leveraging the insights from institutional logics (Friedland & Alford, 1991). While professional investors might follow a market logic, small investors might also consider a community logic (Vismara, 2018). This would explain why ethnic entrepreneurs attract a higher number of investors but are at the end not more likely to secure their target funding.

Future research might expand the assessment of the democratization potential of equity crowdfunding from the demand side (entrepreneurs) to the supply side (investors), thereby delivering a better understanding of the financial inclusion offered by disintermediated entrepreneurial finance. Relatedly, studies are needed with regard to the matching between entrepreneurs and investors. Research in entrepreneurship indicates that investors are attracted to entrepreneurs with whom they share similarities. For instance, coethnicity increases the likelihood that a VC firm invests in a company (Bengtsson & Hsu, 2015). The diverse backgrounds of participants in equity crowdfunding markets permit researchers greater nuance in studying the influence of similarity attraction in funding decisions. While we have investigated democratization along four dimensions of constraints, other aspects are of interest. For instance, the socioeconomic status or the religion of proponents has not been investigated yet. In a preliminary analysis of the videos used to present the offerings in our sample, we could not find any religious symbol. Beautiful people seem to attract more favorable peer-to-peer loans (Ravina, 2008). Given crowdfunding applications gain less publicity (and may be less face-to-face than other means of negotiating to obtain financing), could it democratize for less beautiful people?

Key terms

Access to capital
Age of TMT
Democratization
Ethnic minority
Female leadership
Regional remoteness

Discussion questions

13.1. Are there any differences between the ethnic base, gender, and age of crowdfunded firms versus comparable firms that use junior public capital markets? Explain with reference to empirical evidence. What do you think accounts for this evidence?

13.2. Are regional entrepreneurs helped or hindered by equity crowdfunding? How does regional representation in crowdfunding compare to regional representation of entrepreneurs in junior public capital markets? Explain with reference to empirical evidence. What do you think accounts for this evidence?

13.3. Do you think there is a market failure in access to capital for entrepreneurs? Should or could crowdfunding play a role ensuring equal access to capital for all types of entrepreneurs? What might be some barriers to the use of crowdfunding in ensuring equal opportunities in accessing capital? What might be the appropriate response amongst policymakers to ensure equal access to capital?

Appendix

TABLE 13.A1 Correlation matrix.

	Variables	1	2	3	4	5	6	7	8	9	10	11	12	13	14	15
1	Success	1.000														
2	No. of investors	0.345*	1.000													
3	Female leadership	0.006	−0.058	1.000												
4	Age	−0.118*	−0.157*	0.017	1.000											
5	Ethnical minority	0.073	0.135*	0.082	−0.071	1.000										
6	Metropolitan area	−0.107*	−0.098*	0.062	−0.052	0.140*	1.000									
7	Equity offered	−0.084*	−0.057	0.075*	0.037	−0.146*	0.028	1.000								
8	Target	−0.278*	0.392*	0.107*	0.148*	0.097*	0.084	0.102*	1.000							
9	Firm age	−0.058	−0.084*	−0.014	−0.019	−0.075*	−0.006	0.052	0.018	1.000						
10	TMT size	0.274*	0.249*	−0.043	0.135*	0.079	−0.014	0.004	0.580*	−0.063	1.000					
11	Positive sales	0.083*	0.131*	0.006	0.038	−0.029	0.048	0.020	0.047	0.161*	0.047	1.000				
12	Patents	0.051	0.080*	−0.012	0.004	0.113*	0.061	−0.027	0.008	−0.043	0.067	0.068	1.000			
13	Population	0.109*	−0.052	0.054	−0.028	0.145*	0.199*	−0.033	0.073	−0.036	0.082	−0.032	−0.024	1.000		
14	Female presence	−0.056	0.053	0.343	0.064	0.095	−0.004	0.029	0.026	−0.034	0.309	−0.035	0.047	0.022	1.000	
15	GDP per capita	−0.117*	−0.029	0.043	−0.002	0.144	0.121*	−0.020	0.068	−0.040	0.042	−0.029	−0.026	0.596*	0.043	1.000
16	Unemployment	0.113*	−0.033	0.031	−0.029	0.053	0.177*	−0.056	0.062	−0.021	0.059	−0.032	−0.012	0.632*	−0.013	0.461*

Correlation coefficients calculated on the sample of 167 equity offerings on Crowdcube, and 99 IPOs on the AIM raising more than £300,000 and less than £5 million between 2013 and 2016. Values for Success, Number of investors, and Ethnical minorities refer only to crowdfunding offerings. * represents statistical significance at 5%. *TMT*, Top management team.

Marketplace lending

14.1 Introduction

Marketplace lending refers to online lending from individuals to businesses. It has significantly grown in popularity around the world after the global financial crisis that spanned August 2007 to the latter part of 2009. Marketplace lenders offer fast access to loans without the use of traditional bank intermediaries. The platforms cheaply and efficiently connect between borrowers and lenders, typically in exchange for a 1% borrowing fee.[1]

Some of the main marketplace lending platforms are listed in Table 14.1. Some platforms are focused on marketplace lending (e.g., Zencap), while other platforms enable a variety of different types of loans, including but not limited to person-to-person (P2P) loans. Some platforms service entrepreneurs around the world, such as the Kiva that has a focus on developing regions around the world. Our discussion here is focused on marketplace lending, not P2P loans, for reasons explained in Chapter 1, Introduction.

Marketplace lending platforms enable businesses to borrow up to $500,000, or $1 million, or even $5 million, depending on the platform as shown in Table 14.1. As at July 2019, in the United States, nominal interest rates are normally at least 5% but can be as high as 30%. Loan terms can range from a few months to more than 10 years. Funding time is very quick. An application can take as little as 5 minutes to complete and matches with potential lenders within seconds.[2] The platform is not the lender, but instead the platform connects the borrower (an entrepreneurial firm) with a number of possible individual lenders. As such, marketplace lending is a very novel financial technology (Fintech).

Table 14.1 lists some of the minimum requirements at the different platforms (where that information is available). Typically a business must have been operating for 6 months and have $10,000 in revenues and a suitable minimum credit score. However, there is a notable degree of variation across platforms.

---

[1] Some platforms offer fees as low as 0.5%, while others have fees as high as 10% depending on the loan size and business performance. See https://www.supermoney.com/marketplace-lending/.

[2] https://www.top10bestbusinessloans.com/

TABLE 14.1 Select marketplace lending platforms around the world.

Platform name	Webpage	Nominal yield	Total invested	Companies funded	Founded/ launched	Notable features
Australia						
SocietyOne	https://www.societyone.com.au/marketplace		$600 million +	24,000 +	2012	Australia's first marketplace lender; expect to have done $1 billion in loan by 2020
Canada						
FundThrough	https://www.fundthrough.com/				2014	"FundThrough has since become the US and Canada's fastest growing working capital solution, allowing business owners to access funds tied in outstanding receivables in the click of a button"
Lendified	https://www.lendified.com/				2015	Loans to Canadian businesses of up to $150,000
Lending Loop	https://www.lendingloop.ca/	Starts at 5.9%	$Can 51 million		2014	Borrow $1000–$50,000, no early repayment penalties; Ontario government contributed $3 million over 2 years to loans funded on Lending Loop's platform, funds up to 10% of small business loans, supporting funding of $30 million
Lendmart	https://www.lendmart.com/				2016	Quebec based
Developing countries around the world						
FIINCA	https://finca.org			2.3 million	1984	4.5 million women empowered, microfinance, donations
Kiva	https://www.kiva.org		$1.33 billion	3.3 million	2005	Operates in 78 countries, 18 million lenders (loans start at $25), 96.8% repayment rate (it is a loan, not a donation)
MYC4	Test.myc4.com		€24,349,914	20,475	2006	Africa; 1.9% average rate of return on investment, 5894 investors from 120 countries
Estonia						
Bondora	https://www.bondora.com/en/marketplace-lending	Approximate average 11.6%	€29 + million	72,558 + customers served	2008	€247 million + invested. €29 million + paid out in interest, suggests 11.6% rate
France						
FinexKap					2013	Data from 2017
Lendix	https://en.lendix.com/				2014	Data from 2017
Unilend	https://www.unilend.fr/		€33.9 million	439	2013	

Name	URL	Rate	Volume	Number	Year	Notes
Lendosphere	https://www.lendosphere.com/			70	2014	Dedicated to renewables and environment-friendly projects
Germany						
Lendico	http://www.lendico.com	6.85%			2013	Launched first in Germany with loans €1000–€150,000; expanded into Spain, Poland, Austria, South Africa, The Netherlands, and Brazil
Zencap	https://www.zencap.de/		€14 million	414	March 2014 – November 2015	Acquired by Funding Circle in 2005
Spain						
Loan Book	https://www.loanbook.es/	Rates 4.11% (A – rating, 362 dias) to 7.46 (B rating, 361 dias)			2012	Rates quoted for examples posted on August 2, 2019. LoanBook raised capital for its operations from the UK equity crowdfunding page Crowdcube https://www.crowdcube.com/companies/loanbook/pitches/bwmGEl
Switzerland						
Lend	https://lend.ch/en/nusiness-loan/	Rates 3.50%–12.90%			2016	Terms in months possible for 12, 24, 35, 48, 60; rates quoted for 4-year term
United Kingdom						
Funding Circle	https://www.fundingcircle.com/	Rates start at 4.99%[a]	$10.2 billion	72,000	2010	Acquired German-based marketplace lender Zencap in 2015; also operational in the United States, the United Kingdom, Germany, Spain, and The Netherlands
Zopa	https://www.zopa.com/	7.3%	£4 billion	Hundreds of thousands	2005	£250 million interest collected; offers a wide array of different lending products; marketplace lending is just one line of business
United States						
Fundbox	https://fundbox.com/			100,000 +		Highlights on webpage partnerships with other service providers, including Intuit Quickbooks, FreshBooks, Xero, Harvest, Kashoo, Invoiceasap, Jobber, eBillity, Zoho, Co and Co, Eventbrite, Knowify, paid
Kabbage	https://www.kabbage.com/		$7 billion	185,000		Loan amount: $2k–$250k; time in business: 12 + months; $4.2k in monthly revenue; minimum credit score: none[b]
LendingClub	https://www.lendingclub.com/	4.99%–29.99%	$50 billion + (including P2P and marketplace)	3 million +	2010 P2P Only	4.99%–29.99% for business loans of $500,000–$500,000. Personal loans up to $40,000 rates between 6.95% and 35.89%

(Continued)

TABLE 14.1 (Continued)

Platform name	Webpage	Nominal yield	Total invested	Companies funded	Founded/ launched	Notable features
LendingTree	https://www.lendingtree.com/				2014 marketplace lending[c]	Loan amounts: $2k–$1 million, time in business: 12 + months, require $8K in monthly revenue, minimum credit score: none[e]
Lendio	https://lp.lendio.com/		$1.3 billion	75,000	1998[d]	Loan amount: $1k–$5 million; Time in business: 12 + months; $15k in monthly revenue; minimum credit score: 580[f]
OnDeck	https://www.ondeck.com/	9.99% lowest possible	$12 billion			Loan amount: $5k–$500k; time in business: 12 + months; $10k in monthly revenue; minimum credit score: 600[g]; webpage features local pages for United States, Canada, and Australia
Prosper	https://www.prosper.com/	Depends[h]	$15 billion (including P2P and marketplace)	943,669	2005	First P2P lending platform in the United States
SoFi	https://www.sofi.com		$40 billion	700,000 +	2011	Offers networking events and business coaching for entrepreneurs as well as loans

[a] Advertised rate on US webpage, July 31, 2019. Funding Circle explains on its webpage, "[r]ates may vary according to term and overall creditworthiness. To see what rate your business may qualify for, apply today at no obligation."

[b] https://www.top10bestbusinessloans.com/

[c] https://www.inc.com/kimberly-weisul/new-option-for-business-loans-lending-club.html

[d] https://www.cnbc.com/2014/08/01/lendingtree-an-original-dot-com-darling-grows-up.html#

[e] https://www.top10bestbusinessloans.com/

[f] https://www.top10bestbusinessloans.com/

[g] https://www.top10bestbusinessloans.com/

[h] Prosper states on its webpage for fixed term loans of $2000–$40000, "For example, a three-year $10,000 personal loan with a Prosper Rating of AA would have an interest rate of 5.31% and a 2.41% origination fee for an annual percentage rate (APR) of 6.95%. You would receive $9,759 and make 36 scheduled monthly payments of $301.10. A five-year $10,000 personal loan with a Prosper Rating of A would have an interest rate of 8.39% and a 5.00% origination fee with a 10.59% APR. You would receive $9,500 and make 60 scheduled monthly payments of $204.64. Origination fees vary between 2.41% and 5%. Personal loan APRs through Prosper range from 6.95% (AA) to 35.99% (HR) for first-time borrowers, with the lowest rates for the most creditworthy borrowers. Eligibility for personal loans up to $40,000 depends on the information provided by the applicant in the application form." Note: Funding statistics are from inception to July 2019 based on various searches on the web, either from the platform itself or other media reports of the platform. The list of platforms here is not intended to be exhaustive. Cells left blank where information is not available. P2P, Person-to-person.

This chapter proceeds as follows. Section 14.2 describes the characteristics of borrowers on marketplace lending platforms. Section 14.3 discusses outcomes of marketplace lending for lenders. Section 14.4 considers the impact of marketplace lending on entrepreneurship. Section 14.5 summarizes and concludes the discussion of marketplace lending.

14.2 Characteristics of borrowers

This section[3] makes use of detailed information that was provided by the German Zencap platform (Table 14.1) to describe characteristics of borrowers that make use of marketplace lending. The Zencap platform, based in Berlin, Germany, operated from March 2014 to November 2015 prior to its merger with the UK-based platform Funding Circle. Lenders are presented with detailed financial information of borrowers, including an income statement and a balance sheet. Loans are secured against not only the assets of the business but also a personal guarantee of the borrowers. Loans are possible only between €10,000 and €250,000. Zencap rates all of its loans as either A + , A, B, C, or C − . The interest rate is determined by Zencap. Zencap does extensive due diligence on firms prior to listing to mitigate adverse selection problems (Chapter 2: Overview of agency and signaling theory in crowdfunding). Zencap charges a 1% fee for its services, which applied only if loans are successfully fulfilled (fees are deducted from monthly installment payments).

On Zencap, 23% of the firms were able to raise all of the capital that they had desired, and the average capital raise was 58% relative to capital that was sought. These statistics imply that lenders carry out significant due diligence prior to investing.

For the 414 businesses that borrowed through Zencap, the loans had the following characteristics (Cumming and Hornuf, 2017). The number of lenders per loan was 85 on average (median is 77, minimum is 4, and maximum is 302). The average lender bid was €33,680 on average (median €29,450, minimum €400, and maximum €124,800). The principal amount actually borrowed was on average €72,184 (median €60,000, minimum €10,000, and maximum €250,000). Loan durations were between 6 and 60 months (average 34 months, median 36 months, or 3 years). The nominal yield was on average 6.85% (median 6.57%, minimum 3.13%, and maximum 15.02%).

The 414 businesses that borrowed through Zencap had the following characteristics. The range of employees was between 1 and 300 (average 18 and median 10). Only 16% of these businesses had a female CEO. (And relatedly, 7% of the lenders across all the 414 businesses were female, with the range between 0% and 24%.) The average business had assets of €808,571 (median €295,975, minimum €9000, and maximum €14.6million). Profits ranges from − €346,300 to + €1112,533 (median was €44,100 and average was €66,744).

The Zencap platform assigned ratings of A + to only 5% of the borrows, A to 21% of the borrowers, B to 47% of the borrowers, C to 23% of the borrowers, and C − to 4% of the borrowers.

The 414 businesses that borrowed from lenders through Zencap were in the following industries: accommodation and food service activities 3%; agriculture, forestry, and fishing 2%; arts, entertainment, and recreation 0.1%; construction 9%; electricity, gas, steam, and air conditioning supply 0.1%; financial and insurance activities 3%; human health and

---

[3] This section is based on Cumming and Hornuf (2017).

social work activities 6%; information and communication 7%; manufacturing 11%; other 8%; other services activities 19%; professional, scientific, and technical activities 4%; real estate activities 0.1%; rental and leasing activities 2%; transporting and storage 4%; and wholesale and retail trade, repair of motor vehicles, and motorcycles 21%.

The reasons the businesses borrowed through Zencap were provided as well: asset purchases (12% of businesses), expansion/growth (46%), tax liability (2%), working capital (32%), and other reasons (8%).

Various online resources explain different types of business loans that are feasible with marketplace lending. For example, one popular US-based page[4] explains that businesses can obtain secured loans (by putting up collateral) for annual percentage rates that start at 6%; unsecured loans (with good credit scores) for annual percentage rates that start at 4%,[5] lines of credit (for ongoing working capital expenses) starting at 9%, merchant cash advances (for business with good credit and low risk) starting at 20%, accounts receivable (for outstanding invoices, short term debts) starting at 3%, equipment loans (for equipment necessary to grow a business) starting at 6%, construction loans (expansion or new facility) starting at 2%, and invoice factoring (filing cash gaps) starting at 11%.

14.3 Factors affecting lending success

This section is organized as follows. Section 14.3.1 discuses factors that affect the ability of borrowers to raise the capital that they seek. Section 14.3.2 discusses default rates at marketplace lending pages.

14.3.1 Which loans get funded?

Cumming and Hornuf (2017) show that the vast majority (over 95%) of marketplace funding on Zencap comes within the first 20 days. Within the first 20 days, most of the funding comes within the first couple of days.

Cumming and Hornuf (2017) further show that the Zepcap data strongly support for the importance of simple platform ratings affecting crowd investor investment decisions in terms of funding success and attracting more investors. Platform ratings are not correlated with income statement or balance sheet items. Income and balance sheet outcomes are likewise uncorrelated with borrower success in terms of getting fully funded loans, the time to filling a loan, and the number of borrowers. The analysis in Cumming and Hornuf (2017) further shows that smartphone usage and newsletters, as well as the presence of females, attract more daily capital raises for borrowers, while contemporaneous competition from other borrowers lowers the amount any single borrow raises in a day.

---

[4] https://www.top10bestbusinessloans.com/

[5] On average, we would expect secured loans to be priced lower that unsecured loans due to the extrarisk of unsecured loans, but these are merely that suggested "starting at" rates as per ibid.

14.3.2 Default rates and returns to investors

Statistics on loan default rates are harder to access from marketplace lending webpages, but some information is available. Cumming and Hornuf (2017) report information from Zencap at the time of its merger with Funding Circle 2015 that only 5 of 144 loans were in default. Funding Circle itself had previously been reported in the media to have default rates around 2.8%.[6] To compare with P2P lending, LendingClub reports default rates of 1%–10% for risky borrowers, but the returns offered for riskier borrowers can be as high as 25%.[7] LendingClub reports further that they turn down 90% of the applications for borrowing from the population of individuals that would like to make use of the platform.[8]

Returns to marketplace lending investors have been reported at 5.8% on average after bad debts and fees.[9] There are some differences depending on the platform. The platform Zopa[10] was reported to inform investors to expect returns of 5.0%–5.5% after bad debts and fees, with an average borrowing rate of 7.3%.[11] Similarly, the median rate of return other reputable marketplace lending platforms such as LendingClub has been reported at 5%.[12] Further, Prosper reports a 3%–10% median rate of return on depending on risk tolerance.[13]

Adams (2018) presents data from LendingClub and Prosper, the two largest marketplace platforms in the United States, and compares the rates used to those offered by credit cards (since the unsecured loan terms are similar). Adams concludes from the data that for most all credit ratings, interest rate paid through marketplace lending is substantially lower than that which is paid through credit cards (see Fig. 14.1).

14.4 Impact of marketplace lending on entrepreneurship

Marketplace lending grew dramatically after the global financial crisis that spanned August 2007 to the end of 2009.[14] While the original intent of marketplace lenders may appear consistent with the view that marketplace lenders and banks are substitutes, empirical evidence is consistent with the view that banks and marketplace lenders are

---

[6] https://www.theguardian.com/business/2012/jun/10/peer-to-peer-lenders-future-of-banking

[7] https://www.forbes.com/sites/chrisbarth/2012/06/06/looking-for-10-yields-go-online-for-peer-to-peer-lending/#1dbccd863a8f

[8] https://www.forbes.com/sites/chrisbarth/2012/06/06/looking-for-10-yields-go-online-for-peer-to-peer-lending/#1dbccd863a8f

[9] https://www.theguardian.com/business/2012/jun/10/peer-to-peer-lenders-future-of-banking

[10] https://www.zopa.com/

[11] https://www.theguardian.com/business/2012/jun/10/peer-to-peer-lenders-future-of-banking

[12] https://www.supermoney.com/marketplace-lending/

[13] https://www.supermoney.com/marketplace-lending/

[14] This section is based on Cumming et al. (2018) and Cole, Cumming, and Taylor (2018).

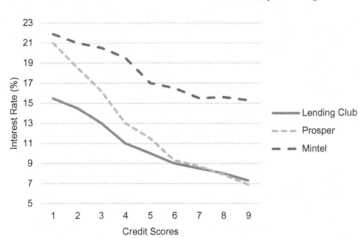

FIGURE 14.1 Marketplace lending (from LendingClub and Prosper) rates versus credit card rates (Mintel). *Source: Based on Adams, R. M. (2018). Do marketplace lending platforms offer lower rates to consumers? In* FEDS notes. *Board of Governors of the Federal Reserve System. <https://www.federalreserve. gov/econres/notes/feds-notes/do-mar- ketplace-lending-platforms-offer-lower- rates-to-consumers-20181022.htm>, for 2017Q4. See Adams for charts over earlier periods with similar dif- ferences between the three options.*

complements.[15] There are five main reasons offered by Cole et al.[16] First, entrepreneurs that have fewer sources of potential capital are more likely to be subjected to hold up agency problems; see Chapter 2, Overview of agency and signaling theory in crowdfunding. Second, having capital from one source can serve as a form of external certification that enables capital more easily from another source. Third, multiple sources enable entrepreneurs to scale up their businesses more easily and grow. Fourth, the community in which an entrepreneur is based is richer if there are more entrepreneurs, which enables community entrepreneurial agglomeration in respect of more business opportunities, more entrepreneurship, and more sources of capital. Finally, when entrepreneurs seek capital, they typically approach multiple sources and are often turned down by one or more sources (Cosh et al., 2009); having multiple sources available thereby encourages more entrepreneurial activity than that which would otherwise be the case.

Marketplace lending restrictions have been in place in the United States at different points in time, including Idaho, Indiana, Iowa, Maine, Mississippi, Nebraska, North Dakota, and West Virginia. Those states have imposed restrictions on LendingClub and Prosper, some of which have since been relaxed (Idaho in 2015, Indiana in 2011, Mississippi in 2013, and Nebraska in 2015). Iowa is the only state that has continuously imposed restrictions on both LendingClub and Prosper. States impose restrictions through origination rebates, licensing restrictions, service reviews, enforcement actions, and several additional hurdles; see Cumming et al. (2018). The restrictions are largely related to how

[15] Cole, R. A., Cumming, D. J., & Taylor, J. (2019). *Does FinTech compete with or complement bank finance?*. SSRN. Available from: <https://ssrn.com/abstract = 3302975> or <https://doi.org/10.2139/ ssrn.3302975>.

[16] Cole, R. A., Cumming, D. J., & Taylor, J. (2019). *Does FinTech compete with or complement bank finance?*. SSRN. Available from: <https://ssrn.com/abstract = 3302975> or <https://doi.org/10.2139/ ssrn.3302975>.

states classify securities,[17] which predated the introduction of marketplace lending, and hence the restrictions enable a nice natural experiment to investigate whether they have a material causal effect on entrepreneurship. Cumming et al. (2018) statistically estimate, using a fuzzy regression discontinuity design, that nonrestricted metropolitan state areas (MSAs) had 120% more marketplace loans than restricted areas, and that a 10% increase in marketplace loans causes a 0.6% increase in new business establishments per capita in an MSA. These economic effects are more pronounced among smaller firms and are not explained by confounding factors. It is noteworthy, however, that there appears to be an increase in the quantity of businesses, while not necessarily an increase in the average quality.

14.5 Summary

This chapter introduced some of the main marketplace lending platforms in selected countries. We explained how some of the platforms work in respect of doing due diligence on entrepreneurial firms, providing ratings on entrepreneurial firms, and the information disclosed on the platform. We offered some, albeit limited, statistics on default rates. We explained the typical rates of interest charged and the possible expected returns to investors after fees and bad debts.

Marketplace lending has grown extensively since the global financial crisis. We reviewed evidence that shows that marketplace lenders operate within the entrepreneurial ecosystem, and on average work as a complement to, and not as a substitute for, traditional banks. Empirical evidence is strongly consistent with the view that marketplace lending spurs on entrepreneurial activity.

Marketplace lending has not been around for an extensive period of time. Further evidence on the determinants of default in marketplace lending across platforms and borrowers would be useful. Also, further evidence as more time passes on the long run performance of firms that use marketplace lending would be useful to better guide entrepreneurs and policymakers on the best features of marketplace lending that would enable successful borrowing.

Key terms

Complements
Default rates
Nominal rate of interest
Lending restrictions
Marketplace lending
MSA
P2P lending
Platform fees
Substitutes

[17] Chapter 19, Crypto regulation, discusses the issue of what constitutes a security in a different but related crowdfunding context.

Discussion questions

14.1. What is the different between P2P lending and marketplace lending? How much do entrepreneurial firms typically borrow through marketplace lending? How do borrowing amounts differ between P2P lending and marketplace lending? What are the default rates and rates of return with marketplace lending versus P2P lending?

14.2. Are detailed financial statements better predictors of funding success in marketplace lending than simple ratings provided by the platform? Why or why not? What does your answer tell you about the sophistication of lenders in marketplace lending platforms and the possible role of financial regulation and disclosure?

14.3. Do marketplace lending platforms substitute for traditional banks? What is the impact of marketplace lending on entrepreneurial activity in terms of quantity and quality? Explain, with reference to theory and evidence.

Crowdfunding Regulation
and Policy

15

Introduction to crowdfunding regulation and policy

15.1 Introduction

Part IV of this book comprises five chapters (Chapters 15—19) on topics pertinent to crowdfunding regulation and policy.

The US Securities Act of 1933 was put in place specifically to deal with problems of improper disclosure and oversight associated with securities offerings, much of which was believed to be tied to the causes of the 1929 stock market crash. Crowdfunding is the antithesis of securities regulation, as it enables the distribution of securities without the accompanying disclosure that is normally required. Professor Jeffrey MacIntosh at the University of Toronto Faculty of Law has colorfully noted "If you utter the word 'crowdfunding' in front of a dusty old-fashioned securities lawyer, make sure you have a fully charged defibrillator on hand. Perhaps a fully equipped contingent of ER doctors and nurses. It won't be pretty."[1]

The demand for equity crowdfunding has been seen through cases such as Oculus Rift, as discussed in Chapter 4, An overview of rewards-based crowdfunding, and Chapter 8, Equity crowdfunding, valuation, and cases, which was funded with rewards crowdfunding and backers did not share in the returns associated with the acquisition exit to Facebook. Similarly, commentators have noted that, prior to the Jumpstart Our Business Startups (JOBS) Act, it was strange to be allowed to bet $5000 at a casino but not be allowed to invest $5000 in an entrepreneurial start-up in the United States. The catch-22 with securities regulation and start-ups is that the cost of regulation is too onerous for the amount of capital that is needed at the start-up stage. Prospectus documents can cost hundreds of thousands of dollars in terms of legal and accounting fees, and fees of other service providers. So if the capital raised is less than costs of prospectus compliance and other regulatory costs, start-ups would never be able to raise capital. As such, there is clearly a demand for equity crowdfunding.

---

[1] See http://business.financialpost.com/fp-comment/extraordinary-popular-delusions-and-the-madness-of-crowd-funding.

But regulation around crowdfunding is likewise needed. To highlight this regulatory need, we begin our examination of crowdfunding regulation in this chapter by presenting some cases of fraud in crowdfunding markets. Section 15.2 gives rationales as to why regulation of crowdfunding is important and necessary. We provide examples of fraud, including fraud amongst rewards and equity crowdfunding campaigns, as well as fraud on behalf of crowdfunding platforms. Further, we explain evidence on adverse selection in crowdfunding. Also, we explain what crowdfunding platforms do (and do not do) and why it is important that they do the things that they should do.

Section 15.3 presents equity crowdfunding rules across a number of different countries. In view of the well-publicized changes in the United States associated with the JOBS Act, we discuss those changes in some detail.

Rules are merely rules without any surveillance and enforcement. Therefore, in Section 15.4 we review evidence on the determinants of fraud in crowdfunding, and how that evidence could guide surveillance and enforcement efforts.

Finally, Section 15.5 concludes and provides a roadmap for the additional chapters in Part IV of this book. In the roadmap we discuss how crowdfunding rules are likely to evolve over time based on marketplace evidence of what marketplace participants demand. We further discuss the importance of forming rules around crowdfunding around other policy initiatives pertinent to the broader entrepreneurial finance and entrepreneurship ecosystem. We explain how crowdfunding rules, cryptocurrency regulation, and other rules pertaining to fintech can affect the evolution of fintech entrepreneurship around the world. These issues are addressed in each of the ensuing chapters in the remainder of Part IV of this book.

15.2 Why do we need crowdfunding regulation?

Empirical evidence is consistent with the view that adverse selection is present in equity crowdfunding markets. For example, Blaseg et al. (2019) present evidence from Germany that shows that entrepreneurial start-ups that are tied to lower quality banks (those that are stressed or face possible failure) are 12% more likely to use equity crowdfunding than those that are not tied to stressed banks. Blasseg et al. also present data consistent with the idea that the riskiest ventures that have bad credit ratings and younger management teams are more likely to use equity crowdfunding that other forms of finance. And further, Blasseg et al. find that the use of equity crowdfunding alongside capital from a distressed bank is associated with entrepreneurial start-ups that themselves are more likely to fail than those that did not use equity crowdfunding. Independent evidence from Walthoff-Borm, Schwienbacher, and Vanacker (2018) confirms the idea that equity crowdfunding is a last resort, and not the first, for many entrepreneurial start-ups.

Cumming et al. (2018a, 2018b) examine platform level data from Canada over the years 2014–17 and find that only 53% of platforms carry out due diligence changes prior to listing a campaign on the platform. Due diligence comprises background checks, site visits, credit checks, cross-checks, account monitoring, and third-party proof on funding projects. Cumming et al. show that due diligence is more commonly applied after the implementation of new crowdfunding regulations in Canada in 2016. Further they show that larger platforms and investing-based (debt and equity crowdfunding) platforms are more likely to carry out due diligence. Further, the data examined in Cumming et al. is consistent with the view that higher amounts of due diligence is associated with a higher percentage of successful capital raises.

In short, empirical evidence is consistent with the view that there are pronounced risks in crowdfunding markets. Moreover, empirical evidence is consistent with the view that regulatory oversight and due diligence mitigate those risks.

Fraud is nevertheless found in crowdfunding markets around the world. Below, we present eight cases of fraud. Four of these cases are from entrepreneurs that used reward-based crowdfunding. Two equity crowdfunding fraud cases are thereafter presented, followed by two cases of fraud perpetrated by crowdfunding platforms and not the entrepreneurs listing on the platform in Sections 15.2.1–15.2.8, respectively. Thereafter in Section 15.2.9 we show an unusual case of a crowdfunded dispute resolution platform, highlighting the apparent market opportunity for profiting off of the apparent growing presence of crowdfunding fraud claims.

15.2.1 iBackPack

iBackPack raised over $720,910 from 4032 backers over three campaigns (the first in 2015, which raised $445,353 from 1946 backers) on Indiegogo[2] and $76,694 from 252 backers in 2016 on Kickstarter.[3] The campaign was well structured with many reward levels, diagrams, pictures, and videos. And the concept is clearly interesting for millennials, offering storage and charging features for iPhones on the go, as evidenced by the multiple campaigns on both Indiegogo and Kickstarter.

Unfortunately, the founder stopped communication with the crowd, removed videos from YouTube, and did not provide updates to the crowd in terms of whether or not the backpacks would be delivered (or even existed). The founder claimed that there was frustration and mistake associated with creating the project due to problems with the storage batteries, such that a safe product could not be created; however, those claims do not appear to be true as others have shown no problems with the batteries.[4] The US Federal Trade Commission investigated in 2018[5] and lawsuit in 2019[6] revealed fraud. Apparently, the founder used the backers' money to buy Bitcoin and pay personal expenses.

15.2.2 Kobe Red—100% Japanese beer fed Kobe beef jerky

The Kobe Red[7] concept is an appealing one. If you have tasted traditional beef jerky and traditional Kobe beef, you can see clear potential for the high quality Kobe beef in

---

[2] https://www.indiegogo.com/projects/ibackpack-wifi-ultra-thin-powerful-batteries.

[3] https://www.kickstarter.com/projects/ibackpack/ibackpack-20-3g-4g-mi-fi-bulletproof-bluetooth-aud.

[4] http://crowdtoolz.com/sorry-ibackpack-backers-you-got-scammed/.

[5] https://www.theverge.com/circuitbreaker/2018/8/29/17793720/ftc-ibackpack-investigation-indiegogo-kickstarter.

[6] https://www.theverge.com/2019/5/6/18534423/ibackpack-ftc-lawsuit-complaint-indiegogo-kickstarter.

[7] https://www.kickstarter.com/projects/kobered/kobe-red-100-japanese-beer-fed-kobe-beef-jerky/description.

improving traditional beef jerky. The Kickstarter campaign attracted a lot of attention, securing pledges totaling $120,309 (and with a mere $2374 goal) from more than 3000 backers.

But Kickstarter closed the campaign just before it ended, so that the funds were never transferred to the founder, a company called "Magnus Fun." Kickstarter closed the project after collective efforts from the crowd (the "wisdom of the crowd"), including a documentary film maker, and comments revealed problems.[8] First, there were no pictures or videos of the founders identifying themselves. Second, the positive comments on the updates part of the Kickstarter campaign page were mainly from new account holders that had only previously backed unsuccessful campaigns. Third, the pledge requests from backers were notably very small relative to the costs of the rewards offerings, if those reward offerings were ever to be delivered.

15.2.3 Skarp Laser Razor

The Skarp Laser Razor originally campaigned on Kickstarter[9] and raised more than $4,005,111 (of a mere $160,000 goal) from 20,632 backers. It is easy to see why the product was popular, as it involved a shaver with a lazer to remove hair.

But was there actually a product? The funding was suspended by Kickstarter after it learned that the prototype product did not actually work (a requirement of Kickstarter). The company was banned by Kickstarter (and bans are never reversed, as highlighted by Kickstarter in the accouchement of this ban).[10]

Surprisingly,[11] after the Kickstarter ban, Skarp Laser Razor then created a new campaign on Indiegogo. The Indiegogo campaign was popular as well, albeit not as popular as the Kickstarter campaign, but nevertheless led to a $507,810 capital raise by 2787 backers in late 2015.[12]

The product was never delivered. Commentators on the web have noted as at October 2018 that the chief technology officer no longer works for Skarp based on a LinkedIn update.[13] Commentators continue to assert that the technology is more a pseudoscience, and the product will never be delivered.[14] It is a remarkable case, as Indiegogo backers appear to have had fair warning but nevertheless gave Skarp more than $500,000.

---

[8] https://money.cnn.com/2013/06/17/technology/kickstarter-scam-kobe-jerky/.

[9] https://www.kickstarter.com/projects/skarp/the-skarp-laser-razor-21st-century-shaving.

[10] https://www.digitaltrends.com/cool-tech/biggest-kickstarter-and-indiegogo-scams/.

[11] https://www.theverge.com/2015/10/13/9518163/laser-razor-kickstarter-banned-indiegogo.

[12] https://www.indiegogo.com/projects/the-skarp-laser-razor-21st-century-shaving#/.

[13] https://www.reddit.com/r/shittykickstarters/comments/9qcz90/skarp_laser_razor_unofficial_update_october_2018/.

[14] https://www.digitaltrends.com/cool-tech/biggest-kickstarter-and-indiegogo-scams/.

15.2.4 Triton

Similar to Skarp, Triton[15] is another pseudoscience product that offered liquid oxygen cylinders as a substitute for traditional scuba breathing gear. The campaign on Indiegogo was popular, leading to more than $900,000 in backing.[16]

But the product could not be made, since it was pseudoscience. And the company failed to consider regulatory approval requirements for the product. In 2016, the company had to acknowledge that the science did not work and had to pay the $900,000 it raised from their backers.[17] The $900,000 was transferred back to the backers prior directly from Indiegogo, since the acknowledgment that the product did not work came prior to the campaign's conclusion (i.e., no funds were ever transferred to the founders).[18]

Nevertheless, the company relaunched their campaign on Indiegogo, raising over $240,000 from a $50,000 funding goal.[19] The company continues to maintain an Indiegogo presence,[20] signaling confidence that they will eventually deliver this new similar product. The case reinforces the issue that, as with the Skarp case, Indiegogo backers can show strong support for promoters of entrepreneurs with proven failed products.

15.2.5 Elio Motors

Unlike the four prior cases of apparent fraud on reward-based crowdfunding platforms, the Elio Motors campaign was an equity crowdfunding campaign on StartEngine.[21] Elio Motors offered an electric car with up to 84 mi/gal at a target base price of $6800,[22] including over 65,000 that reserved a model ahead of time (thereby mixing rewards and equity crowdfunding).[23] The campaign attracted 6345 investors that invested $16,917,576 of a $25.1 million campaign goal.[24]

Unfortunately, the case is a classic case of basic moral hazard (Chapter 2: Overview of agency and signaling theory in crowdfunding). The company used the funds on

---

[15] https://www.indiegogo.com/projects/world-s-first-artificial-gills-oxygen-respirator--2/coming_soon.

[16] https://www.digitaltrends.com/cool-tech/triton-scuba-mask-indiegogo-possibly-hoax/.

[17] https://www.ibtimes.co.uk/triton-artificial-gills-creators-repay-nearly-900k-after-misleading-indiegogo-backers-1553086.

[18] https://www.reddit.com/r/shittykickstarters/comments/4zr6ej/what_happened_to_triton/.

[19] https://www.ibtimes.co.uk/triton-artificial-gills-creators-repay-nearly-900k-after-misleading-indiegogo-backers-1553086.

[20] https://www.indiegogo.com/projects/world-s-first-artificial-gills-oxygen-respirator--2/coming_soon.

[21] https://www.startengine.com/elio-motors; see also https://www.sec.gov/Archives/edgar/data/1661779/000114420418023766/tv492475_partii.htm.

[22] https://www.startengine.com/elio-motors; see also https://www.sec.gov/Archives/edgar/data/1661779/000114420418023766/tv492475_partii.htm.

[23] https://www.digitaltrends.com/cool-tech/biggest-kickstarter-and-indiegogo-scams/.

[24] https://www.startengine.com/elio-motors; see also https://www.sec.gov/Archives/edgar/data/1661779/000114420418023766/tv492475_partii.htm.

suspicious soft expenses (i.e., paychecks) within a few short months.[25] The release date of the product has been delayed for years, and most commentators are skeptical that the product will ever be delivered.[26]

15.2.6 Ascenergy

Ascenergy's[27] crowdfunding case is a similar example of the misuse of funds, as with the Elio Motors case, again highlighting basic moral hazard problems that we introduced in Chapter 2, Overview of agency and signaling theory in crowdfunding. Ascenergy is an oil and gas company that had solicited money on websites including Crowdfunder, Fundable, EquityNet, and Angel.co (AngelList).[28] Ascenergy raised $5,112,473 million equity crowdfunding in 2015 from 90 investors. The SEC accused the company of fraud, asserting that only $2000 was spent on oil and gas, while $3.8 million went to a company for web and mobile app development, $100,000 went to a company controlled by the CEO Joseph "Joey" Galbadon, and $1.2 payments seemed personal in nature, as the SEC stated[29]

> Ascenergy has raised at least approximately $5 million from 90 investors nationwide and internationally. Ascenergy has already spent at least $1.2 million of the offering proceeds, but only a few thousand dollars appear to have been used for oil and gas-related expenses. Instead, a significant part of the $1.2 million has been spent on payments to Galbadon or companies he controls, or for expenses unrelated to the oil & gas business, including, by way of example, foreign travel, fast food restaurants, Apple stores and iTunes, dietary supplements, and personal care products.

The full amount of capital raised had to be repaid with interest, and Gabaldon was held liable for a civil penalty of $320,000, while Ascenergy was liable for a civil penalty of $1,550,000.[30]

At the time of the decision, commentators such as the CEO of Crowdcheck[31] have asserted that platforms are liable in cases like this one only in the even that misleading statements can be attributable to the platform itself, including the content and whether

[25] http://laweconomicscapital.com/2017/01/crowdfunding-fraud-lessons-from-elio-motors/.

[26] http://laweconomicscapital.com/2017/01/crowdfunding-fraud-lessons-from-elio-motors/.

[27] https://www.crowdfundinsider.com/2015/12/77955-the-first-investment-crowdfunding-fraud-what-does-this-mean-for-the-industry/.

[28] https://www.crowdfundinsider.com/2015/11/76712-sec-calls-fraud-on-ascenergy-oil-gas-crowdfunding-scheme/. AngelList allows anyone to create a profile, but no money was raised by Ascenergy on AngelList. SeedInvest and Wefunder turned down Ascenergy's application to raise money on their platforms.

[29] https://www.crowdfundinsider.com/2015/12/77955-the-first-investment-crowdfunding-fraud-what-does-this-mean-for-the-industry/.

[30] https://www.crowdfundinsider.com/2017/08/120747-final-judgement-document-ascenergy-crowdfunding-fraud/.

[31] http://crowdcheck.com/.

it was communicated, and how it was communicated.[32] However, further guidance is provided in Section 15.2.8.

15.2.7 iFunding LLC

The first four[33] cases were examples of entrepreneurs carrying our alleged fraud on rewards crowdfunding platforms, and the fifth and sixth cases were examples of alleged fraud carried out by entrepreneurs raising money on equity crowdfunding platforms. The next two cases involve fraud from portals, not entrepreneurs.

iFunding is a real estate crowdfunding portal. The founders of the portal raised over $3 million from 42 investors across 17 US states to build the portal. The SEC charged the founders on September 26, 2018 with the misappropriation of the funds raised to build the portal.[34] Specifically, the SEC stated[35]

> From at least October 2013 to November 30, 2016, Skelley and Shah misappropriated investor funds. Skelley and Shah used the debit cards to make numerous purchases for personal items and services. These personal items and services included rent, food, beverages, trips, entertainment, dry cleaning, massages, and withdrawals of cash. None of these purchases or cash withdrawals were for iFunding's business operations. Skelley's and Shah's purchases and cash withdrawals were far in excess of any salary or deferred compensation owed to Skelley and Shah.

15.2.8 Dreamfunded

In the United States, under Title III of the JOBS Act, equity crowdfunding portals must be registered with the US Securities and Exchange Commission (SEC) either as a portal or under the more rigorous requirements as broker-dealers. In either case, the portals are obligated to take reasonable measures to protect investors through due diligence checks of the entrepreneurs that promote the sale of securities on their platform, and the information that they share. The Financial Industry Regulatory Authority (FINRA) has investigatory authority under Rule 8210 (as emphasized in the JOBS Act), and DreamFunded was the first time that Ryle 8210 was applied against a crowdfunding portal. FINRA's enforcement action against a crowdfunding portal was carried out on June 5, 2019.[36]

---

[32] https://www.crowdfundinsider.com/2015/12/77955-the-first-investment-crowdfunding-fraud-what-does-this-mean-for-the-industry/.

[33] https://www.sec.gov/litigation/litreleases/2018/lr24288.htm.

[34] https://www.crowdfundinsider.com/2018/09/139540-sec-lawsuit-against-real-estate-crowdfunding-platform-ifunding-alleges-fraud-scheme-to-misappropriate-investor-funds/; https://www.sec.gov/litigation/litreleases/2018/lr24288.htm.

[35] https://www.crowdfundinsider.com/2018/09/139540-sec-lawsuit-against-real-estate-crowdfunding-platform-ifunding-alleges-fraud-scheme-to-misappropriate-investor-funds/; https://www.sec.gov/litigation/litreleases/2018/lr24288.htm.

[36] See http://www.mondaq.com/unitedstates/x/818862/Financial + Services/FINRA + Issues + First + Litigated + Enforcement + Action + Against + Crowdfunding + Portal and https://www.fintechupdate.com/2019/06/finra-issues-first-litigated-enforcement-action-against-crowdfunding-portal/?utm_source = Mondaq&utm_medium = syndication&utm_campaign = View-Original.

The decision banned the founders from FINRA membership and fined $15,900 in hearing costs.[37]

The February 23, 2018 FINRA complaint alleged[38]

DreamFunded had (1) made false or misleading claims to investors about offerings promoted on the portal and about the portal itself, (2) continued to allow access to its platform even after it had reason to believe issuers presented the potential for fraud or investor protection concerns, (3) included issuer communications on its website that contained untrue or misleading facts, (4) lacked a reasonable basis for believing the issuers offering securities through its portal had complied with SEC regulations, (5) failed to provide required notice to investors regarding investment commitments, (6) failed to conduct required background checks, and (7) failed to reasonably supervise the activities of the portal.

FINRA's Funding Portal Rule 200(c)(2) prohibits funding portals from including false or misleading communications on the portal. It is noteworthy that FINRA concluded that requirement does not carry with it a requirement for *intent*.[39]

15.2.9 Dynamite Platforms

Dynamite Platforms[40] is a crowdfunding alternative dispute resolutions (ADR) platform. They offer "quick and effective solutions" to crowdfunding disputes by providing "a roster of mediators and arbitrators" specialized in crowdfunding ADR. Dynamite Platforms takes a percentage fee of "10%–15% of the collected amount, or $250,000, whichever is *higher*". Assessments of cases are free.

The emergence of online ADRs specialized in crowdfunding is interesting, as it highlights that the role of fintech in not merely fundraising but also in the provision of legal services. Further, it shows that the market believes legal costs are sufficiently high and that the provision of legal services can be disrupted in this manner. And just

---

[37] See http://www.mondaq.com/unitedstates/x/818862/Financial + Services/
FINRA + Issues + First + Litigated + Enforcement + Action + Against + Crowdfunding + Portal and
https://www.fintechupdate.com/2019/06/finra-issues-first-litigated-enforcement-action-against-crowdfunding-portal/?utm_source = Mondaq&utm_medium = syndication&utm_campaign = View-Original.

[38] See http://www.mondaq.com/unitedstates/x/818862/Financial + Services/FINRA + Issues +
First + Litigated + Enforcement + Action + Against + Crowdfunding + Portal and https://www.
fintechupdate.com/2019/06/finra-issues-first-litigated-enforcement-action-against-crowdfunding-portal/?
utm_source = Mondaq&utm_medium = syndication&utm_campaign = View-Original.

[39] See http://www.mondaq.com/unitedstates/x/818862/Financial + Services/
FINRA + Issues + First + Litigated + Enforcement + Action + Against + Crowdfunding + Portal and
https://www.fintechupdate.com/2019/06/finra-issues-first-litigated-enforcement-action-against-crowdfunding-portal/?utm_source = Mondaq&utm_medium = syndication&utm_campaign = View-Original. See also http://www.finra.org/sites/default/files/fda_documents/2017053428201%
20DreamFunded%20Marketplace%20CRD%20283594%20and%20Manuel%20Fernandez%20CRD%
206639970%20Extended%20Hearing%20Panel%20Decision%20va.pdf.

[40] http://www.dynamiteplatforms.com/crowdfundingadr/.

as entrepreneurs are matched with investors through platforms, so too can plaintiffs be matched with specialized crowdfunding ADR mediators and arbitrators.

15.3 Equity crowdfunding rules around the world

Equity crowdfunding rules are listed in Table 15.1 for 42 countries around the world, alongside their dates of implementation. Perhaps the most striking thing about Table 15.1 is that most countries (23 of 42) do not have specific crowdfunding rules. Instead, the general securities regulatory framework has been used to govern decision-making. Instead of discussing each of the crowdfunding rules where they have been adopted, here we discuss two countries in particular—the United States and Canada—as they recently introduced new rules as explained later. The interesting thing about comparing Canada and the United States is that the rule changes were adopted roughly at the same time, albeit with some differences that have had profoundly different implications for the market.

Equity crowdfunding in the United States was first legalized at the state level.[41] Kansas first legalized equity crowdfunding under the Invest Kansas Exemption Act (August 2011) followed by Invest Georgia Exemption Act (December 2011), by Idaho (July 2012),[42] Michigan (December 2013), and Wisconsin (November 2013). By 2015, equity crowdfunding was legalized in 17 states,[43] and another 14 states[44] had proposed rules or introduced bills on equity crowdfunding exemptions (Bohliqa, 2015), each with differing levels of exemptions, and the requirement that investors and entrepreneurs had to be residents in the state. Investors had to be accredited in all states (although there are differences as to the wealth or income requirement for accreditation),[45] and some states imposed limits on how much investors could invest into crowdfunded ventures which was also varied by the state.

Nationally, crowdfunding is governed by the JOBS Act, enacted on April 5, 2012. The SEC announced the nationwide adoption of Title III of the JOBS Act on October 30, 2015, which enabled nonaccredited investors to invest in equity crowdfunding projects. Title III of the JOBS Act became effective on May 16, 2016.[46] With the Regulation Crowdfunding (or "Regulation CF") exemption under the rules governing the

---

[41] Johan and Zhang (2019).

[42] Idaho's exemption on equity crowdfunding is based on administrative order.

[43] KS, GA, ID, MI, DC, TX, VT, AL, WA, WI, IN, MD, MR, MA, OR, TN, VA.

[44] NM, MS, CT, FL, HI, IA, KY, MN, NE, NH, NJ, NC, UT, WV.

[45] The one exception was Maine that allowed crowdfunding to nonaccredited investors.

[46] https://www.sec.gov/Archives/edgar/data/1661779/000114420418023766/tv492475_partii.htm.

TABLE 15.1 Overview of equity crowdfunding regulation over the world.

Country	Regulations
Australia	• No specific equity crowdfunding regulation • General securities regulation applicable • Pending proposal: The Corporations Amendment (Crowd-sourced Funding) Bill 2015
Austria	• Specific equity crowdfunding regulation is applicable—the Alternative Financing Act of September 1, 2015 (*Alternativfinanzierungsgesetz—EltFG*)
Belgium	• No specific equity crowdfunding regulation • General securities regulation applicable with several exemptions for crowdfunding, including the Act of April 25, 2014; the Act of July 17, 2013 (amending the Prospectus Act), and the Act on Alternative Investment Funds Managers (AIFM) of April 19, 2014 (implementing AIFM Directive) • Requires a prospectus for every public offering of securities unless they are bellow €300,000 per issuer within 12 months, a maximum of €1000 per project per investors • Registered cooperatives may collect up to €5,000,000
Brazil	• No specific equity crowdfunding regulation • General securities regulation applicable • Brazilian Securities and Exchange Commission published a public hearing on equity crowdfunding regulation in December 2016
Bulgaria	• No specific equity crowdfunding regulation • General securities regulation applicable—Public Offering of Securities Act • Requires a prospectus for every public offering of securities unless they are bellow €100,000

Canada	• Crowdfunding Exemptions are applicable, yet variable from province to province (see Table 15.2):
	  ◦ The start-up crowdfunding exemption (45-316) implemented in 2015 for SMEs to raise a maximum of $250,000 per campaign (maximum two campaigns per year, whereas an individual investor can invest $1500)
	  ◦ The integrated crowdfunding exemption (45-108) implemented in 2016 providing a higher funding ceiling for up to $1.5 million

China	• In 2015, several Chinese regulatory agencies jointly released the Guiding Opinions on Promoting the Healthy Development of Internet Finance that sets out general rules also for equity crowdfunding
Croatia	• No specific equity crowdfunding regulation • The Capital Market Act is strictly applicable • A license from the domestic Financial Services Supervisory Authority is mandatory for providing crowdfunding activities • Prospectus is necessary with certain exemptions
Cyprus	• No specific equity crowdfunding regulation • The Investment Services and Activities and Regulated Markets Law, Law 144(I)/2007 is applicable together with the Alternative Investment Fund Managers Law 56(I)/2013 and the Alternative Investment Funds, Law 131(I)/2014 • License is required for the platform operators under the Business of Credit Institutions Law 66/ • Prospectus is necessary with certain exemptions
Czech Republic	• No specific equity crowdfunding regulation • Act no. 256/2004 Coll., on capital markets, as well as the Act no. 284/2009 Coll., on payment services, are applicable and place a high regulatory burden on the crowdfunding platforms as they would have to be properly licensed by the Czech National Bank and would have to have at least €1,250,000 minimum capital • Prospectus is necessary with certain exemptions

(Continued)

TABLE 15.1 (Continued)

Country	Regulations
Denmark	• No specific equity crowdfunding regulation • Crowdfunding platforms are subject to a license requirement from the Financial Services Authority according to the Danish Securities Trading Act (Consolidated Act no. 831 of June 12, 2014) • Alternative Investment Fund Managers (Act no. 598 of June 12, 2013) and Danish Fundraising Act are also applicable • Prospectus is necessary with certain exemptions
Estonia	• No specific equity crowdfunding regulation • Estonian Securities Market Act is applicable • Crowdfunding platforms, under the Estonian Alternative Investment Funds Managers Directive (AIFMD), are deemed to provide investment services as securities brokers • Prospectus is necessary with certain exemptions
Finland	• Since September 1, 2016 the Finnish Crowdfunding Act is in force that covers specifically the equity crowdfunding • The Act introduces a special registry with the Finnish Financial Supervisory Authority; crowdfunding intermediaries are not required to join the Investors' Compensation Fund and the capital requirement was reduced from €125,000 to €50,000 • Prospectus has to be published only for fundraising securities exceeding €5 million
France	• On October 1, 2014 the Ordinance no 2014-559 introduced the new regulatory framework together with two statutes, (1) IFP for the loan crowdfunding and (2) CIP for equity and bond crowdfunding • Equity platforms must be registered as CIP and the maximum amount that can be raised is €1 million • Since 2015, even the local authorities may use crowdfunding to finance projects
Germany	• In 2015 Germany adopted the Small Investor Protection Act regulating the crowdfunding activities, laying down the licensing requirements, exemptions for platforms from the German financial supervisory authority (BaFin) • The act established two regimes for investments up to €1000 and of more to an absolute €10,000 per investor without differentiating between different types of investors. It further limits the advertisement and specifies the prospectus requirements • Additional changes of the act have been discussed
Greece	• No specific equity crowdfunding regulation • Act no 3606/2007 is applicable for crowdfunding activities as investment services and transaction of investment activities • Prospectus has to be published for the offering exceeding €100,000 within a period of 12 months
Hong Kong	• No specific equity crowdfunding regulation, however, in 2015−16 budget speech the HK Financial Secretary set out the intention to undertake a special crowdfunding regulation
Hungary	• No specific equity crowdfunding regulation • Crowdfunding platforms are subject to investment services requirements under the Hungarian Investment Services Act; license from the Hungarian supervisory authority is required • If a crowdfunding undertaking structures as Alternative Investment Funds (AIF), it must comply with the requirements under the Collective Investment Schemes Act • Prospectus has to be published for the offering exceeding €100,000 within a period of 12 months
Iceland	• No specific equity crowdfunding regulation • General securities regulation are applicable
India	• Equity crowdfunding is illegal according to a consultation paper of SEBI in 2014. However, there have been recent statements that the SEBI plans to introduce a regulatory framework for equity crowdfunding for SMEs

(Continued)

TABLE 15.1   (Continued)

Country	Regulations
Ireland	• No specific equity crowdfunding regulation; AIFMD regulations may be applicable • Prospectus is necessary in the case of a public offering of any transferable securities with certain exemptions
Israel	• The ISA is preparing a new regulation and registry for crowdfunding platforms (offering coordinators). The law should be adopted in 2017
Italy	• Italy adopted in 2012 law no. 221/2012, in 2015 law no. 33/2015 and regulation no. 18592/2013 applicable to equity crowdfunding platforms • The Italian securities market authority (CONSOB) carries out oversight • Equity crowdfunding is limited only to (1) innovative start-ups, (2) innovative SMEs and (3) collective investment undertakings and investment companies, which invest in the innovative start-ups and innovative SMEs • Italian AIFMD does not apply to crowdfunding • Exception from prospectus requirements for public offers through an authorized platform up to €5,000,000
Japan	• Equity crowdfunding is subject to self-regulatory rules of the Japan Securities Dealers Association • In 2014, Japan revised the Japan FIEA and crowdfunding became legal for fundraising not exceeding ¥100 million per issuer and the amount of funds contributed per investor to an issuer must not exceed ¥500,000 per year. The regulation further governs the issues of the nature of the information via website, submission of periodical information, and reporting
Latvia	• No specific equity crowdfunding regulation; however, legislative discussion in place
Lithuania	• A new law on crowdfunding entered into force on December 1, 2016, which governs the requirements for the initiation of crowdfunding activities, prudential requirements for the platform operators, and lays down the conditions for raising funds through crowdfunding • Supervision is carried out by Bank of Lithuania
Luxembourg	• No specific equity crowdfunding regulation; however, legislative discussion in place • Crowdfunding platform would be considered as an AIF and thus the AIFMD could apply and licensing might be required
Malta	• No specific equity crowdfunding regulation • General securities regulation applicable • Crowdfunding platform would be considered as providing an investment service and thus would fall under the Investment Services Act (1994); also the AIFMD Regulation would be also applicable
The Netherlands	• On April 1, 2016, the Dutch Ministry of Finance published the new crowdfunding decree • A platform is considered to be an investment firm and is required to obtain a MiFID license • In regard to prospectus exemption, the threshold has been set to €2,500,000 for crowdfunding platform fundraising, provided that a prescribed warning text is included in any offering
New Zealand	• On April 1, 2014 the regulation of crowdfunding platforms—"CSPs" was introduced • CSPs are required to register and may only raise maximum of NZ $2 million in any 12-month period. They are required to carry out their due diligence and provide issuers with vetted information • The supervisory authority is the Financial Markets Authority provides licenses to CSPs and oversees the market
Poland	• No specific equity crowdfunding regulation • General securities regulation applicable
Portugal	• Since August 24, 2015, the crowdfunding activity is regulated by a law no. 102/2015 • The law requires the crowdfunding platforms to register with the Portuguese Securities Market Commission that also is carrying out supervision

(Continued)

TABLE 15.1 (Continued)

Country	Regulations
	• Platforms are responsible for providing investors with information and must comply with rules in respect of conflict of interest. The law distinguishes between nonaccredited and accredited investors
Romania	• No specific equity crowdfunding regulation • General securities regulation applicable
Russia	• No specific equity crowdfunding regulation • Central Bank of Russia has initiated working group for proposal of crowdfunding regulation
Singapore	• Equity crowdfunding is subject to the Securities and Futures Act, governing both a platform operator as well as an issuer, requiring license for the operators and laying down several advertising restrictions • In 2016, the Consultation Paper of the MAS proposes that equity crowdfunding is restricted to accredited and institutional investors
Slovakia	• No specific equity crowdfunding regulation • General securities regulation applicable
Slovenia	• No specific equity crowdfunding regulation • General securities regulation applicable
Spain	• Law no. 5/2015 of April 27, 2015 to promote the business financing governs crowdfunding activities • Platforms have to register with the market authority (*Comisión Nacional del Mercado de Valores*) • Law differentiates between qualified and nonqualified investors and stipulates the maximum of their respective investments • Exception from prospectus requirements for public offers through an authorized platform up to €5,000,000 in a 12-month period
Sweden	• No specific equity crowdfunding regulation • General securities regulation applicable (MiFID)
Switzerland	• No specific equity crowdfunding regulation • General securities regulation applicable
United Kingdom	• The Financial Services and Markets Act 2000 is applicable for crowdfunding activities, requiring platforms to be licensed • The Act distinguishes between sophisticated and nonsophisticated investors and lays down restrictions for nonsophisticated • The Financial Conduct Authority oversees the crowdfunding activity • In regard to prospectus exemption, the threshold has been set to €5,000,000 for crowdfunding platform fundraising within 12-month period
United States	• Crowdfunding is governed by the Jumpstart Our Business Startups Act, enacted on April 5, 2012 • In 2015 the SEC adopted amendments to Regulation A to the Securities Act 1933 and in May 2016, the SEC introduced new equity crowdfunding rules • Portals have to become members of FINRA and the amounts of possible investments of accredited and nonaccredited investors have been established

CIP, Conseiller en Investissement Participatif; *CSP*, crowdfunding service provider; *FIEA*, Financial Instruments and Exchange Act; *IFP*, Intermédiarie en Financement Participatif; *ISA*, Israel Securities Authority; *MAS*, Monetary Authority of Singapore; *SEBI*, Securities and Exchange Board of India; *SEC*, Securities and Exchange Commission; *SMEs*, small and medium-sized enterprises.
Reproduced from Horváthová, A. (2019). Chapter 28, Crowdfunding: Business and regulatory perspective. In Cumming D. J., & Johan S. (Eds.), Oxford handbook of IPOs. Oxford: Oxford University Press, for which we are much indebted to allowing us to reproduce this table. Horváthová (2019) acknowledges sources as follows: Used data from Current State of Crowdfunding in Europe. (2016). CrowdfundingHub. Amsterdam, The Netherlands; Osborne Clarke Germany. (2016). Review of crowdfunding regulation & market developments. In CrowdFundRES – Unleashing the potential of Crowdfunding for Financing Renewable Energy Projects; *Zhang, B., Baeck, P., Ziegler, T., Bone, J., & Garvey, K. (2016). Pushing boundaries: The 2015 UK alternative finance industry report. Cambridge Centre for Alternative Finance, pp. 31–46 and additional sources found in reference list.*

crowdfunding portals (discussed earlier; see Section 15.2.8). Prior to Regulation CF, from June 2015, companies could raise capital under Regulation A, which afforded an exemption from traditional registration requirements for offerings that did not exceed $50 million in a given 1-year period.[47]

The adoption of these crowdfunding rules in the United States has led to the successful creation of a vibrant marketplace in the United States. See Table 8.1 of this book for a listing of a number of different platforms in the United States and their fundraising volume.

The United States experience sharp contrast with the Canadian experience with the adoption of equity crowdfunding rules. Amazingly, no one has raised money in Canada using the equity crowdfunding exemptions.[48] There are a number of reasons why. Unlike the United States, with a national securities regulator, Canada has a different securities commission in each province. And the crowdfunding exemptions differ across each of the provinces.

As shown in Table 15.2, Canada has three specific crowdfunding exemptions: (1) The "integrated crowdfunding exemption [NI 45-108]," (2) the start-up crowdfunding

---

[47] More specifically, Regulation A + created two distinct fundraising tiers (see, e.g., https://www.moneycrashers.com/equity-crowdfunding-sites-investors-entrepreneurs/ and more directly from the SEC https://www.sec.gov/oiea/investor-alerts-bulletins/ib_regulationa.html):

- "Tier 1 companies can raise up to $20 million in any 12-month period. Each company must provide all prospective investors with a formal offering circular filed with and reviewed by the SEC and applicable state regulators in the company's home jurisdiction. Tier 1 offerings aren't subject to ongoing reporting requirements or audit by independent accountants. The required offering circulars are therefore the most important and complete sources of information about Tier 1 opportunities."
- "Tier 2 companies can raise up to $50 million in any 12-month period. As with Tier 1 offerings, formal offering circulars are required. Tier 2 offerings are subject to ongoing reporting requirements: semiannual reports, annual reports, and reports around certain "enumerated events" such as a change in control or bankruptcy. Tier 2 offerings are also subject to audit by external, independent accountants."

"The SEC defines accredited investors as individuals who consistently earn more than $200,000 per year, couples with consistent combined income of more than $300,000 per year, and individuals whose net worth (excluding primary residence) is at least $1 million."
"There are no limitations on non-accredited investors' access to Tier 1 offerings..."
"There are some limitations on non-accredited investors' access to Tier 2 offerings. Non-accredited investors can invest no more than 10% of their net income (individually or jointly with a spouse) or 10% of their net worth (excluding primary residence) in Tier 2 offerings."

[48] https://www.crowdfundinsider.com/2016/07/88484-dead-in-the-water-canadas-crowdfunding-exemptions/.

TABLE 15.2 A case of regulatory fragmentation and failure: the Canadian crowdfunding exemptions.

	Adoption date	Main issues with the exemption	Manitoba, New Brunswick, Nova Scotia, Quebec, and Saskatchewan	British Columbia	Ontario	Alberta
Start-up crowdfunding exemptions	May-15	The issuer offers the securities during the distribution period that ends no later than 90 days after the date the issuer first offers its securities to purchasers [Section 5(1)(a), MI 45-108] The total proceeds raised by an issuer group under the equity crowdfunding exemption does not exceed $1.5 million within the 12-month period ending on the last day of the distribution period [Section 5(1)(b), MI 45-108] Investors are subject to the following investment limits: an investor that does not qualify as an accredited investor: $2500 per investment; and in Ontario, $10,000 in total in a calendar year An accredited investor other than a permitted client (institutional investors): $25,000 per investment; and in Ontario, $50,000 in total in a calendar year	Yes	Yes	No	No
Integrated crowdfunding exemption	Jan-16	Issuers can raise up to $2 million, but with the added requirement of audited financial statements. The rule requires issuers to provide financial statements which are (1) audited or reviewed by a public accounting firm if the cumulative amount an issuer has raised under any securities exemption since its formation is $250,000 or more but is less than $750,000, or (2) audited if the cumulative amount an issuer has raised under any securities exemptions since its formation is $750,000 or more	Yes	No	No	No
Start-up business exemption	Jun-16	The head office of the issuer must be located in Alberta. The issuer, including other members of its "issuer group," cannot raise in aggregate more than $250,000 per distribution. The issuer group is also limited to two start-up business distributions in a calendar year The aggregate lifetime amount that an issuer group can raise under all start-up business distributions is $1,000,000 Generally, the maximum amount that an issuer can accept as a subscription from an investor in a start-up business distribution is $1500. However, if a registered dealer provides the investor advice that the investment is suitable to the investor, the maximum subscription from that investor is $5000	No	No	No	Yes

exemption[49] [CSA notice 45-316], and (3) the start-up business exemption [ASC Rule

[49] The Crowdfunding exemption in Canada, available from June 2015, allows for the following (as copied from the source: https://ca.practicallaw.thomsonreuters.com/5-622-1385? transitionType = Default&contextData = (sc.Default)&firstPage = true&bhcp = 1):

Crowdfunding exemption

Section 5(1) of *Multilateral Instrument 45-108 — Crowdfunding* (MI 45-108) provides that a *distribution* by an issuer of eligible *securities* of its own issue to a person or company that purchases the security as principal is exempt from the *prospectus* requirements of *Applicable Securities Laws* in Manitoba, Ontario, Quebec, New Brunswick and Nova Scotia, if all of the following apply:

- The issuer offers the securities during the distribution period and the distribution period ends no later than 90 days after the date the issuer first offers its securities to purchasers [Section 5(1)(a), MI 45-108].
- The total proceeds raised by an issuer group under the equity crowdfunding exemption does not exceed $1.5 million within the 12-month period ending on the last day of the distribution period [Section 5(1)(b), MI 45-108].
- Investors are subject to the following investment limits:
- An investor that does not qualify as an *accredited investor*:
  - $2500 per investment and
  - in Ontario, $10,000 in total in a calendar year.
- An accredited investor other than a *permitted client* (institutional investors):
  - $25,000 per investment; and
  - in Ontario, $50,000 in total in a calendar year.
- In Ontario, no investment limits for a permitted client.
    [Sections 5(1)(c) and (d), MI 45-108]
- The issuer must distribute the securities through a single funding portal [Section 5(1)(e), MI 45-108].
- Before the purchaser enters into an agreement to purchase the securities, the issuer makes available to the purchaser, through the funding portal, a crowdfunding offering document that is in compliance with:
  - Section 7 (Certificates) and Section 8 (Right of withdrawal); and
  - Section 9 (Liability for misrepresentation — reporting issuers) or Section 10 (Liability for untrue statement — non-reporting issuers), as applicable.
      [Section 5(1)(f), MI 45-108]
      Section 5(2) of MI 45-108 indicates circumstances when the exemption is not available:
  - The proceeds of the distribution may not be used by the issuer to invest in, merge with or acquire an unspecified business [Section 5(2)(a), MI 45-108].
  - If the issuer is not a reporting issuer and previously distributed securities in reliance on the crowdfunding exemption, it must be in compliance with all of the disclosure requirements in Section 15 (Filing or delivery of distribution materials), Section 16 (Annual financial statements), Section 17 (Annual disclosure of use of proceeds), Section 19 (Period of time for providing ongoing disclosure), Section 20 (Books and records), and in New Brunswick, Nova Scotia and Ontario, Section 18 (Notice of specified key events) [Section 5(2)(b), MI 45-108].
  - If the issuer is a reporting issuer, it must be in compliance with its reporting obligations under securities legislation, including under MI 45-108 [Section 5(2)(c), MI 45-108].
  - If the issuer has previously commenced a distribution under the crowdfunding exemption, it must have closed, been withdrawn or otherwise terminated [Section 5(2)(d), MI 45-108].
      The following are additional requirements in MI 45-108 in order to rely on the exemption:
- The issuer and, if applicable, its parent are incorporated or organized under the laws of Canada or any jurisdiction of Canada.

45-517] that was adopted in Alberta.[50] Canadian issuers can also use the accredited

- The issuer's head office must be located in Canada.
- A majority of the directors of the issuer must be resident in Canada.
- The principal operating subsidiary of the issuer, if any, must be incorporated or organized under either:
  - the laws of Canada or any jurisdiction of Canada; or
  - the laws of the United States of America or any state or territory of the United States of America or the District of Columbia.
- The issuer cannot be an *investment fund*.
- The funding portal must be registered under *National Instrument 31-103 – Registration Requirements, Exemptions and Ongoing Registrant Obligations* (NI 31-103) as either:
  - an *investment dealer* and acts or proposes to act as an intermediary in a distribution of eligible securities through an online platform in reliance on the crowdfunding prospectus exemption; or
  - a *restricted dealer* that is authorized under the terms and conditions of its restricted dealer registration to distribute securities under MI 45-108, acts or proposes to act as an intermediary in a distribution of eligible securities through an online platform in reliance on the crowdfunding prospectus exemption, is not registered in any other registration category, and, in Ontario, is not an affiliate of another registered *dealer*, registered *adviser*, or registered *investment fund manager* (Section 1, MI 45-108).
- A restricted dealer funding portal and a registered individual of the restricted dealer funding portal that distributes securities in reliance on the crowdfunding exemption must comply with all of the following:
  - the requirements of Section 21 and Divisions 2 and 3 of Part 3 of MI 45-108 [Section 21(a), MI 45-108];
  - the terms, conditions, restrictions and requirements applicable to a registered dealer and to a registered individual, respectively, as specified (with exceptions) in Section 21(b), MI 45-108;
  - the requirement to deal fairly, honestly and in good faith with purchasers [Section 21(c), MI 45-108];
  - any other terms, conditions, restrictions or requirements imposed by a securities regulatory authority on the restricted dealer funding portal or on a registered individual of the restricted dealer funding portal [Section 21(d), MI 45-108].
- A registered dealer funding portal and a registered individual of the registered dealer funding portal that distributes securities in reliance on the crowdfunding exemption must comply with all of the following:
  - the requirements in Section 22 and Division 2 of Part 3 of MI 45-108 [Section 22(a), MI 45-108] and
  - the terms, conditions, restrictions or requirements applicable to its registration category and to a registered individual, respectively, under securities legislation [Section 22(b), MI 45-108].

[50] As quoted from Pushor Mitchell, LLP, https://www.pushormitchell.com/2016/08/alberta-securities-commission-introduces-start-up-business-exemption/:
Included among the key conditions of the start-up business exemption are the following:

- The head office of the issuer must be located in Alberta (or, in certain circumstances, a corresponding jurisdiction).
- The issuer must prepare an offering document in the required form, which includes certain information about its business, its management, and the offering, including how it intends to use the funds raised, and the minimum offering amount.
- The issuer, including other members of its "issuer group," cannot raise in aggregate more than $250,000 per distribution. The issuer group is also limited to two start-up business distributions in a calendar year.
- The aggregate lifetime amount that an issuer group can raise under all start-up business distributions is $1,000,000.

investor exemption and the offering memorandum exemption, which is similar to Regulation A + in the United States (described previously).

The different rules in Canada, and their lack of harmonization, coupled with a relatively small population of 37 million people (compared to 327 million in the United States) creates problems of a small deharmonized market, as well as confusion among issuers and investors alike. Further, the capital gaps on issuers and investors make it difficult to justify. Particularly for the integrated crowdfunding exemption, the permanent audited financial statement requirements are a costly barrier for a low capital raise (CAN$2 million in Canada; compared with $20 and $50 million in the United States[51]).

The fact that no one has used the integrated crowdfunding exemption in Canada and scantly anyone has used the start-up crowdfunding exemption in Canada[52] has been

- Generally, the maximum amount that an issuer can accept as a subscription from an investor in a start-up business distribution is $1500. However, if a registered dealer provides the investor advice that the investment is suitable to the investor, the maximum subscription from that investor is $5000.
- If the distribution is made through a funding portal, the portal must be a registered dealer.
- The issuer must provide purchasers with a 48-hour period in which to cancel their agreement to purchase securities.
- The issuer must provide each investor with a specified form clearly explaining certain risks of investing and must obtain an acknowledgment from each investor that they have read and understood the contents of that form.

Importantly, ASC Rule 45-517 does not include a registration exemption. If a person or company is in the business of dealing in securities in Alberta, including as a funding portal, they will be required to comply with the registration requirement.

[51] More specifically, Regulation A + created two distinct fundraising tiers (see, e.g., https://www. moneycrashers.com/equity-crowdfunding-sites-investors-entrepreneurs/ and more directly from the SEC https://www.sec.gov/oiea/investor-alerts-bulletins/ib_regulationa.html):

- "Tier 1 companies can raise up to $20 million in any 12-month period. Each company must provide all prospective investors with a formal offering circular filed with and reviewed by the SEC and applicable state regulators in the company's home jurisdiction. Tier 1 offerings aren't subject to ongoing reporting requirements or audit by independent accountants. The required offering circulars are therefore the most important and complete sources of information about Tier 1 opportunities."
- "Tier 2 companies can raise up to $50 million in any 12-month period. As with Tier 1 offerings, formal offering circulars are required. Tier 2 offerings are subject to ongoing reporting requirements: semiannual reports, annual reports, and reports around certain "enumerated events" such as a change in control or bankruptcy. Tier 2 offerings are also subject to audit by external, independent accountants."

"The SEC defines accredited investors as individuals who consistently earn more than $200,000 per year, couples with consistent combined income of more than $300,000 per year, and individuals whose net worth (excluding primary residence) is at least $1 million."
"There are no limitations on non-accredited investors' access to Tier 1 offerings..."
"There are some limitations on non-accredited investors' access to Tier 2 offerings. Non-accredited investors can invest no more than 10% of their net income (individually or jointly with a spouse) or 10% of their net worth (excluding primary residence) in Tier 2 offerings."

[52] https://www.crowdfundinsider.com/2016/07/88484-dead-in-the-water-canadas-crowdfunding-exemptions/.

noticed by regulators, industry participants, the National Crowdfunding and fintech Association of Canada, and media.[53] There is a current push to harmonize rules; however, the problems with fragmented securities commissions in Canada are not limited to crowd-funding, and despite repeated attempts to harmonize or nationalize securities regulators in Canada,[54] fragmentation persists.

In Chapter 16, Demand-driven crowdfunding regulation, of this book, we examine further evidence from Canada on demand-driven securities regulation based on statistical evidence.

15.4 Surveillance and enforcement

Securities regulation is ineffective without surveillance and enforcement. At the level of stock exchanges, there exist computerized algorithms that detect manipulative trading patterns in real-time.[55] One example is the SMARTS[56] system used at NASDAQ[57] and many other exchanges and regulators around the world. A similar albeit different SMARTS system is likewise used by market participants themselves to monitor trading activity of employees. Algorithms developed by SMARTS can detect problems of pump-and-dump (hyping a stock to only sell it shortly thereafter at a profit) front-running (trading in front of client orders), spoofing (entering orders and deleting them before they execute to give the appearance of a substantial order book), and wash trades (same client reference on both sides of the trade), among other things (Alexander & Cumming, 2020).[58]

But fraud detection on stock exchanges involves various other factors than fraud detection in private financings. For crowdfunding a different type of approach is needed to give rise to prediction models for fraud. If successfully developed, crowdfunding fraud-detection models could be used to better inform regulatory design and surveillance efforts.

One starting point for fraud detection in crowdfunding is the trust triangle or fraud triangle (Albrecht, 2014; Dupont & Karpoff, 2019). In other settings, for example, the Trust Triangle explains the successful development of other forms of private financings, including but not limited to cross-border venture capital transactions (Hain, Johan, & Wang, 2016), for example. The trust triangle puts for the idea that ex ante it is possible to invest in accountability and build trust with other agents with a three pronged approach: (1) *legal liability*, which in the crowdfunding setting would include regulatory rules specific to crowdfunding as well as general securities rules and rules for investor protection,

[53] https://www.crowdfundinsider.com/2019/02/144770-finally-canadian-securities-administrators-announce-intent-to-harmonize-improve-crowdfunding-exemption/.

[54] See, for example, https://www.fin.gc.ca/wise-averties/main_-eng.asp.

[55] For a discussion, see Cumming and Johan (2008, 2018), Cumming, Johan, and Li (2011).

[56] https://www.bloomberg.com/profile/company/0373005D:AU.

[57] https://business.nasdaq.com/market-tech/marketplaces/market-surveillance; NASDAQ acquired SMARTS https://www.marlinllc.com/transactions/recent/smarts-was-acquired-by-nasdaq-omx.

[58] https://www.amazon.ca/Corruption-Fraud-Financial-Markets-Manipulation/dp/1119421772.

(2) *reputation*, which in the crowdfunding setting would include concern with reputation on behalf of crowdfunding platforms and legal and reputational penalties in the event of breaches, and (3) *personal ethics*, which in the crowdfunding setting would include the development of a culture of fair dealing.

Based on the trust triangle, Cumming, Hornuf, Karami, and Schweizer (2016) theorized that fraud in crowdfunding markets would be related to entrepreneur's characteristics, their presence in the crowd, and their campaign structure on the crowdfunding platform. To test this idea, Cumming et al. examined hundreds of thousands of rewards crowdfunding campaigns from Kickstarter and Indiegogo in many countries around the world. It is notable that on a broad definition of fraud (including clearly fraudulent campaigns, such as that of Kobe Red in Section 15.2.2, as well as suspected fraud cases such as those where the promoter stopped communicating with the crowd), there were only 207 fraud cases. This frequency of fraud is lower than that which is observed on public stock exchanges; Cumming, Dannhauser, and Johan (2015) report that approximately 2.5% of companies trading on the New York Stock Exchange and 4.5% of companies trading on NASDAQ experience SEC enforcement actions each year.

The evidence in Cumming, Hornuf, Karmai, and Schweizer (2016) shows four broad classes of factors that are correlated with crowdfunding fraud: the entrepreneurs' characteristics, social media affinity, campaign funding and reward structure, and campaign description. First, fraudsters are typically only using crowdfunding once. Repeat crowdfunders are much less likely to be fraudsters. Second, fraudsters are typically less likely to be on social media such as Facebook, Twitter, and LinkedIn. This evidence is similar to the Kobe Red case (Section 15.2.2) where fraudsters did not identify themselves in videos or photos. Third, fraudulent campaigns have more enticements in their reward structures on average. Incentives to participate can entice the crowd irrespective of the underlying quality of the project. Recall again the Kobe Red case where there were lots of enticements, and the crowd noticed (wisdom of the crowd) that the cost of the rewards seem large relative to the requested level of backing. Finally, Cumming et al.'s evidence shows that fraudsters tend to have poorly worded campaign descriptions. Poorly worded campaigns may be due to the fact that the average fraudster may have been less fortunate with prior experiences in life; alternatively, the lack of personal passion with honestly developing a new idea shows up in part with spending less time and effort on developing a properly worded campaign pitch. In either case, the effect is the same.

Evidence such as that from Cumming et al. (2016) could be developed further to enhance real-time fraud-detection models prior to the completion of crowdfunding campaigns. Fraud-detection models could check for social media presence, unusual reward structures and promises, and use text-mining software to check the quality of text descriptions. There could be other angles through which a surveillance models could be refined developed to assess the likelihood of campaign fraud prior to the completion of a campaign. Such models would better aid due diligence checks on behalf of platforms and better guide securities regulators surveillance and enforcement efforts. For example, with the enormous volume of cases so far that mix empirical outcomes with text and online presence, artificial intelligence tools could be used to fine tune real-time surveillance in crowdfunding. And surveillance along these lines could be linked across markets, that is, across countries and across different types of markets within a country.

Moreover, crowdfunding fraud-prediction models could in turn better inform the development of crowdfunding rules to see where appropriate limits or bans should be set. For example, with a better understanding of the likelihood of the frequency and severity of fraud, a more empirically informed regulator could use fraud-prediction models to more efficiently set capital raising limits like those imposed in Canada, the United States, and elsewhere (Section 15.4). Further work is warranted that better integrates lessons from statistics, artificial intelligence, academics, practice, and policymaking.

15.5 Summary, conclusion, and roadmap for Part IV of this book

This chapter presented a number of different types of crowdfunding fraud cases from rewards and equity crowdfunding, as well as fraud carried about by crowdfunding portal operators. The cases of crowdfunding clearly suggest that crowdfunding risks are pronounced, and as such regulation is needed. We provided an overview of the regulatory structure in 42 countries around the world, and we showed how the introduction of specific crowdfunding rules has led to the successful development of an equity crowdfunding market in the United States, while the contemporaneous introduction of a different set of rules that were fragmented within Canada and more restrictive led to a failed attempt to create an equity crowdfunding market. The sharp distinction for these two closely connected countries in terms of geography, economics, and perhaps to a lesser extent culture shows how regulatory design can profoundly impact crowdfunding success.

We reviewed empirical evidence in this chapter on the frequency of crowdfunding fraud. To date, fraud has been much less common in crowdfunding markets than that which is observed on public stock exchanges. While there may have not yet been enough time that has passed for all of the cases of fraud to come to light, the implication of the dearth of fraud in crowdfunding is striking. Disclosure requirements in securities regulation are extremely expensive and have been put in place to curtail fraud. Concern with crowdfunding has been the raising of capital without proper disclosure. Without exemptions from disclosure requirements, crowdfunding would be impossible because the capital raises are normally less than the costs of disclosure. But the absence of costly disclosure has not given rise to rates of fraud that exist in the public markets that have rules for costly disclosure. To this end, the "wisdom of the crowd" in crowdfunding appears to be working so far.

Much work needs to be done to integrate surveillance efforts and best practices that combine statistics, data mining, academics, artificial intelligence, and policymaking. Although there has only been limited work to date, that work is consistent with the idea that fraud in crowdfunding markets is predictable. With more evidence and resources, refinements could be used to detect fraud on a real-time basis to prevent (or at least mitigate the frequency of) the distribution of capital to fraudulent entrepreneurs at the end of a crowdfunding campaign.

The remaining chapters provide further insights into the causes and consequences of regulation in crowdfunding, and in fintech more generally. Chapter 16, Demand-driven crowdfunding regulation, discusses the rule-formation process in crowdfunding. We consider the traditional race-to-the-top versus race-to-the-bottom question in regulatory competition: do platforms, investors, and entrepreneurs gravitate to regulatory design that accommodates investor protection, or scant regulation? This perspective is instructive to understand how crowdfunding rules may evolve over time and informs regulators on the extent to which they should pay attention to comments from market participants on how crowdfunding regulations should be designed.

Chapters 17–19 take a broader approach that extends beyond rewards and equity crowdfunding. Crowdfunding does not operate on an isolated island separate from other segments in the market. Chapter 17, Public policy towards entrepreneurial finance: spillovers and scale-up, considers how crowdfunding is just one form of entrepreneurial finance. Policies exist not just in terms of regulatory design but also other government spending initiatives to stimulate entrepreneurial finance, including but not limited to angel finance and venture capital. Is crowdfunding a substitute for or a complement with other forms of entrepreneurial finance? We review the evidence in Chapter 17, Public policy towards entrepreneurial finance: spillovers and scale-up, and argue that the best way to stimulate entrepreneurial finance is to consider the portfolio of programs offered in a region and how different forms of finance should be integrated to most efficiently enable small entrepreneurial firms to access capital and scale-up to become successful large firms.

Chapter 18, Regulation and investment in fintech ventures, focuses on fintech more generally, and how fintech investments have evolved around the world. Entrepreneurial fintech start-ups have frequently complained, as noted in widely circulated media, that they face stringent rules that are costly to comply with. Regulatory costs can be relatively "fixed" insofar as compliance costs are at a certain level regardless of whether or not a firm is large or small. Such regulatory costs are therefore relatively more onerous to small firms without the resources to efficiently comply with those costs; for example, regulatory costs/assets is a much smaller ratio for a small firm than a large firm. In some ways, the Canadian experience with crowdfunding regulation described in Section 15.3 is an illustrative example. As such, fintech start-ups may be incentivized to pursue entrepreneurial opportunities in jurisdictions with less regulatory enforcement. Chapter 18, Regulation and investment in fintech ventures, discusses the theory and provides large sample evidence from venture capital fintech investments around the world.

Chapter 19, Crypto regulation, the final chapter in part IV of this book, focuses on the topic of cryptocurrency regulation. Cryptocurrencies are a type of crowdfunding, albeit quite different from the rewards and equity-based crowdfunding and marketplace lending that have comprised the other chapters in this book. In the more common form, cryptocurrencies are an alternative medium of exchange facilitated by blockchain. But cryptocurrencies can also be tied into other forms of crowdfunding and social media. For example, a new venture based in Toronto, Whatrocks Foundation,[59] integrates crowdfunding of social change with empowering consumers to direct advertising dollars. Whatrocks is able to do this using their own cryptocurrency token called Rocks.[60] This innovation linking cryptocurrencies to crowdfunding and impact advertising with empowered consumers has the potential to disrupt digital advertising. Innovations like this one are worth watching as

[59] https://www.whatrocks.co/en/about-whatrocks-foundation.

[60] https://www.whatrocks.co/en/about-whatrocks-foundation. See also https://medium.com/@marclijour/social-innovation-and-the-blockchain-ed862ba75823.

time develops. Chapter 19, Crypto regulation, reviews the fast changing regulatory environment surrounding cryptocurrencies. Policy and practice in crowdfunding are likely to be more closely connected with the evolution of blockchain technologies and regulation and will shape innovations in and around crowdfunding over time.

Key terms

Compliance costs
Detection
Disclosure
Enforcement
Fragmentation
Fraud
Regulatory harmonization
Securities regulation
Surveillance

Discussion questions

15.1. How common is specific crowdfunding regulation around the world? Which countries have successfully introduced crowdfunding regulation that has facilitated market development? Which countries have been less successful with the introduction of crowdfunding regulation? What are some of the factors that comprise a successful regulatory system for crowdfunding versus an unsuccessful system? Among successful systems, are there nevertheless areas of potential improvement in regulatory design?

15.2. How common is fraud in crowdfunding markets? How common is fraud amongst firms listed on stock exchanges? What accounts for differences in rates of fraud in different types of markets for raising capital?

15.3. What affects fraud in crowdfunding? Explain why with reference to theory and evidence. What tools might be used to better detect fraud in crowdfunding?

Demand-driven crowdfunding regulation

Ontario examines ways to loosen crowdfunding rules **The Globe and Mail, November 29, 2012**
Regulators struggle with crowdfunding model ... Ontario looked upon as key to setting pace ... Using our existing regulatory framework to deal with something like equity crowdfunding is like trying to jam a round peg into a square hole **Lawyers Weekly, April 19, 2013 issue**

16.1 Introduction

In selected OECD countries around the world, such as Australia, the United Kingdom, Ireland, France, The Netherlands, and Switzerland, it is possible for entrepreneurs to raise capital by selling equity stakes in their business through crowdfunding or open calls to investors over Internet portals. Other types of crowdfunding platforms include donations, rewards-based, and lending (for a description, see Chapter 1: Introduction; see also Agrawal et al., 2011; Ahlers et al., 2015; Belleflamme et al., 2010, 2012; Bradford, 2012; Burtch et al., 2013; Griffin, 2013; Mollick, 2013; Schwienbacher & Larralde, 2012). In total across all types of crowdfunding models worldwide, there were 39 equity crowdfunding platforms that comprised 7.3% of the 452 platforms, and there was a total of US$ 88 million raised in 2011 from equity crowdfunding and a total of US$ 1441 million raised among all platforms and all crowdfunding models (Ahlers et al., 2015; Crowdfunding Industry Report, 2012). Countries that currently (as at 2013) do not permit equity crowdfunding are contemplating enabling crowdfunding through legislative changes; for example, see the JOBS (Jumpstart Our Business Startups) Act in the United States.

In Canada the Ontario Securities Commission was in 2013 contemplating legislation to permit crowdfunding, largely in response to demand pressure from entrepreneurs and other stakeholders. Empirical evidence is consistent with the view that the adaptability of a country's legal system facilitates access to finance (e.g., Beck, Demirgüç-Kunt, & Levine,

2005; Cumming & Johan, 2008). But whether securities laws should be adaptable to demand pressures to permit crowdfunding is unclear.

Potential benefits associated with equity crowdfunding are highly pronounced. Entrepreneurs may obtain needed capital that would facilitate the existence of their business that would not have been available from other sources, such as banks, angel investors, or venture capital. Indeed, some companies may not exist without having had the option of raising money through crowdfunding. Famous examples of crowdfunding include the pebble watch[1] and the Statue of Liberty.[2] Potential risks associated with equity crowdfunding are likewise very pronounced. For instance, an entrepreneur may squander the proceeds or raise equity capital through crowdfunding and then subsequently issue more shares to himself/herself, thereby diluting the equity stake held by the crowd-investors. Entrepreneurs may simply pay themselves more and not invest in appropriate projects with the money raised. Nevertheless, it is possible to mitigate such risks through conditions imposed on entrepreneurs, portals, and investors, as discussed below.

In view of the pronounced benefits and severe risks with equity crowdfunding, along with the evolving regulatory landscape around the world, the crowdfunding setting provides a fascinating new environment in which to reexamine an old question: is the competitive model of law production one that gives rise to a race to the top or a race to the bottom? The corporate law framework in the United States has been a forum for much debate on the advantages and disadvantages of competitive models of legal production (Bebchuk, 1992; Cumming & MacIntosh, 2000a, 2000b, 2002; Daines, 2001, 2002; Daines & Klausner, 2001; Roe, 2003; Romano, 1985, 1987, 1993) but has not previously been examined in the crowdfunding context. In view of legislative developments in Canada, the United States, and other countries around the world where new crowdfunding models and legislative reforms are being contemplated in 2012 and 2013 and frequently discussed in the media, it is timely and worthwhile to examine the race-to-the-top/race-to-the-bottom debate in the context of crowdfunding.

In this chapter, we present three alternative hypotheses pertaining to the regulation of equity crowdfunding. First, the race-to-the-bottom view posits that portals, entrepreneurs, and investors prefer jurisdictions which offer the least stringent regulation in order to maximize capital that entrepreneurs are able to raise. Second, the neutrality or uniformity view posits that portals, entrepreneurs, and investors are indifferent to the substantive crowdfunding laws. If so, regulators are likely to exhibit a preference for uniformity across jurisdictions or simply adopt models that replicate that of other jurisdictions in order to minimize the cost of law production. Third, the race-to-the-top view posits that portals, entrepreneurs, and investors want strict regulation and mechanisms that mitigate risk.

We test these three competing hypotheses by using crowdfunding survey data gathered by the National Crowdfunding Association of Canada (NCFA) in 2013 Q1. As detailed herein, the data were collected to ascertain whether, first, there were differences in the views about how to mitigate risk in crowdfunding across portals, investors (accredited and otherwise), and start-up entrepreneurs; and second, the intended reasons for seeking

---

[1] http://www.kickstarter.com/projects/597507018/pebble-e-chapter-watch-for-iphone-and-android

[2] http://dailycrowdsource.com/20-resources/projects/169-pulitzer-crowdfunded-the-statue-of-liberty

crowdfunding participation. The data gathered were Canada-wide. The data show some tension toward a race to the bottom insofar as start-ups prefer fewer restrictions on their ability to crowdfund, and portals prefer fewer disclosure requirements and fewer restrictions on free trading of crowdfunded shares. However, this evidence is tempered by the fact that investors demand more disclosure, limits on amounts entrepreneurs can raise, and lower thresholds for audited financial statements, among other things. Based on the ease with which the Internet facilitates cross-jurisdictional investment, we infer from the data that investor demands will give rise to a race to the top in the crowdfunding space.[3]

This chapter is organized as follows. Section 16.2 presents our main testable hypotheses in the context of prior research and the unique crowdfunding institutional setting. The data and summary statistics are presented in Section 16.3. Section 16.4 presents our multivariate empirical tests. The last section concludes, provides suggestions for further research, and discusses policy implications.

16.2 Institutional setting and hypotheses

Equity crowdfunding is the antithesis to traditional models in which entrepreneurs raise capital by preparing a formal prospectus. The costs of preparing a prospectus are large and can reach tens or hundreds of thousands of dollars in terms of legal and accounting fees; for initial public offerings on stock exchanges, prospectus costs can be in the millions (Ritter, 1987). Exemptions from the prospectus requirement are very stringent in most jurisdictions around the world. Exemptions in principle can include limits on the number of solicited investors, on the number of actual investors, and the minimum wealth of the investors.

Without a prospectus, investors are arguably not as well informed. Because the costs of preparing a prospectus may outweigh the benefits, and hence discourage or prevent entrepreneurs from raising external capital, many jurisdictions have permitted equity crowdfunding (such as Australia and select countries in Europe; see the Crowdfunding Industry Report, 2012) and others are contemplating equity crowdfunding, including Canada and the United States. Under equity crowdfunding an Internet portal is used to inform and solicit investment from a wide range of investors who typically do not fit within the traditional wealth levels that would enable a prospectus exemption. Moreover, the number of investors solicited is far beyond the maximum allowable for a prospectus exemption. Hence, some jurisdictions contemplating equity crowdfunding are doing so by introducing a new crowdfunding exemption.

This chapter tests three alternative hypotheses pertaining to regulation of equity crowdfunding. The first view is that entrepreneurs, portals, and their investors prefer less stringent regulation. Securities regulators work to further public interest by supporting investor protection and facilitating market integrity. However, it is noted that securities regulations are not insurance policies against investor losses, and they are not designed to

---

[3] This inference in consistent with recent commentary from the Angel Capital Association in the United States regarding certain provisions in the JOBS Act. See http://venturebeat.com/2013/07/28/why-angels-are-making-a-big-deal-about-the-secs-new-rules-on-advertising-investment-opportunities/.

protect all investors from losing their money in all circumstances (Heminway & Hoffman, 2011). Securities regulators may simply work to offer the regulators sought by lobbyists on behalf of entrepreneurs that seek greater flexibility in ways to raise capital, as suggested by Cary (1974) and Bebchuk (1992). Under this view, entrepreneurs do not want limits on the amount of capital that they can raise. Portals want minimum restrictions on the background and due diligence checks they are required to carry out. Investors want to be able to invest in more projects and not face limits on their ability to invest for they may miss out on profitable opportunities.

Hypothesis 16.1: *Race to the bottom: Portals, entrepreneurs and investors prefer jurisdictions which offer the least stringent regulation.*

From a policy perspective, of course, we worry that such a view is short-lived. A major fraud or scandal would lead to a change in preferences, but not without a major cost or externality imposed on the public taxpayer. Therefore to test for the presence of such a view, it is worthwhile to examine a jurisdiction in which equity crowdfunding has not yet happened.

The second hypothesis posits that entrepreneurs, portals, and investors have little preference on way or the other for the substantive law governing crowdfunding. If so, regulators drafting such laws can do so and meet stakeholder interests by minimizing the cost of legal production by replicating a legislative framework already in place in another jurisdiction. Evidence of the neutrality/uniformity view was found in empirical studies of the Canadian incorporation market by Cumming and MacIntosh (2000a, 2000b, 2002), for example. Corporate codes in different Canadian provinces are near perfect copies of one another and resemble the federal incorporation code in Canada.

Hypothesis 16.2: *Neutrality or uniformity: There is little or no demand for substantive law, and hence the supply of law is likely to reflect a least cost replication of regulations from other jurisdictions.*

The third hypothesis is that the market can figure out on its own what is the best model for governing itself. If regulations are inefficient, in terms of being either too onerous or not onerous enough, the entrepreneurs, portals, and investors will migrate to a different jurisdiction that better meets their needs. Similarly, there is evidence (Daines, 2002; Romano, 1985, 1987) that US corporate laws have evolved out of a competitive model of corporate law production in a way that has led to a race to the top.

Hypothesis 16.3: *Race to the top: Portals, entrepreneurs and investors want strict regulation and mechanisms that most effectively mitigate risk while still enabling capital raising.*

In support of the race-to-the-top view, there is evidence from other jurisdictions such as Australia that disclosure is something that investors pay close attention to in the crowdfunding context. For instance, Chapter 10: Signaling in equity crowdfunding finds evidence that disclosure of firms' financial roadmaps (e.g., preplanned exit strategies such as initial public offerings or acquisitions), internal governance (such as board structure), and risk factors (such as amount of equity offered and the presence of disclaimers) affect fund-raising success. Firms that disclose financing plans and have sound boards of directors with professional curriculum vitae are more likely to raise more money and do it more quickly. Firms that seek to give too much equity end up doing much worse, consistent with theoretical models of selling equity stakes (Myers & Majluf, 1984; see also Leland & Pyle, 1977). By contrast, Chapter 10: Signaling in equity crowdfunding finds evidence that external certification (awards, government grants, and patents) has much less relevance for fundraising success, which can be explained by the fact that if firms had such certification from external bodies and was valuable, the firm would not have to resort to the crowdfunding market to raise external equity.

In further support of the race-to-the-top view, there is evidence from other sources of entrepreneurial finance that reputation matters a great deal to the eventual success of the venture (Nahata, 2008; see also Nahata et al., 2014; Schwienbacher, 2008a, 2008b). As such, we would expect portals that adhere to higher due diligence standards to attract more investors, which, in turn, attract higher quality entrepreneurial ventures.

16.3 Data

Survey data were gathered by the NCFA in order to ascertain perceptions of crowd-funding, and possible ways to mitigate risks. A copy of the survey is available from the NCFA and online.[4]

Surveys were completed online and distributed across Canada to potential investors (accredited and otherwise), investees (start-up entrepreneurs), portals, service providers in 2013 Q1. A total of 144 surveys were completed.

The data are summarized in Table 16.1. The dependent variables used in our empirical models in Section 16.4 are first presented at the top of Table 16.1. The dependent variables included the following:

- What measures, if any, would be the most effective at reducing investor risks and the potential for fraud?
  - Education for issuers and investors
  - Limits on the total amount raised by an issuer and on individual investment size
  - On-going continuous disclosure requirements
  - Prohibiting advertising or sales solicitation except by an authorized portal and issuer's website

---

[4] http://www.ncfacanada.org/. The survey was designed and created by Craig Asano and Brian Koscak of the EMDA. The authors of this chapter were unaware of the survey at the time it was created and did not influence the questions asked and to whom it was distributed. Likewise, Craig Asano and Brian Koscak did not direct or influence the experimental design or results from this chapter but did offer constructive comments for the purpose of providing helpful feedback on the chapter. The findings herein are in no way driven by industry interests for pushing crowdfunding and the like but instead are completely independent and impartial.

TABLE 16.1 Variable definitions.

Variable name	Definition	Mean	Median	Std. dev.	Min.	Max.
Dependent variables						
q14education	14. What measures, if any, would be the most effective at reducing investor risks and the potential for fraud? Education for issuers and investors	3.931	4	0.882	1	5
q14limits	14. What measures, if any, would be the most effective at reducing investor risks and the potential for fraud? Limits on the total amount raised by an issuer and on individual investment size	3.535	3	0.996	1	5
q14disclosure	14. What measures, if any, would be the most effective at reducing investor risks and the potential for fraud? On-going continuous disclosure requirements	3.792	4	0.852	2	5
q14advertise	14. What measures, if any, would be the most effective at reducing investor risks and the potential for fraud? Prohibiting advertising or sales solicitation except by an authorized portal and issuer's website	3.382	3	1.134	1	5
q14portals	14. What measures, if any, would be the most effective at reducing investor risks and the potential for fraud? Portals required to do background checks of each officer, director and significant shareholders of issuers selling securities on its portal	3.708	4	1.044	1	5
q14redemption	14. What measures, if any, would be the most effective at reducing investor risks and the potential for fraud? Purchasers are provided with a rescission/redemption right within a certain number of days	3.625	4	0.938	1	5

(Continued)

TABLE 16.1 (Continued)

Variable name	Definition	Mean	Median	Std. dev.	Min.	Max.
q11atrial	11. (A) Should any crowdfunding exemption in Canada be approved on a trial or limited basis at first? (2 = yes, 1 = undecided, 0 = no)	1.375	2	0.810	0	2
q17freetrade	17. (A) Should crowdfunding securities be free-trading after a period of time? (2 = yes, 1 = undecided, 0 = no)	1.208	1	0.827	0	2
q17freetradetime	17. (B) When should they be eligible for secondary market trading?	21.792	24	7.015	12	36
q12b	12. (B) What is the maximum amount of capital an investor should be able to invest in any 12-month period?	$12,729	$1250	$6601	$1000	$20,000
q15limit	15. What is the aggregate amount of capital that an issuer should be able to raise in any 12-month period?	$2,607,639	$1,750,000	$1,732,972	$250,000	$5,000,000
q16bthresholdaudited	19. (B) Please select an appropriate capital threshold where audited financial statements should be required?	$1,226,389	$1,000,000	$685,411	$100,000	$5,000,000
Explanatory variables						
q99financial	9. What do you believe would motivate an investor to make an investment through crowdfunding? Financial incentives	3.813	4	0.869	1	5
q99nonfinancial	9. What do you believe would motivate an investor to make an investment through crowdfunding? Nonfinancial incentives	3.611	4	0.862	1	5
q99diversify	9. What do you believe would motivate an investor to make an investment through crowdfunding? Diversification of portfolio	3.583	4	0.873	1	5
q99direct	9. What do you believe would motivate an investor to make an investment through crowdfunding? Gain a direct channel to entrepreneurs and owners and in a transparent way	3.938	4	0.813	2	5

(Continued)

TABLE 16.1   (Continued)

Variable name	Definition	Mean	Median	Std. dev.	Min.	Max.
q99network	9. What do you believe would motivate an investor to make an investment through crowdfunding? Networking opportunities within the start-up and the SME community	3.771	4	0.867	2	5
q99support	9. What do you believe would motivate an investor to make an investment through crowdfunding? Support entrepreneurism and the development of innovative products/services	4.167	4	0.845	2	5
q5familiar	5. Are you familiar with the term crowdfunding?	3.021	3	1.387	1	5
startup	4. Please select a stakeholder category that best represents your survey responses: start-up	0.340	0	0.475	0	1
sme	4. Please select a stakeholder category that best represents your survey responses: SME	0.410	0	0.493	0	1
serviceprovider	4. Please select a stakeholder category that best represents your survey responses: potential service provider	0.264	0	0.442	0	1
portal	4. Please select a stakeholder category that best represents your survey responses: potential portal	0.174	0	0.380	0	1
nonaccreditedinvestor	4. Please select a stakeholder category that best represents your survey responses: nonaccredited investor	0.382	0	0.488	0	1
accreditedindividual	4. Please select a stakeholder category that best represents your survey responses: accredited investor	0.139	0	0.347	0	1
accreditedinstitutional	4. Please select a stakeholder category that best represents your survey responses: accredited institutional investor	0.007	0	0.083	0	1
investmentdealer	4. Please select a stakeholder category that best represents your survey responses: investment dealer	0.014	0	0.117	0	1

(Continued)

TABLE 16.1 (Continued)

Variable name	Definition	Mean	Median	Std. dev.	Min.	Max.
portfoliomanager	4. Please select a stakeholder category that best represents your survey responses: portfolio manager	0.028	0	0.165	0	1
exemptmarketdealer	4. Please select a stakeholder category that best represents your survey responses: exempt market dealer	0.042	0	0.201	0	1
alberta	Dummy variable = 1 if respondent based in Alberta	0.111	0	0.315	0	1
ontario	Dummy variable = 1 if respondent based in Ontario	0.472	0	0.501	0	1
bc	Dummy variable = 1 if respondent based in British Columbia	0.181	0	0.386	0	1
quebec	Dummy variable = 1 if respondent based in Quebec	0.076	0	0.267	0	1

The table presents definitions and summary statistics for the main variables in the dataset. Unless otherwise indicated, ranking variables range on a 1–5 scale where 1 = strongly disagree, 2 = disagree, 3 = undecided, 4 = agree, and 5 = strongly agree. Variable names, such as "q14 …", refer to the question numbers used from the National Crowdfunding Association of Canada survey. *SME*, Small- or medium-sized enterprise.

- Portals required to do background checks of each officer, director, and significant shareholders of issuers selling securities on its portal
- Purchasers provided with a rescission/redemption right within a certain number of days

As indicated in Table 16.1, these six variables were measured on a ranking basis (1–5 scale where 1 = strongly disagree, 2 = disagree, 3 = undecided, 4 = agree, and 5 = strongly agree). The highest ranked measure was education, which received an average ranking of 3.931, and the lowest ranked variable was the prohibition on advertising, which received a ranking of 3.382.

In addition, the survey asked the question:

- Should any crowdfunding exemption in Canada be approved on a trial or limited basis at first?

For this variable a response of "yes" was assigned the value 2, "undecided" was assigned the value 1, and "no" was assigned the value "0." The average response was 1.375, and the median response was 2.

Similarly, the survey asked these two related questions:

- Should crowdfunding securities be free-trading securities after a period of time?
  - And when should they be eligible for secondary market trading?

For the first part of the question a response of "yes" was assigned the value 2, "unde-cided" was assigned the value 1, and "no" was assigned the value "0." The average response was 1.208, and the median response was 1. For the second part the average number of months was 21.792, the median was 24 months, the minimum was 12 months, and the maximum was 36 months.

The following three questions are examined as dependent variables:

- What is the maximum amount of capital an investor should be able to invest in any 12-month period?
- What is the aggregate amount of capital that an issuer should be able to raise in any 12-month period?
- What is the appropriate capital threshold where audited financial statements should be required?

For the maximum amount of capital investors should be allowed to invest in a 12-month period, the average reply was $12,729, where the median was $1250, and the range was $1000–$20,000. For the aggregate amount of capital an issuer should be allowed to raise in a 12-month period, the average was $2.608 million, while the average was $1.750 million, and the range was $250,000–$5 million. For the capital raising threshold for which audited financial statements should be required, the average reply was $1.226 million and the median was $1 million.

In our analyses below, we make use of the following explanatory variables that are summarized in Table 16.1. First, we consider this question:

- What do you believe would motivate an investor to make an investment through crowdfunding?
  - Financial Incentives
  - Nonfinancial Incentives
  - Diversification of Portfolio
  - Gain a direct channel to entrepreneurs and owners and in a transparent way
  - Networking opportunities within the start-up and the small- and medium-sized enterprise (SME) community
  - Support entrepreneurism and the development of innovative products/services

This question is ranked with the same ranking scale as the other variables (1–5 scale where 1 = strongly disagree, 2 = disagree, 3 = undecided, 4 = agree, and 5 = strongly agree). Table 16.1 indicates that the highest ranked variable was "support entrepreneurialism" that received an average ranking of 4.167, and the lowest ranking was "diversification of the portfolio" that received an average ranking of 3.583.

Second, we use this question to address the respondent's belief of their expertise with crowdfunding:

- Are you familiar with the term crowdfunding?

We note that the survey was prefaced with an explanation of the term crowdfunding so that respondents would be aware of what they were being asked about. The average ranking for this variable was 3.021 out of 5, and the median ranking was 3, and the full range of 1–5 is observed in the data. As such, we believe the respondents do not represent an overly biased set of people that are crowdfunding experts, but rather they provide an appropriate mix of different levels of experience and understanding of the term crowdfunding.

Finally, we make use of survey data that asked the respondents to select a stakeholder category that best represents themselves as one of the following, and to select the region in which they are primarily located:

- potential portal
- nonaccredited investor
- accredited investor
- accredited institutional investor
- investment dealer
- portfolio manager
- exempt market dealer
- Please select a province/territory—Alberta, Ontario, British Columbia, Quebec, etc.

Based on the data included in Table 16.1, we are able to show that 34% of the respondents were start-ups, 41% were SMEs, 26.4% were potential service providers, 17.4% were potential portals, 38.2% were nonaccredited investors, 13.9% were accredited investors, 0.7% were accredited institutional investors, 1.4% were investment dealers, and 2.8% were portfolio managers. We note that it is possible for overlap across these categories, as respondents may be both SMEs and nonaccredited investors, for example. The potential overlap has no significant implication on our data analyses and interpretations.

Most respondents were from the provinces of Ontario (68), followed by British Columbia (26), Alberta (16), and Quebec (11). There were 23 respondents from the rest of Canada. As the population of Ontario, British Columbia, Alberta, Quebec, and the rest of Canada is 13.5, 4.4, 3.6, 8.1, and 4.9 million, respectively, the surveys are equally representative of the population in the different regions with the sole exception of Quebec which is underrepresented in our sample. The likely explanation for this lower response rate in Quebec is the language and political/cultural differences between Quebec and the rest of Canada. Nevertheless, our empirical findings in the regressions are robust to the inclusion/exclusion of Quebec. These regressions are discussed below in the next section.

16.4 Multivariate regressions

The next section discusses the empirical findings pertinent to the multivariate tests of Hypotheses 16.1–16.3 as summarized in Section 16.2. Our first set of regressions is presented in Table 16.2. In Table 16.2, we examine ordered logit models of the ranking of the importance of different risk reduction measures for Education (Model 1), Limits on Amounts Raised (Model 2), Continuous Disclosure (Model 3), Advertising (Model 4), Portal Due Diligence (Model 5), and Redemption Rights (Model 6). These six different ranking variables are explained as a function of the following variables:

- perceived reasons for crowdfunders' investment
  - Financial, Nonfinancial, Diversification, Networking, and Support Entrepreneurialism

TABLE 16.2 Regression analyses of risk reduction measures.

	Model 1: q14education		Model 2: q14limits		Model 3: q14disclosure		Model 4: q14advertise		Model 5: q14portals		Model 6: q14redemption	
	Coefficient	t-Statistic	Coefficient	t-Statistic	Coefficient	t-Statistic	Coefficient	t-Statistic	Coefficient	t-Statistic	Coefficient	t-Statistic
Perceived reasons for crowdfunders' investment												
q99financial	0.397	1.67*	0.618	2.63***	0.840	3.19***	0.230	0.98	0.086	0.37	0.447	1.80*
q99nonfinancial	0.271	1.10	−0.701	−2.84***	−0.448	−1.75*	0.021	0.09	−0.151	−0.59	0.182	0.72
q99diversify	0.150	0.60	−0.032	−0.13	−0.218	−0.89	0.099	0.41	0.632	2.43**	0.157	0.64
q99direct	0.182	0.58	−0.140	−0.44	0.331	1.03	−0.533	−1.71*	0.416	1.34	0.486	1.58
q99network	0.553	1.86*	−0.068	−0.23	0.039	0.14	0.387	1.39	−0.619	−2.16**	−0.097	−0.36
q99support	0.389	1.24	0.579	1.82*	0.763	2.39**	0.582	1.91*	0.645	2.12**	0.052	0.16
Characteristics of survey respondent												
q5familiar	0.193	1.16	0.170	1.07	0.117	0.70	−0.163	−1.04	0.084	0.53	0.047	0.29
startup	0.090	0.17	−0.925	−1.83*	0.024	0.05	0.780	1.62	0.052	0.11	0.301	0.6
sme	0.068	0.14	−0.639	−1.38	−0.109	−0.22	0.972	2.09**	0.670	1.43	0.662	1.31
serviceprovider	−0.407	−0.84	0.098	0.22	−0.453	−1.00	0.294	0.66	−0.160	−0.36	0.405	0.84
portal	0.426	0.87	−0.176	−0.37	−0.812	−1.65*	−0.226	−0.48	−0.216	−0.47	0.675	1.47
nonaccreditedinvestor	−0.005	−0.01	0.483	1.22	0.962	2.37**	−0.621	−1.64	−0.282	−0.73	0.304	0.75
accreditedindividual	0.382	0.59	0.988	1.49	1.838	2.74***	−0.047	−0.07	−0.115	−0.18	0.145	0.22
accreditedinstitutional	34.306	0.00	0.438	0.19	−0.893	−0.36	0.655	0.3	−3.638	−1.64	2.246	0.99
investmentdealer	0.015	0.01	−1.963	−1.23	−0.555	−0.36	−0.817	−0.44	−1.062	−0.42	0.235	0.18
portfoliomanager	1.201	0.86	−0.100	−0.08	2.763	1.86*	−0.079	−0.07	0.828	0.68	−2.550	−2.10**
exemptmarketdealer	1.066	0.97	0.071	0.08	−1.156	−1.22	−1.614	−1.69*	1.229	1.29	0.730	0.72
alberta	0.181	0.26	0.351	0.53	−1.009	−1.39	−0.839	−1.36	−0.263	−0.42	1.479	2.25**
ontario	−0.261	−0.53	−0.512	−1.11	−0.178	−0.37	0.064	0.15	0.156	0.35	−0.034	−0.07
bc	−0.478	−0.82	−0.924	−1.70*	−1.540	−2.56**	−1.085	−1.95*	−0.627	−1.12	−0.675	−1.16
quebec	0.662	0.80	0.450	0.57	1.184	1.57	−0.278	−0.37	0.572	0.76	−0.126	−0.15
PseudoR2	0.186	0.071	0.182	0.082	0.088	0.120						

The table presents ordered logit estimates of the determinants of perceived benefits for risk reduction to investors. Ordered logit cutoff parameters are not presented for conciseness. Variables are as defined in Table 16.1.
*, **, and *** significant at the 10%, 5%, and 1% level of significance, respectively. *SME*, Small- or medium-sized enterprise.

- characteristics of the survey respondent
  - Familiarity with crowdfunding, Start-up, SME, Service Provider, Portal, Nonaccredited Investor, Accredited Individual Investor, Accredited Institutional Investor, Investment Dealer, Portfolio Manager, and Exempt Market Dealer
- province
  - Alberta, British Columbia, Ontario, Quebec, other provinces

The regressions in Table 16.2 show that risk reduction is closely related to the perceived reasons for the crowdfunders' reasons for investment. First, note that Financial Reasons for Investment are significantly related to Education as a risk reduction measure at the 10% level of significance, Investment Limits at the 1% level, Continuous Disclosure at the 1% level, and Redemption at the 10% level. In terms of the economic significance a 1-point increase in the ranking for Financial Reasons for Investment is associated with an 8.1% increase in the probability of a top rank for Education, a 9.1% increase in probability of the top rank for Investment Limits, an 11.3% increase in the probability of a top rank for Continuous Disclosure, and a 1.5% increase in the probability of a top rank for Redemption.[5] By contrast, Nonfinancial Reasons for Investment is negatively associated with higher ranks for Limits on Investment Limits and Continuous Disclosure, and these effects are significant at the 1% and 10% levels, respectively. In terms of the economic significance a 1-point increase in Nonfinancial Reasons is associated with a 10.3% reduction in the probability of a top rank for Investment Limits and a 6.0% reduction in the probability of a top rank for Continuous Disclosure. Taken together, these findings pertinent to financial versus nonfinancial reasons for investment show that the would-be market participants in Canada are sensitive to the needs for protecting investor interests to a greater degree where such investors are investing for profit that supports the race-to-the-top hypothesis (Hypothesis 16.3).

The regressions indicate that Diversification Reasons for Investment are statistically associated with higher rankings for Portal Due Diligence, and this effect is significant at the 5% level in Model 5. The economic significance is such that a 1-point increase in Diversification is associated with an 11.0% increase in the probability of a top ranking for Portal Due Diligence. Again, this result is intuitive since diversified investors are spread over a large number of investments, by definition, and time constraints require that due diligence be outsourced to a greater degree. In this case, by requiring portals to undertake a higher responsibility for due diligence, investors are better able to diversify their investments across a greater number of crowdfunded projects. As such, this result provides further support for the race-to-the-top hypothesis (Hypothesis 16.3).

Direct Access Reasons for Investment is statistically negatively associated with Advertising Restrictions, and this effect is significant at the 10% level in Model 4. The economic significance is such that a 1-point increase in Direct Access gives rise to a 6.7%

---

[5] Marginal effects are presented for the top rankings only to highlight the size of the effects. Technically, we could present the marginal effects for each of the five rankings, but those added details do not provide much additional insight, and such details would detract from the overall insights (in other words, five times the number of marginal effects would give rise to not seeing the forest through the trees, so to speak).

reduction in the probability of a top rank for Advertising Restrictions. This finding further supports the race-to-the-top view (Hypothesis 16.3) since advertising facilitates the flow of information from entrepreneurs to the would-be investors, thereby enabling investors connect with entrepreneurs.

Networking Reasons for Investment is positively associated with Education and negatively associated with Portal Due Diligence, and these effects are significant at the 10% and 5% levels, respectively. The economic significance is such that a 1-point increase in Networking is associated with an 11.3% increase in the probability of a top rank for Education and a 10.8% reduction in the probability of a top rank for Portal Due Diligence. These findings are intuitive and consistent with the race-to-the-top view since networking is facilitated by educational forums, and investors that network are ones that seek their own information and are thereby able to better and more efficiently carry out their own due diligence.

Support Entrepreneurialism Reasons for Investment is positively associated with Limits on Investment, Continuous Disclosure, Advertising, and Portal Due Diligence, and these effects are significant at the 10%, 5%, 10%, and 5% levels, respectively. The economic significance is such that a 1-point increase in Support Entrepreneurialism gives rise to an 8.5% increase in the probability of a top rank for Limits on Investment, a 10.2% increase in the probability of a top rank for Continuous Disclosure, a 7.3% increase in the probability of a top rank for Advertising, and a 11.3% increase in the probability of a top rank for Portal Due Diligence. Since investors that want to support entrepreneurialism generally may be prone to overinvest without adequate information, be heavily influenced by advertising, and not carry out effective and proper due diligence on their own, these findings support the race-to-the-top view (Hypothesis 16.3).

Overall, the data on reasons for investment are very consistent with effective risk-mitigation strategies tailored to those reasons for investment. In other words the data indicate that the market would work rather efficiently if different jurisdictions attracted different types of investors and different entrepreneurs and portals. All of the findings can be interpreted as consistent with the race-to-the-top view (Hypothesis 16.3).

Our second set of results in Table 16.2 pertains to the characteristics of the market participants. On one hand, four findings pertinent to market participant characteristics are consistent with the race-to-the-top view (Hypothesis 16.3). First, SMEs are 13.0% more likely to have top rank for Advertising Restrictions, and this effect is significant at the 5% level. Second, nonaccredited investors are 14.0% more likely to have top rank for Continuous Disclosure, and this effect is significant at the 5% level. Third, accredited individual investors are 35.2% more likely to have top rank for Continuous Disclosure, and this effect is significant at the 1% level. Fourth, portfolio managers are 58.6% more likely to have top rank for Continuous Disclosure, and this effect is significant at the 10% level.

On the other hand, four findings are consistent with the race-to-the-bottom view (Hypothesis 16.1). First, the data indicate that start-ups are −12.4% less likely to have top rank for Limits on Capital Raising, and this effect is significant at the 10% level of significance. Second, portals are 9.1% less likely to have top rank for Continuous Disclosure, and this effect is marginally significant at the 10% level. Third, portfolio managers are 17.3% less likely to have top rank for redemption, and this effect is significant at the 5% level. Fourth, exempt market dealers are 12.0% less likely to have top rank for Advertising

Restrictions, and this effect is significant at the 10% level. These four findings could be viewed as market participants behaving in their own self-interest in a way that is detrimental to investor's interest, consistent with Hypothesis 16.1. But taken in conjunction with the other findings pertinent to investor characteristics and interests discussed earlier, it is unlikely that markets that mainly serve the interests of start-ups and portals are likely to attract significant retail investor presence, and as such, the supply of capital would be significantly reduced in such markets that narrowly served the interests of select market participants.

Our third set of results in Table 16.2 pertains to regional differences. The data indicate some differences across provinces. Respondents from Alberta show they are 4.3% more likely to have top rank for Redemption, while respondents from British Columbia are 11.2% less likely to have top rank for Limits on Capital Raising, 15.0% less likely to have top rank for Continuous Disclosure, and 10.7% less likely to have top rank for Advertising. These differences are suggestive that there is not a preference for uniformity across provinces, counter to Hypothesis 16.2. Based on the other evidence stated earlier, there is no apparent reason to not let the provinces compete in a way that is consistent with the market for corporate charters in the United States (Romano, 1985, 1993).

The second set of regressions is presented in Table 16.3. It shows two ordered logit models in Models 7 and 8 for Offering Crowdfunding on a Trial Basis (Model 7) and Freely Traded Shares (Model 8). Table 16.3 also presents OLS models of when shares should be freely trading (Model 9), the maximum amount of capital allowed to invest (Model 10), the maximum amount of capital allowed to raise (Model 11), and the capital raising threshold for which audited financial statements should be required (Model 12). Consistent with the regressions in Table 16.2, these variables are regressed on the following explanatory variables:

- perceived reasons for crowdfunders' investment
  - Financial, Nonfinancial, Diversification, Networking, Support Entrepreneurialism
- characteristics of the survey respondent
  - Familiarity with crowdfunding, Start-up, SME, Service Provider, Portal, Nonaccredited Investor, Accredited Individual Investor, Accredited Institutional Investor, Investment Dealer, Portfolio Manager, Exempt Market Dealer
- province
  - Alberta, British Columbia, Ontario, Quebec, other provinces

Models 9 and 10 in Table 16.3 indicate that each 1-point increase in Diversification Reasons for Investment are associated with 2 fewer months until Shares Should be Freely Tradable and $1646 extra Capital Raising Restrictions in a 12-month period, and these effects are both significant at the 5% level of significance. These findings are consistent with Hypothesis 16.3 insofar as diversification is facilitated by less onerous resale restrictions and less idiosyncratic risk associated with a single issuer.

Table 16.3 further shows that Direct Access Reasons for Investment is associated to a 20.0% increase in the probability of Freely Tradable Shares (Model 8, significant at the 5% level), $1536 extra capital allowed for investment in 12-month period (Model 10, significant at the 10% level), $527,294 extra amount raised in a 12-month period (Model 11,

TABLE 16.3 Regression analyses of trial periods, freely tradable shares, and limits on investing, capital raising, and audited financials.

	Model 7: q11atrial		Model 8: q17freetrade		Model 9: q17freetradetime		Model 10: q12b		Model 11: q15limit		Model 12: q16thresholdaudited	
	Coefficient	t-Statistic	Coefficient	t-Statistic	Coefficient	t-Statistic	Coefficient	t-Statistic	Coefficient	t-Statistic	Coefficient	t-Statistic
Perceived reasons for crowdfunders' investment												
q9financial	−0.336	−1.07	−0.341	−1.30	−0.935	−1.18	749.43	1.08	66,658.64	0.35	13,017.24	0.17
q9nonfinancial	−0.425	−1.25	−0.023	−0.09	0.948	1.13	−468.38	−0.64	92,659.79	0.46	−74,454.07	−0.89
q9diversify	−0.333	−1.01	0.255	0.95	−1.979	−2.36**	1645.94	2.25**	−40,641.75	−0.20	−55,650.72	−0.67
q9direct	1.221	3.00***	0.785	2.31**	−0.897	−0.84	1535.50	1.65*	527,293.80	2.05**	−190,267.70	−1.80*
q9network	0.028	0.08	0.002	0.01	−0.362	−0.38	−1248.04	−1.50	150,521.40	0.66	−31,698.40	−0.34
q9support	0.520	1.40	−0.202	−0.59	0.954	0.90	2852.59	3.07***	272,700.30	1.06	220,510.70	2.09**
Characteristics of survey respondent												
q5familiar	0.001	0.00	0.189	1.11	−0.448	−0.79	−466.75	−0.94	−50,943.95	−0.37	−75,938.07	−1.35
startup	−1.017	−1.81*	0.156	0.30	0.105	0.06	−1470.11	−0.98	−25,662.46	−0.06	−7665.40	−0.04
sme	−0.415	−0.81	0.495	1.01	0.385	0.23	−1461.72	−0.98	413,606.40	1.00	−260,118.00	−1.53
serviceprovider	−0.187	−0.37	0.534	1.12	1.685	1.05	1758.51	1.26	−481,479.10	−1.24	151,703.00	0.95
Portal	−0.259	−0.47	1.337	2.37**	−1.552	−0.95	2094.09	1.46	−241,496.60	−0.61	19,459.75	0.12
nonaccreditedinvestor	0.814	1.78*	−0.003	−0.01	−0.416	−0.31	314.55	0.26	560,317.50	1.70*	−339,324.90	−2.50**
accreditedindividual	1.251	1.58	−1.307	−1.93*	−0.723	−0.32	741.54	0.38	−156,153.50	−0.29	−279,290.00	−1.25
accreditedinstitutional	35.405	0.00	31.013	0.00	−12.516	−1.44	1801.74	0.24	425,415.80	0.20	−1,477,569.00	−1.70
investmentdealer	33.388	0.00	−0.480	−0.31	5.688	1.11	2575.43	0.57	2,539,446.00	2.04**	−752,687.40	−1.47
portfoliomanager	−0.915	−0.74	−1.239	−1.02	−0.521	−0.12	−1634.18	−0.44	1,832,786.00	1.79*	858,917.00	2.04**
exemptmarketdealer	−1.672	−1.51	−0.121	−0.12	0.207	0.06	−320.66	−0.11	1,514,151.00	1.90*	−85,318.66	−0.26
alberta	−0.106	−0.14	1.021	1.34	0.649	0.28	494.32	0.25	−794,031.70	−1.43	−328,314.20	−1.43
ontario	−0.693	−1.33	−0.353	−0.74	4.076	2.44**	−561.45	−0.38	−483,354.90	−1.20	−243,407.20	−1.46
bc	−0.635	−0.99	0.379	0.65	3.391	1.69*	−16.74	−0.01	−592,746.90	−1.22	−20,341.25	−0.10
quebec	0.855	0.89	−0.009	−0.01	−0.506	−0.20	2682.19	1.18	−775,120.70	−1.24	−103,707.70	−0.40
Constant					28.635	6.86	−6083.12	−1.66*	−1,315,221.00	−1.30	2,221,942.00	5.34***
Pseudo R^2 (Models 7−10) Adjusted R^2 (Models 10−12)	0.151		0.1205		0.1152		0.21		0.12		0.05	

The table presents ordered logit estimates of the determinants of perceived benefits for a trial period for crowdfunding (Model 7), and whether crowdfunded shares should be freely tradable (Model 8) and OLS estimates of free tradable after a limited period of time in terms of the number of months (Model 9). Ordered logit cutoff parameters are not presented for conciseness. Model 10 presents OLS estimates of the determinants of the aggregated amount of capital an investor should be able to invest in a 12-month period. Model 11 presents OLS estimates of the determinants of the aggregate amount of capital an issuer should be able to raise in the said period. Model 12 presents OLS estimates of the determinants of capital threshold limits for audited financial statements. Variables are as defined in Table 16.1. *, **, and *** significant at the 10%, 5%, and 1% levels of significance, respectively.

significant at the 5% level), and a $190,268 lower threshold for audited financial statements (Model 12, significant at the 10% level). To the extent that investors that seek direct access are more sophisticated investors akin to angel investors that seek to add value to their investees, these findings can be interpreted as consistent with the race-to-the-top Hypothesis 16.3 view. As well, investors that seek direct access are likewise associated with a 21.5% increase in the probability of a Trial Period for crowdfunding (Model 7, significant at the 1% level), which further supports Hypothesis 16.3.

Models 10 and 12 in Table 16.3 indicate that a 1-point increase in Support Entrepreneurialism Reasons for Investment is associated with $2853 extra capital invested in a 12-month period (significant at the 1% level) and a $220,511 higher threshold for audited financial statements (significant at the 5% level). As indicated in conjunction with the findings in Table 16.2, Support Entrepreneurialism as a reasons for investment has the potential to become prone to overinvestment without adequate due diligence, and hence the first finding pertaining to extra capital invested is consistent with the race-to-the-bottom view (Hypothesis 16.1), while the second finding is consistent with the race-to-the-top view (Hypothesis 16.3).

A number of the investor characteristic variables are significant in Table 16.3. Start-ups are 19.4% less likely to be interested in a trial period for crowdfunding (significant at the 10% level), portals are 30.0% more likely to be interested in freely tradable shares (significant at the 5% level), and Portfolio Managers seek $1,832,786 more capital raised and $858,917 higher threshold for audited financial statements. Each of these findings may be interpreted as consistent with the race to the bottom, since they serve their own interests potentially at investors' expense. However, nonaccredited investors are 13.6% more likely to be interested in a trial period for crowdfunding (significant at the 10% level), while accredited individual investors are 30.1% less likely to seek freely tradable shares (significant at the 10% level), suggesting that investors' interest temper the ability of other market participants to act in ways that serve only their own self-interests. Moreover, nonaccredited investors prefer on average $560,318 higher thresholds for amounts of capital that can be raised (significant at the 10% level), which is consistent with the preference of portfolio managers. Further, nonaccredited investors prefer on average a $339,325 lower threshold for audited financial statements (significant at the 5% level). Consistent with the evidence in Table 16.2, the data suggest that investor capital will flow to markets with regulations that are not self-serving to entrepreneurs and portals.

Finally, as in Table 16.2, there is some (albeit not much) evidence of regional differences across Canada. Respondents from Alberta preferred on average 4.1 months longer until shares should be freely tradable (significant at the 5% level), while respondents in British Columbia on average preferred 3.4 months (significant at the 10% level). There were no other evident differences across the regions.

The main findings from the regression evidence are summarized in Table 16.4. Overall, there is more support for Hypothesis 16.3 (race to the top) than Hypothesis 16.1 (race to the bottom). Also, there is some evidence that is inconsistent with uniformity. The data are consistent with the view that investor demands will give rise to a race to the top in crowdfunding markets.

TABLE 16.4 Summary of main findings pertinent to the race-to-the-bottom, neutrality, and race-to-the-top hypotheses.

	Hypothesis 16.1: Race to the bottom	Hypothesis 16.2: Uniformity	Hypothesis 16.3: Race to the top
Model 1: q14education			Yes—financial and network reasons for investment
Model 2: q14limits	Yes—start-ups	No—British Columbia	Yes—financial, nonfinancial, and support entrepreneurialism reasons for investment
Model 3: q14disclosure	Yes—portals	No—British Columbia	Yes—financial, nonfinancial, and support entrepreneurialism reasons for investment, as well as nonaccredited investors and portfolio managers
Model 4: q14advertise	Yes—exempt market dealers		Yes—direct access and support entrepreneurialism reasons for investment, as well as SMEs
Model 5: q14portals			Yes—diversify, networking, and support entrepreneurialism reasons for investment
Model 6: q14redemption	Yes—portfolio managers	No— Alberta	Yes—financial reasons for investment
Model 7: q11atrial	Yes—start-ups		Yes—direct access reasons for investment, as well as nonaccredited investors
Model 8: q17freetrade	Yes—portals		Yes—direct access reasons for investment
Model 9: q17freetradetime		No— Ontario, British Columbia	Yes—Diversification reasons for investment
Model 10: q12b	Yes—support entrepreneurialism reasons for investment		Yes—Diversification and direct access reasons for investment
Model 11: q15limit	Yes—portfolio managers		Yes—direct access reasons for investment, as well as nonaccredited investors
Model 12: q16thresholdaudited	Yes—support entrepreneurialism reasons for investment, as well as portfolio managers		Yes—direct access reasons for investment, as well as nonaccredited investors

The table summarizes the main findings from the regression evidence in Tables 16.2 and 16.3. Variables are as defined in Table 16.1.

16.5 Conclusion

This chapter presented evidence on crowdfunding from a Canadian-wide survey of potential investors, portals, entrepreneurs, service providers, and other market participants in 2013 Q1, prior to any legalized equity crowdfunding in Canada. The data provide insights into the ways in which market participants would allocate capital and jurisdiction shop in the event of any regional differences in the ways in which crowdfunding markets are regulated.

Some of the evidence is consistent with the race-to-the-bottom view insofar as start-ups want fewer limits on the amount of capital they are able to raise each year, and portals want less onerous continuous disclosure requirements and freely tradable shares without time restrictions. However, investors seek more heavily regulated markets, particularly where there are financial reasons for investment and for investors' whose incentives are to support the entrepreneurial community. Such investors seek greater limits on the amount entrepreneurs can raise, lower thresholds for audited financial statements, more education, greater portal due diligence, and other protections to mitigate risks. In effect, as both sides of the market must come together, the data are on balance consistent with the view that capital will flow to better regulated markets that appropriately protect investors and enable entrepreneurs to operate in an environment which facilitates capital raising.

We noted that there were some apparent regional differences in the data, and in conjunction with the other evidence on the race to the top, no apparent reason to not let the provinces compete in terms of offering the best set of regulations and attract both entrepreneurs and investors. Along these lines, in 2013 Q1, the Province of Ontario in Canada was contemplating the introduction of crowdfunding rules. As a first step, this legislative review began with an exhaustive review of current and proposed crowdfunding models around the world by senior staff members at the Ontario Securities Commission. A review document was prepared, and comments were solicited from a wide array of stakeholders in industry. This type of proactive securities regulatory strategy is consistent with the view that regulators are doing their best to serve the interests of all market participants and pushing forward the regulatory landscape to make the Province of Ontario a leading jurisdiction. The data herein are consistent with the view that more successful jurisdictions will attract more investors that feel safe and, hence, attract entrepreneurs that can more efficiently and effectively raise capital, thereby facilitating a race to the top. But further research from other jurisdictions that are contemplating the introduction of crowdfunding legislation is warranted. As the Canadian survey evidence herein shows, one does not need to have crowdfunding put in place in order to empirically study the potential outcomes from crowdfunding. Likewise, further research as the fascinating crowdfunding regulatory landscape changes over time and across jurisdictions could provide much insight into securities regulation more generally.

Key terms

Audited financial statements
Race to the bottom
Race to the top
Redemption
Rescission
Securities regulation
Threshold

Discussion questions

16.1. What types of crowdfunding regulation are most desired by entrepreneurs: limits on investment, limits on capital raising, education, redemption rights, advertising, trials, time period restrictions, other?

16.2. What types of crowdfunding regulation are most desired by investors: limits on investment, limits on capital raising, education, redemption rights, advertising, trials, time period restrictions, other?

16.3. What types of crowdfunding regulation are most desired by portals: limits on investment, limits on capital raising, education, redemption rights, advertising, trials, time period restrictions, other?

16.4. What do your answers to questions 16.1–16.3 imply about the race to the top or race to the bottom in crowdfunding regulation?

Public policy toward entrepreneurial finance: spillovers and scale-up

17.1 Introduction

It is widely recognized that financing constraints are a significant barrier to entrepreneurship and innovation (e.g., Hall, Moncada-Paternò-Castello, Montresor, & Vezzani, 2016; Wilson et al., 2018). Likewise, it is well recognized that there are significant benefits to entrepreneurial activity, including higher levels of patenting, exports, GDP growth, wage growth, and lower levels of unemployment (Audretsch, 2007; Cumming et al., 2014).

In view of the importance of entrepreneurship and innovation to a nation's well-being, many countries around the world have adopted public policies attempting to encourage entrepreneurial activities (Armour & Cumming, 2006; Leleux & Surlemont, 2003). These policies range from government-supported venture capital (VC) funds, tax subsidies, to securities regulation changes that encourage start-ups and R&D activity (Keuschnigg & Nielsen, 2003). Sometimes, government intervention has been successful, such as the creation of VC programs in Europe (Leleux & Surlemont, 2003) and Australia (Cumming & Johan, 2006). But there are various risks associated with government intervention, and the success of such programs supporting entrepreneurial finance has been called into question in numerous countries around the world, particularly in the case of government VC programs (Lerner, 2009).

The traditional approach to public policy toward entrepreneurial finance has been focused on increasing the supply of certain forms of capital. One reason different components of entrepreneurial finance are considered in isolation is that the literature on entrepreneurial finance is highly segmented. Cumming and Vismara (2017) explain that most empirical papers on financing entrepreneurs are based on data from one source of capital. For example, papers on VC use data typically from vendors, such as Thomson Financial, which in turn obtain data from the venture capitalists themselves, and as a result very little can be known from the data about sources of capital for the entrepreneur other than VC. By contrast, there are only a handful of papers that use data from a wide array of sources of finance in the same paper; exceptions include Cosh et al. (2009) for the United Kingdom and Robb and Robinson (2014) for the United States.

This chapter offers a very straightforward message. We argue that this traditional approach of designing and evaluating public policy toward entrepreneurial finance needs revisiting. Instead, public policy toward entrepreneurial finance should play a greater role in mitigating frictions among different sources of capital to facilitate the scale-up of entrepreneurial ventures from birth to becoming successful large enterprises. Our approach is akin to viewing different sources of entrepreneurial finance as a portfolio and exploring how to optimize the portfolio by having different players working together in a successful ecosystem. Portfolio analysis is not new. For example, the view that VC should be considered as part of pension fund investment because VC fits with portfolio analysis has been around since 1979.[1] But to date, public policies dealing with entrepreneurial finance have scantly considered the interaction of different forms of finance. With the growing array and growth of alternative financing vehicles for entrepreneurs, we think the portfolio approach needs more attention in designing public policy toward entrepreneurial finance.

In this chapter, we consider a wide array of new forms of finance and support mechanisms for entrepreneurs including rewards and equity crowdfunding, government grants, incubators, universities, angel investors, private VC, government VC, private equity, private debt, and initial public offerings (IPOs) (Bruton et al., 2015). We review literature on spillovers, or "externalities," associated with different forms of finance. We consider questions that include, but are not limited to, (1) Do government grants to start-ups help promote scale-up finance in crowdfunding, angel, and VC markets?; (2) Do rules promoting crowdfunding positively affect scale-up finance to angels, VCs, and IPOs?; (3) Do subsidies to incubators and angel investors positively affect scale-up finance through VCs?; (4) Does government VC facilitate scale-up through additional private VC and IPOs?; and (5) Are there positive spillovers from the presence of international investors and entrepreneurs?

The evidence evaluated allows us to identify two key structural features or primitives that give rise to barriers that impede complementarities across different forms of finance: excessive ownership dilution and advice. Further, there are two key structural features that give rise to strategic complements across different forms of entrepreneurial finance: signaling and a broadening of opportunities. To build further on the broader goal of stimulating work on the optimal policy mix, we highlight how these primitives could be used to simplify the analysis or at least make the analysis of the optimal policy mix more tractable.

More specifically, the review of the evidence shows the following examples of these primitives at work. First, government grants have an effective signaling effect in spurring scale-up finance depending on their design and the institutional context. For example, the US Small Business Innovation Research (SBIR) program has been very successful in spurring subsequent VC investment (Howell, 2017). However, government grants in Australia have been less successful in spurring equity crowdfunding (Ahlers et al., 2015). Second, recent equity crowdfunding regulation in the United States under the Jumpstart Our Business Startups (JOBS) Act has had unintended consequences for IPOs, including more

---

[1] See the 1979 amendment to the "prudent man" rule of the US Employment Retirement Income Security Act (ERISA), 29 U.S.C. §§ 1001−1461 (1982).

underpricing and fewer IPOs (Chaplinsky, Weiss Hanley, & Moon, 2017). Likewise, evidence from the United Kingdom shows that more dispersed ownership in equity crowdfunding negatively affects a firm's subsequent equity offerings (Signori & Vismara, 2018). As such, policy options to stimulate crowdfunding need to consider incentives to promote firm growth and access to subsequent forms of finance. Third, while angels and incubators are complements such that promoting one helps the other, angels are substitutes with VC (Cumming & Zhang, 2019; Hellmann & Thiele, 2015) and incubators are likewise substitutes with VC (Cumming, Werth, & Zhang, 2019). Put differently, subsidies to angels and incubators will not necessarily stimulate scale-up through subsequent VC due to potential conflicts in the provision of advice, unless the policy encourages strategic cooperation with venture capitalists. Fourth, government VC funds have the potential to displace not only private VC but also other forms of finance, if the design of the government program is ineffective (Cumming and MacIntosh, 2006, 2007). Finally, policies that promote international investors have the potential to significantly enhance scale-up (Chemmanur, Hull, & Krishnan, 2016; Cumming, Sapienza, Siegel, & Wright, 2009; Cumming et al., 2016), although there may be potential costs such as those from reverse knowledge spillovers (Driffield, Love, & Yang, 2014). Also, we highlight areas where there is a dearth of research and how new papers could fill important gaps in our understanding.

This chapter is organized as follows. Section 17.2 provides a motivating example on problematic public policy programs toward entrepreneurial finance. We motivate the need for a different type of framework by highlighting the situation in Canada. Section 17.3 evaluates the importance of spillovers in entrepreneurial finance from one form of finance to another and how that impacts scale-up of entrepreneurial ventures. Also, we discuss the role of public policy in mitigating negative spillovers from one form of entrepreneurial finance or support mechanism to another. Section 17.4 discusses measurements of public policy toward entrepreneurial finance, and how further research on policy mechanisms could address externalities in entrepreneurial finance. Section 17.5 offers concluding remarks and suggests future research topics based on gaps in extant studies and the need to formulate better policy toward entrepreneurial finance.

17.2 Motivating example

Public policy toward business involves substantial expenditures every year. For example, in the province of Ontario, Canada, the annual budget over 2005–12 on business expenditures was CAD$4 billion (Cumming et al., 2017). As of 2012, there were close to 100 distinct programs in Ontario for government support toward business. Typically, the number of programs increases over time because newly elected ministers have incentives to create new programs to show change and progress, but risk political costs resulting from canceling programs, which has for the most part been consistent with the Ontario experience.

The approach to designing public policy toward entrepreneurial finance is one that has been wrought with mistakes in some countries. In practice, there have been substantial challenges in designing effective government programs toward entrepreneurial finance. Government programs have in some cases achieved the exact opposite of their legislative intent. For example, the Canadian Labor Sponsored Venture Capital Corporation (LSVCC) government program led to a reduction in the aggregate supply of VC in Canada by crowding out private VC (Cumming & MacIntosh, 2006). Unlike private VC funds that are structured as limited partnerships and obtain their capital from institutional investors, LSVCCs are tax-subsidized privately run VC funds that obtain their capital from retail investors, akin to mutual funds. The LSVCC program in Canada is very similar to the VC trust program in the United Kingdom (Cumming & Johan, 2013a). Retail investors are incentivized to invest through tax breaks. LSVCCs compete with other nontax subsidized private VC funds for deal flow. The tax incentives to retail investors are sufficiently generous to encourage capital flows regardless of performance. LSVCCs became the dominant form of VC in Canada since the mid-1990s. So, despite their drastic underperformance (Fig. 17.1), investors continue to invest into LSVCCs. LSVCC managers must invest received capital by the end of the next calendar year, which limits due diligence time that can be spent on selecting investees. And with enormous capital inflows and statutory incentives to make those investments, LSVCCs tend to bid up deal prices, lowering rates of return for private investors in the marketplace. As institutional investors are risk averse and overestimate the presence of LSVCCs in the market, Cumming and MacIntosh (2006)

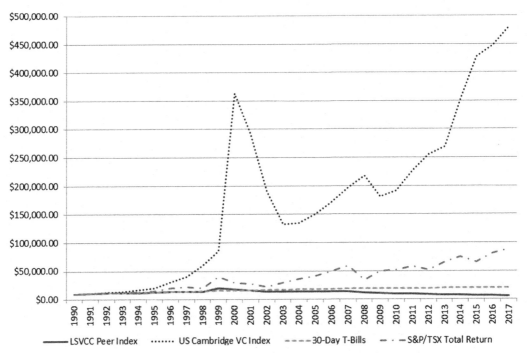

FIGURE 17.1   The performance of $10,000 in Canadian government sponsored venture capital from 1990 to 2017.

LSVCC, Canadian government sponsored venture capital under the Labor Sponsored Venture Capital Tax Credit; *TSX*, Canadian Toronto Stock Exchange Index; *VC*, venture capital. Sources: *Data from The Globe and Mail, and Cambridge Associates LLC.*

and Cumming et al. (2017) found that LSVCCs did not only decrease the supply of VC in Canada (i.e., a one-for-one crowding out effect), but also they actually reduced the aggregate supply of VC in some of the Canadian provinces. The LSVCC program was successfully phased out in Ontario in 2011, after significant opposition (Jacob, Johan, Schweizer & Zhan, 2016; Johan, Schweizer, & Zhan, 2014). But the Canadian federal LSVCC program was scheduled for phase out (planned in 2011 for a 2016 phaseout), only to have it brought back by a newly elected government in 2016.

The Canadian LSVCC case is an interesting example that illustrates the difficulty in removing an ineffective or harmful program. First, governments do not necessarily have competitive advantage over private sectors in either understanding the presence of capital gaps or the ability to solve such apparent problems, and as such any intervention may result in inefficient allocation of resources. Second, private sector institutions may adopt strategies that are contingent on the government support program, which may be inefficient and subject to change in the long run, thereby resulting in long-term operational risk among many private sector institutions. Third, the policy or even the hope of having a policy may be problematic and hence result in agency problems and inefficient lobby efforts (Baumol, 1990). Fourth, it may be costly to adjust the policy depending on how entrenched the policy becomes, market conditions, and the political incentives of the current elected government. Fifth, as there is a wide array of metrics to evaluate public policy, excuses can be made for poorly performing programs by changing the metrics. Policy success may be measured on the basis of financial returns, employment level, employment quality (possibly proxied by wages), employment permanence, economic growth (GDP), quality of economic growth (green or cleantech GDP), patents, patent citations, policy efficiency (such as the time until policies are effective or beneficial institutions mature and can compete without the policy, and the ensuing tax revenues created relative to the government resources spent), and internationalization (attracting foreign investment capital and talented immigrants, and national reputation). With such a wide array, failure in one dimension may be excused by success in another dimension.

The Canadian example highlights the problems associated with segmented policy decisions ignoring interactions among different sources of capital. In Ontario, alongside the phaseout of the LSVCC program announced in 2005 and effective in 2011, a new program was introduced with the idea that one new VC program should replace one removed VC program. As with other areas in public policy, program design in one country tends to resemble programs that have been adopted in other countries. In Ontario in 2008, the provincial government created the Ontario Venture Capital Fund (OVCF) program, which has many similarities to Australia's 1997 Innovation Investment Fund (IIF) program and Pre-Seed Government Venture Capital Fund (PSF) program (Cumming & Johan, 2006). Arguably, with the success of programs like the IIF and PSF, the OVCF strategy is a good one. But simply adopting successful programs from other countries is not necessarily an ideal strategy, as the approach does not consider how it fits with a systematic portfolio of programs supporting entrepreneurs. Moreover, the closing of the IIF program in Australia in 2014 does not render the necessity of cutting the comparable OCVF program in Ontario. Apparently, a plan that accounts for a broader set of factors is of course warranted. As such, a portfolio approach is proposed in the next section.

17.3 Spillovers and scale-up in entrepreneurial finance

This section advances a different framework for understanding optimal public policy design in the entrepreneurial finance arena. The proposed framework is very distinct from the current practices in jurisdictions like Canada as discussed immediately earlier.

The motivating example from Canada highlights the spillovers or "externalities" in entrepreneurial finance. In the Canadian case the spillovers were negative as public funds were used to compete against private funds in the entrepreneurial investment process, thereby resulting in reduced efficiency and improper asset allocation. The externalities are not purely "pecuniary" (i.e., only operate through the price system) such that they manifest in efficiencies only when there are existing frictions (in competitive markets, pecuniary externalities do not create inefficiency; see Greenwald & Stiglitz, 1986). There are also "technological" externalities, where the actions of one investor negatively affect the utility or profit of another (Greenwald & Stiglitz, 1986), due to the fact that various forms of entrepreneurial financiers not only provide financial capital but also take specific actions in monitoring and adding value (Howell, 2017).

In this section, we take a broader look at the wide spectrum of different sources of entrepreneurial finance and the spillovers that exist among them. The spillovers in this section are summarized in Table 17.1 and discussed later. We consider whether or not different forms of finance are complements or substitutes, whether or not agency problems are exacerbated with the presence of more than one form of finance obtained by an entrepreneur, and whether or not growth is accelerated with public policies that encourage complementarities across different forms of entrepreneurial finance and mitigate conflicts of interest.

In this section, we consider different forms of entrepreneurial finance covering rewards and equity crowdfunding, grants, incubators, universities, angel investors, VC, private equity, private debt, and IPOs. We do not evaluate the merits of each source of capital or possible rationales for public support to different sources in isolation.[2] Instead, our focus is on the interaction of these different forms of finance and whether or not there are any positive or negative externalities at this intersection. To the extent that there are externalities, there is a potential role for policy to mitigate problems and foster easier entrepreneurial scale-up through alternative financing channels. We begin with the issue of grants to entrepreneurs, as they are for the most nascent entrepreneurs and highlight the importance of measuring success through scale-up.

17.3.1 Do grants facilitate scale-up through subsequent investment?

Government grants are widely used in countries around the world to encourage the earliest level of entrepreneurial activity. One way to evaluate the success of these grants is to measure the extent to which they encourage individuals in entrepreneurship. That is not

---

[2] Other commentators have carried out analyses of scale-up from specific programs. See for example Aernoudt (2017) and Duruflé, Hellmann, and Wilson (2018) for an assessment of venture debt, and venture capital, respectively, in promoting scale-up of entrepreneurial finance in Europe. This and other work on scale-up, however, does not consider externalities from one form of finance to another.

TABLE 17.1 Summary of prior studies on spillovers in entrepreneurial finance.

	[2] Equity crowdfunding	[3] Government granting agencies	[4] Incubators	[5] Universities	[6] Angel	[7] Private VC	[8] Government VC	[9] Private equity	[10] Private debt (bank or trade credit)	[11] IPO
[1] Rewards crowdfunding	Equity crowdfunding does not crowd out rewards crowdfunding (Cholakova & Clarysse, 2015)	Government grants can work to stimulate crowdfunding (Lehner & Nicholls, 2014); but the success of the project for a community depends on the diversity of the community involvement (Davies, 2015)	Firms in incubators can use crowdfunding to successfully secure external finance (Schwienbacher & Larralde, 2012)	University spinouts can use rewards crowdfunding as a viable means to finance projects (Wieck, Bretschneider, & Leimeister, 2013)	Rewards crowdfunding can spur angel investment (Mason & Harrison, 2015)	Crowdfunding gives rise to higher numbers of subsequent VC deals (Sorenson et al., 2016; Kaminski et al., 2019)	Government programs can use rewards crowdfunding to leverage success (McCahery & Vermeulen, 2014, 2016)	Crowdfunding is needed for early stage; PE focuses on subsequent rounds and later stage investment (Harrison, 2013)	Unknown	Unknown (expect scant overlap due to difference in stage of development)
[2] Equity crowdfunding	–	Government awards do little to spur on the success of equity crowdfunding. (Ahlers et al., 2015)	Social capital through incubators may facilitate equity crowdfunding (Vismara, 2016)	Social capital through universities facilitates equity crowdfunding (Vismara, 2016)	Angel syndicates undermine the democratization of capital associated with equity crowdfunding (Agrawal et al., 2016)	The US JOBS Act has given rise to higher valuations (unicorns) and later stage VC (Chaplinsky et al., 2017) Crowdfunding in the United Kingdom: dispersed ownership means less likely to issue subsequent equity (Signori & Vismara, 2018)	Government programs can use equity crowdfunding to leverage success (McCahery & Vermeulen, 2014, 2016)	Equity crowdfunding helps obtain subsequent PE rounds (Signori & Vismara, 2018)	Unknown	The US JOBS Act caused more underpricing, fewer IPOs (Chaplinsky et al., 2017) Crowdfunding in the United Kingdom: more dispersed ownership firms are less likely to issue subsequent equity (Signori & Vismara, 2018)
[3] Government granting agencies	–	–	Incubators are a critical part of successful government granting programs (Etzkowitz, 2002)	Academic entrepreneurs pursue their own research interests at the expense of creating a fast growing high tech start-up (Meyer, 2003)	Government support for business angel networks is important to limit capital gaps (Mason & Harrison, 2015)	An SBIR award doubles a firm's chances of receiving VC, particularly for more financially constrained firms. Grants reduce investor uncertainty by funding technology prototyping (Howell, 2017)	Government grants in cleantech can spur successful cleantech VC investment for private and public sector VCs (Bürer & Wüstenhagen, 2009)	Unknown (expect scant overlap due to difference in stage of development)	Unknown	Unknown (expect scant overlap due to difference in stage of development)

(Continued)

TABLE 17.1 (Continued)

	[2] Equity crowdfunding	[3] Government granting agencies	[4] Incubators	[5] Universities	[6] Angel	[7] Private VC	[8] Government VC	[9] Private equity	[10] Private debt (bank or trade credit)	[11] IPO
[4] Incubators	–	–	–	A university link a tech park reduces the probability of new venture failure, but also slows time to graduation (Rothaermel & Thursby, 2005)	Early stage business advisory hubs can facilitate access to angel capital (Cumming & Fischer, 2012)	Tech parks and VCs are substitutes: when investing together there is a 5% reduction in the probability of an acquisition, and a 40% increase in the time to an acquisition (Cumming et al., 2019). Tech parks perform worse when they actively license technology (Cumming & Johan, 2013b)	Government VC and incubators are part of the dynamic ecosystem for successful entrepreneurial and innovation environments in Israel (Avnimelech & Teubal, 2006)	Unknown (expect scant overlap due to difference in stage of development)	University spinouts obtain significant debt finance (Wright & Fu, 2015)	There are scant IPOs from incubators (Cohen & Hochberg, 2014)
[5] Universities	–	–	–	–	University spinouts obtain significant angel finance (Wright & Fu, 2015).	University spinouts obtain significant VC finance (Wright & Fu, 2015)	University affiliation spurs on successful pore-seed government investment in Australia (Cumming & Johan, 2009)	University spinouts obtain significant private equity finance (Wright & Fu, 2015)	University spinouts obtain significant debt finance (Wright & Fu, 2015)	Ties to star scientists reduce the time to IPO (Darby & Zucker, 2001). University spin-offs are valued more favorably in IPOs but have worse long-term operating performance (Bonardo et al., 2011)
[6] Angel	–	–	–	–	–	Angels and VCs are substitutes in theory (Hellmann & Thiele, 2015) and evidence (Cumming & Zhang, 2019)	Angel capital is unrelated to the removal of tax-subsidized government VC programs in Canada (Cumming & Johan, 2010)	Angel deals and private equity deals are substitutes (Cumming & Zhang, 2019)	Angel capital and bank debt are substitutes (Cosh et al., 2009)	Angel deals are less likely to IPO than VC and PE deals (Cumming & Zhang, 2019)

[7]	Private VC	—	—	—	—	—	—	Government programs do not crowd out on average in Europe (Leleux & Surlemont, 2003) and Australia (Cumming & Johan, 2006) where the government acts more as a limited partner. Government programs crowd out private VC in Canada where the program gives tax advantages to one type of fund (Cumming & MacIntosh, 2006)	Early stage VC facilitates late stage VC deals and PE deals (Mason & Harrison, 2015)	Venture lending is more suitable for late stage firms with higher liquidation values and less uncertainty regarding outcomes (Tykvová, 2017)	VC spurs successful IPOs in the United States (Gompers & Lerner, 1999; Nahata, 2008) and around the world (Cumming & Johan, 2013a; Nahata et al., 2014)
[8]	Government VC	—	—	—	—	—	—	Government VC structured as tax incentives to labor-sponsored investment funds does not spur more VC or PE investment locally or abroad (Cumming & MacIntosh, 2006)	Government VC funds in Canada are more likely to make use of debt finance (Cumming, 2005)	Tax subsidized government VC programs tend to be negatively associated with IPOs, while programs with governments as limited partners tend to be positively associated with IPOs (Johan, 2010; Cumming & Johan, 2013a)
[9]	Private equity	—	—	—	—	—	—	—	National policies that protect creditor rights attract more private equity investment (Cao, Cumming, Qian, & Wang, 2015)	Private equity significantly improves IPO performance (Cao & Lerner, 2009). Publicly reporting private equity funds have more fairly priced IPOs (Goktan & Muslu, 2018)

(Continued)

TABLE 17.1 (Continued)

	[2] Equity crowdfunding	[3] Government granting agencies	[4] Incubators	[5] Universities	[6] Angel	[7] Private VC	[8] Government VC	[9] Private equity	[10] Private debt (bank or trade credit)	[11] IPO
[10] Private debt	—	—	—	—	—	—	—	—	—	IPOs with high debt have lower valuation uncertainty and are less underpriced compared to VC-backed IPOs. IPOs with high debt levels underperform in the long run, particularly when they do not have VC (Barry & Mihov, 2015)

This table summarizes select prior studies that identify externalities from one source of entrepreneurial finance to another. "—" refers to a redundant part of the matrix as the matrix is symmetrical. *IPOs*, Initial public offerings; *JOBS*, Jumpstart Our Business Startups; *PE*, private equity; *SBIR*, Small Business Innovation Research; *VC*, venture capital.

our aim here. Others have evaluated this goal and have argued quite convincingly that simply encouraging more people to be entrepreneurs might be bad public policy because the average start-up is not innovative and generates merely a few low paying jobs (Shane, 2009).

The other way to evaluate the success of government grants is to ascertain whether or not the government grant can create an amplifying effect that scales up to a high-quality venture, leading to further investments from the private sector. To that end, there is much research that shows various government granting programs have been extremely successful. For example, Howell (2017) shows that the US Department of Energy's SBIR grant program, which grants each winner US$150,000 in the first phase, has positive impacts on entrepreneurial outcomes and improves firm's chances of receiving subsequent VC and improves also probability of realizing positive revenue. Howell (2017) considers the signaling value of SBIR awards, as well as the selection versus value-added effects of such awards. The evidence in Howell (2017) is consistent with the view that the SBIR awards are so effective because they fund technological prototyping, and not necessarily because they are an effective signal.

Government granting programs work in countries outside the United States as well; for example, McKenzie (2017) shows that the YouWin! business plan competition program in Nigeria, which grants each winner approximately US$50,000, substantially increases recipient firms' probability of operating the business, hiring more employees and earning higher sales and profits. Other industry-specific government grants have been shown to be particularly effective for subsequent scale-up, such as grants in cleantech industry, which have had positive impacts on the subsequent success of cleantech VC (Bürer & Wustenhagen, 2009).

Etzkowitz (2002) explains that government granting programs are a critical part of the entrepreneurial ecosystem and need to operate alongside other programs such as incubators that provide coaching to nascent entrepreneurs with scientific skills but little business experience. Similarly, Mason and Harrison (2015) argue that government granting agencies need to operate alongside government support for business angel networks to promote a healthy start-up environment.

But in the case of crowdfunding, government grants may lead to uncertain outcomes. Grants can certainly facilitate the success of rewards crowdfunding (Lehner & Nicholls, 2014). But rewards-based crowdfunding may lead to outcomes that exacerbate social inequality depending on the diversity of participation of the crowd (Davies, 2015). We may infer that entrepreneurs who use a government grant are more likely to scale up to socially optimal outcomes when they secure broad community participation. In the case of equity crowdfunding, government grants have had ambiguous impact on enabling ventures to scale up. Nevertheless, in Australia, government grants are uncorrelated with the equity crowdfunding success in terms of the amount of capital raised and the speed of capital raises (Ahlers et al., 2015).

It is possible that grant design, grant competitiveness, granted amounts, and frequency of award can all play a role in enabling entrepreneurs to scale up to other forms of finance. Grants can be potentially effective in funding prototypes and project designs. As well, grants can create a signaling mechanism to future sources of capital, although the value of the signal may vary depending on the scarcity and quality of grant. Comparative work on the effectiveness of entrepreneurial scale-up resulting from different forms of grants and developing under different institutional contexts is warranted.

17.3.2 Does crowdfunding facilitate scale-up?

Crowdfunding encompasses donations, rewards, lending, and equity platforms that enable individuals and firms to raise money from large numbers of potential donors or investors (Schwienbacher & Larralde, 2012). The global crowdfunding market has more than doubled each year from 2013 to 2016 from $6 billion in 2013 to $16 billion in 2014 to $33 billion in 2015, and estimated at over $65 billion in 2016.[3] Crowdfunding worldwide surpassed angel investment (approximately $25 billion in 2015) in 2015 and is expected to surpass VC (approximately $50 billion in 2015) in 2016 and 2017 based on the growth trends of these different sources of finance.[4]

Over the past decade, rewards-based crowdfunding has been the most important financing channel for entrepreneurs around the world. The two largest platforms are Kickstarter and Indiegogo. These platforms enable entrepreneurs to raise small amounts, typically less than $50,000, and with a range of less than $10,000 and up to $10 million. Crowdfunding can be pursued by the most nascent stage entrepreneurs to fund purely ideas, albeit with the risk that disclosure of an idea on a platform leads to dissemination of the idea and risk of theft. Crowdfunding may also be used by more advanced entrepreneurs: entrepreneurs who reside in incubators and plan to complement the resources they have access to or entrepreneurs who obtain resources from government grants or other support programs, and more generally entrepreneurs that are otherwise further along their path of development than a mere idea (Mason & Harrison, 2015; McCahery & Vermeulen, 2014, 2016; Schwienbacher & Larralde, 2012). Entrepreneurs that demonstrate traction (i.e., demand) for their product through rewards-based crowdfunding mitigate information asymmetry with subsequent investors and attract subsequent angel and VC backing (Colombo & Shafi, 2016). Large sample evidence indicates that rewards-based crowdfunding statistically causes subsequent VC funding in a region (Kaminski, Hopp, & Tykvová, 2019; Sorenson, Assenova, Li, Boada, & Fleming, 2016). Rewards-based crowdfunding does not impede equity crowdfunding (Cholakova & Clarysse, 2015). Overall, prior work is therefore consistent with the view that the externalities with rewards-based crowdfunding are very positive and enable nascent stage entrepreneurs to scale up their business through a variety of subsequent investor types.

There are a number of opportunities brought by equity crowdfunding (Hornuf & Schwienbacher, 2018). First, for small business entrepreneurs, the average project size is approximately $0.3 million in Australia (Ahlers et al., 2015) and $0.5 million in the United States (Cumming, Johan, & Zhang, 2019). By contrast, most VC deals are within the range of $1–$10 million, and many significantly more than $10 million in recent years (Chaplinsky et al., 2017). Second, on average, roughly one-third of the equity crowdfunding projects are fully funded (Ahlers et al., 2015; Cumming, Johan, & Zhang, 2019), which is significantly higher than the proportion of firms that receive VC investment (0.2% of the firms receive VC; Puri & Zarutskie, 2012). Third, there are limited transaction costs in crowdfunding: normally set at a few percentage points of the capital raised depending on the platform.

---

[3] *Source*: Crowdfunder. Aggregate worldwide crowdfunding data for 2016 and 2017 were not yet available at the time of writing this chapter.

[4] *Source*: Crowdfunder. Aggregate worldwide crowdfunding data for 2016 and 2017 were not yet available at the time of writing this chapter.

By contrast, legal fees in angel and VC investment can be quite substantial and comprise a much more significant portion of the capital raised for smaller deals and angel deals in particular. Finally, equity crowdfunding is viewed as being the democratization of capital, without gender or other biases (Guenther et al., 2018). VC, by contrast, is confounded with significant gender effects (Gompers, Mukharlyamov, Weisburst, & Xuan, 2014).

With the rapidly growing equity crowdfunding market, many scholars have investigated the externalities equity crowdfunding may pose on alternative forms of entrepreneurial finance. On one hand, in theory, there may be complementarities between equity crowdfunding and angel and VC investors. Angels and venture capitalists may have incentives to participate in equity crowdfunding to diversify their deal sourcing means, thereby creating a new revenue generating channel. Further, angels and venture capitalists may want to build a relationship with start-ups from an earlier stage, as this relationship may result in fruitful larger investments later on. As with rewards crowdfunding, equity crowdfunding is an instrument to test market traction of the start-up.

There are potentially some complementarities between equity crowdfunding and other sources of entrepreneurial finance. For example, the social capital entrepreneurs obtain through an affiliation with government agencies and incubators may enable more successful equity crowdfunding, thereby rendering positive externalities between incubators, government granting programs, and equity crowdfunding (McCahery & Vermeulen, 2014, 2016; Vismara, 2016).

On the other hand, there are frictions between equity crowdfunding and angel capital. Agrawal et al. (2016) note that the participation of angel investor syndicates in online crowdfunding platforms tends to undermine the original intent of crowdfunding markets, particularly as angel groups have distinct investment practices (Bonini, Capizzi, & Zocchi, 2019). That is, crowdfunding enables the democratization of capital to entrepreneurs. But the presence of online angel investor syndicates shifts the focus from crowdfunding entrepreneurs to crowdfunding lead investors in angel syndicates as the crowd is much more inclined to align with reputable lead investors (Agrawal et al., 2016).

As well, there are potential costs associated with equity crowdfunding in respect of generating subsequent VC investment and IPOs. First, the dispersion in ownership may dissuade subsequent angel or VC investors from participating in a deal. Signori and Vismara (2018) find evidence that the extent of ownership dispersion in equity crowdfunding is negatively correlated with subsequent equity offerings in the United Kingdom. Second, in the United States the JOBS Act has enabled nationwide equity crowdfunding since May 2016. In order to make equity crowdfunding more attractive and not merely legal, the Securities and Exchange Commission also eased the reporting requirements of entrepreneurial firms; in particular, it increased the number of shareholders from 500 to 2000 before public reporting requirements become effective and lowered disclosure obligations for IPO firms in their first 5 years subsequent to the IPO (Chaplinsky et al., 2017). In particular, these changes in United States have been shown to cause the rise of large "unicorn" VC investments with over $1 billion valuations prior to IPOs, given the different reporting standards and incentives to avoid being public.[5] Further, the changes increased

---

[5] https://www.marketwatch.com/story/the-government-tried-to-encourage-ipos-but-it-helped-create-the-age-of-the-unicorn-2017-12-26. "You can have nearly unlimited private investors, they can raise huge amounts of money, ergo the birth of the unicorn... In a convoluted way, the JOBS act is directly responsible for the rise of the unicorn and the depression of the IPO market."

the costs of capital associated with being a publicly listed firm, increased IPO underpricing, and reduced the number of IPOs (Chaplinsky et al., 2017). Overall, therefore, there is reason to be concerned with negative externalities associated with equity crowdfunding, and we would not expect equity crowdfunding in the way it has been designed in the United States to spur subsequent scale-up investment through IPOs.

Signori and Vismara's (2018) evidence from the United Kingdom and Chaplinaky et al.'s (2017) evidence from the United States suggest some scope for policy to mitigate frictions between equity crowdfunding and other financing channels and to better enable scale-up through follow-on equity investment. The biggest concern is about large ownership dispersion in the very early stage of a firm's life cycle: it leads to excessive reporting and disclosure problems for an entrepreneur. A possible solution is treating crowdfunded shares as legally distinct from other equity issuances in regards to reporting obligations so that there are not overly perverse incentives that have changed the dynamics of VC and IPOs as in the United States Further, crowdfunded shares could have tied with their mandated drag along provisions that enable entrepreneurs to secure additional finance in subsequent offerings, which can be subject to achieving a hurdle rate for crowdfunding investors. Other possible solutions should be contemplated among policymakers to ensure that equity crowdfunding does not impose externalities that discourage scale-up finance.

Crowdlending has potential to facilitate scale-up investment as well, but there is scant research on the interaction between crowdlending and other forms of subsequent finance. Evidence to date shows that crowdlending markets function quite well, where information gleaned from the crowd is more effective at evaluating borrower quality than traditional mechanisms such as credit rating scores (Iyer et al., 2015). Hence, while adverse selection may be pronounced among small borrowers without a significant track record, it appears that crowdlending is a more effective means of finance than traditional modes of lending. Further research is warranted on the performance of companies and their subsequent financing success in scale-up after crowdlending.

Separate from crowdlending, as identified in Fig. 17.1, venture lending appears to complement VC (Tykvová, 2017). There is evidence that lending to private firms enables entrepreneurial growth and survival (Cole & Sokolyk, 2018), but VC appears to play a more pronounced role than banks in stimulating entrepreneurial development (Cole, Cumming, & Li, 2016). Further research is needed on the interplay between private debt and other sources of entrepreneurial finance.

17.3.3 Scaling up from incubators, universities, and angel investors

Early stage incubators and technology parks (hereafter "incubators"[6]) provide a wide array of services to resident entrepreneurs, including at times direct financing (Cumming & Johan, 2013b). Incubators that more actively engage in claiming ownership over technologies developed as a resident of incubator, and offer services to license that technology to others, typically have resident entrepreneurial firms that are less

---

[6] Related literature makes important distinctions about different types of incubators as distinct from technology parks. For the purpose of our discussion, we treat them as the same, without loss of meaning insofar as they involve externalities with various sources of entrepreneurial finance.

successful (Cumming & Johan, 2013b). Incubators that provide coaching and advice to entrepreneurs, by contrast, are more often able to foster entrepreneurial firms that secure subsequent financing such as angel investment (Cumming & Fischer, 2012). The evidence on the positive impact of advice from incubators and angel investors holds, even after controlling for the nonrandom assignment of different types of firms to incubators, at least insofar as available data enable such selection effects to be controlled for (Cumming & Fischer, 2012).

Incubators have a variety of incentives to maximize returns and/or reputation and size, which at times may come in conflict with other sources of capital. With a large sample of firms in the Crunchbase dataset, Cumming et al. (2019) find evidence that firms that simultaneously have VC and incubator support are much less likely to achieve a successful acquisition exit, and the time to exit is significantly prolonged. In particular, when venture capitalists invest in firms residing in incubators, there is a 5% reduction in the probability of an acquisition and a 40% increase in the time to acquisition, all other things being equal (Cumming et al., 2019).

When incubators are associated with universities, by contrast, there is pronounced reduction in the probability of bankruptcy, although the time to exit from the incubator is substantially longer (Rothaermel & Thursby, 2005; see also Lockett et al., 2005). While these effects indeed may be attributable to the inherent nature of firms started at universities, and additional work that benchmarks selection versus value-added effects on topic could be helpful to sort out the joint impact of universities and incubators. University spin-offs also obtain significant angel finance, VC, and private equity (Wright & Fu, 2015). Ties to star scientists have been shown to reduce the time to IPO (Darby & Zucker, 2001). Further, university spin-offs are valued more favorably in IPOs, albeit with worse long-term operating performance (Bonardo, Paleari, & Vismara, 2011), possibly due to conflicting objectives associated with maximizing operating performance and engaging in scientific research.

Overall, therefore, the evidence is consistent with the view that incubators and universities are important vehicles that successfully enable scale-up with subsequent forms of finance. There are some potential conflicts of interest between entrepreneurs and incubators that engage more often in licensing technology, and between university spin-offs and university-based scientists that pursue research endeavors at the expense of maximizing financial returns. Governance structures through financial contracts and boards of directors can be put into place to mitigate these potential problems.

Angel investors, by contrast, are associated with more pronounced conflicts of interest with others in start-up scaling up. Prior work has quite consistently shown that angel investors and venture capitalists are substitutes (Cumming & Zhang, 2019; Goldfarb, Hoberg, Kirsch, & Triantis, 2013; Hellmann & Thiele, 2015). Angels are less likely than venture capitalists to have successful exits such as IPOs and acquisitions (Cumming & Zhang, 2019). Venture capitalists often view the equity involvement of an active angel investor negatively and conflicts also arise from the active advice from angels alongside venture capitalists.

In view of the evidence that incubators and venture capitalists are substitutes (Cumming et al., 2019) and that angels and venture capitalists are substitutes (Cumming & Zhang, 2019; Goldfarb et al., 2013; Hellmann & Thiele, 2015), public policies that subsidize angels and incubators may be in conflict with policy goals of scaling up entrepreneurial growth through VC investment and IPOs. Policy incentives to angels and incubators could be redesigned to incentivize exit through the next investor who will provide scale-up finance for the entrepreneur. Angels and incubators that benefit from public subsidies should ideally benefit only when they promote the overall entrepreneurial ecosystem, and part of that ecosystem includes facilitating entrepreneurial scale-up.

17.3.4 Private venture capital, government venture capital, and scale up

Private venture capital, especially for reputable VC funds, carries a clear positive signal in IPO and has the potential to mitigate underpricing and facilitate long-term IPO performance (Gompers & Lerner, 1999; Jeppsson, 2018; Nahata, 2008; Nahata et al., 2014). More transparent VC and private equity funds that publicly report their activities have realized even superior IPO performance (Goktan & Muslu, 2018). Public policies that encourage more transparent reporting of VC and private equity backed activities also limit misinformation provided to institutional investors for short-term fundraising gains (Cumming & Walz, 2010; Johan & Zhang, 2015). Public policies that encourage more transparent VC and private equity funds therefore enhance the overall size of VC markets, IPO performance and facilitate financial scale-up for entrepreneurs.

Government VC, by contrast, has had a less successful track record (Lerner, 2009). Government VC funds that are organized as tax subsidized mutual fund–like entities to attract retail investors have not been successful and have in fact crowded out private investment thereby frustrating the legislative objective of scaling up entrepreneurial growth (see Fig. 17.1 and accompanying text in Section 17.2). Government VC funds that are organized as limited partnerships where government investors receive financial returns only after private sector limited partners achieve their preset hurdle rate of return have been more successful, such as in the case of the Australian IIF program and the Australian PSF program (Cumming & Johan, 2006). The superior organizational and governance structure with the government as a limited partner relative to tax subsidized retail VC funds enables and incentivizes more and better advice to investee firms and thereby is associated with better operating performance of investee firms (Cumming & Johan, 2006). Further research is warranted on the extent to which government VC funds enable scale-up, and under what conditions.

17.3.5 International investors

Should policymakers subsidize or promote international investors in entrepreneurial finance? On the positive side, there is evidence from VC suggesting that firms are much better off in terms of their success with exiting and scale-up when they have both domestic and international investors (Chemmanur et al., 2016; Cumming et al., 2009, 2016; Hain et al., 2016). On the downside, however, there are dampened economic benefits to the sponsoring country if the company migrates to a new country, which happens quite frequently in the case of international VC (Cumming et al., 2009). An additional potential negative effect involves reverse knowledge spillovers. That is, collaboration with an external partner can give rise to the knowledge generated or gained being used to the advantage of either the collaborator or other affiliated firms in different markets and at the expense of the domestic firm (Driffield et al., 2014).

17.3.6 Summary of lessons learned: structural features (primitives) directing externalities

The evidence reviewed in the prior Sections 17.3.1–17.3.5 can be best summarized by highlighting four primitives, two of which enhance complementarities across different forms of finance and two of which impede complementarities across different forms of finance. The first primitive involves excessive ownership dilution, which can impede accessing subsequent forms of finance. For example, the evidence suggests that equity crowdfunding with nontrivial ownership dilution can impede subsequent investment. Indeed, if ownership dilution is overly aggressive with equity crowdfunding, the entrepreneurial project may fail at the equity crowdfunding stage itself (Ahlers et al., 2015). Ownership dilution reduces the flexibility of the company to obtain subsequent capital and increases administrative costs in corporate communications to large numbers of small investors (Signori & Vismara, 2018). Further, ownership dispersion can increase corporate transparency in a way that is too premature for the strategic operation and progress of an innovative entrepreneurial project (McCahery & Vermeulen, 2016).

The second primitive involves the provision of advice. Advice from one type of investor may come into conflict with that from another type of investor, particularly when the advice mixes the strategic objectives of that of the investor with the best interests of the investee company. For these reasons, prior work shows angel investors and venture capitalists are not complements (Cumming & Zhang, 2019; Hellmann & Thiele, 2015) and technology parks, angel investors, and venture capitalists are not complements (Cumming et al., 2019).

The third primitive involves signaling. To be effective, signals must be costly if the signal comes from the entrepreneurial firm (Ahlers et al., 2015), or hard to obtain if the signal comes an external certification provider such as through a government award (Howell, 2017). Effective signals mitigate information asymmetries faced by subsequent investors and therefore enable better decision-making by subsequent investors and a better matching of quality entrepreneurs with their investors.

The fourth and final primitive involves the broadening of opportunities, or lowering the barriers of "distance." Earlier, we discussed distance as a geographic measure. A broader geographic scope of investors broadens the geographic reach of the entrepreneurs' business opportunities (Cumming et al., 2016; Hain et al., 2016). But it is worth adding here that a broadening of opportunities may not only involve geographic distance but also involve minimizing costs associated with other types of institutional distance, including cultural, cognitive, and regulatory distance. A lowering of any form of institutional distance created through barriers of language, culture, regulation, and other impediments can enhance the positive spillover value associated with alternative forms of capital (Cumming et al., 2017) regardless if it is the same geographic area or a broadened geographic area. For example, Cumming and Fischer (2012) show that advice provided through publicly funded incubators in Ontario, Canada, significantly enables entrepreneurs to overcome various impediments of institutional distance and obtain strategic networks and angel investment to further grow their business within their own region.

17.4 Measuring and achieving impact

Different types of subsidies, such as direct grant, tax credit, incubator support, and entrepreneurial training programs, are often implemented by governments around the world to enhance small business development. However, empirical analyses exhibit mixed evidence on the impact of government programs on small business development. And academics have faced pronounced challenges in evaluating the quality of public support programs toward VC. For example, Lerner (2009) evaluated the success of European government VC funds on the basis of research that measures the success of a government program as the ratio of early to late stage VC. This type of measure relied on by Lerner (2009) is clearly misguided, as it gives rise to rankings of European VC market quality with countries such as Hungary, Austria, and Iceland as the best VC markets in the world and the United Kingdom as the worst VC market in the world (Cumming & Johan, 2013a).[7]

An additional problem with measuring impact of policy in entrepreneurial finance and designing the optimal set of programs is the number of measures that have been used. A large number of metrics becomes problematic because poorly performing programs can be excused by changing the evaluation criteria. While it is relatively easy to measure firm-level performance owing to government subsidy, it is less straightforward to evaluate the impact of government subsidy on social welfare in general. As government subsidy is ultimately funded by taxpayers, the effectiveness of government subsidy is an important topic attracts broad attention from policymakers, practitioners, and academic scholars.

The effectiveness of government subsidies has traditionally been evaluated by the following four indicators: employment (the number and quality of new jobs), economic growth (GDP growth), efficiency (including R&D, patents, and the building of sustainable businesses that will not need the policy support in the long term), and international impact (exports). Each of these indicators is complicated by the potential spillovers or side effects of government subsidy. As discussed earlier, positive spillovers occur when public subsidy fosters growth in related areas, but often spillovers are negative. Additional research is needed to better understand how to measure spillovers across different policy outcomes (returns, leveraging private investment, more jobs, more new companies, internationalization, and others).

Moreover, additional research is needed to better understand the policy levers that minimize negative externalities, reduce conflicts of interest across different sources of finance, and facilitate scale-up. Theoretical work has examined optimal capital gains versus employment tax policies to encourage the quality of investor advice and to maximize the number of entrepreneurs (Keuschnigg & Nielsen, 2003). Tax practice can likewise

---

[7] See also https://corpgov.law.harvard.edu/2013/04/11/measuring-the-effectiveness-of-public-policy-towards-venture-capital/

encourage securities to be used in VC finance (Gilson & Schizer, 2003). There is empirical consensus that small business tax relief programs do not encourage scale-up (Chen & Mintz, 2011). But more empirical work would be helpful in examining specific influences on different types of investors in entrepreneurial finance. Also, more empirical work on the role of tax versus direct government expenditure programs and regulations (including securities law, bankruptcy law, and labor regulations) in fostering scale-up is needed in regards to their roles in coordinating scale-up across different sources of entrepreneurial finance.

17.5 Conclusion

The evolving relationship between public policy and entrepreneurial finance needs to be considered in light of new technology, the changing nature of marketplaces, and the options open to entrepreneurs to achieve financial scale-up. This chapter proposed a new approach to evaluating public policy toward entrepreneurial finance. We motivated a need for policymakers to have a new framework on promoting entrepreneurial finance by discussing the policy decisions made in Canada.

The approach we take in this chapter is to recognize some very recent advances in entrepreneurial finance scholarship. The literature in entrepreneurial finance has been extremely segmented over the years. For example, academic work on VC typically involves data only from venture capitalists without recognizing or addressing other sources of capital available to entrepreneurs before, during and after VC. Indeed, there exist large spillovers to other areas in entrepreneurial finance. Rarely does a dataset involve more than one form of finance, as the data in academic studies typically are derived from the source of capital and not the entrepreneur. Only more recently have we seen work that has started to examine the interplay between one source of finance with another. This work shows that spillovers across different sources of finance are large, and sometimes negative. The central proposition in this chapter is that these negative externalities could be mitigated through policy responses.

We summarized two key primitives that impede complementarities across different forms of entrepreneurial finance: excessive ownership dilution and advice. There are two key primitives that enhance complementarities: signaling and a broadening of opportunities. These primitives can be used to simplify the analysis or at least make the analysis of the optimal policy mix more tractable.

This chapter is a first step at identifying the array of spillovers across different sources of entrepreneurial finance. Further work is needed to better understand the nature of externalities in and across different industries, in and across different regions, and across different sources of capital. It is possible that policy responses are more effective in specific industries such as cleantech where capital gaps are potentially more pronounced. Likewise, there could be different policy responses depending on the legal structure, cultural institutions, and economic environment in different countries. These related topics would help shed light on optimal public policy toward entrepreneurial finance.

Key terms

Acquisition
Agency problems
Angel finance
Banks
Complements
Grants
Incubator
Initial public offering
Merger
Private debt
Scale-up
Substitutes
Trade credit
Venture capital

Discussion questions

17.1. Does rewards crowdfunding in some ways impede follow-on finance? Explain with reference to theory and evidence. Is your answer different for different types of follow-on finance?

17.2. Does equity crowdfunding in some ways impede follow-on finance? Explain with reference to theory and evidence. Is your answer different for different types of follow-on finance?

17.3. How do your responses to questions 17.1 and 17.2 inform government policy and regulatory design for crowdfunding and other forms of entrepreneurial finance?

17.4. Does it help an entrepreneur to have another type of finance prior to crowdfunding? If so, why? If not, why not?

17.5. Does it help an entrepreneur to be connected with an incubator or university to enable successful crowdfunding? Why or why not? Explain with reference to agency and signaling theory, and discuss existing evidence.

18

Regulation and investment in fintech ventures

... without the financial crisis and the popular anger it spawned against the whole banking system, there would be no fintech[1] ***"Fintech's Wakeup Call," Bloomberg, February 22, 2016.***

"After the 2008 crisis, banks faced additional capital adequacy requirements and also came under fire for non-compliance on existing rules. So while fintech startups are still subject to many of the same rules as their traditional counterparts, they don't have the added burdens that come with litigation, fines and other penalties that several large institutions have had to deal with in recent years."
"An Inside Look At Fintech Marketplace Lenders"[2] ***—Forbes, February 27, 2016***

18.1 Introduction

Recent research has shown that corporate governance issues are fundamentally different in young entrepreneurial firms than in large, well established ones, and that these issues may vary across countries (Armitage, Sarkar, & Talaulicar, 2017; Bjørnskov & Foss, 2013; Djankov, La Porta, Lopez-De-Silanes, & Shleifer, 2002; Luo & Junkunc, 2008; Wright, Westhead, & Ucbasaran, 2007). While the latter has been studied extensively, the former has recently attracted much interest in connection with entrepreneurial firms active on a global scale (Zahra, 2014). Firms may obtain a comparative advantage when located in countries with more favorable regulation, since it can reduce the costs and enable developing innovations that are more difficult to implement in countries with more stringent regulation (Blind, 2012; Bozkaya & Kerr, 2014; Braun, Eidenmüller, Engert, & Hornuf, 2013; Dharmapala & Khanna, 2016; Hornuf & Schwienbacher, 2017a, 2017b; Levine, Lin, & Shen, 2015; Wang & Wang, 2012). Empirical evidence suggests that differential enforcement of

---

[1] http://www.bloomberg.com/gadfly/articles/2016-02-22/fintech-funding-will-suffer-as-banks-tighten-reins

[2] http://www.forbes.com/sites/falgunidesai/2016/02/27/an-inside-look-at-fintech-marketplace-lenders/#13a2143d89ac

law may drive the structure of corporate governance and patterns of start-up activity. In this paper, we examine a specific industry—"fintech" or financial technology—to see whether or not differential enforcement of banking rules around the world affects the financing patterns of fintech start-ups, including the shareholder structure and type of investors participating in the financing. We further examine the impact on these firms to go public.

Recent years have seen an increasing amount of hype about fintech, and venture capital (VC) fintech in particular, around the world. The hype in some camps is sufficient to remind some practitioners of the dot com bubble from 1998 to 2000. For example, at a March 2016 seminar at the law offices of McCarthy Tétrault in Toronto, one senior practitioner was overheard saying that some of the junior roundtable participants should "settle down!" because "they are not old enough to remember the dot com bubble."

The new fintech wave is also driven by ventures and no longer just by investments by incumbents in internal projects. According to Accenture (2015), the worldwide investment volume in fintech ventures has amounted to USD 12.21 billion in 2014 and is likely to be far larger in 2015. This new wave has been attributed by some researchers and practitioners to the financial crisis for at least two reasons (Arner, Barberis, & Buckley, 2015; Kelly, 2014). First, this has let many skilled employees of banks and other financial institutions to leave their job (or even be fired) and seek new opportunities by undertaking entrepreneurial initiatives, leading to an increased supply of investments opportunities by VC funds (and thus increased demand for VC by fintech projects). Second, as incumbents have been subject to stronger regulation and scrutiny by regulators since the start of the financial crisis, fintech ventures that develop products and services that are outside the scope of financial regulators (such as crowdfunding platforms and alternative payment systems) have become more attractive relative to incumbents. A striking example are crowdfunding platforms that are often structured so that many of the services that are subject to strong regulatory oversight are either outsourced to other service suppliers (e.g., PayPal for payments) or not offered at all (e.g., they may not provide "investment advises" as a mean to avoid compliance to MiFiD regulation). Thus many platforms are able to operate under light regulation and in some countries any significant license is absent (Hornuf & Schwienbacher, 2017a, 2017b). Another illustrative example relates to alternative payments systems. This may have spurred more investments into fintech ventures, hoping it will reduce the costs of financial intermediation for the economy as a whole (Philippon, 2016).

We investigate whether the financial crisis has changed investment behavior made by VC funds in fintech ventures, and how. More specifically, in this paper we address the issue of whether or not there has been a change in the pattern of fintech VC investments since the financial crisis. In the spirit of the Bloomberg quote above, we expect that there is a spike in fintech VC. In the view of differential enforcement of banking rules around the world for large established organizations versus start-ups, as documented by Forbes and quoted above, we expect the rise in fintech is more pronounced in countries that do not have a major financial center where fintech start-ups are more able to flourish with less risk of regulatory oversight. Similarly, we expect smaller VC funds with less experienced management to have a greater spike in fintech investments as such fund managers are less likely to see the hype in the context of recent history of booms and busts such as that experienced in the dot com bubble or the recent financial crisis. In view of the apparent boom and tendency to overinvest in the latest fads, we expect that fintech investments on average are less likely to result in successful initial public offering (IPO) and acquisition exits and are more likely to be written off.

To test these propositions, we extract all VC investments from VentureXpert from January 1, 1990 to December 31, 2015 and record as fintech ventures all VC investments active in the financial services industry, leading to a final sample of 2678 investment rounds in 747 distinct fintech ventures. Similarly we obtain a sample of 277,994 VC investments in nonfintech ventures during the same time period that we use as control group.

The data examined are consistent with our expectations. Controlling for other things being equal, we estimate that round investment amounts for fintech went up in the full sample. We observe investment rounds at higher levels for the subsample of deals done by independent VCs, but no material change for corporate or financial institution affiliated VCs. Fintech VC round investment amounts went up by a small amount among large VC funds, and by a much larger amount among small VC funds. Fintech VC round investment amounts significantly increased in countries without a major financial center but were unchanged in countries with a major financial center. Also, controlling for other things being equal, we observe round syndicate size went up for fintech VC for full sample, and the subset of early stage rounds, and the subsample excluding early stage rounds. Further, fintech VC round syndicate size increased more for small VC funds than large VC funds. Round syndicate size for fintech increased substantially in countries without a major financial center but was unchanged in countries with it. Finally, the data indicate that controlling for other things being equal, fintech VC deals are less likely to be write-offs if they originated after the financial crisis, except for investments made in ventures located in countries without a major financial center. In these cases, we observe a substantial increase in the probability of having write-offs for fintechs after the financial crisis.

This paper is related to a growing literature on booms and busts in VC, and regional analyses of VC. First, with respect to booms and busts in general, booms and busts in VC investment have been documented by Gompers and Lerner (1999), Cumming, Fleming, and Schwienbacher (2005), and Buzzacchi, Scellato, and Ughetto (2015), among others. Second, region specific patterns of VC activity have been documented by Bertoni, Colombo, and Quas (2015) and Bozkaya and Kerr (2014) for Europe. International analyses of VC investment patterns linked to differences in institutional settings have been examined, among others, by Bertoni and Groh (2014), Bonini, Alkan, and Salvi (2012), Dai and Nahata (2016), Guler and Guillén (2010), Johan et al. (2014), Li and Zahra (2012), Schwienbacher (2007), Schertler and Tykvová (2012), Tykvova and Schertler (2014), and Wang and Wang (2012). Prior work has not examined investment VC investment cycles of fintech. This extension is not trivial, as we are able to examine whether enforcement of financial regulation can spur investment activity into start-ups, as well as whether or not and how the VC cycle can seemingly and surprisingly repeat itself despite repeated booms and bust cycles. An exception is the work by Haddad and Hornuf (2019), who examine economic and technological determinants of fintech start-ups, without, however, examining the investment cycle or the impact of the recent financial crisis.

This paper is organized as follows. The next section reviews related literature and develops testable hypotheses. Thereafter we present the data, summary statistics, and multivariate analyses. The last section offers concluding remarks and policy implications.

18.2 Hypotheses

There are costs and benefits associated with developing a start-up fintech company that is away from a financial center. On the benefit side, there is a dearth of enforcement banking rules in countries without a major financial center, which in turn encourages innovation and exploitation of risky opportunities for fintech start-ups.[3] The reason why enforcement is more pronounced in regions with major financial centers is that there are economies of scale in prudential supervision (Cassard, 1994). Fintech start-ups thereby benefit in the spirit of regulatory arbitrage with differential enforcement of banking rules. However, there are also costs of being away from a financial center, and one of these costs is being less well connected with the main industry players. For instance, there is a gain to entrepreneurs from being close to Silicon Valley where significant human and financial resources are located. Similarly, fintech ventures may have an advantage of being located in New York or London (United Kingdom) as opposed to Louisiana.

A number of prior studies link weaker regulation with innovation and entrepreneurial risk-taking. First, Saxenian (2000) argues that a key reason why Silicon Valley developed into a vibrant and highly innovative tech area as we know it today is because of the weaker labor regulation in California as opposed to other US states. It reduced failure costs of start-ups, in case they needed to lay off employees at short notice. Similarly, it created a more liquid labor market so that the cost for employees associated with increased risk of being fired was mitigated by the higher chances of finding a new job quickly in the highly liquid labor market in the Silicon Valley. The more employer-favorable the labor market regulation are, the more it encourages innovation and entrepreneurial risk-taking. Comparing across countries, Bozkaya and Kerr (2014) find consistent evidence in the Europe, and Wang and Wang (2012) find consistent evidence across other countries including Asia.

Second, Dharmapala and Khanna (2016) document a positive stock market reaction to the announcement of already listed companies in the United States that opt for the weaker disclosure and compliance obligations under the Jumpstart Our Business Startups (JOBS) Act of 2012. That is, companies that are recently listed on the stock market and that fall in the category of "emerging growth companies," as defined in the JOBS Act, may comply with the weaker regulation of the JOBS Act. The fact that the choice to opt for the weaker regulation leads to a positive stock market reaction means the extra expected costs of weaker investor protection are lower than the cost savings associated with reduced needs for the company to disclose and comply with the more stringent securities regulation.

Third, Levine et al. (2015) find that cross-border acquisitions generate lower abnormal returns in countries with stronger labor-protection regulations due to higher costs related to such regulation. Stronger labor protection also leads to fewer cross-border acquisitions in these countries. Assuming these cross-border acquisitions being value-creating, they find that tougher labor regulation reduces efficiency.

---

[3] See supra, note 2 and accompanying text. Relatedly, others have documented that financial enforcement is more pronounced in and directed from regions that have a major financial center; see, for example, Schroeder (2001).

Fourth, minimum capital requirements can strongly impact choices of newly incorporated firms. In an empirical study of five different European countries that made significant changes in the minimum capital requirements for newly incorporate firms, Braun et al. (2013) find that the reduction or abolishment of minimum capital requirements increased entrepreneurship activities and thus ultimately risk-taking by entrepreneurs.

Fifth, Hornuf and Schwienbacher (2017a, 2017b) argue that tailored regulation is needed to encourage equity crowdfunding, which would not be able to develop well under strict securities regulation that applies to large, established firms. This leads to establishing weaker investor protection under equity crowdfunding (so that transaction costs are reduced) than under the issuance of new shares by large firms (who can afford the higher transactions costs associated with stronger investor protection and information disclosure requirements).

Sixth, using macro-level OECD data, Blind (2012) studies the impact of different forms of regulation (economic, social, and institutional regulations) on innovation. While the literature often attributes ambivalent effects of regulation on innovation, Blind shows that regulations that generate compliance costs deter innovation, while regulations that create extra incentive effects encourage innovation. Several examples are provided by Blind in the theoretical analysis, and the empirical evidence is consistent.

In sum, there is substantial prior theory and evidence that is consistent with the view that strong regulation and enforcement offers better investor protection, but at higher transaction costs. Compliance is costly, which deters risk-taking and may particularly affect risky start-ups. We therefore expect that growth in fintech VC activity will be more pronounced in countries without strong enforcement of banking rules.

Hypothesis 18.1: *Growth in fintech VC investment has been more pronounced in countries without a major financial center since the global financial crisis.*

Next, VCs in countries without a major financial center are less likely to be experienced (Nahata et al., 2014; Schertler & Tykvová, 2012; Schwienbacher, 2008a, 2008b) since there are fewer exit opportunities. This lack of exit opportunities reduces investments. VC experience is a key determinant of VC success, as the networks, due diligence, and value-added services provided by VCs (such as providing strategic, financial, human resource, and marketing advice, and facilitating connections to customers, suppliers, accountants, and lawyers and investment banks) is substantially higher among experienced VCs (Hege et al., 2009; Nahata, 2008; Nahata et al., 2014). Inexperienced VCs are more likely to overinvest in boom periods and invest without the knowledge of prior investment cycles (Gompers & Lerner, 1999) and hence be subjected to problems in subsequent busts (Nahata, 2008; see also Chaplinsky & Gupta-Mukherjee, 2009, Nahata et al., 2014; Nielsen, 2008, 2010, among others). The boom in fintech, therefore, is more likely to be amongst inexperienced VCs, and less likely to result in successful exit outcomes.

Hypothesis 18.2: *Growth in fintech VC investment has been more pronounced among less experienced VCs since the global financial crisis.*

Hypothesis 18.3: *Fintech VC investments are less likely to result in successful exit outcomes, particularly since the global financial crisis.*

18.3 Data

We collect all VC investments from the VentureXpert database from January 1, 1990 to December 31, 2015. To ensure that we only focus on true VC deals, we exclude investment rounds that are categorized as "Buyout/Acquisition," "Real Estate," and "Other." We classify VC investments with "Company VE Primary Industry Sub-Group 1" to be "Financial Services" as fintech investments. We obtain a final sample of 2678 investment rounds in 747 distinct fintech ventures. A manual check on a selected number of individual cases included in the category confirms our classification, even though the sample of fintechs is large. Similarly we obtain a sample of 277,994 round investments in nonfintech ventures that comprises all remaining industry sectors. We further collect different macroeconomic data related to GDP from the World Bank database.

To assess whether a venture is located in a country with a major financial center, we rely on the 2015 Global Financial Centres Index 18 (GFCI 18) that is computed by the Z/Yen Group Limited on an annual basis. While this index captures the overall market capitalization of stock markets and banks, it takes a more comprehensive perspective. It also includes competitiveness of the center, among others. While some considered factors are quantitative measures taken from various sources such as the World Bank, the OECD, and the Economist Intelligence Unit, others are assessed through thousands of questionnaire responses received. More specifically, the GFCI provides ratings for financial centers calculated by a "factor assessment model" that uses these two distinct sets of measures. We rely on this index as it better captures the type of proxy than restricting to, say, the size of the public equity market, since fintech activities covers the full spectrum of financial activities (not just stock market activities). We consider the following list of countries to have a major financial center: United Kingdom (London), United States (New York; San Francisco; Washington, DC; Chicago; and Boston), China (Hong Kong), Singapore (Singapore), Japan (Tokyo), South Korea (Seoul), Switzerland (Zurich and Geneva), Canada (Toronto), Germany (Frankfurt), and Australia (Sydney). The dummy variable *Financial Center* takes a value of 1 for ventures located in any of these countries, and 0 for all the others. While the index is provided annually, we only use the values of 2015, since the definition of the index varies almost every year. This ensures comparability over the time period in terms of definition of a financial center.[4] All the variables are defined in Table 18.A1.

---

[4] We do not rely on measures of financial development often used in other studies (e.g., ratio of stock market capitalization over GDP, banking concentration, bank branch density, and rule of law), since they often lead some of the small countries to be the most developed ones, such as Luxembourg. This is not what we want to capture. Others such as indices from the World Bank's Doing Business Database (e.g., the strength of legal rights index) are also broader than just the financial industry. Our interest is the size and overall attractiveness of the financial center (such as New York and London), for which the index used here is more appropriate. Also, many of these alternative indices are time-invariant, thus their effects are captured with our fixed effects. Moreover, we do not include a variable for enforcement costs, such as those used in Cumming, Groh, and Johan (2018). The reasons for such an exclusion are that Cumming et al.'s (2018) measure is for Europe only and a subset of years relative to our sample here and covers to a significant degree enforcement of trading rules on stock exchanges, while our focus is pertinent to privately held entrepreneurial start-ups and fintech companies.

The summary statistics are provided in Table 18.1. Average round amounts in fintech ($17,937,200), however, have been larger than nonfintech ($13,279,000). Syndicate size is on average larger for nonfintech (4.6 syndicated partners on average) than fintech (3.2). Fintech start-ups are older on average (7.5 years) than nonfintech (5.1 years). For the entire sample years a greater proportion of fintech deals are in the expansion stage (49.6%) versus nonfintech (40.9%), while relatively more nonfintech deals are in the seed, start-up, and later stages (7.6%, 27.3%, and 24.2%, respectively) than their fintech counterparts (5.9%, 23.0%, and 21.6%, respectively).

A higher proportion of fintech deals exit as IPOs (30.0%) than nonfintech deals (22.1%). A lower proportion of fintech deals exit as trade sales (51.2%) relative nonfintech deals (61.4%). There is no statistically significant difference in the proportion of deals that exit as write-offs between fintechs (15.7%) and nonfintechs (14.5%).

The country distribution shows fintech is mostly in the United States (62.8%), followed by the United Kingdom (6.2%), China (6.3%), Canada (1.8%), and France (1.8%). The country distribution shows that nonfintech is mostly in the United States (75.9%), Canada (3.9%), the United Kingdom (3.5%), France (3.0%), and China (2.9%).

Financial (bank-affiliated) VCs are more likely to finance fintech (10.2%) than nonfintech (6.6%), while private limited partnerships are more likely to finance nonfintech (65.0%) than fintech (63.6%) and corporate VCs are more likely to finance nonfintech (7.7%) than fintech (5.8%). Older VC firms are more likely to finance fintech (average age is 21.8 years) than nonfintech (average age is 20.2 years). Similarly, fintech ventures are more often financed by larger VC funds (average fund size of USD 395.3 million) than nonfintech ventures (USD 292.0 million).

Table 18.A2 provides summary statistics of all fintech deals by country of origin for the two main dependent variables [*ln(Round Amount)* and *Syndicate Size (No. Investors)*]. It offers a comprehensive picture of the distribution of our international sample of fintech deals. Statistics are reported for all fintech deals, and for the subsamples of fintech deals after (*Post-Crisis = 1*) and before (*Post-Crisis = 0*) the financial crisis. Deals tend to be concentrated in a small set of countries, mainly large ones. However, no specific country outlier strikes out from this table. Still, in the multivariate analyses, we will include country dummies to control for any time-invariant country specificities.

Fig. 18.1 shows that the round investment size (i.e., the amount invested in a single round) dramatically increased after the financial crisis for fintech in nonfinancial centers relative to nonfintech and relative to financial centers. Fintech VC round amounts increased to 40 from 2007 to 2015 (starting from a benchmark of 0 at 2007) among nonfinancial centers versus financial centers and stayed at 0 among nonfintech investments for nonfinancial centers versus financial centers. Similarly, Fig. 18.2 shows that the number of rounds for fintech increased in financial centers relative to nonfintech and to financial centers. The number of fintech VC investment rounds increased to 50 from 2007 to 2015 (starting from a benchmark of 0 at 2007) among nonfinancial centers versus nonfinancial centers and stayed at 0 among nonfintech VC for nonfinancial centers versus financial centers. This evidence in Figs. 18.1 and 18.2 is consistent with Hypothesis 18.1.

Fig. 18.3 shows that the number of investment rounds increased significantly after the financial crisis for fintech for small funds relative to nonfintech, and relative to large funds, consistent with Hypothesis 18.2. Among small funds, fintech was more than twice

TABLE 18.1 Summary statistics of the sample.

Variable	Full sample			Fintech sample only	Nonfintech sample only	Diff. mean test
	Mean	Median	Std. dev.	Mean	Mean	P-Value
Start-up characteristics						
Post-Crisis (dummy)	0.3412	0.0000	0.4741	0.3170	0.3414	.008
Fintech Startup (dummy)	0.0096	0.0000	0.0977	1.0000	0.0000	—
Round Amount (× 1000 USD)	13,323.8	6000.0	39,161.4	17,937.2	13,279.0	.000
ln(Round Amount)	8.5001	8.6995	1.6260	8.5672	8.4995	.032
Syndicate Size (No. Investors)	4.5392	4.0000	3.2081	3.1538	4.5527	.000
Startup Age (in years)	5.1569	4.0000	8.7989	7.5358	5.1338	.000
Seed-Stage Dev. (dummy)	0.0759	0.0000	0.2648	0.0586	0.0760	.001
Early-Stage Dev. (dummy)	0.2726	0.0000	0.4453	0.2296	0.2730	.000
Expansion-Stage Dev. (dummy)	0.4096	0.0000	0.4918	0.4955	0.4087	.000
Later-Stage Dev. (dummy)	0.2419	0.0000	0.4283	0.2162	0.2422	.002
IPO Exit (dummy)	0.2216	0.0000	0.4153	0.3000	0.2209	.000
Trade Sale Exit (dummy)	0.6129	1.0000	0.4871	0.5118	0.6137	.000
Successful Exit (dummy)	0.8345	1.0000	0.3717	0.8118	0.8347	.029
Bankruptcy Exit (dummy)	0.1453	0.0000	0.3524	0.1567	0.1452	.249
Startup Country: USA (dummy)	0.7527	1.0000	0.4314	0.6281	0.7539	.000
Startup Country: Canada (dummy)	0.0385	0.0000	0.1925	0.0183	0.0387	.000
Startup Country: United Kingdom (dummy)	0.0348	0.0000	0.1832	0.0616	0.0345	.000
Startup Country: China (dummy)	0.0298	0.0000	0.1699	0.0631	0.0294	.000
Startup Country: France (dummy)	0.0295	0.0000	0.1691	0.0176	0.0296	.000
VC fund characteristics						
Financial VC Fund (dummy)	0.0665	0.0000	0.2491	0.1019	0.0661	.000
Private VC Fund (dummy)	0.6497	1.0000	0.4771	0.6355	0.6499	.122
Corporate VC Fund (dummy)	0.0772	0.0000	0.2668	0.0579	0.0773	.000
VC Firm Age (in years)	20.2090	15.0000	18.0797	21.8096	20.1935	.000
Fund Size (million USD)	293.01	106.60	945.00	395.26	292.00	.000
Market conditions						
GDP (in USD)	9.6895	10.2848	5.3009	7.9656	9.7062	.000
GDP per Capita (in USD)	38.4823	38.1139	12.3711	31.4577	38.5506	.000
GDP Growth	2.8160	2.6660	2.2646	3.7273	2.8071	.000
No. Obs.	277,994			2678	275,316	

The table shows summary statistics for the full sample and for different subsamples (fintech vs nonfintech, postcrisis vs precrisis). The number of observations reported in the last line corresponds to the number for most of the variables. For some variables, fewer observations are available. For the variables, IPO Exit, Trade Sale Exit, Successful Exit, and Bankruptcy Exit, statistics are reported for the subsample of exited ventures only.

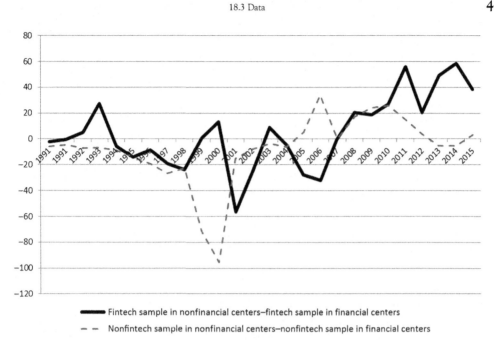

FIGURE 18.1   Total size of all VC rounds, scaled 2007 = 0. *VC*, Venture capital.

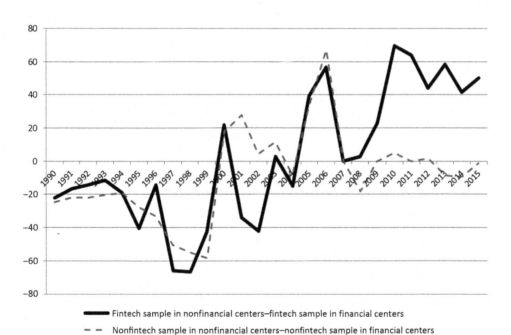

FIGURE 18.2   Number of VC rounds, scaled 2007 = 0. *VC*, Venture capital.

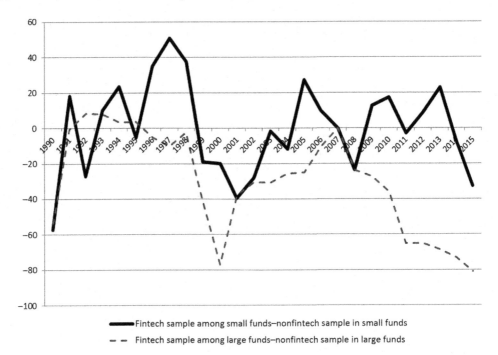

FIGURE 18.3   Number of investment rounds, scaled 2007 = 0.

as important relative to nonfintech, as compared to large funds, over the 2007 to 2015 period for the number of round investments. Similarly, Fig. 18.4 shows that the annual volume of VC investments increased dramatically for fintech for small funds relative to large funds and relative to nonfintech, again consistent with Hypothesis 18.2. Among small funds, fintech was more than twice as important relative to nonfintech, as compared to large funds, over the 2007 to 2015 period for the volume of round investments.

18.4 Multivariate analyses

Our multivariate analyses proceed as follows. First, we present analyses of the impact of the financial crisis on VC round investment amounts in Table 18.2 to establish the broad patterns in the fintech after the financial crisis around the world as a base case without testing specifically for differences in countries as predicted by Hypotheses 18.1 and 18.2. Thereafter, in Tables 18.3—18.5 examine subsets of the data to directly test Hypotheses 18.1 and 18.2. Finally, in Table 18.6, we provide an analysis of exits to test Hypothesis 18.3.

Table 18.2 presents OLS regressions of the determinants of round amounts (in natural logarithm) with an analysis for fintech relative to nonfintech after the financial crisis. Our main variable of interest is therefore the interaction term *Post-Crisis × Fintech*. Several other explanatory variables are included to control for alternative factors. The inclusion of fixed effects helps controlling for different common effects across industry, stage of

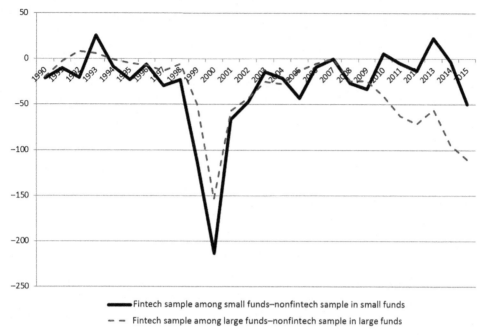

FIGURE 18.4   Annual volume of round investments, scaled 2007 = 0.

development, and country of start-up that may not be captured by our other variables. Among other things, it is meant to capture possible differences in the economies of scale and scope across countries, and differences in time-invariant business laws, level of corruption, and misreporting practices across countries (Djankov et al., 2002; Johan & Zhang, 2015).

The data examined are consistent with our expectations that fintech investments increased after the financial crisis. Controlling for other things being equal, we estimate that round investment amounts for fintech went up, relative to the average amounts for all investments in the sample, by 3.2%−3.7% for the full sample (Models 3 and 4), relative to the average deal sizes in the sample.[5] Fintech went up by 3.0%−3.4% for the subset of early stage VC fintech deals (Models 5 and 6), and by 2.7%−3.2% for the early/seed stage rounds excluded (Models 7 and 8).

Table 18.3 presents an analysis of round investment amounts by type of VC fund. Round investment amounts for fintech postcrisis went up by 5.4% in countries without a major financial center (Model 2) but were unchanged in countries with a major financial

---

[5] The economic significance from the marginal effects is calculated as the ratio of the coefficient to the average value in Table 18.1. For example, from Model 3, the calculation is 0.3133/8.5001 = 3.7%. Note that while the dependent variable is transformed in natural logs, the variable of interest (*Post-Crisis* × *Fintech*) is the interaction of two dummy variables; hence, it is a binary variable. As such, the impact of this explanatory variable on the dependent variable is akin to shifting the intercept, which has a straightforward economic interpretation.

TABLE 18.2 Determinants of round investment amounts.

Variable	Full sample				Early/seed-stage rounds only		Early/seed-stage pounds excluded	
	(1)	(2)	(3)	(4)	(5)	(6)	(7)	(8)
Start-up characteristics								
Post-Crisis (dummy)	−0.1364	−0.0999	−0.1398	−0.1030	−0.1214	−0.0819	−0.1409	−0.1019
Fintech Startup (dummy)	0.0353	0.5278***	−0.0622	0.4419***	0.0991	0.3644*	−0.1185	0.4545**
Post-Crisis × Fintech			0.3133***	0.2733***	0.2946**	0.2597**	0.2759**	0.2272**
Startup Age (in years)	−0.0111***	−0.0088***	−0.0011***	−0.0088***	−0.0065	−0.0069	−0.0114***	−0.0087***
VC fund characteristics								
Financial VC Fund (dummy)	0.6345***	0.6359***	0.6344***	0.6359***	0.7702***	0.7661***	0.5624***	0.5663***
Private VC Fund (dummy)	0.4794***	0.4674***	0.4794***	0.4674***	0.6105***	0.5926***	0.3943***	0.3845***
Corporate VC Fund (dummy)	0.8071***	0.7821***	0.8067***	0.7818***	0.8302***	0.8031***	0.7671***	0.7395***
VC Firm Age (in years)	0.0048***	0.0046***	0.0048***	0.0046***	0.0068***	0.0066***	0.0038***	0.0036***
Market conditions								
GDP (in USD)	0.0164	0.0129	0.0164	0.0129	0.0095	0.0073	0.0195	0.0162
GDP per Capita (in USD)	0.0204***	0.0205***	0.0205***	0.0205***	0.0141**	0.0148**	0.0244***	0.0238***
GDP Growth	0.0799*	0.0811*	0.0799*	0.0811*	0.0556	0.0618*	0.0933*	0.0922*
Industry Dummies	No	Yes	No	Yes	No	Yes	No	Yes
Stage of Dev. Dummies	Yes	Yes	Yes	Yes	Partial	Partial	Partial	Partial
Startup Country Dummies	Yes	Yes	Yes	Yes	Yes	Yes	Yes	Yes
No. Obs.	277,994	277,994	277,994	277,994	96,874	96,874	181,120	181,120

The table shows OLS regressions on the determinants of investment amounts. The dependent variable is *ln(Round amount)*, where *Round Amount* is the value in USD (×1000). Standard errors are clustered by year of investment. Significance levels: *, **, and *** for 10%, 5%, and 1%, respectively.

TABLE 18.3 Determinants of round investment amounts.

Variable	Major financial center (1)	No major financial center (2)	Financial VCs (3)	Private VCs (4)	Corporate VCs (5)	Small VC funds (6)	Large VC funds (7)	Younger VC firms (8)	Older VC firms (9)
Start-up characteristics									
Post-Crisis (dummy)	−0.1548	0.2739	−0.0219	−0.2295	−0.0107	−0.3192	−0.0185	−0.2072	0.0246
Fintech Startup (dummy)	0.3938**	0.6952**	0.7236**	0.3845***	−0.3014	0.1979	0.4799**	0.4730***	0.3218
Post-Crisis × Fintech	−0.0232	0.4607**	−0.0016	0.3931***	−0.4767	0.7737***	0.1741**	0.4167**	0.1041
Startup Age (in years)	−0.0122***	−0.0019*	−0.0112***	−0.0090**	−0.0144***	−0.0152***	−0.0075***	−0.0083**	−0.0091***
VC fund characteristics									
Financial VC Fund (dummy)	0.6937***	0.4506***	—	—	—	0.4811***	0.7674***	0.6417***	0.6814***
Private VC Fund (dummy)	0.4702***	0.4558***	—	—	—	0.3656***	0.5320***	0.4630***	0.5075***
Corporate VC Fund (dummy)	0.7955***	0.6341***	—	—	—	0.7443***	0.7853***	0.8890***	0.6856***
VC Firm Age (in years)	0.0044***	0.0054***	0.0053***	0.0053***	0.0005	0.0074***	0.0019***	−0.0063*	0.0030***
Market conditions									
GDP (in USD)	0.0094	0.1716	0.1086***	0.0301*	−0.0175	0.0338	−0.0078	0.0310	−0.0151
GDP per Capita (in USD)	0.0254***	−0.0102	0.0012	0.0234***	0.0170**	0.0236***	0.0162**	0.0220***	0.0215**
GDP Growth	0.0902*	0.0371*	0.0934**	0.0746*	0.0914**	0.0849*	0.0708**	0.0830*	0.0746*
Industry Dummies	Yes	Yes	Yes	Yes	Yes	Yes	Yes	Yes	Yes
Stage of Dev. Dummies	Yes	Yes	Yes	Yes	Yes	Yes	Yes	Yes	Yes
Startup Country Dummies	Yes	Yes	Yes	Yes	Yes	Yes	Yes	Yes	Yes
No. Obs.	247,958	30,036	18,484	180,621	21,448	62,973	215,021	139,482	138,512

The table shows OLS regressions on the determinants of investment amounts. The dependent variable is *ln(Round amount)*, where *Round Amount* is the value is USD ($\times 1000$), where *Round Amount* is the value is USD 100 million. Younger (Older) VC firms (Models 8 and 9) are classified based on the cutoff level of 15 years between time of investment and the VC firm's incorporation date. Small (Large) VC funds (Models 6 and 7) are classified based on the cutoff level of USD 100 million. Standard errors are clustered by year of investment. Significance levels: *, **, and *** for 10%, 5%, and 1%, respectively.

TABLE 18.4 Robustness analyses on the determinants of round investment amounts.

Variable	Non-US ventures in financial centers only	Non-US ventures in nonfinancial centers only	US ventures in financial centers only (state level)	US ventures in nonfinancial centers only (state level)	High Internet usage	Low Internet usage	High mobile phone subscription rate	Low mobile phone subscription rate
	(1)	(2)	(3)	(4)	(5)	(6)	(7)	(8)
Start-up characteristics								
Post-Crisis (dummy)	0.404**	0.274	0.176	0.281	0.373	−0.357	0.267	−0.172
Fintech Startup (dummy)	1.036***	0.695**	0.193	0.579**	0.184	0.461***	0.293	0.512**
Post-Crisis × Fintech	−0.890***	0.461**	0.263	−0.0947	−0.181	0.401***	−0.318	0.360***
Startup Age (in years)	−0.00396*	−0.00193*	−0.0235***	−0.0140***	−0.00269	−0.0148***	−0.00164	−0.0153***
VC fund characteristics								
Financial VC Fund (dummy)	0.720***	0.451***	0.563***	0.775***	0.459***	0.650***	0.508***	0.649***
Private VC Fund (dummy)	0.669***	0.456***	0.334***	0.482***	0.516***	0.455***	0.482***	0.461***
Corporate VC Fund (dummy)	0.981***	0.634***	0.617***	0.824***	0.745***	0.774***	0.801***	0.767***
VC Firm Age (in years)	0.00167	0.00536***	0.00396***	0.00682***	0.00162	0.00506***	0.00407**	0.00466***
Market conditions								
GDP (in USD)	0.0495**	0.172	−0.883	−1.738**	−0.188	0.0820***	0.0480	−0.00777
GDP per Capita (in USD)	0.0104*	−0.0102	0.353	0.651**	0.0196*	0.00606	0.00759	0.0304***

GDP Growth	0.0741***	0.0371*	0.114*	0.112*	0.0565*	0.0736	0.00471	0.0894*
Industry Dummies	No	Yes	Yes	Yes	Yes	Yes	Yes	Yes
Stage of Dev. Dummies	Yes	Yes	Yes	Yes	Yes	Yes	Yes	Yes
Startup Country Dummies	Yes	Yes	No	No	Yes	Yes	Yes	Yes
No. Obs.	38,707	30,036	131,853	77,398	33,968	244,026	35,830	242,164

The table shows OLS regressions on the determinants of investment amounts. The dependent variable is ln(Round amount), where Round Amount is the value is USD ($\times$ 1000). In Models 3 and 4, US states with a financial center are New York (New York), California (San Francisco), District of Columbia (Washington, DC), Illinois (Chicago), and Massachusetts (Boston), following the definition of the country-level list of US states (see definition of *Financial Center* in Table 18.A1). Models 5 and 6 show results for the subsamples of observations for which the country's Internet Usage is above and below 75%. Models 7 and 8 show results for the subsamples of country's Mobile Phone Subscription is above and below 100. The Standard errors are clustered by year of investment. Significance levels: *, **, and *** for 10%, 5%, and 1%, respectively.

TABLE 18.5 Determinants of round syndicate size.

Variable	Full sample	Early/seed-stage rounds only	Early/seed-stage rounds excluded	Small VC funds	Large VC funds	Younger VC firms	Older VC firms	Large financial center	No large financial center
	(1)	(2)	(3)	(4)	(5)	(6)	(7)	(8)	(9)
Start-up characteristics									
Post-Crisis (dummy)	−0.310	0.281	−0.640***	−0.550***	−0.299	−0.280	−0.305	−0.359*	0.200
Fintech Startup (dummy)	0.346	0.323	0.258	0.275	0.376	0.197	0.332	0.298	0.718
Post-Crisis × Fintech	1.077***	0.833**	1.202**	1.444***	1.030**	0.502	1.686***	0.432	1.154***
Startup Age (in years)	−0.061***	−0.022***	−0.063***	−0.059***	−0.062***	−0.058***	−0.063***	−0.066***	−0.028***
VC fund characteristics									
Financial VC Fund (dummy)	0.871***	0.661***	0.971***	0.537***	0.954***	1.087***	0.407***	1.011***	0.165
Private VC Fund (dummy)	0.471***	0.392***	0.526***	0.263**	0.500***	0.675***	0.023	0.524***	0.088
Corporate VC Fund (dummy)	1.165***	0.845***	1.326***	0.913***	1.203***	1.291***	0.750***	1.251***	0.473***
VC Firm Age (in years)	0.007***	0.008***	0.007***	0.013***	0.006***	0.008***	−0.016***	0.007***	0.007***
Market conditions									
GDP (in USD)	−0.049**	0.018	−0.089***	−0.052**	−0.041	−0.061**	−0.040*	−0.060**	−0.125
GDP per Capita (in USD)	0.006	−0.010*	0.014	0.012	0.004	0.004	0.009	0.013	−0.019**
GDP Growth	0.046	0.042	0.049	0.046	0.042	0.027	0.061	0.047	0.034
Industry Dummies	Yes	Yes	Yes	Yes	Yes	Yes	Yes	Yes	Yes
Stage of Dev. Dummies	Yes	Yes	Yes	Yes	Yes	Yes	Yes	Yes	Yes
Startup Country Dummies	Yes	Yes	Yes	Yes	Yes	Yes	Yes	Yes	Yes
No. Obs.	277,994	96,874	181,120	62,973	215,021	138,512	139,482	247,958	30,036

The table shows Poisson regressions on the determinants of syndicate size. The dependent variable is the number of investors involved in the financing of a given round. Reported coefficient values are marginal effects. Standard errors are clustered by year of investment. Significance levels: *, **, and *** for 10%, 5%, and 1%, respectively.

TABLE 18.6 Determinants of exit outcomes.

Variable	Full sample			Ventures located in country with a major financial center			Ventures not located in country with a major financial center		
	IPO Exit	Successful Exit	Bankruptcy Exit	IPO Exit	Successful Exit	Bankruptcy Exit	IPO Exit	Successful Exit	Bankruptcy Exit
	(1)	(2)	(3)	(4)	(5)	(6)	(7)	(8)	(9)
Start-up characteristics									
Post-Crisis (dummy)	0.1421**	0.0625***	− 0.0519***	0.1524***	0.0635***	− 0.0558***	0.0313	0.0476***	− 0.0056**
Fintech Startup (dummy)	− 0.1192*	0.0197	− 0.0055	− 0.1168	− 0.0007	− 0.0031	− 0.1165	0.0583	0.0190***
Post-Crisis × Fintech	0.0074	0.0828***	− 0.0462***	0.0329	0.0810***	− 0.0502***	0.0381	0.0748***	0.0328**
Market conditions									
GDP at Exit (in USD)	− 0.0052***	0.0027***	0.0008*	− 0.0030*	0.0017*	0.0004	0.0787***	− 0.0034	− 0.0027*
GDP per Capita at Exit (in USD)	− 0.0077***	− 0.0017***	0.0005	− 0.0093***	− 0.0011	0.0001	− 0.0077***	− 0.0022***	0.0003***
GDP Growth at Exit	0.0182***	0.0043*	− 0.0017	0.0121**	0.0030	− 0.0017	0.0321***	0.0082***	− 0.0007
Early-Stage VC Fund	− 0.0554***	0.0062	0.0103***	− 0.0550***	0.0013	0.0133***	− 0.0461	0.0306**	0.0011
Industry Dummies	Yes	Yes	Yes	Yes	Yes	Yes	Yes	Yes	Yes
No. Obs.	14,593	14,593	14,593	12,564	12,564	12,564	2029	2029	2029

The table shows Probit regressions on the determinants of exit outcomes as measure of success. The dependent variable "IPO Exit" is a dummy variable equal to 1 for exited ventures that made an IPO. "Successful Exit" that made either an IPO or a trade sale (TS), and "Bankruptcy Exit" that went bankrupt. The variable "Early-Stage VC Fund" is a dummy variable taking the value of 1 if at least one participating VC fund has an early stage investment mandate, and 0 otherwise. Reported coefficient values are marginal effects. Standard errors are clustered by year of investment. Significance levels: *, **, and *** for 10%, 5%, and 1%, respectively.

center (Model 1), consistent with Hypothesis 18.1. Here, we are unable to test the prediction in a single regression due to the inclusion of country fixed effects (which would eliminate the variable *Financial Center*, since it is invariant over time within countries).

Table 18.3 also shows that round investment amounts went up for fintech postcrisis by 4.6% for independent VCs (Model 4) but there was no change for corporate VCs (Model 5) or financial institution affiliated VCs (Model 3).[6] Round investment amounts for fintech postcrisis went up by 2.0% among large VC funds (Model 7), and 9.1% among small VC funds (Model 6), consistent with Hypothesis 18.2. To offer further support to Hypothesis 18.2, we use a second measure of experience, which is fund size. We define small VC funds as those with a fund size less than USD 100 million. We obtain similar conclusions with an alternative measure of experience (we consider VC firms with age less than 15 years as "young" and the others as "old"), namely age of the VC firms; indeed, the impact on fintech in the postcrisis period is only significant for the younger VC firms (Models 8 and 9).

Table 18.4 presents robustness analyses of fintech rounds investment amounts excluding the United States (Models 1 and 2), and within the United States only at the state level (Models 3 and 4). Showing robustness without the United States is important, since about 75% of the sample is the investment made in these countries (Table 18.1). As for the second one, we there provide an analysis at the US state level (see accompanying note in Table 18.4 for more details), where we expect no significant difference due to the same regulation applied across all US states. Thus a lack of finding for the US state level analysis offers support to our story. The evidence in Models 1 and 2 is consistent with Table 18.3 and shows a pronounced increase in fintech after the financial crisis among countries without a financial center and not in countries with a financial center, consistent with Hypothesis 18.1. By contrast, within the United States, there is no material difference in state-level investments depending on whether or not the state had a financial center (as defined in Table 18.4) in Models 3 and 4. This evidence in Models 3 and 4, in the context of Models 1 and 2, and in Tables 18.2 and 18.3, supports our analysis at the country level where financial regulation and enforcement takes place. There are scant differences in the enforcement of banking regulations within a country, but marked differences in enforcement of banking regulations across countries. Hence, the marked differences in fintech VC after the crisis are observed across countries where there is, and is not, a major financial center, consistent with Hypothesis 18.1.

One possibly alternative explanation for the results obtained is that the impact on fintech postcrisis, being more pronounced in certain countries than others, may be due to differences in the level of democratization of digitalization. Countries where digitalization is more widely spread among the population may be more attractive for fintech start-ups, since the adoption rate of their products and services may in turn be higher. To check the plausibility of this alternative explanation, we run different subsample analyses for country-year observations where digitalization differs significantly. We use two measures of democratization of digitalization. One is the degree of internet usage (Models 5 and 6)

---

[6] Our sample also includes a few investments by government-affiliated VC funds. Given the same number of deals, we are not able to examine this category separately. However, performing the analysis on the full sample excluding government-affiliated VC funds does not affect results.

and the other is the subscription rate of mobile phones (Models 7 and 8). High degree of digital adoptions is associated with a greater internet usage and higher mobile phone subscription rate in the population. To ensure that we capture the digitalization trend of the most recent years that match the fintech emergence, we take a cutoff of 90% of the distribution of these variables. Note also that these variables are time-varying, which means that observations of a given country are generally found in both subsamples (the more recent observations are more likely to be in the high digitalization subsample). However, we obtain the opposite results, in which the effect of the interaction term is only significant and positive when digitalization is low. This offers no support for this alternative explanation.

Table 18.5 presents an analysis of syndicate size. Controlling for other things being equal, round syndicate size went up for fintech after the financial crisis, relative to the average syndicate size in the full sample, by 23.7% for full sample (Model 1), by 18.3% for early stage rounds (Model 2), 26.5% excluding early stage rounds (Model 3), 31.8% for small VC funds (Model 4), 22.7% for large VC funds (Model 5), and 37.1% for older VC firms. Also, the data indicate that syndicate size went up by 25.4% in countries without a large financial center (Model 9), and unchanged in countries with a large financial center (Model 8), consistent with Hypothesis 18.1 on investment behavior postcrisis.

Table 18.6 presents an analysis of exit outcomes. There, we control for market conditions at the time of exit, and whether a VC fund with an early stage investment mandate participated in the financing of the VC-backed start-up. The data for the full sample indicate that controlling for other things being equal, fintech VC deals are 4.6% less likely to be write-offs if they originated after the financial crisis (Model 3), but 8.3% more likely to be either an IPO or a trade sale (Model 2), consistent with Hypothesis 18.3. We find similar impacts on exit outcomes for fintech after the crisis amongst the countries with a major financial center (Models 4–6). Focusing on the exits of ventures located in a country without a major financial center (Models 7–9), there is a material increase in liquidations postcrisis for fintech, as the effect is now positive and economically large. The probability is now higher by 3.3% (Model 9), and a slight reduction in the probability of successful exits (IPOs or trade sales).

Overall, the data indicate that changes in fintech investments are more pronounced in countries without a major financial center after the crisis (Table 18.3), and that these ventures are more likely to fail after the crisis relative to nonfintech ventures (Table 18.6). We note that we could have added other variables to the exit regressions, such as syndication. In Table 18.5, we noted that fintech deals are more likely to be syndicated in regions without a financial center. Syndication of VC investment can facilitate larger investment amounts and is often associated with more value-added advice by investors (Casamatta, 2003; Casamatta & Haritchabalet, 2007; Gompers & Lerner, 1999; Sevilir, 2010). Including syndication is arguably endogenous to exit performance, and as such we do not include syndication as explanatory variable in Table 18.6. But doing so only strengthens our results that fintech deals performed worse after the financial crisis in regions without a financial center, particularly relative to the expected performance in view of investment syndication and relative to performance of comparable investments in regions with a financial center. As robustness check, we further run Heckman probit regressions that control for the possible nonrandomness of the sample of exited ventures. Indeed, the set of ventures that were started before and after the financial crisis may not be the same if exits through some of the routes take longer. We find that even after controlling for this possible self-selection bias, fintech ventures started after the financial crisis and have significantly higher risks of failing if located away from a major financial center. Thus these extra tests confirm our earlier conclusion.

18.5 Alternative explanations and future research

We use the GFCI 18 as computed by the Z/Yen Group as a main focus of international difference in banking regulatory enforcement. The advantages with this index are that (1) it is specific to the finance industry (unlike the World Bank Doing Business Indices, for example, that are not industry specific), (2) we can examine a stable set of countries over time to enable us to track what is going on in one consistent set of countries versus another, and (3) it pertains to financial regulation enforcement, which appears to be the most pertinent based on industry insights from Forbes and others (see Footnote 2 and accompanying text above). There are hundreds of indices to measure differences across countries including but not limited to the World Bank indices. We believe our index is directly appropriate for our research question. Perhaps future research with better and more fine-tuned data will come to other insights with other country groupings.

There could be alternative explanations for the patterns that we observe in the data. First, as pointed out before, there may be differences in the democratization of digitalization in developed versus developing countries. Our analysis however provides no support for this alternative explanation, although clearly it is a necessary condition for making fintech investments attractive from the market perspective. A greater adoption of digital products and services will ensure greater market prospects for fintechs. Second, the term fintech covers the entire scope of services and products traditionally provided by the financial services industry (Haddad & Hornuf, 2019). It comprises several areas such as finance and investment, operations and risk management, payments and infrastructure, data security and monetization, and customer interface. As such, some of the results may be sensitive to the nature of fintech start-ups at a level that is more granular than what we observe with the industry classifications in the SDC Platinum VentureXpert dataset. Third, there may be economics of scale and scope in fintech to different degrees in developed versus developing countries.

These potential explanations, and possibly others, are not immediately obvious with the data that we have access to. Nevertheless, we have included fixed effects for industry, stage of development, and start-up country domicile in our regression specifications to capture many of these unobserved potential effects. Also, we use an approach akin to difference-in-differences specification to compare before and after the critical event, which further controls for these competing explanations insofar as they remain stable over time. We welcome and encourage future research on topic with more detailed data, if they become available, to shed more light on the issues that we examined for the first time in this paper.

18.6 Conclusion

Fintech start-ups have been able to raise significant amounts of capital in the most recent years. We provide evidence that this change is more pronounced amongst smaller, private independent limited partnership VCs and in countries without a major financial center. This pattern is consistent with a differential enforcement of rules pertaining to financial institutions, where enforcement is more likely for major financial institutions and not start-ups, and hence fintech start-ups are more likely to receive larger financing in countries without a major financial center. At the same time, these ventures are more likely to fail. Taken together, these findings may suggest inefficient VC investments in some regions of the world.

Syndicate sizes for fintech VCs have likewise become larger after the financial crisis, which would normally imply that fintech deals would do better. But the evidence to date shows that fintech deals are substantially less likely to be acquired after the financial crisis, and more likely to result in liquidation. The data thus point to exuberance in fintech VC investment, and a short memory of other recent boom and bust cycles in VC.

The data suggest a number of practitioner and policy implications. First, VCs should be concerned about excessive pushes into hot industries, fueled in part by media hype. With too much money chasing too few quality deals, there may be a commensurate reduction in their average quality, consistent with our evidence on fintech exits herein. Second, policymakers should be aware that differential enforcement of financial regulations can spur economic activity in different directions that are away from the watchful eye of regulators. Public policies spurring VC investment patterns have been documented by Armour and Cumming (2006), Kanniainen and Keuschnigg (2003, 2004), and Keuschnigg and Nielsen (2003, 2004). However, prior work has not examined the intersection of enforcement policies and government programs. The evidence in this paper suggests that further work is warranted. Fintech VC is a burgeoning area because financial regulators are prone to focus on large financial institutions. Regulators could be given incentives to pay attention to the broader marketplace to not only protect consumers but also to ensure that innovations and new technologies are efficiently developed and not a response to differential regulatory oversight.

Key terms

Compliance
Corporate venture capital
Disclosure
Early stage
Exit
Expansion stage
Financial center
Financial crisis
Financial venture capital

Fintech
Initial public offering
Later stage
Private venture capital
Regulation
Seed
Start-up
Syndication
Trade sale
Venture capital

Discussion questions

18.1. In which countries around the world are fintech ventures financed by venture capitalists more common? In which countries has the growth in the number of fintech ventures been more common since the global financial crisis? Explain why, with reference to theory and evidence.

18.2. Are fintech investments in countries with more regulatory oversight more or less successful on average? Explain why, with reference to theory and evidence.

18.3. How does the experience and reputation of the venture capital investor affect your responses to questions 18.1 and 18.2? Explain why, with reference to theory and evidence.

Appendix

TABLE 18.A1 Definition of variables.

Variable	Definition
Start-up characteristics	
Post-Crisis (dummy)	Dummy variable equal to one if the round investment takes place in 2008 or later
Fintech Startup (dummy)	Dummy variable equal to one if the VentureXpert variable "Company VE Primary Industry Sub-Group 1" is "Financial Services," and 0 otherwise (*Source*: SDC Platinum VentureXpert)
Round Amount ($\times$ 1000 USD)	Total amount invested by VCs in a given round, in thousands of USD (*Source*: SDC Platinum VentureXpert)
ln(Round Amount)	Natural logarithm of the variable "Round amount"
Syndicate Size (No. Investors)	Number of VC funds participating in the financing round (*Source*: SDC Platinum VentureXpert)

(Continued)

TABLE 18.A1 (Continued)

Variable	Definition
Startup Age (in years)	Age in years of the venture at time of the financing round (*Source*: SDC Platinum VentureXpert)
Seed-Stage Dev. (dummy)	Dummy variable equal to one if the venture's financing round is in the seed stage, and 0 otherwise (*Source*: SDC Platinum VentureXpert; companystagelevel1 == "Startup/Seed")
Early-Stage Dev. (dummy)	Dummy variable equal to one if the venture's financing round is in the early stage, and 0 otherwise (*Source*: SDC Platinum VentureXpert; companystagelevel1 == "Early Stage")
Expansion-Stage Dev. (dummy)	Dummy variable equal to one if the venture's financing round is in the expansion stage, and 0 otherwise (*Source*: SDC Platinum VentureXpert; companystagelevel1 == "Expansion")
Later-Stage Dev. (dummy)	Dummy variable equal to one if the venture's financing round is in the later stage, and 0 otherwise (*Source*: SDC Platinum VentureXpert; companystagelevel1 == "Later Stage")
IPO Exit (dummy)	Dummy variable equal to one if the exit from the venture was through an IPO, and 0 otherwise (*Source*: SDC Platinum VentureXpert; companysituation == "Went Public" or "In Registration")
Trade Sale Exit (dummy)	Dummy variable equal to one if the exit from the venture was through a trade sale, and 0 otherwise (*Source*: SDC Platinum VentureXpert; companysituation == "Acquisition" or "Merger" or "Pending Acquisition")
Successful Exit (dummy)	Dummy variable equal to one if the exit from the venture was through either an IPO or a trade sale, and 0 otherwise (*Source*: SDC Platinum VentureXpert)
Bankruptcy Exit (dummy)	Dummy variable equal to one if the exit from the venture was through a liquidation, and 0 otherwise (*Source*: SDC Platinum VentureXpert; companysituation == "Bankruptcy - Chapter 11" or "Bankruptcy - Chapter 7" or "Defunct")
Startup Country: USA (dummy)	Dummy variable equal to one if the venture is located in the United States, and 0 otherwise (*Source*: SDC Platinum VentureXpert)
Startup Country: Canada (dummy)	Dummy variable equal to one if the venture is located in Canada, and 0 otherwise (*Source*: SDC Platinum VentureXpert)
Startup Country: United Kingdom (dummy)	Dummy variable equal to one if the venture is located in the United Kingdom, and 0 otherwise (*Source*: SDC Platinum VentureXpert).
Startup Country: China (dummy)	Dummy variable equal to one if the venture is located in China, and 0 otherwise (*Source*: SDC Platinum VentureXpert)
Startup Country: France (dummy)	Dummy variable equal to one if the venture is located in France, and 0 otherwise (*Source*: SDC Platinum VentureXpert)
VC fund characteristics	
Financial VC Fund (dummy)	Dummy variable equal to one if the VC fund is affiliated to a financial institution, and 0 otherwise (*Source*: SDC Platinum VentureXpert; variable fundtypeshort == "FINCORP" or "IBANK")

(Continued)

TABLE 18.A1   (Continued)

Variable	Definition
Private VC Fund (dummy)	Dummy variable equal to one if the VC fund is a private limited partnership fund, and 0 otherwise (*Source*: SDC Platinum VentureXpert; variable fundtypeshort == "PRIV")
Corporate VC Fund (dummy)	Dummy variable equal to one if the VC fund is affiliated to a nonfinancial corporation, and 0 otherwise (*Source*: SDC Platinum VentureXpert; variable fundtypeshort == "CORPVEN")
VC Firm Age (in years)	Age in years of the VC firm at time of the financing round (*Source*: SDC Platinum VentureXpert)
Fund Size	Size of the VC fund in millions of USD (*Source*: SDC Platinum VentureXpert)
Market conditions	
Financial Center (dummy)	Dummy variable equal to one if the venture is located in the United Kingdom (London), the United States (New York, San Francisco, Washington DC, Chicago, Boston), China (Hong Kong), Singapore (Singapore), Japan (Tokyo), South Korea (Seoul), Switzerland (Zurich, Geneva), Canada (Toronto), Germany (Frankfurt) or Australia (Sydney), and 0 otherwise (*Source*: 2015 Global Financial Centres Index 18 (GFCI 18) computed by the Z/Yen Group Limited)
GDP (in USD)	Gross domestic product in billions of USD (in current prices) in the year of the financing round (*Source*: World Bank; subject code == NGDPD)
GDP per Capita (in USD)	Gross domestic product per capita in USD (in current prices) in the year of the financing round (*Source*: World Bank; subject code == NGDPDPC)
GDP Growth	Annual percentages of constant price GDP are year-on-year changes in the year of the financing round (*Source*: World Bank; subject code == NGDP_RPCH)
GDP at Exit (in USD)	Gross domestic product in billions of USD (in current prices) in the year of exit (*Source*: World Bank; subject code == NGDPD)
GDP per Capita at Exit (in USD)	Gross domestic product per capita in USD (in current prices) in the year of exit (*Source*: World Bank; subject code == NGDPDPC)
GDP Growth at Exit	Annual percentages of constant price GDP are year-on-year changes in the year of exit (*Source*: World Bank; subject code == NGDP_RPCH)
Internet Usage	Individuals using the Internet, in % of population (*Source*: World Bank)
Mobile Phone Subscriptions	Mobile cellular subscriptions, per 100 people (*Source*: World Bank)

TABLE 18.A2 Summary statistics of dependent variables, by country.

Country (in alphabetical order)	No. Obs. fintech deals	Mean of *ln(Round Amount)*			Mean of *Syndicate Size* (No. Investors)		
		All	Post-Crisis	Pre-Crisis	All	Post-Crisis	Pre-Crisis
Algeria	1	8.306	–	8.306	1.000	–	1.000
Australia	35	8.808	10.373	8.344	2.257	3.750	1.815
Bahrain	1	10.916	10.916	–	1.000	1.000	–
Belgium	3	5.373	–	5.373	1.667	–	1.667
Bolivia	1	8.006	–	8.006	1.000	–	1.000
Brazil	11	8.424	8.267	9.999	3.364	3.600	1.000
Bulgaria	1	8.975	–	8.975	1.000	–	1.000
Burkina Faso	1	5.182	–	5.182	1.000	–	1.000
Cambodia	1	8.103	8.103	–	1.000	1.000	–
Canada	49	5.848	4.117	6.349	3.041	3.545	2.895
Chile	1	8.038	–	8.038	1.000	–	1.000
China	169	9.752	9.841	9.701	2.645	3.484	2.159
Colombia	1	9.210	9.210	–	1.000	1.000	–
Costa Rica	1	9.903	–	9.903	1.000	–	1.000
Cyprus	1	8.987	8.987	–	1.000	1.000	–
Denmark	2	10.653	10.653	–	2.000	2.000	–
Egypt	2	7.090	7.090	–	2.000	2.000	–
Finland	3	6.862	–	6.862	1.667	–	1.667
France	47	8.271	8.587	7.994	3.638	2.909	4.280
Germany	4	6.878	–	6.878	1.000	–	1.000
Ghana	2	8.059	8.517	7.601	1.000	1.000	1.000
Greece	1	4.787	–	4.787	1.000	–	1.000
Guatemala	1	7.653	–	7.653	1.000	–	1.000
Hungary	2	6.516	2.534	10.498	1.000	1.000	1.000
India	267	9.276	9.481	8.489	3.487	3.736	2.527
Indonesia	4	9.688	9.903	9.616	2.500	1.000	3.000
Ireland	26	8.575	8.775	8.549	3.615	3.000	3.696
Israel	5	8.130	8.746	7.719	2.200	1.000	3.000
Italy	6	9.129	–	9.129	1.667	–	1.667

(Continued)

TABLE 18.A2 (Continued)

Country (in alphabetical order)	No. Obs. fintech deals	Mean of *ln(Round Amount)*			Mean of *Syndicate Size (No. Investors)*		
		All	Post-Crisis	Pre-Crisis	All	Post-Crisis	Pre-Crisis
Japan	19	5.994	5.067	6.667	1.105	1.000	1.182
Kazakhstan	1	9.210	9.210	–	1.000	1.000	–
Kenya	6	8.587	9.192	7.378	2.000	2.000	2.000
South Korea	33	7.797	8.884	7.727	3.545	2.000	3.645
Lebanon	3	9.122	8.700	9.966	1.667	2.000	1.000
Luxembourg	1	8.366	8.366	–	1.000	1.000	–
Malaysia	2	9.945	–	9.945	2.000	–	2.000
Mexico	13	8.784	8.784	–	4.385	4.385	–
Mongolia	2	9.306	–	9.306	2.000	–	2.000
Mozambique	4	6.716	8.352	6.171	1.000	1.000	1.000
The Netherlands	20	8.024	9.511	7.859	1.300	1.000	1.333
New Zealand	4	8.542	8.233	9.469	1.500	1.667	1.000
Nigeria	3	8.473	9.210	8.105	1.000	1.000	1.000
Norway	4	9.111	–	9.111	1.500	–	1.500
Pakistan	1	7.550	7.550	–	1.000	1.000	–
Paraguay	1	8.132	8.132	–	1.000	1.000	–
Poland	5	9.311	10.916	8.241	1.400	2.000	1.000
Portugal	3	7.663	7.663	–	1.000	1.000	–
Romania	4	5.724	–	5.724	1.000	–	1.000
Russia	10	8.507	8.726	8.361	1.200	1.500	1.000
Saudi Arabia	1	10.916	10.916	–	1.000	1.000	–
Sierra Leone	3	9.477	9.477	–	3.000	3.000	–
Singapore	9	10.536	7.496	10.916	4.556	1.000	5.000
South Africa	1	8.517	–	8.517	1.000	–	1.000
Spain	3	6.494	8.248	5.617	1.000	1.000	1.000
Sweden	4	7.778	–	7.778	1.000	–	1.000
Switzerland	9	8.008	7.350	10.309	3.444	3.857	2.000
Thailand	4	5.960	5.960	–	4.000	4.000	–
Togo	1	9.798	–	9.798	1.000	–	1.000

(Continued)

TABLE 18.A2 (Continued)

Country (in alphabetical order)	No. Obs. fintech deals	Mean of *ln(Round Amount)*			Mean of *Syndicate Size (No. Investors)*		
		All	Post-Crisis	Pre-Crisis	All	Post-Crisis	Pre-Crisis
Ukraine	3	5.478	7.223	4.605	1.667	1.000	2.000
United Kingdom	165	8.862	8.311	9.169	3.788	4.797	3.226
United States	1682	8.465	8.600	8.426	3.229	2.842	3.343
Uzbekistan	1	8.144	8.144	–	1.000	1.000	–
Vietnam	4	9.219	9.116	9.254	1.000	1.000	1.000

The table presents sample means of the two main dependent variables [*ln(Round Amount)* and *Syndicate Size (No. Investors)*] of all fintech deals, by country of origin. The sample used here is restricted to the countries with at least one fintech deal. Statistics are reported for all fintech deals and for the subsamples of fintech deals after (*Post-Crisis* = 1) and before (*Post-Crisis* = 0) the financial crisis. "No. Obs." gives the number of fintech deals in each country in the sample.

19

Crypto regulation

19.1 Introduction

Blockchain has recently emerged as a secure, peer-to-peer platform for verifying digital events and validating transactions in an increasingly decentralized economy. It facilitates security verification, background checks, and payments, even of small amounts. Entrepreneurs benefit from the creation of transparent and accountable supply chains, and the reduction of background checks for identity verification. Perhaps most importantly for entrepreneurs, several barriers to entry for individuals and firms with good, but unfunded, ideas are further lowered as they have been in recent years with the new, less regulated methods of raising capital and seeking financing (Ahlstrom, Cumming, & Vismara, 2018a).

Yet with blockchain and related technologies such as cryptocurrency, there are also some concerns that have arisen alongside this important new technology with respect to security and the required regulation, especially given the very nascent nature of this technology and its potential for disruption. Thus in this chapter, we explain the regulatory and security issues around blockchain and initial coin offerings (ICOs) in an increasingly decentralized economy. We examine ICO structures, and how this crowdfunding mechanism has the promise for economic innovation. We explain how fraud may be carried out within the context of these innovative asset classes and the evolving regulatory struggles. Given the value that entrepreneurship can generate for economies and societies (Ahlstrom, 2010), it is crucial that these financial innovations are better understood so as to facilitate their regulation and development (Crafts, 2006; Spulber, 2008).

In the spring of 2016 an entity called the decentralized autonomous organization (DAO) became one of the most successful crowdfunded entities in history, with an ICO that raised more than US$150 million worth of ether, a cryptocurrency, in less than 30 days (Popper, 2016a). The DAO, funded through ether by equity investors situated globally, was not registered as a legal entity in any sovereign jurisdiction and, additionally, had no employees. As such, it did not have within its "structure," a board of directors, a chief executive officer, or a management team (Dale, 2016). The rationale behind the crowdfunding was the creation of new software applications, but before the venture could be executed, it was hit with a cyberattack that effectively drained DAO of a third of the capital

433

raised (Popper, 2016b). It was soon made clear that the ICO initiated by DAO violated a long list of securities laws. Many entrepreneurs, while appreciating the desire to find exemptions from registration under the US Securities Act of 1933, and to raise money with security "tokens," argued that a new structure was needed to accomplish both goals: raise capital and launch a successful blockchain protocol.

Across the globe, another digital venture investment fund from India called GainBitCoin guaranteed its investors a monthly return of 10% on their crypto-token investment. The scheme was a multilevel-marketing scheme that aimed to extract the liquid bitcoin from the investors and provide returns in the form of another cryptocurrency called the MCAP. The value of the MCAP is negligible to the market. The mastermind of the scheme, one Amit Bhardwaj, was arrested by the Enforcement Directorate and charged with defrauding investors to the tune of $300 million through this nouveau Ponzi scheme (Anupam, 2018).

Along with cryptocurrency investment funds DAO and GainBitCoin, multiple ICOs (also called token sales) are still being launched worldwide. In 2017 these ICOs raised a collective $5.6 billion, of which only 48% were successful (Williams-Grut, 2018). In late May 2017, SingularityNet, a decentralized marketplace for artificial intelligence (AI), raised $36 million in 30 seconds (Alois, 2017). Bancor, a company that is developing a cryptocurrency exchange platform, raised in excess of $153 million in just 3 hours (Suberg, 2017).

As investors risk their unsecured capital investments, the market participants started questioning the silence of the regulators. In July 2017 the question was answered by the Securities and Exchange Commission (SEC) of the United States, in a report detailing its findings after its investigation in the DAO. In the report the SEC stated that the method used to raise equity in the DAO was in fact not a currency, but a security.[1] This report used the 70-year-old Howey Test, in which it is indicated that ICOs are subject to federal securities law as they primarily profit from the efforts of others. In May 2017 the SEC chairman mentioned that the usage of the term coin/token does not circumvent the fact that capital is eventually raised from the public, classifying it as a security and not a currency (Roberts, 2018).[2]

The scale of these fintech marketplace developments clearly creates new avenues not only for entrepreneurial financing but also for financial fraud (Ahlstrom et al., 2018a). Thus in this chapter, we explain the current issues and overview some of the regulatory developments and highlight current regulatory uncertainty. Hence, the chapter is organized as follows. Sections 19.2 and 19.3 provide an overview of blockchain and ICOs, respectively, in terms of the new technology, the evolving regulatory process, and regulatory needs. Sections 19.4 and 19.5 provide more details about crypto and cybersecurity fraud, respectively. Section 19.6 discusses regulatory developments in selected countries around the world and different paces of regulatory development. A discussion of the implications of managing crypto risks, challenges, and regulatory uncertainty follows in the last two sections.

---

[1] See https://www.sec.gov/news/press-release/2017-131.

[2] See also https://www.cnbc.com/2018/03/07/the-sec-made-it-clearer-that-securities-laws-apply-to-cryptocurrencies.html.

19.2 Blockchain

A person or a group of persons (depending on what you believe) under the name of Satoshi Nakamoto[3] published a white paper that introduced the world to the bitcoin, a decentralized cryptocurrency system that is neither produced nor regulated by any government.[4] It introduced a cryptographically proven electronic payment system, allowing parties to transact directly without an intermediary (Arslanian & Fischer, 2019). The technology aimed to move the focus from centralized institutions to peer-to-peer transactions in the market with the equanimity of control distribution as a key goal. The peer-to-peer architecture of the technology itself, as well as its open-source accessibility and privacy, ensures, through encryption, the direct exchange of value between parties without interference from banks, governments, and other intermediaries. From an underground unknown currency, bitcoin has now become a globally recognized asset, with bitcoin futures contracts being traded on the Chicago Mercantile Exchange Inc. (CME) and the CBOE Futures Exchange (CFE), holding a market cap more than $136 billion.[5] Bitcoin is both a cryptocurrency and a worldwide payment system. It is based on a technology called the bitcoin blockchain. Blockchain is a distributed public ledger that uses a cryptographic consensus protocol known as "proof of work" to allow the exchange of value between two parties. It is a ledger that can be used to virtually record any type of transaction, from cryptocurrency transfers to medical records to real estate chains of title. It is set up as a peer-to-peer network that allows its participants to agree on the state of the ledger at any given time by reaching consensus through a mathematical protocol. Owing to the fact that every individual participant works to ensure that the blockchain is accurate and secure, it is not dependent on the actions of any single central authority (Tapscott & Tapscott, 2016). The blockchain aims to solve the double-spend problem—the problem that until that time had prevented the widespread use of digital currencies. Although the blockchain is pseudonymous, it is not truly anonymous. The anonymity is removed in the transactional purchase of the cryptocurrency with the national fiat currency (Extance, 2015). These exchanges that facilitate such transactions are regulated under the national law and are subject to national know your client (KYC) and antimoney laundering requirements. However, some operators that keep the proceeds of their transactions in cryptocurrency or exchange the cryptocurrency via cash or a private transaction are still impervious to regulation.

19.3 Initial coin offerings

ICOs are a new form of crowdoffering in which participants exchange fiat currencies or existing cryptocurrency tokens for entity-specific tokens (Amsden & Schweizer, 2018).

---

[3] https://www.economist.com/the-economist-explains/2015/11/02/who-is-satoshi-nakamoto

[4] L.S. (2 November 2015). Who is Satoshi Nakamoto?. *Economist*. Available from <https://www.economist.com/the-economist-explains/2015/11/02/who-is-satoshi-nakamoto>.

[5] See Commodities Futures Trading Comm'n v. McDonnell, 287 F. Supp. 3d 213, 226, 228 (E.D.N.Y. 2018); Press Release No. 7731-18, U.S. Commodity Futures Trading Comm'n, CFTC Staff Issues Advisory for Virtual Currency Products (21 May 2018).

ICOs have exploded as the preferred mechanism used by blockchain entities to raise funds. Bellevatis, Cumming, and Vanacker (2019) provide theoretical rationales and empirical evidence from 73 countries over 2013–17 for the view that the cross-country diffusion of ICOs depends on governmental financial regulators, the media, and academic institutions as they affect the institutional legitimacy of ICOs. They also show that bans on ICOs in China and South Korea have internationally mobile governance implications that affect the diffusion of ICOs in other countries. This spillover in diffusion and effects of regulation from one country to the next shows that a harmonized and coordinated approach to regulation is appropriate, as these markets are internationally integrated, and the effect of regulations is not limited to national borders.

ICOs are often compared with initial public offerings (IPOs), with which companies sell stock shares to the public for the first time. Both of them are used to raise equity for budding companies, both produce substantial amounts of cash, and both have the potential to make company founders instantly wealthy. This is where the similarity lies. On the flip side, IPOs are heavily regulated (Carpentier et al., 2012). In the United States, the Securities Act of 1933 and the Securities Exchange Act of 1934 subject firms seeking to raise funds to registration, ongoing compliance, and disclosure requirements. These regulations ensure that firms raising funds provide truthful, sufficient, and accurate information. Owing to the extensive and exhaustive complex requirements of an IPO, the launching of the same requires a monthslong process that requires hiring an investment bank and legal counsel. The acts require every security offered to the public in the United States to be either registered with the SEC or meet one of the several complex enumerated exemptions from registration.

In the traditional world of raising capital, companies with exciting ideas for new products or services first have to build a prototype or beta to demonstrate to investors the validity of the idea. Post the demonstrated functionality of the product, and usually post a certain level of adaptation, a company can seek out venture funding to further develop or scale the idea. Entrepreneurs are then forced to give up significant equity in their own creations in exchange for early seed round capital. This limits those entrepreneurs with ideas who do not have a network of wealthy accredited investors. It also limits who can invest as most early round fundraising are limited to wealthy accredited investors. ICOs stand for a substantial shift in the way ideas are developed and commercialized. They allow developers with strong ideas for new applications/products/services on the blockchain to raise funds from those who would ultimately utilize the product/service built.

The issued tokens in an ICO do not grant the purchasers any form of equity or ownership interest in the issuing company. Instead, most ICOs issue some form of an application token or crypto asset that has some utility within the software program being developed. These tokens can be used to power decentralized applications built on the blockchain or to purchase products or services in the issuing entity decentralized software of protocol. Although primarily designed to be used as payment within the issuing entity blockchain ecosystem, app tokens may also operate as an independent store of value that can be traded through online cryptocurrency exchanges. Therefore ICOs are less like IPOs and more akin to preorders, with investors purchasing assets that would have value within the issuing entity system once the system is actually built, if at all.

ICOs also differ from IPOs in that, to date, they largely have not complied with any registration or disclosure requirements under the US securities laws (Arnold et al., 2019; Day & Osborne, 2018). Some of these ICOs have raised immense sums of money (Rohr & Wright, 2018). Some ICOs are launched by companies with no established track record, no history of bringing a viable product to the marketplace. There have been ICOs—such as the DAO's token sale—launched by developers without ever forming a corporation or other legal entity. Other ICOs have completed multimillion dollar fundraisers by marketing tokens that are explicitly held out as having no "rights, uses, purpose, attributes, functions, or features" (Williams-Grut, 2018).

19.4 Types of cryptocurrency frauds and regulatory uncertainty

19.4.1 Fictitious assets

Digital assets, unregistered with the regulatory authorities, promise substantial returns (Roberts, 2017). However, these assets are neither registered with the regulatory authorities nor securitized by the firm. Hence, with the absence of a registered prospectus certifying the security, information about the management, or financial statements, the asset being sold to the public lacks credibility.

With the substantial increase in the issuance of crypto-securities and the absence of a clear common understanding of the industry or the issues, regulators are understandably rushing toward securing the interests of the investors with significant effort toward the regulation and regularization of the ICOs. To illustrate, we refer to the SECs and Commodity Futures Trading Commissions cryptocurrency hearing in February 2018 which established that every ICO that the SEC had seen so far would be considered a security, only recently to be refuted and negated with the exclusion of the bitcoin and ether as neither securities nor currencies (Oyedele, 2017). The continual advent toward the incorporation and inclusion of regulation for the world's fastest growing industry has left many dazzled, dazed, and confused. On February 11, 2019 the SEC issued guidelines on ICOs in an attempt to formalize the sector and confirmed, among other things, that ICOs are a security regardless of how it is referred to as marketplace participants, issuers, and promoters.[6]

However, legal scholars have raised concerns about regulatory uncertainty with different types of crypto assets (Clements, 2019a, 2019b). Digitized securities are clearly within the realm of securities regulation, while decentralized crypto assets, asset tokens, and multipurpose utility tokens are not necessarily within the realm of securities regulation, as graphically summarized by Clements (2019a) reproduced here in Fig. 19.1.

The rationale behind the negation of addressing the crypto assets as a currency is the decentralization of the issuing authority, negating the possibility of the asset being addressed as a general ledger—which is the accepted mode of payment for debt and can be used to trade within the economy backed by the central bank of the government.

---

[6] https://www.mooncatchermeme.com/u-s-regulator-the-sec-has-reiterated-guidelines-on-icos-as-efforts-to-formalize-the-sector-continue/

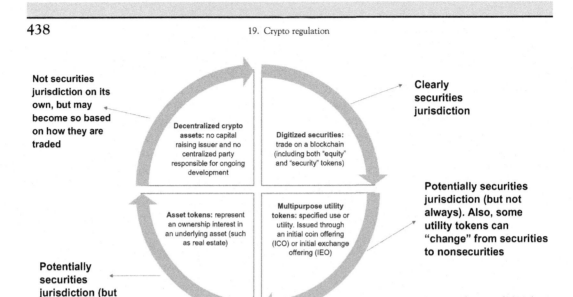

Not securities jurisdiction on its own, but may become so based on how they are traded

Clearly securities jurisdiction

Decentralized crypto assets: no capital raising issuer and no centralized party responsible for ongoing development

Digitized securities: trade on a blockchain (including both "equity" and "security" tokens)

Potentially securities jurisdiction (but not always). Also, some utility tokens can "change" from securities to nonsecurities

Asset tokens: represent an ownership interest in an underlying asset (such as real estate)

Multipurpose utility tokens: specified use or utility. Issued through an initial coin offering (ICO) or initial exchange offering (IEO)

Potentially securities jurisdiction (but not always)

Source: Clements (2019a)

FIGURE 19.1   Crypto assets: evolution of form and jurisdictional uncertainty.

The rationale behind the negation of the digital assets as a security is the absence of a third party that is expecting to seek a return on the investment—the absence of which negates the assets being a security. The SECs analysis, however, has been received without much criticism. The reasons are substantive. There is not much historical understanding of the industry, and, hence, not many legal experts working toward the regulatory aspects of the same. The limited knowledge of the disruptive nature of the technology is another reason. Lawyers tend to accommodate newer technology in older frameworks. The SECs report on the DAO was not just a onetime investigation. The report on the DAO was a message by the SEC to future ICOs that it is on alert, and it has the resources to not just investigate but also to enforce. The SECs scrutiny into the ICO industry threatens future fundraisers with legal implications. The so-called promise of democratization without substantive implementation is under threat as the increased regulatory constraints would impose substantial compliance requirements as the SEC expands upon investigative and enforcement challenges regarding the ICOs, such as tracing of money, international scope, and the ability to freeze cryptocurrency assets.

It is important for investor protection that crypto assets be within securities regulation jurisdiction. The US Securities Act of 1933 governs the issue of new securities in the public domain. The act requires that investors receive financial and other significant information concerning securities being offered for public sale and prohibits deceit, misrepresentations, and other fraud in the sale of securities. The regulations safeguard the disclosure of pertinent financial information regarding the security being offered for sale in the United States by firms raising funds for outside investors. In the case of an ICO, none of these companies have filed any registration with the SEC as they do not consider their offering a security. In the absence of any formal documentation, the investment in these assets is held at the mercy of the companies issuing the ICO, with the SEC unable to hold the company accountable. The SEC in recent disclosures has indicated that the ICOs are similar to securities being issued via other exchanges and need to be registered with the agency. Compliance is not only to ensure the protection of the investor's capital but also to ensure the growth of the industry, and innovation brought about through the capital raising mechanism.

19.4.2 Fake investment funds/advisors

With asset management one of the key drivers for the growth, many cryptocurrency investment funds have propped up trying to entice investors with unsubstantiated substantial returns. Most of these schemes run on multilevel-marketing schemes that induce the investor into not only contributing toward the scheme but also participating in the business to increase returns. As the bitcoin futures have been listed on the CME and CFE, the increase and decrease in the price of the asset can be bet against in the market, increasing the investors' interest toward the asset. The inclusion of the bitcoin on these established exchanges lures investors into the purchase of the asset as assumptions of legitimacy are made.

With a clear classification of cryptocurrencies as securities and this being within the domain of securities regulators, the next step would be the regulation of the investment funds and their advisors. In the United States, for example, the Investment Company Act of 1940 regulates the organization of companies, including mutual funds, which engage primarily in the investing, reinvesting, and trading securities. The act requires these companies to disclose information about the fund and its investment objectives, as well as the investment company structure and operations, to the investing public. The same act also regulates investment advisors, requiring firms or sole practitioners compensated for advising others about securities investments to register with the SEC and conform to regulations designed to protect investors. To the extent that ICOs are weakly regulated, their investment funds and advisors are likewise scantly within registration compliance. The SEC eventually would ensure the regulation of these funds in accordance with the rules and regulations of the two acts regulating the nondigital securities.

19.4.3 Unregulated manipulated crypto-exchanges

Market manipulation is a deliberate creation of a false price for a product, security, commodity, or currency. With minimal regulation binding these assets, and the assets being traded on portals that are also not bound with much regulation, investors may be exposed to multiple counts of market manipulation. Not unlike more traditional securities or commodities exchanges, there are numerous instances in the past where market manipulative if not fraudulent trades are carried out on portals, including but not limited to churning and ramping. Researchers found that just one person was able to drive the price of the bitcoin up from $100 to $1000 with the use of bots (Gandal, Hamrick, Moore, & Oberman, 2018). Some of these exchanges may also not adhere to the filing of the prerequisite KYC documentation. With the absence of the regulatory oversight, these exchanges operating on a global scale act as money laundering schemes and move money across geographic boundaries without much regulation. In 2006 the operators of a US-based exchange called GoldAge Inc. were indicted "on charges of operating an illegal digital currency exchange and money transmittal business". They were charged with transmitting $30 million to digital currency accounts owned by clients' limited identification documentation, with transaction fees of up to $100,000 (US Department of Justice National Drug Intelligence Center, 2008).

19.5 Cybersecurity fraud

Ownership of cryptocurrency has led to a demand for methods of storage. Cryptocurrency is stored in forms of "cryptocurrency wallets," where sensitive information is encrypted and securely stored (Bauer & Ahmad, 2017). There are desktop wallets, mobile app wallets, and online wallets, also known as an "exchange." The exchange provider stores the encrypted information on behalf of the owner, although exchanges are considered the storage method, most vulnerable to theft or fraud and may not be subject to regulatory oversight (FINRA 2018). Bauer and Ahmad (2017) identified a few popular methods utilized by cybercriminals or hackers.

19.5.1 Exchange hacks

Exchanges are counterintuitive to the decentralized nature of cryptocurrency (Valdivia, Del-Valle-Soto, Rodriguez, & Alcaraz, 2019). Their vulnerability can be exemplified by the Mt. Gox hack in 2014, and approximately 25,000 investors lost approximately 650,000 bitcoins (approximate value of $400 million). Investors had no recourse as exchanges not only unregulated but also uninsured (Bauer & Ahmad, 2017). The cryptocurrencies' anonymity and encryption is thus a double-edged sword. A study funded by the US Department of Homeland Security found that 33% of the bitcoin trading platforms have been hacked (Gandal et al., 2018).

Cryptocurrency hacks significantly reduce the price discovery of the hacked currency (Corbet, Cumming, Lucey, Peat, & Vigne, 2018). Moreover, cryptocurrency hacks increase both the volatility of the hacked currency and cross-cryptocurrency correlations (Corbet et al., 2018). Significant regulation, surveillance, and enforcement are needed to protect all cryptocurrencies, in view of the disruption they cause internally and spillovers to other related crypto markets. It is consistent with the shift toward a global approach to financial regulation (see also Chan & Milne, 2019).

Cryptocurrency hacks also give rise to abnormal returns in the hours prior to the actual hacking event, but those abnormal returns revert to zero at the time of the public announcement of the hack (Corbet et al., 2018). This evidence suggests that current regulatory and surveillance efforts are too slow to be an effective protection for investors.

In the future, regulation and computerized market surveillance (Aitken, Cumming, & Zhan, 2015a; Aitken, Cumming, & Zhan, 2015b; Cumming & Johan, 2008, 2019; Cumming et al., 2011, 2015) could be improved in crypto marketplaces. To this end a number of stylized facts identified from studies of the volatility and price discovery process from cryptocurrencies provide guidance as to some of the pronounced issues that are distinct from other securities trading (Corbet et al., 2018). For example, cryptocurrencies exhibit weekend-volatility effects, which suggest that pronounced surveillance is needed in traditional aftermarket trading period. Similarly, intraday volatility is significantly influenced by international trading times, which suggests that significant cross-market surveillance would help detect market manipulation in crypto markets. Moreover, it is influenced by periods of substantial volatility in the markets for oil and exchange rates, which indicates that significant cross product surveillance would help detect market manipulation in crypto markets.

19.5.2 Social media identity hacking

The ubiquitous use of social media has led to innovative methods of identity theft. It is unfortunately extremely simple for hackers to obtain information such as e-mail addresses, mobile phone numbers, and personal details such as pet names and childhood nicknames (common passwords use by online users). Exchanges that unfortunately rely on the traditional two-factor identification will thus be vulnerable to hackers seeking to transfer cryptocurrency held in investors' wallets. The stolen cryptocurrency can then be converted to real currency or other encrypted cryptocurrencies (Bauer & Ahmad, 2017).

19.5.3 Ransomware

Since 2016 cybersecurity experts have noted an increase in ransomware attacks. Liska (2019) noted 46 attacks in 2016, 38 in 2017, and 53 in 2018. In the first quarter of 2019, 21 attacks have been reported. After a more recent attack on the city of Riviera Beach, Florida in June 2019, city official paid hackers 65 bitcoin $592,000 in digital currency (Mazzei, 2019). Bauer and Ahmad (2017) highlighted two ransomware attacks that gained worldwide attention, WannaCry and Petya, and they find that the same modus operandi is used where the computer systems of a company, or city, are held hostage, and data will only be released upon payment of a ransom. The peer-to-peer architecture of the cryptocurrency or rather the direct exchange of value between hostages without interference from other intermediaries enables payment of ransom remotely and anonymously.

19.5.4 Cryptojacking

Bauer and Ahmad (2017) identify a method used by hackers to "mine" cryptocurrencies. Hackers use malware to hijack a mobile device or computer by using its processing power to mine a cryptocurrency. Not only are owners of these devices unaware of the cryptojacking but also even websites may oblivious to their role in the distribution of the malware. Other more nefarious sites encourage the distribution to share in the profit of the mining.

19.5.5 Taxation fraud

Tax havens enable taxpayers to conceal earnings from home country tax authorities by offering an environment with little taxation, where the activity is usually not subject to information exchange because of strict bank secrecy regulations (Westhuizen, 2017). Worldwide, revenue loss as a result of unattributed earnings adds up to $255 billion, with $40–$70 billion for the United States alone (Brunson, 2012; Marian, 2013). As a result, there is considerable international pressure for the tax havens to minimize their taxation of income earned by foreign investors (Dharmapala & Hines, 2009). Cryptocurrencies, while having no "jurisdiction" per se, possess the two crucial elements of a traditional tax haven: the absence of jurisdiction of operation and anonymity (Marian, 2013). Therefore they would not be subject to taxation at source.

Marian (2013) suggests that the concealment of earnings may be further extended. One example is the usage of tax-exempt buying agents to exchange financial contract obligations. Under the swap the agent receives bitcoin, buys a security with legal currency value, and any dividends earned would be paid in bitcoin value to the swap holder. Losses or gains would be paid the same way. At all times, the bitcoin holder would be untraceable, and the agent would also have no tax liability because of his tax-exempt status. Currently, the US Internal Revenue Service (IRS) has through IRS Notice 2014–21 categorized cryptocurrency as property. General taxation principles applicable to property transactions apply to transactions using virtual currency (VC). According to the notice a taxpayer receiving VC as income must declare it as income calculated at fair market value at the date of payment or receipt. Any transaction of the VC with respect to a property has to be adjusted with respect to its adjusted cost base and gain or loss depending upon the fair market value at the time. Any gain or loss on the exchange of the cryptocurrency is considered capital gains on the asset. Currently, the IRS Criminal Investigation Division is training its agents to detect cryptocurrency wallets in its efforts to minimize tax fraud and evasion (IRS, 2018).

There are of course many other possible illegal uses including criminal money laundering and terrorism. Organizations such as Al-Sadaqah are targeting Muslims in the West to raise capital to supply fighters with resources in Syria (Stalinsky, 2018). As the potential for illegality is real, regulation and surveillance are needed. Some regulatory trends are discussed in the subsequent section.

19.6 Current international regulatory trends

To illustrate the differing pace of regulatory development across markets, we highlight key issues in selected jurisdictions (apart from the U.S., which has been discussed above).

19.6.1 Canada

While Canada allows the usage of digital currency to buy goods and services on the Internet, and its usage in stores that accept digital currencies, digital currencies are not considered legal tender. Canada still only considers banknotes and coins issued by the

Bank of Canada as legal tender. Digital currencies are, however, considered a commodity and are subject to the barter rules of the Income Tax Act (Al-Shikarchy, Baum, & Gheorghiu, 2017). It allows digital currency to be bought and sold on exchanges. Digital currencies are subject to the Income Tax Act, and GST/HST also applies to the fair market value of any goods or services bought using digital currency. In that regard, goods purchased using digital currency must be included in the seller's income for tax purposes.[7]

19.6.2 India

In January 2018, Arun Jaitley, the Finance Minister of India, declared the bitcoin as not being legal tender. Being a VC, and having no physical attributes, the Indian government deemed to be neither currency nor coin, thus without the formal authorization by the Reserve Bank of India to enable the VC to be used as a medium of exchange. This is not terribly surprising as the very nature of the VC would make the country's stringent currency control measures ineffectual (Nupur, 2018). Having said that, India has determined that the growth in capital from the asset class will be taken into consideration as capital gains. The Income Tax Department, the Securities and Exchange Board of India, and the Ministry of Finance have sought details from various crypto-exchanges about their transactions (Jain & Kumar, 2018). India has currently banned the usage of cryptocurrency as an asset class by both businesses and financial institutions. The conversion of Indian currency to cryptocurrency is illegal within India. The conversion between different ICOs is, however, still allowed.

19.6.3 China

The Chinese government has decided to stifle the cryptocurrency industry by completely not recognizing of VCs, banning the trading of VCs and the issuance of ICOs. In September 2017, seven central government regulators issued the Announcement on Preventing Financial Risks from ICOs (ICO Rules) for purposes of investor protection (Pilarowski & Yue, 2017). The ICO Rules essentially prohibit the exchanges from dealing with VC, converting VC into legal tender, and setting prices for VC. This, however, has led to capital raising from domestic Chinese investors by platforms relocated to Hong Kong and other offshore centers (Perper, 2018). China is, however, known to have the highest number of bitcoin miners in the world (Huang, 2018).

19.6.4 United Kingdom

With its threat to leave the European Union, the United Kingdom was impacted by political and economic uncertainty that motivated many UK platforms to relocate to Paris, Amsterdam, and Frankfurt. The UK Financial Conduct Authority announced that it would

---

[7] Government of Canada at https://www.canada.ca/en/financial-consumer-agency/services/payment/digital-currency.html.

be working with the UK Treasury Committee in order to analyze the risks and opportunities related to cryptocurrencies and blockchain technologies (Tomzack, 2018).

19.6.5 Norway and Sweden

Norway, like many other jurisdictions, considers the Bitcoin a taxable asset, but not as a currency. Norway Bank is, however, moving toward the direct integration of the currency (Mandelli, 2017). Similarly, Sweden has embraced the technology and plans to launch its own currency called the E-Krona.

19.6.6 The European Union

In January 2019 the European Union released a set of guidelines for ICOs.[8] There are clear differences across European countries, but these guidelines will help to harmonize policies and regulations pertaining to ICOs and crypto assets. Future research could empirically examine the implications of the introduction of these guidelines on marketplace volatility and uncertainty, among other things, when more time has passed, and data are available (see also (Corbet et al., 2018) for earlier work that predates these guidelines). Regulatory approaches and their effects on markets in other regions around the world could likewise be examined in more detail in future work.

19.7 Contributions

This chapter contributes to the nascent research on new financing techniques and their growing importance (Cumming, Deloof, Manigart, & Wright, 2019). It also adds to research on regulation and encouraging innovation (Butenko & LaRouche, 2015). Effective regulation is crucial to encouraging innovation (Spulber, 2008), though as Butenko and LaRouche (2015) highlight, regulation and effective enforcement often lag behind innovation.

The law and technology literature shows potential for harmful innovation, while the law and economic literature is more concerned with identifying market failures and the flow of information, and motivating innovation (Butenko & LaRouche, 2015; Crafts, 2006). In the case of the rapidly changing cryptocurrency market and other entrepreneurial applications of blockchain technology, there is a need for a sort of intersection of the law and technology with the law and economics literatures. Blockchain applications are not exogenous to the regulatory process, which creates a need for law and economics perspectives. However, these applications are not all necessarily positive, particularly as they may better enable financing of illegal activities and other illegal market misconduct, which requires law and technology perspectives and the regulation of innovation.

At this early stage of legal and institutional developments, there is much research that needs to be done to better understand the appropriate legal and surveillance/enforcement

---

[8] https://www.esma.europa.eu/sites/default/files/library/esma50-157-1391_crypto_advice.pdf

regimes that will minimize negative externalities from blockchain applications while not stifling innovation. Further, additional work on international cooperation and harmonization of regulation is needed, as financial innovations with blockchain are clearly designed with little regard to national borders. Some of the regulatory changes reviewed here could be the subject of future empirical studies on the causes and consequences of financial regulation in blockchain and cryptocurrencies. Moreover, the blockchain and cryptocurrency markets offer a natural setting for intersecting the law and technology and law and economics literatures as advocated by Butenko and LaRouche (2015). Inclusive institutions are critical for technological development and economic growth (Acemoglu & Robinson, 2012; Ahlstrom, Yang, Wang, & Wu, 2018b; Tomizawa, Zhao, Bassellier, & Ahlstrom, 2019). More work is needed to better understand how laws and institutions enable the most economic growth at the minimal expected costs with Blockchain and cryptocurrencies.

19.8 Conclusion

This chapter reviewed the SEC's initial statements on ICOs, and subsequent pronouncements and the evolving legal framework. Enforcement is problematic with the existing regulatory framework, and there is a greater need for collaboration between government agencies and developers to establish an ecosystem that integrates investor protection and investment.

On the positive side, the distributed ledger technology backed by the blockchain industry is set to revolutionize the world in effectively mitigating trust constraints while reducing transaction costs. The crowdfunding for software development has already reduced the distance between venture capitalists and ventures. The ability for an entrepreneur to increase millions of dollars in equity within days shows the interest of the general public toward not just the venture but also the equity stake or tokens received in return. The ever-expansive interest is reflective of the world's interest in the asset class and the world's trust in the asset class.

On the negative side, the inherent nature of the crypto assets can facilitate fraud. There are multiple cases of investors losing their capital from investing in the nouveau offerings, resulting in the much-evaded and much-negated skepticism toward the industry. Despite these concerns, there is much regulatory uncertainty. Debate even continues regarding the categorization of crypto assets as currency or securities (Agrawal, 2018; Clements, 2019a). The Pecora Commission in the post−1930s' Depression and Dodd−Frank in the post-2008 Financial Crisis are examples of how regulation and solid institutions substantially helped in avoiding (or mitigating) economic crises. The inherent "trust" nature of the technology backing the crypto assets should not determine or undermine the regulation's guarding the industry for decades. At the end of the day the conversion of fiat currency to any asset is guarded by various securities laws governing the industry. These laws ensure the protection of not just the investors' capital but also the extreme volatility and possible future economic ripple effects that can be caused.

If blockchain and its ancillary technologies can be regulated and managed, it may be that it will enable a whole new wave of entrepreneurs and engineers to build and implement this infrastructure and facilitate faster advances along this key technological trajectory (Dunbar & Ahlstrom, 1995). The major opportunities in the blockchain may be comparable to the Internet of the 1990s, with new Amazon and Alibaba waiting to be founded and built up. In the next 5 years, we will see a number of critical innovations and their applications emerge come from it.

Given that cryptocurrencies such as bitcoin operate independently of geographic location or central banks, blockchain can thus allow entrepreneurs from virtually anywhere in the world access to startup funds and developmental capital. What microfinance and other disruptive funding methods started (Bonini, Capizzi, & Cumming, 2019; Newman, Schwarz, & Ahlstrom, 2017), blockchain technology can bring much further along. Blockchain can be a major facilitator of entrepreneurship, which is a crucial part of a growing economy (Tomizawa et al., 2019). It needs a regulatory framework that will protect investors and firms alike (Peng, Ahlstrom, Carraher, & Shi, 2017), while not discouraging needed innovation and continuing the facilitation of entrepreneurial financing.

Key terms

Blockchain
Cryptocurrency
Cryptojacking
Cybersecurity
Fictitious assets
Hacking
Initial coin offerings
Ransomware

Discussion questions

19.1. Why do we need cryptocurrencies? Are cryptocurrencies a security for the purposes of securities regulation? Why or why not? Explain, with reference to different types of cryptocurrencies and the ongoing regulatory debate.

19.2. Describe some types of cryptocurrency frauds, and cybersecurity frauds. Give some examples from recent cases. What do they imply for regulating cryptocurrency and crowdfunding?

19.3. How are cryptocurrencies different from traditional forms of crowdfinancing? How might cryptocurrencies be used alongside other forms of traditional crowdfunding, such as in the case of Whatrocks?[9] Can you think of other potential links between cryptocurrencies and different types of crowdfunding that might be developed in the future?

---

[9] See Section 15.5.

## PART V

Conclusion

Summary, conclusion, and looking forward

Crowdfunding has enormous potential for entrepreneurs around the world to access capital to finance a wide array of new ideas. The exponential growth in crowdfunding around the world (Chapter 1: Introduction) highlights the trend toward crowdfunding as one of the most important forms of finance for entrepreneurs around the world in a variety of different cultural and regulatory settings (Chapter 3: Overview of institutional contexts and empirical methods). And crowdfunding offers the potential for a democratized access to capital (Chapter 13: Does equity crowdfunding democratize access to entrepreneurial finance?), enabling different types of entrepreneurs to better achieve access to capital.

As with other forms of finance, there are potential risks due to information asymmetries between entrepreneurs, portals, and backers or investors (Chapter 2: Overview of agency and signaling theory in crowdfunding). But throughout this book, we described mechanisms through which these information asymmetries and agency costs can be mitigated to optimize the potential for crowdfunding. For example, there is a role for crowdfunding portals to do due diligence, and portals that carry out more due diligence have better financing outcomes (Chapter 4: An overview of rewards-based crowdfunding). Crowdfunding portals can likewise structure their portals to maximize outcomes. For example, by offering different funding mechanisms, such as the "keep-it-all" versus the "all-or-nothing" mechanisms on Indiegogo, portals enable entrepreneurs to signal their quality and more efficiently raise capital (Chapter 5: Crowdfunding models: keep-it-all versus all-or-nothing). And other types of innovations, such as the voting process on WiSeed, offer an effective screening process from the wisdom of the crowd, which, in turn, is a useful predictor of crowdfunding success (Chapter 8: Equity crowdfunding, valuation, and cases). The use of "soft information," such as text and videos, can be designed in ways to tailor specific funding needs such as that for cleantech projects (Chapter 6: Crowdfunding cleantech) and internationalization (Chapter 7: Crowdfunding to internationalize).

With cases, such as that of Oculus Rift (Chapter 4: An overview of rewards-based crowdfunding), we have seen the importance of allowing entrepreneurs and investors to

Crowdfunding
DOI: https://doi.org/10.1016/B978-0-12-814637-8.00020-2

access equity crowdfunding. There have been many successful cases in equity crowdfunding (Chapter 8: Equity crowdfunding, valuation, and cases), including but not limited to ReWalk's campaign on OurCrowd and subsequent public listing on NASDAQ. Differences across crowdfunding platforms allow entrepreneurs and their investors to pick the right governance model that works best for them such as the possibility to invest alongside a professional angel investor or venture capitalist (Chapter 9: Equity crowdfunding and governance). Crowdfunding campaigns can be designed in a way whereby entrepreneurs can make the use of costly signals to convey their quality to the crowd and predictably improve their chances of success in equity crowdfunding (Chapter 10: Signaling in equity crowdfunding). For example, we showed on the basis of theory and empirical evidence that entrepreneurs show not give up too much equity capital, since doing so lowers chances of success as seen from data from ASSOB in Australia and Crowdcude in the United Kingdom (Chapter 10: Signaling in equity crowdfunding, and Chapter 12: Cash-flow and control rights in equity crowdfunding). And entrepreneurs likewise can elect into selling nonvoting equity shares thereby creating dual class ownership structures (Chapter 12: Cash-flow and control rights in equity crowdfunding). Various choices about the type of equity campaign offered enable different types of retail and professional investors (Chapter 12: Cash-flow and control rights in equity crowdfunding) and from different regions (Chapter 11: Are equity crowdfunders sensitive to distance?), and into entrepreneurial startups from a variety of different segments of the population (Chapter 13: Does equity crowdfunding democratize access to entrepreneurial finance?). Entrepreneurs firms and their investors may alternatively elect into the rapidly growing marketplace lending area. Despite some concerns with the role of simple ratings by marketplace lending platforms versus the role of detailed financial information in driving investor decisions, marketplace lending has had a very strong positive impact on the rate of new entrepreneurial startups (Chapter 14: Marketplace lending).

There have been a number of cases of crowdfunding fraud (Chapter 15: Introduction to crowdfunding regulation and policy). The presence of fraud of course leads to regulatory concerns. But the extent of fraud is not as common as what we might have expected. Crowdfunding fraud cases as a percentage of crowdfunding campaigns are much lower than securities fraud cases relative as a percentage of publicly traded companies (Chapter 15: Introduction to crowdfunding regulation and policy).

Many countries around the world have introduced specific crowdfunding regulations. These regulations typically limit the amount of capital that can be raised in a 12-month period, and likewise the amount of money investors can invest. As well, some regulations impose requirements for audited financial statements. We have seen how the introduction of regulatory systems in some countries has given rise to vibrant equity crowdfunding markets, such as that in the United States, while other regulatory systems designed at the same time have given rise to no entrepreneurs using equity crowdfunding such as that in Canada (Chapter 15: Introduction to crowdfunding regulation and policy). Regulation and regulatory oversight, or the lack thereof, has the potential to spur on fintech entrepreneurship (Chapter 18: Regulation and investment in fintech ventures). Regulations should be designed keeping in mind the needs of the marketplace (Chapter 16: Demand-driven crowdfunding regulation). Regulations and public policy should likewise reflect on the broader ecosystem of other forms of entrepreneurial finance such as angel investment and venture capital (Chapter 17: Public policy toward entrepreneurial finance: spillovers and scale-up). And as innovation progresses into links with crowdfunding and cryptocurrencies (Chapter 19: Crypto regulation), a more integrated framework of oversight is likely needed in coming years. Crowdfunding has enormous potential, and public policy and regulation that is well designed can keep this potential on track to enable the financing of new innovations to the benefit of entrepreneurs, portals, investors, and society at large.

References

Accenture. (2015). *The future of fintech and banking: Digitally disrupted or reimagined?* Accenture Consulting. Available from: <https://www.accenture.com/us-en/insight-future-fintech-banking.aspx>.

Acemoglu, D., & Robinson, J. A. (2012). *Why nations fail: The origins of power, prosperity, and poverty.* New York: Crown Publishing.

Ackerlof, G. A. (1970). The market for "lemons": Quality uncertainty and the market mechanism. *Quarterly Journal of Economics, 84,* 488–500.

Ackerman, P. L., & Humphreys, L. G. (1990). Individual differences theory in industrial and organizational psychology. *Handbook of Industrial and Organizational Psychology, 1,* 223–282.

Adams, R. M. (2018). Do marketplace lending platforms offer lower rates to consumers? In: *Board of Governers of the Federal Reserve System, FEDS notes.* <https://www.federalreserve.gov/econres/notes/feds-notes/do-marketplace-lending-platforms-offer-lower-rates-to-consumers-20181022.htm>.

Aernoudt, R. (2017). Executive forum: the scale-up gap: And how to address it. *Venture Capital: An International Journal of Entrepreneurial Finance, 19*(4), 361–372.

Afonso, G., Kovner, A., & Schoar, A. (2014). *Trading partners in the interbank lending market. Staff reports, no. 620.* New York: Federal Reserve Bank of New York.

Afuah, A., & Tucci, C. L. (2012). Crowdsourcing as a solution to distant search. *Academy of Management Review, 37*(3), 355–375.

Aggarwal, R., Prabhala, N. R., & Puri, M. (2002). Institutional allocation in initial public offerings: Empirical evidence. *Journal of Finance, 57*(3), 1421–1442.

Aghion, P., & Bolton, P. (1992). An incomplete contracts approach to financial contracting. *Review of Economic Studies, 59,* 473–494.

Agrawal, N. (2018). *SEC Chairman Clayton: Bitcoin is not a security.* <https://coincenter.org/link/sec-chairman-clayton-bitcoin-is-not-a-security>.

Agrawal, A., Catalini, C., & Goldfarb, A. (2016). Are syndicates the killer app of equity crowdfunding? *California Management Review, 58*(2), 111–124.

Agrawal, A., Catalini, C., & Goldfarb, A. (2011). The geography of crowdfunding. In: *National Bureau of Economic Research working paper.* Available from SSRN: <http://ssrn.com/abstract = 1692661>.

Agrawal, A., Catalini, C., & Goldfarb, A. (2013). Some simple economics of crowdfunding. *Innovation Policy and the Economy, 14,* 63–97.

Agrawal, A., Catalini, C., & Goldfarb, A. (2015). Crowdfunding: Geography, social networks, and the timing of investment decisions. *Journal of Economics and Management Strategy, 24*(2), 253–274.

Agrawal, A., Catalini, C., & Goldfarb, A. (2016). Are syndicates the killer App of equity crowdfunding? *California Management Review, 58*(2), 111–124.

Aguilar, F. X., & Cai, Z. (2010). Exploratory analysis of prospects for renewable energy private investment in the U.S. *Energy Economics, 32*(6), 1245–1252.

Aguilera, R. V., Filatotchev, I., Gospel, H., & Jackson, G. (2008). An organizational approach to comparative corporate governance: Costs, contingencies, and complementarities. *Organization Science, 19*(3), 475–492.

Ahearne, A. G., Griever, W. L., & Warnock, F. E. (2004). Information costs and home bias: An analysis of US holdings of foreign equities. *Journal of International Economics, 62,* 313–336.

Ahlers, G. K., Cumming, D. J., Günther, C., & Schweizer, D. (2015). Signaling in equity crowdfunding. *Entrepreneurship Theory and Practice, 39*(4), 955–980.

Ahlstrom, D. (2010). Innovation and growth: How business contributes to society. *The Academy of Management Perspectives, 24,* 11–24.

Ahlstrom, D., & Bruton, G. D. (2006). Venture capital in emerging economies: Networks and institutional change. *Entrepreneurship Theory and Practice, 30*, 299−320.

Ahlstrom, D., Cumming, D. J., & Vismara, S. (2018a). New methods of entrepreneurial firm financing: Fintech, crowdfunding and corporate governance implications. *Corporate Governance: An International Review, 26*, 310−313.

Ahlstrom, D., Yang, X., Wang, L., & Wu, C. (2018b). A global perspective of entrepreneurship and innovation in China. *Multinational Business Review, 26*, 302−318.

Aitken, M., Cumming, D. J., & Zhan, F. (2015a). High frequency trading and end-of-day price dislocation. *Journal of Banking and Finance, 59*, 330−349.

Aitken, M., Cumming, D. J., & Zhan, F. (2015b). Exchange trading rules, surveillance, and suspected insider trading. *Journal of Corporate Finance, 34*, 311−330.

Akerlof, G. A. (1970). The market for" lemons": Quality uncertainty and the market mechanism. *Quarterly Journal of Economics*, 488−500.

Albrecht, S. W. (2014). Iconic fraud triangle endures. *Fraud Magazine, 29*, 46−52.

Aldrich, H., & Waldinger, R. (1990). Ethnicity and entrepreneurship. *Annual Rev. Sociology, 16*(1), 111−135.

Alexy, O., Block, J., Sandner, P., & Ter Wal, A. (2012). Social capital of venture capitalists and start-up funding. *Small Business Economics, 39*, 835−851.

Alois, J. D. (2017). *Fastest ICO ever? SingularityNet raises $36 million in 60 seconds.* Available from: <https://www.crowdfundinsider.com/2017/12/126315-fastest-ico-ever-singularitynet-raises-36-million-60-seconds/>.

Al-Shikarchy, M., Baum, S., & Gheorghiu, L. (2017). *Gowling WLG, Canadian taxation of cryptocurrency ... so far.* Lexology. Available from: <https://www.lexology.com/library/detail.aspx?g = 6283077e-9d32-4531-81a5-56355fa54f47> (accessed 22.07.19).

AltFi.com. (2015). *AltFi data analytics.* <http://analytics.altfidata.com/data/analytics/volume>.

Amit, R., Brander, J., & Zott, C. (1998). Why do venture capital firms exist? Theory and Canadian evidence. *Journal of Business Venturing, 13*(6), 441−466.

Amsden, R., & Schweizer, D. (2018). *Are blockchain crowdsales the new 'Gold Rush'? Success determinants of initial coin offerings.* Available from SSRN: <https://ssrn.com/abstract = 3163849> or <https://doi.org/10.2139/ssrn.3163849>.

Anupam, S. (2018). *Who is Amit Bhardwaj? The real story behind $300 mn Bitcoin Ponzi schemes and more.* Available from: <https://inc42.com/buzz/who-is-amit-bhardwaj-the-real-story-behind-300-mn-bitcoin-ponzi-schemes/>.

Armitage, S., Sarkar, S., & Talaulicar, T. (2017). Corporate governance challenges in emerging economies. *Corporate Governance: An International Review, 25*, 148−154.

Armour, J., & Cumming, D. (2006). The legislative road to Silicon Valley. *Oxford Economic Papers 58*, 596−635.

Arner, D. W., Barberis, J., & Buckley, R. P. (2015). The evolution of Fintech: A new post-crisis paradigm. *Georgetown Journal of International Law, 47*, 1271.

Arnold, L., Brennecke, M., Camus, P., Fridgen, G., Guggenberger, T., Radszuwill, S., Rieger, A., Schweizer, A., & Urbach, N. (2019). Blockchain and initial coin offerings: Blockchain's implications for crowdfunding. In H. Treiblmaier, & R. Beck (Eds.), *Business transformation through blockchain* (pp. 233−272). Basingstoke, Cham: Palgrave.

Arrow, K. J. (1998). What has economics to say about racial discrimination? *Journal of Economic Perspective, 12*(2), 91−100.

Arslanian, H., & Fischer, F. (2019). *The rise of bitcoin. The future of finance.* Cham: Palgrave Macmillan.

Assenova, V., Best, J., Cagney, M., Ellenoff, D., Karas, K., Moon, J., Neiss, S., Suber, R., & Sorenson, O. (2016). The present and future of crowdfunding. *California Management Review, 58*, 125−135.

Audretsch, D. (2007). Entrepreneurship capital and economic growth. *Oxford Review of Economic Policy, 23*(1), 63−78.

Autio, E., Kenney, M., Mustar, P., Siegel, D., & Wright, M. (2014). Entrepreneurial innovation: The importance of context. *Research Policy, 43*(7), 1097−1108.

Avnimelech, G., & Teubal, M. (2006). Creating venture capital industries that co-evolve with high tech: Insights from an extended industry life cycle perspective of the Israeli experience. *Research Policy, 35*(10), 1477−1498.

Backes-Gellner, U., & Werner, A. (2007). Entrepreneurial signaling via education: A success factor in innovative start-ups. *Small Business Economics, 29*, 173−190.

Baeyens, K., Vanacker, T., & Manigart, S. (2006). Venture capitalists' selection process: The case of biotechnology proposals. *International Journal of Technology Management, 34*(1-2), 28–46.

Baker, H. K., Nofsinger, J. R., & Weaver, D. G. (2002). International cross-listing and visibility. *Journal of Financial and Quantitative Analysis, 37*(3), 495–521.

Barnett, C. (2015). *Trends show crowdfunding to surpass VC in 2016.* Available from: <https://www.forbes.com/sites/chancebarnett/2015/06/09/trends-show-crowdfunding-to-surpass-vc-in-2016/2/#4cc9dbbb666f>.

Barry, C. B., & Mihov, V. T. (2015). Debt financing, venture capital, and the performance of initial public offerings. *Journal of Banking and Finance, 58*, 144–165.

Bartus, T., & Roodman, D. (2014). Estimation of multiprocess survival models with CMP. *The Stata Journal, 14*, 756.

Bauer, S., & Ahmad, I. (2017). *The lawyers daily.* Available from: <https://www.wolfelawyers.com/resources/Cryptocurrency-and-Cybersecurity---The-Implications---The-Lawyer%27s-Daily.pdf> (accessed 17.11.17).

Baum, J. A., & Silverman, B. S. (2004). Picking winners or building them? Alliance, intellectual, and human capital as selection criteria in venture financing and performance of biotechnology startups. *Journal of Business Venturing, 19*, 411–436.

Baum, J. R., Locke, E. A., & Smith, K. G. (2001). A multidimensional model of venture growth. *Academy of Management Journal, 44*, 292–303.

Baumol, W. J. (1990). Entrepreneurship: Productive, unproductive, and destructive. *Journal of Political Economy, 98*, 893–921.

Baumol, W. J. (2002). *The free-market innovation machine: Analyzing the growth miracle of capitalism.* Princeton University Press.

Bayus, B. (2013). Crowdsourcing new product ideas over time: An analysis of the Dell IdeaStorm Community. *Management Science, 59*, 226–244.

Bebchuk, L. A. (1992). Federalism and the corporation: The desirable limits on state competition in corporate law. *Harvard Law Review, 105*, 1435–1510.

Bebchuk, L. A., & Kastiel, K. (2017). The untenable case for perpetual dual-class stock. *Virginia Law Review, 103*(4), 585–631.

Bebchuk, L. A., Kraakman, R., & Triantis, G. (2000). *Stock pyramids, cross-ownership, and dual class equity: The mechanisms and agency costs of separating control from cash-flow rights. Concentrated corporate ownership* (pp. 295–318). National Bureau of Economic Research, Inc, NBER chapters.

Beck, T., Demirgüç-Kunt, A., & Levine, R. (2005). Law and firm's access to finance. *American Law and Economics Review, 7*, 211–252.

Becker, G. (1957). *The economics of discrimination.* Chicago, IL: University of Chicago Press.

Becker, J., & Myers, S. L. (June 11, 2015). Russian groups crowdfund the war in Ukraine. New York Times.

Bell, R. G., Filatotchev, I., & Rasheed, A. A. (2012). The liability of foreignness in capital markets: Sources and remedies. *Journal of International Business Studies, 43*(2), 107–122.

Belleflamme, P., Lambert, T., & Schwienbacher, A. (2010). Crowdfunding: An industrial organization, working paper.

Belleflamme, P., Lambert, T., & Schwienbacher, A. (2013). Individual crowdfunding practices. *Venture Capital: An International Journal of Entrepreneurial Finance, 15*(4), 313–333.

Belleflamme, P., Lambert, T., & Schwienbacher, A. (2014). Crowdfunding: Tapping the right crowd. *Journal of Business Venturing, 29*(5), 585–609.

Bellevatis, C., Cumming, D. J., & Vanacker, T. (2019). *The cross-country diffusion of new entrepreneurial practices: The case of Initial Coin Offerings, working paper.* Auckland Business School, Florida Atlantic University, and Ghent University.

Bengtsson, O., & Hsu, D. H. (2015). Ethnic matching in the U.S. venture capital market. *Journal of Business Venturing, 30*, 338–354.

Bergh, D. D., Connelly, B. L., Ketchen, D. J., & Shannon, L. M. (2014). Signaling theory and equilibrium in strategic management research: An assessment and a research agenda. *Journal of Management Studies, 51*(8), 1334–1360.

Berglöf, E. (1994). A control theory of venture capital finance. *Journal of Law, Economics, and Organization, 10*, 247–267.

Bernstein, S., Korteweg, A. G., & Laws, K. (2017). Attracting early stage investors: Evidence from a randomized field experiment. *Journal of Finance, 72*, 509–538.

Bertoni, F., & Groh, A. F. (2014). Cross-border investments and venture capital exits in Europe. *Corporate Governance: An International Review, 22*(2), 84–99.

Bertoni, F., Colombo, M. G., & Grilli, L. (2013). Venture capital investor type and the growth mode of new technology-based firms. *Small Business Economics, 40*, 527–552.

Bertoni, F., Colombo, M. G., & Quas, A. (2015). The patterns of venture capital investment in Europe. *Small Business Economics, 45*(3), 543–560.

Bjørnskov, C., & Foss, N. (2013). How strategic entrepreneurship and the institutional context drive economic growth. *Strategic Entrepreneurship Journal, 7*(1), 50–69.

Blaseg, D., Cumming, D., & Koetter, M. (2019). Equity crowdfunding: Lemons or lollipops? *Entrepreneurship Theory and Practice*, conditionally accepted.

Blind, K. (2012). The influence of regulations on innovation: A quantitative assessment for OECD countries. *Research Policy, 41*(2), 391–400.

Block, J., Hornuf, L., & Moritz, A. (2018). Which updates during an equity crowdfunding campaign increase crowd participation? *Small Business Economics, 50*(1), 3–27.

Block, J. H., Colombo, M. G., Cumming, D. J., & Vismara, S. (2018). New players in entrepreneurial finance and why they are there. *Small Business Economics, 50*(2), 239–250.

Bloomberg New Energy Finance. (2010). *Crossing the Valley of Death: Solution to the next generation clean energy project financing gap, June 2010 white paper.* <http://bnef.com/PressReleases/view/119>.

Bloomberg New Energy Finance. (2012). *Global trends in renewable energy investment.* Frankfurt School UNEP Collaborating Centre for Climate & Sustainable Energy Finance. Frankfurt School of Finance & Management gGmbH.

Blossfeld, H.-P., Golsch, K., & Rohwer, G. (2007). *Event history analysis with STATA.* Mahwah, NJ: Lawrence Erlbaum Associates.

Boeh, K. K., & Dunbar, C. G. (2013). *Post IPO withdrawal outcomes. SSRN working paper.*

Bohliqa, A. (2015). A study of the U.S. intrastate crowdfunding exemptions. In: *Portland international conference on management of engineering and technology (PICMET)* (pp. 961–967).

Bonardo, D., Paleari, S., & Vismara, S. (2011). Valuing university-based firms: The effects of academic affiliation on IPO performance. *Entrepreneurship Theory and Practice, 35*(4), 755–776.

Bonini, S., Capizzi, V., & Zocchi, P. (2019). The performance of angel-backed companies. *Journal of Banking & Finance, 100*, 328–345.

Bonini, S., Alkan, S., & Salvi, A. (2012). The effects of venture capitalists on the governance of firms. *Corporate Governance: An International Review, 20*(1), 21–45.

Bonini, S., Capizzi, V., & Cumming, D. J. (2019). Emerging trends in entrepreneurial finance. *Venture Capital: An International Journal of Entrepreneurial Finance, 21*, 133–136.

Boudreau, K. J., & Jeppesen, L. B. (2015). Unpaid crowd complementors: The platform network effect mirage. *Strategic Management Journal, 36*(12), 1761–1777.

Bozkaya, A., & Kerr, W. (2014). Labor regulations and European venture capital. *Journal of Economics & Management Strategy, 23*(4), 776–810.

Bradford, S. C. (2012). Crowdfunding and the Federal Securities Laws. *Columbia Business Law Review, 2012*(1), 1–150.

Brau, J. C., & Fawcett, S. (2006). Initial Public Offerings: An Analysis of Theory and Practice. *Journal of Finance, 61* (1), 399–436.

Braun, R., Eidenmüller, H., Engert, A., & Hornuf, L. (2013). Does charter competition foster entrepreneurship? A difference-in-difference approach to European Company Law Reforms. *Journal of Common Market Studies, 51*, 399–415.

Brüderl, J., & Preisendörfer, P. (1998). Network support and the success of newly founded businesses. *Small Business Economics, 10*, 213–225.

Bürer, M. J., & Wustenhagen, R. (2009). Which renewable energy policy is a venture capitalist's best friend? Empirical evidence from a survey of international clean energy investors. *Energy Policy, 37*, 4997–5006.

Brunson, S. D. (2012). Repatriating tax-exempt investments: Tax havens, blocker corporations, and unrelated debt-financed income. *Northwestern University Law Review, 106*, 225.

Brush, C. G., Greene, P. G., & Hart, M. M. (2001). From initial idea to unique advantage: The entrepreneurial challenge of constructing a resource Base. *The Academy of Management Executive, 15*, 64–78.

Brush, C. G., Carter, N. M., Gatwood, E. J. Greene, P. G., & Hart, M. (2004). *Gatekeepers of venture growth: A Diana Project report on the role and participation of women in the venture capital industry*. Kansas City, MO: The Kauffman Foundation.

Bruton, G., Khavul, S., Siegel, D., & Wright, M. (2015). New financial alternatives in seeding entrepreneurship: Microfinance, crowdfunding, and peer-to-peer innovations. *Entrepreneurship Theory and Practice, 39*(1), 9–26.

Burtch, G., Ghose, A., & Wattal, S. (2014). Cultural differences and geography as determinants of online prosocial lending. *MIS Quarterly, 38*(3), 773–794.

Burtch, G., Ghose, A., & Wattal, S. (2013). An empirical examination of the antecedents and consequences of contribution patterns in crowd-funded markets. *Information Systems Research, 24*(3), 499–882.

Burtch, G., Ghose, A., & Wattal, S. (2015). The hidden cost of accommodating crowdfunder privacy preferences: A randomized field experiment. *Management Science, 61*(5), 949–962.

Busenitz, L. W., Fiet, J. O., & Moesel, D. (2005). Signaling in venture capitalists—New venture team funding decisions: Does it indicate long-term venture outcomes? *Entrepreneurship Theory and Practice, 29*, 1–12.

Butenko, A., & LaRouche, P. (2015). Regulation for innovativeness or regulation of innovation? *Law, Innovation and Technology, 7*, 52–82.

Buzzacchi, L., Scellato, G., & Ughetto, E. (2015). Investment stage drifts and venture capital managerial incentives. *Journal of Corporate Finance, 33*, 118–128.

Cameron, L. D., Brown, P. M., & Chapman, J. G. (1998). Social value orientations and decisions to take pro-environmental action. *Journal of Applied Social Psychology, 28*(8), 675–697.

Campbell, A. A., Cherry, C. R., Ryerson, M. S., & Yang, X. (2016). Factors influencing the choice of shared bicycles and shared electric bikes in Beijing. *Transportation Research Part C: Emerging Technologies, 67*, 399–414.

Cao, J., Cumming, D. J., Qian, M., & Wang, X. (2015). Cross border LBOs. *Journal of Banking and Finance, 50*, 69–80.

Carlson, R. (1972). Understanding women: Implications for personality theory and research. *The Journal of Social Issues, 28*, 17–32.

Carpentier, C., Cumming, D. J., & Suret, J. (2012). The value of capital market regulation: IPOs versus reverse mergers. *Journal of Empirical Legal Studies, 9*, 56–91. Available from https://doi.org/10.1111/j.1740-1461.2011.01247.

Carter, S., & Rosa, P. (1998). The financing of male and female-owned businesses. *Entrepreneurship and Regional Development, 10*(3), 225–241.

Cary, W. (1974). Federalism and corporate law: Reflections upon Delaware. *Yale Law Journal, 83*, 663–705.

Casamatta, C. (2003). Financing and advising: Optimal financial contracts with venture capitalists. *Journal of Finance, 58*, 2059–2085.

Casamatta, C., & Haritchabalet, C. (2007). Experience, screening and syndication in venture capital investments. *Journal of Financial Intermediation, 16*, 368–398.

Cassard, M. (1994). *The Role of Offshore Centers in International Financial Intermediation*. Washington, DC: International Monetary Fund, IMF working papers series, WP/94/107-EA.

Catalini, C., Fazio, C. & Murray, F. (2016). *Can equity crowdfunding democratize access to capital and investment opportunities? SSRN working paper*.

Cavalluzzo, K. S., Cavalluzzo, L. C., & Wolken, J. D. (2002). Competition, small business financing, and discrimination: evidence from a new survey. *Journal of Business, 75*(4), 641–679.

Cefis, E., & Marsili, O. (2005). A matter of life and death: Innovation and firm survival. *Industrial and Corporate Change, 14*, 1167–1192.

Certo, S. T. (2003). Influencing initial public offering investors with prestige: Signaling with board structures. *Academy of Management Review, 28*(3), 432–446.

Chakraborty, S., & Swinney, R. (2019). Signaling to the crowd: Private quality information and rewards based crowdfunding. *Manufacturing & Service Operations Management*, forthcoming.

Chan, K. K., & Milne, A. (2019). The global legal entity identifier system: How can it deliver? *Journal of Risk and Financial Management, 12*(1), 39. Available from https://doi.org/10.3390/jrfm12010039.

Chan, K., Covrig, V., & Ng, L. (2005). What determines domestic bias and foreign bias? Evidence from mutual fund equity allocations worldwide. *Journal of Finance, 60*, 1495–1534.

Chaplinsky, S., & Gupta-Mukherjee, S. (2009). *The rise of M&A exits in venture capital: Implications for capital recovery, Darden working paper.*

Chaplinsky, S., Weiss Hanley, K., & Moon, S. K. (2017). The JOBS Act and the costs of going public. *Journal of Accounting Research, 55*(4), 795–836.

Chemla, G., & Tinn, K. (2017). Learning through crowdfunding. In: *CEPR discussion papers 11363, C.E.P.R. discussion papers.*

Chemmanur, T. J., & Jiao, Y. (2012). Dual class IPOs: A theoretical analysis. *Journal of Banking & Finance, 36*(1), 305–319.

Chemmanur, T. J., Hull, T. J., & Krishnan, K. (2016). Do local and international venture capitalists play well together? The complementarity of local and international venture capitalists. *Journal of Business Venturing, 31,* 573–594.

Chen, D., & Mintz, J. (2011). Small business taxation: Revamping incentives to encourage growth. University of Calgary, *SPP Papers, 4*(7), 1–31.

Cholakova, M., & Clarysse, B. (2015). Does the possibility to make equity investments in crowdfunding projects crowd out reward-based investments? *Entrepreneurship Theory and Practice, 39*(1), 145–172.

Chung, S., Singh, H., & Lee, K. (2000). Complementarity, status similarity and social capital as drivers of alliance formation. *Strategic Management, 21,* 1–22.

Clarysse, B., Wright, M., Bruneel, J., & Mahajan, A. (2014). Creating value in ecosystems: Crossing the chasm between knowledge and business ecosystems. *Research Policy, 43*(7), 1164–1176.

Clements, R. (2019a). *Crypto-Assets: Current research and public policy issues. Working paper.* Calgary: University of Calgary School of Public Policy.

Clements, R. (2019b). *Regulating Fintech in Canada and the United States: Comparison, challenges, and opportunities. Publications SPP research paper 12* (p. 20) Calgary: University of Calgary School of Public Policy.

Cleves, M. A., Gould, W. W., & Gutierrez, R. G. (2008). *An introduction to survival analysis using STATA.* TX: STATA Press Publication.

Cohen, L. (2009). Loyalty-based portfolio choice. *Review of Financial Studies, 22,* 1213–1245.

Cohen, S., & Hochberg, Y. V. (2014). *Accelerating startups: The seed accelerator phenomenon.* Available from SSRN: <https://ssrn.com/abstract = 2418000>.

Cole, R. A., & Sokolyk, T. (2018). Debt financing, survival, and growth of start-up firms. *Journal of Corporate Finance, 50,* 609–625.

Cole, R. A., Cumming, D. J., & Taylor, J. (2019). Does FinTech compete with or complement bank finance? *SSRN.* Available from https://doi.org/10.2139/ssrn.3302975.

Cole, R. A., Cumming, D. J., & Li, D. (2016). Do banks or VCs spur small firm growth? *Journal of International Financial Markets, Institutions and Money, 41,* 60–72.

Coleman, S. (2000). Access to capital: A comparison of men and women-owned small businesses'. *Journal of Small Business Management, 38*(3), 37–52.

Colombo, M., & Shafi, K. (2016). *Does reward-based crowdfunding help firms obtain venture capital and angel finance? Working paper.* Available from SSRN: <http://ssrn.com/abstract = 2785538>.

Colombo, M. G., Croce, A., & Grilli, L. (2013). ICT services and small businesses' productivity gains: An analysis of the adoption of broadband internet technology. *Information Economics and Policy, 25,* 171–189.

Colombo, M. G., Franzoni, C., & Rossi-Lamastra, C. (2015). Internal social capital and the attraction of early contributions in crowdfunding projects. *Entrepreneurship Theory and Practice, 39*(1), 75–100.

Connelly, B. L., Certo, S. T., Ireland, R. D., & Reutzel, C. R. (2011). Signaling theory: A review and assessment. *Journal of Management, 37,* 39–67.

Corbet, S., Cumming, D. J., Lucey, B. M., Peat, M., & Vigne, S. (2018). *Investigating the dynamics between price volatility, price discovery, and criminality in cryptocurrency markets, working paper.* DCU Business School, Florida Atlantic University, Trinity Business School, University of Sydney, and Queen's Management School.

Corwin, S. A., & Schultz, P. (2005). The role of IPO underwriting syndicates: Pricing, information production, and underwriter competition. *Journal of Finance, 60*(1), 443–486.

Cosh, A., Cumming, D. J., & Hughes, A. (2009). Outside entrepreneurial capital. *Economic Journal, 119*(540), 1494–1533.

Coval, J. D., & Moskowitz, T. J. (1999). Home bias at home: Local equity preference in domestic portfolios. *Journal of Finance, 54,* 2045–2073.

Coval, J., & Moskowitz, T. (2001). The geography of investment: Informed trading and asset prices. *Journal of Political Economy, 109,* 811–841.

Crafts, N. (2006). Regulation and productivity performance. *Oxford Review of Economic Policy, 22,* 186–202.

Crifo, P., & Forget, V. D. (2013). Think global, invest responsible: Why the private equity industry goes green. *Journal of Business Ethics, 116*(1), 21–48.

CrowdfundingHub. (2016). *Current state of crowdfunding in Europe.* Amsterdam, The Netherlands: CrowdfundingHub.

Crowdsourcing, LLC. (2012). *Crowdfunding IndustryReport: Market trends, composition and crowdfunding platforms.* Crowdsourcing, LLC.

Crowdsourcing, LLC. (2013). *Crowdfunding IndustryReport: Market trends, composition and crowdfunding platforms.* Crowdsourcing, LLC.

Cumming, D. J. (2008). Contracts and exits in venture capital finance. *Review of Financial Studies, 21,* 1947–1982.

Cumming, D. J., & Dai, N. (2010). Local bias in venture capital investments. *Journal of Empirical Finance, 17*(3), 362–380.

Cumming, D. J., & Fischer, E. (2012). Publicly funded business advisory services and entrepreneurial outcomes. *Research Policy, 41,* 467–481.

Cumming, D. J., & Hornuf, L. (2017). *Marketplace lending of SMEs. Working paper.* Florida Atlantic University and University of Trier.

Cumming, D. J., & Johan, S. A. (2006). Provincial preferences in private equity. *Financial Markets and Portfolio Management, 20,* 369–398.

Cumming, D. J., & Johan, S. A. (2007). Advice and monitoring in venture finance. *Financial Markets and Portfolio Management, 21,* 3–43.

Cumming, D. J., & Johan, S. A. (2008). Global market surveillance. *American Law and Economics Review, 10,* 454–506.

Cumming, D. J., & Johan, S. A. (2009). Pre-seed government venture capital funds. *Journal of International Entrepreneurship, 7,* 26–56.

Cumming, D. J., & Johan, S. A. (2010). Phasing out an inefficient venture capital tax credit. *Journal of Industry, Competition and Trade, 10,* 227–252.

Cumming, D. J., & Johan, S. A. (2013a). *Venture capital and private equity contracting: An international perspective.* (2nd ed.). San Diego, CA: Elsevier Science Academic Press.

Cumming, D. J., & Johan, S. A. (2013b). Demand driven securities regulation: Evidence from crowdfunding. *Venture Capital: An International Journal of Entrepreneurial Finance, 15,* 361–379.

Cumming, D. J., & Johan, S. A. (2013c). Technology parks and entrepreneurial outcomes around the World. *International Journal of Managerial Finance, 9*(4), 279–293.

Cumming, D. J., & Johan, S. A. (2016). Crowdfunding and entrepreneurial internationalization. In N. Dai, & D. Siegel (Eds.), *Entrepreneurial finance: Managerial and policy implications.* The World Scientific Publishers, Chapter 5.

Cumming, D. J., & Johan, S. A. (2019). Capital-market effects of securities regulation: Prior conditions, implementation, and enforcement revisited. *Finance Research Letters,* forthcoming.

Cumming, D. J., & MacIntosh, J. (2000a). The determinants of R&D expenditures: A study of the Canadian biotechnology industry. *Review of Industrial Organization, 17*(4), 357–370.

Cumming, D. J., & MacIntosh, J. (2000b). The role of interjurisdictional competition in shaping Canadian corporate law. *International Review of Law and Economics, 20*(2), 141–186.

Cumming, D. J., & MacIntosh, J. (2002). The Rationales underlying reincorporation and implications for Canadian corporations. *International Review of Law and Economics, 22*(3), 277–330.

Cumming, D. J., & MacIntosh, J. (2006). Crowding out private equity: Canadian evidence. *Journal of Business Venturing, 21,* 569–609.

Cumming, D. J., & MacIntosh, J. (2007). Mutual funds that invest in private equity? An analysis of Labour Sponsored Investment Funds. *Cambridge Journal of Economics, 31*(3), 445–487.

Cumming, D. J., & Vismara, S. (2017). De-segmenting research in entrepreneurial finance. *Venture Capital, 19* (1–2), 17–27.

Cumming, D. J., & Walz, U. (2010). Private equity returns and disclosure around the world. *Journal of International Business Studies, 41*(4), 727–754.

Cumming, D. J., & Zambelli, S. (2017). Due diligence and investee performance. *European Financial Management*, 23, 211−253.

Cumming, D.J., & Zhang, Y. (2016). Are crowdfunding platforms active and effective intermediaries? Working paper.

Cumming, D. J., & Zhang, M. (2016). *Angel investors around the world*, Journal of International Business Studies, 50(5), 692−719. Available from SSRN: <https://ssrn.com/abstract = 2716312>.

Cumming, D. J., Sapienza, H. J., Siegel, D. S., & Wright, M. (2009). International entrepreneurship: managerial and policy implications. *Strategic Entrepreneurship Journal*, 3(4), 283−296.

Cumming, D. J., Schmidt, D., & Walz, U. (2010). Legality and venture capital governance around the world. *Journal of Business Venturing*, 25(1), 54−72.

Cumming, D. J., Fischer, E., & Peridis, T. (2015). Publicly funded business advisory services and entrepreneurial internationalization. *International Small Business Journal*, 33, 824−839.

Cumming, D.J., Hervé, F., Manthé, E., Schwienbacher, A. (2017). Hypothetical investment bias, Working paper.

Cumming, D.J., Hornuf, L., Karami, M., & Schweizer, D. (2017). Disentangling crowdfunding from fraudfunding. Working paper.

Cumming, D.J., Meoli, M., & Vismara, S. (2017). Investors' choice between cash and voting rights: evidence from dual-class equity crowdfunding. Working paper.

Cumming, D. J., Leboeuf, G., & Schwienbacher, A. (2017). Crowdfunding cleantech. *Energy Economics*, 65, 292−303.

Cumming, D. J., Fleming, G., & Schwienbacher, A. (2005). Liquidity risk and venture finance. *Financial Management*, 34, 77−105.

Cumming, D. J., Fleming, G., & Schwienbacher, A. (2009). Corporate relocation in venture Capital finance. *Entrepreneurship Theory and Practice*, 33, 1121−1155.

Cumming, D. J., Johan, S. A., & Li, D. (2011). Exchange trading rules and stock market liquidity. *Journal of Financial Economics*, 99(3), 651−671.

Cumming, D. J., Johan, S. A., & Zhang, M. (2014). The economic impact of entrepreneurship: Comparing international datasets. *Corporate Governance: An International Review*, 22(2), 162−178.

Cumming, D. J., Dannhauser, B., & Johan, S. A. (2015). Financial market misconduct and agency conflicts: A synthesis and future directions. *Journal of Corporate Finance*, 34, 150−168.

Cumming, D. J., Leung, T. Y., & Rui, O. (2015). Gender diversity and securities fraud. *Academy of Management Journal*, 58(5), 1572−1593.

Cumming, D. J., Hornuf, L., Karami, M & Schweizer, D. (2016). Disentangling crowdfunding from fraudfunding. In: *Max Planck Institute for Innovation and Competition research paper no. 16-09.*

Cumming, D., Knill, A., & Syvrud, K. (2016). Do international investors enhance private firm value? Evidence from venture capital. *Journal of International Business Studies*, 47(3), 347−373.

Cumming, D. J., Henriques, I., & Sadorsky, P. (2016). Cleantech' venture capital around the world. *International Review of Financial Analysis*. Available from https://doi.org/10.1016/j.irfa.2016.01.015.

Cumming, D. J., Walz, U., & Werth, J. C. (2016). Entrepreneurial spawning: experience, education, and exit. *Financial Review*, 51(4), 507−525.

Cumming, D. J., Hervé, F., Manthé, E., & Schwienbacher, A. (2017). Identifying start-up success: Testing-the-waters policy with hypothetical investment. In: *Working paper, presented at the 2nd emerging trends in entrepreneurial finance conference.* Available from SSRN: <https://ssrn.com/abstract = 3114526 or https://doi.org/10.2139/ssrn.3114526>.

Cumming, D. J., Filatoctchev, I., Knill, A., Reeb, D., & Senbet, L. (2017). Law, finance, and the international mobility of corporate governance. *Journal of International Business Studies*, 48, 123−147.

Cumming, D. J., Johan, S. A., & MacIntosh, J. (2017). A drop in an empty pond: Canadian public policy towards venture capital. *Journal of Industrial and Business Economics*, 44, 103−117.

Cumming, D. J., Johan, S. A., & Zhang, Y. (2019). The role of due diligence in crowdfunding platforms, Journal of Banking & Finance, forthcoming.

Cumming, D. J., McGowan, D., Farag, H. & Johan, S. A. (2018). The digital credit divide: The effect of marketplace lending on entrepreneurship, working paper. In: *Presented at the European Finance Association annual conference.* 2019. University of Birmingham and Florida Atlantic University.

Cumming, D., Groh, A. P., & Johan, S. (2018). Same rules, different enforcement: Market abuse in Europe. *Journal of International Financial Markets, Institutions and Money*, 54, 130−151.

Cumming, D. J., Meoli, M., & Vismara, S. (2019). Investors' choice between cash and voting rights: evidence from dual-class equity crowdfunding. *Research Policy, 48*(8), 103740.

Cumming, D., Werth, J. C., & Zhang, Y. (2019). Governance in entrepreneurial ecosystems: Venture capitalists vs. technology parks. *Small Business Economics, 52*(2), 455–484.

Cumming, D. J., Deloof, M., Manigart, S., & Wright, M. (2019). New directions in entrepreneurial finance. *Journal of Banking & Finance, 100,* 252–260.

Cumming, D. J., Leboeuf, G., & Schwienbacher, A. (2019). Crowdfunding models: Keep-it-all vs. all-or-nothing. *Financial Management,* 1–30. Available from https://doi.org/10.1111/fima.12262.

Dai, N., & Nahata, R. (2016). Cultural differences and cross-border venture capital syndication. *Journal of International Business Studies, 47,* 140–169.

Dai, N., Jo, H., & Kassicieh, S. (2012). Cross-border venture capital investments in Asia: Selection and performance. *Journal of Business Venturing, 27,* 666–684.

Daines, R. M. (2001). Does Delaware law improve firm value? *Journal of Financial Economics, 62,* 525–558.

Daines, R. (2002). The incorporation choices of IPO firms. *New York University Law Review, 77,* 1559–1611.

Daines, R. M., & Klausner, M. (2001). Do IPO charters maximize firm value? Antitakeover protection in IPOs. *Journal of Law, Economics, & Organization, 17,* 83–120.

Dale, B. (2016). *The DAO: How the employee less company has already made a boatload of money.* Available from: <http://observer.com/2016/05/dao-decentralized-autonomous-organizatons/>.

Darby, M., & Zucker, L. G. (2001). *Change or die: The adoption of biotechnology in the Japanese and U.S. pharmaceutical industries, Research on Technological Innovation* (7, pp. 85–125).

Davies, R. (2015). Three provocations for civic crowdfunding. *Information, Communication & Society, 18*(3). Available from http://www.tandfonline.com/doi/abs/10.1080/1369118x.2014.989878?journalCode = rics20.

Davila, A., Foster, G., & Gupta, M. (2003). Venture capital financing and the growth of startup firms. *Journal of Business Venturing, 18,* 689–708.

Davis, J. (2016). *The Vanishing American Corporation.* Oakland, CA: Berrett-Koehler Publishers, Inc.

Day, Z., & Osborne, C. (2018). *SEC pursues dozens of companies in cryptocurrency ICO crackdown.* Available from: <https://www.zdnet.com/article/sec-pursues-dozens-of-companies-in-cryptocurrency-ico-crackdown/>.

Deephouse, D. L., & Carter, S. M. (2005). An examination of differences between organizational legitimacy and organizational reputation. *Journal of Management Studies, 42*(2), 329–360.

DeMeza, D., & Webb, D. (1987). Too much investment: A problem of asymmetric information. *Quarterly Journal of Economics, 102*(2), 281–292.

Dewally, M., Ederington, L. H., & Fernando, C. S. (2013). Determinants of trader profits in commodity futures markets. *Review of Financial Studies, 26,* 2648–2683.

Dharmapala, D., & Hines, J. R. (2009). Which countries become tax havens? *Journal of Public Economics, 93*(9–10), 1058–1068.

Dharmapala, D., & Khanna, V. (2016). The costs and benefits of mandatory securities regulation: Evidence from market reactions to the JOBS Act of 2012. *Journal of Law, Finance and Accounting, 1,* 139–186.

DiMaggio, P. J., & Powell, W. W. (1983). The iron cage revisited: Institutional isomorphism and collective rationality in organizational fields. *American Sociological Review, 48,* 148–160.

Disdier, A., & Head, K. (2008). The puzzling persistence of the distance effect on bilateral trade. *Review of Economics and Statistics, 90,* 37–48.

Djankov, S., La Porta, R., Lopez-De-Silanes, F., & Shleifer, A. (2002). The regulation of entry. *Quarterly Journal of Economics, 117,* 1–37.

Doms, M., Lewis, E., & Robb, A. (2010). Local labor force education, new business characteristics, and firm performance. *Journal of Urban Economics, 67,* 61–77.

Downes, D. H., & Henkel, R. (1982). Signaling and the valuation of unseasoned new issues. *Journal of Finance, 37,* 1–10.

Driffield, N., Love, J. H., & Yang, Y. (2014). Technology sourcing and reverse productivity spillovers in the multinational enterprise: Global or regional phenomenon? *British Journal of Management, 25*(S1), S24–S41.

Duarte, J., Siegel, S., & Young, L. (2012). Trust and credit: The role of appearance in peer-to-peer lending. *Review of Financial Studies, 25*(8), 2455–2484.

Dunbar, R., & Ahlstrom, D. (1995). Seeking the institutional balance of power: Avoiding the power of a balanced view. *Academy of Management Review, 20,* 171–192.

Dupont, Q., & Karpoff, J. M. (2019). The trust triangle: Laws, reputation, and culture in empirical finance research. *Journal of Business Ethics*, forthcoming.

Duruflé, G., Hellmann, T., & Wilson, K. (2018). *From start-up to scale-up: Examining public policies for the financing of high-growth ventures* (pp. 179–219).

Dushnitsky, G., & Zunino, D. (2019). The role of crowdfunding in entrepreneurial finance. *Handbook of Research on Crowdfunding*, 2019. Chapter 3, pages 46–92.

Dushnitsky, G., Guerini, M., Piva, E., & Rossi-Lamastra, C. (2016). Crowdfunding in Europe: determinants of platform creation across countries. *California Management Review*, *58*(2), 44–71.

Eagly, A. H., Karau, S. J., & Makhijani, M. G. (1995). Gender and the effectiveness of leaders: a meta-analysis. *Psychological Bulletin*, *117*, 125–145.

Epstein, L. G., & Schneider, M. (2008). Ambiguity, information quality, and asset pricing. *Journal of Finance*, *63*, 197–228.

Estrin, S., Gozman, D., & Khavul, S. (2018). The evolution and adoption of equity crowdfunding: Entrepreneur and investor entry into a new market. *Small Business Economics*, *51*(2), 425–439.

Etzkowitz, H. (2002). Incubation of incubators: Innovation as a triple helix of university-industry-government networks. *Science and Public Policy*, *29*(2), 115–128.

Extance, A. (2015). The future of cryptocurrencies: Bitcoin and beyond. *Nature*, *526*, 21–23.

Fabowale, L., Orser, B., & Riding, A. (1995). Gender, structural factors, and credit terms between Canadian small businesses and financial institutions. *Entrepreneurship Theory and Practice*, *19*(4), 41–65.

Faccio, M., & Lang, L. H. (2002). The ultimate ownership of Western European corporations. *Journal of Financial Economics*, *65*, 365–395.

Fagenson, E. (1993). Personal value systems of men and women: Entrepreneurs versus managers. *Journal of Business Venturing*, *8*(5), 409–430.

Fairlie, R. W., & Robb, A. (2007). Why are black-owned businesses less successful than white-owned businesses? The role of families, inheritances, and business human capital. *Journal of Labor Economics*, *25*(2), 289–323.

Fairlie, R. W., Morelix, A., Reedy, E. J., & Russell, J. (2016). *The Kauffman index of startup activity: National trends*. Kansas City, MO: The Ewing Marion Kauffman Foundation.

Farmer, R. E., & Winter, R. A. (1986). The role of options in the resolution of agency problems: a comment. *Journal of Finance*, 1157–1170.

Farrell, J., & Rabin, M. (1996). Cheap talk. *Journal of Economic Perspectives*, *10*(3), 103–118.

Feng, L., & Seasholes, M. S. (2004). Correlated trading and location. *Journal of Finance*, *59*, 2117–2144.

Filatotchev, I., & Wright, M. (2017). Methodological issues in governance research: An editor's perspective. *Corporate Governance: An International Review*, *25*(6), 454–460.

FINRA Staff & BBB Institute. (2018). *Storing and securing cryptocurrencies*. Available from: <http://www.finra.org/investors/highlights/storing-and-securing-cryptocurrencies> (accessed 19.07.19).

Fleming, L., & Sorenson, O. (2016). Financing by and for the masses. *California Management Review*, *58*(2), 5–19.

Florida, R., & Smith, F. (1994). Venture capital formation, investment, and regional industrialization. *Annals of the Association of American Geographers*, *83*, 434–451.

Franke, N., Gruber, M., Harhoff, D., & Henkel, J. (2006). What you are is what you like—Similar biases in venture capitalists' evaluations of start-up teams. *Journal of Business Venturing*, *21*, 802–826.

Freear, J., Sohl, J. E., & Wetzel, W. E., Jr. (1994). Angels and non-angels: Are there differences? *Journal of Business Venturing*, *9*, 109–123.

French, K. R., & Poterba, J. M. (1991). Investor diversification and international equity markets. *American Economic Review*, *81*, 222–226.

Fried, V. H., & Hisrich, R. D. (1994). Toward a model of venture capital investment decision making. *Financial Management*, 28–37.

Friedland, R., & Alford, R. R. (1991). Bringing society back. In W. W. Powell, & P. J. DiMaggio (Eds.), *Symbols, practices and institutional contradictions. The new institutionalism in organizational analysis* (pp. 232–263). Chicago, IL: University of Chicago Press.

Gajda, O., & Mason, N. (2013). *Crowdfunding for impact in Europe and the USA, European crowdfunding white paper*. Available from: <www.europecrowdfunding.org>.

Gandal, N., Hamrick, J. T., Moore, T., & Oberman, T. (2018). Price manipulation in the bitcoin ecosystem. *Journal of Monetary Economics, Volume 95*, 86–96.

Garcia, D., & Strobl, G. (2011). Relative wealth concerns and complementarities in information acquisition. *Review of Financial Studies, 24,* 169–207.

Ghosh, S., & Nanda, R. (2010). Venture capital investment in the clean energy sector. In: *Harvard Business School working paper, 11-020.*

Gilson, R., & Schizer, D. (2003). Venture capital structure: A tax explanation for convertible preferred stock. *Harvard Law Review, 116,* 875–916.

Goktan, M. S., & Muslu, V. (2018). Benefits of public reporting: Evidence from IPOs backed by listed private equity firms. *Journal of Corporate Finance, 50,* 669–688.

Goldfarb, B. D., Hoberg, G., Kirsch, D. & Triantis, A. J. (2013). Are angels different? An analysis of early venture financing. In: *Robert H. Smith school research paper no. RHS 06-072.* Available from SSRN: <https://ssrn.com/abstract = 1024186> or <https://doi.org/10.2139/ssrn.1024186>.

Gompers, P. A., & Lerner, J. (1999). *The Venture Capital Cycle.* Cambridge, MA: MIT Press.

Gompers, P. A., Ishii, J., & Metrick, A. (2010). Extreme governance: An analysis of dual-class firms in the United States. *Review of Financial Studies, 23*(3), 1051–1088.

Gompers, P. A., Mukharlyamov, V., Weisburst, E., & Xuan, Y. (2014). *Gender effects in venture capital.* Available from SSRN: <https://ssrn.com/abstract = 2445497>.

Graham, J. R., & Harvey, C. R. (2001). The Theory and Practice of Corporate Finance: Evidence from the Field. *Journal of Financial Economics, 60*(2–3), 187–243.

Granovetter, M. (1973). The strength of weak ties. *American Journal of Sociology, 78,* 1360–1380.

Granovetter, M. (1983). The strength of weak ties: A network theory revisited. *Sociological Theory, 1,* 201–233.

Green, R. (1984). Investment incentives, debt, and warrants. *Journal of Financial Economics, 13,* 115–136.

Greenberg, J., & Mollick, E. R. (2017). Activist choice homophily and the crowdfunding of female founders. *Administrative Science Quarterly, 62*(2), 341–374.

Greene, P., Brush, C., Hart, M., & Saparito, P. (2001). Patterns of venture capital funding: is gender a factor? *Venture Capital, 3,* 63–83.

Greenwald, B. C., & Stiglitz, J. E. (1986). Externalities in economies with imperfect information and incomplete markets. *The Quarterly Journal of Economics, 101*(2), 229–264.

Griffin, Z. J. (2013). Crowdfunding: Fleecing the American masses. *Journal of Law, Technology & the Internet, 4*(2), 375–410.

Grilli, L., & Murtinu, S. (2014). Government, venture capital and the growth of European high-tech entrepreneurial firms. *Research Policy, 43*(9), 1523–1543.

Grinblatt, M., & Keloharju, M. (2000). The investment behavior and performance of various investor types: A study of Finland's unique data set. *Journal of Financial Economics, 55,* 43–67.

Grossman, S. J. (1981). The informational role of warranties and private disclosure about product quality. *Journal of Law and Economics, 24,* 461–483.

Guenther, C., Johan, S. A., & Schweizer, D. (2018). Is the crowd sensitive to distance? How investment decisions differ by investor type. *Small Business Economics, 50*(2), 289–305. Available from https://doi.org/10.1007/s11187-016-9834-6.

Guiso, L., Sapienza, P., & Zingales, L. (2009). Cultural biases in economic exchange? *Quarterly Journal of Economics, 124,* 1095–1131.

Guler, I., & Guillén, M. F. (2010). Institutions and the internationalization of US venture capital firms. *Journal of International Business Studies, 41,* 185–205.

Haddad, C., & Hornuf, L. (2019). The emergence of the global fintech market: Economic and technological determinants. *Small Business Economics, 53*(1), 81–105.

Hain, D., Johan, S. A., & Wang, D. (2016). Determinants of cross-border venture capital investments in emerging and developed economies: The effects of relational and institutional trust. *Journal of Business Ethics, 138,* 743–764.

Hall, B. H., Moncada-Paternò-Castello, P., Montresor, S., & Vezzani, A. (2016). Financing constraints, R&D investments and innovative performances: New empirical evidence at the firm level for Europe. *Economics of Innovation and New Technology, 25*(3), 183–196.

Ham, J. C. (1982). Estimation of a labour supply model with censoring due to unemployment and underemployment. *Review of Economic Studies, 49,* 335–354.

Hamilton, J. (2011). Historical oil shocks. In: *NBER working paper no. 16790.*

Harrison, R. (2013). Crowdfunding and the revitalisation of the early stage risk capital market: catalyst or chimera. *Venture Capital: An International Journal of Entrepreneurial Finance, 15*(4), 283–287.

Harrison, R., Mason, C., & Robson, P. (2010). Determinants of long-distance investing by business angels in the UK. *Entrepreneurship & Regional Development, 22*, 113–137.

Hart, O. (1995). Corporate governance: some theory and implications. *Economic Journal, 105*(430), 678–689.

Hart, S., & Milstein, M. (1999). Global sustainability and the creative destruction of industries. *Sloan Management Review, 41*(1), 23–33.

Hau, H., & Rey, H. (2008). Home bias at the fund level. *American Economic Review, 98*, 333–338.

Heckman, J. J. (1979). Sample selection bias as a specification error. *Econometrica, 47*, 153–162.

Hege, U., Schwienbacher, A., & Palomino, F. (2009). Venture capital performance: The disparity between Europe and the United States. *Finance, 30*(1), 7–50.

Hellmann, T., & Thiele, V. (2015). Friends or foes? The interrelationship between angel and venture capital markets. *Journal of Financial Economics, 115*(3), 639–653.

Heminway, J. M., & Hoffman, S. R. (2011). Proceed at your peril: Crowdfunding and the Securities Act of 1933. *Tennessee Law Review, 78*(879), 2011.

Henderson, B. J., Pearson, N. D., & Wang, L. (2015). New evidence on the financialization of commodity markets. *Review of Financial Studies, 28*(5), 1285–1311.

Henriques, I., Husted, B. W., & Montiel, I. (2013). Spillover effects of voluntary environmental programs on greenhouse gas emissions: Lessons from Mexico. *Journal of Policy Analysis & Management, 32*(2), 296–322.

Herzenstein, M., Andrews, R. L., Dholakia, U. M., & Lyandres, E. (2008). The democratization of personal consumer loans? Determinants of success in online peer-to-peer lending communities. *Boston University School of Management Research Paper, 14*(6), 1–36.

Hildebrand, T., Puri, M., & Rocholl, J. (2017). Adverse incentives in crowdfunding. *Management Science, 63*(3), 587–608.

Hoang, H., & Antoncic, B. (2003). Network-based research in entrepreneurship: A critical review. *Journal of Business Venturing, 18*, 165–187.

Hofstede, G. (1980). *Culture's consequences.* Newbury Park, CA: Sage Publications.

Hofstede, G. (1991). *Cultures and organizations: Software of the mind.* Berkshire, England: McGraw-Hill.

Hofstede, G. (2001). *Culture's consequences: Comparing values, behaviors, institutions and organizations across nations* (2nd ed). Thousand Oaks, CA: Sage.

Hofstede, G. (2011). Dimensionalizing cultures: The Hofstede model in context. *Online Readings in Psychology and Culture, 2*, 1–26.

Hofstede, G., Hofstede, G. J., & Minkov, M. (2010). *Cultures and organizations: Software of the mind* (3rd ed.). New York: McGraw-Hill.

Holmstrom, B., & Milgrom, P. (1991). Multitask principal – Agent analyses: Incentive contracts, asset ownership, and job design. *Journal of Law, Economics & Organization, 7*, 24–52.

Hong, H., Kubik, J. D., & Stein, J. C. (2004). Social interaction and stock-market participation. *Journal of Finance, 59*, 137–163.

Hornuf, L. & Schwienbacher, A. (2014). The emergence of crowdinvesting in Europe. In: *Discussion papers in economics.* University of Munich, Department of Economics. Available from: <ssrn.com/abstract = 2481994>.

Hornuf, L., & Schwienbacher, A. (2017a). Internet based entrepreneurial finance: Lessons from Europe. *California Management Review, 60*, 150–175.

Hornuf, L., & Schwienbacher, A. (2017b). Should securities regulation promote equity crowdfunding? *Small Business Economics, 49*(3), 579–593.

Hornuf, L., & Schwienbacher, A. (2018). Market mechanisms and funding dynamics in equity crowdfunding. *Journal of Corporate Finance, 50*, 556–574.

Hornuf, L., Schmitt, M., & Stenzhorn, E. (2018). Equity crowdfunding in Germany and the UK: Follow-up funding and firm failure. *Corporate Governance: An International Review, 26*, 331–354.

Hortacsu, A., Martinez-Jerez, F. A., & Douglas, J. (2009). The geography of trade in online transactions: Evidence from eBay and MercadoLibre. *American Economic Journal: Microeconomics, 1*, 53–74.

Horváthová, A. (2019). Crowdfunding: Business and regulatory perspective. In D. J. Cumming, & S. Johan (Eds.), *Oxford handbook of IPOs.* Oxford: Oxford University Press, Chapter 28.

Howell, S. T. (2017). Financing innovation: Evidence from R&D grants. *American Economic Review, 107*(4), 1136–1164.

Huang, Z. (2018) This could be the beginning of the end of China's dominance in bitcoin mining. Available from: <https://qz.com/1172632/chinas-dominance-in-bitcoin-mining-under-threat-as-regulators-hit-where-it-hurts-electricity/>.

Huang, R., & Zhang, D. (2011). Managing underwriters and the marketing of seasoned equity offerings. *Journal of Financial and Quantitative Analysis, 46,* 141–170.

Huang, R., Shangguan, Z., & Zhang, D. (2008). The networking function of investment banks: Evidence from private investments in public equity. *Journal of Corporate Finance, 14,* 738–752.

Huberman, G. (2002). Familiarity breeds investment. *Review of Financial Studies, 14,* 659–680.

Hunter, J. E. (1986). Cognitive ability, cognitive aptitudes, job knowledge, and job performance. *Journal of Vocational Behavior, 29,* 340–362.

Inchauspe, J., Ripple, R. D., & Trück, S. (2015). The dynamics of returns on renewable energy companies: A state-space approach. *Energy Economics, 48,* 325–335.

Internal Revenue Service. (2018). *IRS: Criminal investigation annual report 2018.* Available from: <https://www.irs.gov/pub/irs-utl/2018_irs_criminal_investigation_annual_report.pdf> (accessed on 22.07.19).

Isenberg, D. (2012). The road to crowdfunding hell. *Harvard Business Review.* Available from: <https://hbr.org/2012/04/the-road-to-crowdfunding-hell>.

Ivković, Z., & Weisbenner, S. (2005). Local does as local is: Information content of the geography of individual investors' common stock investments. *Journal of Finance, 60,* 267–306.

Ivković, Z., Sialm, C., & Weisbenner, S. (2008). Portfolio concentration and the performance of individual investors. *Journal of Financial and Quantitative Analysis, 43,* 613–655.

Iyer, R., Khwaja, A. I., Luttmer, E. F. P., & Shue, K. (2015). Screening peers softly: Inferring the quality of small borrowers. *Management Science, 62*(6), 1554–1577.

Jacob, M., Johan, S. A., Schweizer, D., & Zhan, F. (2016). Corporate finance and the governance implications of removing government support programs. *Journal of Banking and Finance, 63,* 35–47.

Jain, R., & Kumar, M. (2018). *India sends tax notices to cryptocurrency investors as trading hits $3.5 billion.* Available from: <https://www.reuters.com/article/us-markets-bitcoin-india-taxes/india-sends-tax-notices-to-cryptocurrency-investors-as-trading-hits-3-5-billion-idUSKBN1F8190>.

Janis, I. L. (1982). *Groupthink: Psychological studies of policy decisions and fiascoes.* Boston, MA: Houghton Mifflin.

Jääskeläinen, M., Maula, M., & Seppä, T. (2006). Allocation of attention to portfolio companies and the performance of venture capital firms. *Entrepreneurship Theory and Practice, 30,* 185–206.

Jensen, M. C. (1986). Agency costs of free cash flow, corporate finance, and takeovers. *American Economic Review, 76,* 323–329.

Jensen, M. C. (2001). Value maximization, stakeholder theory, and the corporate objective function. *European Financial Management, 7,* 297–318.

Jensen, M. C. (2004). The agency costs of overvalued equity and the current state of corporate finance. *European Financial Management, 10,* 549–566.

Jensen, M. C., & Meckling, W. H. (1976). Theory of the firm: managerial behaviour, agency costs and ownership structure. *Journal of Financial Economics, 3,* 305–360.

Jeppsson, H. (2018). Initial public offerings, subscription precommitments and venture capital participation. *Journal of Corporate Finance, 50,* 650–668.

Johan, S. A. (2010). Listing standards as a signal of IPO preparedness and quality. *International Review of Law and Economics, 30*(2), 128–144.

Johan, S. A., & Zhang, M. (2015). *Reporting bias in private equity: Reporting frequency, endowments, and governance.* Working paper.

Johan, S. A., & Zhang, Y. (2019). *Quality revealing or overstating? Analysis on qualitative startup information in equity crowdfunding.* Working paper. Available from SSRN: <https://ssrn.com/abstract = 3291905> or <https://doi.org/10.2139/ssrn.3291905>.

Johan, S. A., Knill, A., & Mauck, N. (2013). Determinants of sovereign wealth fund investment in private equity. *Journal of International Business Studies, 44,* 155–172.

Johan, S. A., Schweizer, D., & Zhan, F. (2014). The changing latitude: Labor-sponsored venture capital corporations in Canada. *Corporate Governance: An International Review, 22*(2), 145–161.

Johnson, S., La Porta, R., Lopez-da-Silanes, F., & Shleifer, A. (2000). Tunneling. *American Economic Review, 90,* 22–27.

Kaminski, J., Hopp, C., & Tykvová, T. (2019). New technology assessment in entrepreneurial financing – Does crowdfunding predict venture capital investments? *Technological Forecasting and Social Change, 139,* 287–302.

Kanniainen, V., & Keuschnigg, C. (2003). The optimal portfolio of start-up firms in venture capital finance. *Journal of Corporate Finance, 9*, 521–534.

Kanniainen, V., & Keuschnigg, C. (2004). Start-up investment with scarce venture capital support. *Journal of Banking and Finance, 28*, 1935–1959.

Karlsson, A., & Nordén, L. (2007). Home sweet home: Home bias and international diversification among individual investors. *Journal of Banking & Finance, 31*, 317–333.

Kelly, G. (2014). *The digital revolution in banking, G30 occasional paper 89.* Available from: <http://www.centerforfinancialstability.org/research/OP89.pdf>.

Keuschnigg, C. (2004). Taxation of a venture capitalist with a portfolio of firms. *Oxford Economic Papers, 56*, 285–306.

Keuschnigg, C., & Nielsen, S. B. (2003). Tax policy, venture capital and entrepreneurship. *Journal of Public Economics, 87*, 175–203.

Keuschnigg, C., & Nielsen, S. B. (2004). Start-ups, venture capitalists and the capital gains tax. *Journal of Public Economics, 88*, 1011–1042.

Kim, J., & Park, K. (2016). Financial development and deployment of renewable energy technologies. *Energy Economics, 59*, 238–250.

Kim, K., & Viswanathan, S. (2014). *The experts in the crowd: The role of reputable investors in a crowdfunding market.* Available from SSRN: <http://ssrn.com/abstract = 2258243>.

Kolympiris, C., Seele, R., & Kalaitzandonakes, N. (2015). Geographic distance between venture capitalists and investees and the strength of quality signals. *Industrial and Corporate Change, 27*(1), 189–220.

Kotlar, J., Signori, A., De Massis, A., & Vismara, S. (2018). Financial wealth, socioemotional wealth and IPO underpricing in family firms: A two-stage gamble model. *Academy of Management Journal, 61*(3), 1073–1099.

Kountouris, Y., & Remoundou, K. (2016). Cultural influence on preferences and attitudes for environmental quality. *Kyklos, 69*, 369–397.

Kumar, S., Managi, S., & Matsuda, A. (2012). Stock prices of clean energy firms, oil and carbon markets: A vector autoregressive analysis. *Energy Economics, 34*(1), 215–226.

Kuppuswamy, V., & Bayus, B. L. (2017). Does my contribution to your crowdfunding project matter? *Journal of Business Venturing, 32*, 72–89.

Kuppuswamy, V., & Bayus, B. L. (2018). Crowdfunding creative ideas: The dynamics of project backers in kickstarter. In D. Cumming, & L. Hornuf (Eds.), *The economics of crowdfunding: start-ups, portals, and investor behavior* (pp. 151–182). London: Palgrave McMillan, Chapter 8.

Kutner, M. H., Nachtsheim, C. J., Neter, J., & Li, W. (2005). *Applied linear statistical models* (5th ed.). New York: McGraw-Hill.

La Porta, R., Lopez-de-Silanes, F., Shleifer, A., & Vishny, R. W. (1997). Legal determinants of external finance. *Journal of Finance, 52*(3), 1131–1150.

La Porta, R., Lopez-de-Silanes, F., Shleifer, A., & Vishny, R. W. (1998). Law and finance. *Journal of Political Economy, 106*, 1113–1155.

La Porta, R., Lopez-de-Silanes, F., Shleifer, A., & Vishny, R. W. (2002). Investor protection and corporate valuation. *Journal of Finance, 57*(3), 1147–1170.

La Porta, R., Lopez-da-Silanes, F., & Shleifer, A. (2006). What works in securities laws? *Journal of Finance, 61*(1), 1–32.

Lai, S., & Teo, M. (2008). Home-biased analysts in emerging markets. *Journal of Financial & Quantitative Analysis, 43*, 685–716.

Lang, L. (2014). *Can crowdfunding lead to a start-up export boom in 2015?* Available from: <http://www.virgin.com/entrepreneur/can-crowdfunding-lead-to-a-start-up-export-boom-in-2015>.

Latané, B., Williams, K., & Harkins, S. (1979). Many hands make light the work: The causes and consequences of social loafing. *Journal of Personality and Social Psychology, 37*(6), 822–832.

Lauga, D., & Ofek, E. (2009). Market research and innovation strategy in duopoly. *Marketing Science, 28*(2), 373–396.

Lee, L. (1978). Unionism and wage rates: A simultaneous equations model with qualitative and limited dependent variables. *International Economic Review, 19*, 415–433.

Lee, L. F. (1992). Amemiya's generalized least squares and tests of overidentification in simultaneous equation models with qualitative or limited dependent variables. *Econometric Reviews, 11*(3), 319–328.

Lee, S. Y. (2011). Why the accredited investor standard fails the average investor? *Review of Banking & Financial Law, 31*, 987–1013.

Lee, M. O., & Vouchilas, G. (2016). Preparing to age in place: Attitudes, approaches, and actions. *Housing and Society*, *43*(6), 69–81.

Lee, N., Sameen, H., & Cowling, M. (2015). Access to finance for innovative SMEs since the financial crisis. *Research Policy*, *44*, 370–380.

Lehner, O. M., & Nicholls, A. (2014). Social finance and crowdfunding for social enterprises: A public–private case study providing legitimacy and leverage. *Venture Capital: An International Journal of Entrepreneurial Finance*, *16*(3). <http://www.tandfonline.com/doi/full/10.1080/13691066.2014.925305?src = recsys>.

Leland, H. E., & Pyle, D. H. (1977). Informational asymmetries, financial structure, and financial intermediation. *Journal of Finance*, *32*, 371–387.

Leleux, B., & Surlemont, B. (2003). Public versus private venture capital: Seeding or crowding out? A Pan-European analysis. *Journal of Business Venturing*, *18*, 81–104.

Lerner, J. (1995). Venture capitalists and the oversight of private firms. *Journal of Finance*, *50*, 301–318.

Lerner, J. (2009). *Boulevard of broken dreams: Why public efforts to boost entrepreneurship and venture capital have failed – And what to do about it*. Princeton University Press.

Lerner, J., Hardymon, F., & Leamon, A. (2012). *Venture capital and private equity: A casebook* (5th ed.). Wiley.

Levie, J., & Gimmon, E. (2008). Mixed signals: Why investors may misjudge first time high technology venture founders. *Venture Capital*, *10*, 233–256.

Levine, R., Lin, C., & Shen, B. (2015). *Cross-border acquisitions and labor regulations (no. w21245)*. National Bureau of Economic Research.

Lewis-Kraus, G. (April 30, 2015). ZPM espresso and the rage of the jilted crowdfunder: What happens when a kickstarter project fails to launch? *New York Times*.

Li, Y., & Zahra, S. A. (2012). Formal institutions, culture, and venture capital activity: A cross-country analysis. *Journal of Business Venturing*, *27*(1), 95–111.

Lillard, L. A., Brien, M. J., & Waite, L. J. (1995). Premarital cohabitation and subsequent marital dissolution: A matter of self-selection? *Demography*, *32*, 437–457.

Lin, T. C., & Pursiainen, V. (2018). Fund what you trust? Social capital and moral hazard in crowdfunding. In: *The University of Hong Kong working paper*.

Lin, M., & Viswanathan, S. (2015). Home bias in online investments: An empirical study of an online crowdfunding market. *Management Science*, *62*(5), 1393–1414.

Lin, M., Prabhala, N., & Viswanathan, S. (2009). *Social networks as signaling mechanism: Evidence from online peer-to-peer lending, working paper*.

Liobikienė, G., Mandravickaitéb, J., & Bernatonienéc, J. (2016). Theory of planned behavior approach to understand the green purchasing behavior in the EU: A cross-cultural study. *Ecological Economics*, *125*, 38–46.

Lipton, M. (1977). *Why poor people stay poor: Urban bias in world development*. Cambridge, MA: Harvard University Press.

Liska, A. (2019). *Early findings: Review of state and local government ransomware attacks*. Available from: <https://www.recordedfuture.com/state-local-government-ransomware-attacks/> (accessed 22.07.19).

Lockett, A., Murray, G., & Wright, M. (2002). Do UK venture capitalists still have a bias against investment in new technology firms? *Research Policy*, *31*(6), 1009–1030.

Lockett, A., Siegel, D., Wright, M., & Ensley, M. D. (2005). The creation of spin-off firms at public research institutions: Managerial and policy implications. *Research Policy*, *34*(7), 981–993.

Long, C. (2004). Information costs in patent and copyright. In: University of Virginia Legal working paper series 5.

Luo, Y., & Junkunc, M. (2008). How private enterprises respond to government bureaucracy in emerging economies: the effects of entrepreneurial type and governance. *Strategic Entrepreneurship Journal*, *2*(2), 133–153.

Lévesque, M., & Minniti, M. (2006). The effect of aging on entrepreneurial behavior. *Journal of Business Venturing*, *21*, 177–194.

Malmendier, U., & Shanthikumar, D. (2007). Are small investors naive about incentives? *Journal of Financial Economics*, *85*, 457–489.

Mandelli, A. (2017). *Norway's largest online bank adopts direct bitcoin integration*. Available from: <https://www.ccn.com/banking-bitcoins-age-norway-bank-adopts-direct-bitcoin-integration/>.

Manes, S., & Andrews, P. (1993). *Gates: How Microsoft's Mogul reinvented an industry—And made himself the richest man in America*. New York: Doubleday.

Manigart, S., & Wright, M. (2013). Venture capital investors and portfolio firms. *Foundations and Trends in Entrepreneurship*, *9*(4–5), 365–570.

Manso, G. (2011). Motivating innovation. *Journal of Finance*, *66*(5), 1823–1860.

Marcus, A. A., Ellis, S., & Malen, J. (2012). Conferring legitimacy: Takeoff in clean energy venture capital investments. In: *Paper presented at Academy of Management meetings*. Boston, MA.

Marian, O. (2013). Are cryptocurrencies super tax havens. *Michigan Law Review First Impressions, 112,* 38.

Marom, D., Robb, A., & Sade, O. (2016). Gender dynamics in crowdfunding (kickstarter): Evidence on entrepreneurs, investors, deals and taste-based discrimination. In: *Investors, deals and taste-based discrimination*.

Mason, C. M., & Harrison, R. T. (2015). Business angel investment activity in the financial crisis: UK evidence and policy implications. *Environment and Planning C: Politics and Space, 33*(1). Available from http://journals.sagepub.com/doi/abs/10.1068/c12324b.

Massa, M., & Simonov, A. (2006). Hedging, familiarity and portfolio choice. *Review of Financial Studies, 19,* 633−685.

Massolution (2015) 2015 CF The crowdfunding industry report. Available at: http://reports.crowdsourcing.org/index.php?route = product/product&product_id = 54.

Massolution. (2015). *2015 CF crowdfunding industry report.* <http://crowdsourcing.org/l/20898>.

Mazzei, P. (2019). Hit by ransomware attack, Florida City agrees to pay hackers $600,000. *New York Times.* Available from: <https://www.nytimes.com/2019/06/19/us/florida-riviera-beach-hacking-ransom.html> (accessed 22.07.19).

McCahery, J. A., & Vermeulen, E. P. M. (2014). Conservatism and innovation in venture capital contracting. *European Business Organization Law Review, 15*(2), 235−266.

McCahery, J. A., & Vermeulen, E. P. M. (2016). Venture capital 2.0: From venturing to partnering. *Annals of Corporate Governance, 1*(2), 95−173.

McKenzie, D. (2017). Identifying and spurring high-growth entrepreneurship: Experimental evidence from a business plan competition. *American Economic Review, 107*(8), 2278−2307.

Megginson, W. L. (2004). Towards a global model of venture capital? *Journal of Applied Corporate Finance, 16,* 89−107.

Megginson, W., & Weiss, K. (1991). Venture capital certification in initial public offerings. *Journal of Finance, 46*(3), 879−903.

Meyer, M. (2003). Academic entrepreneurs or entrepreneurial academics? Research-based ventures and public support mechanisms. *R&D Management, 33*(2), 107−115.

Michael, S. C. (2009). Entrepreneurial signaling to attract resources: The case of franchising. *Managerial and Decision Economics, 30,* 405−422.

Milgrom, P. R. (1981). Good news and bad news: Representation theorems and applications. *Bell Journal of Economics, 12,* 380−391.

Milosevic, M. (2018). Skills or networks? Success and fundraising determinants in a low performing venture capital market. *Research Policy, 47*(1), 49−60.

Mäkelä, M. M., & Maula, M. V. J. (2006). Interorganizational commitment in syndicated cross-border venture capital investments. *Entrepreneurship Theory and Practice, 30,* 273−298.

Modigliani, F., & Miller, M. (1958). The cost of capital, corporation finance and the theory of investment. *American Economic Review, 48*(3), 261−297.

Mohammadi, A., & Shafi, K. (2018). Gender differences in the contribution patterns of equity-crowdfunding investors. *Small Business Economics, 50*(2), 275−287.

Mollick, E. R. (2013). Swept away by the crowd? Crowdfunding, venture capital, and the selection of entrepreneurs. In: *Venture capital, and the selection of entrepreneurs*.

Mollick, E. R. (2014). The dynamics of crowdfunding: Determinants of success and failure. *Journal of Business Venturing, 29,* 1−16.

Mollick, E. (2014). The dynamics of crowdfunding: An exploratory study. *Journal of Business Venturing, 29*(1), 1−16.

Mollick, E. R. & Kuppuswamy, V. (2014). After the campaign: Outcomes of crowdfunding. In: *UNC Kenan-Flagler research paper, (2376997)*.

Mollick, E., & Nanda, R. (2015). Wisdom or madness? Comparing crowds with expert evaluation in funding the arts. *Management Science, 62*(6), 1533−1553.

Mollick, E., & Nanda, R. (2016). Wisdom or madness? Comparing crowds with expert evaluation in funding the arts. *Management Science, 62*(6), 1533−1553.

Mollick, E., & Robb, A. (2016). Democratizing innovation and capital access. *California Management Review, 58*(2), 72−87.

Mondria, J., & Wu, T. (2010). The puzzling evolution of the home bias, information processing and financial openness. *Journal of Economic Dynamics and Control, 34,* 875–896.

Morck, R., & Yeung, B. (2003). Agency problems in large family business groups. *Entrepreneurship Theory and Practice, 27*(4), 367–382.

Moritz, A., & Block, J. H. (2016). Crowdfunding: A literature review and research directions. In D. Brüntje, & O. Gajda (Eds.), *Crowdfunding in Europe* (pp. 25–53). Springer International Publishing.

Moritz, A., Block, J. H., & Lutz, E. (2015). Investor communication in crowdfunding: A qualitative-empirical study. *Qualitative Research in Financial Markets, 7,* 309–342.

Morse, A. (2015). Peer-to-peer crowdfunding: Information and the potential for disruption in consumer lending. *Annual Review of Financial Economics, 7,* 463–482.

Muñoz, F., Vargas, M., & Marco, I. (2014). Environmental mutual funds: Financial performance and managerial abilities. *Journal of Business Ethics, 124*(4), 551–569.

Myers, S., & Majluf, N. (1984). Corporate financing and investment decisions when firms have information that investors do not have. *Journal of Financial Economics, 13,* 187–221.

Nahata, R. (2008). Venture capital reputation and investment performance. *Journal of Financial Economics, 90,* 127–151.

Nahata, R., Hazarika, S., & Tandon, K. (2014). Success in global venture capital investing: do institutional and cultural differences matter? *Journal of Financial and Quantitative Analysis, 49*(4), 1039–1070.

Nambisan, S. (2017). Digital entrepreneurship: Toward a digital technology perspective of entrepreneurship. *Entrepreneurship Theory & Practice, 41*(6), 1029–1055.

Nambisan, S., Lyytinen, K., Majchrzak, A., & Song, M. (2017). Digital innovation management: Reinventing innovation management research in a digital world. *MIS Quarterly, 41*(1), 223–238.

Newman, A., Schwarz, S., & Ahlstrom, D. (2017). Microfinance and entrepreneurship: An introduction. *International Small Business Journal: Researching Entrepreneurship, 35,* 787–792.

Nielsen, K. M. (2008). Institutional investors and private equity. *Review of Finance, 12,* 185–219.

Nielsen, K. M. (2010). The return to direct investment in private firms: New evidence on the private equity premium puzzle. *European Financial Management, 17,* 436–463.

North, D. C. (1990). *Institutions, institutional change and economic performance.* Cambridge, UK: Cambridge University Press.

Nupur, A. (2018). *Arun Jaitley has just killed India's cryptocurrency party.* Available from: <https://qz.com/india/1195316/budget-2018-busts-bitcoin-arun-jaitley-has-just-killed-indias-cryptocurrency-party/>.

Ordanini, A., Miceli, L., Pizzetti, M., & Parasuraman, A. (2011). Crowd-funding: Transforming customers into investors through innovative service platforms. *Journal of Service Management, 22,* 443–470.

Osborne Clarke Germany. (2016). Review of crowdfunding regulation & market developments. In: *CrowdFundRES – Unleashing the potential of crowdfunding for financing renewable energy projects.*

Oviatt, B. M., & McDougall, P. P. (1994). Toward a theory of international new ventures. *Journal of International Business Studies, 25*(1), 45–64.

Oyedele, A. (2017). US regulators just gave the green light to bitcoin futures trading. *Business Insider.* <http://www.businessinsider.com/bitcoin-price-futures-trading-exchanges-cftc-2017-12>.

Parker, S. C. (2009). *The economics of entrepreneurship.* Cambridge: Cambridge University Press.

Parwada, J. T. (2008). The genesis of home bias? The location and portfolio choices of investment company start-ups. *Journal of Financial & Quantitative Analysis, 43,* 245–266.

Peng, M. W., Ahlstrom, D., Carraher, S. M., & Shi, W. S. (2017). An institution-based view of global IPR history. *Journal of International Business Studies, 48,* 893–907.

Penrose, E. T. (1959). *The theory of the growth of the firm.* New York: John Wiley.

Pernick, R., & Wilder, C. (2007). *The Cleantech revolution: The next big growth and investment opportunity.* New York: Harper Collins Publishers.

Perper, R. *China is moving to eliminate all cryptocurrency trading with a ban on foreign exchanges.* (2018). Available from: <https://www.businessinsider.com/china-eliminates-all-cryptocurrency-trading-2018-2>.

Petersen, M. (2009). Estimating standard errors in finance panel data sets: Comparing approaches. *Review of Financial Studies, 22,* 435–480.

Petkova, A. P. (2012). From the ground up: Building young firms' reputations. In M. L. Barnett, & T. G. Pollock (Eds.), *The Oxford handbook of corporate reputation* (pp. 383–401). Oxford, UK: Oxford University Press.

Philippon, T. (2016). *The fintech opportunity (no. w22476)*. National Bureau of Economic Research.

Pilarowski, G., & Yue, L. (September 21, 2017). China bans initial coin offerings and cryptocurrency trading platforms. *China Regulation Watch.* Available from: <http://www.pillarlegalpc.com/en/news/2017/09/21/china-bans-initial-coin-offerings-and-cryptocurrency-trading-platforms/> (accessed 22.07.19).

Piva, E., & Rossi-Lamastra, C. (2018). Human capital signals and entrepreneurs' success in equity crowdfunding. *Small Business Economics, 51*(3), 667−686.

Podolny, J. M. (1993). A status-based model of market competition. *American Journal of Sociology, 98*, 829−872.

Polzin, F., Toxopeus, H., & Stam, E. (2018). The wisdom of the crowd in funding: information heterogeneity and social networks of crowdfunders. *Small Business Economics, 50*(2), 251−273.

Pope, D. G., & Sydnor, J. R. (2011). What's in a picture? Evidence of discrimination from Prosper.com. *Journal of Human Resources, 46*(1), 53−92.

Popper, N. (2016a). *A venture fund with plenty of virtual capital, but no capitalist.* <https://www.nytimes.com/2016/05/22/business/dealbook/crypto-ether-bitcoin-currency.html?_r = 1>.

Popper, N. (2016b). *A hacking of more than $50 million dashes hopes in the world of virtual currency.* Available from: <https://www.nytimes.com/2016/06/18/business/dealbook/hacker-may-have-removed-more-than-50-million-from-experimental-cybercurrency-project.html>.

Porter, M. E. (2000). Location, competition, and economic development: Local clusters in a global economy. *Economic Development Quarterly, 14*, 15−34.

Powell, W., Koput, K., Bowie, J., & Smith-Doerr, L. (2002). The spatial clustering of science and capital: Accounting for biotech firm-venture capital relationships. *Regional Studies, 36*, 291−305.

Prokop, J., & Wang, D. (2018). Is there a gender gap in equity crowdfunding? In: *Proceedings of the INFINITI conference on international finance 2018.*

Puri, M., & Zarutskie, R. (2012). On the lifecycle dynamics of venture-capital- and non-venture-capital-financed firms. *Journal of Finance, 67*(6), 2247−2294.

Radford, J. S. (2016). The emergence of gender inequality in a crowdfunding market: an experimental test of gender system theory. In: *SSRN working paper.*

Rao, D. (2013). *Forbes.* <http://www.forbes.com/sites/dileeprao/2013/07/22/why-99-95-of-entrepreneurs-should-stop-wasting-time-seeking-venture-capital/print/> (accessed 11.11.15).

Rau, P. R. (2018). Law, trust, and the development of crowdfunding. Working Paper, University of Cambridge.

Ravina, E. (2008). Beauty, personal characteristics and trust in credit markets. Working Paper, presented at the American Law & Economics Association Annual Meetings. *American Law & Economics Association annual meetings.*

Riding, A., & Swift, C. (1990). Women business owners and terms of credit: some empirical findings of the Canadian experience. *Journal of Business Venturing, 5*(5), 327−340.

Ritov, I., Gati, I., & Tversky, A. (1990). Differential weighting of common and distinctive components. *Journal of Experimental Psychology: General, 119*, 30−41.

Ritter, J. R. (1987). The costs of going public. *Journal of Financial Economics, 19*, 269−281.

Ritter, J. R. (1998). Initial public offerings. In D. Logue & J. Seward (Eds.), *Warren Gorham & Lamont handbook of modern finance.* Warren, Gorham & Lamont, New York: New York.

Ritter, J. R. (2003). Differences between European and American IPO markets. *European Financial Management, 9*, 421−434.

Ritter, J. R. (2013). Re-energizing the IPO market. *Journal of Applied Finance, 24*(1), 37−48.

Ritter, J. R., Signori, A., & Vismara, S. (2013). Economies of scope and IPO activity in Europe. In Mario Levis, & Silvio Vismara (Eds.), *Handbook of research on IPOs* (pp. 11−34). Cheltenham: Edward Elgar.

Robb, A. M., & Robinson, D. (2014). The capital structure decisions of new firms. *Review of Financial Studies, 27*, 153−179.

Roberts, J. J. (2017). Why tech investors love ICOs—And lawyers don't. *Fortune.* Available from: <http://fortune.com/2017/06/26/ico-initial-coin-offering-investing/>.

Roberts, J. J. (2018). Is the SEC gunning for Ethereum and Ripple? Fat chance. *Fortune.* Available from: <http://fortune.com/2018/05/01/sec-and-cryptocurrency-regulations/>.

Roe, M. J. (2003). Delaware's competition. *Harvard Law Review, 117*, 588−646.

Rohr, J. & Wright, A. (2018). Blockchain-based token sales, initial coin offerings, and the democratization of public capital markets. In: *Cardozo Legal Studies research paper no. 527; University of Tennessee Legal Studies research paper no. 338*. Available from SSRN: <https://ssrn.com/abstract = 3048104> or <https://doi.org/10.2139/ssrn.3048104>.

Roma, P., Petruzzelli, A. M., & Perrone, G. (2017). From the crowd to the market: The role of reward-based crowdfunding performance in attracting professional investors. *Research Policy, 46*(9), 1606–1628.

Romani, S., Grappi, S., & Bagozzi, R. P. (2016). Corporate socially responsible initiatives and their effects on consumption of green products. *Journal of Business Ethics, 135*(2), 253–264.

Romano, R. (1985). Law as a product: Some pieces of the incorporation puzzle. *Journal of Law, Economics, and Organization, 1*, 225–283.

Romano, R. (1987). The state competition debate in corporate law. *Cardozo Law Review, 8*, 709–757.

Romano, R. (1993). *The Genius of American Corporate Law*. Washington, DC: The AEI Press.

Roodman, D. (2011). Fitting fully observed recursive mixed-process models with CMP. *The Stata Journal, 11*(2), 159–206.

Rosenbaum, P., & Rubin, D. B. (1983). The central role of the propensity score in observational studies for causal effects. *Biometrika, 70*(1), 41–55.

Rosenbaum, P. R., & Rubin, D. B. (1985). Constructing a control group using multivariate matched sampling methods that incorporate the propensity score. *The American Statistician, 39*(1), 33–38.

Ross, S. A. (1978). Some notes on financial incentive-signaling models, activity choice and risk preferences. *Journal of Finance, 33*, 777–792.

Rossi, A., & Vismara, S. (2017). What do crowdfunding platforms do? A comparison between investment-based platforms in Europe. *Working paper*.

Rossi, A., & Vismara, S. (2018). What do crowdfunding platforms do? A comparison between investment-based platforms in Europe. *Eurasian Business Review, 8*(1), 93–118.

Rothaermel, F. T., & Thursby, M. (2005). Incubator firm failure or graduation?: The role of university linkages. *Research Policy, 34*(7), 1076–1090.

Roxas, M. L., & Stoneback, J. Y. (2004). The importance of gender across cultures in ethical decision-making. *Journal of Business Ethics, 50*, 149–165.

Ruiz, R. (June 11, 2015). F.T.C. reaches settlement in a kickstarter scheme. *New York Times*.

Sadorsky, P. (2011). Some future scenarios for renewable energy. *Futures, 43*, 1091–1104.

Sadorsky, P. (2012). Correlations and volatility spillovers between oil prices and the stock prices of clean energy and technology companies. *Energy Economics, 34*(1), 248–255.

Sapienza, H. J., Manigart, S., & Vermeir, W. (1996). Venture capitalist governance and value added in four countries. *Journal of Business Venturing, 11*(6), 439–469.

Saxenian, A. (2000). *Regional advantage: Culture and competition in Silicon Valley and route* (p. 128) Cambridge, MA: Harvard University Press.

Scarlata, M., & Alemany, L. (2010). Deal structuring in philanthropic venture capital investments: financing instrument, valuation and covenants. *Journal of Business Ethics, 95*, 121–145.

Schertler, A., & Tykvová, T. (2012). What lures cross-border venture capital inflows? *Journal of International Money and Finance, 31*(6), 1777–1799.

Schjoedt, L., Monsen, E., Pearson, A., Barnett, T., & Chrisman, J. J. (2013). New venture and family business teams: Understanding team formation, composition, behaviors, and performance. *Entrepreneurship Theory and Practice, 37*, 1–15.

Schroeder, W. R. (2001). Money laundering: A global threat and the international community's response. *FBI Law Enforcement Bulletin, 70*, 1–9.

Schumpeter, J. (1942). *The process of creative destruction (capitalism, socialism and democracy)*. Harper and Row.

Schwartz, A. A. (2014). Teenage crowdfunding. *University of Cincinnati Law Review, 83*, 515.

Schweizer, D., & Zhou, T. (2017). Do principles pay in real estate crowdfunding? *The Journal of Portfolio Management, 43*(6), 120–137.

Schwienbacher, A. (2007). A theoretical analysis of optimal financing strategies for different types of capital-constrained entrepreneurs. *Journal of Business Venturing, 22*, 753–781.

Schwienbacher, A. (2008a). Innovation and venture capital exits. *Economic Journal, 118*(533), 1888–1916.

Schwienbacher, A. (2008b). Venture capital investment practices in Europe and in the United States. *Financial Markets and Portfolio Management, 22*(3), 195–217.

Schwienbacher, A. (2018). Entrepreneurial risk-taking in crowdfunding campaigns. *Small Business Economics, 51*(4), 843−859.

Schwienbacher, A., & Larralde, B. (2012). Crowdfunding of small entrepreneurial ventures. In D. Cumming (Ed.), *Handbook of entrepreneurial finance*. Oxford University Press.

Scott, R. W. (1995). *Institutions and organizations*. Thousand Oaks, CA: Sage.

Seasholes, M., & Zhu, N. (2010). Individual investors and local bias. *Journal of Finance, 65*, 1987−2010.

Sevilir, M. (2010). Human capital investment, new firm creation and venture capital. *Journal of Financial Intermediation, 19*, 483−508.

Shaheen, S., Guzman, S., & Zhang, H. (2010). Bikesharing in Europe, the Americas, and Asia. Transportation research record. *Journal of the Transportation Research Board, 2143*(1), 159−167.

Shane, S. (2009). Why encouraging more people to become entrepreneurs is bad public policy. *Small Business Economics, 33*(2), 141−149.

Shane, S., & Cable, D. (2002). Network ties, reputation, and the financing of new ventures. *Management Science, 48*(3), 364−381.

Shane, S., & Venkataraman, S. (2000). The promise of entrepreneurship as a field of research. *Academy of Management Review, 25*, 217−226.

Signori, A., & Vismara, S. (2018). Does success bring success? The post-offering lives of equity-crowdfunded firms. *Journal of Corporate Finance, 50*, 575−591.

Silverman, B. S., & Baum, J. A. C. (2002). Alliance-based competitive dynamics in the Canadian biotechnology industry. *Academy of Management, 45*, 791−806.

Sinnott, R. W. (1984). Virtues of the haversine. *Sky and Telescope, 68*, 159.

Smart, S. B., Thirumalai, R. S., & Zutter, C. J. (2008). What's in a vote? The short-and long-run impact of dual-class equity on IPO firm values. *Journal of Accounting and Economics, 45*(1), 94−115.

Sohl, J. (1999). The early-stage equity market in the USA. *Venture Capital, 1*, 101−120.

Sorenson, O., & Stuart, T. (2001). Syndication networks and the spatial distribution of venture capital investments. *American Journal of Sociology, 106*, 1546−1588.

Sorenson, O., Assenova, V., Li, G. C., Boada, J., & Fleming, L. (2016). Expand innovation finance via crowdfunding. *Science, 354*(6319), 1526−1528.

Spence, M. (1973). Job market signaling. *Quarterly Journal of Economics, 87*(3), 355−374.

Spence, M. (2002). Signaling in retrospect and the informational structure of markets. *American Economic Review, 92*, 434−459.

Spulber, D. F. (2008). Unlocking technology: Antitrust and innovation. *Journal of Competition Law, 4*, 915−966.

Stalinsky, S. (2018). *The imminent release of Telegram's cryptocurrency, ISIS's encryption app of choice − An international security catastrophe in the making*. Available from: <https://www.memri.org/reports/imminent-release-telegrams-cryptocurrency-isiss-encryption-app-choice-%E2%80%93-international>.

Stanko, M. A., & Henard, D. H. (2017). Toward a better understanding of crowdfunding, openness and the consequences for innovation. *Research Policy, 46*(4), 784−798.

Steinhoff, R. H. (2015). The next British invasion is securities crowdfunding: How issuing non-registered securities through the crowd can succeed in the United States. *University of Colorado Law Review, 86*, 661.

Stengel, G. (2015). Women-owned businesses: A tale of two types of entrepreneurs. *Forbes [Online]*. Available from: <http://www.forbes.com/sites/geristengel/2015/08/26/women-owned-businesses-a-tale-of-two-types-of-entrepreneurs/#1de811693e8c>.

Stiglitz, J. E., & Weiss, A. (1981). Credit rationing with imperfect information. *American Economic Review, 71*, 393−410.

Stock, J., Wright, J., & Yogo, M. (2002). A survey of weak instruments and weak identification in generalized method of moments. *Journal of Business and Economic Statistics, 20*(4), 518−529.

Strange, R., Filatotchev, I., Buck, T., & Wright, M. (2009). Corporate governance and international business. *Management International Review, 49*(4), 395−407.

Strausz, R. (2017). A theory of crowdfunding: A mechanism design approach with demand uncertainty and moral hazard. *American Economic Review, 107*(6), 1430−1476.

Stuart, T. E., Hoang, H., & Hybels, R. C. (1999). Interorganizational endorsements and the performance of entrepreneurial ventures. *Administrative Science Quarterly, 44*(2), 315−349.

Stulz, R. (1999). Globalization, corporate finance, and the cost of capital. *Journal of Applied Corporate Finance, 12*(3), 8−25.

Suberg, W. (2017). *Singularity NET announces $36 million ICO funding for AI platform expansion.* Available from: <https://cointelegraph.com/news/singularitynet-announces-36mln-ico-funding-for-ai-platform-expansion>.

Sulaeman, J. (2014). Do local investors know more? Evidence from mutual fund location and investments. *Quarterly Journal of Finance, 4,* 1450010.

Suominen, K., & Lee, J. A. (2015). Bridging trade finance gaps: State-led innovations to bolster exporting by small and medium-sized firms. In: *Brookings-Rockefeller project on state and metropolitan innovation.* Available from: <http://www.brookings.edu/~/media/Research/Files/Reports/2015/01/08%20export%20finance/RF_ExportFinance_Jan7.pdf>.

Surowiecki, J. (2005). *The wisdom of crowds.* Anchor.

Tapscott, D., & Tapscott, A. (2016). *Blockchain revolution: How the technology behind bitcoin is changing money, business and the world.* London: Portfolio Penguin.

Teo, M. (2009). The geography of hedge funds. *Review of Financial Studies, 22,* 3531−3561.

Terza, J. V. (1998). Estimating count models with endogenous switching: Sample selection and endogenous treatment effects. *Journal of Econometrics, 84,* 129−154.

Tesar, L., & Werner, I. (1995). Home bias and high turnover. *Journal of International Money and Finance, 14,* 467−492.

Tesar, L., & Werner, I. (1998). The internationalization of securities markets since the 1987 crash. In: *Brookings-Wharton papers on financial services.* The Brookings Institution.

The World Bank. (2013). *Crowdfunding's potential for the developing world.* <http://www.infodev.org/infodev-files/wb_crowdfundingreport-v12.pdf>.

Timmis, J. (2013). *Internet adoption and firm exports in developing economies.* Nottingham Centre for Research on Globalisation and Economic Policy, University of Nottingham.

Tirole, J. (1998). *The theory of industrial organization.* Cambridge, MA: MIT Press.

Tomizawa, A., Zhao, L., Bassellier, G., & Ahlstrom, D. (2019). Economic growth, innovation, institutions, and the great enrichment. *Asia-Pacific Journal of Management.* Available from https://doi.org/10.1007/s10490-019-09648-2.

Tomzack, A. (2018). *Cryptocurrency regulation to be welcoming for business − United Kingdom.* Available from: <https://ethereumworldnews.com/cryptocurrency-regulation-to-be-welcoming-for-business-united-kingdom/>.

Tunali, I. (1986). A general structure for models of double selection and an application to a joint migration/earnings process with remigration. *Research in Labor Economics, 8B,* 235−283.

Tykvová, T. (2017). When and why do venture-capital-backed companies obtain venture lending? *Journal of Financial and Quantitative Analysis, 52*(3), 1049−1080.

Tykvova, T., & Schertler, A. (2014). Does syndication with Local Venture capitalists moderate the effects of geographical and institutional distance? *Journal of International Management, 20*(4), 406−420.

Unger, J. M., Rauch, A., Frese, M., & Rosenbusch, N. (2011). Human capital and entrepreneurial success: A meta-analytical review. *Journal of Business Venturing, 26,* 341−358.

United States District Court, E.D. New York (2018). *Commodity Futures Trading Commission, Plaintiff, v. Patrick K. McDonnell, and CabbageTech, Corp. d/b/a Coin Drop Markets, defendants* (213, 226, 228 pp.). Available from: <https://www.leagle.com/decision/287180197fsupp3d21314> (accessed 19.07.19).

U.S. Department of Justice National Drug Intelligence Center. (2008). *Money laundering in digital currencies.* Available from: <https://www.justice.gov/archive/ndic/pubs28/28675/28675p.pdf>.

Valdivia, L. J., Del-Valle-Soto, C., Rodriguez, J., & Alcaraz, M. (2019). Decentralization: The failed promise of cryptocurrencies. *IT Professional, 21,* 33−40.

Van de Ven, W. P. M. M., & Van Pragg, B. M. S. (1981). The demand for deductibles in private health insurance: A probit model with sample selection. *Journal of Econometrics, 17,* 229−252.

Van Nieuwerburgh, S., & Veldkamp, L. (2009). Information immobility and the home bias puzzle. *Journal of Finance, 64,* 1187−1215.

Vanacker, T., Heughebaert, A., & Manigart, S. (2014). Institutional frameworks, venture capital and the financing of European new technology-based firms. *Corporate Governance: An International Review, 22*(3), 199−215.

Verheul, I., & Thurik, R. (2001). Start-up capital: does gender matter? *Small Business Economics, 16*(4), 329−346.

Vismara, S. (2016). Equity retention and social network theory in equity crowdfunding. *Small Business Economics, 46*(4), 579−590.

Vismara, S. (2018). Information cascades among investors in equity crowdfunding. *Entrepreneurship Theory and Practice, 42*(3), 467−497.

Vismara, S., Paleari, S., & Ritter, J. R. (2012). Europe's second markets for small companies. *European Financial Management, 18,* 352−388.

Vitell, S. J., Nwachukwu, S. L., & Barnes, J. H. (1993). The effects of culture on ethical decision making: An application of Hofstede's typology. *Journal of Business Ethics, 12,* 753−760.

Vulkan, N., Åstebro, T., & Sierra, M. F. (2016). Equity crowdfunding: A new phenomena. *Journal of Business Venturing Insights, 5,* 37−49.

Walthoff-Borm, X., Schwienbacher, A., & Vanacker, T. (2017). Equity crowdfunding. First resort or last resort? Working paper.

Walthoff-Borm, X., Vanacker, T., & Collewaert, V. (2017). Equity crowdfunding, shareholder structures, and firm performance. Working paper.

Walthoff-Borm, X., Schwienbacher, A., & Vanacker, T. (2018). Equity crowdfunding: First resort or last resort? *Journal of Business Venturing, 33*(4), 513−533.

Walthoff-Borm, X., Vanacker, T. R., & Collewaert, V. (2018). Equity crowdfunding, shareholder structures, and firm performance. *Corporate Governance: An International Review, 26*(5), 314−330.

Wang, L., & Wang, S. (2012). Economic freedom and cross-border venture capital performance. *Journal of Empirical Finance, 19,* 26−50.

WCED: The World Commission on Environment and Development. (1987). *Our common future.* New York: Oxford University Press.

Wei, Z., & Lin, M. (2016). Market mechanisms in online peer-to-peer lending. *Management Science, 63*(12), 4236−4257.

Westhead, P., & Howorth, C. (2006). Ownership and management issues associated with family firm performance and company objectives. *Family Business Review, 19,* 301−316.

Westhuizen, C. (2017). *Future digital money: The legal status and regulation of bitcoin in Australia. Working paper.* The University of Notre Dame Australia.

Wieck, E., Bretschneider, U., & Leimeister, J. M. (2013). Funding from the crowd: An Internet-based crowdfunding platform to support business set-ups from universities. *International Journal of Cooperative Information Systems, 22.* Available from https://doi.org/10.1142/S0218843013400078.

Williams-Grut, O. (2018). *Only 8% of ICOs were successful last year.* Available from: <https://www.businessinsider.com/how-much-raised-icos-2017-tokendata-2017-2018-1>.

Wilson, N., Wright, M., & Kaceer, M. (2018). The equity gap in knowledge-based firms. *Journal of Corporate Finance, 50,* 626−649.

World Bank. (2013). Crowdfunding's potential for the developing world. In: *infoDev, Finance and Private Sector Development Department.* Washington, DC: World Bank.

Wright, M., & Fu, K. (2015). University spin-outs: What do we know and what are the policy implications? Evidence from the UK. *Journal of Innovation Management, 3*(4), 5−15.

Wright, M., Clarysse, B., Lockett, A., & Binks, M. (2006). University spin-out companies and venture capital. *Research Policy, 35,* 481−501.

Wright, M., Westhead, P., & Ucbasaran, D. (2007). The internationalization of SMEs and international entrepreneurship: A critique and policy implications. *Regional Studies, 41*(7), 1013−1029.

Wüstenhagen, R., Wuebker, R., Bürer, M. J., & Goddard, D. (2009). Financing fuel cell market development: Exploring the role of expectation dynamics in venture capital investment. In S. Pogutz, A. Russo, & P. Migliavacca (Eds.), *Innovation, markets, and sustainable energy: The challenge of hydrogen and fuel cells* (pp. 118−137). Cheltenham (UK) and Lyme, CT (US): Edward Elgar.

Younkin, P., & Kashkooli, K. (2016). What problems does crowdfunding solve? *California Management Review, 58* (2), 20−43.

Younkin, P., & Kuppuswamy, V. (2017). The colorblind crowd? Founder race and performance in crowdfunding. *Management Science, 64*(7), 3269−3287.

Younkin, P., & Kuppuswamy, V. (2019). Discounted: The effect of founder race on the price of new products. *Journal of Business Venturing, 34*(2), 389−412.

Yu, S., Johnson, S., Lai, C., Cricelli, A., & Fleming, L. (2017). Crowdfunding and regional entrepreneurial investment: An application of the CrowdBerkeley Database. *Research Policy, 46*(10), 1723–1737.

Zacharakis, A. L., & Meyer, G. D. (2000). The potential of actuarial decision models: Can they improve the venture capital investment decision? *Journal of Business Venturing, 15*, 323–346.

Zahra, S. A. (2014). Public and corporate governance and young entrepreneurial firms. *Corporate Governance: An International Review, 22*(2), 77–83.

Zellweger, T. M. (2007). Time horizon, costs of equity capital, and generic investment strategies of firms. *Family Business Review, 20*(1), 1–15.

Zhang, T., & Acs, Z. (2018). Age and entrepreneurship: Nuances from entrepreneur types and generation effects. *Small Business Economics, 51*(4), 773–809.

Zhang, B., Baeck, P., Ziegler, T., Bone, J., & Garvey, K. (2016). Pushing boundaries: The 2015 UK alternative finance industry report (pp. 31–46). Cambridge Centre for Alternative Finance.

Zook, M. (2002). Grounded capital: Venture financing and the geography of the internet industry, 1994-2000. *Journal of Economic Geography, 2*, 151–177.

Further Reading

Aghion, B. A., & Gollier, C. (2000). Peer group formation in an adverse selection model. *Economic Journal, 110*, 632–643.

Allison, T. H., Davis, B. C., Webb, J. W., & Short, J. C. (2017). Persuasion in crowdfunding: An elaboration likelihood model of crowdfunding performance. *Journal of Business Venturing, 32*, 707–725.

Anand, A. (2018). Governance complexities in firms with dual class shares. *Annals of Corporate Governance, 3*(3), 184–275.

Andrieu, A., & Groh, A. (2012). Entrepreneurs' financing choice between independent and bank-affiliated venture capital firms. *Journal of Corporate Finance, 18*, 1143–1167.

Ang, J. (2014). Innovation and financial liberalization. *Journal of Banking and Finance, 47*, 214–229.

Anglin, A. H., Short, J. C., Drover, W., Stevenson, R. M., McKenny, A. F., & Allison, T. H. (2018). The power of positivity? The influence of positive psychological capital language on crowdfunding performance. *Journal of Business Venturing, 33*, 470–492.

Asongu, S., & Nwachukwu, J. (2016). Mobile phones in the diffusion of knowledge and persistence in inclusive human development in Sub-Saharan Africa. *Information Development, 33*, 289–302.

Åstebro, T. (2002). The return to independent invention: evidence of unrealistic optimism, risk seeking or skewness loving? *The Economic Journal, 113*(484), 226–239.

Audretsch, D. B., & Mahmood, T. (1994). Firm selection and industry evolution: The post-entry performance of new firms. *Journal of Evolutionary Economics, 4*, 243–260.

Baker, T., & Nelson, R. E. (2005). Creating something from nothing: Resource construction through entrepreneurial bricolage. *Administrative Science Quarterly, 50*(3), 329–366.

Barasinska, N., & Schäfer, D. (2014). Is crowdfunding different? Evidence on the relation between gender and funding success from a German peer-to-peer lending platform. *German Economic Review, 15*(2), 436–452.

Barber, B. M., & Odean, T. (2008). All that glitters: The effect of attention and news on the buying behavior of individual and institutional investors. *Review of Financial Studies, 21*, 785–818.

Belleflamme, P., Omrani, N., & Peitz, M. (2015). The economics of crowdfunding platforms. In: *CORE and Louvain School of Management, Paris School of Business, and University of Mannheim working paper.*

Berea, A., Goldfarb, B., Kirsch, D., & Rand, B. (2016). *Crowdfunding success and social media: A data-driven analysis. Working paper.* University of Maryland.

Berger, A. N., & Udell, G. F. (1998). The economics of small business finance: The roles of private equity and debt markets in the financial growth cycle. *Journal of Banking & Finance, 22*(6), 613–673.

Berman, J. (2014). *I backed Oculus Rift on Kickstarter and all I got was this lousy T-shirt.* Available from: <https://www.huffingtonpost.com/2014/03/26/oculus-rift-kickstarter_n_5034511.html>.

Bernile, G., Cumming, D. J., & Lyandres, E. (2007). The size of venture capital and private equity fund portfolios. *Journal of Corporate Finance, 13*, 564–590.

Bertoni, F., Colombo, M. G., & Grilli, L. (2011). Venture capital financing and the growth of high-tech start-ups: Disentangling treatment from selection effects. *Research Policy, 40*, 1028–1043.

Bester, H. (1985a). The level of investment in credit markets with imperfect information. *Journal of Institutional and Theoretical Economics, 141*, 503–515.

Bester, H. (1985b). Screening versus rationing in credit markets with imperfect information. *American Economic Review, 75*(4), 850–855.

Black, B. S., & Gilson, R. J. (1998). Venture capital and the structure of capital markets: Banks versus stock markets. *Journal of Financial Economics, 47*, 243–277.

Blanding, M. (2013). *Crowdfunding a poor investment? Working knowledge.* Available from: <https://hbswk.hbs.edu/item/crowdfunding-a-poor-investment>.

Bloodgood, J. (2013). Crowdsourcing: Useful for problem solving, but what about value capture? *Academy of Management Review, 38*(3), 455–465.

Bolero Crowdfunding (2016). Crowdfunding in België [Crowdfunding in Belgium]. Available at: https://newsroom.kbc.com/white-paper-over-crowdfunding.

Bonini, S., Capizzi, V., Valletta, M., & Zocchi, P. (2018). Angel network affiliation and business angels' investment practices. *Journal of Corporate Finance, 50*, 592–608.

Brinckmann, J., Salomo, S., & Gemuenden, G. (2011). Financial management competence of founding teams and growth of new technology-based firms. *Entrepreneurship Theory and Practice, 35*, 217–243.

Butticè, V., Colombo, M. G., & Wright, M. (2017). Serial crowdfunding, social capital, and project success. *Entrepreneurship Theory and Practice, 41*(2), 183–207.

Caliendo, M., & Kopeinig, S. (2008). Some practical guidance for the implementation of propensity score matching. *Journal of Economic Surveys, 22*, 31–72.

Cho, Y. J. (1986). Inefficiencies from financial liberalization in the absence of well-functioning equity markets. *Journal of Money, Credit, and Banking, 18*(2), 191–199.

Cohen, J. E., & Lemley, M. A. (2001). Patent scope and innovation in the software industry. *California Law Review, 89*, 1–57.

Cole, R. A., & Sokolyk, T. (2016). Who needs credit and who gets credit? Evidence from the surveys of small business finances. *Journal of Financial Stability, 24*, 40–60.

Colombo, M. G., & Piva, E. (2012). Firms' genetic characteristics and competence-enlarging strategies: A comparison between academic and non-academic high-tech start-ups. *Research Policy, 41*, 79–92.

Conti, A., Thursby, M., & Rothaermel, F. T. (2013). Show me the right stuff: Signals for high tech startups. *Journal of Economics & Management Strategy, 22*(2), 341–364.

Cook, D. O., Kieschnick, R., & McCullough, B. D. (2008). Regression analysis of proportions in finance with self-selection. *Journal of Empirical Finance, 15*, 860–867.

Cumming, D. J. (2006a). Adverse selection and capital structure: Evidence from venture capital. *Entrepreneurship Theory and Practice, 30*, 155–184.

Cumming, D. J. (2006b). The determinants of venture capital portfolio size: Empirical evidence. *Journal of Business, 79*, 1083–1126.

da Cruz, J. V. (2018). Beyond financing: Crowdfunding as an informational mechanism. *Journal of Business Venturing, 33*, 371–393.

Davidson, W. N., III, & Worrel, D. L. (1988). The impact of announcements of corporate illegalities on shareholder returns. *Academy of Management Journal, 31*, 195–200.

Davis, B. C., Hmieleski, K. M., Webb, J. W., & Coombs, J. E. (2017). Funders' positive affective reactions to entrepreneurs' crowdfunding pitches: The influence of perceived product creativity and entrepreneurial passion. *Journal of Business Venturing, 32*, 90–106.

De Rassenfosse, G., & Fischer, T. (2016). Venture debt financing: Determinants of the lending decision. *Strategic Entrepreneurship Journal, 10*, 235–256.

Dew, N., & Sarasvathy, S. D. (2007). Innovations, stakeholders & entrepreneurship. *Journal of Business Ethics, 74*, 267–283.

Diamond, D. (1989). Reputation acquisition in debt markets. *Journal of Political Economy, 97*(4), 828–862.

Diamond, D. (1992). Monitoring and reputation: The choice between bank loans and directly placed debt. *Journal of Political Economy, 99*(4), 689–721.

Dorfleitner, G., Priberny, C., Schuster, S., Stoiber, J., Weber, M., & Kammler, J. (2016). Description-text related soft information in peer-to-peer lending – Evidence from two leading European platforms. *Journal of Banking and Finance, 64*, 169–187.

Dou, Y., Ryan, S. G., & Zou, Y. (2017). The effect of credit competition on banks' loan loss provisions. *Journal of Financial and Quantitative Analysis, 53*(3), 1195–1226.

Dyck, A., Morse, A., & Zingales, L. (2010). Who blows the whistle on corporate fraud? *Journal of Finance, 65,* 2213–2253.

Ehrlich, I. (1973). Participation in illegitimate activities: A theoretical and empirical investigation. *Journal of Political Economy, 81,* 521–565.

Espenlaub, S., Khurshed, A., & Mohamed, A. (2015). Venture capital exits in domestic and cross-border investments. *Journal of Banking & Finance, 53,* 215–232.

Fischel, D. R. (1982). Use of modern finance theory in securities fraud cases involving actively traded securities. *Business Lawyer, 38,* 1–20.

FTC. (2015). *Crowdfunding project creator settles FTC charges of deception: Defendant spent backers' money on personal expenses.* Available from: <https://www.ftc.gov/news-events/press-releases/2015/06/crowdfunding-project-creator-settles-ftc-charges-deception> (accessed 02.05.16).

Fulghieri, P., & Sevilir, M. (2009). Size and focus of a venture capitalist's portfolio. *Review of Financial Studies, 22,* 4643–4680.

Gerasymenko, V., De Clercq, D., & Sapienza, H. J. (2015). Changing the business model: Effects of venture capital firms and outside CEOs on portfolio company performance. *Strategic Entrepreneurship Journal, 9*(1), 79–98.

Giannetti, M., Liao, G., You, J., & Yu, X. (2017). *The externalities of corruption: Evidence from entrepreneurial activity in China.* Available from SSRN: <http://ssrn.com/abstract = 3049901>.

Gino, F., Ayal, S., & Ariely, D. (2009). Contagion and differentiation in unethical behavior: The effect of one bad apple on the barrel. *Psychological Science, 20,* 393–398.

Giot, P., & Schwienbacher, A. (2007). IPOs, trade sales and liquidations: Modelling venture capital exits using survival analysis. *Journal of Banking & Finance, 31,* 679–702.

Giudici, G., Guerini, M., & Rossi-Lamastra, C. (2018). Reward-based crowdfunding of entrepreneurial projects: The effect of local altruism and localized social capital on proponents' success. *Small Business Economics, 50*(2), 307–324.

Gompers, P. A. (1996). Grandstanding in the venture capital industry. *Journal of Financial Economics, 42,* 133–156.

Greenwald, B. C., Stiglitz, J., & Weiss, A. (1984). Informational imperfections in the capital markets and macroeconomic fluctuations. *American Economic Review, 74*(1), 194–199.

Gulati, R., & Higgins, M. C. (2003). Which ties matter when? The contingent effects of interorganizational partnerships on IPO success. *Strategic Management Journal, 24,* 127–144.

Hainz, C. (2018). Fraudulent behavior by entrepreneurs and borrowers. In D. J. Cumming, & L. Hornuf (Eds.), *The economics of crowdfunding* (pp. 79–99). Cham: Palgrave Macmillan.

Hall, J., & Vredenburg, H. (2003). The challenges of innovating for sustainable development. *Sloan Management Review, 45*(1), 61–69.

Hazen, T. L. (2012). Crowdfunding or fraudfunding? Social networks and the securities laws – Why the specially tailored exemption must be conditioned on meaningful. *North Carolina Law Review, 90,* 1735–1770.

Heinkel, R. (1982). A theory of capital structure relevance under. Imperfect information. *Journal of Finance, 37*(5), 1141–1150.

Herzenstein, M., Dholakia, U. M., & Andrews, R. (2011). Strategic herding behavior in peer-to-peer loan auctions. *Journal of Interactive Marketing, 25,* 27–36.

Herzenstein, M., Sonenshein, S., & Dholakia, U. M. (2011). Tell me a good story and I may lend you money: The role of narratives in peer-to-peer lending decisions. *Journal of Marketing Research, 48,* 138–149.

Hilgert, M. A., Hogarth, J. M., & Beverly, S. G. (2003). Household financial management: The connection between knowledge and behavior. *Federal Reserve Bulletin Board of Governors of the Federal Reserve System (U.S.),* 309–322.

Hodas, N. O., & Lerman, K. (2013). Attention and visibility in an information-rich world. In: *Proceedings of the 2nd international ICME workshop on social multimedia research.*

Holmes, R. M., Jr, Miller, T., Hitt, M. A., & Salmador, M. P. (2013). The interrelationships among informal institutions, formal institutions, and inward foreign direct investment. *Journal of Management, 39*(2), 531–566.

Hornuf, L., & Neuenkirch, M. (2017). Pricing shares in equity crowdfunding. *Small Business Economics, 48,* 795–811.

Jiang, T. (2013). Cheating in mind games: The subtlety of rules matters. *Journal of Economic Behaviour and Organization, 93,* 328–336.

Karpoff, J. M., Lee, D. S., & Martin, G. S. (2008a). *The consequences to managers for cooking the books, Journal of Financial Economics* (88, pp. 193–215).

Karpoff, J. M., Lee, D. S., & Martin, G. S. (2008b). The consequences to managers for financial misrepresentation. *Journal of Financial Economics, 85*, 66–101.

Keynes, J. M. (1936). *The General Theory of Employment Interest and Money*. London: Macmillan and Co.

Kieschnick, R., & McCullough, B. D. (2003). Regression analysis of variates observed on (0,1): Percentages, proportions and fractions. *Statistical Modelling, 3*, 193–213.

Kim, K., & Hann, I.-H. (2015). Does crowdfunding democratizes access to finance? A geographical analysis of technology projects. In: *A geographical analysis of technology projects (October 13, 2015). Robert H. Smith school research paper*.

King, G., & Zeng, L. (2001a). Logistic regression in rare events data. *Political Analysis, 9*, 137–163.

King, G., & Zeng, L. (2001b). Improving forecasts of state failure. *World Politics, 53*, 623–658.

Kitchens, R., & Torrence, P. D. (2012). The JOBS Act—Crowdfunding and beyond. *Economic Development Journal, 11*, 42.

Klöhn, L., Hornuf, L., & Schilling, T. (2016). The regulation of crowdfunding in the German Small Investor Protection Act: Content, consequences, critique, suggestions. *European Company Law, 13*, 56–66.

Lacker, J. M., & Weinberg, J. A. (1989). Optimal contracts under costly State falsification. *Journal of Political Economy, 97*, 1345–1363.

Lehner, O. M. (2013). Crowdfunding social ventures: A model and research agenda. *Venture Capital, 15*, 289–311.

Lester, R. H., Certo, S. T., Dalton, C. M., Dalton, D. R., & Cannella, A. A. (2006). Initial public offering investor valuations: An examination of top management team prestige and environmental uncertainty. *Journal of Small Business Management, 44*(1), 1–26.

Levine, R., Lin, C., & Xie, W. (2018). Corporate resilience to banking crises: The roles of trust and trade credit. *Journal of Financial and Quantitative Analysis, 53*(4), 1441–1477.

Liang, T. P., Wu, S. P. J., & Huang, C. C. (2019). Why funders invest in crowdfunding projects: Role of trust from the dual-process perspective. *Information & Management, 56*(1), 70–84.

Lin, M., Prabhala, N. R., & Viswanathan, S. (2013). Judging borrowers by the company they keep: Friendship networks and information asymmetry in online peer-to-peer lending. *Management Science, 59*(1), 17–35.

Lusardi, A., & Mitchell, O. S. (2007). Baby boomers retirement security: The role of planning, financial literacy and housing wealth. *Journal of Monetary Economics, 54*, 205–224.

Lusardi, A., & Mitchell, O. S. (2008). Planning and financial literacy: How do women fare? *American Economic Review, 98*, 413–417.

Lusardi, A., & Mitchell, O. S. (2011). Financial literacy around the world: An overview. *Journal of Pension Economics & Finance, 10*(4), 497–508.

Manigart, S., & Struyf, C. (1997). Financing high technology startups in Belgium: An explorative study. *Small Business Economics, 9*(2), 125–135.

Mann, H., Garcia-Rada, X., Hornuf, L., & Tafurt, J. (2016a). What deters crime? Comparing the effectiveness of legal, social, and internal sanctions across countries. *Frontiers in Psychology (Cognitive Science), 7*. Available from https://doi.org/10.3389/fpsyg.2016.00085.

Mann, H., Garcia-Rada, X., Hornuf, L., Tafurt, J., & Ariely, D. (2016b). Cut from the same cloth: Similarly dishonest individuals across countries. *Journal of Cross-Cultural Psychology, 47*, 858–874.

Massolution. (2013). *2013 CF crowdfunding industry report*. <http://crowdsourcing.org/l/20898>.

Mazar, N., Amir, O., & Ariely, D. (2008). The dishonesty of honest people: A theory of self-concept maintenance. *Journal of Marketing Research, 45*, 633–644.

McGinnis, L. P., & Gentry, J. W. (2009). Underdog consumption: An exploration into meanings and motives. *Journal of Business Research, 62*, 191–199.

McKenny, A. F., Allison, T. H., Ketchen, D. J., Short, J. C., & Ireland, R. D. (2017). How should crowdfunding research evolve? A survey of the Entrepreneurship Theory and Practice Editorial Board. *Entrepreneurship Theory and Practice, 41*(2), 291–304.

Milde, H., & Riley, J. (1988). Signaling in credit markets. *Quarterly Journal of Economics, 103*(1), 101–129.

Milfront, T. L., & Schultz, P. W. (2016). Culture and the natural environment. *Current Opinion in Psychology, 8*, 194–199.

Modigliani, F., & Miller, M. (1963). Corporate income taxes and the cost of capital: a correction. *American Economic Review, 53*(3), 433–443.

Mohammadi, A., & Shafi, K. (2017). *How wise are crowd? A comparative study of crowd and institutions, Academy of Management proceedings* (1, p. 13707). Briarcliff Manor, NY: Academy of Management.

Mollick, E. R. (2018). Crowdfunding as a font of entrepreneurship: Outcomes of reward-based crowdfunding. In D. J. Cumming, & L. Hornuf (Eds.), *The economics of crowdfunding* (pp. 133–150). Cham: Palgrave Macmillan.

Nair, M., & Cachanosky, N. (2017). Bitcoin and entrepreneurship: Breaking the network effect. *Review of Austrian Economics, 30*, 263–275.

Narayanan, M. (2017). Investor compensation in investment crowdfunding. In: Academy of Management proceedings, 13675.

Parhankangas, A., & Renko, M. (2017). Linguistic style and crowdfunding success among social and commercial entrepreneurs. *Journal of Business Venturing, 32*, 215–236.

Pauly, M. V. (1968). The economics of moral hazard: Comment. *American Economic Review*, 531–537.

Perino, M. A. (1998). Fraud and federalism: Preempting private state securities fraud causes of action. *Stanford Law Review, 50*, 273–338.

Poole, M. S., & Van de Ven, A. H. (1989). Using paradox to build management and organization theories. *Academy of Management Review, 14*(4), 562–578.

Prasad, D., Bruton, G. D., & Vozikis, G. (2000). Signaling value to business angels: The proportion of the entrepreneur's net worth invested in a new venture as a decision signal. *Venture Capital, 2*, 167–182.

Ramos, J., & González, B. (2018). Crowdfunding and employment: An analysis of the employment effects of crowdfunding in Spain. In D. Brüntje, & O. Gajda (Eds.), *Crowdfunding in Europe state of the art in theory and practice* (pp. 97–114). Cham: Springer.

Rauch, A., & Frese, M. (2007). Let's put the person back into entrepreneurship research: A meta-analysis on the relationship between business owners' personality traits, business creation, and success. *European Journal of Work and Organizational Psychology, 16*, 353–385.

Rezaee, Z. (2005). Causes, consequences, and deterence of financial statement fraud. *Critical Perspectives on Accounting, 16*, 277–298.

Robb, A. M., & Coleman, S. (2014). *Financing high growth women-owned enterprises: Evidence from the United States. ICSB world conference proceedings* (p. 1) International Council for Small Business (ICSB).

Ryan, R. M., O'Toole, C. M., & McCann, F. (2014). Does bank market power affect SME financing constraints? *Journal of Banking & Finance, 49*, 495–505.

Sahlman, W. A. (1990). The structure and governance of venture-capital organizations. *Journal of Financial Economics, 27*(2), 473–521.

Scheaf, D. J., Davis, B. C., Webb, J. W., Coombs, J. E., Borns, J., & Holloway, G. (2018). Signals' flexibility and interaction with visual cues: Insights from crowdfunding. *Journal of Business Venturing, 33*(6), 720–741.

Serrano-Cinca, C., Gutiérrez-Nieto, B., & López- Palacios, L. (2015). Determinants of default in P2P lending. *PLoS One, 10*(10), e0139427.

Shalvi, S., Gino, F., Barkan, R., & Ayal, S. (2015). Self-serving justifications doing wrong and feeling moral. *Current Directions in Psychological Science, 24*, 125–130.

Sharma, A., & Kesner, I. F. (1996). Diversifying entry: Some ex ante explanations for post-entry survival and growth. *Academy of Management Journal, 39*, 635–677.

Short, J. C., Ketchen, D. J., McKenny, A. F., Allison, T. H., & Ireland, R. D. (2017). Research on Crowdfunding: Reviewing the (Very Recent) Past and Celebrating the Present. *Entrepreneurship Theory and Practice, 41*(2), 149–160.

Siering, M., Koch, J., & Deokar, A. V. (2016). Detecting fraudulent behavior on crowdfunding platforms: The role of linguistic and content-based cues in static and dynamic contexts. *Journal of Management Information Systems, 33*, 421–455.

Sila, V., Gonzalez, A., & Hagendorff, J. (2016). Women on board: Does boardroom gender diversity affect firm risk? *Journal of Corporate Finance, 36*, 26–53.

Simmonds, A. R., Sagat, K. A., & Ronen, J. (1992). Dealing with anomalies, confusion and contradiction in fraud on the market securities class actions. *Kentucky Law Journal, 81*, 123–186.

Sorenson, O., & Audia, P. G. (2000). The social structure of entrepreneurial activity: Geographic concentration of footwear production in the United States, 1940–1989. *American Journal of Sociology, 106*, 424–462.

Stanko, M. A., & Henard, D. H. (2016). How crowdfunding influences innovation. *MIT Sloan Management Review*, *57*, 15.

Statista. (2018). Available from: <https://www.statista.com/outlook/335/100/crowdfunding/worldwide# markettransactionValue>.

Stinchcombe, A. L. (1965). Social structures and organizations. In: *Handbook of organizations*. Chicago, IL: Rand McNally.

Sufi, A. (2007). Information asymmetry and financing arrangements: Evidence from syndicated loans. *Journal of Finance*, *62*, 629–668.

Thompson, S. B. (2011). Simple formulas for standard errors that cluster by both firm and time. *Journal of Financial Economics*, *99*, 1–10.

Townsend, R. (1979). Optimal contracts and competitive markets with costly state verification. *Journal of Economic Theory*, *21*, 265–293.

Van Rooij, M., Lusardi, A., & Alessie, R. (2011). Financial literacy and stock market participation. *Journal of Financial Economics*, *101*, 449–472.

Vismara, S. (2019). Sustainability in equity crowdfunding. *Technological Forecasting and Social Change*, *141*, 98–106.

Vismara, S., Benaroio, D., & Carne, F. (2017). Gender in entrepreneurial finance: Matching investors and entrepreneurs in equity crowdfunding. In Albert Link (Ed.), *Gender and entrepreneurial activity* (pp. 271–288). Cheltenham: Edward Elgar.

Wessel, M., Thies, F., & Benlian, A. (2015). A lie never lives to be old: The effects of fake social information on consumer decision-making in crowdfunding. In: *ECIS 2015 completed research papers (Spring 5-29-2015)*. Available from: <http://aisel.aisnet.org/cgi/viewcontent.cgi?article = 1200&context = ecis2015_cr>.

Wette, H. (1983). Collateral in credit rationing in markets with imperfect information: Note. *American Economic Review*, *73*(3), 442–445.

Winborg, J., & Landström, H. (2001). Financial bootstrapping in small businesses: Examining small business managers' resource acquisition behaviors. *Journal of Business Venturing*, *16*(3), 235–254.

Wright, M., Lockett, A., Pruthi, S., Manigart, S., Sapienza, H., Desbrieres, P., & Hommel, U. (2004). Venture capital investors, capital markets, valuation and information: US, Europe and Asia. *Journal of International Entrepreneurship*, *2*(4), 305–326.

Wright, M., Wilson, N., Gilligan, J., Bacon, N., & Amess, K. (2016). Brexit, private equity and management. *British Journal of Management*, *27*(4), 682–686.

Wright, M., Pruthi, S., & Lockett, A. (2005). International venture capital research: From cross-country comparisons to crossing borders. *International Journal of Management Reviews*, *7*(3), 135–165.

Wu, F., & Huberman, B. (2007). Novelty and collective attention. *Proceedings of the National Academy of Sciences of the United States of America*, *104*(45), 17599–17601.

Yi, S. K. M., Steyvers, M., Lee, M. D., & Dry, M. J. (2012). The wisdom of the crowd in combinatorial problems. *Cognitive Science*, *36*(3), 452–470.

Yung, C. (2009). Entrepreneurial finance and costly due diligence. *The Financial Review*, *44*(1), 137–149.

Index of cases

Index

Printed in the United States
By Bookmasters